K of Sale
due on 10/16

Campbell Co. Courthouse
York Street
in Newport

340 York Street
Newport KY
41071

applicable
stickers

REAL ESTATE TRANSACTIONS

ASPEN PUBLISHERS

Real Estate Transactions

Problems, Cases, and Materials

Third Edition

ROBIN PAUL MALLOY

E.I. White Chair and Distinguished Professor of Law
Vice Dean of the College
Director, Center on Property, Citizenship, and Social Entrepreneurism (PCSE)
College of Law, Syracuse University

JAMES CHARLES SMITH

John Byrd Martin Professor of Law
University of Georgia

Wolters Kluwer
Law & Business

AUSTIN BOSTON CHICAGO NEW YORK THE NETHERLANDS

Aspen Publishers
Attn: Permissions Department
76 Ninth Avenue, 7th Floor
New York, NY 10011-5201

To contact Customer Care, e-mail customer.care@aspenpublishers.com, call 1-800-234-1660, fax 1-800-901-9075, or mail correspondence to:

Aspen Publishers
Attn: Order Department
PO Box 990
Frederick, MD 21705

Printed in the United States of America.

1 2 3 4 5 6 7 8 9 0

ISBN 978-0-7355-6257-8

Library of Congress Cataloging-in-Publication Data

Malloy, Robin Paul, 1956-
Real estate transactions : problems, cases, and materials/Robin Paul Malloy, James Charles Smith.—3rd ed.
p. cm.
Includes index.
ISBN 978-0-7355-6257-8
1. Vendors and purchasers—United States—Cases. 2. Real property—United States—Cases. I. Smith, James Charles, 1952- II. Title.
KF665.A4M35 2007 2006032733
346.7304′37—dc22

About Wolters Kluwer Law & Business

Wolters Kluwer Law & Business is a leading provider of research information and workflow solutions in key specialty areas. The strengths of the individual brands of Aspen Publishers, CCH, Kluwer Law International and Loislaw are aligned within Wolters Kluwer Law & Business to provide comprehensive, in-depth solutions and expert-authored content for the legal, professional and education markets.

CCH was founded in 1913 and has served more than four generations of business professionals and their clients. The CCH products in the Wolters Kluwer Law & Business group are highly regarded electronic and print resources for legal, securities, antitrust and trade regulation, government contracting, banking, pension, payroll, employment and labor, and healthcare reimbursement and compliance professionals.

Aspen Publishers is a leading information provider for attorneys, business professionals and law students. Written by preeminent authorities, Aspen products offer analytical and practical information in a range of specialty practice areas from securities law and intellectual property to mergers and acquisitions and pension/benefits. Aspen's trusted legal education resources provide professors and students with high-quality, up-to-date and effective resources for successful instruction and study in all areas of the law.

Kluwer Law International supplies the global business community with comprehensive English-language international legal information. Legal practitioners, corporate counsel and business executives around the world rely on the Kluwer Law International journals, loose-leafs, books and electronic products for authoritative information in many areas of international legal practice.

Loislaw is a premier provider of digitized legal content to small law firm practitioners of various specializations. Loislaw provides attorneys with the ability to quickly and efficiently find the necessary legal information they need, when and where they need it, by facilitating access to primary law as well as state-specific law, records, forms and treatises.

Wolters Kluwer Law & Business, a unit of Wolters Kluwer, is headquartered in New York and Riverwoods, Illinois. Wolters Kluwer is a leading multinational publisher and information services company.

To Celia Sacco Malloy with love and appreciation for enduring so much, and for giving me the strength and character to succeed in a less than perfect world.

R.P.M.

For Donna, Nicole, and Kristin in gratitude for your gifts of love and understanding.

J.C.S.

Summary of Contents

Contents

Preface

We like to say that real estate covers a lot of ground. And, as marathon runners, we like to believe we cover that ground better than anyone else in the market. Our aim is to equip students to cross the finish line, prepared for success in the competitive environment of the real world. To this end, we put together a "training program" with three main ingredients.

First, we place transactions in their market context, taking pains to explain how various sales and finance markets work. Once students understand how markets operate — how banks, developers, and investors make money — they can then understand what drives transactions: the motivations of the parties, the risks involved, and the ways that parties use the law to advance their interests. Second, we integrate issues of professional responsibility into our materials, illustrating the stresses of legal practice and the areas in which real estate attorneys most often encounter trouble. Because we want students to see that professional responsibility is not merely an abstraction, we weave discussions of ethical problems into the study of actual cases. Third, we include problem sets throughout the book to enhance the learning of legal analysis and lawyering skills. Our goal is to balance theory and practice by emphasizing what successful transaction lawyers do on a daily basis.

Our overarching goal has been to make the materials comprehensible yet challenging. We assume the student knows nothing beyond the rudiments of property and contract law. Each chapter includes text that highlights the pertinent general rules and transactional considerations. In addition to the text, we present cases and problems that illustrate how the key rules play out in practice. Our selection of cases is designed to highlight the transactional nature of underlying legal problems and the economic dimensions of the parties' exchange. The problems reinforce, and test the scope of, principles addressed in the text and in the cases. We've also found that the problems provide a rich starting point for the discussion of lawyering strategies and transactional tactics.

The practice of real estate law is document intensive; thus, we have provided basic documents and problems on a CD that accompanies this book. These documents and problems can be tailored to fit the needs and objectives of individual users.

Although a few chapters in our book separately address residential and commercial transactions, we see these areas as closely interrelated. As a consequence, the text, cases, and problems throughout the book show many issues arising in residential and commercial contexts. Our materials also emphasize how modern real estate transactions cross a wide range of subject matters within the standard law school curriculum. The student will encounter problems that might have arisen in many other courses, among them contracts, commercial law, torts, corporations or business organizations, constitutional law, land use, and environmental law. As is true throughout the book, our goal is to help students see how real estate transactions fit into a "big picture" so that they can begin to appreciate the rich multidimensional context in which they will practice.

While we view the course in real estate transactions as primarily focused on the private market for exchange and finance, we also address questions of access to housing and mortgage opportunities. These matters are important in part because future lawyers must know something about the nature of the clients they are likely to serve. In general, their clients will represent a privileged class of people. Students should understand this fact, and they should also see how the subject of "market failures" raises questions of social policy, civil rights, and potential market opportunities.

This edition of the book is significantly shorter than the second edition and has noticeably larger fonts, thereby offering streamlined coverage for easier classroom use. Every chapter has been updated to include new cases and the latest information on law, markets, and ethics. And, as our revised table of contents reveals, we stay true to the core components of our first and second editions. The result is a better and leaner "training guide" for success on the road ahead.

We could not have prepared this book without the help and support of many people. First and foremost, we thank our family members and friends. In addition, we wish to acknowledge those people who have made special contributions to the success of our project. In particular, we appreciate the advice and assistance of Carol McGeehan and Melody Davies. For research assistance we thank Eric Sarabia and Jason Mintz. Eric also worked on gathering statistics on mortgage lending and housing markets, and Jason, after graduation, became the Program Director for the Center on Property, Citizenship, and Social Entrepreneurism at Syracuse, and assisted in the editing process. We also thank the many people who have used our book, and, in particular, Patrick Bauer, Daniel Bogart, Carol Brown, John Lovett, John Martinez, Patrick Randolph, and Paul Zolan for taking the time to send us specific suggestions for the new edition of this book.

Happy Trails,

Robin Paul Malloy

James Charles Smith

Robin

Jim

The successful practice of law, like marathon running, requires a commitment to preparation, hard work, and the relentless pursuit of excellence.

Acknowledgments

The authors gratefully acknowledge the permissions granted to reproduce the following materials.

Books and articles

Epperson, K. Q., & K. A. Sullivan, Title Examination Standards: A Status Report, 4 Probate & Property 16 (Sept./Oct. 1990). Copyright © 1990 by the American Bar Association. All rights reserved. Reprinted by permission of the authors and the publisher.

McCormack, J. L., Torrens and Recording: Land Title Assurance in the Computer Age, 18 Wm. Mitchell L. Rev. 61 (1992). Reprinted by permission of the author and the publisher.

Natelson, R. G., Modern Law of Deeds to Real Property 151-158 (1992). Reprinted by permission of Aspen Law & Business, a division of Aspen Publishers, Inc.

Simes, L. M., & C. B. Taylor, Model Title Standards 14, 16-17, 36-38 (1960). Reprinted by permission of the University of Michigan.

Williams, M. G., & H. J. Onsrud, What Every Lawyer Should Know About Title Surveys, in Land Surveys: A Guide for Lawyers 49-62 (2d ed. 2000). Copyright © American Bar Association. All rights reserved. Reprinted by permission of the authors and the publisher.

Illustrations

Bala Plaza photograph, by Cathy Seidler-Coenen.

Smith, James Charles, photograph by Action Sports International, Tucker, GA.

Survey for Rupard by McLeroy, B (Aug. 16, 1995). Reprinted by permission.

Trump World Tower photograph, reprinted by permission of the Trump Organization.

REAL ESTATE TRANSACTIONS

1
Market Context for Real Estate Transactions

Successful transactional lawyers are familiar with much more than the bodies of law that govern their areas of practice. The law provides the basic tools of lawyering, but the lawyer is an expert who needs to understand how the law fits into the larger process of social exchange. This larger process encompasses human factors as the lawyer constantly interacts and deals with clients and other people. The practice of real estate law is people oriented. In addition, to comprehend the role of the lawyer in the social enterprise of real estate transactions, one must understand the market or business context in which the various actors pursue their assorted goals.

The goal of this chapter is to introduce some important concepts that will assist you in understanding the market context for a transactional real estate practice. In going over this material it is important to keep in mind that a transactional practice is goal oriented. Whereas many first year courses are primarily about learning definitions and concepts of a given legal subject matter, a transactions course is about employing a variety of legal tools to accomplish a specific goal. In a transaction the client does not want to know that you can recite the different estates in land. The client wants to accomplish a specific objective, such as acquiring land and building a shopping mall. In achieving that objective there may be parts of the transaction that require the attorney to know the various estates. There may also be a need to use contract law, the Uniform Commercial Code, corporate law, tax law, securities law, and mortgage law. Therefore, in a transactions course one needs to learn to bring many areas of law together to accomplish a given objective.

A transactional approach to real estate embraces three key areas of concern: the *perspective, purpose,* and *planning* of the transaction.

1. *Perspective* involves thinking about the transaction from the point of view of the various parties to the exchange. The parties have

alternative expectations and desires, which often are compatible, but sometimes are in competition.

2. *Purpose* involves developing a clear understanding of the *subject matter* of the exchange and its ultimate *objective.* Usually the objective is mutually shared by the parties.
3. *Planning* involves putting together a strategy for achieving the client's purpose. The transactional lawyer plans the transaction by trying to employ the most appropriate tools to protect the client and achieve a positive outcome.

If you keep these three key elements in mind as you study the cases and problems throughout the book, you will begin to develop an appreciation of what makes a person a successful and valuable transactional lawyer.

A. VALUE AND MARKET CHOICE

Our starting point is the simple concept of *value.* All real estate transactions involve the process of capturing or creating value. The various parties to the transactions we discuss in this book participate because they believe that the successful conclusion of their undertaking will make them better off than they were before the exchange. The parties are typically looking for profits, equity appreciation, or cash flow from their involvement in a real estate transaction. Sometimes, however, the economic benefits of a transaction are indirect motivators for an exchange. For instance, the benefits or values may relate to gaining control or autonomy, as in moving out of an apartment and into a single-family home; or a buyer may not expect a great deal of equity appreciation from buying a particular piece of real estate but may instead seek the tax benefits of the deal. This is often a motivating factor for high-income people to purchase expensive homes so that they can get tax benefits for such things as interest paid on the home mortgage. Whatever the particular circumstances are for a given transaction, it is clear that most real estate transactions are pursued for basic economic considerations of self-interest. This concept is simple and straightforward. To illustrate this, just ask yourself why you, as a lawyer, will facilitate the real estate transaction for the client. Generally, the lawyer is there for the same reason as everyone else — to earn a fee and to benefit from the business. The important thing to remember is that everyone else in the transaction is there for a similar reason.

When one considers that the motivation for a transaction is based on a desire to capture and create value, one must also understand the process for making a decision to engage in a particular exchange. In general, people will seek to cover their costs and to derive additional benefits from an exchange. Some of the potential benefits will be easier to quantify than others. The key concerns for the lawyer in representing a client involve using the law to: (a) identify various components of cost, including risk; (b) manage these costs; and (c) protect client expectations with respect to revealed value preferences.

A person who seeks value by entering into a real estate transaction is making a *market choice.* Like most other market transactions, a real estate transaction is undertaken or completed by choice because it makes sense for a number of reasons, including ones that are purely economic. Market factors are what motivate people to engage in real estate transactions. Developers, landlords, lenders, and other parties engage in transactions as a market choice because they hope to capture or create value. Consequently, if the potential for gain is eliminated from real estate activities, people won't be interested in doing them.

B. ACCOUNTING PROFIT AND ECONOMIC PROFIT

Market choices relate closely to the idea of profit. A desirable market choice is one that will be *profitable,* but the meaning of this term can vary with different circumstances. Not all motivations for doing a transaction are easily quantifiable, therefore, it may be difficult to do a cost and benefit analysis of an anticipated exchange.

Profit from an exchange is typically considered in two different ways. These include *accounting profits* and *economic profits.* Accounting profits are based on covering the cost of a transaction. Economic profits measure the amount of accounting profit against the comparative return that could have been earned from undertaking an alternative transaction of comparable risk. Generally, a client will expect a transaction to cover the accounting costs and return an accounting profit. In the long-run, a client's commitment to a particular type of business activity will also be influenced, in part, by the potential for economic profits.

C. RISK AND RETURN

For every market choice, there is a relationship between risk and return. The return may be described as value that is created and captured or as accounting profit or economic profit, with the latter term implying that there are alternative market choices bearing similar risk. The crucial relationship between risk and return is understood easily by thinking about something as simple as a savings account at the bank. As savers of money, we all want the best return on our investment. If one bank is paying us 3 percent to deposit our money and another is paying us 10 percent, we are likely to move our money to the location where we capture the most value. This is simple and straightforward, but what if the risks are different? How might one respond if the bank offering a 3 percent return on savings accounts was 100 percent insured by the federal government and therefore, the saver knew she couldn't lose her money, if the other bank paying 10 percent was not insured and was rumored to have some financial problems? In confronting this market choice, one has to consider the relationship between the risk and the rate of return offered by each bank. The riskier investment choice must provide a higher rate of return to attract investment. The potential investor is forced to weigh her aversion to risk against her desire for higher potential returns.

Imagine a buyer and a seller negotiating over various contract terms and over the purchase price of a particular property. As will be brought out in this book, many contract terms are about identifying and adjusting risk. Examples of a few types of risk that are important to real estate contract negotiation are potential environmental problems, title defects, structural defects in buildings, zoning and land use problems, and financing contingencies. Favorable contract terms will create value for the party benefited by such terms.

Problem 1A

Your client, Damian, has spotted a home, owned by Susannah, that he's interested in buying. It's a ten-year-old house, which appears to be in good condition, for which Susannah is asking $280,000. The house has stucco-siding, and Damian is concerned because he has heard that a number of houses in his community have had problems with defective stucco siding, necessitating expensive reconstruction work. Damian has just made an offer to buy the house for $270,000, with the provision that Susannah warrant that the siding presently has no defects, coupled with an indemnity whereby Susannah will pay all costs incurred by Damian to repair or replace the siding if that becomes necessary at any time during the next six years.

(a) What effect will Damian's request for the stucco warranty and indemnity have on Susannah's perception of risk and return?

(b) Suppose that Susannah objects to the stucco provision, but Damian insists that he won't buy the house unless it goes into the parties' contract. How might Susannah signal to Damian the value she attaches to not having the provision in the contract?

D. VALUE, UTILITY, AND COMPARATIVE ADVANTAGE

Discussions of market choice often include the terms *value*, *utility*, and *comparative advantage*, and therefore it is useful to examine these related ideas. First, let's look more closely at the concept of value. We have said that one helpful way to understand a real estate transaction is to think of it in terms of various parties attempting to capture or create value from their efforts. To appreciate this, we need to have some useful concept of what we mean by the term *value.* In simple economic terms, value is related to a concept called utility. *Utility* is a measure of how much an individual values a particular good, service, or activity. One can measure utility by observing the trade-offs that people make in the assorted choices of daily living. Some people work long hours to increase their income, whereas others forgo added income from work by pursuing more leisure time. In observing the trade-off between work and leisure, one sees the relative utility that different people get from alternative ways to use their time (time being a scarce commodity and therefore valuable). Utility analysis tries to measure how much value or enjoyment a person gets from a particular thing or activity. In most cases it is easiest to rely on some tangible or outward proxy or device for measuring the degree of utility represented by any given set of trade-offs between competing opportunities. Generally, money is used as a proxy, with a person's willingness to pay equated to the utility she derives from the activity or transaction. For instance, if John will pay $200,000 for a particular property and Morgan will only pay $180,000 for the same property, we can say that John values the property more than Morgan or that John has a higher utility for the property.

When considering John's and Morgan's utility for the property, we must keep in mind that there is a problem with using price as a proxy for utility, because it assumes that all people have a meaningful way of registering their preferences in the marketplace. The difficulty stems from the fact that resources and bargaining power in our society are not equally distributed. Therefore, it may be true that John will pay $200,000 for a property for which Morgan will offer only $180,000, but it may also be true that Morgan would be willing to pay as much as $250,000 for that property if she had access to better credit. Limited by credit constraints and buying power, Morgan is unable to register, in dollar terms, her full level of personal preference for this particular property. Thus, the price proxy on which our market system operates is not a perfect measure of utility in terms of willingness to pay, but rather serves as a proxy for the combined notion of willingness and ability to pay. Consequently, we should always consider accessibility to credit and the distribution of resources before jumping to any significant conclusions about the actual preferences and values of particular market actors.

Likewise, social policy concerning real estate matters must be understood against a market backdrop that produces exchanges motivated not only by the desires of the actors but also by the resources they already control. As a result, prior accumulated wealth has a major influence on market activities. The distribution of wealth has an important impact on the types of products offered in the real estate market; moreover, there is evidence that it affects access to credit and housing markets based on race and gender.

As real estate lawyers, we are often called on to determine the legal reliability and completeness of essential information underlying the client's judgments and expectations. We are also engaged to structure transactions so as to protect the value of the client's plans. To do this we must truly understand the market choices and preferences that shape the client's market outlook and transactional motivation. In this context, the *value* of the lawyer rests in her ability to facilitate the client's investment expectations. The lawyer is selling an expertise, or *comparative market advantage,* in understanding the legal rules and infrastructure necessary to protect the client's expectations and to complete the desired transaction. The client is treating law and the legal system as a commodity. The law is a product that forms a necessary part of a successful real estate transaction, and the lawyer is hired to provide a level of skill and confidence in the delivery of this product that exceeds the performance of nonlawyers. This added level of skill is the lawyer's comparative advantage in facilitating the transaction, and it is generally thought that these skills increase with time and experience. Thus, more senior lawyers and lawyers with a specialized practice gain more expertise and advantage over others, and consequently command higher fees for their services.

Although the lawyer has a comparative advantage or expertise in the delivery of legal services, clients involved in commercial real estate generally perceive themselves as having a comparative advantage in their sector of business. Part of the lawyer's job is to protect that advantage and adequately constrain the client's liabilities with respect to matters outside the client's area of perceived advantage.

Market activities and functions are broken down along lines of comparative advantage based on an individual's or an entity's expertise in doing specific tasks more efficiently and cost-effectively than others. The real estate lawyer, quite frequently, is hired to facilitate the demarcation of these lines or functions, and she is expected to do so in a way that gives maximum advantage to the client while assuring minimal exposure for loss. In other words, the lawyer is called on not only to facilitate the client's market transactions, but also to define both the client's role and the particular aspects of the market structure in which the transaction will take place.

E. CATEGORIES OF COSTS

In pursuing real estate transactions, parties incur four specific types of costs: *transaction, out-of-pocket, opportunity,* and *sunk costs.* These categories of cost affect market choice, and they also directly or indirectly influence the calculation of damages in the event that a transaction runs into difficulty.

Transaction costs are the costs associated with undertaking a particular exchange. They are the costs of collecting information, negotiating, cooperating, and regulatory compliance. It is important to keep in mind that as a lawyer engaged to assist the client in legal matters related to an exchange, you too are a transaction cost from the client's perspective. One goal of a person confronted with transaction cost, as well a goal of a legal system concerned with facilitating market exchanges, is to reduce the costs of transactions.

Out-of-pocket costs are actual expenses incurred in doing a project, whereas *opportunity costs* are associated with the market choices one gives up to pursue the selected choice. In every transaction, each party has both an out-of-pocket cost and an opportunity cost. When a person gives value in exchange for another item, the value surrendered is the out-of-pocket cost, which might be cash, land, legal rights, or something else. In simple terms, consider John's payment of $200,000 to purchase a property. The $200,000 is his out-of-pocket cost. John's opportunity cost, however, includes all the other things he might have done with that $200,000 but which he must now forgo, such as buying a boat or investing in the stock of a new venture capital group. Having made a choice to purchase a particular real property, John will measure his accounting profits or losses by the return he gets from the property, and he will measure his economic profits or losses with reference to the return he might have earned from other investments. Although accounting profits will likely keep John out of bankruptcy and in the market for the short run, competitive economic profits are necessary for the long-term viability of real estate markets relative to other investments and alternative capital market choices.

Sunk costs are a special type or category of out-of-pocket costs. They are costs that cannot be recovered when a party abandons a course of action. The problem with sunk costs is deciding at what point, and under what conditions, one should stay in or exit from a transaction. To answer this question, one needs to evaluate the potential costs and consequences of both staying in and getting out of a deal. The decision involves legal consequences, such as damages or penalties, as well as business considerations, such as the ability to pursue other transactions in the future. Staying in an exchange that has gone sour means one will continue to invest resources in a transaction that is no longer expected to generate the returns that initially made it seem attractive. New information about the marketplace or the project may have changed the expectations for profit, but the disappointed investor also knows that she has already committed a lot of money and resources to the undertaking. This confronts the investor with the difficult choice of whether it makes more sense to invest additional time and resources in an effort to turn a project around or simply to abandon the undertaking in a way that best limits the losses, including legal exposure.

F. TRANSACTIONAL MISBEHAVIOR

As clients try to get out of contractual commitments, seek to renegotiate terms, or just plain attempt to get more than they bargained for, we uncover the problem of *transactional misbehavior.* Transactional misbehavior occurs when a party to a transaction tries to change the dynamics of the deal after the deal has been struck. To understand transactional misbehavior, we must recall that there is a direct relationship between risk and price. In market terms, the greater the risk assumed by a given party, the higher rate of return that party will expect as a reward for engaging in the activity. Recall our example of putting money in a no-risk government-insured savings account for a guaranteed 3 percent rate of return. Compare this situation to an offer by a real estate developer that promises a 30 percent return on money invested but admits that there is only a 20 percent chance of success. If asked to consider these two choices, an investor has to think carefully about the potential returns as well as her own aversion to risk.

In a given transaction, if an investor can have a beneficial (self-serving) after-the-fact effect on the expected rates of return or associated risks, then she has an incentive to misbehave. This means that parties can have an incentive to act differently after entering an agreement as compared to their conduct prior to the undertaking. In short, the underlying premise of transactional misbehavior is that each party to a transaction has an economic incentive to modify the initial allocation of risks so as to enhance her own rate of return. This premise hinges on an understanding that the parties entered into a legally enforceable agreement that locks in a specific set of risk assumptions and market expectations. Once locked into a negotiated price and risk relationship, each party can, in effect, improve her position or rate of return by acting in a way that shifts the calculus in her favor.

The goal of good transactional lawyering is to recognize the potential for transactional misbehavior, and to structure the transaction to reduce the risk of such behavior. By reducing the opportunities for transactional misbehavior, the lawyer enhances the opportunity to protect the client's transactional expectations.

G. RENT-SEEKING BEHAVIOR

Real estate transactions are only partially concerned with property per se as tangible, physical matter. Much transactional value comes from the legal and financial markets that make them possible. Parties sometimes try to capture or create value by engaging in *rent-seeking* behavior. The basic proposition is that law and legal regulations are a primary source of the economic value of real property, and this law is not frozen or static. People are "rent seeking" when they discover or manipulate legal opportunities in the pursuit of economic gain. In so doing, they treat law as a commodity in which, like other commodities, they invest. For instance, the market value of a vacant piece of real estate may depend more on the zoning laws that define its permitted uses than on any other factor. Consequently, much value can be created for a particular property by effecting a favorable zoning use classification. Thus, it makes economic sense to invest money to effect a change in the property's zoning status. Generally, excluding other cost considerations, a person should be willing to spend almost as much money on changing an unfavorable zoning rule as she estimates that a favorable rule will add to the value of the property.

Rent-seeking behavior is often a species of transactional misbehavior. Although rent-seeking activities may take different forms, they often consist of a party trying to gain a special advantage over competitors.

H. CATEGORIES OF MARKET RISK

Throughout our discussion up to now, we have referred to the concept of risk as an important factor to consider in planning every real estate transaction. Risk is one component of cost in evaluating a transaction. At this point we'll develop a more specific understanding of the nature of risk and its major forms by elaborating two significant categories of market risk: *temporal risk* and *transactional risk.*

1. Temporal Risk

Temporal risk concerns a variety of risk factors related to time. These risks can relate to past, present, or future information about a property or a transaction. Very few activities in a complex society can be done simultaneously, and consequently almost all real estate transactions are carried out over a period of time. There will be time for negotiating before entering into any specific agreements, there will be time involved in carrying out the terms of an agreement, and there will be time after the closing of a transaction when legal obligations may still be outstanding. Time as a factor in a transaction affects both value and risk. The effect of time on monetary value, often referred to by the phrase "the time value of money," is very important. Stated simply, this means that a dollar today is worth more than a dollar tomorrow.

There are a number of reasons for this, but the easiest explanation is the effect of inflation. We know that in periods of inflation as time passes, the purchasing power of a dollar falls. It still is a dollar, but it takes more dollars to acquire or control the same goods and resources. If, for example, we assume an inflation rate of 15 percent per year, a dollar today would be worth only 85 cents one year from now; stated differently, what one could buy for a dollar today would cost $1.15 one year from now. One can easily see that inflation has opposite effects on borrowers and lenders. A borrower enjoys the advantages of inflation by getting money today and paying back in the future with dollars that are worth less. At the same time, a lender naturally has quite the opposite view of this situation.

Another important element of time-value risk relates to the old adage "a bird in the hand is worth two in the bush." This simply means that having one's money or performance now is better than merely having an expectation that it will be available at some date in the future. This is true for a number of reasons; but consider one simple point. The promise to pay or to perform in the future always involves a risk of nonperformance, therefore it is often best to have the other party perform first. In this way one enhances her opportunity to receive actual performance rather than a mere right to sue for nonperformance at a later date.

Having considered the relationship between time and value, it is important to look more closely at temporal risk related to past, present, and future informational concerns. *Past* or *historical risk* refers to an inability to be certain about historical information upon which particular business judgments rely in calculating the desirability of a current transaction. For instance, in approving a borrower for a loan, a bank would consider the credit history of the borrower. In making a decision about the borrower's credit risk, the bank would invest in historical information. The bank would hope that the past information would shed some light on the borrower's likely conduct in the future. The bank would probably include a credit check among the reports it commissioned in its effort to evaluate the risk of a loan. The credit report provides a great deal of information about the borrower and her payment history to a wide variety of creditors over a period of years. Although such a report can be useful, it might contain an error. Errors could be of a type favorable to the borrower (not picking up past credit problems) or harmful to her (reporting on credit problems that do not in fact exist). Errors against the borrower can cost her a good rate on a loan, and errors in her favor can cost the bank money by causing it to underprice the risk of its loan. In each case, there is a risk of inaccuracy concerning information about the past. This is historical risk.

The second category of temporal risk concerns *present risk*. Present risk centers on information relied on for purposes of establishing the presence or absence of specific conditions that would affect the property or the transaction. We may, for instance, want an inspection of the improvements on the property to make sure that the improvements comply with all current building and zoning codes and regulations. Here, we have at least two initial areas where error can arise. First, we may make a mistake in our reading of the codes and regulations and thereby fail to apply the appropriate standard in measuring compliance. Second, even if we properly determine the code rules and regulations, we may misapply the standard by not measuring or calculating accurately. For instance, a zoning code that requires a certain number of parking spaces for a building may use a formula based on the building's net square footage of useable space. First, we would need to find this regulation and figure out what was meant by *net square footage*; second, we would need to apply that formula to the property and then check the actual spaces for compliance with the number from the formula. As one can imagine, actual codes can be very confusing about the way square footage is to be measured and about what types of areas count as parking spaces. Consequently, errors can be made about the present status of the property. A similar problem can confront us when we do a home inspection. We might have a termite inspection done, which we are told reveals no active infestation, and then discover later that this determination was erroneous. Likewise, we might have an environmental audit of property to determine whether it is free of any hazardous waste problems, and these results may be flawed. Results may be flawed because the testing was improperly performed or simply because not all testing or sampling is completely accurate. Therefore, a party can do all that is economically practical to reduce this area of risk and still end up with erroneous information.

Finally, we have the problem of *future risk*— the risk of not being able to predict the future. We can make educated guesses, but there is always a risk that our expectations about the future will be inaccurate; just look at how often government budget projections are wrong because of failed assumptions about future inflation rates, interest rates, and employment rates. Future risk also presents problems in the form of revisions to prior information. The future may reveal new information about historical conclusions, thereby revealing their inaccuracy. Likewise, the future may reveal that determinations about the present status of the property were incorrect. Such is the case when the presence of termites is revealed after closing on a property despite the pre-closing inspection report to the contrary. Future risk, therefore, not only concerns the inability to correctly predict the future, but also encompasses the problem of new information that changes the calculus of prior decisions.

New information or any variation from the expectations and assumptions of a party going into a transaction will change the value of the exchange to that party. These risks, if they materialize, will change the value of the deal and influence the incentives and motivations of the party affected.

2. *Transactional Risk*

In addition to temporal risk, there are also transactional risks, which include *investor or ownership risk*, *marketplace risk*, *credit risk*, and *transfer risk*. Each category of risk should be understood and appreciated if one is to analyze a real estate transaction properly. Sometimes these areas of risk analysis will overlap or be difficult to separate. The important point is that the lawyer must have a general understanding of the nature of transactional risk so that she can properly approach and manage an exchange.

Investor or *ownership risk*, which is sometimes called *entrepreneurial risk*, defines the position of a person who is an equity stakeholder in property. Simple elements of ownership risk involve liability for environmental problems that affect the property and tort liability for injuries that occur to certain categories of visitors to the property. Ownership risk also includes contract liability of an owner contracting for goods and services or the construction of improvements that will benefit the property. The owner as entrepreneur also takes on the risk of depreciating value of property and the risk that a construction project may be unsuccessful. If a project is unsuccessful or if an owner becomes liable as a result of her activity, there will be a cost or a loss.

The other side of this coin, however, is the potential for profit and gain if the real estate appreciates in value. The owner of real property is the one who benefits when property values rise. If the value of a home or commercial property appreciates, the owner wins the reward. The owner will also receive the benefit if any valuable minerals are discovered on the property.

A second key category of transactional risk involves the marketplace. *Marketplace risks* are those associated with general market forces that can affect the profitability of any given transaction. This type of risk is different from investor or ownership risk, because it affects all market participants and is generally not property-specific. The parties' structure of a transaction is often governed by their expectations concerning market forces. Changes in those expectations during the life of a transaction may dramatically alter the value of the exchange to each party. All the parties have to make some guesses — one hopes educated and informed guesses — about the future state of the market and plan their transaction around specified parameters. (In some respects, because market risk involves problems of future information, it is also properly considered a form of temporal risk, as discussed earlier.) Examples of marketplace risk are the risk of inflation or a general downturn in the economy.

In addition to affecting value, market factors can also affect liquidity. *Liquidity* is the measure of how quickly a person can exchange her investments for cash or other assets. Cash is very liquid because it is easy to exchange for other things. Likewise, most publicly traded stocks are considered liquid because there is a large and ready market for them. In contrast, liquidity for real estate can vary widely and can change over time. When it takes six months to a year to sell a piece of real estate, it would not be considered a very liquid investment. As market conditions fluctuate, a risk is imposed on real estate transactions because market changes will affect the liquidity of a particular holding.

Credit risk is another element of transactional risk. The most obvious area of credit risk involves financing transactions, but it arises in other transactions whenever payment and performance are not simultaneous. A lender who extends credit should be concerned about two primary risk areas: the borrower's *ability* to pay and *willingness* to pay. Assessing ability to pay requires an investigation into the income, credit history, and net worth of the borrower as well as an investigation into the stability of the borrower's income flow and employment. Additionally, in a commercial undertaking the borrower's past record or experience with similar types of activities is important. Although assessing the ability to pay might be thought of as a purely historical inquiry, it also has a forward-looking element. Often the ability to pay is related to market risk, because changes in the market may affect a person's income or employment. During an economic downturn, people on commission income or in particular industries may experience a decline in money resources or outright lose their jobs. Even in times of economic growth, some sectors of the economy do worse than others.

Credit risk involves more than just the risk of *inability* to pay or perform; it also involves a party's *willingness* to pay and perform. Everyone who extends credit knows that some people have the means or ability to pay and yet do not pay. Nonsimultaneous performance by all parties to a transaction, therefore, means that credit is extended with the possibility of future unwillingness to perform.

Transactional risk also includes a variety of potential problems that can arise from the actual mechanics of transfer — *transfer risk*. Whether it is the purchase and sale agreement between seller and buyer or the loan agreement between borrower and lender, the concept is the same. Risk arises from the process of transfer because of the possibility that any particular promise, warranty, or representation made by one party to another party may prove to be untrue or unenforceable, or at least not live up to the expectation of the party meant to be benefited. It can also arise from mistakes in document preparation, from errors in recording, or as a consequence of lost documentation. The more complex the transaction and the longer the period of time over which the transaction is to be conducted, the higher the level of risk.

I. LAWYER AS RISK MANAGER

Understanding the market risks associated with a real estate transaction illuminates the role and function of the lawyer. To a large extent the lawyer is hired to identify and manage the wide assortment of risks that can and should be anticipated in a particular transaction. The lawyer, of course, is supposed to be the expert on the law and may not be an expert in the many areas of market risk that may affect the viability of any given transaction. As a consequence, the lawyer must use her knowledge of the law to structure a managed approach to the variety of risks that may arise and to protect, as much as possible, the client's value expectations from the transaction. As a manager of risk, the lawyer must use the law to define clearly and fully the relationship and expectations of the parties. The lawyer must also be skilled at identifying areas of risk and concern, and at implementing effective methods for addressing them.

Problem 1B

Malloy and Smith are novice real estate developers in a coastal area in the State of Georgia. They investigate unimproved residential lots being offered for sale by a real estate broker. The lots are one acre in size and are located in a new development in which several very large homes are currently being built. Malloy and Smith both decide to buy a lot for their own personal use. On February 1, each contracts to buy a one-acre lot for $1 million. Each plans to subdivide his lot into two half-acre lots—one to sell to a market buyer and one to retain, where he will build a three-story vacation home with approximately 7,000 square feet. They plan to put the homes at a setback from the water of 100 feet. They expect to pay about $900,000 to build each home, and each is certain that the improved lots will be priced at $2.5 million by the time the homes are finished, and the unimproved half-acre lots will themselves be worth $800,000. After accounting for other expenses such as architecture fees, title work, and legal fees, each anticipates that the return on the investment will be around 30 percent at the time of completion of construction. Similar investment opportunities are currently returning 15 percent.

While Malloy and Smith are working out their plans to acquire the two lots, the Georgia Coastal Planning Commission is reviewing the progress of coastal land development under regulations pertaining to coastal land management and preservation.

On May 1, Malloy and Smith, having secured financing from Coastal Bank and Trust, close on their respective contracts, paying the $1 million per lot pursuant to their development plans. On July 1, of the same year, and prior to Malloy and Smith subdividing the lots and starting construction, the Georgia Coastal Planning Commission issues new regulations restricting development within the coastal area where the Malloy and Smith lots are located. The new regulations are designed to reduce the impact on coastal areas by restricting the size and density of new residential construction. The new regulations require all residential housing to be on a lot with a minimum size of one acre. The regulations also restrict the type of housing to one level ranch housing of a size no greater than 2,500 square feet. All housing and improvements must be set back from the water by at least 150 feet.

Malloy and Smith are extremely upset about the new regulations as the regulations dramatically affect their expectations. What were the expectations of Malloy and Smith going into the original residential development project and then later in purchasing the two lots? What kind of things might you be able to identify as their out-of-pocket costs, opportunity costs, sunk costs, and transaction costs? Under their original expectations, what did they see as their accounting profit relative to their economic profit? What types of precautionary steps might a lawyer take in advising a person such as Malloy or Smith when developing ocean-front property? What steps can and should be taken to acquire current and accurate information about the status of the property, and about any proposed legislation that may be in the works? What steps can be taken to reduce the risk of potential loss during the time it takes to acquire and develop a tract of land? How might a third-party lender, such as Coastal Bank and Trust, address the risks posed by potential land use regulations?

J. TYPES OF REAL ESTATE LAW PRACTICE

There are many types of real estate practice, but most real estate lawyers tend to think of the field as divided into two major market segments: residential and commercial. The legal work encountered in these two market segments is generally similar in nature but different in scope. There are also regional variations in what work is typically handled by lawyers in law firm settings rather than by other professionals. Each type of real estate practice must be sensitive to its own market context. In the past, there was not as drastic a split between residential and commercial real estate practices, and the knowledge needed for a real estate practice was often thought to be finite and circumscribed. Real estate practitioners could fare quite well if they could do title work and draft, with reasonable proficiency, standard types of instruments used in the jurisdiction where they practiced—deeds, leases, promissory notes, mortgages, oil and gas leases, and conveyances of other property interests. Their basic title work consisted in reviewing title to properties in accordance with local procedures and solving title defects and other title problems. Depending on local custom, this involved searching recorded instruments at the county courthouse, issuing title opinions, ordering and reviewing title abstracts, obtaining and reviewing title insurance, or some combination of these tasks. In rural and small urban areas, lawyers often combined real estate with probate and trust work. Because they represented individuals in connection with estate planning, they could rely on getting legal work when those clients wanted to buy or sell real estate, sign a lease, or obtain a loan secured by land. The lawyer might also represent a local bank in connection with its real estate work. This type of practice is why the ABA section for real estate practitioners became known as the Real Property, Probate & Trust Law Section, and why its journal is known as the *Real Property, Probate & Trust*

Law Journal. This old-line type of practice can still be found in some places, but it is no longer predominant and it is not the mainstream in urban areas. The practice of real estate has changed because the real estate business has changed. Now there is a significant difference between the scope of a residential and a commercial real estate practice. Residential practitioners are finding that many of their transactional activities are being taken over by an influx of competent, market-savvy nonlawyers, thus changing the nature and profitability of a residential practice. At the same time, commercial real estate lawyers have also been under pressure to change. Today increased specialization, interdisciplinary thinking, and the development of market expertise are needed to practice commercial real estate law.

We can better understand the differences between modern residential and commercial practices by briefly describing their basic market contexts. A residential real estate practice involves home sales (including single-family homes, condominiums, and cooperatives) and purchase financing. Occasionally the residential practitioner handles other matters as well, such as refinancing home loans, leasing, subdivision covenants, homeowners' associations, and nuisance disputes. In residential transactions, the lawyer is likely to represent one of three parties: buyer, seller, or lender. In some cases, the lawyer will represent more than one party, but this raises ethical problems concerning dual representation (this is discussed in detail in future chapters). A lawyer in a residential practice may be employed prior to or after a contract of purchase and sale has been entered into by the parties. Obviously, it is better to educate your clients to engage you to represent them before any contracts are signed. The contract is the main blueprint for the entire transaction, and the lawyer has the best opportunity for successful risk management when she is involved at the outset. If a client sees a lawyer after the contract has been entered into, there is much less that can be done for the client, because many risks and obligations have already been expressly or implicitly covered (or omitted) by the agreement. If both parties (buyer and seller) have attorneys prior to contracting, there is ample opportunity for negotiation. This situation, the presence of multiple lawyers in the residential setting, depends in part on local custom and to a large extent on the level of sophistication of the homebuyer or seller and the value of the property. One is more likely, for example, to find multiple lawyers involved in the sale of a $3 million home than a $120,000 home.

Although residential transactions sometimes involve substantial precontract negotiation between the buyer and the seller, usually very little is negotiated beyond the terms stated in a series of printed forms. This is also true with residential financing. Most residential mortgage financing is done on standardized forms with little or no room for negotiation with the lender. The lender will typically carry several types of mortgages that are structured to appeal to different market and risk motivations, but other than selecting the type of standard financing form offered, there is generally no negotiation concerning the terms of any given choice. For example, a lender may offer a choice between a 30-year or 15-year fixed rate mortgage and several differently priced adjustable rate mortgages, but the specific legal terms of all of these choices will be fixed by a standardized form. Lenders typically view residential transactions as low-profit activities with high administrative costs, so they seek efficiency and profit by using standard forms and concentrating on volume.

In most parts of the country, lawyers share the field of residential practice with nonlawyers. Real estate brokers, title companies, and escrow-closing agencies are among the types of nonlawyers who generally compete for a significant portion of the work. In many parts of the country these nonlawyers can fill in simple contract forms, assist buyers in the selection of a mortgage, and often prepare most or all of the closing documents. As a consequence, the residential market has become very competitive for lawyers; unless they have a niche with very wealthy clients, the key to success has become high volume and a standardized practice (just as for lenders). Many such lawyers employ paralegals to do most of the transactional work in an effort to keep costs down. Similarly, in today's computerized world, costs can be reduced by using one or more of the many highly effective software packages that generate the standard forms and documents used in a residential closing. Even title information, in the more populated parts of the country, is fully available online, thus reducing the cost of a simple residential title search. As a consequence of the intrusion of nonlawyers, the standardization of the practice, and the slim profit margins, there are generally fewer real estate lawyers involved in residential transactions today than in the past.

A commercial real estate practice builds on the basic contract, property, and mortgage law foundations of a residential transaction. It is much more interdisciplinary in nature than a residential practice, and it requires a greater understanding of financial and market information. Commercial real estate activities are national and international in scope and involve complex financial and development vehicles. The underlying object of these transactions is property, but commercial transactions are fully integrated commercial undertakings. They require the real estate lawyer to be competent in areas that transcend the traditional principles of contract, property, and mortgage law. Now, the commercial real estate lawyer must deal with law related to a number of other subjects, including taxation; corporations; business associations; securities; bankruptcy; the environment; land use and zoning; takings; torts; administrative law; the full range of the Uniform Commercial Code (UCC), with special concern for Article 2 Sales, 2A Leasing, 3 and 4 Commercial Paper and Fund Transfers, and 9 Secured Transactions; antitrust; and antidiscrimination regulations, including the Americans with Disabilities Act. She must also have an understanding of market forces, basic finance, and accounting. The commercial real estate lawyer prepares many contracts and documents that are not strictly real estate in nature. Some non–real-estate contracts might include partnership agreements, building management contracts, utility service agreements, cable television contracts, construction contracts, and mortgage securitization agreements, among others. Although some commercial real estate lawyers specialize in particular aspects of the practice, all must have an understanding of the connection between their specialty and the bigger picture that makes up the client's overall objective.

Given the changing nature of real estate law, driven by the tremendous financial market integration that has occurred in the past few years, it is safe to say that today even a residential practitioner must fully understand the workings of the commercial real estate market. This is because commercial real estate projects (subdivisions, condominiums, etc.) end up being the subject of residential sales, and residential mortgage markets are affected by activities in commercial lending markets. It is impossible to be a knowledgeable residential practitioner if you do not understand the bigger context in which a residential transaction is situated. At the same time, the commercial real estate lawyer must first encounter and learn the basics of a residential transaction if she is eventually to understand the scope and complexity of commercial real estate development and financing. The basic residential transaction contains all the essential elements necessary for understanding commercial real estate development. In the commercial setting, however, the basic problems become more complex because the number of parties, legal interests, and market factors increases.

K. LAWYERS' PROFESSIONAL RESPONSIBILITIES

Understanding real estate transactions in a market context raises certain questions about the professional responsibility of a lawyer. First and foremost is the question of the lawyer's role in the transaction. Should the lawyer in a real estate transaction be merely an instrument for the client's will and manipulation for a favorable market position? Or are there ethical limitations that make it inappropriate for her to act in a way that maximizes the client's return no matter what? The lawyer cannot function as a mere economic actor seeking to maximize profit, because the lawyer is subject to a code of professional conduct, which incorporates values and obligations that may not always be consistent with the client's market objectives. Still, there are issues of just how far a lawyer should or can go in promoting a client's business objectives. The idea of the lawyer as zealous advocate incorporates the marketplace image of an unrelenting fighter or tool of the client's desires. In contrast is the view of the lawyer as an officer of the court with public duties. Existing within this tension is a further question: Does the lawyer's role change with the context of the setting in which she is engaged? In other words, does a lawyer have as much support for zealous advocacy in the pursuit of a client's market interests as our society tends to allow in the defense of a client accused of a serious crime? Stated differently, should zealous advocacy mean different things in a market context than it does in a criminal law context and, if so, why? These are difficult questions for which there are no easy answers. Keep these questions in mind while thinking about the different types of real estate practice.

A discussion of the market context for real estate transactions would be incomplete if we did not say a few words about the manner in which lawyers expect to get paid for the legal services they provide. Legal fees are a subject covered by the ABA *Model Rules of Professional Conduct.* Under these rules, lawyers are expected to charge clients reasonable fees based on such factors as the complexity of the work, the amount of effort and expertise required, the likelihood that other employment opportunities will be forgone by taking on the matter, the significance of or the amount involved in the matter, the time limitation imposed, and any special reputational skills or talents possessed by the attorney. In all cases, it is best to think of work done for a client as a professional employment contract, thus indicating the desirability of reducing the arrangement to writing as would be prudent in other contractual contexts.

This written agreement generally takes the form of a fee agreement letter addressed to the client that explains the legal services to be provided in exchange for compensation. Although this agreement is often drafted in the form of a letter, it is advisable to have the client sign off on the letter, indicating that she understands and agrees to the terms. The fee agreement letter should be prepared early in the relationship, and the manner of earning compensation should be clearly defined, such as by a set rate per hour, a percentage based on the value of the transaction, a flat fee, or some other basis. The letter should also indicate when compensation is expected to be paid: at the completion of the transaction, every 30 days, or in some other manner. It is important to identify the manner in which late fees and overdue payment will be handled. The taking of a retainer should also be spelled out, and provisions for costs (copies, express mail charges, travel, filing fees, title searches, etc.) should also be addressed if costs are to be treated as separate from the professional fee. If the fee will include added or bonus payment for a successful outcome, then this too should be specifically stated; indeed, under Model Rule 1.5(c), contingency fee and bonus fee agreements *must* be written. In short, one of the first obligations owed to a client is a clear explanation of the professional services that you are competent to provide and a clear statement of the manner in which you expect to be paid. Having this understanding in writing will avoid many problems later on.

BOHN v. CODY
Supreme Court of Washington, 1992
119 Wash. 2d 35, 832 P.2d 71

JOHNSON, Justice. Lucille and Landis Bohn loaned money to their daughter after discussing aspects of the proposed loan with their daughter's attorney. After their daughter failed to repay the loan, the Bohns sued the attorney. The attorney moved for summary judgment on the theory that he owed no duty of care to the Bohns, because the Bohns were neither his clients nor were they within the class of third parties to whom an attorney would owe a duty of care. The trial court found that no duty of care existed and dismissed the Bohns' claims in contract and negligence. The trial court also dismissed the Bohns' claim that the attorney had violated the former attorney disciplinary rule regarding conflicts of interest. The Court of Appeals affirmed.

On the issue of duty, we reverse. Although we agree with the courts below that no attorney/client relationship was formed under these circumstances, genuine issues of material fact exist as to whether Bohn was within the class of nonclients to whom an attorney owes a duty of care. We affirm the dismissal of the claim alleging violation of the disciplinary rules.

I

The transaction at issue here had its roots in a foreclosure proceeding involving Dian and Marville Follett. The Folletts had purchased a house on a real estate contract and had subsequently failed to make a $15,000 balloon payment. George Cody represented the Folletts in defending the foreclosure action. The trial judge in the foreclosure action imposed a deadline of June 30, 1982 (plus a 5-day grace period) for the Folletts to pay the entire balance due under the contract.

Dian Follett was unable to obtain a commercial loan to cover the amount owed. She then approached her parents, Lucille and Landis Bohn, to borrow from them the necessary sum. Cody was not involved in these negotiations between the Folletts and the Bohns.

On June 30, 1982, Lucille Bohn met alone with Cody to discuss the situation. According to Cody, he told Lucille Bohn at the outset that he represented the Folletts in this matter, not the Bohns. Lucille Bohn does not dispute these statements. . . .

Lucille Bohn told Cody that she and her husband were willing to advance the necessary amount only if they could have "absolute security." Cody said he would prepare an assignment of the right to receive the deed from the contract vendors — the Heatheringtons — but added that he could do so only after obtaining the Folletts' approval. Lucille Bohn asked whether she would receive a "free and clear" deed. Cody responded that the deed would be free and clear of any liens resulting from the *Heatheringtons'* ownership of the property. Cody did not say whether any liens could have arisen from the *Folletts'* ownership interest. The Bohns contend that although the information in Cody's statement was technically accurate, it was misleading in its failure to fully address the question asked.

On July 2, 1982, Cody met with Lucille Bohn and Dian Follett. They had further discussions about the amount due under the contract. Later that day, Lucille Bohn posted approximately $50,000 — representing her and her husband's life savings — with the court registry on behalf of the Folletts. . . .

Later in July, the Heatheringtons' attorney made out a deed to the Folletts rather than to the Bohns. Lucille Bohn told Cody of this fact, and Cody indicated he would take care of it. Lucille Bohn offered to pay for his services in this regard. Cody stated, however, that he was doing so on behalf of the Folletts and that he was not acting as the Bohns' attorney. On July 29, Cody sent a letter to the Heatheringtons' attorney demanding that a deed be executed in favor of the Bohns. In this letter, Cody stated that he was "authorized to take court action to enforce the proper preparation and delivery of the deed. . . ." On August 5, the Heatheringtons issued a new deed naming the Bohns as grantees.

A few days later, Lucille Bohn learned that Internal Revenue Service (IRS) liens already encumbered the property. The IRS had filed the liens in order to collect unpaid taxes from the Folletts. These liens apparently were in place at the time when Cody discussed the deed with Bohn, but Cody denies knowing of the liens at that time and the Bohns do not argue that Cody actually knew of the liens. The Bohns do contend, however, that Cody should have known that such liens were possible. They point out that Cody represented the Folletts between 1980 and June 1981 with respect to tax disputes, and that even after June 1981 Cody had reason to suspect that the Folletts' tax difficulties continued.

Later in August, Lucille Bohn again approached Cody and insisted on paying Cody for his services. Cody told her that she owed nothing, but when she persisted, he suggested that she pay $50. Bohn paid him this amount but Cody used it to credit the Folletts' account.

The IRS subsequently sold the house to another couple. The Bohns were unable to redeem the house and consequently lost their interest in it. The Folletts never repaid the money to the Bohns.

The Bohns sued Cody for negligence, breach of contract and violation of the attorney disciplinary rules. Their complaint alleges that when Cody first met with Lucille Bohn he should have (1) advised her to seek independent counsel; (2) informed her of his potential conflict of interest in the transaction; (3) recommended that she obtain a title report; or (4) indicated that although the deed would be free of any liens against the Heatheringtons' interest, it could still be subject to any liens against the Folletts' interest. Lucille Bohn stated in an affidavit that she believed that Cody was acting as her attorney at all times relevant to this case.[1] . . .

II

. . . .

A. Existence of Attorney/Client Relationship

Determining whether an attorney/client relationship exists necessarily involves questions of fact. *See* 48 Am. Jur. Proof of Facts 2d, *Existence of Attorney-*

1. The Bohns have not alleged that Cody acted fraudulently or with intent to harm them.

Client Relationship 525 (1987); 1 R. Mallen & J. Smith, *Legal Malpractice* §11.2 (3d ed. 1989). . . .

The essence of the attorney/client relationship is whether the attorney's advice or assistance is sought and received on legal matters. *See* 1 R. Mallen & J. Smith §11.2 n.18; 7 Am. Jur. 2d *Attorneys at Law* §118 (1980). The relationship need not be formalized in a written contract, but rather may be implied from the parties' conduct. . . .

Cody told Lucille Bohn at the outset of their very first meeting that he could not act as her attorney in this matter, as he was already representing the Folletts. Lucille Bohn has not challenged this statement. Moreover, Cody reemphasized this point when he told Lucille Bohn later in the conversation that he would prepare the necessary documentation only upon obtaining the Folletts' approval.

Lucille Bohn maintains that despite these clear disclaimers she still believed that Cody was acting as her attorney. She argues that her belief was reasonably held because Cody gave her legal advice and performed legal services for her. First, she contends that he answered (though not fully) her questions concerning the effect of the assignment of the right to receive the fulfillment deed. An attorney/client relationship is not created, however, merely because an attorney discusses the subject matter of a transaction with a nonclient. *See* 1 R. Mallen & J. Smith §11.2. Second, she points out that Cody prepared the assignment paperwork. Yet an attorney for one party to a transaction does not become the other party's attorney merely because he prepared the documents formalizing the transaction. *See* 1 R. Mallen & J. Smith §8.2.

Lucille Bohn also relies on the letter Cody wrote seeking reissuance of the fulfillment deed to the Bohns. This letter, however, was written approximately 4 weeks after the conversations were held that form the basis for the Bohns' action. The important consideration here is the reasonableness of Lucille Bohn's belief at the time of the allegedly tortious acts. The occurrence of subsequent events has no bearing on this issue, for we are not concerned with whether Cody was acting as her attorney at a later time, and the letter gives no indication that he was acting as the Bohn's attorney at any prior time.

In light of Cody's disclaimers of any attorney/client relationship and in light of the Bohns' inability to show that Cody acted inconsistently with these statements, we conclude that Lucille Bohn's subjective belief was not reasonably based on the attending circumstances, and no attorney/client relationship was formed. Reasonable finders of fact could reach no other conclusion on the record here presented.

B. ATTORNEY'S DUTIES TOWARD THIRD PARTIES

Even in the absence of an attorney/client relationship, however, liability could still exist in this case. We next turn to whether Cody owed a duty of care to the Bohns even though they were not his clients.

Traditionally, a rule of strict privity limited an attorney's liability for malpractice. Under this rule, a malpracticing attorney could be held liable only to the attorney's own clients. *See* Stangland v. Brock, 109 Wn.2d 675, 680, 747 P.2d 464 (1987).

Privity of contract, however, is no longer required in all cases. Under certain circumstances, an attorney may be held liable for malpractice to a party the attorney never represented. Two theories provide the basis for this expanded liability. *Stangland,* at 680. First, an attorney may be held liable for negligence toward third party beneficiaries of an attorney/client relationship. *Stangland,* at 681; Bowman v. John Doe, 104 Wn.2d 181, 188, 704 P.2d 140 (1985). Second, an attorney may be held liable under a multifactor balancing test developed in California. This test involves analysis of the following six factors:

> the extent to which the transaction was intended to affect the plaintiff; the foreseeability of harm to the plaintiff; the degree of certainty that the plaintiff suffered injury; the closeness of the connection between the defendant's conduct and the injury; the policy of preventing future harm; and the extent to which the profession would be unduly burdened by a finding of liability. The inquiry under this multi-factor test has generally focused on whether the attorney's services were intended to affect the plaintiff.

(Citations omitted.) *Stangland,* at 680; *see also Bowman,* at 187-88.

Under the multifactor test, genuine issues of material fact exist as to whether Cody owed a duty of care to the Bohns. Each factor of that test will be examined separately.

1. Intent to affect the Bohns. A reasonable factfinder could infer from the evidence that Cody intended to affect the Bohns when he discussed the consequences of the proposed security arrangement for the $50,000 loan. An inference can reasonably be drawn from the evidence that Cody only told a portion of the truth in order to increase the likelihood that the Bohns would loan the money to the Folletts.

2. Foreseeability of harm. A reasonable factfinder could also infer that Cody's misleading statements would foreseeably harm the Bohns. First, given Lucille Bohn's apparent inexperience in financial affairs and given that she was lending money to her own daughter, it was certainly foreseeable that she would rely on Cody's statements about the fulfillment deed rather than seek verification elsewhere. Moreover, Cody was fully aware of the Folletts' recent financial difficulties, having represented them in at least two actions against their creditors. He knew that the Folletts had not been able to arrange conventional financing and that the IRS was having difficulties collecting payments from the Folletts in the year immediately preceding his misleading statements. Given this knowledge, a factfinder could find it foreseeable that Cody's statements would harm the Bohns.

3. Certainty of harm. The Bohns lost $50,000 — their life savings — in this transaction.

4. Proximity of harm. The Bohns' harm was proximately caused by the combination of the Folletts' failure to repay the money they borrowed and the failure of the fulfillment deed to provide any security. Based on the record so far developed in this case, we conclude that although Cody was not responsible for his clients' failure to repay the Bohns, he was directly responsible for the Bohns' reliance on the ineffective security and he had reason to know that the Folletts' financial situation was such that the security might actually be needed. Under these facts, Cody's conduct is proximately connected to the Bohns' harm.

5. Policy of preventing harm. This factor weighs strongly in favor of finding a duty. Based on the record so far developed in this case, we conclude the misleading nature of Cody's statements would justify imposing a duty of care, taking into account the amount of money here at stake, the foreseeability of the damages that the Bohns could suffer in this transaction, the foreseeability of their reliance, the familial relationship between the Folletts and the Bohns, and Lucille Bohn's express statements to Cody that she would make the loan only if she received absolute security. The policy of preventing harm under these circumstances is strong indeed.

6. Burden on the legal profession. Balanced against the importance of providing a remedy to those harmed by attorneys is the recognition that imposing liability could place an undue burden on practicing attorneys. Attorneys have a duty of zealously representing their clients within the bounds of the law. When their clients have opposing interests with third parties, attorneys are supposed to represent their clients' interests over the interests of others.

Imposing liability in the present case will not unduly burden an attorney's duty to represent his or her own clients. Under the extreme facts of this case, we hold simply that an attorney should advise the unrepresented party to seek independent counsel before the attorney discusses the transaction with that party. It was not enough in this case that Cody told Bohn that he was not acting as her attorney. This information does not sufficiently convey to the general public the adversarial stance an attorney must take toward those having interests different from the client's own interests. Moreover, if the attorney undertakes to tell part of the story to an unrepresented party with whom the attorney's client is doing business, the attorney must take reasonable steps to tell the whole story, not just the self-serving portions of it.

Because a duty could still exist between Cody and the Bohns, the Bohns' contract and negligence causes of action were improperly dismissed.

Problem 1C

Review the facts of Bohn v. Cody. What do you believe Cody could have done to reduce the risk of liability in this situation? What specific planning and transactional management steps might you take to reduce your own exposure to the risk of liability when dealing with client and nonclient participants in a transaction?

2
Real Estate Brokers

Real estate brokers perform the critical task of finding the parties for the deal. Usually the parties have never met and do not know each other until the broker brings them together. The broker thus plays the role of transactional intermediary in the market for property sale and exchange, but the broker does not simply disappear once the parties are found. Instead, the broker continues to facilitate the transaction by assisting the parties with matters such as contract negotiation, inspections of the property, and financing arrangements.

Brokers are information specialists; the primary service they offer is market information, which has great value because of brokers' training and experience and the systems they have created to share market data. They have access to information that the parties need about properties and the terms at which prospective participants are willing to deal. Brokers also have information about other market transactions that can provide guidance in determining the market value for a particular deal.

All 50 states regulate the business of real estate brokerage in order to create and maintain professional standards and to protect members of the public who interact with brokers. A state administrative agency, often called the *real estate commission* or the *department of real estate,* is responsible for enforcing the laws pertaining to brokers. There are two levels of licenses. A *broker* has a "full" license, and although he may work as an employee of a brokerage firm, he is qualified, just like an attorney, to "hang out his own shingle." In contrast, a real estate *salesperson* has a license that permits him to act as a broker only under the supervision of a licensed broker. Many states require that a broker first work as a salesperson before obtaining a broker's license.

Slightly more than half of the active brokers and salespersons in the United States are members of the National Association of Realtors (NAR), a trade association founded in 1908. The term *realtor,* which NAR has trademarked, means an NAR member, although in popular parlance it is often used as a synonym for *broker*. All the state associations of real estate brokers and most local real estate boards are members of NAR.

Brokers earn their living by collecting commissions. For a sale transaction, the commission is a percentage of the sales price. Other methods of compensating brokers are possible, such as a flat fee or payment on an hourly basis for time spent, but these are rarely used. In residential real estate sales, commissions paid to brokers who provide a full range of services (as opposed to "discount brokers," who are a small part of the market in most communities) typically range from 5 to 7 percent of the sales price. Sellers sometimes think such commissions are too high. After all, a 6 percent commission on a house sold for $200,000 is the tidy sum of $12,000. For this reason, a good number of homeowners try to sell without using a broker, a practice sometimes identified by the acronym FSBO (pronounced *fizzbo*)—for sale by owner. Many times FSBO attempts fail, either because the seller fails to attract a buyer or because the seller finds a buyer but agrees to less advantageous terms than a professional broker would have obtained.

In sale transactions, the broker's client is usually the seller. When a property owner hires a broker to sell his property, their contract is known as a *listing*. Typically, it is a written contract; usually it is better for both parties that they put the terms of the brokerage in writing. Indeed, some states have passed a special statute of frauds that requires a written broker's contract and bars a broker from recovering on an oral brokerage arrangement. In other states, an oral listing contract, if proven, is enforceable.

Four types of listing agreements for selling property are presently in common use. Under an *open listing* (nonexclusive listing), the broker earns his commission if he procures a ready, willing, and able buyer for the property. Other brokers can be engaged by the seller, in which event the first one to procure a buyer earns the commission. In addition, the seller can sell his property by himself, without a broker's help, in which event no commission is payable.

The *exclusive agency* agreement contains a promise by the seller not to engage another broker during the term of the agreement. The broker is the exclusive agent with respect to the listed property. If the owner sells using another agent, the exclusive agent is still entitled to his commission. Like the open listing, however, the owner may sell by his own efforts and thereby avoid a commission.

The *exclusive right to sell agreement* (or exclusive listing) is the most protective of the broker's expectation of earning the commission. The seller is obligated to pay the commission if any buyer purchases the property during the term of the agreement. It does not matter whether the broker procures the buyer, whether another broker finds the buyer, or whether the buyer and seller meet without the assistance of any broker.

The fourth type of agreement, the *net listing*, is less common than the other three types. The commission is not specified as a percentage, and the seller agrees to pay the broker all amounts received in excess of a set price established by the broker and the seller. The word *net* means the seller is guaranteed a net amount of sales proceeds, but that is also the limit of what the seller can get from the sale. The broker typically has discretion with respect to setting the listing price and will seek to sell at a higher price and pocket the difference. For example, the agreement might say the seller is to receive a net price of $100,000, and the broker might set an initial asking price of $110,000.

Many brokers are members of a *Multiple Listing Service* (MLS), which facilitates the sharing of listings among the MLS members. Real estate markets are by definition geographically local, and so are MLSs, which typically are citywide, countywide, or metropolitan. Each member broker submits new listings to the MLS, which compiles a directory or database with information pertaining to all current listings. The MLS broadens the market exposure for listed properties, which may benefit the seller. A potential buyer who contacts any member broker has the opportunity to see and consider any of the MLS properties. Almost all listings turned in to MLSs are exclusive right to sell listings. MLSs concentrate on residential properties, but most services also accept listings for vacant land and commercial properties.

The seller does not pay a higher commission by virtue of the listing going into a MLS. The broker who enters into the listing agreement with the seller is known as the *listing broker.* If a customer of another member broker buys the property, that broker is known as the *selling broker* or *cooperating broker.* The MLS agreements require a division of the standard commission between the listing broker and the selling broker. Often the division is 50 percent to each broker, but this can vary according to the local MLS regulations.

Problem 2A

Five years ago, Jack and Karen Sutter bought a three-bedroom house located at 1510 Cedar Avenue, Pine City. Having outgrown their home, the Sutters are ready to sell and trade up to a newer, more expensive residence. They do not know a broker in Pine City. One of Karen's friends sold a home recently, and Karen contacted her friend's broker, Betty Baxter.

What type of commission agreement will Betty want? What type of commission agreement will Jack and Karen want? For each party, what are the advantages and disadvantages of each type of brokers' contract? Should Jack and Karen try to negotiate a low commission rate? What other terms in the brokers' contract are important to the parties?

A. BROKERS' DUTIES TO CLIENTS

When a person hires a broker, their relationship is governed chiefly by the law of contracts and the law of agency. With respect to his client, the broker, just like the lawyer, is a fiduciary. Though there are many other aspects of fiduciary relationships that may bear on the broker-client relationship, three primary duties often come into play: the broker's *duty of loyalty*, the broker's *duty of disclosure*, and the broker's *duty of confidentiality*.

Loyalty encompasses traits such as honesty and fidelity. The broker should do his utmost to protect the client and advance the client's interest. The client wants to engage in a real estate transaction to create value, and it is the broker's role to assist in creating value by using his time, experience, and knowledge. In selling property, one aspect of loyalty concerns property value and price. The seller wants to sell at the highest price possible, and the broker is charged with the duty of obtaining a sufficient sales price.

Closely related to loyalty is the broker's duty of disclosure. When a broker learns facts or other information that are material to the client's position or interests, the broker should promptly tell the client. The broker must keep the client informed.

The duty of confidentiality is the flip side of the disclosure duty. In the course of representing a client, the broker gains information about the client's objectives and the property that, absent the client's consent, should not be disclosed to third parties. Sometimes the client's interest is simply privacy, but often the information has economic value.

To whom does the broker owe the duties of loyalty, disclosure, and confidentiality? Usually the identity of the broker's principal or client is plain and clear, but this is not always the case. Most of the time, the broker represents the seller. The broker met the seller prior to the buyer's coming on the scene, and usually the broker and the seller have signed a listing agreement that details their agency relationship, the commission arrangements, and other matters related to the undertaking.

There are several reasons why the identification of agency relationships sometimes gets complicated or obscured. First, *dual agency* is permissible in most states. This means a broker may lawfully represent both the seller and the buyer in the same transaction, provided that the broker discloses the dual agency to both parties who consent to the arrangement. Dual agency poses obvious problems, such as the potential for conflicting duties of loyalty, disclosure, and confidentiality. Nevertheless, the practice is allowed; because of its risks, however, many brokers have adopted the policy of not engaging in dual agency relationships.

Second, brokers do very many things to facilitate transactions, and the context of any dispute that arises may affect the issue of who represents whom. A broker who is clearly the seller's agent for the primary duty of selling the property may act as the buyer's agent with respect to a collateral task. For example, if a broker helps the buyer obtain financing, with respect to this work the broker may be the buyer's agent. With respect to some chores, such as preparing documents required for the closing, the broker may be a dual agent of both parties.

Third, agent relationships tend to get confused when two brokers, a listing broker and a selling broker, are involved with the same transaction. This happens in a large percentage of residential sales within the MLS system. The listing broker is clearly the seller's agent. It is the position of the selling broker, or cooperating broker, that clouds matters. The selling broker is the agent who deals directly with the prospective buyer, typically showing the buyer a number of properties that may suit his needs. This broker tries hard to find just the right house for the buyer, who often gets the justifiable impression that the broker is on his side, working for him. Yet the traditional rule is that the selling broker, just like the listing broker, is the seller's agent, even though the seller and the selling broker may meet for the first time at closing or may never meet. The selling broker is considered the listing broker's *subagent,* who is engaged by the listing broker to help perform his task. This view is reinforced by the scheme for compensating the selling broker. The buyer does not pay the selling broker; instead, the listing broker shares part of his commission with the selling broker.

The traditional subagency rule has been widely criticized on two grounds: first, that buyers are misled into thinking that the selling broker is *their* agent; and second, that buyers deserve representation at the critical stage of selecting a property and negotiating the terms of a purchase contract. Presently, more than 40 states mandate a written disclosure, either by statute or by broker's regulation. The disclosure forms vary widely from state to state. Most states expressly permit not only seller's agents but also buyer's agents (discussed later) and, with consent of both parties, dual agency.

Over the years, the percentage of homebuyers who hire buyers' brokers has risen steadily, as the obvious advantages have become better known. This is partially due to market specialization, with many brokers choosing to concentrate on buyer representation and advertise their services as such. Moreover, statutorily required disclosures of agency relationships have raised awareness among homebuyers that they have a choice in the matter.

A recently touted alternative to the formation of agency relationships with seller and buyer is the device known as *transaction brokerage* or *nonagency brokerage.* Under this arrangement, the broker sells services but has no formal agency relationship with either party. The broker's role is described as facilitator, intermediary, or middleman. Transaction brokerage avoids the creation of fiduciary duties, thereby implying that the broker should not become an advocate for, or give advice to, either party. The primary advantage of transaction brokerage from the broker's perspective is risk reduction. Beginning in the late 1990s, many states passed statutes that define transaction or nonagency brokerage and authorize brokers, upon proper disclosure, to enter into such relationships.

DUBBS v. STRIBLING & ASSOCIATES

Court of Appeals of New York, 2001
96 N.Y.2d 337, 728 N.Y.S.2d 413, 752 N.E.2d 850

GRAFFEO, J. At issue is whether a real estate broker breached a fiduciary duty owed a principal. For the reasons that follow, we conclude that the Appellate Division properly dismissed plaintiffs' breach of fiduciary duty claim.

Because the complaint was dismissed on a motion for summary judgment, the facts are viewed in the light most favorable to the plaintiffs. Plaintiffs placed their Manhattan cooperative apartment on the market in 1994 as an "open listing." Under this arrangement, any real estate broker who located a purchaser for the property would be entitled to a commission from plaintiffs. Defendant Stribling & Associates, a real estate brokerage firm, through its agents, defendant Avery Chappel-Smith (a licensed salesperson) and defendant Judith Durham (a licensed broker), showed plaintiffs' apartment to several prospective purchasers. Plaintiffs confided to Chappel-Smith and Durham that they would have preferred to retain their apartment and purchase the adjacent apartment, combining the two into one residence. Because the owner of the adjacent apartment was unwilling to sell, plaintiffs had decided to sell their apartment and purchase a larger property.

After showing plaintiffs' apartment on several occasions to potential purchasers, Chappel-Smith and her husband decided to submit an offer to purchase the apartment themselves. Durham presented the proposal to plaintiffs, indicating that the brokerage commission to which defendants would have been entitled had they located a third-party purchaser would be waived because Chappel-Smith was an agent of the brokerage firm. Durham cautioned plaintiffs to contact their neighbor one more time to make certain purchase of the adjacent apartment was not a viable option before they accepted Chappel-Smith's offer. Plaintiffs maintained that they advised their neighbor to "name her price" but she again declined to sell.

Accordingly, in December 1994 plaintiffs entered into a written contract with Chappel-Smith and her husband for the sale of their apartment. In the section of the standard form contract which identifies the broker involved in the transaction, the parties inserted the word "none." Paragraph 12.2 of the contract, a provision referencing the seller's obligation to pay the broker the commission owed under a separate agreement between the seller and the broker, was crossed-out in its entirety. Indeed, because the apartment was an "open listing," plaintiffs had not entered into a separate agreement with defendants when the apartment was placed on the market and, the commission having been waived, no written brokerage agreement was created when plaintiffs contracted to sell to Chappel-Smith.

The purchase contract also provided for delay of the closing for several months to allow plaintiffs time to find a new home. In the months that followed, Durham and Chappel-Smith showed plaintiffs several properties but plaintiffs eventually located an apartment through another brokerage firm, entering into a written purchase contract for that property in March 1995. The closing on the sale of plaintiffs' apartment to Chappel-Smith and her husband occurred on May 30, 1995. Plaintiffs then acquired title to their new apartment.

Approximately three weeks prior to the May 30 closing, Chappel-Smith had reached an oral agreement with plaintiffs' neighbor to purchase the apartment adjacent to plaintiffs, with the same desire to combine the two apartments. Plaintiffs were not advised that the neighboring apartment had been placed on the market or that Chappel-Smith intended to purchase it and they remained unaware of this turn of events when they consummated the sale of their apartment to Chappel-Smith. On June 5, 1995, Chappel-Smith and her husband entered into a written contract to purchase the adjacent apartment.

When plaintiffs discovered the arrangement between Chappel-Smith and their former neighbor, they commenced this action alleging, among other claims, that defendants breached a fiduciary duty when they failed to inform plaintiffs that the adjacent apartment had been placed on the market. On defendants' motion for summary judgment made after extensive discovery, Supreme Court dismissed the complaint. The Appellate Division affirmed and plaintiffs appeal as of right on a two-Justice dissent. We now affirm.

In New York, it is well settled that a real estate broker is a fiduciary with a duty of loyalty and an obligation to act in the best interests of the principal. *See* Northeast Gen. Corp. v. Wellington Adv., 82 N.Y.2d 158, 163, 604 N.Y.S.2d 1, 624 N.E.2d 129 (clarifying the distinction between a broker and a finder); Wendt v. Fischer, 243 N.Y. 439, 154 N.E. 303. The broker/principal relationship and accompanying fiduciary duty can be severed by agreement of the parties or by unilateral action of the principal. *See* Midcourt Bldrs. Corp. v. Eagan, 31 N.Y.2d 728, 337 N.Y.S.2d 527, 289 N.E.2d 564 (broker/vendor relationship terminated when the vendor issued a written notice of cancellation of sales authorization). Where a broker's interests or loyalties are divided due to a personal stake in the transaction or representation of multiple parties, the broker must disclose to the principal the nature and extent of the broker's interest in the transaction or the material facts illuminating the broker's divided loyalties. "[T]he disclosure to be effective must lay bare the truth, without ambiguity or reservation, in all its stark significance." Wendt v. Fischer, *supra*, 243 N.Y. at 443, 154 N.E. 303 (citations omitted).

Applying these principles to this case, we conclude that defendants were entitled to summary judgment. Certainly, as a broker who endeavored to obtain a personal interest in the principals' property, Chappel- Smith had a duty to inform plaintiffs of her intent to purchase their apartment and to disclose any information that could reasonably bear on plaintiffs' consideration of her offer. She clearly fulfilled this obligation for there is no evidence in the record that Chappel-Smith withheld any relevant information that was in her possession at the time she and her husband entered into the 1994 purchase contract with plaintiffs.

Additionally, defendants demonstrated by reference to the December 1994 purchase contract that plaintiffs had agreed that no broker would be involved in facilitating completion of the transaction. Plaintiffs did not counter this documentary evidence with any proof to the contrary. After making full disclosure — consistent with her fiduciary duty — Chappel-Smith entered into a purchase contract with plaintiffs, placing her on the opposite side of an arm's length transaction. Under these circumstances, Chappel-Smith could no longer be considered plaintiffs' broker. Indeed, in the purchase contract itself plaintiffs expressly recognized that the preexisting broker/principal relationship had been discontinued. Thus, plaintiffs had no reasonable basis to expect defendants to continue to act as fiduciaries with respect to sale of their apartment. *See* Midcourt Bldrs. Corp. v. Eagan, *supra*. We note further that defendants had no involvement in plaintiffs' March 1995 contract for purchase of their new apartment — a property they located through a different broker.

Finally, in opposing summary judgment, plaintiffs speculated that Chappel-Smith may have known of their neighbor's intent to sell her apartment prior to May 1995 when the neighbor listed the property with several brokers. They did not, however, offer proof in evidentiary form countering the sworn statements of defendants and the neighbor indicating otherwise. The neighbor testified at an examination before trial that she did not decide to sell her property until early May 1995. Defendants averred that they did not learn the property was available until the neighbor placed it on the market on May 8 or 9, five months after plaintiffs executed the purchase contract with Chappel-Smith and two months after plaintiffs contracted for their new apartment. Thus, the admissible evidence in the record indicates that, by the time defendants learned the neighbor's property was available, they were no longer working for plaintiffs and plaintiffs were no longer seeking an apartment.

To the extent plaintiffs' breach of duty claim is predicated on an allegation that Chappel-Smith used to her personal advantage confidential information plaintiffs imparted to her concerning the manner in which the two apartments could be joined, it was properly dismissed. Plaintiffs failed to rebut defendants' proof that this construction option was not confidential or exclusive for as early as 1991 a floor plan showing precisely how two similar apartments in plaintiffs' building had been combined was on file at defendants' brokerage firm and available for use by any of its agents.

Under the circumstances, we conclude plaintiffs failed to raise a material question of fact warranting a trial on the breach of fiduciary duty claim. Defendants' application for summary judgment dismissing the complaint was, therefore, properly granted.

Accordingly, the order of the Appellate Division should be affirmed, with costs.

Problem 2B

Bill and Tricia Nelson just learned that they're moving out of state in two months, when Tricia will start a new job. They listed their house for sale with Bonnie, a broker who promptly turned the listing in to the local multiple listing service. The listing agreement specifies a price of $270,000, but when the Nelsons signed the listing agreement, they told Bonnie that they would gladly take $240,000 for the house.

(a) Bonnie is approached by an interested prospective buyer, who inquires as to whether the sellers will accept less than the asking price of $270,000. What should Bonnie say? Can she tell the buyer that he can get the property for $240,000?

(b) Alfred Hanes is interested in buying a home, so he contacts Rick Carson, a residential broker, to find out what's available. Rick arranges with Bonnie to show the Nelsons' house to Alfred. What duties does Rick have to Alfred? Should he disclose that the property can be bought for less than $270,000? Should he disclose that the Nelsons plan to move soon and for this reason may have extra motivation to accept a low offer?

(c) Alfred told Rick that he went through bankruptcy three years ago and has a bad credit rating, which he is seeking to improve. Should Rick disclose this to the Nelsons if Alfred makes an offer for the property?

B. BROKER'S RIGHT TO A COMMISSION

In most sales transactions, the broker is paid his commission at closing, with the seller using part of the price paid by the buyer for this purpose. When the broker is paid this way, the legal question of when the broker earned the commission does not arise. The issue becomes important only if, for some reason, after the broker finds a potential buyer, the sale does not go forward to close.

In this type of situation, the general rule followed by a majority of American jurisdictions is favorable to the broker. The broker earns his commission when he produces a customer who is ready, willing, and able to purchase upon terms acceptable to the owner. This is interpreted to mean that the broker finishes his undertaking prior to closing, when he presents his client, the owner, with an acceptable written offer to purchase.

In spite of the general rule, sellers frequently defeat brokers' claims for commissions on sales that fail to close. One well-recognized exception to the general rule involves conditions set forth in the contract of sale. Most contracts have express conditions that, if not satisfied, give one or both parties the right to terminate the contract. If the sale fails to close due to an unsatisfied condition, the broker is generally not entitled to a commission.

Sellers have also won many cases based on express contract. The basic rule that the commission is earned when a buyer is found is subject to modification by the parties. The broker and the seller are free to replace the implied rule with an express provision of their own. A savvy seller would negotiate for a term making closing an express condition to payment of the commission. Sellers, however, infrequently do this. For residential sales, they almost never are represented by a lawyer in connection with the listing agreement, and for commercial sales, they also often forgo legal representation at this stage. As a result, brokers generally control the terms of the listing agreement, using standardized agreements prepared by local or state brokers' associations or in-house forms prepared by or for the broker's office.

Beginning with New Jersey in Ellsworth Dobbs, Inc. v. Johnson, 236 A.2d 843 (N.J. 1967), a number of courts have protected sellers simply by overruling the traditional doctrine. Under the new minority rule, for the broker to earn the commission, not only must he find a ready, willing, and able buyer, but also the sale must close. If the buyer defaults, no commission is payable. There is one exception to the new rule. If the failure to complete the sale is caused by the seller's wrongful default or interference, then a commission is payable. The reasoning is that the seller should not be able to deprive the broker of his commission by refusing to go forward. This rule is an emerging trend, although most states still follow the traditional rule. In states following the trend, it is sometimes not clear whether the parties retain freedom of contract to replace the new implied rule with a pro-broker term. For example, can the broker expressly contract for the traditional rule, with the seller thus waiving the benefit of the new rule? One judicial view disallows such a contract on public policy grounds, reasoning that such a contract is unconscionable due to an inequality of bargaining position and knowledge between broker and customer. The *Ellsworth Dobbs* court took this position.

When considering a commission dispute, the presence of earnest money or a down payment paid by the buyer is an additional consideration to bear in mind. If a buyer defaults after signing a contract, the earnest money is often forfeited to the seller. Many brokers' listing contracts expressly give the broker the right to take all or part of the commission out of the forfeited earnest money. This approach helps the seller, in that the seller does not have to come up with funds out-of-pocket to pay the commission. However, it may surprise a seller who did not pay close attention to the clause, which typically appears as boilerplate in the listing contract, the sales contract, or both.

Occasionally, the seller's agent or subagent has sought damages against a buyer who defaulted after signing a contract with the agent's principal. The theory is that the buyer's wrongful conduct has deprived the broker of the commission that he would have collected. Traditionally, the lack of an express contract barred such claims, based on the notion that liability should be predicated on privity. In addition, the broker had the alternative remedy of collecting the commission from the seller, even though the transaction had not closed. In turn, the seller who coughed up the commission generally had an action against the defaulting buyer for consequential damages.

Under the modern trend that insulates the seller from liability for the commission when the buyer defaults, it is much harder for the broker to collect a commission from the seller for a sale that does not close. Thus, there is greater incentive for brokers to pursue defaulting buyers. With the demise of the doctrine of privity in much of our law, some states have permitted brokers to recover based on contract and tort theories. Under contract analysis, an implied contract is found if the broker performs some services for the buyer. In exchange, the buyer has impliedly promised the broker that she will complete the transaction. Alternatively, recovery is justified by calling the broker a third-party beneficiary of the purchase agreement between the buyer and the seller. Under tort analysis, the defaulting buyer has engaged in tortious interference with contract. This is especially likely to succeed when the broker, such as a subagent who serves as a cooperating broker, has a working relationship with the buyer. The reasoning is that the buyer who defaults has tortiously interfered with the listing contract, pursuant to which the broker was to earn a commission. This deprives the broker of his prospective economic advantage.

HILLIS v. LAKE

Supreme Judicial Court of Massachusetts, 1995
421 Mass. 537, 658 N.E.2d 687

Greaney, J. The plaintiffs [Duane Hillis and John Brady], partners in a real estate brokerage firm, brought this action in the Superior Court to recover a commission on a sale of real estate. The complaint asserted claims of breach of contract, quantum meruit, and a violation of G.L. c.93A, §11 (1994 ed.). The case was tried before a judge sitting without a jury. The judge concluded that the plaintiffs were entitled to a commission with interest and, on her finding of a violation of G.L. c.93A, an award of attorney's fees. The Appeals Court reversed the judgment. . . . We also conclude, in substantial agreement with the reasoning of the Appeals Court, that the plaintiffs were not entitled to a commission. . . . We also take the opportunity to state that Bennett v. McCabe, 808 F.2d 178 (1st Cir. 1987), on which the plaintiffs rely, and which supports their position, is not a correct statement of Massachusetts law on the point with which we are concerned.

. . . Donald Lake, and his wife, Joanna, in their capacity as trustees of Lakeland Park Trust (defendants), were the owners of a parcel of real estate in Peabody which they had purchased in 1984, with the intent of developing the land as an industrial park. Before purchasing the property, Lake had it examined for the presence of hazardous materials as defined by G.L. c.21E. Hazardous materials were not found. Lake also owned a construction company, and his intention in developing the park was to build to suit for prospective tenants. John Brady, a partner in a commercial real estate firm, met Lake in 1986, while Brady was seeking a suitable site for a building for his client, Federal Express. An agreement was concluded between Lake and Federal Express, which became one of the first tenants of the industrial park.

After this successful collaboration, at Lake's request, Brady became the exclusive broker for the industrial park. The agreement between Lake and Brady was oral. It was understood that Lake was only interested in tenants for whom he would construct a building, and who, after construction was completed, might lease or purchase outright the resulting structure. Brady's commissions were to be five percent of the gross sale price.

First Agreement

Around April, 1988, Brady received an inquiry from the vice-president of Patriot Properties, Inc. (Patriot), who indicated that the company wanted to construct an office building. Brady showed the property in Peabody to principals of the company, and he arranged a meeting between Lake and Patriot's principals. On June 14, 1988, a purchase and sale agreement was executed between Patriot and the defendants for the purchase of land and a building constructed to Patriot's specifications. The purchase price was set at $1,810,000. The agreement provided for a broker's commission of $54,300, payable "if and provided the Closing occurs as herein described."[4] With a $400,000 construction mortgage from the Bank of New England in hand, Lake's construction company commenced construction of the building. At all times, Patriot's principals intended to seek additional investors in the project. It was anticipated that Patriot's principals would own a thirty-seven and one-half percent interest in the project and two other investors would own the remainder.

The purchase and sale agreement obligated Patriot to provide a mortgage commitment letter to the defendants. By a letter dated September 28, 1988, First American Bank issued a financing commitment in the amount of $1,410,000. A condition of the commitment was a requirement that, at the option of the bank, it would be provided with evidence that the property did not contain any hazardous materials. In response to this requirement, the defendants and Patriot executed an addendum to the purchase and sale agreement, in which the defendants warranted that the property was free of hazardous materials.[5] The bank, nonetheless, insisted on an inspection,

4. Brady had agreed to reduce his commission to three percent of the purchase price. The plaintiffs did not sign the purchase and sale agreement.

5. In signing the addendum, Patriot acknowledged receipt of a copy of the report on the G.L. c.21E inspection that had been conducted in 1984, in conjunction with the defendants' purchase of the property. Patriot also agreed to assume the cost of further inspections for hazardous materials.

which disclosed the presence of contamination in the ground water.[6] The bank withdrew its financing commitment, and the investors other than Patriot also withdrew from participation in the project. Patriot, however, which had been occupying the already completed building rent free for several months, remained interested in completing the purchase.

Second Agreement

By June, 1989, Patriot had located another investor, Ro-Jo Realty Trust, whose principals agreed to acquire a twenty-five percent interest in the project. As had been the case under the first agreement, Patriot's principals would acquire a thirty-seven and one-half percent interest in the project. To conclude the transaction, Lake himself agreed to acquire the remaining thirty-seven and one-half percent interest in the project. A joint venture was formed, known as the Five Lakeland Park Partners, which became the sole beneficiary of a newly organized trust, the Five Lakeland Park Trust.

Each of the three partners contributed a share in the initial capitalization ($500,000) of the project in proportion to his, or its, interest in the project. On June 13, 1989, the building and land were sold by the defendants to Five Lakeland Park Trust for $1,810,000. The parties did not obtain financing for the deal from a third party. Lake himself financed the transaction. The buyer paid $400,000 in cash, and executed a mortgage note to the defendant in the amount of $1,410,000, secured by a purchase money mortgage on the property. An agreement concluded simultaneously with the sale provided that:

> [i]f, on or before [June 12, 1991] the Seller delivers to the Buyer a report of a qualified environmental scientist or engineer . . . stating that there is no evidence of hazardous waste or oil . . . present on the Property . . . the Buyer shall exercise its best efforts to pay the unpaid principal balance and accrued interest due on the [mortgage note] as soon as is reasonably practical. . . . If the Seller has not delivered the Report . . . to the Buyer on or before [June 12, 1991], the Buyer, at its option, may elect to require the Seller to repurchase the Property from the Buyer for the sum of [$1,810,000].

The defendants used the $400,000 in cash received at the time of the sale to pay off the construction mortgage held by the Bank of New England. From June 13, 1989, through approximately October 3, 1991, monthly payments were made by Five Lakeland Park Trust on the mortgage notes. Lake contributed his pro rata share to these payments. At the end of two years, the defendants were not able to produce certification that the contamination

6. It was subsequently determined that gasoline had leaked from an underground tank installed by Federal Express in connection with its business operation in the industrial park. The judge made no finding that the defendants knew about the leak or about contamination from any other source, and no such finding would have been warranted.

on the property had been cleaned up. In keeping with the June 13, 1989, agreement, the defendants repurchased the property and discharged the mortgage. The $400,000 cash contribution was refunded to the investors in proportion to their shares in the project. The plaintiffs received no commission on the June 13, 1989, sale of the property.

Based on these facts, the judge concluded that the sale contemplated in the first agreement "did not close in accordance with the parties' contract only because of the seller's inability to back up its promise that the land was free of toxic materials such as gasoline." This lapse on the defendants' part was sufficient, in the judge's view, to require payment of a broker's commission to the plaintiffs. We do not agree that the conditions for payment of a broker's commission were met.

1. "When a broker is engaged by an owner of property to find a purchaser for it, the broker earns his commission when (a) he produces a purchaser ready, willing and able to buy on the terms fixed by the owner, (b) the purchaser enters into a binding contract with the owner to do so, and (c) the purchaser completes the transaction by closing the title in accordance with the provisions of the contract." Tristram's Landing, Inc. v. Wait, 367 Mass. 622, 629, 327 N.E.2d 727 (1975), *quoting* Ellsworth Dobbs, Inc. v. Johnson, 50 N.J. 528, 551, 236 A.2d 843 (1967). The third requirement was not met here because no closing occurred under the first agreement.

The requirement that the sale actually be consummated, however, is subject to an exception. We have said that a broker has an enforceable claim when the first two requirements are met but "the failure of completion of the contract results from the wrongful act or interference of the seller." *Id.* . . .

The exception does not apply to this case. The defendants had not agreed to remove hazardous materials from the property. As the Appeals Court observed:

> The Addendum provided that the failure of the defendants' representation was an occasion only for Patriot's right to terminate the agreement, not for a claim to damages for a wilful default in the obligations of the defendants. Any failure of the defendants' representation was to be regarded as the same as the failure of Patriot, for example, to obtain a mortgage commitment letter: each event was an occasion to terminate the transaction without fault by or liability to either party.

38 Mass. App. Ct. at 229, 646 N.E.2d 1081. We agree with this analysis. The judge did not find, and no such finding would have been warranted on the evidence, that the failure of the sale was the product of any bad faith or wrongful interference by the defendants. We conclude that the failure of the first agreement was not caused by any wrongful conduct on the defendants' part.

2. As the Appeals Court correctly recognized, the plaintiffs would still be entitled to a commission "if the second agreement was merely different from

the first agreement in form, not substance, and if there was a closing on that agreement, or a wilful default by the defendants." 38 Mass. App. Ct. at 229, 646 N.E.2d 1081. *See* Bonin v. Chestnut Hill Towers Realty Corp., 392 Mass. 58, 66, 466 N.E.2d 90 (1984) (commission due when transaction, "while different in form, conformed in substance to the terms of the agreement"); Morad v. Haddad, 329 Mass. 730, 734-735, 110 N.E.2d 364 (1953) (same). Here, the second agreement differed substantially from the first agreement, and the difference rendered the second agreement substantially less favorable to the defendants than the first agreement had been.

Under the first agreement, the defendants would have been guaranteed a return of $1,810,000 minus the cost of their investment in the project. That investment would have consisted only of some portion of the original purchase price of the property and the approximately $400,000 cost of constructing the building to Patriot's specifications. Any risk of default by the purchaser would have rested with the bank which loaned the funds to Patriot and its fellow investors to make the purchase. In contrast, the second agreement required that the defendants assume virtually all of the financial risk associated with the project. The financial risk to the defendants under the second agreement was twofold. Because the defendants were the holders of the mortgage on the property, the risk of default by the purchaser fell wholly on the defendants. In addition, the sale under the second agreement was contingent: if the defendants were unable to provide assurance, within two years, that contamination on the property had been eliminated, the sale would be rescinded. That these financial risks to the defendants were significant is proved by the fact that the sale was rescinded in 1991. Moreover, under the second agreement, instead of an outright conveyance of the entire property, Lake was required to retain a thirty-seven and one-half percent interest in the project, which might or might not have proved profitable, but which created additional financial risks and apparently was not an investment envisioned during the discussions between Brady and Lake.[7] Clearly, the second agreement, which would appear attributable to some desperation on the defendants' part, differed in substance from the first agreement. Thus, we agree with the Appeals Court that the plaintiffs were not entitled to a commission on the basis of the sale under the second agreement.[8]

7. Under the agreement between Brady and Lake, the defendants would have been required to pay a commission in the absence of an outright sale if a tenant was found who was willing (like Federal Express) to enter into a long-term lease on a building constructed to the prospective lessor's specifications. The second agreement was not analogous to a long-term lease.

8. The plaintiffs place weight on a June 2, 1989, letter written by Lake to Brady that terminated the parties' brokerage agreement. In the letter, Lake also indicated that he intended to pay any commissions due to the plaintiffs and noted: "We have already discussed Patriot Properties and that commission will be paid as soon as possible." There was conflicting testimony on the content of the discussion between Lake and Brady to which the letter referred. As the Appeals Court noted, "[i]n particular, it is unclear whether, or the extent

3. We comment briefly on Bennett v. McCabe, 808 F.2d 178 (1st Cir. 1987). In that case, the parties executed a purchase and sale agreement for the purchase of a motel. The real estate broker received a ten percent deposit from the buyer which was held in escrow pending the closing. Prior to the closing, the parties discovered a defect in title which no one knew of previously. When the seller was unable to correct the defect in a timely manner, the seller asked the broker to return the deposit to the prospective purchaser. The broker declined and brought an action in the United States District Court for the District of Massachusetts seeking to recover a broker's commission. The District Court granted summary judgment for the defendants on the basis of Tristram's Landing v. Wait, *supra.* The United States Court of Appeals for the First Circuit reversed. The Court of Appeals detected a "gray area" in the *Tristram's Landing* decision concerning a default by a seller that did not amount to wrongful acts or interference. *Id.* at 181. The Court of Appeals held that the seller would be liable for a broker's commission even if the seller's default was innocent, concluding that this court would adopt this conclusion if it were faced with facts like those in the *Bennett* case. *Id.* at 182. In so doing, the Court of Appeals assumed that this court would prefer a "bright line rule" which would award a broker the commission when the seller defaults on a binding purchase and sale agreement whether the default is innocent or motivated by bad faith. *Id.* at 183-184.

The *Bennett* decision does not state Massachusetts law correctly. . . . In circumstances like those present in this case and in the *Bennett* case, the broker is not entitled to a commission unless it appears that the closing is prevented by wrongful conduct on the seller's part. . . .

4. The judgment is reversed, and a new judgment is to enter in favor of all defendants on the counts in the plaintiffs' complaint.

Problem 2C

Ted and Karen Troop list their four-bedroom colonial for sale with Brandy, a local broker. On January 10 they sign an exclusive listing agreement, with a term of four months, a selling price of $180,000, and a commission of 5 percent. On February 23, Brandy presents a contract from Sam for $168,000, along with a check for $3,000 of earnest money made payable to a local title company. The Troops accept the contract and sign

to which, the restructured deal of June 12th was fully formed on June 2d, and, if so, what impact the new structure was to have on the plaintiffs' right to a commission." 38 Mass. App. Ct. at 225-226 n.9, 646 N.E.2d 1081. In view of our conclusion that, as a matter of law, the plaintiffs were not entitled to a commission in the circumstances present here, we give no significance to Lake's ambiguous promise to pay.

it, but the transaction never closes. In which of the following situations has Brandy earned a commission? If Brandy has earned a commission, when is it payable?

(a) The reason the transaction never closes is that Sam changes his mind and defaults.

(b) The reason the transaction never closes is that Sam has a poor credit history, and even though he has a high-paying job, he is turned down for a mortgage loan.

(c) The reason the transaction never closes is that the Troops change their mind about selling their house. They negotiate a rescission with Sam, which provides for the return of his earnest money plus the Troops' payment to Sam of an additional $1,000.

(d) The reason the transaction never closes is that the title search discloses an easement on the property, to which Sam objects.

C. BROKERS AND LAWYERS

1. Unauthorized Practice of Law

The core of a broker's work in helping a client to sell or buy real estate consists of marketing and negotiation, but it often goes beyond these measures. Many of the steps required to complete a sale have legal aspects. To be licensed, one of the subjects brokers must study and pass an examination on is real estate law. The line between a broker's expertise as a market intermediary and as an advisor on matters that may have legal consequence is sometimes difficult to define. If a broker is not to engage in the practice of law, a line must be drawn somehow and somewhere. This gives rise to several questions. What are a broker's proper activities, and when has he engaged in the unauthorized practice of law? May the broker draft the contract of sale? Help the buyer obtain financing? Perform title clearing work? Prepare deeds and other closing documents?

Over the years, many state and local bar associations have challenged broker practices as constituting the unauthorized practice of law. Consequently, courts have struggled with the problem of defining the limits on the broker's role. Earlier courts often prohibited brokers from completing any instruments that affect the legal rights of sellers and buyers, whether standard forms or not. Most states now permit brokers to prepare standard-form contracts of sale for customers, at least in some circumstances. In many states, the standard contracts must be approved by a bar association or a licensed attorney. The following three tests are widely used today to define the scope of brokers' services with respect to document preparation:

Contracts Versus Conveyances Test. The broker may prepare the contract of sale or earnest money contract between the parties and other ancillary documents, such as a loan application or escrow instructions, but he may not prepare closing instruments that convey interests in land.

Simple-Complex Test. If the transaction is simple and straightforward, a broker is permitted to select standard-form instruments and assist the parties in filling in blanks. The broker cannot furnish documents for a complex transaction or an unusual feature of a simple transaction, such as creation of an easement.

Incidental Test. Broker drafting of instruments is authorized if it is incidental to the broker's business and the party pays no separate charge for this service.

In re OPINION NO. 26 OF THE COMMITTEE ON THE UNAUTHORIZED PRACTICE OF LAW

Supreme Court of New Jersey, 1995
139 N.J. 323, 654 A.2d 1344

Per Curiam. We again confront another long-simmering dispute between realtors and attorneys concerning the unauthorized practice of law. . . . Since our decision today permits sellers and buyers in real estate transactions involving the sale of a home to proceed without counsel, we find it necessary to state the Court's view of the matter at the outset. The Court strongly believes that both parties should retain counsel for their own protection and that the savings in lawyers fees are not worth the risks involved in proceeding without counsel. All that we decide is that the public interest does not require that the parties be deprived of the right to choose to proceed without a lawyer. . . .

I. Proceedings Below

Opinion No. 26 of the Committee on the Unauthorized Practice of Law, 130 N.J.L.J. 882 (March 16, 1992), was issued in response to an inquiry, one of many, from the New Jersey State Bar Association. The inquiry sought a determination of whether the South Jersey practice constituted the unauthorized practice of law. That practice, described in detail later, concerns the sale of a home generally financed by a purchase money mortgage. The essence of the South Jersey practice is that from the beginning of the transaction to the end, neither seller nor buyer is represented by counsel. Every aspect of the transaction is handled by others, every document drafted by others, including the contract of sale, affidavit of title, bond and mortgage. The Committee on the Unauthorized Practice of Law (the Committee) . . . ruled that the ordering of a title search by the broker, the preparation of conveyancing and other documents by title officers, their clearing of title questions, and indeed the activities of both broker and title officers at the closing itself, where neither buyer nor seller was represented by counsel, that all of these activities constituted the unauthorized practice of law. The decision was interpreted widely as prohibiting the South Jersey practice, in effect prohibiting a seller and buyer from proceeding with the sale of a home without counsel.

. . . Given the concerns of both potential sellers and buyers, as well as those of brokers and title officers, and given the fact that the South Jersey practice had continued for so long, we stayed the effect of Opinion No. 26 pending review by this Court.

Following briefing and oral argument by those interested in the matter—the organized bar, brokers, title officers—we remanded the matter to develop a fuller record, referring it to Judge Edward S. Miller, as Special Master, for that purpose. After sixteen days of hearing, Judge Miller rendered his report to us. While personally strongly favoring a requirement that sellers and buyers be represented by counsel, Judge Miller recommended essentially that we allow the South Jersey practice to continue subject to certain conditions. . . .

Judge Miller found that there had been no proof of actual damage resulting from the South Jersey practice, or more accurately that whatever problems existed did not in the aggregate exceed those in matters where the parties were represented by counsel. . . .

. . . Our decision today, substantially in accord with Judge Miller's recommendations, affirms portions of Opinion No. 26 and reverses others. Specifically, we rule as follows: a real estate broker may order a title search and abstract; an attorney retained by a title company or a real estate broker may not prepare conveyance documents for a real estate transaction except at the specific written request of the party on whose behalf the document is to be prepared; a title company may not participate in the clearing of certain legal objections to title; and the practice of conducting closings or settlements without the presence of attorneys shall not constitute the unauthorized practice of law. We hold further, however, that unless the broker conforms to the conditions set forth later in this opinion, all participants at the closing who have reason to believe those conditions have not been complied with will be engaged in the unauthorized practice of law, and any attorney with similar knowledge so participating in such a transaction will have committed unethical conduct.

II. The South Jersey Practice

Although the variations are numerous, the South Jersey practice complained of typically involves residential real estate closings in which neither buyer nor seller is represented by counsel, and contrasts most sharply with the North Jersey practice if one assumes both parties are represented there. Obviously, that is not always the case: the record shows that about sixty percent of the buyers and about sixty-five percent of the sellers in South Jersey are not represented by counsel. In North Jersey, only one half of one percent of buyers, and fourteen percent of sellers, proceed without counsel.

In North Jersey, when both seller and buyer are represented by counsel, they sign nothing, agree to nothing, expend nothing, without the advice of competent counsel. If, initially without counsel, they sign a contract of sale prepared by the broker, they ordinarily then retain counsel who can revoke that contract in accordance with the three-day attorney review clause. They are protected, and they pay for that protection. The seller in North Jersey spends on average $750 in attorneys' fees, and the buyer in North Jersey spends on average $1,000. The buyer in South Jersey who chooses to proceed without representation spends nothing. The South Jersey seller whose attorney does no more than prepare the deed and affidavit of title, usually without even consulting with the seller, spends about $90. South Jersey buyers and sellers who are represented throughout the process, including closing, pay an average of $650 and $350, respectively.[2] Savings obviously do not determine the outcome of this case; they are but one factor in the mix of competing considerations.

The typical South Jersey transaction starts with the seller engaging a broker who is ordinarily a member of the multiple listing system. The first broker to find an apparently willing buyer gets in touch with the seller and ultimately negotiates a sale price agreeable to both. The potential buyer requires financing arrangements which are often made by the broker. Before the execution of any sales contract the broker puts the buyer in touch with a mortgage company to determine if the buyer qualifies for the needed loan. At this preliminary stage, no legal obligations of any kind are likely to have been created, except for those that arise from the brokerage relationship itself.

Assuming the preliminary understanding between the seller and buyer remains in effect, the broker will present the seller with the standard form of contract used in that area (usually a New Jersey Association of Realtors Standard Form of Real Estate Contract). That form includes, pursuant to our opinion in New Jersey State Bar Association v. New Jersey Association of Realtor Boards, 93 N.J. 470, 461 A.2d 1112 (1983), notice that the attorney for either party can cancel the contract within three business days. If the seller signs the contract, and does not within three days retain counsel, the seller will have become legally bound to perform numerous obligations without the benefit of any legal advice whatsoever, some of which may turn out to be onerous, some costly, some requiring unanticipated expense, and some beyond the power of the seller to perform, with the potential of substantial liability for such nonperformance. Many sellers will not understand just what those obligations are, and just what the risks are. Not only has the seller not retained a lawyer, the only person qualified to explain those

2. It is suggested that although the parties under the South Jersey practice save the cost of counsel, the savings may be offset to some extent because they nonetheless pay others for services attorneys in North Jersey customarily provide.

risks. Worse yet, the only one the seller has had any contact with in the matter is the broker, whose commission depends entirely on consummation of the transaction, and whose interest is primarily—in some cases it is fair to say exclusively—to get the contract signed and the deal closed.

After the seller signs the contract, the broker delivers it to the buyer for execution. The buyer may not know if the description of the property is precisely that assumed to be the subject of the purchase. The buyer may have no idea if the title described in the contract is that with which he would be satisfied, no sound understanding of what the numerous obligations on the part of the seller mean, and no fair comprehension of whether all of the possible and practical concerns of a buyer have been addressed by the contract. No lawyer is present to advise or inform the buyer; indeed, there is no one who has the buyer's interest at heart, only the broker, whose interests are generally in conflict with the buyer's. Although the record does not dispose of the issue, and although Judge Miller explicitly left it undecided, he noted concern that the broker, through his or her actions, may lead the buyer to believe that the broker is looking out for the buyer's interests. Therefore, without independent advice, the buyer signs the contract. If no attorney is retained within three days, the buyer is bound by all of its terms.

For both seller and buyer, it is that contract that substantially determines all of their rights and duties. Neither one of them can be regarded as adequately informed of the import of what they signed or indeed of its importance. At that point the broker, who represents only the seller and clearly has an interest in conflict with that of the buyer (the broker's interest is in consummation of the sale, the buyer's in making certain that the sale does not close unless the buyer is fully protected) performs a series of acts on behalf of the buyer, and is the only person available as a practical matter to explain their significance to the buyer. The broker orders a binder for title insurance, or a title commitment to make sure that the *buyer* is going to get good title. The buyer has no idea, and hopefully never will have, whether the broker ordered the right kind of title search, a fairly esoteric question that only an experienced attorney can determine.

The broker also orders numerous inspection and other reports, all primarily of interest to the buyer, to make certain that not only is the title good, but that there are no other problems affecting the premises, the house and their use. Those reports can have substantial legal consequences for both seller and buyer. For example, at what threshold dollar amount of required repairs should the seller (or the buyer) be able to cancel the contract? At what dollar amount should the buyer ignore the repairs? At what dollar amount should the buyer be able to compel the seller to make the repairs, and within what time frame? At this stage of the transaction the help of a lawyer could be invaluable, and the advice of a broker problematic.

The seller in the meantime is happy to hear from no one, for it suggests there are no problems. Eventually, the seller is told that a deed will be arriving drafted by an attorney selected by the broker; the instrument that our decisions clearly require may be drafted only by the seller's attorney. Cape May County Bar Assn. v. Ludlam, 45 N.J. 121, 211 A.2d 780 (1965). Of course, the purpose of that ruling was to assure competent counsel in the drafting of such a uniquely legal document, but "competent" always meant counsel who understood the entire transaction. In South Jersey, the attorney selected by the broker, while theoretically representing the seller, may be primarily interested in the broker, the source of the attorney's "client" and the likely source of future "clients," and consequently primarily interested in completing the sale. That attorney is likely to prepare a deed satisfactory to the title company—in fact that attorney often does not even contact the seller. He or she may have no idea of anything in the contract of sale other than the description of the land and the fact that a certain kind of deed is required. No advice on the substance of the transaction comes from such an attorney even though the seller may get the impression that, since an attorney drafted the deed, the seller's interests are somehow being protected. In fact, the only protection those interests ever received, other than those that happened to appear in the form contract, is in the numbers inserted in that contract, the total purchase price, the down payment, and the closing date, for those are probably the only terms of that contract fully understood by the seller.

The buyer's position is even worse when the closing occurs. The seller will at least know that he or she got paid. Legal training is not required for that fact, even though there is no practical assurance that the seller will not thereafter be sued. The buyer, on the other hand, wants something that is largely incomprehensible to almost all buyers, good and marketable title, one that will not result in problems in the future. What the buyer gets before closing is a "title binder," a piece of paper that may suggest something about the quality of the seller's title, but that is very much in need of explanation for any substantial understanding of its meaning. The title company is required to mail to the unrepresented buyer notice of any exceptions or conditions associated with the title insurance policy. N.J.S.A. 17:46B-9. This notice, which must be sent five days prior to the closing, must also notify the buyer of the right to review the title commitment with an attorney. *Ibid.* If the buyer chooses not to retain an attorney, there is no one to give the buyer that understanding other than the broker and the title agent. The broker's knowledge will often be inadequate, and the conflicting interest apparent. The title company similarly has a conflicting interest, for it too is interested in completion of the transaction, the *sine qua non* of its title premium. But the title company is also interested in good title, for it is guaranteeing that to the mortgage company, as well as to the buyer. "Good title," however, may be one on which the title company and the mortgagee are willing to take a risk, but one on which a buyer might or should not be willing to, if the buyer knew what the risk was. Again, there is no one to tell the buyer what those risks are, and in some cases the explicit exceptions found in a title policy, those matters that the title company will not guarantee, are of the greatest importance. The significance of those matters is conceded by all to be something that only attorneys can give advice on, and it is contended by all that they never give such advice. Yet such exceptions exist, and title still closes, and the buyer is totally unrepresented by counsel. One must assume that somewhere, somehow, the buyer is satisfied that there is nothing to worry about, leading to the inescapable conclusion that either the broker or the title officer provides some modicum of assurance or explanation.

The day for closing arrives and everyone meets, usually at the offices of the title company. Seller and buyer are there, each without an attorney; the broker is there, and the title officer is there, representing both the title company and the mortgagee. The funds are there. And the critical legal documents are also on hand: the mortgage and the note, usually prepared by the mortgagee; the deed, along with the affidavit of title, prepared by the attorney selected by the broker or by the title company; the settlement statement, usually prepared by the title company, indicating how much is owed, what deductions should be made for taxes and other costs, and what credits are due; and the final marked-up title binder, which evidences the obligation of the title company to issue a title policy to the buyer, and which at that point is probably practically meaningless to the buyer. All are executed and delivered, along with other documents, and the funds are delivered or held in escrow until the title company arranges to pay off prior mortgages and liens.

It would take a volume to describe each and every risk to which the seller and buyer have exposed themselves without adequate knowledge. But it takes a very short sentence to describe what apparently occurs: the deal closes, satisfactory to buyer and seller in practically all cases, satisfactory both at the closing and thereafter.

III. The Unauthorized Practice of Law

As noted above, this transaction in its entirety, the sale of real estate, especially real estate with a home on it, is one that cannot be handled competently except by those trained in the law. The most important parts of it, without which it could not be accomplished, are quintessentially the practice of law. The contract of sale, the obligations of the contract, the ordering of a title search, the analysis of the search, the significance of the title search, the quality of title, the risks that surround both the contract and the title, the extent of those risks, the probability of damage, the obligation to close or not to close, the closing itself, the settlement, the documents there exchanged, each and every one of these, to be properly understood must be explained by an attorney. And the documents themselves, to be properly drafted, must be drafted by an attorney. Mixed in with these activities are many others that clearly do not require an attorney's knowledge, such as the ordering of inspection and other reports, and the price negotiation. But after that, even though arguably much can be accomplished by others, practically all else, to be done with full understanding, requires the advice of counsel.

As this Court's prior treatment of the subject shows, the prohibition against non-lawyers engaging in activities that are the practice of law is not automatic.[3] Having answered the question whether the practice of law is involved, we must decide whether the public interest is served by such prohibition. Not every such intrusion by laypersons into legal matters disserves the public: this Court does not wear public interest blinders when passing on unauthorized practice of law questions. We have often found, despite the clear involvement of the practice of law, that non-lawyers may participate in these activities, basing our decisions on the public interest in those cases in allowing parties to proceed without counsel. . . .

In a case involving some of the same questions now before us, New Jersey State Bar Association v. Northern New Jersey Mortgage Associates, 22 N.J. 184, 123 A.2d 498 (1956), . . . defendants, in the business of searching titles, acting as agents for title companies, and handling the closing of transactions involving sellers, buyers, and mortgagees, admitted that they prepared bonds, mortgages and other instruments connected with titles and mortgage loans, and that the services performed incidental to closing included the giving of legal advice in connection with those transactions. . . .

After remand and plenary hearing, this Court [reviewed] the trial court's dismissal of the charge that defendants were engaged in the unauthorized practice of law. New Jersey State Bar Assn. v. Northern N.J. Mortgage Assocs., 32 N.J. 430, 161 A.2d 257 (1960). In passing on the issues the Court repeated again that the restrictions against the practice of law by non-lawyers "are designed to serve the public interest by protecting 'the

3. Our use of the word "non-lawyers" or "laypersons" here and elsewhere is not intended to cover all cases of unauthorized or impermissible practice of law. Title officers are often lawyers, but since they do not represent the buyer, their performance of legal functions for the buyer has no more legitimacy than the actions of laypersons. *Cf.* Stack v. P.G. Garage, 7 N.J. 118, 80 A.2d 545 (1951) (layperson cannot be retained to practice law even though legal work done by lawyer).

We note that some of the cases in this area conclude that the practice of law, although performed by lawyers, is nevertheless unauthorized where the attorneys are employed by the title company, a corporation, the conclusion seemingly based on the observation that corporations may not practice law. *See* New Jersey State Bar Assn. v. Northern New Jersey Mortgage Assocs., 32 N.J. 430, 437, 161 A.2d 257 (1960). Rather clearly, however, the basic evil is that the person performing the legal service is in no sense doing it for the *party*, but rather in the interest of the employer, the title company, neither of them (the lawyer or the title company) representing the party, be it seller, buyer or lender. Even if the title organization entity consisted of but one individual, not a corporation, but one attorney, even one who actually did all of the legal work, that practice of law would be unauthorized, impermissible, for it is only an attorney retained by and actually representing the client who is authorized to practice law on the client's behalf. What is involved is not simply the license to practice, but the professional duty of loyalty that is included in the concept of permissible representation. Depending on the circumstances, attorneys who act purportedly on behalf of those they do not represent may be engaged in the unauthorized practice of law, or unethical professional conduct, or both.

unwary and the ignorant from injury at the hands of persons unskilled or unlearned in the law.' " *Id.* at 436, 161 A.2d 257 (citation omitted). . . .

The message is clear: not only is the public interest the criterion for determining what is the unauthorized practice of law, but in making that determination practical considerations and common sense will prevail, not impractical and technical restrictions that may hamper or burden the public interest with no reasonable justification. . . . The title company . . . claimed that on the basis of the entire record its activities did not constitute the unauthorized practice of the law. By then the measuring rod was clear, for the title company's contention was that "the public policy of this State" compelled that conclusion. Id. at 447, 161 A.2d 257. The Court disagreed, but not with the standard against which the issue would be determined, for it found that by enjoining the practices involved in the case "the public interest will not be disserved but on the contrary will be significantly advanced." *Ibid.* There, the public interest consisted of removing "unwarranted charges imposed by the Title Company on purchasers" and encouraging "parties to obtain the important protection of independent counsel." . . .

In what is undoubtedly the clearest example of the dominating influence of the public interest in this area, we decided in *New Jersey Association of Realtor Boards, supra,* that real estate brokers may draft contracts for the sale of residential property if the contract contains a prominent clause informing the parties of their right, through counsel, to cancel it within three days. While our decision took the form of the approval of a settlement reached between the brokers and the bar, our approval was explicitly based on a finding by Justice Sullivan, sitting as the trial judge, that the settlement was in the public interest, a finding with which we concurred. . . .

Finally, we note that our own Rules recognize certain exceptions to what used to be the absolute prohibition against the practice of law by non-lawyers. Rule 1:21-3(a) allows law school graduates to appear in court to answer the calendar call for the firm employing them, obviously a practical recognition of the benefits measured against the minimal risks. Rule 1:21-3(b) is broader, allowing third-year law school students and graduates to appear before a court or an agency as part of a program approved by this Court, the programs generally aimed at supplying needed legal resources to public agencies and to organizations serving the disadvantaged. Another aspect of the public interest involved in this latter exemption is the better training of law school students . . .

Our holding today, therefore, accords with the Court's consistent treatment of this issue. Although technically we have overruled the holding of *Northern New Jersey Mortgage Associates, supra,* 32 N.J. 430, 161 A.2d 257,[4] that

4. Our holding in this case allows a title company, under certain conditions, to prepare bonds and mortgages not only when it is a party to the transaction (as lender or mortgagee) but when requested to do so, acting on behalf of the mortgagee; the final judgment approved by this Court in *Northern New Jersey Mortgage Associates, supra,* prohibits the latter. *See* New Jersey State Bar Assn. v. Northern N.J. Mortgage Assocs., 34 N.J. 301, 169 A.2d 150 (1961) (modifying

case applied precisely the same standard in passing on the challenged conduct before it—the public interest. As we view it, the real difference is found in the differing records before the Court in the two cases, for in that case the public interest in allowing the challenged practices to continue was apparently nowhere demonstrated, and certainly not with the force of the record before us. Indeed, since the practice challenged apparently related solely to one firm located in North Jersey, and not to the South Jersey practice, it may have seemed that such showing would be irrelevant. More than that, at the time of our decision in that case, we had not yet ruled that brokers could prepare contracts of sale, a change which has affected the entire landscape in this area.

In this case, the record clearly shows that the South Jersey practice has been conducted without any demonstrable harm to sellers or buyers, that it apparently saves money, and that those who participate in it do so of their own free will presumably with some knowledge of the risk; as Judge Miller found, the record fails to demonstrate that brokers are discouraging the parties from retaining counsel, or that the conflict of interest that pervades the practice has caused material damage to the sellers and buyers who participate in it. . . .

Of decisive weight in our determination is the value we place on the right of parties to a transaction to decide whether or not they will retain counsel. We should not force them to do so absent persuasive reasons. Given the importance in our decision of the assumption that the parties have chosen not to retain counsel, and without coercion have made that decision, we have attached a condition to the conclusion that the South Jersey practice does not constitute the unauthorized practice of law. The condition is designed to assure that the decision is an informed one. If that condition is not met, the brokers (and title officers, if aware of the fact) are engaged in the unauthorized practice of law, and attorneys with knowledge of that fact who participate are guilty of ethical misconduct. . . .

. . . We do *not* conclude that the public is better off without lawyers in the South Jersey practice. As stated several times above, we firmly believe the parties should retain counsel. We decide only that given the history and experience of the South Jersey practice, the public interest will not be disserved by allowing the parties, after advance written notice of their right to retain counsel and the risk of not doing so, to choose to proceed without a lawyer; we decide only that the public interest does not require that the protection of counsel be forced upon the parties against their will. Our required disclosure notice goes beyond that of other cases, reflecting our

---

the initial injunction entered after our decision in the same case, 32 N.J. at 430, 161 A.2d 257, in order to conform with that decision). Our holding in this case allows the title company, and others, to participate in the preparation of various legal instruments, including conveyances, under certain conditions; the final judgment in *Northern New Jersey Mortgage Associates, supra,* 32 N.J. at 430, 161 A.2d 257, prohibits it. Our holding permits title companies to take certain legal steps to remove certain kinds of objections to title or to cure defects therein; the final judgment in *Northern New Jersey Mortgage Associates, supra,* prohibits it.

determination to assure that the parties who decide not to retain lawyers know the conflicting interests of others and know that there are risks of proceeding without one.

There is a point at which an institution attempting to provide protection to a public that seems clearly, over a long period, not to want it, and perhaps not to need it — there is a point when that institution must wonder whether it is providing protection or imposing its will. It must wonder whether it is helping or hurting the public.[5] We have reached that point in this case. Although we have strong doubts, the evidence against our doubt requires that we allow this practice to continue with some form of added protection, recognizing, however, that like the attorney-review clause, the added protection may not be effective.

IV. Conclusion and Conditions

We premise our holding on the condition that both buyer and seller be made aware of the conflicting interests of brokers and title companies in these matters and of the general risks involved in not being represented by counsel. We shall ask the Civil Practice Committee to recommend to us practical methods for achieving those aims. Presumably, that Committee will want to form a subcommittee including those who have been involved with this problem for many years. Obviously, the best way to achieve the goal is to have a knowledgeable disinterested attorney sit down with both buyer and seller and carefully explain both the conflict factor and the risk factor, but we doubt if that would be practical. Pending the report of that Committee and our action on it, we have decided to adopt an interim notice requirement that the broker must comply with. If that notice is not given, the broker will be engaged in the unauthorized practice of law. Furthermore, anyone who participates in the transaction, other than buyer and seller, knowing that the notice has not been given when and as required, will also be engaged in the unauthorized practice of law. As for any attorney who, under the same circumstances, continues to participate in the transaction, that attorney will also be subject to discipline for unethical conduct. At the commencement of the closing or settlement, the title officer in charge shall inquire of both buyer and seller whether, how, and when, the notice was given, and shall make and keep a record of the inquiry and the responses at that time.

The interim notice that we require is attached as Appendix A.[6] It is a written notice, and it shall be attached to the proposed contract of sale as its

5. We note that in Arizona, after its Supreme Court prohibited brokers from preparing real estate sales contracts, the people approved a constitutional amendment that provided that licensed real estate brokers "shall have the right to draft or fill out and complete" real estate documents, including deeds, mortgages, and contracts of sale. Ariz. Const. art. XXVI, §1.

6. We note that title companies are required to disclose to the buyer the desirability of seeking counsel to review title exceptions. N.J.S.A. 17:46B-9. This disclosure was revised as of

cover page. The notice may be appropriately revised if the broker represents the buyer or is a dual agent, one who represents both seller and buyer. Whenever a broker presents either buyer or seller with the proposed contract, that cover page shall be so attached, and the broker shall personally advise the buyer or seller at that point that he or she must read it before executing the contract. If the contract is not personally delivered by the broker to the buyer or seller, the broker must make certain, prior to such delivery, that buyer and seller have been so informed, and must do so by speaking to them personally or by phone.

Assuming such notice is given in accordance with the terms and conditions mentioned above, we hold that attendance and participation at the closing or settlement where neither party has been represented by counsel, or where one has not been so represented, does not constitute the unauthorized practice of law; that brokers may order abstracts, title binders, and title policies; that an attorney retained by the broker to draft a deed and/or affidavit of title for the seller may do so but only if the attorney personally consults with the seller; regardless of the prior restriction, any attorney retained by the broker for that purpose, or any attorney acting for the title company, may draft any of the documents involved in the transaction upon written request of the party, be it buyer, seller, lender, mortgagee, bank, or others;[7] that the title company may participate in clearing up those minor objections which Judge Miller refers to as categories one and two: standard exceptions such as marital status and money liens customarily paid at closing, but not those classified as categories three and four: easements, covenants or other serious legal objections to title.

Other equally important protections for buyer and seller should exist. Any broker participating in a transaction where buyer and seller are not represented should have the experience and knowledge required at least to identify a situation where independent counsel is needed. Under those circumstances the broker has a duty, in accordance with the standards of that profession, to inform either seller or buyer of that fact. N.J.A.C. 11:5-1.23(a), (f). Presumably, the same duty applies to any title officer, whether or not an attorney, but especially if an attorney, who becomes aware of the need of either party for independent counsel. In addition to whatever potential action might be taken by the bodies that regulate brokers and title officers, as well as by their own associations, their failure to inform exposes them to the risk of civil liability for resulting damages. . . .

August 1, 1994 to include the warning that the title company does not represent the buyer and cannot offer legal advice. However, because this disclosure does not address the role of the broker, and is only required to be mailed five days prior to closing, we believe it does not provide adequate protection for the buyer. . . .

We are aware of the adoption of N.J.A.C. 11:5-1.43, effective July 1, 1995, requiring certain written disclosures in real estate transactions. 27 N.J.R. 705 (Feb. 21, 1995). We do not find those disclosures inconsistent with our interim notice.

7. Of course, the title company may continue to prepare non-conveyance documents such as the settlement statement.

In addition, Judge Miller recommended the following, all of which we refer to the Civil Practice Committee for review and report: any unrepresented buyer or seller must execute a written waiver of the right to have counsel; both the broker and title agent must urge buyers and sellers to retain attorneys; the parties conducting a closing must be under the supervision of a public entity; brokers should be required to carry adequate liability insurance.

Concerning the prior paragraph, we believe that the disclosure required in this opinion, or such disclosure as the Civil Practice Committee may recommend, may render such added protection unnecessary. While we are concerned about, and determined to afford, adequate protection for buyers and sellers, we do not want to burden the real estate transaction process with detailed requirements that do not add measurable protection. . . .

The decision of the Committee, Opinion No. 26, is affirmed in part, and reversed in part, and judgment entered declaring the rights of the participants in New Jersey residential real estate transactions in accordance with this opinion.

Appendix A

NOTICE

To Buyer and Seller:
You Must Read This Notice Before Signing the Contract

The Supreme Court of New Jersey requires real estate brokers to give you the following information before you sign this contract. It requires us to tell you that you must read all of it before you sign. Here is the information for both buyer and seller:

1. I am a real estate broker. I represent the seller. I do not represent the buyer. The title company does not represent either the seller or the buyer. Furthermore, both the seller and the buyer should know that it is in my financial interest that the house be sold and that the closing be completed. My fee is paid only if that happens. The title company has the same interest, for its insurance premium is paid only if that happens.
2. I am not allowed, and I am not qualified, to give either the seller or the buyer any legal advice. Neither the title company nor any of its officers are allowed to give either the seller or buyer any legal advice. Neither of you will get any legal advice at any point in this transaction unless you have your own lawyer. If you do not hire a lawyer, no one will represent you in legal matters either now, or at the closing. I will not represent you and the title company and its officers will not represent you in those matters.

3. The contract attached to this notice is the most important part of the sale. It determines your rights, your liabilities, and your risks. It becomes final when you sign it — unless it is cancelled by your lawyer within three days — and when it does become final you cannot change it, nor can any attorney you may hire thereafter change it in any way whatsoever.
4. The buyer especially should know that if he or she has no lawyer, no one will be able to advise him or her what to do if problems arise in connection with the purchase of this property. Those problems may be about various matters, including the seller's title to the property. They may affect the value of the property. If either the broker or title company sees that there are problems and that because of them you need your own lawyer, they should tell you. However, it is possible that they may not recognize the problems or that it may be too late for a lawyer to help. Also, they are not your lawyers, and they may not see the problem from your point of view.
5. Whether you, seller or buyer, retain a lawyer is up to you. It is your decision. The purpose of this notice is to make sure you have some understanding of the transaction, the risks, who represents whom, and what their interests are, when you make that decision. The rules and regulations concerning brokers and title companies prohibit each of them from suggesting that you are better off without a lawyer. If anyone makes that suggestion to you, you should carefully consider whose interest they are serving. The decision whether to hire a lawyer to represent your interests is yours and yours alone.

Problem 2D

Stan is selling his house to Patricia. The closing, conducted by a title company officer, is attended by both parties, the listing broker, and the selling broker. Neither party is represented by an attorney. Patricia says, "I want to know whether there are covenants and restrictions on the property." The listing broker says, "Yes, haven't you seen them?" and hands her a copy of the recorded neighborhood covenants (eight pages in length). Patricia asks whether she can put a swimming pool in the backyard.

(a) Assume the sale takes place in New Jersey after the decision in *In re Opinion No. 26* and that the contract has the interim notice attached, which the brokers properly explained to the parties. How should the broker(s) respond?

(b) Assume the sale takes place in another state that has no specific law on point. How should the broker(s) respond?

2. *Lawyers Acting as Brokers*

Statutes that provide for the regulation of brokers typically provide exemptions for certain persons—for instance, persons representing themselves, fiduciaries, auctioneers, and newspapers. Attorneys are exempt in almost all states, but the scope of the exemption varies. Some states confer on attorneys a total exemption from the licensing requirements, allowing them to collect commissions for finding buyers or arranging other transactions. In most states, the exemption is limited to brokerage services that are incidental to the attorney's law practice. Thus, an attorney can sell or rent property only for clients for whom his primary work is the provision of legal services.

In re ROTH

Supreme Court of New Jersey, 1990
120 N.J. 665, 577 A.2d 490

Per Curiam. This is an attorney-disciplinary matter. Respondent, Lee B. Roth, was found to have violated our ethics rules by attempting to obtain a real estate commission in a transaction in which he also served as the attorney for a prospective buyer of residential real estate. The case impels us to determine the appropriate ethics standards governing an attorney who undertakes to represent a client as both attorney and real estate broker in the same transaction.

The charges in this case were brought before the District XIII Ethics Committee (DEC), which found that respondent's conduct in representing a client as both an attorney and real estate broker reflected adversely on his fitness to practice law in violation of Disciplinary Rule (DR) 1-102(A)(6), which provided that "[a] lawyer shall not . . . [e]ngage in any other conduct that adversely reflects on his fitness to practice law." . . .

I

Respondent has been a member of the New Jersey bar since 1962 and is a well-respected authority on real estate law. Although at the time this matter arose respondent had taken the course to become a real estate broker and had passed the examination administered to real estate salespeople, he was not a licensed real estate broker. In January 1984, a paralegal employed in respondent's law firm became interested in purchasing a house she had seen for sale located in Flemington, New Jersey. The listing price for the house was $123,900. The paralegal asked respondent to assist her in purchasing the house and in finding a way of lowering the purchase price. Respondent told her that he would act as both her lawyer and broker in the transaction, and that as the selling real estate broker, he would be entitled to a fifty-percent share of the commission, which he would apply to a reduction in the purchase price.

Respondent's client subsequently communicated with the real estate agency owned by Carl D. Bayuk, who was the listing broker. She expressed interest in the property and stated that respondent would act both as her attorney and as the selling real estate broker. Because he was confused about respondent's dual role as attorney and broker, Bayuk called respondent directly, and respondent explained to Bayuk that, as an attorney, he, respondent, was authorized to sell real estate without a broker's license and that he would be entitled to half of the six-percent commission.

On January 20, 1984, respondent's client made a written offer of $114,000 to the sellers expressly conditioned on "the assumption that you have agreed to pay your real estate broker six percent (in this case $6,840) and that your real estate broker will divide the commission with our lawyer, who agrees that that commission be credited against the purchase price." That offer was rejected, as was a second offer, conditioned on the identical terms, for $118,500. Shortly thereafter, the property was sold to another buyer for the full listing price.

The listing real estate broker, Bayuk, subsequently filed an ethics complaint against respondent. At the hearing before the DEC, respondent stated that he had advised both his client and Bayuk that he would act as the attorney and the selling real estate broker. He testified that he did not intend to benefit personally from the arrangement and that his share of the real estate commission was to have been applied on behalf of his client to reduce the purchase price of the property.

The DEC found that respondent had not performed any brokerage services and therefore was not entitled to any brokerage commission. . . . [On appeal the Disciplinary Review Board] also concluded that respondent had violated [DR 1-102(A)(6)] and recommended that respondent be publicly reprimanded.

II

It is not unlawful or unethical per se for an attorney to engage in the business of a real estate broker. The Advisory Committee on Professional Ethics has concluded that an attorney who is also licensed as a broker may conduct business in both fields, so long as he or she separates the two. *See, e.g.,* Opinion 124, 91 N.J.L.J. 108 (1968). As the DEC noted below, "There would appear to be no impediment to respondent engaging in the real estate brokerage business upon obtaining a proper license and upon taking appropriate steps to separate such a brokerage business from his practice of law." An attorney who is not so licensed may also perform brokerage activities. Although the law governing the licensing of real estate brokers,

N.J.S.A. 45:15-1 to -42, provides in pertinent part that "no person shall engage either directly or indirectly in the business of a real estate broker or salesman . . . without being licensed," it exempts certain classes of people, including attorneys, from that requirement. N.J.S.A. 45:15-4. Thus attorneys are authorized to engage in the business of a real estate broker or salesperson without being licensed as such. The primary question posed in this matter, however, is not whether respondent could lawfully undertake to perform brokerage activities, but whether in this transaction he compromised his professional responsibilities as an attorney by engaging in such dual activities and seeking dual compensation. . . .

Our courts have had few occasions to examine the statutory "attorney" exemption of N.J.S.A. 45:15-4. In Spirito v. New Jersey Real Estate Commission, 180 N.J. Super. 180, 434 A.2d 623 (1981), the Appellate Division rejected the notion that the statutory exemption makes an attorney's license the equivalent of a real estate broker's license. The court declined to grant a real estate broker's license to an attorney who claimed a right to the license by virtue of the statutory exemption. It held that an attorney is not entitled to a broker's license without meeting the apprenticeship and licensing requirements of the real estate licensing law, N.J.S.A. 45:15-1 to -42. . . .

. . . [A]n attorney who does not hold a license under Title 45 but seeks to act as both a broker and a lawyer for the same client in the same transaction, must confine any broker's services to those that are obviously minor, incidental, ancillary, and subordinate to the legal services entailed in the client's representation. An unlicensed attorney who acts in a substantial capacity as a broker acts beyond the authority conferred by law under Title 45, and to that extent acts improperly as an attorney and in a manner that reflects adversely on the legal profession. DR 1-102(A)(6). . . .

In determining whether brokerage services may fairly be characterized as incidental to legal services, the compensability of such brokerage services is highly relevant. Common sense and ordinary experience tell us that an attorney who performs sufficient work as a broker to be entitled to a commission for those services would not be acting as broker in a manner only incidental to the normal practice of law. Conversely, an attorney performing brokerage services that are really only incidental to his or her work as a lawyer would not be entitled to a commission because . . . those incidental services would be substantially less significant than the "activities normally associated with a real estate broker." We therefore hold that an attorney whose actions as a broker are undertaken pursuant to the "attorney" exemption to the licensing law, N.J.S.A. 45:15-4, may perform brokerage services that are only incidental to the normal practice of law, which cannot be the basis for a claim of compensation as a broker. . . .

We acknowledge that it may be difficult to assess the professional mix of attorney and brokerage services in a given transaction to determine with any degree of confidence whether the latter is really only incidental to the former. Nevertheless, attorneys are expected and required to make that evaluation. Attorneys are held to a higher standard of ethical propriety than are members of the general public. . . . Accordingly, we conclude that an attorney is ethically obligated to perform only those brokerage services that are incidental or ancillary to the performance of legal services in a given transaction on behalf of the same client. It follows that in such situations, an attorney may not be independently and separately compensated for brokerage services.

III

. . . In addressing the areas of overlap between real estate brokers and attorneys, we have sought to draw a fairly bright line of separation. New Jersey State Bar Association v. New Jersey Association of Realtor Boards, 93 N.J. 470, 461 A.2d 1112 (1983), exemplifies that concern. Just as we there guarded against brokers engaging in the unauthorized practice of law, here we concern ourselves with attorneys who engage in inappropriate or improper brokerage activities. Regardless of whether he or she is licensed as a broker, when an attorney seeks a real estate commission for his or her efforts on behalf of a client, the danger of conflict, actual, potential, or perceived, is great. . . .

As noted, respondent was not a licensed broker at the time he sought to obtain a portion of the broker's commission. Had he been licensed, however, his actions would have been prohibited by N.J.S.A. 45:15-17(i). That statutory provision proscribes "[c]ollecting a commission as a real estate broker in a transaction, when at the same time representing either party in a transaction in a different capacity for consideration." In Mortgage Bankers Association of New Jersey v. New Jersey Real Estate Commission, 200 N.J. Super. 584, 491 A.2d 1317 (1985), *rev'd and remanded,* 102 N.J. 176, 506 A.2d 733 (1986), the Appellate Division concluded that N.J.S.A. 45:15-17(i) prohibits a broker who receives a commission from the seller in a real estate transaction from also earning consideration for assisting the buyer in obtaining mortgage financing. In *Mortgage Bankers,* the court was concerned by the potential for a conflict of interest in situations involving dual compensation for dual representation. "We are thus persuaded that . . . the legislature's intent was to permit dual representation by consent but only if there was no dual compensation therefor." 200 N.J. Super. at 600, 491 A.2d 1317. We see no lessened obligation when the dual representation and dual compensation involves that of broker and lawyer.

Although respondent testified that he did not intend to profit from the commission, the application of his commission on behalf of his client in this fashion might nevertheless have constituted an indirect benefit to respondent. Had the sale occurred, respondent's actions would arguably have been tantamount to his actually receiving a commission, notwithstanding his gift over to his client.

In sum, we conclude that an unacceptable conflict of interest is created if an attorney who is not licensed as a real estate broker claims or accepts a commission for participating as a broker in the purchase or sale of real estate if the attorney also represents one of the parties in the transaction. That conflict, however, may be overcome if the brokerage activities are incidental to the legal services rendered and do not generate any entitlement to compensation. We agree with amicus New Jersey Real Estate Commission that an attorney's real estate activities "must be limited to only those necessary to fulfill his legal representations of a client, but in no sense is he an actual real estate broker, nor should he be compensated as such."

IV

We are satisfied that an attorney who seeks to obtain a commission for brokerage services in connection with legal services rendered in the same transaction for the same client will have violated our ethics rules. In this case, respondent's conduct violated DR 1-102(A)(6); his conduct "reflects adversely on his fitness to practice law." Under our more recent Rules of Professional Conduct, we conclude that activities similar to respondent's would violate our Rules of Professional Conduct, prohibiting attorneys from representing clients in cases "involving conflict or apparent conflict," RPC 1.7(c), and in cases in which representation will result in a violation of "other law," RPC 1.16(a)(1).

An attorney who in the future violates the ethics standards as explained herein will assuredly be subject to professional discipline. We note that in the present case, however, respondent did not act nefariously or with venality. His dual role as attorney and broker was fully disclosed to all interested parties at the outset of respondent's involvement. He expressly informed complainant that he intended to apply his share of the commission to reduce the purchase price for his client. . . . Moreover, as amicus New Jersey State Bar Association emphasizes, there was no clear precedent governing or proscribing respondent's actions. That amicus also points out that other states, contrary to our own approach, *see, e.g.*, N.J.S.A. 45:15-17(i), permit attorneys to share commissions.

Both the dearth of relevant opinions and the lack of clear legislative or regulatory mandate support the perception that there was no "clear prohibition" of respondent's actions. We therefore conclude that respondent acted in the good-faith belief that his conduct did not violate disciplinary standards. Under these circumstances, this opinion is efficacious both to explain the nature of the underlying ethical misconduct and to discourage its repetition. Accordingly, we see no reason grounded in the public's confidence in the legal profession to impose formal discipline. [Citations omitted.]

Problem 2E

Ken and Norma Miller are ready for retirement. Two years ago they purchased their mountain hideaway where they will move later this year. It's time to sell their home in the city, where they have lived for 18 years, and they want to hire a broker named Fred (some close friends were happy with Fred's work). They bought the house for $102,000, and it's probably worth about $440,000 now. Although you're still in law school, they ask you whether they should hire an attorney prior to signing a listing agreement. What is your response?

Problem 2F

Gracie recently graduated from law school and is practicing real estate law. Though admitted to the state bar, she is not a licensed broker. The state Real Estate License Act has an attorney exemption, which provides: "nor shall this Act be construed to include in any way services rendered by an attorney at law."

Through a newspaper ad, Gracie finds a two-bedroom house at an asking price of $200,000. She calls the advertised phone number, reaching Steve, the listing broker. The property is listed with the local multiple listing service, with a total commission of six percent to be split equally between the listing broker and selling broker. Gracie sees the house and loves it. She drafts a contract of sale, offering $200,000, but with a provision stating: "Purchaser declares that she is representing herself as broker. Accordingly, Purchaser hereby claims a right to the three percent commission customarily paid to selling brokers." The contract of sale, as is typical in the community, has a signature blank for the brokers to sign. Gracie fully signs the contract and submits it to Steve. He not only refuses to sign the contract but also refuses to forward it to the owner, Carl. Gracie therefore contacts Carl directly. Carl wants to accept the offer, but Steve insists that the offer is improper and unethical. One week later, Carl terminates his listing agreement with Steve, alleging that Steve violated his duties of loyalty. Carl promptly sells the house to Gracie for $191,000, and the parties close the transaction without using the services of any broker. Steve sues both Carl and Gracie, claiming they are jointly and severally liable for a 6 percent commission. What result?

3
Preparing to Contract

Contract law is an important cornerstone in the foundation of any real estate transaction. Real property law is a second cornerstone, interfacing with contract law in every transaction. The parties must come to some understanding as to what will be exchanged and how and when the exchange will proceed. They must agree on the subject of their contract, which is often much more complicated than it might seem at first. Precise identification of the property under consideration involves issues of physical quantity and the legal quality of the estate. For example, as to quantity there may be questions of exactly how many acres or square feet the buyer should get; what fixtures and personal property stay with the property; and whether air, water, and mineral rights are included or excluded. As to quality of the estate, matters of fee simple versus life estates or long-term tenancy arrangements may come into play. Besides identifying the subject of the exchange, the parties must address many other issues in their negotiations, such as financing, title protection, and environmental and zoning compliance. There will be need for definitions, representations, warranties, conditions, inspections, investigations, and consequences in the event of any variety of planned or unplanned happenings.

In Chapter 1 we discuss a variety of risk factors that can have an effect on the potential value of a real estate transaction. We also discuss the relationship between risk and price. At this point, we must take a moment to recall these concepts as we consider the dynamics of contract preparation. The relationship between price and risk is such that the more risk a party has, the less valuable the transaction is to it. Risk, in this sense, is like a cost. When the contract terms allocate more risk to the buyer, the purchase price must be lowered. When more risk is allocated to the seller, the seller will desire an upward adjustment in the sales price. Thus, the buyer and the seller have inverse relationships in the trade-off between risk and price.

This trade-off is illustrated by the diagram in Figure 3-1. In this diagram, price is on the horizontal axis and risk is on the vertical axis. The intersection of the horizontal and vertical axis is marked as point zero, reflecting a point of zero risk and zero price impact. Moving out along the price axis shows a rise in price from 0 to 20. Moving out along the risk axis shows a rise in risk factors from 0 to 20. The downward-sloping line for the buyer illustrates the idea that a buyer will be willing to pay a higher price for a property when the seller takes on more and more of the risk associated with the transaction. At the same time, it illustrates that the buyer will pay a lower price if she has to take on a lot of risk. A buyer would have a high degree of risk, for example, in the case of an "as is" sale. Similarly, the upward-sloping seller's line depicts the relationship between risk and price for the seller. The greater the risk to a seller, the higher the selling price; the lower the risk, the lower the selling price. The parties can negotiate trade-offs anywhere along these lines. Moreover, different people might have different tolerances to risk or different abilities to effectively manage or lower risk or its consequences. In such situations, the parties may find it mutually beneficial to allocate risk to the least risk-averse party or the best risk avoider and have the least impact on cost and price. These kinds of trade-offs will be an important part of the contract preparation period. This is especially true in transactions in which the parties do not already know each other well, because they will need to invest time through the negotiation process to learn about each other's risk/price trade-off schedules.

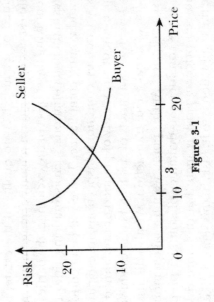

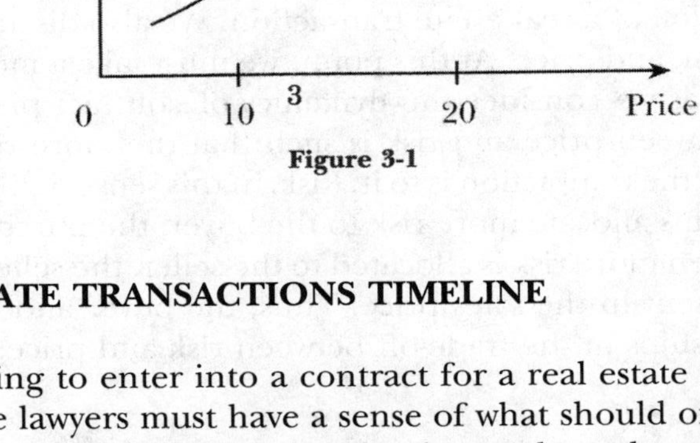

Figure 3-1

A. REAL ESTATE TRANSACTIONS TIMELINE

In preparing to enter into a contract for a real estate transaction, the parties and the lawyers must have a sense of what should or might happen after the contract is signed. They need to know where they are going. Thus, an overview of the entire contract process will help us develop a feel for the different stages involved. The diagram that follows depicts a timeline of contracting activities, broken down into four functional stages.

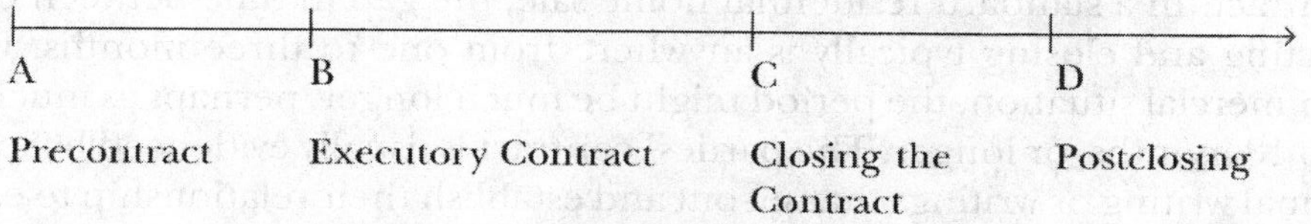

Figure 3-2

Understanding the "big picture" shown by this timeline will lead to effective lawyering. The good lawyer must negotiate and assess a transaction in the precontract stage with an understanding of all that might possibly follow. To best advise a client and to draft a complete and advantageous contract, the lawyer must contemplate and address all that might go wrong or become problematic at a later time during the covered relationship. To do this, one must first get a firm grasp of the issues, rules, and concerns that arise in each individual stage and then appreciate how they relate to the other stages. Ultimately, everything that is learned must be brought back to the precontract stage as a basis for informing the lawyer about the matters that must be discussed and clarified so that the transaction will proceed smoothly and without any unfavorable surprises for the client. We will now briefly discuss the dynamics that generally characterize each of the four stages.

Time Period "A → B"

The precontract stage is characterized by information gathering and negotiation. The parties engage in activities designed to get information on a possible transaction. They explore market possibilities and the viability of alternative market choices.

Precontract negotiation begins when the potential parties have identified each other. During the course of negotiation, temporal risk concerning information continually challenges both parties. One must gather good information in order to assess the value of the transaction, and both the buyer and the seller are trying to maximize the informational advantage while hoping that the other side is not withholding important material to the contrary. Each side must seek to discover as much as possible on her own and also confront the issue of when it may be advantageous or obligatory to disclose particular information to the other party. The law may or may not be clear as to what has to be disclosed, when disclosure is required, and who must do the disclosing.

Time Period "B → C"

After completing the precontract negotiation stage, either the parties have aborted their plans to go forward or they have struck a deal, thereby entering the "executory contract" period. This period runs from the moment of entering into the contract until the moment of "closing" the contract. In a standard residential home sale, the gap in time between contracting and closing typically is anywhere from one to three months. In a commercial situation, the period might be much longer, perhaps as much as 6 to 18 months, or longer. The parties' contract is usually evidenced by some formal writing or writings that set out and establish their relationship to each other and to the property, and during the executory contract period the parties undertake to accomplish the tasks and fulfill the promises identified in their contract. The doctrine of *equitable conversion* applies at the time of fully executing the contract document. Under the doctrine of equitable conversion, title is split with the legal title remaining in seller and the equitable title in the buyer.

Time Period "C → D"

The parties complete their contractual undertakings by means of an activity known as *closing* or *settlement,* which puts an end to the executory contract stage. It is a time when the title that was split by the doctrine of equitable conversion is brought back together and is vested in the buyer as owner of the full interest conveyed by the seller. The closing is typically a meeting scheduled at the office of the lender, one of the attorneys, or the title company.

The actual process of closing can vary with the state or community where the property is located or the particular circumstances of the transaction. In many parts of the country, most closings are conducted as ceremonies where everybody gathers at a prearranged meeting time. In other areas, however, an alternative arrangement called an *escrow closing* is commonly used, which dispenses with the need for everyone to be physically present at once. With an escrow, each party can show up separately to deposit papers and money in escrow, with the closing officer having the responsibility of finishing the closing when everything is complete.

All the activity at closing centers around the formal acts of the buyer delivering the purchase price to the seller and the seller delivering the instrument of conveyance to the buyer. At closing the *doctrine of merger* applies. The doctrine of merger provides that all promises prior to the closing are merged into the final documents taken at closing. Thus, warranties in the instrument of conveyance replace the warranties that were in the contract.

Time Period "D → "

The last stage in the real estate transaction is the postclosing period. This is the stage that reminds us that "the job isn't over until the paperwork is done." At the end of the closing meeting there will be many executed documents. Some of these documents, such as the warranty deed and any mortgage, will have to be recorded in the public records. In addition, certain things, like issuance of the final title insurance policy, cannot be completed until the necessary closing documents are officially available from the public records. All of this means that there are still parts of the deal to be completed after the formal closing. During this period, things can go wrong. Documents may get lost before being properly recorded, or documents may get misfiled or filed with the wrong attachments. These problems will delay the preparation of final title work and can seriously impair the completion of the transaction.

B. UNDERSTANDING THE CONSEQUENCES OF SIMPLE RULES

In preparing to contract, the lawyer must think carefully about the practical implications of simple legal rules. It is not enough simply to know the rules that govern real estate transfers; one must be able to respond to the implications behind the rules and take appropriate steps in contracting for any exchange. As an example of this process, consider one of the most basic rules of real property conveyancing. To have a valid conveyance of real property, the law requires that there be both a grantor and a grantee. The grantor is the party transferring the property, and the grantee is the party receiving the transfer or grant. This is a straightforward and easily understood rule that any person can memorize, but what is its implication for real estate contracting?

Problem 3A

Assume that Margaret contracts to purchase a major real estate property from GSPM, Inc. for $15 million. As the lawyer for Margaret, what will you want to examine and provide for in the purchase contract to assure the client that GSPM is a grantor capable of entering into an enforceable contract and conveying the property? Specifically identify documents and records you will want to receive and review.

Now assume that the various documents of transfer from GSPM were signed by Gina, the president and a 50 percent shareholder of the company. There is only one other shareholder, Giovanni, and he also holds 50 percent of the shares. Prior to closing with Margaret, the company had been in continuous existence for 10 years. Recently, but prior to closing, it failed to pay annual taxes and fees. If this issue comes to light at closing, what arguments might one use to support or defeat the ability of GSPM to properly transfer the property to Margaret? Instead of corporate president, what other type of status might apply to Gina, and how might this affect the validity of any transfer?

In both of the situations above, be sure to address the way in which each party to the transaction might view the situation. Think about the steps one would take at the contracting stage to reduce the risk of a bad outcome at closing.

C. LETTERS OF INTENT, OPTIONS, AND CONTRACT ENFORCEABILITY

Sometimes people negotiate about a transaction and exchange written information without intending to enter into a binding agreement. There will be many occasions when people exchange various offers and counteroffers or when they submit in writing some, but not all, terms of a proposed offer. The more complex the transaction, the more likely that various written pieces of information will be exchanged so that the parties can make progress toward reaching an overall basis for agreement. The exchanges of such information raise some common legal problems. The first problem is identifying the point in time when mere negotiations become a binding contract. Another is to determine whether the writing is a contract for a real estate transfer or merely an option to purchase at a later date, on specific terms, when and if the option is exercised. Finally, problems arise concerning the *statute of frauds* and the *parol evidence rule.*

The parol evidence rule prohibits the admission of prior written or prior or contemporaneous oral evidence that adds to or is inconsistent with the final written agreement between the parties. This assumes that the parties intended the final written agreement to be fully integrated. Such a presumption is usually implied unless there is clear evidence to the contrary. Many standard written contracts include a term stating that the document is the full and complete agreement between the parties. Such a provision is an *integration clause* and is meant to raise the parol evidence bar.

The statute of frauds prohibits the enforcement of oral agreements unless there is a writing signed by the party to be charged. The writing must generally set out essential terms such as the identification of the property to be exchanged, the price, and the names of the parties. These two legal doctrines are often related. A contract for the sale of real estate must be in writing, but the nature, extent, and scope of the required writing are often in dispute. Similarly, the writing may not state all the terms of the exchange, and the parties may be in disagreement about many details. Sometimes the parties will disagree about the very purpose of a writing. One party may assert that it forms the basis of an enforceable contract, while the other believes that it merely embraces some preliminary points of negotiation.

In a fundamental way, the key objectives of the letter of intent and the option contract are similar. Both arrangements seek a result that temporarily takes a property off the market while giving the buyer more time to consider the merits and demerits of a possible purchase. With a letter of intent, the parties generally proceed with an expectation that a very limited time will pass between the expression of intent to do a deal and the actual formulation of a binding contract to proceed with such an undertaking. In addition, the letter of intent is usually given without financial consideration. In contrast, an option is usually granted on the basis of money paid in exchange for taking the property off the market while the buyer contemplates the desirability of going forward. Options, therefore, generally express by their terms uncertainty as to the ultimate sale and purchase of the property. Letters of intent, in contrast, do not generally express such contingency, which heightens the risk that they will serve as evidence of an actual contract of sale and purchase.

Given the risk associated with letters of intent, it is often wise to avoid using them, but one may find that particular commercial clients like the idea of being able to do "handshake" deals, to be papered in detail by lawyers at a later time. Some clients also like the idea of getting a seller to hold a property off the market without paying an option fee. Consequently, a lawyer may have to use the letter-of-intent approach simply because her clients demand it. This is fine as long as the client is made aware of the potential risks associated with the use of a letter of intent.

GMH ASSOCIATES, INC. v. PRUDENTIAL REALTY GROUP
Superior Court of Pennsylvania, 2000
752 A.2d 889

CAVANAUGH, J. [O]n May 13, 1996, appellant, Prudential Realty Group (hereinafter "Prudential" and/or "Seller"), entered into a Letter of Interest (LOI) with appellee, GMH Associates (hereinafter "GMH" or "Buyer"), for the sale of commercial real estate in Montgomery County known as Bala Plaza (the Property).[2] The LOI contained certain terms and conditions previously discussed between the parties regarding the contemplated sale of the Property, including the following: the Property would be sold "AS IS" for a purchase price of $109.25 million; Buyer had begun "due diligence" and would complete same by 5 p.m. on July 3, 1996; the parties would endeavor to execute a formal, written contract of sale by that date; and

2. Prudential held title to the Property. Prudential's agent charged with handling the details of the transaction was Devon Glenn. Appellant, CB Commercial Real Estate Group was the entity Prudential used to market the Property. Appellant Douglas Joseph is CB Commercial's agent. Gary Holloway is the CEO and sole shareholder of appellee Buyer, GMH. Bruce Robinson is GMH's Chief Financial Officer.

the transaction would close on July 19, 1996.[3] The LOI contained the following clause in large, bold print:

> NOTWITHSTANDING THAT EITHER OR BOTH PARTIES MAY EXPEND SUBSTANTIAL EFFORTS AND SUMS IN ANTICIPATION OF ENTERING A CONTRACT, THE PARTIES ACKNOWLEDGE THAT IN NO EVENT WILL THIS LETTER BE CONSTRUED AS AN ENFORCEABLE CONTRACT TO SELL OR PURCHASE THE PROPERTY AND EACH PARTY ACCEPTS THE RISK THAT NO SUCH CONTRACT WILL BE EXECUTED.

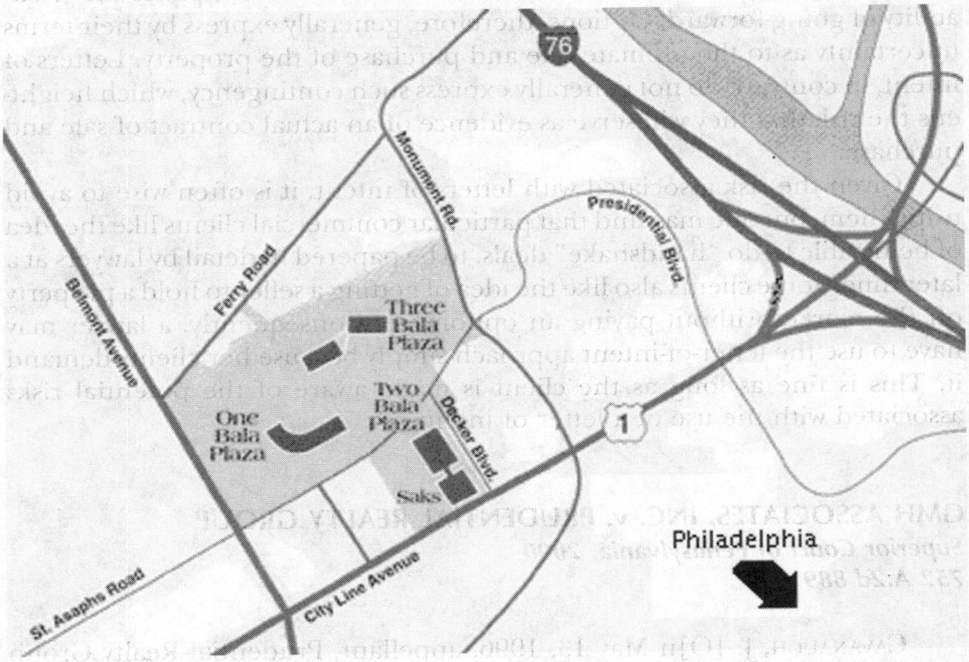

Bala Plaza map

Immediately below the bold print the LOI stated that "each party shall be free to terminate negotiations with the other for any reason whatsoever, at any time prior to the execution of the Contract without incurring liability to the other." The LOI further stated:

> Any Contract which may be negotiated shall not be binding on Seller until it has been approved by the senior corporate officers and the Law Department of Seller and by the Finance Committee of Seller's Board of Directors. Such

3. The record shows that in the weeks preceding the execution of the LOI, Buyer had inspected the Property and had begun conducting its "due diligence," i.e., its review of matters relating to, *inter alia*, title, land use, applicable zoning laws, profitability of existing and prospective leases and physical condition of the Property.

approvals are conditions precedent to the Seller's obligation to perform under the terms of the Contract, and may be withheld for any reason or for no reason.

Saks store and Two Bala Plaza office building.

At trial, it was established that Seller told Buyer that in exchange for Buyer's execution of the LOI, Seller would take the property "off the market." The record is also clear that both parties were aware, prior to executing the LOI, that Buyer was negotiating a master lease/purchase option agreement with a prospective tenant, the Allegheny Health and Education Research Foundation (hereinafter "Allegheny" or "AHERF"). Under this prospective agreement, on the same day Seller would convey the Property to Buyer, Allegheny would purchase the ground beneath a portion of Bala Plaza from Buyer for $6.2 million and would enter into a long-term lease with Buyer for office space in one of the Bala Plaza buildings.[4]

In late May or early June of 1996, Allegheny informed Buyer that it would be unable to negotiate the lease/purchase transaction for 90 days. . . . At the same time, Buyer notified Seller that its due diligence had uncovered some $3 million in capital improvements the Property required. Thus, Buyer sought to obtain a $3 million credit toward, or reduction below, the stated LOI purchase price.

On July 1st, Seller verbally agreed to Buyer's request to extend the closing date to July 31st. At the same time, Buyer suggested an "earn-out"

4. The court found that Seller knew that Buyer "was in a 'Catch-22' situation[,]" *i.e.*, Buyer did not have resources to pay the full purchase price contained in the LOI unless Buyer entered into and received proceeds from the prospective lease/purchase agreement with Allegheny, but Allegheny would not enter into the lease/purchase agreement unless Buyer could assure Allegheny that the Property was off the market.

proposal to Seller. Under the terms of this proposal, Buyer would forward to Seller, sometime after closing, a portion of the proceeds Buyer expected to receive as the result of executing the lease/purchase option with Allegheny. In early July, Buyer's verbal offer for the property was $103 million in cash at closing plus a post-closing "earn out" payment of $3.25 million after Buyer concluded its lease/purchase agreement with Allegheny. The remaining $3 million of the LOI purchase price would be deemed a capital improvements credit. Thus, the unconditional LOI purchase price of $109.25 million would not actually be met. Seller's net receipt of cash would be less than the LOI purchase price by an amount equal to the proposed capital improvements credit despite the provision of the LOI that the property was to be sold "AS IS."

In mid-July, Buyer increased its cash at closing offer to $103.5 million and lowered its capital credit request to $2.5 million. On July 30th, Seller's agent, Devon Glenn, asked Buyer to put the "earn-out" proposal in writing. Upon receiving same, Seller requested Buyer to give "teeth" to the proposal. The trial court found that by "teeth," Seller meant it wanted to be able to realize a percentage of any profit Buyer might get from consummating the Allegheny lease/purchase transaction. Buyer declined to put "teeth" into the "earn-out" proposal and on August 12, 1996, Glenn took the Buyer's purchase offer of $103.5 million cash at closing with a subsequent potential "earn-out" payment of $3.25 million to Prudential's investment committee for approval. The committee rejected Buyer's purchase offer that same date.

From the time the parties executed the LOI, Seller repeatedly assured Buyer that the property was off the market and that Buyer was the only prospective purchaser. The court found that Seller did, in fact, keep the Property "off the market at least from May 13, 1996 until August 12, 1996." After August 12th, Seller continued to negotiate with Buyer and continued to assure Buyer that it was not "shopping the deal" to other prospective purchasers, when, in fact, Seller allowed the Government of Singapore Investment Corporation (GSIC) to tour the Property on August 21st to determine whether GSIC had any interest in purchasing the Property. For a period of approximately three weeks thereafter, Seller conducted negotiations with both prospective purchasers, GMH and GSIC, without telling either entity about its negotiations with the other.

When Seller rejected GMH's latest proposal on August 12th, Seller told GMH that it was not interested in an "earn out" proposal and would require an all cash offer. Thus, on August 16th, GMH made a new oral offer of $105.5 million, all cash at closing. Seller did not immediately act thereon because GSIC was also expected to make an offer. On August 27th, an internal memorandum of Seller stated that "we will have GSIC's offer by the end of the week . . . we should be prepared to consider both proposals from GMH and GSIC and respond accordingly by Friday."

On August 30th, GSIC forwarded a letter of intent to Seller offering to purchase the Property for $108.5 million, all cash at closing. That date, Seller rejected GMH's $105.5 million all cash offer, but untruthfully continued to assure GMH that there existed no other bidder. . . .

[On] September 10th, Joseph told Robinson that "there were three people interested in the property and he was concerned they were going to put in bids on the property". . . .

Joseph, at that time, advised Robinson that GMH's next offer had to be in writing and did not disclose to GMH that GSIC had already submitted a written $108.5 million bid on the Property. Immediately after speaking with Joseph, Robinson called the leasing agent for the Property, Janet Giuliani. Giuliani informed Robinson that GSIC had toured the Property.

The next day, September 11th, Mr. Holloway and Mr. Robinson decided that they would meet Seller's "offer" of $107.25 million. Also that date, before putting their "acceptance" of Seller's "offer" in writing, the pair met with representatives of Allegheny. The meeting had been called by Allegheny. At the beginning of the meeting, Holloway told the Allegheny representatives that "GMH had a deal with Prudential, that GMH and Prudential had agreed to a price, and GMH was moving toward closing." At the conclusion of the meeting, Allegheny told GMH that they had an agreement in principle to the lease/purchase transaction but that further negotiations were necessary to resolve some outstanding issues, namely "clarification from GMH on when GMH would be able to put tenants into the Bala buildings and whether GMH was able to give Allegheny an additional $10 [per square foot] allowance [on a 185,000 square foot space] for tenant improvement."[8] The court found these issues did not appear to be material or significant to the ultimate completion of the GMH/Allegheny transaction.

Later in the day, Mr. Robinson called Mr. Joseph to inform him that GMH had "accepted" Prudential's "offer" of $107.25 million and would put the acceptance in writing. Joseph suggested that the writing be in a letter of interest format. Thus, on September 11th, Robinson forwarded a letter to Devon Glenn which stated, in pertinent part:

> This letter summarizes certain revised terms and conditions which we have discussed regarding the sale of [the Property] by Prudential Insurance Company of America ("Seller") to GMH Associates, Inc. ("Purchaser").
>
> 1. Purchase Price. The Purchase Price for the Property will be $107,250,000 ("Purchase Price") payable as follows:
>
> (a) $1,000,000 in immediately available funds . . . upon full execution of the contract for the sale and purchase of the property . . .
>
> (b) The balance of the Purchase Price would be paid upon closing . . .
>
> 2. Due Diligence and Inspection Contingencies
>
> (a) Both Purchaser and Seller acknowledge that there is an outstanding environmental issue . . . Purchaser and Seller both agree to have their

8. Thus, it appears that Allegheny wanted to negotiate a $1.85 million credit from GMH toward tenant improvements.

respective representatives meet in order to come to a mutually agreeable resolution to this issue. . . .

All other terms and conditions of the letter of interest dated May 13, 1996 between Purchaser and Seller shall remain in full force and effect except for the items mentioned above, and the contract and closing dates of which shall now be changed to October 31, 1996.

If you are in agreement with the above please so indicate by signing the enclosed copy of this letter in the space provided below and return to us as soon as possible.

Sincerely Yours,
GMH ASSOCIATES, INC.

By: [*Signature*]
Bruce F. Robinson

AGREED TO AND ACCEPTED:
By: ______________________
Name:
Title:
Date Executed:

On September 12th, Devon Glenn called Joseph Grubb, GSIC's agent. Glenn informed Grubb that Prudential had received an offer from GMH that was a "higher net number than GSIC's offer."[9] Mr. Glenn further told Grubb that if GSIC agreed to pay $806,158 toward tenant improvements and brokerage commissions (TIBCs) then Prudential would sign GSIC's letter of intent. GSIC agreed to the proposal which, as the trial court found, made GSIC's "offer approximately $500,000 more than GMH's number, including TIBCs."

That same date, Glenn and Joseph informed Holloway and Robinson that Prudential had rejected GMH's bid and had agreed to sell the Property to GSIC.

GMH subsequently sued Prudential, CB Commercial Real Estate and Douglas Joseph. The complaint alleged Breach of Contract, Breach of Duty to Negotiate in Good Faith, and Promissory Estoppel against Prudential. It further alleged Fraudulent Misrepresentation, Fraudulent Nondisclosure, and Civil Conspiracy against all defendants. . . .

Following a non-jury trial, the court found for GMH on all its claims and awarded damages to GMH for lost profits in the amount of $20,340,623. It also awarded GMH $10,000,000 in punitive damages — $7,000,000 assessed against Prudential and $3,000,000 assessed against CB Commercial. . . .

9. As the trial court explained: The reason GMH's $107.25 million number was a higher net number than GSIC's $108.5 million number was because, in its LOI, GMH agreed to pay tenant improvements and broker's commissions, which were $1.6 million. GSIC had no such provision in its offer. Therefore, comparing "apples to apples," GMH's number was $107.25 [million] plus $1.6 million, or $108,850,000, and GSIC's was $350,000 less.

The trial court authored a lengthy opinion in support of its determination. Among other things, the court concluded that GMH and Prudential entered into an enforceable oral contract for the sale of the Property on September 11th; that Prudential defrauded GMH and failed to negotiate in good faith in procuring the oral contract; that GMH relied to its detriment on Prudential's representations; that Prudential breached the September 11th oral contract with GMH when it subsequently sold the property to GSIC; and that GMH was entitled to damages in the nature of lost profits.

Prudential now appeals, contending that the court's verdict is not sustainable under any of the causes of action GMH presented. We agree.

A. Breach of Contract

Contrary to the trial court's determination, we find that no oral contract for the sale of the Property arose. . . .

It appears the court's conclusion that an enforceable oral contract was formed between the parties was based, in part, on its finding that $107.25 million was Prudential's "will sell" price. The court found Mr. Robinson credible and credited his testimony that on September 9th, Devon Glenn asserted he could "close the deal" at a purchase price of $107.25 million; that the price quoted was "not a moving target" and represented the "number that we will sell the property to you for." Further the court found that GMH "met" Prudential's "will sell" offer on the basis of the content of the September 11th letter of interest, which stated that the purchase price would be $107.25 million. Thus, the court implicitly found that on September 9th, Prudential orally "offered" to sell the Property to GMH for $107.25 million and that on September 11th, GMH "accepted" Prudential's offer, in writing, by forwarding the letter of interest containing the agreed upon purchase price. Based on these findings, the court concluded that an enforceable oral contract for the sale of the Property arose on September 11th.

We find that the court's determination was legal error. First, we cannot agree that Glenn's statements to Robinson on September 9th constituted an offer to sell. . . . Robinson testified that during his conversation with Glenn on September 9th, Glenn said "I'm not saying you can't *offer* a lower number and that we won't *accept* a lower number. However, if you want to make sure you get the property, you must *offer* the $107,250,000 because that's the number I know *I can get the deal approved at.*" We find that Prudential, through Glenn, was soliciting an offer from GMH which would then be taken to Prudential's decision makers for approval and acceptance.

Assuming *arguendo* that Glenn's statements on September 9th did, in fact, constitute an offer to sell the property for a sum certain, we would find the offer was revoked the next day when Joseph informed Robinson that there were other likely bidders competing for the Property; that GMH's next offer had to be in writing; and that GMH's next offer ought to be its best offer. It is hornbook law that an offeree's power to accept an offer is terminated by a revocation of the offer by the offeror. First Home Savings Bank, FSB v. Nernberg, 436 Pa. Super. 377, 648 A.2d 9, 15 (Pa. Super. 1994); Restatement (Second) of Contracts §36 (1981).

Moreover, GMH's purported acceptance of Prudential's offer, made via the unexecuted letter of interest dated September 11th, included a clause stating that the parties would agree to discuss an open and apparently unresolved environmental issue regarding the property. . . . We additionally note that, on its face, the unexecuted letter of interest, which the court concluded was GMH's "acceptance," does not purport to be an acceptance at all, but, in fact, is drafted as an offer. We conclude that GMH's offer to buy the Property was rejected by Prudential and that no contract was formed.

Further, it is clear that the parties always intended and agreed that any binding transaction between them for the conveyance of the Property would be accomplished by a written contract. This intention is stated and agreed to by the parties in the executed LOI of May 13th and is adopted by reference in GMH's unexecuted September 11th letter of interest.

Our supreme court has recently reiterated that "where the parties have agreed orally to all the terms of their contract, and a part of the mutual understanding is that a written contract embodying these terms shall be drawn and executed by the respective parties, such oral contract may be enforced, though one of the parties thereafter refuses to execute the written contract." Shovel Transfer & Storage, Inc. v. PLCB, 559 Pa. 56, 66, 739 A.2d 133, 138 (1999) (*quoting* Ketchum v. Conneaut Lake Co., 309 Pa. 224, 163 A. 534, 535 (1932)). *See also* Mazzella v. Koken, 559 Pa. 216, 224, 739 A.2d 531, 536 (1999) ("where the parties have agreed on the essential terms of a contract, the fact that they intend to formalize their agreement in writing but have not yet done so does not prevent enforcement of such an agreement"). Relying on decisional precedent which embodies this proposition, the trial court concluded that an enforceable contract arose on September 11th despite the fact that no written contract was ever executed. . . . We find that the court's conclusion in this regard was error.

The essential terms that must be identified and agreed to in order to form a valid contract for the sale of real estate are the naming of the specific parties, property and consideration or purchase price. *See* Detwiler v. Capone, 357 Pa. 495, 502, 55 A.2d 380, 385 (1947). . . . We conclude that there was no mutual assent between the parties as to essential terms or the subject matter of the transaction and that all issues surrounding the structure of the proposed transaction had not been closed.

First, the original LOI contemplated a $109.25 million all cash at closing purchase price. At the same time that GMH informed Prudential that there was a "glitch" in procuring Allegheny's involvement, it also informed Prudential that its due diligence had uncovered $3 million in necessary capital improvements. Despite the LOI's "AS IS" language, GMH sought a $3 million capital improvements credit. . . the evidence is that when

GMH's "earn out" proposal was rejected and the parties began to focus on an all cash price, the parties were still $1.5 million apart on the amount of any capital improvements credit. The evidence does not suggest that gap was ever closed. Thus, we conclude that an essential term, namely, the purchase price amount, as affected by the capital improvements credit, had never been agreed to by the parties and thus that no enforceable contract arose.

Second, the September 11th "acceptance" letter of interest specifically incorporated the terms of the original LOI of May 13th. The May 13th LOI provided that "the parties have not attempted in this letter to set forth all essential terms of the subject matter of this transaction, and such essential terms shall be the subject of further negotiations." Moreover, the September 11th letter expressly provided that the parties would continue to negotiate regarding an unresolved environmental issue. Because recognized issues remained unresolved, no mutual assent existed sufficient to bind the parties.

Third, the executed LOI of May 13th contained an express condition precedent that was never met. The parties agreed that any written contract they might negotiate would not bind Seller unless it was approved by Seller's senior corporate officers, law department and board finance committee. It is undisputed that no corporate approval was given to the terms of the Buyer's September 11th proposal and thus, we conclude that no enforceable contract arose. . . .

B. Fraud

The trial court concluded that "Prudential obtained the oral agreement of September 11th by fraud." Specifically, the court found as fact that all defendants, between August 15th and September 12th, continually assured GMH that Prudential was not negotiating with other prospective buyers, when in fact, Prudential was actively negotiating with GSIC during that period. The court concluded that these assurances were fraudulent misrepresentations. Similarly, the court concluded that after August 15th, the defendants' failure to inform GMH that Prudential was negotiating with GSIC amounted to fraudulent nondisclosure of the fact that the Property was no longer "off the market." Thus, the court concluded that the oral contract of sale created on September 11th, was procured through fraud.

Initially, because we find that no contract was created, we correspondingly conclude that no fraud was committed in its alleged procurement. However, even if the elements of an oral contract had been created on September 11th, we would nonetheless be constrained to conclude that defendants' collective failure to disclose, between August 15th and September 12th, that the Property was no longer "off the market," as well as their affirmative statements that GMH was the exclusive bidder, were immaterial to the transaction at hand, *i.e.*, GMH's decision to offer $107.25 million and Prudential's decision to reject that offer. Thus, we would conclude that no fraud was committed. . . .

C. Duty to Negotiate in Good Faith

The court determined that Prudential breached a duty to negotiate in good faith by failing to keep the Property off the market.

Our courts have not determined whether a cause of action for breach of duty to negotiate in good faith exists in Pennsylvania. Jenkins v. County of Schuylkill, 441 Pa. Super. 642, 658 A.2d 380, 385 (1995). The Third Circuit Court of Appeals has predicted that Pennsylvania would recognize such an action. *See* Flight Systems, Inc. v. EDS Corp., 112 F.3d 124, 129 (3d Cir.1997) (*citing* Channel Home Centers v. Grossman, 795 F.2d 291, 299 (3d Cir.1986)).

This court has previously quoted the following principle with approval: "The full extent of a party's duty to negotiate in good faith can only be determined, however, from the terms of the letter of intent itself." *Jenkins*, 658 A.2d at 385 (*quoting* A/S Apothekernes Laboratorium For Specialpraeparater v. I.M.C. Chemical Group, Inc., 873 F.2d 155, 158-59 (7th Cir.1989)). . . .

Here, the parties' May 13th LOI expressly provided that either party could terminate negotiations at any time for any reason without incurring liability to the other prior to the execution of a written contract. It did not contain any provision regarding the duty to negotiate in good faith. Further, the LOI included no provision regarding the Property's "off the market" status. Thus, we conclude, if our courts were to recognize the existence of such a cause of action, that the duty to negotiate in good faith was not breached in this case by Prudential's failure to keep the property "off the market" or to reveal that it was entering negotiations with GSIC.

D. Promissory Estoppel

The doctrine of promissory estoppel allows a party, under certain circumstances, to enforce a promise even though the promise is not supported by consideration. . . .

The trial court found that the doctrine of promissory estoppel applied to GMH's claims that (1) Prudential promised to keep the Property off the market while negotiations with GMH continued; and (2) Prudential promised to sell the Property to GMH for $107.25 million.

We conclude the court erred in finding these "promises" were enforceable for the same reasons we find that no contract arose and that no fraud was committed. First, the parties agreed that the Property would stay off the market, *inter alia*, as long as GMH was meeting the deadlines it proposed to Prudential. The Property was, in fact, off the market for three months, but GMH could not close within that time. . . . Since Prudential kept the Property off the market for three months during which time the proposed transaction was not consummated, we do not find the doctrine of promissory estoppel available to bind it to continue to keep the Property off the market seemingly indefinitely.

Second, we find that any offer Prudential made on September 9th, to sell the Property to GMH for $107.25 million, was revoked by Prudential's representations of September 10th. Thus, we conclude that there existed no enforceable "promise" to sell the property to GMH for a sum certain. . . .

G. Conclusion

For the foregoing reasons, we find that the court's verdict is not sustainable under any of the causes of action set forth by GMH. Accordingly, we reverse the judgment entered in favor of GMH and remand with directions to enter judgment notwithstanding the verdict in favor of appellants. Jurisdiction is relinquished.

Problem 3B

Jim and Kathy are contemplating the exchange of a small winery business owned by Kathy. The business includes 15 acres of land on which there are varietal grapevines, a wine production facility, and an inventory storage area with adjoining tasting room. The negotiated price for the entire operation is $5.2 million. The parties have reached agreement on the terms of the deal, with the exception of the financing. Kathy insists on a cash deal with no financing contingency in the contract. Jim knows that he needs financing of about $2 million. Jim goes to Cabernet Bank & Trust (CB&T) to get a loan prior to formally executing a contract with Kathy. Jim tells CB&T about his discussions with Kathy and of his needs for money. CB&T prepares a standard form "Letter of Intent to Finance" for Jim. The letter is addressed to Jim and signed by the Vice President of Lending Operations. The letter states that CB&T has made a review of Jim's plans to acquire certain property for a wine business and that it would be able and willing to finance the acquisition of both the land and the improvements on the terms of $2 million borrowed at the market rate for the bank's preferred corporate clients, terms to be as set out in the bank's standard wine industry lending forms, specifics to be inserted at a later date. Jim takes the letter and decides to sign on to the all-cash deal proposed by Kathy.

After Jim signs the contract with Kathy, CB&T, pointing to a decline in the wine market, refuses to make more than $1.4 million available to Jim. As a result, Jim is unable to close the contract with Kathy. Jim sues CB&T for breach of its contract to lend him $2 million. What arguments and issues might confront each party in this situation?

Problem 3C

After reviewing the form Letter of Intent that follows, consider how you might have used this form in working with the parties involved in problem 3B above. Try drafting a letter of intent for the underlying sale between Kathy and Jim, as well as between Jim and the lender. How might the letter differ if you were representing the buyer rather than the seller, and vice versa? How might it differ as between Jim and the lender? What if you were the only lawyer involved in these transactions and you had been asked to represent both parties? Do you see any difficulty or problems with this form letter? Do you think that in the absence of any further writings, you could give a legal opinion to your client assuring her that the letter of intent you have drafted will not be construed as a complete and binding contract?

In the alternative, assume that this form Letter of Intent is used between your client Jim, the buyer, and Kathy the seller of the property. Assume that in using this form the parties fill in all of the blanks, including a price term of $5.2 million. Three days after this Letter of Intent is signed, Kathy enters a binding contract of sale with a third party, Giovanni. In this contract, Giovanni agrees to pay Kathy $6 million for the property. Jim calls you and is upset about losing such a great deal. Jim wants you to sue Kathy on the grounds that she was already contractually bound to sell the property to Jim for $5.2 million. Jim wants the property, or in the alternative the $800,000 extra that was paid by Giovanni for the property. Jim argues that the extra $800,000 rightfully belongs to him because he had a binding contract under the letter of intent prior to the contract between Giovanni and Kathy. How will you argue the case for Jim, and what do you anticipate as responses from Kathy and Giovanni?

FORM LETTER OF INTENT

Date: __________

[Name] __________

[Address] __________

Re: ("Property") __________

Dear [Name] __________:

The following is to serve as a Letter of Intent to acquire from you that certain Property located at __________; described as:

1. *Buyer* [Name] __________:

2. *Seller* [Name] __________:

3. *Purchase Price*. Purchase price shall be the sum of __________ DOLLARS ($ ______), which shall be payable:

A. __________ DOLLARS ($ __________) cash deposit to be deposited with an escrow agent, selected by Buyer, said deposit to be deposited in

an interest-bearing account, interest accruing to the benefit of the Buyer. Said deposit to be paid upon execution of a formal Contract to Purchase, executed by both parties.

B. ___________ DOLLARS ($) ___________ payable in cash at closing.

4. *Acceptance of Letter of Intent*: Seller shall have until the _______ day of ____ , 20____ to accept this Letter of Intent, by delivering written notice of acceptance to Buyer by said date at [Address, City, State] _____________.

5. *Contract of Sale*: Within ten (10) days of your acceptance of this Letter of Intent by written notice to the Buyer specified above, the parties will enter into a contract embodying the terms of this Letter of Intent, and such other provisions as the parties and/or their counsel deem necessary or appropriate.

6. *Rights of Inspection*: Seller shall furnish Buyer upon execution of the Contract of Sale, copies of any mortgages or liens encumbering the subject property, a current rent roll, copies of all leases and contracts pertaining to the property, a current survey, and profit and loss operating statements relative to the property for the years ___________. Buyer shall have twenty (20) days from the date of delivery of said documents to review the same. In addition, Buyer shall have twenty (20) business days from the date of execution of the Contract of Sale within which to inspect the property and all improvements thereon, and to conduct a termite inspection of the improvements on the property. If the Seller is not notified in writing prior to the termination of the twenty (20) business day period that Buyer wishes to terminate the Contract of Sale, the earnest money deposit will be forfeited to Seller and will be non-refundable.

7. *Closing*: Closing with respect to the sale will take place on or before the _____ day of ____ , 20____.

8. *Formal Agreement*: The provisions of this Letter of Intent are subject to the execution of a formal agreement by the parties within a specified time in Paragraph 5 above and this Letter of Intent shall not be binding on Buyer or Seller until complete execution of such Purchase and Sale Agreement by the parties which said Purchase and Sale Agreement shall embody the above provisions and contain acceptable covenants and agreements concerning title, survey, closing procedures and expenses, notices, remedies, and such other items as may be deemed necessary or appropriate.

Please confirm that the foregoing is acceptable to you so that we may proceed to prepare a formal Purchase and Sale Agreement for your submission and review.

Very truly yours,

____
Signature

4

Executory Contracts

The executory contract period of a real estate transaction is a busy time for the parties, full of risk and activity. The time period generally begins at the moment the parties reach an agreement, usually memorialized in the execution of a formal writing. Typically, it ends at the closing of the contract with the satisfactory completion of all the various contractual undertakings of each party. Thus, the time horizon we are considering is the duration of the parties' contractual relationship with each other.

Identifying the specific points of opening and closure to the contract is not always a clean and easy matter. Sometimes it can be outright messy. As we discuss in Chapter 3, it is not always clear when the parties have reached the point of having entered into an enforceable agreement. Moreover, even when the parties attempt to write out a formal contract of purchase and sale, they are sometimes unsuccessful. Thus, what sometimes looks like the moment of agreement between the parties may still be only the potential for such a legally recognizable relationship. At the other end of the time span, the difficulties inherent in determining the commencement of a contract can also arise when trying to pinpoint the ending of that relationship. Sometimes the parties to an agreement will intentionally leave certain aspects of their contractual relationship open beyond what otherwise passes as the closing ceremony. Likewise, the courts have developed legal doctrines that can prolong some aspects of a contractual relationship beyond the formalities of the closing process. Despite these "gray areas," it is still useful to begin the study of this time period by thinking of it as a specific time horizon with specific and measurable moments of commencement and closure.

During the executory contract period, the parties are busy performing their obligations. It is a time that allows for more detailed investigation of the property and for the gathering of evidence to demonstrate one's own compliance with the contract.

A. EXECUTING AN ENFORCEABLE CONTRACT

The main purpose of the contract in a real estate transaction is to arrange for the orderly transfer of an interest in real property to the buyer in exchange for the money or other consideration given to the seller. In its most simple formulation, one might think in terms of a deed conveying title swapped for cash.

1. The Need for a Writing

A basic legal rule is that an agreement for the purchase and sale of real property must comply with the *statute of frauds.* The requirements for a writing to satisfy the statute are often muddy, both because the legal rules suffer from indeterminacy and because the disputes are fact-specific. Statute of frauds defenses are often raised in connection with the many modern real estate transactions that go awry and end up in court. Usually this happens when parties forgo the assistance of lawyers in planning their transaction. High volumes of litigation have generally failed to resolve the lack of clarity concerning the requirements of the statute.

To satisfy the statute of frauds the writing must include essential terms such as the names of the parties, the description of the property, and the intent to buy and sell. It need not include all contract terms, and thus the *parol evidence rule* may be a factor when considering the enforceability of alleged contract terms that are not part of the written agreement.

The writing must be signed by the party to be charged. The *Electronic Signatures in Global and National Commerce Act,* 15 U.S.C. §§7001 to 7031, passed by Congress in 2000, expands our understanding of "signing" the "document." It adds an additional wrinkle to the need for a writing and for analysis of an exchange under the statute of frauds. By this Act, Congress authorized electronic signatures. For this reason, the Act is sometimes referred to as the *E-sign Act.* The Act has a broad scope. It applies to any transaction in or affecting interstate or foreign commerce, including contracts, sales, leases, or other dispositions of personal and real property. The Act preempts any state law to the contrary; it operates notwithstanding "any statute, regulation, or other rule of law." *Id.* §7001(a). Thus, a traditional state statute of frauds, which may be interpreted to require a traditional writing, is preempted. The Act validates an electronic signature for purposes of a variety of transactions. This means that a seller could send a contract proposal for the sale of real estate to a buyer as an e-mail attachment and the buyer could form a legally binding commitment by e-mailing back an approval that is meant to signify intent to be bound. In addition, telephone calls are electronic communications, and thus voice mail or a message left on an answering machine may operate as a legal signature. Naturally, there are continuing issues of when a signature or a mark, even an electronic mark, signifies intent to be bound, and there are issues to be raised about the authenticity of an e-signature.

Some oral contracts for the purchase and sale of real property can be enforced on the theory of *part performance* or *equitable estoppel*. In each case, there must be proof of an oral agreement between the parties. In the alternative, a claim may be raised on the theory of *promissory estoppel*, which is a contract substitute. As a contract substitute, one would not have to prove an underlying oral contract using this theory, but would have to demonstrate the facts supporting detrimental reliance.

Problem 4A

Dana and Jim, a married couple, own property in northern New York. On August 1, Jim enters a contract to sell the property to Donnatella. The contract calls for a purchase price of $300,000 and the delivery of good and marketable fee simple title to be conveyed by general warranty deed at a closing to be held on November 1. Jim and Dana, husband and wife, hold title as tenants by the entireties. Dana is not a party to the contract with Donnatella. Jim executed the contract with Donnatella while Dana was out of town on a lecture tour to promote her latest book. Jim thought that the price offered by Donnatella for the property was at least $20,000 above the price he would have expected. He felt he could not wait on the deal and assumed his wife would go along with the transaction when she discovered what a great price they were going to get.

(a) By November 1, it becomes clear that Jim has miscalculated the value of his property. During the time of the executory contract, inflation has risen because of the outbreak of military conflicts in Asia and the resulting instability of international financial markets. At the same time, plans have been announced for a Japanese manufacturing facility to be transplanted to an area near the subject property. Current estimates are that the property is worth somewhere between $350,000 and $370,000. At closing, Dana refuses to join in the deed of conveyance and refuses to recognize the contract of sale. What, if anything, might you recommend that Donnatella do, and what potential problems await her?

(b) Assume that during the executory contract period Donnatella discovers that she has paid too much for the property. Furthermore, property values in the area have been on a steady decline as a result of high unemployment and the departure of several major businesses. Donnatella does a little research and discovers that Jim is not the sole owner of the property, but instead owns it with Dana. Donnatella informs Jim that she does not consider the contract binding and lets him know that she will not close on the deal. The next day, Dana adds her signature to the contract already executed by Jim and Donnatella. Jim delivers the contract, with Dana's recently added signature, to Donnatella, along with evidence of an appropriate deed signed by both Dana and himself which will be delivered at closing. Donnatella says this comes too late and is ineffective. Must Donnatella proceed or pay damages? What issues confront the various parties?

(c) How can a person like Donnatella be certain that all the proper and necessary parties have executed the contract of purchase and sale? What can she do to avoid the problems and risks of the above situation? Is there a reasonable, low-cost way to proceed to cover this risk? Should someone like Jim be held to his promise to deliver good and marketable title or pay damages if he cannot perform? Is the conduct of the parties predictable in the above situations when one considers the market context of the transaction?

2. *Other Requirements for an Enforceable Contract*

In addition to the statute of frauds requirement of a writing for the sale of real property, we must remember that the entire domain of contract law generally applies to real estate transactions. This means that there will be issues of adequate consideration, offer, acceptance, unconscionability, anticipatory repudiation, breach, warranty, and damages, among others. This is important to keep in mind because it is easy to forget when the subject matter of a contract is real property. For instance, the law governing deeds, leases, titles, mortgages, foreclosures, liens, real covenants, and priority rights can be very different from that governing contract law or the law applicable to personal property. The underlying law applicable to your subject matter can nonetheless generally be the subject of contract. This means that when parties to a transaction structure their relationship, they are given the opportunity to impose obligations and benefits on each other in a manner prescribed by contract law principles. To do this effectively, however, requires a working knowledge of the relevant property law so that the appropriate risks, obligations, and consequences of a proposed transaction can be accounted for in the parties' agreement. Thus, a person needs to know the types of deeds that are available to convey real property and also the rules and consequences, under real property law, related to those deeds before he can intelligently invoke contract law to structure a relationship involving the property.

In today's real estate markets, most transactions will include some non-real property elements, which means that the contract of purchase and sale will have to account for more than just real property law. Even in the simplest residential home sale, for example, the transfer of basic appliances such as a stove or refrigerator is covered under the law pertaining to the sale of goods, and the transfer of the furnace and central air conditioning units might well fall into yet another classification as fixtures. Some forms of residential housing offer even more complication. The purchase and sale of a cooperative apartment, for instance, actually involves the transfer of stock, which is considered personal property subject to a security interest under Article 9 of the Uniform Commercial Code, rather than a real estate mortgage.

Problem 4B

A contract for purchase and sale is generally freely assignable. Your client, John, comes to your office and shows you a copy of a contract under which Tom is to purchase improved real estate from Diane for $300,000. John says that Tom no longer wants the property and is willing to assign the contract to him for $10,000, which means the property will cost him $310,000 in total. John feels the price is a very good deal and wants to accept Tom's offer. You review the contract for all the essential terms and find no serious problems. The contract was signed two weeks ago and is scheduled to close in 60 days. It includes a number of provisions related to financing, title, zoning, and building and occupancy permits. As John's attorney, what special risks do you see that are peculiar to taking this assignment? Does John need a written assignment from Tom? What kinds of provisions should be included in the assignment agreement? To protect John adequately, is it necessary to do more than bargain with Tom?

Problem 4C

Yoshi seeks to contract for the sale of his house to Marnin. The contract calls for a total sales price of $325,000. Included in the sale are certain items of personal property, including a stove, a refrigerator, a dining room table with chairs, a Persian rug, a freezer, and an alarm system. Yoshi's draft of the contract requires him to convey the property by good and proper general warranty deed. Marnin objects and says he wants a bill of sale for the personal property. Yoshi turns to you, his lawyer, and asks for advice. Yoshi wants you to explain why Marnin would make such a request. Yoshi also wants to know what you think his response should be.

THE FLORIDA BAR v. BELLEVILLE
Supreme Court of Florida, 1991
591 So. 2d 170

PER CURIAM. We have this case on complaint of The Florida Bar for review of a referee's report recommending that Walter J. Belleville, an attorney licensed in Florida, be found not guilty of alleged ethical violations. . . .

In the summer of 1988, Belleville was retained as counsel for Bradley M. Bloch. Bloch had entered into an agreement with James F. Cowan to purchase property owned by the latter. Cowan was an elderly man, eighty-three years of age, who had a third-grade education. While the evidence showed that Cowan had substantial prior experience in selling real estate when he was younger, neither party to this cause disputes that the various written documents alleged to constitute the agreement overwhelmingly favored the buyer, Mr. Bloch. Cowan, in fact, has subsequently disputed that he ever agreed to some of the terms embodied in these documents.[1]

Although Cowan and Bloch had negotiated only for the sale of an apartment building, the documents stated that Cowan was selling both the apartment building and his residence, which was located across the street from the apartments. The referee specifically found that Cowan had no intention of selling his residence and did not know that it was included in the sale. The record substantially supports this finding, which accordingly must be accepted as fact by this Court. The Fla. Bar v. Bajoczky, 558 So. 2d 1022 (Fla. 1990).

It is unclear whether Belleville knowingly participated in his client's activities or merely followed the client's instructions without question. Whatever the case, Belleville drafted the relevant documents to include the legal description of Cowan's house in the instruments of sale. Cowan then apparently signed the documents without realizing he was transferring title to his house. No one at the closing explained the significance of the legal description to him. Belleville only sent a paralegal to the closing and did not attend it himself. In fact, he had never met Cowan to this point in time.

In exchange for the apartment and his residence, Cowan received only a promissory note, not a mortgage. The loan thus was unsecured. This note provided for ten percent interest amortized over twenty-five years. However, the first payment was deferred for four months with no apparent provision for interest to accumulate during this time, and the note by its own terms will become unenforceable upon Cowan's death. Finally, the documents called for Cowan to pay the closing costs, which Bloch and Belleville construed as including Belleville's attorney fee of $625.

When Cowan received the promissory note and closing documents, he realized that their terms varied from the agreement he thought he had entered. Cowan contacted an attorney, who wrote a letter to Belleville explaining the points of disagreement. The next day, Bloch attempted to evict Cowan from his home.

The referee recommended no discipline based on his conclusion that Belleville owed no attorney-client obligation to Cowan. The Board of Governors of The Florida Bar voted to appeal this decision, and the Bar now seeks a thirty-day suspension.

While it is true that the factual findings of a referee may not be disturbed unless clearly and convincingly wrong, *Bajoczky*, we do not find that the present case turns on a dispute about the facts. The essential facts are not in question; and Belleville himself concedes with some understatement that "Mr. Cowan did not have a particularly good deal as a result of his negotiations with Mr. Bloch." Rather, the disagreement in this case is over

1. The Florida Bar has not charged Belleville with any fraud-related violation, and we accordingly express no opinion as to whether such a violation occurred.

Belleville's guilt and the appropriate discipline, if any. This is a question entirely of law that we must decide. As former Chief Justice Ehrlich has noted, a referee's recommendation "is a recommendation and nothing more. It does not carry the authority or weight of a finding of fact by the referee." *Bajoczky,* 558 So. 2d at 1025.

Based on the facts, we cannot accept the referee's recommendation about guilt and punishment. The referee's factual findings established that Cowan had negotiated to sell the apartment, that he did not intend to sell anything other than the apartment, and that he did not know that the documents of sale would result in the loss of his residence. It also is clear Belleville should have harbored suspicions about the documents he was preparing, because the documents established on their face a transaction so one-sided as to put Belleville on notice of the likelihood of their unconscionability.

When faced with this factual scenario, we believe an attorney is under an ethical obligation to do two things. First, the attorney must explain to the unrepresented opposing party the fact that the attorney is representing an adverse interest. Second, the attorney must explain the material terms of the documents that the attorney has drafted for the client so that the opposing party fully understands their actual effect. When the transaction is as one-sided as that in the present case, counsel preparing the documents is under an ethical duty to make sure that an unrepresented party understands the possible detrimental effect of the transaction and the fact that the attorney's loyalty lies with the client alone. R. Regulating Fla. Bar 4-1.7. . . .

For the foregoing reasons, we adopt the referee's findings of fact but reject the recommendations regarding guilt and discipline. The violation Belleville committed is a serious one. . . . Accordingly, we grant the request of the Florida Bar. Walter J. Belleville is hereby suspended from the practice of law for a period of thirty days, commencing on January 6, 1992. . . . Judgment for costs in the amount of $1,220.30 is entered against Belleville in favor of the Florida Bar.

B. EQUITABLE CONVERSION AND ALLOCATION OF RISK

One of the most significant legal consequences of entering a binding contract between the buyer and the seller of real property involves the doctrine of *equitable conversion.* In simple terms, this doctrine splits title to the property between the seller and the buyer at the moment the contract is signed. The seller is still the owner of the property and is said to retain *legal title* to the realty, while the buyer is said to acquire *equitable title.* This splitting of the title by way of the doctrine of equitable conversion has a number of legal consequences. To start with, it means that the buyer has an interest in the property even though the contract has not been fully performed. Both parties have the right to deal with their respective interests—that is, to buy, sell, assign, pledge, mortgage, devise, and insure, among other things. A seller may not want the buyer to have such abilities because they could affect the ultimate risk of completing a successful transaction. For similar reasons, a buyer may want to limit the seller's right to transfer his legal title and interest in the property to a third party while the contract remains executory.

Another important consequence of equitable conversion relates to risk allocation during the executory contract period. The basic problem is to determine who should be responsible for a loss to the property during this time period when title is split between the expectant owner with equitable title and the seller with legal title. Common situations involve the destruction of building improvements by fire, hurricane, or similar natural disasters. Also included are disputes over special taxes or assessments levied after the signing of the contract but before the closing and actual transfer of title. Similar problems arise when there is a zoning change or a public condemnation proceeding implemented with respect to the property during this time. These and many other scenarios raise the question of which party should pay the cost or take the loss as a result of actions, events, or information that affect the value of the property during this stage of the transaction. The same type of question would arise if some new discovery enhanced the value of the property during this time period, such as the discovery of gold. In such a case, who gets the benefit of this value-enhancing benefit?

The rules that have developed generally start with the proposition that at the moment of equitable conversion, the buyer takes on the risks associated with anything that happens during the executory period. Over the years, courts were confronted with a variety of fact patterns that made them reevaluate the application of the risk allocation function of the doctrine. The courts took a number of approaches that included putting the risk on the party in possession or control of the property or assigning risk after the fact to the party who might have been the least-cost avoider. Most courts retained the basic pro-seller risk rule, but modified it around the edges to protect buyers under some circumstances. Most notably, equitable conversion operates to transfer the risk of loss to the buyer only if the contract is specifically enforceable at the time of the loss. Based on this precept, courts have often come up with reasons why, in retrospect, specific performance may be said not to have been available to the seller. Perhaps the seller had unperformed contract obligations, or there were title defects that had not yet been cured, or the buyer had not yet obtained financing as specified in an express contract condition.

In most states, common-law rules presently govern risk of loss, but there is one significant legislative reform. The Uniform Vendor and Purchaser Risk Act (UVPRA), drafted by contracts scholar Samuel Williston, may well be the most succinct uniform act in American legal history. The Act in its entirety states:

Uniform Vendor and Purchaser Risk Act (1935)

Section 1. Risk of Loss.

Any contract hereafter made in this State for the purchase and sale of realty shall be interpreted as including an agreement that the parties shall have the following rights and duties, unless the contract expressly provides otherwise:

(a) If, when neither the legal title nor the possession of the subject matter of the contract has been transferred, all or a material part thereof is destroyed without fault of the purchaser or is taken by eminent domain, the vendor cannot enforce the contract, and the purchaser is entitled to recover any portion of the price that he has paid;

(b) If, when either the legal title or the possession of the subject matter of the contract has been transferred, all or any part thereof is destroyed without fault of the vendor or is taken by eminent domain, the purchaser is not thereby relieved from a duty to pay the price, nor is he entitled to recover any portion thereof that he has paid.

Section 2. Uniformity of Interpretation.

This act shall be so interpreted and construed as to effectuate its general purpose to make uniform the law of those states which enact it.

Section 3. Short Title.

This act may be cited as the Uniform Vendor and Purchaser Risk Act.

Beginning in the 1930s, 12 states, including California and New York, enacted the UVPRA, some with minor modifications.

With the variety of rule choices for risk of loss that have developed, both judicial and statutory, only one thing is certain. A cautious lawyer does not subject his client to the risk of guessing which of the many rules a future court would apply to any particular case. The most important risk allocation rule for the practicing lawyer is that the parties are free to address the issues in their contract. This means that counsel for the parties should draft liberally with specific provisions addressing all manner of foreseeable risk. Generally, many types of risk are foreseeable, including fire, earthquake, hurricane, tornado, zoning changes, environmental regulation changes, bankruptcy, death, and interest rate changes, to name a few.

Each party to a real estate contract has an *insurable interest,* and this is generally true regardless of how the party's contract allocates risk of loss. When a property loss occurs during the contract executory period and one or both parties have insurance covering the relevant risk, one might suppose there would be little trouble and both parties could easily proceed to consummate the deal. Unfortunately, this is not so. Courts often have great trouble sorting things out when there is an insured loss and the parties' contract does not specifically address insurance matters. Ideally, the party who has the risk of loss should obtain insurance, but this doesn't always happen. The most common scenario is the seller having property insurance but the buyer assuming the risk of loss, either under the implied doctrine of equitable conversion or under an express contract provision. A standard principle of insurance law states that an insurance contract is a personal contract between the insurance company and the insured, giving rise to no third-party rights. Following this characterization, the traditional judicial response was to ignore the seller's insurance policy when the contract was silent on the matter, permitting the seller to collect insurance proceeds *and* enforce the contract against the buyer for the full price. Although some states still follow this rule, most states perceive this outcome as a windfall for the seller coupled with a devastating, undeserved loss to the buyer, and thus they have reformed their laws to protect the buyer under these circumstances. The insurance proceeds are held in trust by the seller for the buyer, and if the transaction goes forward to close, the buyer receives a credit on the price equal to the proceeds minus the amount of the insurance premium previously paid by the seller. This device of an implied trust overrides the maxim that insurance is a personal contract of indemnity, in effect making the insurance proceeds into a substitute res that runs with the land.

HOLSCHER v. JAMES
Supreme Court of Idaho, 1993
124 Idaho 443, 860 P.2d 646

SILAK, Justice. . . .

FACTS AND PROCEDURAL BACKGROUND

On March 29, 1989, the Jameses and Holschers entered into a purchase agreement whereby the Jameses agreed to purchase from the Holschers a cabin and five acres. Under the terms of the purchase agreement, the Jameses deposited $500 as earnest money towards the purchase price of $50,000. The purchase agreement specified May 1, 1989, as the closing date for the transaction. Paragraph 13 of the purchase agreement also provided that "[s]hould the premises be materially damaged by fire or other causes, prior to closing this sale, this agreement shall be voidable at the option of the Buyer."

On April 5, 1989, the Jameses entered into an insurance binder with State Farm to insure the cabin. The insurance binder provided $50,000 coverage on the cabin and $35,000 coverage on the contents of the cabin. A section of the binder form entitled "other int[erests]" provided for the listing of parties other than the named insured who, by virtue of some interest in the covered property, would have a beneficial interest in the insurance. In this section of the binder, the State Farm agent listed the name and address of Ernest Holscher. The binder stated that its effective date was April 5, 1989, and the Jameses made their first premium payment that same day. The amount of the premium was calculated to pay for coverage beginning on April 5th. The Holschers did not themselves purchase any insurance coverage for the cabin.

Also on April 5, 1989, pursuant to the purchase agreement, the Jameses took possession of the property and began moving their personal belongings into the cabin. On April 11, the Jameses moved more of their belongings into the cabin. At about 5 p.m. or 6 p.m. on the 11th, the cabin caught fire and was destroyed. The district court found that the fire was not the fault of either party, and the parties do not dispute that finding. Prior to May 1, the date set for closing, the Jameses notified the Holschers that, because the cabin had been destroyed, they were exercising their option under paragraph 13 to void the purchase agreement.

The Holschers subsequently sued the Jameses and State Farm seeking to recover the value of the cabin. At trial, two issues were submitted to the jury for determination: (1) whether the Holschers were intended beneficiaries of the insurance binder between the Jameses and State Farm, and (2) the fair market value of the cabin at the time it was destroyed. The jury returned a verdict finding that the Holschers were not intended beneficiaries of the insurance binder, and that the fair market value of the cabin was $36,125. The district court entered judgment on the jury's verdict in favor of State Farm, concluding that the Holschers were not third-party beneficiaries, and therefore that they had no claim under the James/State Farm insurance binder.

Two equitable issues were tried to the court: (1) whether the purchase agreement should be reformed, based on mutual mistake, to provide that the Jameses bore the risk of loss prior to closing, and (2) whether the doctrine of equitable conversion applied to shift the pre-closing risk of loss to the Jameses. The district court concluded that reformation of the purchase agreement was inapplicable in this case based on its finding that there was no mutual mistake regarding allocation of the risk of loss or the obligation to insure the property prior to closing because the parties never even considered, much less reached an agreement upon, those issues. The district court did not determine the second issue, whether equitable conversion applied to shift the risk of loss to the Jameses.

However, the district court entered judgment in favor of the Holschers based on two other conclusions: (1) that State Farm was liable to the Jameses for the value of the cabin, and (2) that the Jameses were liable to the Holschers for the value of the cabin. The court concluded that State Farm was liable to the Jameses by applying the doctrine of equitable conversion to determine that the Jameses had an insurable interest in the cabin, and therefore, under the insurance binder, they were entitled to the insurance proceeds after the cabin was destroyed. The court reached its second conclusion, that the Jameses were liable to the Holschers for the value of the cabin, based on its construction of paragraph 13 of the purchase agreement. The court construed paragraph 13 to mean that if the premises were materially damaged prior to closing, the Jameses were entitled to seek equitable rescission of the contract from the court. From this the district court reasoned that the Jameses could not avail themselves of the equitable remedy of rescission unless they restored the Holschers to their pre-contract position. Based on its two conclusions, the district court ordered State Farm to pay the Jameses the proceeds of the insurance on the cabin, and then ordered that the Jameses pay the insurance proceeds to the Holschers before they could void the purchase agreement.

Issues on Appeal

The appeal and cross-appeal of the parties require us to address three issues: (1) whether the district court erred in its application of the doctrines of equitable conversion and equitable rescission; (2) whether the district court erred in entering judgment on the jury's finding that the Holschers were not third-party beneficiaries of the James/State Farm insurance binder. . . . We address each of these issues in turn.

Analysis

I. Applicability of Equitable Conversion and Equitable Rescission

The parties raise three issues regarding the application of equitable conversion and rescission. The Holschers assert that the district court erred by not applying equitable conversion to conclude that the risk of loss was on the Jameses at the time of the fire. State Farm asserts that the district court erred because it did apply equitable conversion to conclude that the Jameses had an equitable, and thus insurable, interest in the cabin at the time of the fire. Finally, the Jameses claim that the district court erred by applying the doctrine of equitable rescission to conclude that they were liable to the Holschers for the value of the cabin.

A. Whether the District Court Should Have Applied Equitable Conversion to Conclude that the Jameses Bore the Risk of Loss Prior to Closing.

This Court has explained the doctrine of equitable conversion as follows:

> The doctrine of equitable conversion is a fiction resting upon the fundamental rule of equity that equity regards that as done which ought to be done. Under the doctrine, an equitable conversion takes place when a contract for the sale of real property becomes binding on the parties. The purchaser is then treated in equity as having an interest in realty, and the vendor an interest in personalty, that is, the right to receive the purchase money.

First Security Bank of Idaho v. Rogers, 91 Idaho 654, 657, 429 P.2d 386, 389 (1967). Thus, when equitable conversion applies, the contract purchaser is deemed the equitable owner of the realty, and assumes the risk of loss on the property. Rector v. Alcorn, 241 N.W.2d 196, 200 (Iowa 1976). The Holschers assert that the district court should have applied equitable conversion to place the risk of loss of the cabin on the Jameses, as purchasers and equitable owners of the property. For the following reasons, we disagree.

The doctrine of equitable conversion applies only if "nothing in the contract states otherwise." Rush v. Anestos, 104 Idaho 630, 634, 661 P.2d 1229, 1233 (1983); *Rector,* 241 N.W.2d at 200. Thus, equitable conversion does not apply if the effect would be to shift the risk of loss to a buyer contrary to the terms of the parties' agreement. *Id.* In this case, paragraph 13 of the parties' purchase agreement provided: "Should the premises be materially damaged by fire or other causes, prior to closing this sale, this agreement shall be voidable at the option of the Buyer." We construe this provision as placing the risk of loss prior to closing on the Holschers. In a factually similar case, Georgia's Supreme Court held that when a provision in a purchase agreement allows the buyer to cancel the agreement if the premises are destroyed prior to closing, the effect of that provision is to allocate to the seller the risk of loss prior to closing. Phillips v. Bacon, 245 Ga. 814, 267 S.E.2d 249 (1980). *See also* Bishop Ryan High School v. Lindberg, 370 N.W.2d 726 (N.D. 1985); *Rector,* 241 N.W.2d at 201. The same reasoning applies here. Paragraph 13 absolved the Jameses from assuming the risk of any material damage to the property prior to closing, leaving that risk upon the Holschers. It would be inconsistent and illogical to say that the Jameses had the right to void the purchase agreement if the premises were materially damaged prior to closing, but also hold them responsible to pay for any pre-closing damages to the property. Such a construction would essentially take away the very right conferred upon the Jameses by paragraph 13. Because we construe paragraph 13 of the parties' purchase agreement as placing the pre-closing risk of loss on the Holschers, we hold that the district court did not err in refusing to apply the doctrine of equitable conversion to shift the pre-closing risk of loss to the Jameses.

B. Whether the District Court Erred by Applying Equitable Conversion to Conclude that the Jameses Had an Insurable Interest in the Cabin Prior to Closing.

State Farm challenges the district court's conclusion that it was liable to the Jameses under the insurance binder, contending that the Jameses lacked an insurable interest in the cabin at the time of the loss, and I.C. §41-1806 prohibits any person from enforcing a contract of insurance against an insurer unless that person has an insurable interest in the insured property. By applying the doctrine of equitable conversion, the district court concluded that the Jameses had equitable ownership of, and thus an insurable interest in, the cabin at the time of the loss. The arguable lack of an insurable interest in the Jameses is not conclusive, however, under I.C. §41-1806, for it is the Holschers, not the Jameses, who are seeking to enforce the insurance contract against State Farm. The Holschers assert coverage in their own right as intended third-party beneficiaries of the insurance binder, not as derivative beneficiaries of the Jameses' rights under the binder. State Farm has not asserted that the Holschers lacked an insurable interest in the property at the time of the loss. Because the Jameses are not seeking to enforce the insurance contract against State Farm, we need not decide whether they had an insurable interest in the cabin at the time of the loss.

C. Whether the District Court Erred in Applying Equitable Rescission to Conclude that the Jameses Were Liable for the Value of the Cabin.

The district court construed paragraph 13 of the purchase agreement as giving the Jameses the right to seek equitable rescission of the contract from the court in the event that the premises were materially damaged prior to closing. Based on this determination, the district court concluded that the Jameses could not "equitably rescind" the purchase agreement unless they restored the Holschers to their pre-contract position. The legal meaning and effect of contract terms are questions of law which we review freely. Barr Development, Inc. v. Utah Mortg. Loan Corp., 106 Idaho 46, 47, 675 P.2d 25, 26 (1983).

Paragraph 13 gave the Jameses the right *under the contract* to void the contract at *their option* if the premises were materially damaged prior to closing. They did not need to apply to the court and prove the elements essential to a decree of equitable rescission before they could void the contract. Once the premises were materially damaged, the Jameses' right to void the contract was "at law," under the terms of the contract. They could simply refuse to close. A right provided by contract is, by definition, legal and not equitable. Equitable remedies are not dependent upon contractual authorization, but apply precisely because there is no adequate remedy at law under the contract's terms, and because sufficient grounds to invoke equity, such as mutual mistake, fraud, or impossibility, are present. We hold that under paragraph 13 of the parties' purchase agreement, the Jameses had the legal right to void the contract once the premises were materially damaged, and their choice to exercise that right was not dependent on their satisfaction of the elements required for the application of equitable rescission. Accordingly, the district court erred in concluding that the Jameses were obliged to restore the value of the cabin to the Holschers.

II. THIRD-PARTY BENEFICIARY STATUS OF THE HOLSCHERS UNDER THE JAMES/STATE FARM INSURANCE BINDER

At trial, the Holschers submitted as evidence a copy of the insurance binder between the Jameses and State Farm to show that they were intended third-party beneficiaries of that agreement. The Holschers asserted that the listing of Ernest Holscher in the section of the binder entitled "other interests" unambiguously demonstrated that they were intended beneficiaries of the insurance coverage, and therefore no extrinsic evidence was admissible to prove otherwise. The district court, however, over the Holschers' objection, allowed the insurance agent who executed the insurance binder to testify that he did not intend the Holschers to be beneficiaries of the binder prior to closing. The agent testified that he listed Ernest Holscher on the binder under the section entitled "other interests" only because he was told the Holschers would become mortgagees at the time of closing and he wanted to have their name and address so he could send them a copy of the policy insuring their mortgagee interest after the transaction closed. The district court concluded that the insurance binder was ambiguous as to the Holschers' beneficiary status at the time of the loss, and submitted the issue to the jury for resolution. The jury found that the Holschers were not intended beneficiaries of the insurance binder, and the district court entered judgment on that verdict. The Holschers contend that the district court should not have submitted this issue to the jury, but should have ruled as a matter of law that they were intended beneficiaries of the insurance binder. . . .

> It has long been the rule of this Court that a contract should be construed most strongly against the party preparing it. Furthermore, in cases involving . . . insurance contracts, where the language of the contractual provision may be given one of two meanings, one of which permits recovery and the other forbidding it, the contract is to be construed in favor of the insured.

Toevs v. Western Farm Bureau Life Insurance Co., 94 Idaho 151, 153, 483 P.2d 682, 684 (1971). . . .

Because the insurance binder listed the Holschers as having a beneficial interest in the insurance with April 5, 1989, as the effective date of coverage, and because the binder contained no words limiting the coverage either to the Holschers' mortgagee interest in the property or to their post-closing losses, we hold that the insurance binder unambiguously provided the Holschers with a beneficial interest in the insurance to cover whatever insurable interest they had in the property as of April 5, 1989. We will not read into the binder a time or nature-of-interest limitation which State Farm did not deem important enough to write into the binder. We hold as a matter of law that the Holschers were third-party beneficiaries under the insurance binder, and that this beneficial interest was limited only to the extent of their insurable interest in the cabin under I.C. §41-1806. . . .

Conclusion

We hold that the parties' purchase agreement placed the pre-closing risk of loss on the Holschers, and allowed the Jameses to void the agreement at their option once the premises were materially damaged prior to closing. Accordingly, we reverse the district court's judgment holding the Jameses liable to the Holschers. We further hold that the Holschers were intended third-party beneficiaries of the insurance binder between the Jameses and State Farm, and therefore the Holschers are entitled to judgment against State Farm for the proceeds of that insurance. The Holschers are also entitled to an award of reasonable attorney fees against State Farm. We remand the case to the district court for modification of the judgment with respect to State Farm and for further proceedings consistent with this opinion.

Costs and attorney fees on appeal are awarded to the Holschers against State Farm.

Problem 4D

(a) Buyer and seller are negotiating a contract for purchase and sale of a seven-year-old single-family house. They have exchanged various contract language to cover a number of risks and contingencies. One provision being discussed is specifically titled a "Risk of Loss" clause. It reads as follows:

> The risk of loss or damage to the Property by casualty or condemnation prior to the Closing Date is Seller's. If the Property is damaged by some casualty prior to the Closing Date, Seller agrees to the cost of repairing or restoring the Property, up to a value which does not exceed thirty percent (30%) of the valuation of the Property so damaged. Should aggregate damage exceed thirty percent (30%) of the Purchase Price hereof, then this Agreement may be rescinded at the option of either party.

What comments, criticisms, or changes might you want to make if you represented the buyer? The seller? Or would this language be adequate for most cases?

(b) Suppose a lawyer represented the seller in this transaction and the buyer was known to be without counsel. What obligation should the attorney have to the unrepresented party? Might the attorney be betraying his role as zealous advocate for his own client if he explains too much to the other party? How much information should be explained to meet the requirements of the *Belleville* decision excerpted earlier in this chapter? How might an attorney best protect himself from being held accountable to the nonclient while not violating an obligation to his actual client?

Problem 4E

Gary owns a one-acre parcel of property with a four-bedroom home on it. He contracts to sell it to Jean for $400,000. They value the lot at about $100,000 and the structure at $300,000. According to the terms of the contract, "The owner of the Property shall have the risk of loss during the executory contract period." During the executory contract period, while Gary is in possession, the house burns to the ground as a result of a fire that was not caused by either party.

(a) If Gary has $300,000 of insurance on the property (to cover the value of the improvements to the land) and Jean does not have any insurance, does Jean have to proceed under the contract? Is she entitled to the insurance proceeds if she pays the contract price? Does Gary have any obligation to rebuild the structure? If Gary sought to rebuild the structure, would it have to be an exact duplicate of the prior home, or could he use lower-cost or different materials? Who, if anyone, would supervise and approve the work?

(b) If Jean has $300,000 of insurance to cover the improvements but Gary does not (he previously cancelled his policy), should Jean be able to pocket the money and walk away from the transaction?

(c) What if both parties have insurance, but neither one has an adequate policy of coverage? Assume Gary has kept his policy in force, but has not updated it for several years, so his coverage is only $225,000 for the improvements. Jean has also insured the property, but took a deal on a low-cost policy that covers less than 100 percent of a loss by fire, so she can only get a maximum of $275,000. In this case, what should each party's obligation be and why? Should the insurance companies have to pay out a total of $500,000 under their policies even though the property loss is $300,000?

(d) In the above situations, who is meant to be benefited by the insurance? Should the presence of insurance coverage be relevant to the questions of contract interpretation and the allocation of risk? Does the contract term drafted by the parties clarify the problem in any of the foregoing situations? Would it make a difference in the above situations if the jurisdiction had enacted the Uniform Vendor and Purchaser Risk Act?

C. MAJOR CONTRACT CONDITIONS

During the executory contract period, there are many ways to allocate risk between the parties. In addition to the use of implied rules such as equitable conversion, risk can be allocated by express promises or covenants as well as by warranties, representations, and conditions. Contract covenants allocate risk by mapping out the parties' mutual expectations and obligations. Covenants can also reduce risk by assigning specific tasks to each party. The seller may, for example, undertake or promise to get title search work done on the property, while the buyer agrees that it is his responsibility to file for any needed permits.

In addition to covenants or promises for contractual undertakings, a number of contract warranties and representations will likely be made between the parties. Such contract provisions are designed to address areas of informational risk. A seller, for instance, tells a buyer that the house he is selling is free of radon gas problems and that it is located in "Elite School District #1." If this information is important to the buyer, he might want to have the contract address it specifically. The buyer may want a contract provision that says, "Seller hereby represents and warrants that this property is free of any and all radon gas problems meaning that any government calibrated reading levels would register at '0'; and, Seller further represents and warrants that the property is located within the Elite School District #1 and eligible for all of the benefits thereof." By putting these express provisions in the contract, the buyer gains a direct cause of action against the seller should the information prove to be false. It also provides some basis for arguing that the particular items of information were material to the buyer's decision to purchase the property. If the information proves to be incorrect, the buyer may have a cause of action for breach of warranty.

Contracts of purchase and sale contain many conditions (conditions are often called "contingencies" in real estate contracts). In drafting contracts, conditions serve to allocate risk and establish an orderly timing for the performance of specific tasks. They also help to reduce economic exposure and cost by sometimes allowing one party to hold back on certain actions or expenses until the other party has first accomplished a preliminary prerequisite or objective. Should the preliminary objective fail to occur, no further action or investment may be required. A typical contract condition will make the buyer's obligation to go forward with a purchase conditional on being approved for an appropriate home mortgage loan. This means that if the buyer cannot get such a loan, the buyer does not have to proceed under the contract toward closing. Similarly, when a contract has such a mortgage loan condition, the seller will usually make his obligation to obtain costly title information conditional upon the buyer first being approved for a loan.

Not all conditions provide for termination of the contract in the event that a condition does not occur. Generally, though, the major conditions related to financing, title, and land use will provide for such a termination. Other conditions may spell out different consequences in the event that they fail to take place. Contract conditions can be used to order other rights and obligations between the parties even as they proceed with an exchange.

Timing issues may be resolved by resort to the classification of conditions. Does language create a condition precedent, a condition subsequent, or simultaneous conditions, or is it merely poor drafting that results in no condition at all?

With respect to conditions and other performance requirements under a contract, the time for performance will generally be strictly enforced if there is a date certain stated in the contract, and the contract provides that "time is of the essence." To enforce strict compliance with stated dates, one must avoid taking steps that might be interpreted as evidence of waiver or estoppel with respect to time being of the essence.

If a contract term is interpreted as establishing a condition precedent or a simultaneous condition, the parties will generally be released from any further obligations; but if the contract language in question is interpreted as a covenant, there may be a different result. In the case of a breached covenant, when the breach does not destroy the entire value of the exchange, the parties may be obligated to proceed under the contract with only an allowance for the breach of the promise or warranty. The allowance might be in the form of a price abatement or an award of damages to account for the diminished value of a given performance, but the end result is that, unlike the case of an unmet condition, performance may still be required.

Whenever the buyer and the seller begin the process of drafting a contract, they must keep in mind the effects their agreement may have on third parties. Prior to executing the purchase and sale agreement, for instance, the seller probably has already entered into an agreement with a broker to sell his property. To a certain extent, the seller may have already committed himself to undertakings with the broker that will not be subject to alteration in the purchase and sale contract. Answering the question of what happens under the contract between the buyer and the seller does not always tell one what happens with respect to third parties like the broker.

Contract conditions often pose a special risk for the seller. If a signed contract prevents the seller from dealing with any other parties and yet leaves the buyer with plenty of room to escape from the contract by the use of conditions, the buyer will be getting something similar to an option on the property without having to pay the seller. The buyer can have his cake and eat it too—he ties up the property but still has the freedom to exit the transaction. Consequently, when sellers appreciate this risk, they sometimes negotiate contracts that provide either for a short time limit on a certain condition or for some agreed-to amount to be paid to the seller if the contract does not close.

In the next part of this chapter, we consider the condition for mortgage financing in more detail. In Chapters 8 and 9, we discuss contract conditions related to marketable title, including the provision for the preparation of a survey. Taken together, the conditions for mortgage financing, title examination, and survey preparation are probably the most important examples of the use of contract conditions in the residential transaction. The lessons to be learned from these examples can be applied to many other contract areas one will encounter when participating in more complex real estate transactions.

In most real estate transactions, the exchange will require some form of financing. The buyer seldom does a transaction for all cash, although this is sometimes the case. Usually, the buyer does not have all the necessary cash but has some money on hand plus the credit to borrow the remaining capital. When a buyer undertakes to borrow funds in the financial markets or from the seller, there will be a charge for the extension of credit. The value of the transaction must, therefore, cover the cost of financing. Additionally, the cost of credit for any particular real estate investment must be weighed against alternative investment opportunities. Thus, the buyer must think in terms of both the accounting and economic profit potential from the proposed investment. Tax motivations may also play a factor in determining the profitability of an exchange. Similarly, the buyer's asset and liquidity position may restrict or limit the availability of credit even in a situation where additional borrowing might prove to be profitable.

To understand the buyer's position more clearly, one should start with the rule that in the absence of any contract financing terms, the transaction would most likely be construed to be an "all-cash" exchange. An *all-cash exchange* means that the buyer undertakes to buy the property at the stated price and takes on all the risk of having the full amount of money in hand at closing.

When the buyer attempts to draft a financing condition into a purchase and sale agreement, his objective may very well differ from that of the seller. The seller would like the language to be written broadly so as to make almost any offer of financing sufficient to satisfy the condition, thereby obligating the buyer to complete the deal. The buyer, in contrast, would generally benefit from a much more narrowly drafted provision that restricts acceptable financing to a set of specifically feasible and profitable parameters. The provision should describe more loan characteristics than just the principal amount to be borrowed. The buyer should identify the initial and maximum interest rate he is willing to accept. A deal may be profitable at 9 percent interest and unprofitable at 9½ percent interest. Likewise, the term of the loan should be clarified, because a 30-year loan is different from a 15-year loan in ways that bear on the economics of a deal. The term of a loan affects the monthly payments, total interest costs, and tax implications of a transaction. If the specified financing terms cannot be satisfied, the buyer would be relieved from any further obligation under the contract. In thinking about this dynamic between the buyer and the seller, it must be remembered that the seller is not engaged in a cost-free exercise. The moment the seller enters into a contract with a buyer, equitable conversion takes place and the buyer has a legally recognizable interest in the property. The buyer's interest restricts the ability of the seller to deal with the property.

LOUISIANA REAL ESTATE COMMISSION v. BUTLER

Court of Appeal of Louisiana, 2005
899 So. 2d 151

EZELL, Judge. This is a concursus matter arising out of a contract to buy a home. The buyers, Dr. Brett Butler and his wife, Elizabeth, appeal the decision of the trial court awarding the sellers, Dr. Edward Crocker and his wife Trudy, a $12,500 deposit for the failure to complete the transaction. For the following reasons, we affirm the decision of the trial court.

The Crockers owned a home in Lake Charles which was listed for sale through ERA Moffett Realty. Through their own realtor, the Butlers found the home and eventually submitted a purchase agreement, offering to buy the home for the sum of $770,000. The agreement was signed by both parties, and a deposit of $12,500 was given by the Butlers. The contract stated that the sale was contingent on the Butlers obtaining financing for the home, the amount of which was "to be determined," at an eight and one half percent interest rate. The Butlers applied for a loan through Red River Bank. The loan was denied. Thereafter, the Butlers sought the return of their deposit. The Crockers refused. Based on this dispute, the Louisiana Real Estate Commission filed this concursus proceeding in the trial court below. The trial court found that no specific amount of funding was set out by the contract as a condition, only that the desired interest rate be secured. Noting that there was no evidence that the rate was not obtained, the trial court found that the Crockers were entitled to keep the deposit. From this decision, the Butlers appeal. . . .

The general rules of contract interpretation are found in Articles 2045 through 2057 of the Louisiana Civil Code. . . . "In case of doubt that cannot be otherwise resolved, a provision in a contract must be interpreted against the party who furnished its text." La. Civ. Code art. 2056.

The agreement to purchase or sell in this matter contained two pertinent provisions. The first provision, paragraph two, stated[1]:

> THIS SALE is conditioned upon the ability of the PURCHASER(s) to borrow upon this property as security the sum of $ **To Be Determined** by a Mortgage loan or loans at an initial Fixed rate of interest not to exceed **8½** per annum payable in equal monthly installments, or upon such other terms that may be acceptable to PURCHASER, so long as such terms create no additional cost to seller and do not affect the closing date.

The other provision, included in paragraph seven, states that "PURCHASER represents that PURCHASER has the funds necessary to satisfy Purchasers obligations, including the down payment, under this Agreement."

The Butlers contend that because they applied for a loan of ninety percent of the value of the home and were rejected that they have met the requirements of the contract. We disagree. Nowhere within the four corners of the contract is listed any specific monetary amount the Butlers must have obtained loan approval for. On the contrary, the only condition set for by the document is that a loan be approved at an eight and one half percent interest rate. There is no evidence that they could not obtain financing at some amount at the desired rate. If the Butlers had wanted to require a specific amount of financing, they could have simply inserted whatever amount they

1. Bold emphasis indicates handwritten portions of the agreement.

desired into the blank where they wrote instead "to be determined." Taken in conjunction with the provision in paragraph seven which represents that the Butlers had sufficient funds to complete the transaction, including any down payment, it is clear that the Butlers failed to meet the obligations set out for them in the contract. Moreover, if there was any ambiguity in the contract, as the party who furnished the text in question, the "to be determined" provision in the contract must be interpreted against the Butlers. La. Civ. Code art. 2056. There is no error in the trial court's ruling awarding the Crockers the deposit.

The Butlers next assert that the agreement should be declared null and void for lack of consent, as a mutual misunderstanding existed as to the loan amount they would seek. This is based on Mr. Butler's self serving assertion that, at the time the contract was signed, he only intended to put forth a ten percent down payment and seek financing for the remainder. However, as noted above, if he had actually intended to set a limit as to the maximum amount he would finance, he, as the writer of the contract, could simply have inserted the ninety percent amount into the contract. Furthermore, Charmayne Crawford, one of the realtors handling the sale, testified that forty percent of all purchase agreements contain the "to be determined" language and that she felt, based on the language, that the Butlers would have no trouble obtaining funds, but were only seeking a set interest rate. There is no evidence in the record of a mutual misunderstanding as to the terms of the contract. . . .

For the above reasons, we affirm the decision of the trial court. Costs of this appeal are assessed against Brett and Elizabeth Butler.

Problem 4F

Teresa and José contract for the purchase and sale of a property. Teresa agrees to buy the property on the condition that she can obtain suitable financing in the amount of $180,000, which will be a 90 percent loan against the contract price of $200,000. Teresa goes to Big Bank for a loan and is told that the bank valued the property at $170,000 and, therefore, would loan only $153,000 (90 percent) against the property. As a result, Teresa must back out of the purchase. A week later José sells the property to Mary Ann for $240,000. Big Bank discovers that it made an error in its appraisal. What, if anything, do you think Teresa should be able to do, and what might have been done to protect against this outcome?

Problem 4G

Buyer and Seller enter a contract for the purchase and sale of a single-family residential home. As a condition to purchase, Buyer drafts a contract term to deal with inspection of the home for any defects. The parties agree on language that they put in their contract. The contract provision reads as follows:

> Purchaser reserves the right to have the Property inspected. All inspections shall be made within 10 business days of the date of this contract. Inspections shall be at the expense of the Purchaser and shall be made by qualified and licensed inspectors and contractors within this state. Inspections may include but are not limited to heating, cooling, electrical, plumbing, roof, walls, ceilings, floors, foundation, basement, crawl space, well, septic, water analysis, and wood-eating infestations. If the Purchaser does not make a written objection within 17 business days from the date of this contract Purchaser will be deemed to have accepted the Property. Objections must be accompanied by copies of the written inspection reports. If an inspection report reveals a major problem with the Property the seller can either fix the problem at its own expense or if seller elects not to fix the problem either party can terminate the contract.

(a) Under the contract in this case, the price of the home is $150,000. Buyer has an inspection done, and it is reported that there is a leak in the roof, termite damage to a structural beam, and a wet area in the basement. The estimated cost to repair all these items is $1,000. Under the inspection provision of the contract, should Buyer be able to terminate this contract?

(b) If Buyer mails a written objection to Seller on the 16th business day after entering the contract but it is not delivered to Seller until the 19th business day, is it an effective objection?

(c) Assume that Buyer submits a timely objection to Seller. The objection is based on a termite inspection that reports damage to a roof support beam and recommends replacement of the beam at a cost of $700. On receipt of this objection, Seller hires a separate qualified and licensed inspector who reports evidence of prior termite activity in the identified beam but goes on to say that the activity is old and has left the beam structurally sound. Consequently, Seller's inspector concludes that the beam is not in need of replacement or repair. Seller presents its report to Buyer, refuses to make a repair, and insists that Buyer close on the contract. What result?

(d) Assume that the property is located in Syracuse, New York, where the winters are long, cold, and very snowy. The transaction is taking place in the winter and Buyer is getting inspections during February. At this time of the year, the ground has been frozen hard for several months, and there is three feet of snow on the ground. Buyer has the home inspected for radon gas emissions and detects a level slightly above the federal government guidelines for this type of naturally occurring radioactive gas. Buyer makes a timely objection to Seller. A radon abatement system could cost between $1,000 and $1,500 to install. Seller responds with a copy of a radon test report done in the summer months that indicates a radon level below the federal government guidelines. If both tests were done properly, what might explain this difference? Can Buyer terminate the contract if Seller refuses to install an abatement system? What if, instead of repairing or correcting the problem, Seller takes $1,000 off the sale price; can Buyer be forced to close on the contract?

(e) Assume a wintertime transaction in Minnesota with freezing temperatures. The home inspector informs Buyer that the air conditioning system cannot be tested without risk of serious damage when outside temperatures are below 50°F. Buyer goes forward with the contract and closes on the deal in March. By June, the outside temperature is warm enough to try out the central air conditioning and Buyer learns for the first time that the system does not work. What do you think Buyer can do or should be able to do at this point? How could Buyer have protected himself under the terms of the inspection contract provision as written?

5

Condition of the Property

When contracting for the purchase and sale of real property, one must be concerned with the condition of the subject real estate. The contract must address matters that relate to both the quantity and the quality of the property being exchanged. The parties want to have a degree of certainty regarding the amount of land or improvements being transferred as well as the physical characteristics of the property. This is important because both matters will affect the value and, therefore, the appropriate price of the transaction. This may seem easy and straightforward, but there are many potential problem areas in the context of a real estate transaction.

A. QUANTITY

PERFECT v. McANDREW

Court of Appeals of Indiana, 2003
798 N.E.2d 470

SHARPNACK, Judge. Clyde and Ella Mae Perfect (the "Perfects") appeal the trial court's judgment granting specific performance of a contract to sell real estate to Michael E. McAndrew. . . .

The relevant facts follow. In the spring of 1999, McAndrew became interested in purchasing real estate in Dearborn County, Indiana from the Perfects.[1] Based upon acreage listed in the deed conveying the property to the Perfects, the Perfects thought that the property consisted of 81.1 acres. On April 20, 1999, McAndrew offered to purchase the real estate from the Perfects for $250,000. The offer described the property as "Anderson Rd,

1. The property is actually owned only by Ella Mae Perfect. However, Ella Mae gave Clyde authority to handle the transaction for her. For purposes of this opinion, we will refer to the Perfects as the owners of the property.

81.1 acres owned by Perfects." On April 21, 1999, the Perfects countered with a purchase price of $252,500. On April 23, 1999, McAndrew, his wife, and Ashley Howe and Betsy Bates, real estate agents with StarOne Realtors, met with Clyde Perfect to view the property and its boundaries. Clyde could not walk the property because of an injury to his knee. However, he rode his tractor along much of the boundary while the others walked. When they encountered an area that Clyde could not traverse with his tractor, Clyde described the remaining boundaries to the McAndrews and the real estate agents. The McAndrews and the real estate agents then walked the remaining boundaries. McAndrew never had any conversations with the Perfects regarding the acreage of the property. After inspecting the property, McAndrew accepted the Perfects' counteroffer of $252,500.

The contract provided, in part, that:

> [McAndrew] shall apply for financing within 10 calendar days after acceptance of this Contract and will make a diligent effort to obtain financing. If [McAndrew] or [McAndrew's] lender does not notify Listing REALTOR or [the Perfects], in writing, that a loan commitment has been obtained, denied or waived by May 20, 1999, then [the Perfects] may, by written notice to selling REALTOR or [McAndrew], terminate this Contract.

The contract also provided for the following contingencies:

1. Satisfactory septic approval (to [McAndrew]).
2. Satisfactory to [McAndrew] survey to be [paid] by [McAndrew] and [the Perfects] equally.
3. Satisfactory to [McAndrew] verification of easements on property.
4. [The Perfects] to remove all debris—junk around barn area and along property line as discussed.
5. Satisfactory to [McAndrew] verification of lot lines A.S.A.P.

On May 11, 1999, McAndrew advised Bates that he had secured a loan. McAndrew received a written loan commitment on May 21, 1999, and signed the commitment on May 25, 1999. On approximately June 20, 1999, the Perfects removed the junk and debris from the property. The survey was completed on June 24, 1999, and indicated that the property contained 96.2815 acres rather than 81.1 acres. After receiving the survey, Clyde "was quite surprised and thought about it for a while and decided [he] didn't want to give away 15 acres."

On July 8, 1999, the Perfects attempted to renegotiate the contract with three different proposals: (1) McAndrew would purchase the 96.2815 acres for an additional $35,000; (2) McAndrew would purchase 81 acres for $230,000 and the Perfects would keep 15.30 acres with west frontage on Anderson Road; or (3) McAndrew would purchase sixty acres on the east side of the property for $200,000. McAndrew rejected the new proposals and sought to close on the property pursuant to the contract. On August 4, 1999, the Perfects sent a letter to Howe attempting to terminate the contract because McAndrew had failed to provide a timely written notice of a loan commitment. Prior to this letter, the Perfects had not advised McAndrew or Howe of any problems regarding the timeliness of McAndrew's loan commitment. The Perfects then refused to convey the property to McAndrew.

McAndrew filed a complaint against the Perfects for specific performance. . . .

I

The first issue is whether the trial court's finding that the parties intended an "in gross" sale of real estate is clearly erroneous. The Perfects argue that the trial court erred when it determined that the parties intended an in gross sale of the property because: (1) the property was discussed in terms of 81.1 acres, not 81.1 acres "more or less;" (2) all of the parties were surprised to discover that the property was actually 96.2815 acres and surprise is not an element contemplated by in gross sales; and (3) the parties' actions demonstrated that acreage was important to the bargain. McAndrew argues that nothing indicated that the sale of the land was based upon a price per acre and the phrase "more or less" in describing the acreage is not determinative of whether the sale is an in gross sale or a price per acre sale. Further, McAndrew argues that the parties' actions demonstrated that the acreage of the property was not important to the bargain.

In general, where property is "sold in lump, and for a gross sum," such that "it appears by words of qualification, as 'more or less,' that the statement of the quantity of acres in the deed is mere matter of description and not of the essence of the contract, the buyer takes the risk of the quantity" so long as there is no fraud, concealment, or misrepresentation. Tyler v. Anderson, 106 Ind. 185, 189, 6 N.E. 600, 601 (Ind. 1886); *see also* Cravens v. Kiser, 4 Ind. 512, 513 (1853) ("Where land is sold by metes and bounds, and estimated to contain a specific quantity, or for 'more or less,' and a gross sum is paid for the entire tract, the vendee will not be entitled to an abatement in price should the number of acres fall short of the estimated quantity," unless there is fraud or concealment on the part of the vendor.). However, where property is "sold at so much per acre, and there is a deficiency in the number [of acres] conveyed, the purchaser will be entitled to a compensation." Hays v. Hays, 126 Ind. 92, 94, 25 N.E. 600, 601 (1890) (holding that the purchaser was entitled to compensation where the property was sold at $100 per acre and estimated to contain 28 40/100 acres but actually contained only 23 40/100 acres). . . .

The Perfects argue that . . . because the contract here did not contain the phrase "more or less," the sale here was a per acre sale. McAndrew responds that the sale was an in gross sale despite the lack of the phrase "more or less." In *Hays*, our supreme court discussed the use of the phrase "more or less" and concluded that:

> The question of quantity, in its most complicated form, usually arises in sales of land in compact bodies, sold under some specific name, or by particular description, and as containing, by estimation, a given number of acres, or a given number of acres more or less. The difficulty arises in determining whether the sale was intended to be in gross or by the acre. If in gross, the mention of the quantity of acres after another and certain description, whether by metes and bounds, or other known specifications, is not a covenant or agreement as to the quantity to be conveyed. In such cases the statement of acreage is regarded as mere matter of description, and not of contract. *But the terms "by estimation," "more or less," or other expressions of similar import, added to a statement of quantity, can only be considered as covering inconsiderable or small differences, one way or the other, and do not, in themselves, determine the character of the sale.* Even where the sale has been in gross, and not by the acre, if it appear that the estimated number of acres was in fact the controlling inducement, and that the price, though a gross sum, was based upon the supposed area, and measured by it, equity will interfere to grant relief, and rescind the contract on the ground of gross mistake.

Hays, 126 Ind. at 93, 25 N.E. at 600 (citation omitted) (emphasis added). Thus, while the phrase "more or less" may assist in determining if the sale was an in gross sale or a price per acre sale, the language is not determinative.

. . . Here, the contract described the land as "Anderson Rd, 81.1 acres owned by Perfects." Before accepting the Perfects' counteroffer, McAndrew walked the property with Clyde, and Clyde pointed out the boundaries. McAndrew never had any conversations with the Perfects regarding the acreage of the property. In fact, Clyde testified that he never discussed the acreage with McAndrew and did not counteroffer with a price per acre. Thus, there is no evidence that the parties ever discussed a per acre price for the property. There is also no indication that the estimated acreage was the controlling inducement in the contract. Although the contract describes the property as "Anderson Rd, 81.1 acres owned by Perfects," the evidence indicates that the estimated acreage was merely a manner of describing the property. The evidence indicates that the parties contemplated a sale of the entire tract for a lump sum, not a price per acre.

II

The next issue is whether the trial court's finding that there was no mutual mistake of fact is clearly erroneous. The trial court found that "on the issue of what land was intended to be bought and sold there was a meeting of the minds. There was no ambiguity, no fraud, no misrepresentation, and no equitable circumstances that would indicate otherwise." The

Perfects argue that the trial court's finding is clearly erroneous because this "is a classic example where mutual mistake of fact renders the contract voidable by either party." The Perfects argue that the parties thought that the property was 81.1 acres and that the parties were surprised to learn that the property actually contained 96.2185 acres. McAndrew argues that the acreage was not the "essence of the agreement," and, thus, no mutual mistake of fact exists.

The doctrine of mutual mistake provides that "where both parties share a common assumption about a vital fact upon which they based their bargain, and that assumption is false, the transaction may be avoided if because of the mistake a quite different exchange of values occurs from the exchange of values contemplated by the parties." [Bowling v. Poole, 756 N.E.2d 983, 988-989 (Ind.Ct.App.2001)], 756 N.E.2d at 988-989 (*quoting* Wilkin v. 1st Source Bank, 548 N.E.2d 170, 172 (Ind. Ct. App. 1990)). . . .

[H]ere, there is no evidence that the parties were mistaken about the actual tract of land to be sold. In fact, Clyde testified that "there wasn't any question about which piece of property [they] were dealing for. The only question [was] how many acres it really [was]." There is also no evidence that the exact acreage was the essence of the parties' agreement. [I]t is not enough that McAndrew and the Perfects were mistaken about the acreage. Rather, to constitute a mutual mistake of fact, the fact complained of must be one that is "of the essence of the agreement" and "must be such that it animates and controls the conduct of the parties." *Bowling,* 756 N.E.2d at 989. . . . Consequently, we cannot say that the trial court's finding that no mutual mistake of fact existed here is clearly erroneous.

III

The next issue is whether the trial court's judgment improperly added a provision to the contract. The Perfects argue that the clear contract language requires the sale of 81.1 acres but the trial court ordered the sale of 96.2185 acres, thus adding a term to the written contract. McAndrew argues that the trial court did not add a new term to the contract. Rather, according to McAndrew, the trial court correctly determined that the Perfects intended to sell and McAndrew intended to buy the entire tract. . . .

Here, although the trial court did not specifically find the "Anderson Rd, 81.1 acres owned by Perfects" language to be ambiguous, it considered extrinsic evidence in interpreting the language. The description of the property is ambiguous because it could be interpreted to mean the entire tract of land on Anderson Road owned by the Perfects or to mean only 81.1 acres of the land. Because the description is ambiguous, the trial court appropriately considered extrinsic evidence regarding the transaction. The extrinsic evidence indicated that the parties intended that the Perfects sell and McAndrew purchase the entire tract, not just 81.1 acres. Further, the evidence indicated that the sale was an in gross sale and not a price per acre sale.

See supra Part I. Consequently, the trial court did not add a term to the contract, but rather properly interpreted an ambiguous contract with the aid of extrinsic evidence.

For the foregoing reasons, we affirm the trial court's judgment in favor of McAndrew on his complaint for specific performance.

Problem 5A

Angie wants to purchase a ranch. She needs enough land for her cattle and horses, and she needs good fenced-in property, grazing lands, fresh water and improvements, including a main house, a bunkhouse for hired hands, and several barns and storage buildings. Angie locates a nice tract of land being offered for sale by Jim Bob. Jim Bob has what he describes as an 11,000-acre ranch for sale. He has owned and worked the ranch for 35 years. Angie examines the ranch and rides it on horseback to get a real feel for it. One part of the property has a small lake on it that will be excellent for livestock use and irrigation purposes. Near the lake is some top-grade grazing land. These two areas make up about 7,000 acres. Other parts of the ranch include the building areas, some lesser grazing lands, and some low-quality rock flats of little use to the ranch. The rock flats are about 1,000 acres, but Jim Bob will not do the deal unless Angie takes the entire spread. Before signing the contract for purchase and sale, Jim Bob shows Angie a government map of the area. The ranch is shown on the map and listed as having 11,000 acres. Angie, who has bought and sold many properties in her time, signs the contract to purchase the land at $3,300,000 for "11,000 acres more or less." Angie does not have a survey prepared, but one week prior to closing with Jim Bob she learns that an adjoining property owner has obtained a survey, which reveals that some of the land the government had thought was within the old Jim Bob ranch is actually owned by the adjoining owner. In fact, it turns out that Jim Bob owns, and Angie will get, only 7,000 acres. Angie is understandably upset.

(a) Can Angie rescind her contract with Jim Bob based on this new information?

(b) If a court were to reduce the price, would it be fair simply to give Angie a pro rata reduction based on the shortfall of 4,000 acres times a per-acre value of $300? (11,000 acres times $300 per acre is $3,300,000.)

(c) Would it make any difference in parts (a) and (b) if the neighboring survey was prepared after Jim Bob and Angie closed their deal, and Angie then objected?

(d) What more should Jim Bob and Angie have done in their process of contracting? Try to draft a contract provision that: (1) seeks to avoid the problem; and (2) calculates any set-off should one be needed at a future date.

(e) Assume instead that after the contract is signed, it is discovered that the property really has 15,000 acres, or 4,000 more than Jim Bob thought he owned. Does this change your analysis and concerns?

(f) Would it make any difference in part (e) if Angie had paid for a survey that revealed the extra 4,000 acres to her, but she did not relay this information to Jim Bob, who thought it was only 11,000 acres?

B. QUALITY

Issues of property quality are also important to the parties in an exchange. Quality issues arise in many different situations. Primary areas of concern include the structural soundness of improvements, the environmental safety of improvements and land, and the availability of amenities such as utilities and access. These problem areas are discussed later in this section. In Chapters 8 through 12 we explore a number of issues related to the quality of title.

1. *Express Allocations of Risk of Quality*

ALIRES v. McGEHEE

Supreme Court of Kansas, 2004
277 Kan. 398; 85 P.3d 1191

LUCKERT, J. Tim and Loretta Alires purchased a house from James and Dorothy McGehee and sued when the basement leaked. After a bench trial, the district court found that the McGehees had fraudulently misrepresented the condition of the house. The district court entered judgment in favor of the Alireses for $25,621.68. The McGehees appealed, and a majority of the Court of Appeals panel reversed. The majority found the evidence did not establish that the McGehees made untrue statements about the basement with the intent to deceive or fraudulently induce the sale or that the Alireses were justified in relying on the alleged misrepresentations. Alires v. McGehee, No. 88,514, unpublished opinion filed September 12, 2003. This court granted the Alireses' petition for review. . . .

FACTS

The fact that the basement leaked was discovered very soon after the Alireses purchased the house in September 2000. Mr. Alires watered the front lawn and then discovered water leaking into the basement. The basement leaked twice more in October 2000, once during a rainstorm and once when a main water line broke in the alley behind the house.

The McGehees, as sellers, had made several representations regarding the condition of the basement. Mr. Alires testified that, upon first touring the home, he asked Mrs. McGehee whether the basement leaked and she said, "No." The McGehees' real estate agent, Janie Rine, who showed the house to the Alireses, testified that she heard this exchange.

In addition, Mrs. McGehee completed and signed a seller's property disclosure statement, which contained the question: "Has there ever been leaking or seepage in the basement or crawl space?" She answered: "Yes," and in the space provided for explanation wrote: "Repaired broken pipe."

At trial Mrs. McGehee testified to instances of water leakage in the basement which she had not disclosed on the seller's property disclosure statement. She testified that she had discovered water stains on carpet in two different rooms in the basement during the last 2 to 3 years. She believed moisture had come in through the basement windows, and this was the reason the McGehees had their patio repaired. On another occasion, a broken water heater had leaked in the utility room. Mrs. McGehee also testified about the broken water pipes in a bathroom which were mentioned in the seller's disclosure statement. She stated that she simply forgot to mention the other incidences of water leakage in the disclosure. Mrs. McGehee explained that she underwent surgery for a brain tumor in 1998 and her short-term memory was affected. She also testified her husband had a massive stroke in 1985, just before the couple purchased the house, which caused him to have difficulty speaking. Therefore, he was not involved in providing information to the buyers.

Mr. Alires testified that, had he known the history of leaking in the basement, he would not have purchased the house. Rine confirmed that she knew Mr. Alires was particularly concerned about leaky basements.

Mr. Alires also testified that as soon as he discovered that the basement leaked, he called Rine who in turn contacted Mrs. McGehee. According to Mr. Alires, Rine said Mrs. McGehee told her there was a crack around the foundation and that the McGehees avoided watering too close to the house. Rine testified that when she called Mrs. McGehee to tell her about the leaking, Mrs. McGehee responded that there was no warranty on the house and that the McGehees did not water close to the house. A few days later, Mrs. McGehee told Rine that they had no problems watering near the foundation. Rine also explained that Mrs. McGehee never said there was a crack in the foundation, but that there had been a crack in the ground near the foundation and the McGehees had concrete work done as a result.

The contractor who performed the concrete work in May 1999 testified that he removed and replaced a crumbling patio and put in a sidewalk around the house. He explained that the existing patio was sloping toward the house and causing a water leak. His work established a grade so that water would flow away from the house.

Robert Smith, owner of a basement and foundation repair company, testified that the concrete in the Alireses' house was deteriorating and showed both angular and horizontal cracking, which indicated inward wall movement. Smith observed that the brick and mortar on the outside of the house showed stair-step type cracks. He also observed cracking inside where the walls were not covered.

However, his inspection was not conducted until after the home was purchased even though, in the original contract, the Alireses reserved the right to conduct mechanical, structural, and wood infestation inspections of the house. If defects were found, the McGehees agreed to pay up to $250 for repairs. If the cost of repairs exceeded that amount, either the Alireses or the McGehees could pay the excess amount or the contract could be canceled. The contract specifically provided that the house was being purchased "as is." The contract also included a waiver of all claims arising because of any patent defects in the property, stating:

> If inspections are not performed regarding all or part of the property, Buyer is bound by whatever information an inspection would have revealed, and waives any claim, right or cause of action relating to or arising from any condition of the property that would have been apparent had inspections been performed.

In an addendum to the contract covering certain repairs to be made before closing, the Alireses agreed to waive the inspections. Mr. Alires testified that he did not have the foundation inspected because he trusted Mrs. McGehee's representation that the basement did not leak. He agreed that, had such an inspection been done, a determination about the condition of the basement could have been made before closing.

At some point, the McGehees attempted to back out of the sales contract because Mrs. McGehee was concerned about finding a new place to live. The Alireses refused to allow the cancellation of the contract, and the sale went forward.

After hearing the evidence, the trial court determined that Mrs. McGehee knew the basement leaked, failed to disclose the fact to the Alireses, and misrepresented the nature of past water problems. The trial court recognized the contractual provisions regarding inspections, including the waiver for claims arising from defects which would have been detected by inspection. However, the court entered judgment for the Alireses, finding that Mrs McGehee had superior knowledge and an obligation to disclose the past leakage problem when she knew the Alireses were not having an inspection performed.

Court of Appeals Decision

On appeal, a majority of the Court of Appeals panel reversed. The majority noted that Mrs. McGehee had attempted to back out of the sales contract at one point, but the Alireses would not agree to the cancellation. The majority therefore concluded that the McGehees could not have had any intent to deceive or fraudulently induce the Alireses to purchase the house. . . .

Did the Court of Appeals Erroneously Conclude That the McGehees Had No Intent to Deceive and That the Alireses Were Not Justified in Relying upon the McGehees' Statements?

. . . The Alireses' argument is persuasive. The evidence showed that Mrs. McGehee attempted to back out of the sale at one point because she was concerned about finding a new place to live. She never mentioned the other basement leaks or corrected her prior misstatements. The fact that Mrs. McGehee later wanted out of the deal has no bearing on whether her misrepresentations, made before the Alireses entered into the contract, were made with the intent to deceive or with reckless disregard for the truth. . . . Therefore, the Court of Appeals erroneously determined that there was no intent to deceive.

Next, the majority ruled that the Alireses were not justified in relying on the alleged misrepresentations because the seller's disclosure statement contained a section specifically allowing the Alireses to note any important representations being relied upon and the Alireses wrote nothing in that section. The dissent aptly noted this write-in section was for representations not mentioned in the "above" section of the contract, the section where the McGehees disclosed the basement leakage caused by a broken pipe but not the other incidences of leakage. The dissent characterized this as a partial disclosure, citing Sparks v. Guaranty State Bank, 182 Kan. 165, 168, 318 P.2d 1062 (1957), for the premise that when a person makes an equivocal, evasive, or misleading statement which is literally true but fails to disclose the whole truth, that person has made an affirmative misrepresentation.

Again, we agree with the dissent. The seller's disclosure form was integrated into the contract, and one of the alleged fraudulent representations was contained within the disclosure form itself. There was no need for the Alireses to write in the representation on which they were relying because Mrs. McGehee's representation that the basement had leaked only when broken pipes needed repairing was already listed.

However, this does not dispose of the issue of reasonable reliance and the other issues raised by the McGehees on appeal. . . .

Did the District Court Err in Ruling in Favor of the Alireses?

. . . Our review of the record reveals substantial competent evidence to support the findings of the trial court that Mrs. McGehee made untrue statements of fact and knew the statements were untrue.

Next, the McGehees argue that, as part of the real estate contract, they bargained for limited liability by including provisions that the Alireses purchased the house "as is," obtained the right to have the house inspected for structural defects, and, if they elected not to have an inspection, waived any claim for defects which would have been apparent had an inspection been performed. Alternatively, the McGehees argue that there could not have been reasonable reliance upon the alleged misrepresentation, as a matter of law, because of the disclaimer or waiver provisions.

The seller's property disclosure statement, which was integrated into the contract, stated: "The Seller discloses the following information with the knowledge that even though this is not a warranty, prospective Buyers may rely on this information in deciding whether, and on what terms, to purchase the subject real property." At the end of the disclosure statement was a buyer's acknowledgment and agreement, signed by the Alireses, which provided:

> 1. I acknowledge that I have read and received a signed copy of the Seller's Property Disclosure Statement from the Seller, the Seller's agent, or transaction broker.
> 2. I have carefully inspected the property. Subject to any inspections allowed under my contract with Seller, I agree to purchase the property in its present condition only, without warranties or guarantees of any kind by Seller or any real estate licensee concerning the condition or value of the property.
> 3. I agree to verify any of the above information that is important to me by an independent investigation of my own. I have been advised to have the property examined by professional inspectors.
> 4. I acknowledge that neither Seller nor any real estate licensee involved in this transaction is an expert at detecting or repairing physical defects in the property. I state that no important representations concerning the condition of the property are being relied upon by me except as disclosed above or as fully set forth as follows:______________________.

As previously discussed, the partial disclosure regarding past water leakage was included in the "disclosed above" section. However, the Court of Appeals did not discuss other contract provisions regarding the issues of reliance and waiver of claims. Conspicuously displayed at the top of the disclosure form was the following: "THIS STATEMENT . . . IS NOT A WARRANTY OF ANY KIND BY THE SELLER(S) OR ANY REAL ESTATE LICENSEE IN THIS TRANSACTION, AND SHOULD NOT BE ACCEPTED AS A SUBSTITUTE FOR ANY INSPECTIONS OR WARRANTIES THE BUYER MAY WISH TO OBTAIN."

The contract also contained the following paragraph regarding inspections:

> Buyer and Seller agree that the real estate licensees involved in this transaction are not experts regarding whether any environmental or health hazards, defects in the mechanical equipment or systems, structural defects, or damage from wood destroying insects exists in and on the property. Buyer and Seller should seek expert advice and obtain inspections to determine if hazards, defects or damage exist in and on the property. If inspections are not performed regarding all or part of the property, Buyer is bound by whatever information an inspection would have revealed, and waives any claim, right or cause of action relating to or arising from any condition of the property that would have been apparent had inspections been performed. Unless otherwise provided in paragraphs relating to specific inspections, Buyer accepts the

property in its current condition. This shall not be deemed a waiver or modification of any implied warranties which may exist.

. . . [T]he buyers in this case, the Alireses, not only contractually assumed a duty to inspect the property and failed to have the property inspected, but the Alireses agreed that if they failed to have inspections performed, they waived "any claim, right or cause of action relating to or arising from any condition of the property that would have been apparent had inspections been performed." Thus, in order to prove their case, it was incumbent upon the Alireses to provide evidence that, even if an inspection had been performed, the water leakage problems in the basement would not have been apparent. The Alireses provided no such evidence. To the contrary, under cross-examination, Mr. Alires admitted that, had an inspection been done, a determination about the condition of the basement could have been made before closing.

Still, the Alireses assert that this waiver should not be given effect because it was induced by the misrepresentation. This brings into question whether their reliance upon the representation was reasonable. This court has previously addressed a similar factual situation. In Munkres v. McCaskill, 64 Kan. 516, 68 P. 42 (1902), a case cited in the McGehees' reply brief, the parties entered into an agreement to exchange land subject to a stipulation that the contract should not be binding until each party had investigated the property of the other and each assumed the responsibility to make a full, fair, and complete examination of the property to be satisfied as to the truth or falsity of the representations made by the other and the advisability of making the exchange. The *Munkres* court held that after one of the parties made the examination, signified satisfaction, and closed the trade by exchanging title papers, such party could not rescind the contract upon the ground that the party was induced to make the contract in reliance upon false representations made by the other party, unless the other party fraudulently prevented the making of a full, fair, and complete examination of the property.

Under the facts of this case, the buyer of real estate could not reasonably rely upon representations of the seller when the truth or falsity of the representation would have been revealed by an inspection of the subject property and the misrepresentations were made prior to or as part of the contract in which the buyer contracted for the right to inspect, agreed that the statements of the seller were not warranties and should not replace the right of inspection, declined inspection, and waived any claims arising from defects which would have been revealed by an inspection. There is no showing in the record that the subsequent contract addendum which contained the waiver of the right to inspect was induced by any additional misrepresentations of the seller. Thus, although we disagree with the analysis of the Court of Appeals, we reach the same conclusion that the Alireses were not justified in their reliance upon the misrepresentations of Mrs. McGehee. . . .

We affirm the Court of Appeals decision reversing the judgment of the district court.

Problem 5B

Hernandes is buying a home from Gorky. The property is located in a region of the country known to have problems with wood-destroying organisms such as termites. In the written contract of purchase, Hernandes bargains for a home inspection, including a termite inspection, and further extracts a representation from Gorky that the property is free of all wood-destroying organisms. Prior to closing, the home inspection and termite reports are delivered to Hernandes, and these reports indicate the presence of no wood-destroying organisms. The reports, however, also contain standard form disclaimers and qualifiers related to the inaccessibility of certain parts of the premises and to the fact that internal walls and structures cannot be seen with a visual check. The parties close the transaction. About one month later, Hernandes notices little black droppings along some of the edge boards of the house, and a close inspection of some "dust" build-up reveals the presence of additional droppings. During the regularly scheduled pest control service visit, Hernandes consults with the pest control servicer. Hernandes is told that these droppings are evidence of termite activity in the home. This is followed up a week later by a more detailed examination of the property by the pest control company, at which time termite damage is discovered in some of the structural beams and braces of the home. The company estimates, based on the discovered damages, that the termites have most likely been present for about a year. They add, however, that this is sometimes difficult to determine.

(a) Should Hernandes be able to sue Gorky or the pre-closing home inspector for loss of value or damages as a result of the termite activity? What factors should be considered?

(b) What if we learn that all home inspection companies use the same report form with the same standard disclaimers as the one given to Hernandes prior to closing?

(c) What if the home inspector doing the pre-closing termite inspection worked for the same company that later confirmed the presence of the termite activity? Would it make any difference if the company could show that the later-discovered evidence of activity would not have been found under the practices of most other companies' inspectors either?

(d) If Gorky is held liable for any damages to Hernandes, should Gorky be able to sue the preclosing termite inspector? On what theory would this be possible, and what are the defenses to any such theory of liability?

(e) Can you identify the terms you would want drafted into a contract to avoid this type of problem, or at least to reduce the risk of a similar issue confronting one of your clients? Draft a contract provision that incorporates and addresses your concerns. Is your language likely to be acceptable to the other side?

(f) How might an "as-is" term be used in this type of situation?

(g) How might the rule related to a patent versus a latent defect figure in an analysis of this type of problem?

2. *Disclosing Inaccurate Information*

PETRILLO v. BACHENBERG
Supreme Court of New Jersey, 1995
139 N.J. 472, 655 A.2d 1354

POLLOCK, J. The issue is whether under the circumstances of this case the attorney for the seller of real estate owes a duty to a potential buyer. Plaintiff, Lisa Petrillo, alleges that because of the negligence of defendant Bruce Herrigel, an attorney, she received a misleading copy of a percolation-test report that induced her to sign a contract to purchase property. At the close of plaintiff's case, the Law Division concluded that Herrigel did not owe a duty to plaintiff to provide a complete and accurate report. The Appellate Division reversed, 263 N.J. Super. 472, 623 A.2d 272 (1993). It determined that an attorney for a seller has a duty not to provide misleading information to potential buyers who the attorney knows, or should know, will rely on the information. We granted Herrigel's petition for certification, 134 N.J. 566, 636 A.2d 523 (1993), to determine whether he owed such a duty to plaintiff. We now affirm the judgment of the Appellate Division.

I

In 1987, Rohrer Construction (Rohrer) owned a 1.3-acre tract of undeveloped land in Union Township, Hunterdon County. Herrigel represented Rohrer in the sale of the property. Rohrer hired Heritage Consulting Engineers (Heritage) to perform percolation tests concerning a contract of sale to Land Resources Corporation (Land Resources). Percolation tests reveal, among other things, the suitability of soil for a septic system. Union Township requires two successful percolation tests for municipal approval of a septic system.

In September and October 1987, Heritage provided Rohrer and Herrigel with copies of reports describing two series of percolation tests. The first report, dated September 24, 1987, revealed that of twenty-two tests, only one had been successful. A November 3, 1987, report showed that of eight tests conducted in October, one had been successful.

Rohrer's contract with Land Resources failed. Subsequently, Rohrer listed the property with a local real estate broker, Bachenberg & Bachenberg, Inc. In October 1988, William G. Bachenberg, Jr. (Bachenberg) of Bachenberg & Bachenberg, Inc. asked Herrigel for information concerning the listing. Herrigel told Bachenberg that "he had some perc results," and sent him a two-page document consisting of one page from each of the two Heritage reports. The first page was page one from the September 24, 1987, report; it reflected one successful test and five unsuccessful tests. The second page was culled from the November 3, 1987, report; it listed one successful and one unsuccessful test. Read together, the two pages appear to describe a single series of [eight] tests, two of which were successful. In fact, the property had passed only two of thirty percolation tests. The document, subsequently described as the "composite report," became part of Bachenberg's sales packet. . . .

Bachenberg listed the property for sale at $160,000. In February 1989, Petrillo expressed an interest in purchasing the property to build and operate a child day-care facility. That month, at their first meeting, Bachenberg gave Petrillo a sales packet, which included the composite report.

In June 1989, Petrillo agreed to pay Bachenberg his asking price. Herrigel represented Bachenberg in negotiating the terms of the contract with Petrillo's attorney. Nothing in the record indicates that Herrigel informed Petrillo's attorney of the test results that had been omitted from the composite report. At the insistence of Petrillo's attorney, the contract provided Petrillo with forty-five days to conduct independent soil and water tests, including percolation tests. The contract provided further that Petrillo could rescind if the percolation tests were not satisfactory to her.

In August 1989, Petrillo hired an engineering firm, Canger & Cassera, to conduct soil tests and site planning. Based on the composite report, Canger & Cassera recommended that they start site-planning work simultaneously with the conduct of percolation tests by a sub-contractor, PMK, Ferris & Perricone (PMK). PMK conducted six percolation tests, all of which failed. Consequently, PMK concluded that the site was inadequate for a septic system. Canger & Cassera stopped working on the preliminary site plan. On August 22, 1989, Petrillo notified Bachenberg that the contract was null and void.

In response, Bachenberg contracted with Heritage to design a septic system that would satisfy the municipality. Heritage designed the system, which the Hunterdon County Board of Health approved. Petrillo, however, refused to accept the design, and requested permission to conduct additional percolation tests. Bachenberg denied her request. During the course of their negotiations, Herrigel sent Petrillo the complete copies of the September 24 and November 3 Heritage reports.

The parties could not settle their differences. Bachenberg refused to return Petrillo's $16,000 down payment, claiming that she had breached the contract. Petrillo sued . . . for the return of the down payment and for the costs of her engineering fees. . . .

In the complaint, Petrillo alleged, among other things, that Herrigel's failure to provide the complete Heritage reports violated a duty that he owed to her. She claimed further that the violation had caused her to incur engineering expenses that she would not have incurred if she had known all the facts. Specifically, she contended that if she had known that the property had passed only two of thirty percolation tests, she would not have signed the contract or hired Canger & Cassera and PMK.

At the close of plaintiff's case, the trial court dismissed Petrillo's complaint against Herrigel. The court concluded that Petrillo had not alleged facts sufficient to support a duty extending from Herrigel to her. . . .

Before us, however, is the Appellate Division's reversal of the dismissal of Petrillo's claims against Herrigel for negligent misrepresentation. The Appellate Division determined that a seller's attorney owes a duty to a non-client buyer "who the attorney knows or should know would rely on the attorney in his or her professional capacity." 263 N.J. Super. at 483, 623 A.2d 272. It stated that "a buyer of real estate has a cause of action against an attorney for the seller who provides misleading information concerning the subject of the transaction." *Id.* at 487, 623 A.2d 472. The court concluded that a jury could have found that when Herrigel gave Bachenberg the composite report, Herrigel should have known that Bachenberg would provide the report to a prospective purchaser, such as Petrillo, who would rely on the report in deciding whether to purchase the property. *Ibid.*

II

As a claim against an attorney for negligence resulting in economic loss, Petrillo's claim against Herrigel is essentially one for economic negligence. Formerly, the doctrine of privity limited such claims by non-clients against attorneys and other professionals. Jay M. Feinman, *Economic Negligence: Liability of Professionals and Businesses to Third Parties for Economic Loss* 29 (1995). More recently, other doctrines have replaced privity as a means of limiting a professional's duty to a non-client. *See, e.g.,* Biakanja v. Irving, 49 Cal. 2d 647, 320 P.2d 16 (1958) (adopting a "balance of factors" test).

The determination of the existence of a duty is a question of law for the court. Wang v. Allstate Ins. Co., 125 N.J. 2, 15, 592 A.2d 527 (1991); Strachan v. John F. Kennedy Memorial Hosp., 109 N.J. 523, 529, 538 A.2d 346 (1988). Whether an attorney owes a duty to a non-client third party depends on balancing the attorney's duty to represent clients vigorously, Rules of Professional Conduct, Rule 1.3 (1993), with the duty not to provide misleading information on which third parties foreseeably will rely, Rules of Professional Conduct, Rule 4.1 (1993). *See also* Restatement of the Law Governing Lawyers §73 comment b (Tentative Draft No. 7, 1994) (discussing rationale for imposing duty to non-clients); Stephen Gillers, *Regulation of Lawyers* 656–64 (3d ed. 1992) (discussing duty to non-clients); Geoffrey C. Hazard, Jr. & W. William Hodes, *The Law of Lawyering* §1.1:203, §2.3:102 (2d ed. 1990) (same). Because this matter arises on the grant of defendant Herrigel's motion to dismiss, we accord Petrillo the benefit of all favorable inferences that may be drawn from her proofs. R. 4:37-2(b); Bozza v. Vornado, Inc., 42 N.J. 355, 357, 200 A.2d 777 (1964).

Although we have not previously addressed the issue of attorney liability to third parties, the Appellate Division has recognized that attorneys may owe a limited duty in favor of specific non-clients. In Stewart v. Sbarro, 142 N.J. Super. 581, 585, 362 A.2d 581, *certif. denied,* 72 N.J. 459, 371 A.2d 63 (1976), an attorney for the buyers of a corporation agreed to obtain the buyers' signatures on a bond and mortgage indemnifying the sellers against liability for existing corporate debt. The attorney failed to obtain the required signatures. As a result, the debt was unsecured, rather than secured. *Id.* at 586-87, 362 A.2d 581. When the buyers filed a bankruptcy petition, the sellers sued their own attorney, the buyers, and the buyers' attorney for the unpaid debt. The Appellate Division determined that the buyers' attorney could be liable in negligence for breaching a duty to the sellers. *Id.* at 593, 362 A.2d 581. It reasoned that when an attorney should foresee that a third party may rely on the attorney's promise to act, a duty attaches. *Ibid.*

Similarly, in Albright v. Burns, 206 N.J. Super. 625, 503 A.2d 386 (1986), the Appellate Division held that an attorney was liable to a decedent's estate when the attorney knowingly facilitated improper transactions involving the holder of the decedent's power of attorney. The court stated that "a member of the bar owes a fiduciary duty to persons, though not strictly clients, who he knows or should know rely on him in his professional capacity." *Id.* at 632-33, 503 A.2d 386.

More recently, in R. J. Longo Construction Co. v. Schragger, 218 N.J. Super. 206, 527 A.2d 480 (1987), the Appellate Division considered a case involving township attorneys who had prepared bid documents for a sewer-construction contract. The attorneys had failed to obtain certain easements mentioned in the bid package. *Id.* at 207-08, 527 A.2d 480. Consequently, the successful bidder, plaintiff, R. J. Longo Construction Co. (Longo), which had begun construction on notice to proceed from the town, was forced to stop work. As a result, Longo suffered losses and sued the attorneys. *Id.* at 208, 527 A.2d 480. The trial court dismissed the claims against the township attorneys because of the absence of privity. *Ibid.* The Appellate Division reversed. It held that Longo was an intended third-party beneficiary of the defendant attorneys' employment contracts with the township. *Id.* at 210, 527 A.2d 480. The court determined that the attorneys owed the contractor a fiduciary duty and that they were liable for the foreseeable consequences of their negligent misrepresentations on which plaintiff reasonably and foreseeably relied. *Id.* at 209-10, 527 A.2d 480.

Other jurisdictions similarly have relaxed traditional privity requirements when an attorney induces specific non-clients to rely on the attorney's representations. For example, in Greycas, Inc. v. Proud, 826 F.2d 1560, 1561-62 (7th Cir. 1987), *cert. denied,* 484 U.S. 1043, 108 S. Ct. 775, 98 L. Ed. 2d 862 (1988), Greycas, a finance company, agreed to lend funds to an Illinois borrower if the borrower provided an attorney's opinion letter stating that the borrower's collateral was not subject to prior liens. The borrower asked an attorney, his brother-in-law, to prepare the needed opinion letter. *Id.* at 1562. The attorney prepared the letter based solely on the borrower's representations and submitted it to Greycas, which promptly issued the funds. *Ibid.* After the borrower defaulted, Greycas learned that most of the borrower's collateral was subject to superior liens and that the loan was largely unsecured. *Ibid.* Greycas sued the attorney for negligent misrepresentation. The court concluded under Illinois law that the attorney owed Greycas a duty not to negligently misrepresent the status of the borrower's collateral notwithstanding the lack of privity. *Id.* at 1564-65 [citations omitted].

The New York Court of Appeals has likewise held that an attorney may owe a duty to specific non-clients who rely on the attorney's representations. *See* Prudential Insurance Co. of America v. Dewey Ballantine, Bushby, Palmer & Wood, 80 N.Y.2d 377, 590 N.Y.S.2d 831, 605 N.E.2d 318 (1992). In *Prudential,* a lender sued a borrower's attorney for negligently preparing an opinion letter that was provided to the lender as a condition to a debt restructuring. An attorney could be liable to a non-client for negligent misrepresentation, the court conceded, if the nature of the relationship between the attorney and the non-client was "so close as to approach that of privity." *Id.*, at 377, 590 N.Y.S.2d at 833, 605 N.E.2d at 320. The court stated the criteria for finding a duty:

> (1) an awareness by the maker of the statement that it is to be used for a particular purpose; (2) reliance by a known party on the statement in furtherance of that purpose; and (3) some conduct by the maker of the statement linking it to the relying party and evincing its understanding of that reliance.

Id., at 384, 590 N.Y.S.2d at 834-35, 605 N.E.2d at 321-22 (citing Credit Alliance Corp. v. Arthur Andersen & Co., 65 N.Y.2d 536, 493 N.Y.S.2d 435, 483 N.E.2d 110 (1985)). The court concluded that the attorney knew that the lender would rely on the opinion letter and intended to induce that reliance. *Id.*, 590 N.Y.S.2d at 8, 605 N.E.2d at 322. *See also* Vereins- und Westbank, AG v. Carter, 691 F. Supp. 704, 708-16 (S.D.N.Y. 1988) (holding under New York law that lawyer owes duty to non-clients to whom lawyer furnishes legal opinion on behalf of client).

Thus, when courts relax the privity requirement, they typically limit a lawyer's duty to situations in which the lawyer intended or should have foreseen that the third party would rely on the lawyer's work. *See* Feinman, *supra,* at 131-34. For example, a lawyer reasonably should foresee that third parties will rely on an opinion letter issued in connection with a securities offering. *See* Norman v. Brown, Todd & Heyburn, 693 F. Supp. 1259, 1265 (D. Mass. 1988) ("As a general matter, tax opinion letters are drafted so that someone can rely upon them."). The purpose of a legal opinion letter is to induce reliance by others. If an attorney foresees or should foresee that reliance, the resulting duty of care can extend to non-client third parties [citations omitted].

In other contexts, courts have imposed a duty on an attorney who prepares an instrument with the intent that third parties will rely on it. Thus, in Molecular Technology Corp. v. Valentine, 925 F.2d 910, 915-17 (1991), the Sixth Circuit Court of Appeals determined that a lawyer who prepared a private offering statement for his client's corporate debentures owed a duty of care to potential investors whom the attorney knew, or should have known, would rely on the statement. The court held that Michigan law "imposes a duty in favor of all those third parties who defendant knows will rely on the information and to third parties who defendant should reasonably foresee will rely on the information." *Id.* at 916 [citation omitted].

Likewise, in Century 21 Deep South Properties, Ltd. v. Corson, 612 So. 2d 359 (Miss. 1992), a buyer of real property sued alleging negligence of the attorney for the seller, who had conducted a title search on which the buyer had detrimentally relied. The Mississippi Supreme Court held that "an attorney performing title work will be liable to reasonably foreseeable persons who, for a proper business purpose, detrimentally rely on the attorney's work." *Id.* at 374.

Similarly, section 73 of the proposed Restatement of the Law Governing Lawyers, *supra*, pertaining to "duty to certain non-clients," provides:

> For the purposes of liability . . . , a lawyer owes a duty to use care . . . (2) To a non-client when and to the extent that the lawyer or (with the lawyer's acquiescence) the lawyer's client invites the non-client to rely on the lawyer's opinion or provision of other legal services, the non-client so relies, and the non-client is not, under applicable law, too remote from the lawyer to be entitled to protection. . . .

We also recognize that attorneys may owe a duty of care to non-clients when the attorneys know, or should know, that non-clients will rely on the attorneys' representations and the non-clients are not too remote from the attorneys to be entitled to protection. The Restatement's requirement that the lawyer invite or acquiesce in the non-client's reliance comports with our formulation that the lawyer know, or should know, of that reliance. No matter how expressed, the point is to cabin the lawyer's duty, so the resulting obligation is fair to both lawyers and the public.

III

The imposition on attorneys of defined liability to third parties comports with general principles of tort law. . . .

IV

The objective purpose of documents such as opinion letters, title reports, or offering statements, and the extent to which others foreseeably may rely on them, determines the scope of a lawyer's duty in preparing such documents. . . .

Here, Herrigel did not prepare an opinion letter. Giving Petrillo the benefit of all reasonable inferences, however, we infer that Herrigel extracted information from existing percolation-test reports, created the composite report, and delivered the report to a real estate broker. Our initial inquiry, as with an opinion letter or comparable document, is to ascertain the purpose of the report.

Although Herrigel may have intended that the composite report would demonstrate only that the property had passed two percolation tests, his subjective intent may not define the objective meaning of the report. The roles and relationships of the parties color our assessment. In making that assessment, we cannot ignore the fact that Herrigel is an attorney who, in connection with his client's efforts to sell the property, provided the report to a real estate broker. We infer that when he delivered the report to Bachenberg, Herrigel knew, or should have known, that Bachenberg might deliver it to a prospective purchaser, such as Petrillo. Herrigel did nothing to restrict a prospective purchaser's foreseeable use of the report. In neither the report, a covering letter, nor a disclaimer did Herrigel even hint that the report was anything but complete and accurate.

Significantly, Herrigel's involvement continued after he delivered the report to Bachenberg. After Bachenberg purchased the property, Herrigel acted as his lawyer and negotiated the terms of the contract for the sale of commercial property to Petrillo. Although compiling an engineering report to help a client sell real estate may not be part of a lawyer's stock-in-trade, representing the seller of real estate is a traditional legal service. By representing Bachenberg on the sale to Petrillo, Herrigel confirmed the continuity of his involvement as a lawyer. On these facts, Herrigel's continuing involvement permits the inference that the objective purpose of the report was to induce a prospective purchaser to buy the property. His involvement supports the further inference that Herrigel knew that Bachenberg intended to use the report for that purpose.

Furthermore, a purchaser reading the composite report reasonably could conclude that the property had passed two of [eight], not two of thirty, percolation tests. Based on that conclusion, a purchaser reasonably could decide to sign a purchase contract, although the purchaser would not have signed the contract if he or she had seen the complete set of percolation reports. So viewed, Herrigel should have foreseen that Petrillo would rely on the total number of percolation tests in deciding whether to sign the purchase contract. In sum, a jury reasonably could infer that the composite report misrepresented material facts.

By providing the composite report to Bachenberg and subsequently representing him in the sale, Herrigel assumed a duty to Petrillo to provide reliable information regarding the percolation tests. Herrigel controlled the risk that the composite report would mislead a purchaser. Fairness suggests that he should bear the risk of loss resulting from the delivery of a misleading report. We further conclude that Herrigel should have foreseen that a prospective purchaser would rely on the composite report in deciding whether to sign the contract and proceed with engineering and site work.

Herrigel easily could have limited his liability. Most simply, he could have sent complete copies of both reports to Bachenberg. Alternatively,

Herrigel could have sent a letter to Bachenberg stating that the property had passed two successful percolation tests as required by Union Township. Or he could have stated either in a letter to Bachenberg or in the composite report that the report evidenced only that the property had yielded two successful percolation tests and that no one should rely on the report for any other purpose. Because Herrigel did nothing to limit the objective purpose of the composite report, he should have foreseen that Petrillo, as a prospective purchaser, would rely on the facts set forth in the report. Accordingly, Herrigel's duty extends to Petrillo. . . .

. . . The recognized duty hardly constitutes lawyers as "guarantors of the accuracy of surveys or other similar experts' reports that they merely transmit [as claimed by the dissent *infra*]." We do not hold that Herrigel guaranteed the accuracy of the tests. Our holding goes no further than to state that Herrigel had a duty not to misrepresent negligently the contents of a material document on which he knew others would rely to their financial detriment. In many situations, lawyers, like people generally, may not have a duty to act, but when they act, like other people, they should act carefully.

The judgment of the Appellate Division is affirmed.

Stein, J., concurring. [Concurring opinion omitted.]

Garibaldi, J., dissenting. The majority imposes on an attorney a duty of care to a non-client broader than that imposed on an attorney under the proposed Restatement of the Law Governing Lawyers §73 (Tentative Draft No. 7, 1994), under the Restatement (Second) of Torts §552 (1977), and under our case law, including Rosenblum v. Adler, 93 N.J. 324, 461 A.2d 138 (1983). Such an extension will lead to defensive lawyering; it will make legal services more cumbersome, more costly, and less accessible to clients. . . .

Problem 5C

Abby is negotiating to purchase an office building from Jesse, the current owner who bought the building 20 years ago. Based on land values and cash flow from current leases along with other economic indicators, Abby offers $17.5 million for the property. Jesse considers this a fair offer and accepts the deal. The contract includes a provision allowing Abby to have the building inspected for "structural soundness" and to have the standard inspections for mechanicals in the building, such as the electric, heating, cooling, plumbing, elevators, fire alarms, and so on.

The inspections are completed and the deal is closed. About a year after owning the property, Abby decides to refurbish and renovate some of the office space so that it will be more appealing to tenants. In the course of the renovation work, the presence of asbestos is discovered. On closer examination, it turns out that the entire building contains asbestos, which was applied as a fire retardant at the time of the original construction. The law requires that the asbestos be removed, at an estimated cost of $1.8 million.

(a) Should Abby be able to recover anything from Jesse?

(b) Assume that Abby discovers the asbestos prior to closing the transaction. She tries to back out of the deal, but Jesse wants to enforce the contract. What are the parties' arguments? Who should prevail and why?

(c) Assume that Debbie is the attorney for Jesse and that she is aware of the high probability of asbestos being in the building based on her review of some of the original building construction blueprints. Debbie advises Jesse to avoid raising the issue or undertaking to confirm her suspicions for fear that it will "open a can of worms" and that the client's best interest will not be served thereby. Further assume that, based on some court decisions from other jurisdictions, Debbie feels that the language of "structural soundness" does not imply environmental or health issues. During the contract negotiations, nothing is said about the asbestos issue and Debbie negotiates hard for the "structural soundness" language. Might Debbie be found to have a duty of some sort to Abby? What if Debbie knew that Abby and her lawyers were concerned about such issues even if they never specifically asked a direct question concerning the presence or absence of asbestos? What if Abby, in the presence of Debbie, asked Jesse a direct question about the presence of asbestos on the property and Jesse replied, "Don't worry about it. I did a detailed examination a year ago and there is no problem. Your only concern should be to confirm the structural soundness of the building, which I think you will find more than satisfactory." Knowing Jesse's statement to be false, would Debbie have any duty to Abby at that time? What would be the appropriate action for Debbie to take with Jesse?

3. *Material Defects and Duty to Disclose*

a. Statutory Duty to Disclose

Statutes and regulations at both the federal and state level increasingly bear on issues of quality of real property being sold, especially when it is sold by developers or merchants. At the local level, for example, a home seller who builds a house with material violations of the building code may be required, at the buyer's insistence, to remedy the defect.

At the federal level, one significant law bearing on property quality is the Interstate Land Sales Full Disclosure Act, 15 U.S.C. §§1701-1720. Adopted by Congress in 1968, the Act applies to the sale of unimproved lots in subdivisions with 25 or more lots. Builders' sales of completed new homes are not subject to the Act. Although the principal application of the Act is to residential properties, it also covers developers who plan industrial and commercial subdivisions. Jurisdiction under the Act is triggered whenever the developer uses any of the means of interstate commerce, including mail and advertising that circulates in more than one state. Basically, the Act is a disclosure statute, requiring the developer to file a registration known as a *statement of record* for approval by the government before offering any lots for sale. As part of marketing, the developer must give each prospective purchaser a detailed "property report" that contains required disclosures about the lots and the overall real estate development. Because the Act is designed to protect lot buyers, it has antifraud provisions and provides penalties for violations. Under general notions of contract law, a representation made by the developer in the property report may be enforceable by purchasers. One significant buyer remedy for a developer's violation of the Act is the buyer's statutory right to revoke her lot purchase contract at any time within two years after signing the contract. The Act and its regulations are quite complicated, and compliance by developers may be costly in terms of legal and administrative expense. The main point to keep in mind is that merchant sellers must consider whether the Act applies to their project or whether they are entitled to one of the Act's full or partial exemptions. Lot buyers, in contrast, should be aware of their rights to information and remedies under the Act. Three cases to look at on this topic are Hester v. Hidden Valley Lakes, Inc., 495 F. Supp. 48 (N.D. Miss. 1980); Gibbes v. Rose Hill Plantation Development Co., 794 F. Supp. 1327 (D.S.C. 1992); and Tomlinson v. Village Oaks Development Co., 2003 U.S. Dist. LEXIS 8488 (S.D. Ind. 2003). And, for a case dealing with a state disclosure act, *see* Woods v. Pence 708 N.E.2d 563 (Ill. App. 1999) (dealing with the Illinois Residential Real Property Disclosure Act).

b. Implied Duty to Disclose

VAN CAMP v. BRADFORD

Court of Common Pleas of Ohio, Butler County, 1993
63 Ohio Misc. 2d 245, 623 N.E.2d 731

MICHAEL J. SAGE, Judge. This matter comes before this court on three motions filed by the defendants. The defendants in this case are Connie Bradford, the original owner/seller; Campbell Realty World (hereinafter "Realty World"), the . . . listing agency; William Campbell, the owner of Realty World; Martin Patton, the agent of Realty World; West Shell Realtors, Inc., the cooperating agency (hereinafter "West Shell"); and Robert Hoff, the cooperating agent of West Shell. Counsel have agreed that these motions are to be treated as Civ.R. 56(C) motions for summary judgment.

I

This case arises from the sale of a residence located at 6027 Arcade Drive, Fairfield, Ohio. On or about October 30, 1991, a renter's daughter was raped at knifepoint in the residence owned by defendant Bradford. On

The house purchased by Kitty Van Camp

or about December 20, 1991, another rape occurred in a neighboring home at 2499 E. Highland Drive; that same day, defendant Bradford listed the house for sale with defendant Realty World.

Plaintiff Kitty Van Camp submitted a written offer to purchase the home on February 4, 1992. Before closing and during a walk-through inspection of the premises with defendant Bradford, and defendant Patton and defendant Hoff present, plaintiff noticed bars on the basement windows. In response to plaintiff's inquiry regarding the purpose and necessity of the bars on the windows, defendant Bradford stated that a break-in had occurred sixteen years earlier, but that there was currently no problem with the residence. Plaintiff stated that she would like to remove the bars for cosmetic purposes, but Bradford advised her not to do so, as it was in plaintiff's best interests to leave the bars in place.

The closing on the property took place on February 21, 1992. At this time, the perpetrator of the crimes was still at large. While moving into the home, a neighbor informed plaintiff that the daughter of the last occupant had been raped in October, and that another brutal rape had occurred shortly before Christmas, in 1991. Two more rapes occurred in June and August 1992 at a nearby home, 5886 Coachmont Drive, Fairfield. Plaintiff's house was burglarized on April 8, 1992, and threatening phone calls were received by plaintiff in July 1992. Police reports submitted by plaintiff confirm that all of these crimes did in fact take place.

Plaintiff, after being informed of the rapes in her home and the surrounding neighborhood, confronted defendant Campbell, who acknowledged that he, defendant Patton, and defendant Hoff were all aware of the rapes, including the rape at the subject property.

Plaintiff filed her complaint on May 25, 1992, alleging that the defendants knew of the unsafe character of the residence and neighborhood, failed to disclose, and concealed these material facts, which would have influenced her decision to buy the property. Plaintiff seeks damages from all defendants for mental stress and anguish, for the decreased value of the property, for fraud and negligence, and for equitable relief.

The defendants have filed for summary judgment, arguing primarily that the doctrine of caveat emptor is a complete defense in a suit seeking recovery for the "stigma" attached to or the "psychological impairment" of a piece of property. Defendants also claim that a cause of action for property defects that are neither a physical or legal impairment does not exist in Ohio.

II

The rule that a seller is generally under no duty to disclose material facts about the subject matter of a sale unless a specific exception exists originates from the doctrine of *caveat emptor.* Powell, *The Seller's Duty to Disclose in Sales of Commercial Property* (Summer 1990), 28 Am. Bus. L.J. 245, at 248. At least since 1956, the principle of *caveat emptor* has been consistently applied in Ohio to sales of real estate relative to conditions discoverable by the buyer, or open to observation upon an investigation of the property. Traverse v. Long (1956), 165 Ohio St. 249, 135 N.E.2d 256. One of the earliest Ohio cases upholding this principle held that since repairs to an area of filled-in land were clearly visible upon inspection, the plaintiffs knew of the defect and *caveat emptor* was an applicable defense to their claim. *Id.* Similarly, in 1974, the Franklin County Court of Appeals held that since the seller generally has no affirmative duty to disclose patent material defects, the defendants were not liable for failing to disclose that the residence in question was serviced by well water and not city water, since the well itself and the defects in the well were both readily observable. Klott v. Assoc. Real Estate (1974), 41 Ohio App. 2d 118, 121, 322 N.E.2d 690, 692.

Five years later, however, the Supreme Court of Ohio held that latent defects do give rise to a duty on the part of the seller, and constitute an exception to the application of *caveat emptor.* Miles v. McSwegin (1979), 58 Ohio St. 2d 97, 100, 388 N.E.2d 1367, 1369. When latent defects are coupled with misrepresentations or concealment, the doctrine of *caveat emptor* does not preclude recovery for fraud. Finomore v. Epstein (1984), 18 Ohio App. 3d 88, 481 N.E.2d 1193. Fraudulent concealment exists where a vendor fails to disclose sources of peril of which he is aware, if such a source is not discoverable by the vendee. *Klott,* 41 Ohio App. 2d at 121, 322 N.E.2d at 692. Thus, the Supreme Court of Ohio held that the plaintiffs could sue for termites discovered after the real estate agent made the representation that the house was a "good solid home," especially since the seller was personally aware of the problem prior to the sale. *See Miles.* The nature of the defect and the ability of the parties to determine through a reasonable inspection that a defect exists are key to determining whether or not the defect is latent. *Id.*, 58 Ohio St. 2d at 101, 388 N.E.2d at 1369.

In the 1983 case of Kaye v. Buehrle, the Summit County Court of Appeals affirmed a directed verdict in favor of the defendants and upheld the validity of a real estate "as is" disclaimer clause. Kaye v. Buehrle (1983), 8 Ohio App. 3d 381, 457 N.E.2d 373. Such disclaimer clauses bar suit for passive nondisclosure, but will not protect a defendant from positive misrepresentation or concealment. *Id.* The court found, however, that the defendants did not make any statement or false representation regarding the condition of the basement, which suffered extensive flooding after the plaintiffs purchased the property.

The following year, the Cuyahoga County Court of Appeals held that *caveat emptor* did not preclude the purchaser of two tracts of land from recovering for fraud due to a latent defect in the form of a blemished title, since a misrepresentation had accompanied the latent defect. *See Finomore.* The plaintiff in that case testified that the owner had told him that the lots were "free and clear," yet the evidence indicated that a small mortgage on the property was outstanding at the time of the sale. . . .

Virtually all of the case law regarding the buyer's duties under *caveat emptor* focuses on physical property defects. Thus, the case at bar is unique in that it presents issues regarding duty and liability for a so-called psychological defect in the property, namely, that the property was rendered unsafe for habitation by the plaintiff due to the serious crimes that had occurred in and near the residence.

The stigma associated with the residence at 6027 Arcade Drive is analogous to the latent property defects that have become an exception to the strict application of *caveat emptor*. Due to the intangible nature of the defect at issue here, a prospective buyer would have been unable to determine from a walk-through of the house in 1992 that it was the site of a serious, unsolved violent crime. Clearly, any psychological stigma that may be attached to a residence is even more undiscoverable than the existence of termites in a home, *see Miles,* or a defect in the title to the property, *see Finomore,* both of which have been deemed latent defects despite the fact that they could have been discovered through a professional inspection or title search.

Defendants' argument that the defect at issue here was readily discoverable lacks merit. Checking police records in order to ascertain the relative safety of a neighborhood or a particular residence would not be an action undertaken by even the most prudent of purchasers. When viewed in conjunction with a potential misrepresentation or concealment on the part of defendant Bradford regarding the relative safety of the home, the latent nature of the defect at issue here renders the defense of *caveat emptor* inapplicable.

III

The case sub judice raises the question whether Ohio should recognize a cause of action for residential property tainted by stigmatizing events that have occurred on and near the premises. The only reported case involving a psychological property defect was heard in California by the Third District Court of Appeals, and involved a house that had been the site of multiple murders ten years prior to its sale to the plaintiff. Reed v. King (1983), 145 Cal. App. 3d 261, 193 Cal. Rptr. 130. The Third District held that the plaintiff buyer did have a cause of action capable of surviving the seller's motion to dismiss. The determinative issue in that case was whether the failure to disclose the murders was material. *Id.* . . .

Clearly defining the cause of action for stigmatized property is necessary in order to protect the stability of contracts and prevent limitless recovery for insubstantial harms and irrational fears: misrepresentation, concealment or nondisclosure of a material fact by a seller of residential property in response to an affirmative inquiry is evidence of a breach of duty on the part of the seller. After inquiry, if the buyer justifiably relied on the misrepresentation or nondisclosure, or was induced or misled into effecting the sale to his/her detriment and damage, the buyer has met the burden of proof required to withstand a summary judgment motion.

Fraud may be committed by suppression or concealment, as well as by expression of a falsehood [citation omitted]. Even an innocent misrepresentation may, under the appropriate circumstances, justify rescission in the interests of fairness [citation omitted].

The misrepresentation, however, must be regarding a material fact. . . .

The misrepresentation or nondisclosure of the seller must cause justifiable reliance on the part of the buyer, and damage must result as a consequence of the fraudulent transaction. Both of these requirements will serve as effective limitations on seller liability and will function to prevent the bringing of meritless claims. In determining whether reliance is justifiable, courts consider the various circumstances involved, such as the nature of the transaction, the form and materiality of the representation, the relationship of the parties, the respective intelligence, experience, age, and mental and physical condition of the parties, and their respective knowledge and means of knowledge. *Finomore,* 18 Ohio App. 3d at 90, 481 N.E.2d at 1195. When a fiduciary relationship exists, as between a realty agent and a client, the client is entitled to rely upon the representations of the realty agent. *Id.*; *see, also, Foust.* In the absence of a fiduciary relationship, the law requires a person to exercise proper vigilance in his dealings, so that where one is put on notice as to any doubt as to the truth of a representation, the person is under a duty to reasonably investigate before relying thereon. *Id.*, 4 Ohio App. 3d at 165, 446 N.E.2d at 1124. The prevailing trend in misrepresentation cases, however, is to place a minimal duty on the buyer to investigate and discover the true facts about the property. *See* Powell, *supra,* at 258.

A seller who is under a duty to disclose facts and fails to do so will be held liable for damages directly and proximately resulting from his silence [citation omitted]. A person injured by fraud is entitled to such damages as will fairly compensate him for the wrong suffered. . . .

The defendants in this case have argued that the prevailing trend across the nation regarding property disclosure is evidenced by the nondisclosure statutes that have been enacted in twenty states and the District of Columbia. . . .

These statutes generally state that sellers of real estate are not liable for failing to disclose stigmatizing events, such as the fact that a homicide, suicide, felony or death by AIDS occurred in the residence. Ohio has not adopted a nondisclosure statute of this nature.

It is the opinion of this court that the nondisclosure statutes as enacted in other states still require a good faith response to an inquiry regarding a potential psychological impairment: these statutes were enacted solely to insulate sellers from liability for any failure to voluntarily and automatically disclose information regarding potential stigmas associated with property. . . .

Nondisclosure statutes are not designed to allow sellers to make false representations regarding property defects in response to affirmative questioning by the buyer. . . .

Thus, since the nondisclosure statutes of other states merely protect sellers from the burden of voluntary disclosure regarding psychological defects, and since several states have specific provisions designed to uphold honesty in residential sales transactions, the duty described in this opinion is well within the range delineated and envisioned by other state legislatures.

VI

A cause of action for stigmatized property, as previously defined and limited, is warranted in the case at bar. . . .

Construing the evidence in the light most favorable to the plaintiff, the court finds that the plaintiff has met her initial burden of proof. . . .

Reasonable minds could construe the plaintiff's question regarding the bars on the basement windows as an affirmative inquiry directed at ascertaining the safety of the premises, and defendant Bradford's statements regarding the reason for the bars to be a misrepresentation or a nondisclosure of their current purpose. Upon the plaintiff's inquiry, defendant Bradford was simply required to tell the truth. A more difficult case would arise had there been no evidence to indicate that the plaintiff had solicited information regarding the safety of the residence.

Further, both the plaintiff and defendant Bradford are single mothers with teenage daughters. This fact alone may be sufficient to make disclosure of the rape a material fact with regard to the sale of the property at Arcade Drive, or at least may be sufficient to demonstrate that defendant Bradford should have known that the plaintiff was "peculiarly disposed" to attach importance to the subject of female-targeted crimes. Thus, a potential misrepresentation in response to plaintiff's affirmative inquiry regarding a material fact placed a duty of honesty upon the seller, and plaintiff has shouldered her initial burden in coming forward.

Numerous questions of material fact remain regarding the conversation that took place between plaintiff and defendant Bradford, and these questions preclude a granting of summary judgment. . . .

By contrast, however, the court finds as a matter of law that the inquiry of plaintiff was directed solely to the homeowner, defendant Bradford: she alone responded to plaintiff's question regarding the safety of the residence. The real estate defendants had no duty to affirmatively speak up and disclose their knowledge of the crimes simply because they were in the room at the time the inquiry was made. . . .

Problem 5D

Giorgio is interested in buying a home from Clara. The home is located in the town of Dewitt, a suburb of the city of Syracuse, New York. The home has a mailing address of Fayetteville, New York, which is an adjoining suburb. It is a spacious three-bedroom, four-bath home on an acre of land with three fireplaces and all the amenities that Giorgio has been looking for. The asking price is $260,000, but Giorgio is confident he can get it for $240,000. In fact, he ends up with a contract to purchase at his offer price.

(a) Assume that during one of the times Giorgio looks at the home, he asks about the size of the rooms and total square footage. Clara replies that the total is 3,000 square feet. After moving in Giorgio determines that the home is 2,600 square feet. Should Giorgio have a cause of action against Clara? Does Clara's state of mind (intent) affect your view? What if Clara said she didn't know but the broker volunteered the 3,000-square-foot number? Would the broker be liable? What if the broker knew it was 2,600 but Clara said 3,000, and the broker remained silent (did not correct the error)? What if Giorgio never asked about the square footage but it was erroneously stated on the multiple listing service description of the home? Would it be vital that Giorgio prove he read the erroneous description? How can a broker or seller provide the buyer with information about the home without worrying about the problems of unintended errors or about what has to be disclosed?

(b) What if Giorgio asks about the school district that his home is located in? The home is in Dewitt but has a mailing address of Fayetteville. Clara has no children so she is uncertain. The broker says, "They are both very good school districts, but since your mailing address is Fayetteville, it's a pretty safe bet that you are in that school district." Giorgio, not having any children himself, takes that as a good enough answer. Ten months later, Giorgio decides to sell the house and he has a prospect who is very interested. The prospect is a young family currently living in a smaller home in Fayetteville. They want to buy a bigger home, but they want to keep their children in the same school district. They tell Giorgio they want to buy the home for $243,000 and Giorgio agrees to sell. They plan to meet later that night to draw up the written contract. That night, Giorgio gets a call from the family saying they decided not to buy the house because they called the Fayetteville school district and were told that the house is located just across the district boundary line and therefore is within the Dewitt school district. Six months pass and Giorgio has had no other prospects even look at this house. Can Giorgio recover from the broker? What if the broker who was there and made the comment was Clara's listing broker and not Giorgio's broker? Would that make any difference?

(c) Assume Clara is an HIV-infected person in the later stages of the disease and she is selling the home in order to move into a hospice. The contract with Giorgio is a good deal for her. Furthermore, her companion of ten years who lived with her in the home died of AIDS at home about three months earlier. One day while Giorgio is viewing the home with Clara's broker in preparation for moving in, and while Clara is out, the broker says, "You know it's too bad that Clara's friend died of AIDS in this house and now Clara is preparing herself for the same fate. It's sad, but I suppose you should know that about the place before you move in." Giorgio decides not to go ahead with the deal. Clara sues her broker for breach of privacy, disclosure of confidential information, and damages for a lost sale. Should Clara be able to recover? Did the broker have a duty to disclose? What if the broker was responding to conversation but not a direct question, such as if Giorgio had been saying, "I can't wait to move out here to the suburbs, I'm sick of the city with its drug users, crack houses, and other things. . . . I'm scared to death that half the people in my neighborhood have AIDS because there are so many junkies sharing needles over at this abandoned housing project." What if a fear of AIDS, even an unfounded one, is shown to have a substantial impact on the value of a property?

(d) Assume that the house, Clara, the school district, and everything else are all in good shape. About a week prior to entering the contract with Giorgio, Clara gets a notice from the town zoning board informing her that a local not-for-profit organization has bought the house two doors down from Clara's. They have applied to turn the home into a group residence for five teenage boys and girls with mental and physical disabilities. One trained adult supervisor will be on location 24 hours a day. The notice says the board has granted preliminary approval for the zoning modification, with a public hearing scheduled two weeks from now. Does Clara have to disclose this to Giorgio?

(e) Assume that a week after entering the contract, the town tax authority sends Clara a notice of special assessment. Clara and her neighbors are being assessed $2,000 per lot to pay for the installation of new sewer lines that will directly benefit each home on her street. Is nondisclosure of the tax notice material if the sewer work in fact adds value to the house? If the assessment is made against the property during the executory contract period, who should pay the $2,000 cost?

4. *Implied Warranties*

Express warranties are traditional elements of a real estate transaction because they form a part of the parties' bargain in fact. *Implied warranties* arise from the situation or context in which a transaction takes place. As the term indicates, the implied warranty is read into an exchange on the basis of reasonable or fair expectations given the nature of the exchange. The implied warranty has been more problematic in real estate sales where, up until the 1950s, *caveat emptor* was clearly the ruling doctrine.

Since the 1950s, we have witnessed the gradual decline of the doctrine of *caveat emptor*. Courts have increasingly analogized a home sale to a sale of goods, thereby creating implied warranty protections for homebuyers and home dwellers. This implied warranty protection has been extended, in some cases, beyond the physical structure of the home to include such things as the quality of the water and soil related to the home. The cases in this area have recognized that housing markets and the methods of housing production and sales have changed over the years. Now most homes are mass-produced using prefabricated materials and, thus, home building very much resembles other forms of commercial product production. These market changes have exerted considerable pressure on real estate law to abandon old common-law principles in favor of new approaches that comport with modern commercial realities. This shift should also serve to alert lawyers to a related legal matter. As real estate development is increasingly seen as a commercial production process—similar to that of many other complex products such as automobiles—it not only becomes subject to more general contract and commercial law principles, but it also opens the door to tort law implications. Products liability, strict liability, damages for emotional distress, and punitive damages seem more and more appropriate for application to real estate transactions as our society becomes increasingly comfortable with the idea of conceptualizing real estate development as similar to other forms of commercial manufacturing and production.

The movement toward treating real estate development like other forms of commercial production is not just a process occurring in the courts. There are legislative measures addressing this area as well. A number of states, for instance, have passed statutes that read warranties into the sale of new housing, and some states have disclosure statutes that require sellers of used homes to inform buyers of material latent defects known to the seller.

The homebuilding industry has also responded to issues of property quality. Many builders offer their own express warranties to buyers of new homes, but more significant are standardized warranties given or guaranteed by third parties. The most prominent such warranty is backed by the Residential Warranty Corporation (RWC), founded in 1981, with headquarters in Harrisburg, Pennsylvania. It offers warranties on new homes, including manufactured homes, as well as remodeling projects.

In addition to the warranties for new homes, many realty companies offer insurance on used homes to help relieve buyers' fears of unknown problems with the home they are thinking of purchasing. Although this adds some cost to the transaction, it gives the buyer a vehicle for fixing certain home repair problems without cost during the covered time period, which is usually one year. One key problem with both the new and used warranty programs is that the actual insurance policy must be read carefully to see what types of repairs are covered and what types are excluded.

Problem 5E

Sejal contracts to buy a home from Juan. One of the reasons she wants to buy the property is because it is located in a high-growth area where values are expected to rise dramatically. Sejal sees the home as both a place to live and a good investment. She knows that, like other investments, a home purchase can be risky, but home ownership may also provide the investor with a profitable return. The contract price is $225,000. Juan has been in the house for only six months. He purchased it new for $210,000 from the developer, Ajax Construction Co. Juan is selling because he got a job transfer and soon will move to another state. At the time Juan bought the house, he obtained a mortgage loan of $180,000 from Big Bank. He used this to pay for the home. Juan's mortgage loan was a special type of mortgage known as a shared appreciation mortgage, or SAM. This type of mortgage allowed him to get a below-market rate of interest on his loan in exchange for giving Big Bank a 30 percent share in any equity appreciation in the home that occurred during the term of the mortgage. The SAM makes it possible for the bank to profit from the lower than market rate of interest on the loan by allowing it to share in some of the potentially profitable returns of home ownership. To keep the paperwork on the sale simple, Sejal agrees to assume Juan's SAM from Big Bank. This means that she takes over the promise to pay the remaining amount owed on the mortgage according to its terms. Because Sejal is a good credit risk, Big Bank releases Juan from the SAM and looks only to Sejal to make good on all of the obligations under the SAM.

After being in the home for about four months, Sejal becomes aware of certain defects in the property. There are three defects that she learns about: (1) a Carrier heating and cooling system fails to work properly, making the home very uncomfortable; (2) as a result of settling, a number of cracks occurred in the foundation and the floor; and (3) it is discovered that the developer located the house on the lot in violation of zoning setback restrictions in force at the time of construction and at the time of Sejal's ownership. The setback regulation provides that no improvements shall be placed on any lot that will be closer than 40 feet from the front property line. Ajax built the home 30 feet from the front property line.

Given these three categories of defects, which, if any, should Sejal be able to pursue under a breach of warranty theory against Ajax? As against Juan? If Juan is liable to Sejal for anything, should he be able to sue Ajax? If Juan had not sold the property to Sejal, would he have been able to successfully sue Ajax for these defects? Should Ajax be able to separate the Carrier heating and cooling system problems from the other issues by asserting that the system is movable equipment and, therefore, not part of the real property? In any event, may/must Sejal sue Carrier as the manufacturer for any defect?

Assume that Juan cannot be located and that Ajax has gone out of business. Can Sejal sue Big Bank to recover for any of her losses as a result of these defects? How might your answer be affected, if at all, if you learned through discovery that Big Bank also did the commercial financing for Ajax when it developed and built the homes in this subdivision, including the home that Juan bought and resold to Sejal?

6
Closing the Contract

Closing the contract of purchase and sale represents the culmination of the earlier stages of the transaction. In some respects, it is actually a two-phase process. The first phase consists of everything that goes into preparing for the completion of the exchange as contracted. The second phase involves the paperwork that is required postclosing, such as the recording of documents in the public records. In each phase there are a number of concerns that require the attorney's attention.

From the buyer's point of view, the primary document is the deed of conveyance, which has to be examined for the quantity and quality of estate transferred and for any typographical errors that could result in title problems, such as a mistyped legal description or an incorrect spelling of the grantor or grantee's name.

Six important elements of conveyance must be complied with and accomplished at closing. To have an effective conveyance: (1) the deed must be in writing, (2) it must name a grantor and a grantee, (3) it must adequately describe the real property to the exclusion of all others, (4) there must be an intent to convey by the grantor, (5) there must be actual or constructive delivery, and (6) the grantee must accept the deed. Recording of the document is not required to create the interest. Recording is done to protect the grantee's interest from various third parties. We discuss recording in Chapter 10.

Problem 6A

Leilani owned 500 acres of land in Hawaii. Because she was growing old and her husband had died, she wanted to give her land to her two sons, Kalani and Akoni. Leilani went to the stationery store and found a simple form deed. She bought and prepared two separate deeds. In one, she granted 100 acres to her older son, Kalani, who had left home years ago to become a successful attorney in a distant city. In the other, she granted the remaining 400 acres to

Akoni, who had stayed at home and helped her through her trials with old age and illness. Without telling anyone what she had done, she placed the deed instruments in her bank safety deposit vault. Two years later she died and her safety deposit box was opened.

(a) Should this be considered a completed conveyance?

(b) What other area of law might Kalani argue governs this transfer that might give him a bigger share in the property?

(c) Would it make any difference if two months before her death, Leilani had given Akoni the key to her safe deposit box and said, "I know my time is short. Take this—there is something I want you to have."

(d) Assume that Leilani delivered the respective deeds to each son prior to her death and that the conveyance to each is effective. As it turns out, Kalani discovers that his property is contaminated with some subsurface chemical waste, and it is estimated that it will cost $1 million to clean up the soil. Kalani decides to make a gift to his brother without disclosing the environmental problem. He drafts an appropriate deed and delivers it to Akoni with a note attached saying, "Mother always liked you best, so, here, enjoy the whole thing." Is Akoni now stuck with the additional land and its environmental liabilities? What should Akoni do?

Problem 6B

Shane is preparing for his first solo closing. He has sat in on a number of closings while at his law firm, but this time he will go it alone. The deal is considered a simple transaction, involving a $300,000 single-family home being purchased directly from the developer in a new subdivision. Shane is going to the closing to represent the bank that is providing the mortgage financing for the purchase. At the closing, a number of documents are presented for review and are executed to effectuate the conveyance, implement the mortgage, and otherwise satisfy the purchase and sale contract as well as the loan commitment agreement. The vice president of the developer corporation is present at the closing, and she signs the deed and other documents that have to be executed by the seller. The loan officer for the bank asks Shane if the vice president's signature will be appropriate. All the other deals done out of this subdivision and financed with this bank had documents executed by the president. The bank loan officer worries that an improper deed might affect the bank's mortgage. Everyone in the closing room is anxious to get the deal over with and the vice president says that the president is out of town so she decided to do this sale herself to accommodate the buyer. The seller's broker remarks that he doesn't understand the concern; he has seen more senior lawyers close deals with the signature of any corporate officer.

(a) Should Shane have anything to worry about? If Shane says the signature of the vice president is not sufficient, the bank will not release the money. If Shane says the signature is okay, the bank will release the funds.

(b) Assume that Shane says, "Go ahead, no problem." The deal gets funded and then a problem is discovered. If the buyer was not represented by an attorney at closing, should the buyer be able to hold Shane liable on the grounds that the buyer thought Shane was representing his interest because Shane was considering the validity of the deed from the seller to buyer? What, if anything, can or should Shane do to reduce this risk of misunderstanding? Should the buyer in such a situation be able to sue the lender on the grounds that the lender's consideration and ultimate action in favor of proceeding confirmed to the buyer the soundness of the transaction? In other words, did the bank's conduct in this context serve as an implied, if not an express, stamp of approval upon which the buyer should be entitled to rely?

A. MULTIPLE REPRESENTATION

AMERICAN BAR ASSOCIATION
MODEL RULES OF PROFESSIONAL CONDUCT (2002)

RULE 1.7 CONFLICT OF INTEREST: CURRENT CLIENTS

(a) Except as provided in paragraph (b), a lawyer shall not represent a client if the representation involves a concurrent conflict of interest.

A concurrent conflict of interest exists if:

(1) the representation of one client will be directly adverse to another client; or

(2) there is a significant risk that the representation of one or more clients will be materially limited by the lawyer's responsibilities to another client, a former client, or a third person or by a personal interest of the lawyer.

(b) Notwithstanding the existence of a concurrent conflict of interest under paragraph (a), a lawyer may represent a client if:

(1) the lawyer reasonably believes that the lawyer will be able to provide competent and diligent representation to each affected client;

(2) the representation is not prohibited by law;

(3) the representation does not involve the assertion of a claim by one client against another client represented by the lawyer in the same litigation or other proceeding before a tribunal; and

(4) each affected client gives informed consent, confirmed in writing.

In re LANZA
Supreme Court of New Jersey, 1974
65 N.J. 347, 322 A.2d 445

PER CURIAM. The Bergen County Ethics Committee filed a presentment with this Court against respondent, Guy J. Lanza, who has been a practicing member of the bar of this State since 1954.

The Committee specifically found that respondent's conduct violated DR5-105. This Disciplinary Rule forbids an attorney to represent adverse interests, except under certain very carefully circumscribed conditions.[1]

In April or May of 1971, Elizabeth F. Greene consulted respondent with respect to the sale of her residence property in Palisades Park, New Jersey. Mr. Lanza agreed to act for her. In due course a contract, apparently prepared by a broker, was signed by Mrs. Greene as seller as well as by the prospective purchasers, James and Joan Connolly. The execution and delivery of the contract took place in Mr. Lanza's office, although he seems to have played little or no part in the negotiation of its terms. By this time he had agreed with the Connollys that he would represent them, as well as Mrs. Greene, in completing the transaction. The testimony is conflicting as to whether or not Mrs. Greene had been told of this dual representation at the time she signed the contract. Mr. Lanza says that she had been told, but according to her recollection she only learned of this at a later date from Mrs. Connolly. In any event it is quite clear that respondent agreed to act for the purchasers before discussing the question of such additional representation with Mrs. Greene.

The contract as originally drawn provided for a closing date in late July, 1971. At Mrs. Greene's request this date was postponed to September 1. A short time later, circumstances having again changed, Mrs. Greene found that she would now prefer the original date. This proved satisfactory to the purchasers but Mr. Connolly told Mrs. Greene that at this earlier date he would not have in hand funds sufficient to make up the full purchase price of $36,000. Of this sum he would lack $1,000. He suggested, however, that the parties might close title upon the earlier date if Mrs. Greene would accept, as part of the purchase price, a check for $1,000 postdated approximately 30 days. Mrs. Greene was personally agreeable to this. She consulted respondent who advised her that he saw no reason why she should not follow this course.

The closing accordingly took place late in July and in accordance with the foregoing arrangement, Mrs. Greene received, as part of the purchase

1. The Disciplinary Rules of the Code of Professional Responsibility became effective in New Jersey on September 13, 1971. Respondent's criticized conduct took place earlier in the year and hence was governed by the Canons of Professional Ethics then in force. Canon 6, the predecessor of DR 5-105, read as follows:

> 6. Adverse Influences and Conflicting Interests
>
> It is the duty of a lawyer at the time of retainer to disclose to the client all the circumstances of his relations to the parties, and any interest or connection with the controversy, which might influence the client in the selection of counsel.
>
> It is unprofessional to represent conflicting interests, except by express consent of all concerned given after a full disclosure of the facts. Within the meaning of this canon, a lawyer represents conflicting interests when, in behalf of one client, it is his duty to contend for that which duty to another client required him to oppose.
>
> The obligation to represent the client with undivided fidelity and not to divulge his secrets or confidences forbids the subsequent acceptance of retainers or employment from others in matters adversely affecting any interest of the client with respect to which confidence has been reposed.

price, Mr. Connolly's check in the sum of $1,000 dated August 31, 1971. Shortly after this latter date she deposited the check for collection and it was returned because of insufficient funds. When questioned, Mr. Connolly said that after he and his wife had taken possession of the property they discovered a serious water condition in the cellar. He added that Mrs. Greene had made an explicit representation that the cellar was at all times dry. For this reason he refused to make good the check, saying that it would cost him $1,000 to rectify the condition in the cellar. Mrs. Greene denied that she had ever made any representation whatsoever. She immediately got in touch with respondent who did nothing effective on her behalf. She then retained other counsel and has subsequently initiated legal proceedings against the Connollys.

We find respondent's conduct to have been unprofessional in two respects. In the first place, the way in which he undertook the dual representation failed to meet the standards imposed upon an attorney who elects to follow such a course. In the second place, after the latent conflict of interests of the two clients had become acute, he nevertheless continued to represent both parties. At that point, rather than going forward with the matter as he did, he should have withdrawn altogether. . . .

. . . [A]fter respondent learned that the purchasers would not be able to pay the full purchase price in cash at the time of closing title [, at] that point adequate representation of the seller required that her attorney first strongly insist on her behalf that cash be forthcoming. Failing this, and if the seller persisted in her wish to close upon the earlier date, her attorney should have vigorously urged the execution and delivery to her of a mortgage from the purchasers in the amount of $1,000, or of other adequate security, in order to protect her interest pending receipt of the full cash payment. We think it fair to assume that had respondent not found himself in a position of conflicting loyalties, his representation of the seller would have taken some such course. . . .

A client cannot foresee and cannot be expected to foresee the great variety of potential areas of disagreement that may arise in a real estate transaction of this sort. The attorney is or should be familiar with at least the more common of these and they should be stated and laid before the client at some length and with considerable specificity. Of course all eventualities cannot be foreseen, but a great many can. Here respondent was representing Mrs. Greene, a seller of property. Generally a seller who has entered into a mutually binding contract of sale is principally interested in securing the full purchase price to which he or she is entitled. As counsel experienced in this field of practice well knows, to allow a purchaser to take possession of the premises in question before the entire consideration has been received, either in the form of cash or purchase money mortgage, will often prove contrary to the seller's best interests. So it was here.

For the reasons set forth above, we deem respondent's conduct to merit censure. He is hereby reprimanded.

PASHMAN, J. (concurring). . . .

While the majority and the Advisory Committee on Professional Ethics, in its Opinion 243, 95 N.J.L.J. 1145 (1971), have opined that the line can be drawn at negotiation or preparation and execution of the sales contract, *i.e.*, dual representation is not available in these situations, I believe that such a limiting boundary is wholly imaginary and fails to fully deal with the whole gamut of conflicts which runs throughout the entire spectrum of the buyer-seller and even the institutional lender situation.

It is virtually impossible for one attorney in any manner and under any circumstances to faithfully and with undivided allegiance represent both a buyer and seller. This concurrence, therefore, stands for the position of the majority and further holds that dual representation in a buyer-seller situation should be totally forbidden. The reasons for this seem to me fairly obvious. In this type of transaction, it is most certainly in the public interest to safeguard and protect both parties from any abuses, whether they be ill-advised or inadvertent. The potential conflict in home buying or selling may never come to fruition. However, when it does surface, both sides explode in anger and accusations. The attorney will then withdraw, leaving the situation no better than when it occurred and, for that matter, probably a bit worse. This is not fair to either party.

It is my contention that neither buyer nor seller can ever possibly fully appreciate all the complexities involved. That is precisely the reason why full disclosure and informed consent are illusory. What most people typically do is rely upon the representation of their attorney when he reassures them that everything will be properly handled. However, the attorney is, unfortunately, not a clairvoyant who can foresee problem areas, although he realizes that there is certainly the potential for genuine conflict. Even where his motives are of the highest, as they usually are, and in good faith believes that he can effect a meeting of the minds, he really is not sure. . . .

While the present case dealt with the problem of full disclosure or more accurately the lack thereof, the potential for damage always existed and in fact actualized itself in the case of Mr. Lanza. Any attorney or client who is foolhardy enough to believe that a buyer-seller situation is relatively problem free, is looking for trouble. . . .

Problem 6C

Nancy is a young associate in a large law firm. She is in the real estate department and is handling part of a transaction for one of the partners in the firm. The client is a major developer and is in the process of acquiring a significant piece of property. The deal is for $11 million. The closing will take place in the law firm's conference room and is scheduled for 4:00 P.M. on Friday. The attorney for the seller is Tanya, a senior partner in another large firm in town. Tanya arrives late for the closing, and once they get started Nancy finds that several points of the deal still remain unresolved, despite careful pre-closing planning and earlier conversations during the day. As a result of these factors, Nancy and Tanya don't finish the closing paperwork until 7:00 P.M. that night. Because it is too late to take the documents directly to the recording office, Tanya turns to Nancy and says, "I will leave the documents in your able hands for recording first thing bright and early Monday morning." Nancy says, "Sure, let's just get it over with so we can go home." Tanya looks at Nancy again and says, "You will undertake to hold the documents over the weekend and record them first thing Monday morning." Nancy says, "Yes." Then Tanya leaves and Nancy finishes up additional work at the office.

On Monday morning, Nancy is in the office at 6:30 A.M. and is getting some work done while waiting to go to the recording office when it opens at 9:00 A.M. Around 8:50 A.M., the senior partner comes into the office and asks Nancy if she has recorded the documents on the deal with Tanya. Nancy is explaining that she was not able to do it on Friday when the partner interrupts and says, "Good, don't record them. The client just called, mad as can be, saying that Tanya and her clients pulled a fast one on the soil test information and he doesn't want to finish the deal until things get reworked. It seems this all broke loose over the weekend. Lucky break for us, because the client is adamant that we not record in order to preserve the strongest position we can." By the time this is all explained, it is about 9:20 A.M. and the phone rings for Nancy. It is Tanya, checking to see if Nancy has fulfilled her obligation to record the documents as promised.

(a) What should Nancy's obligation be? Does she have an ethical obligation to Tanya or to the firm's client or to both?

(b) What should Nancy do if the partner says, "Look, the firm made no promises to Tanya, and this client is worth a good $1 million in billables per year to the firm. You know what the client wants, and I want the client to be happy. Just get it resolved and don't tell me anything more about *your* problems."

B. DOCTRINE OF MERGER

Closing is the time when we must also deal with the *doctrine of merger.* Basically, this doctrine provides that everything that came before closing is merged into the documents exchanged at closing. As a consequence, all rights, warranties, and obligations from the executory contract are no longer operative between the parties. The contract is no longer "executory"; at closing, it is "executed." Any causes of action based on the pre-closing contracts or negotiations no longer exist. Once closing occurs, the parties are left with only those rights, warranties, and promises expressed in the closing documents.

EMBASSY GROUP, INC. v. HATCH

Court of Appeals of Utah, 1993
865 P.2d 1366

BILLINGS, Presiding Judge. Plaintiff/appellant Embassy Group, Inc. appeals from a judgment denying its claims for breach of contract, fraud, mutual mistake, and unjust enrichment and quieting title to property in defendants/appellees Daryl and Maureen Hatch. We affirm.

FACTS

This dispute centers on the purchase price of Lot 33 of Bridlewood Subdivision in Bountiful, Utah. Embassy argues that the asking price was $99,000, but that its predecessor accepted the Hatches' offer to purchase Lot 33 for $80,000. Daryl Hatch, on the other hand, contends he agreed to purchase Lot 33 for $40,000.

. . . In early 1986, Shim Investments, Embassy's predecessor in interest,[1] obtained three Bridlewood Subdivision lots totaling approximately two acres. At the time of acquisition, the property was valued at approximately $99,000. The three lots were subsequently combined into one lot known as Bridlewood Subdivision Lot 33. During the summer of 1986, Daryl Hatch negotiated the purchase of Lot 33 with Mark Wahlquist, Shim's agent. Wahlquist was employed by Granada, Inc., a real estate acquisition and development company.

Two standard Earnest Money Agreement and Offer to Purchase forms (Agreements), memorializing the arrangement between the parties, were introduced into evidence at trial. The first, signed only by Maureen Hatch and dated September 12, 1986, describes the property as "a portion of Bridlewood Subdivision Lot #33 See exhibit A." No such exhibit was attached. The total purchase price is indicated as $40,000, with $100 as the earnest money deposit and $39,900 as the balance to be paid through a trust deed note. The second Agreement, bearing the same date, differs materially from the first only in its payment terms. The breakdown of the $40,000 purchase price is as follows: $100 as the earnest money deposit, $20,000 as the cash down payment at closing, and $19,900 as the balance to be paid "from the long term loan on the home to be built on the lot." Both Agreements contain two clauses relevant to the resolution of this dispute. With respect to the vesting of title, they provide, "Title shall vest in

1. Shim assigned to Embassy all of its claims against the Hatches.

Buyer as follows: As specified at closing." Additionally, both contain an abrogation clause indicating, "Execution of a final real estate contract, if any, shall abrogate this Agreement."

Closing on the property occurred on November 25, 1986. Wahlquist directed the preparation of the closing documents. The Hatches paid the $20,000 down payment and executed a Trust Deed Note for $20,000 in which they promised to pay that amount upon obtaining long-term financing or on November 25, 1987, whichever came first. To secure the $20,000 indebtedness, the Hatches executed a Deed of Trust naming Associated Title Co. as the trustee for all of Lot 33. Keith Sorenson, Vice President of Granada, executed a Special Warranty Deed conveying all of Lot 33 to the Hatches for the sum of $10, which was held in escrow by Associated Title. After the closing, the Hatches proceeded to build a home on Lot 33.

In July 1987, the Hatches' lender paid the $20,000 Trust Deed Note. That same day, at Granada's behest, Associated Title transferred the Deed of Trust for all of Lot 33 to the Hatches.

Embassy later became the successor in interest to Shim Investments, retaining C. Dean Larsen as its president. Larsen contacted the Hatches requesting payment of $40,000, the amount he claimed they owed on the purchase of the lot. The Hatches refused, arguing they agreed to purchase the lot for $40,000 and had paid the full purchase price. Consequently, Embassy commenced this action seeking recovery for breach of contract, fraud, mutual mistake, and unjust enrichment.

At trial, Embassy's witnesses testified the arrangement intended by the parties was a two-step purchase of all of Lot 33 for $80,000. Wahlquist testified that the Agreements conveyed only a portion of Lot 33 for $40,000, and that this two-step purchase was arranged to accommodate the Hatches. The completed Agreements purportedly memorialized only the first portion of the arrangement. Larsen testified he approved the sale for $80,000.

Daryl Hatch denied any such two-step arrangement existed. He testified that he had agreed to purchase the entire lot for $40,000 and knew nothing of the $80,000 agreement described by Wahlquist. Maureen Hatch testified that she was not involved with the negotiations and that she did not know of any terms or agreements other than those she and her husband signed.

The trial court found all of the witnesses credible. Nevertheless, the court concluded that Embassy had not met its burden of proof and denied all of its claims for relief. In its findings, the court focused on the closing documents to support its denial of relief:

> 7. All of the written documentation concerning the sale of Lot 33 to the Defendants indicates that the purchase price was $40,000. . . .
>
> 14. The Earnest Money Agreement and all of the loan and closing documents prepared by the Plaintiffs indicate that the purchase price of Lot 33 was $40,000.

Therefore, the court ordered legal and equitable title to Lot 33 to vest solely in the Hatches. This appeal followed. . . .

I. The Doctrine of Merger

The precise legal basis of the trial court's decision to vest title to all of Lot 33 in the Hatches is not clearly stated. However, the court's underlying findings of fact and the undisputed facts in the record allow us to affirm the court's decision based on the doctrine of merger.

The Utah Supreme Court has explained the doctrine of merger as follows:

> The doctrine of merger . . . is applicable when the acts to be performed by the seller in a contract relate only to the delivery of title to the buyer. Execution and delivery of a deed by the seller then usually constitutes full performance on his [or her] part, and acceptance of the deed by the buyer manifests his [or her] acceptance of that performance even though the estate conveyed may differ from that promised in the antecedent agreement. Therefore, in such a case, the deed is the final agreement and all prior terms, whether written or verbal, are extinguished and unenforceable.

Stubbs v. Hemmert, 567 P.2d 168, 169 (Utah 1977) (footnotes omitted). . . .

The two Agreements upon which Embassy relies contain abrogation clauses. The unambiguous language of the deed vests title in the Hatches for the consideration paid at the time of delivery. Under the general doctrine of merger, the trial court was correct in rejecting prior oral or written terms and enforcing the transfer of title reflected in the deed, "even though the estate conveyed may [have] differ[ed] from that promised in the antecedent agreement." *Stubbs,* 567 P.2d at 169.[4]

II. Exceptions to Merger

The merger doctrine is not without its exceptions, which include fraud, mistake, and the existence of collateral rights in the contract of sale. Secor v. Knight, 716 P.2d 790, 793 (Utah 1986). Ambiguity in the final contract may also warrant the introduction of parol evidence to remedy the ambiguity. Verhoef v. Aston, 740 P.2d 1342, 1344 (Utah App. 1987). We consider each exception in turn.[6]

4. The employees of Embassy's predecessor, as sellers, were experienced in real estate transactions, and they conveyed title to all of Lot 33 at their own risk.

6. We do not address the ambiguity issue in detail. The relevant ambiguity is ambiguity between the final document and other contemporaneous writings on the same subject. Verhoef v. Aston, 740 P.2d 1342, 1344 (Utah App. 1987). In the instant case, the terms of the final conveyance are clearly and unambiguously reflected in the closing documents. There can be no question as to their meaning; they reflect the exchange of the entire Lot 33 for the sum of $40,000.

A. FRAUD

Proof of fraud militates against application of merger; "[h]owever, in order to prevail on a claim of fraud, all the elements of fraud must be established by clear and convincing evidence." Secor v. Knight, 716 P.2d 790, 794 (Utah 1986). The trial court found no factual basis for Embassy's claim of fraud. . . . Nothing in the record suggests the court's findings on fraud are clearly erroneous. . . .

B. MISTAKE

Mistake also bars application of merger. However, not every mistake will suffice; rather, a mistake precludes merger when "one of the parties demonstrates a *mutual* mistake in the drafting of the contractual documents has occurred." Grahn v. Gregory, 800 P.2d 320, 327 n.8 (Utah App. 1990), *cert. denied,* 843 P.2d 516 (Utah 1991) (emphasis added); *cf.* Verhoef v. Aston, 740 P.2d 1342, 1343-44 (Utah App. 1987) (affirming trial court's refusal to reform uniform real estate contract or to award recovery when parties disagreed as to purpose of additional payment).

The Utah Supreme Court has required that "when a party denies merger due to mistake, he [or she] has the burden to show mistake *by clear and convincing evidence.*" Neeley v. Kelsch, 600 P.2d 979, 981 (Utah 1979). The party denying merger must demonstrate that (1) the instrument does not conform to the intent of both parties, (2) the claimant was mistaken as to the content of the instrument and the other party knew of the mistake but kept silent, or (3) the claimant was mistaken as to actual content due to "'fraudulent affirmative behavior.'" Mabey v. Kay Peterson Constr. Co., 682 P.2d 287, 290 (Utah 1984) (*quoting* Jensen v. Manila Corp. of the Church of Jesus Christ of Latter-Day-Saints, 565 P.2d 63, 64-65 (Utah 1977)).

Our review of the record supports the trial court's finding that Embassy did not present clear and convincing proof that both parties intended a purchase price of $80,000 but mistakenly conveyed the entire lot for $40,000. The testimony of Embassy's witnesses that the purchase price was $80,000 was directly contradicted by the testimony of Daryl Hatch, whom the trial court found credible. Nor was there a showing that Embassy was mistaken and that the Hatches were aware of the mistake but kept silent about it. In fact, the trial court determined that Daryl Hatch was not aware that Embassy's predecessors believed the purchase price was $80,000. Finally, the trial court found no fraud, and by implication we conclude that fraudulent affirmative behavior was similarly lacking.

C. COLLATERAL RIGHTS

The collateral rights exception applies when the seller's performance involves some act collateral to the conveyance of title, with the result that those obligations "survive the deed and are not extinguished by it."

Stubbs v. Hemmert, 567 P.2d 168, 169 (Utah 1977). Thus, when the contract of sale contains terms collateral to the conveyance of title, the deed cannot be said to be the intended performance of those terms, which necessarily survive after the conveyance. Secor v. Knight, 716 P.2d 790, 793 (Utah 1986).

Collateral terms may take various forms. For example, the supreme court found collateral terms to exist in *Stubbs,* where the earnest money and exchange agreement required the seller to remove certain equipment from the property at issue. The court held that the agreed-upon removal was collateral to the conveyance and hence that it survived the delivery of the deed; accordingly, the supreme court affirmed the trial court's admission of the earnest money agreement to prove the term. *Stubbs,* 567 P.2d at 170.

The supreme court has likewise defined those instances in which collateral rights are not implicated. Relevant to the instant case is the *Secor* court's conclusion that "covenants relating to title and encumbrances are not considered to be collateral because they relate to the same subject matter as the deed." *Secor,* 716 P.2d at 793. Applying merger, the *Secor* court held that the buyers were subject to restrictive covenants not present in the earnest money agreement but alluded to in the warranty deed, which referred to "restrictions of record." *Id.* at 792-94. In other words, because the restrictions related directly to title, they bound the buyers, despite the absence of those covenants in the merged earnest money agreement. *Id.*

In the present case, the disputed size and price of Lot 33 cannot be viewed as collateral because those terms relate directly to title and conveyance. The provisions for transfer of title were as follows: The Earnest Money Agreement stated that title would vest in the buyers as specified at closing, the Special Warranty Deed conveyed title to all of Lot 33 to the Hatches, and the Deed of Trust named Associated Title as the trustee for the property pending the Hatches' payment of the remaining $20,000 obligation. Taken together, these documents provided that title to all of Lot 33 would vest in the Hatches upon their payment of the Trust Deed Note, which occurred in July 1987 and represented the final installment of the $40,000 purchase price. These terms are clearly central to the conveyance and cannot be viewed as collateral in any way. *See id.* at 793.

III. Conclusion

Because we have found no exception that precludes application of the merger doctrine in the instant case, we therefore conclude that the conveyance at closing of all of Lot 33 for the sum of $40,000 represents the final merged agreement of the parties. Accordingly, we affirm the trial court's judgment vesting title to Lot 33 in the Hatches.

Problem 6D

Sophia owned 40 acres of rural property. On November 1, she contracted to sell ten acres of the property to Bartelo for $250,000, with closing specified to take place on or before February 15. The parties signed an earnest money contract, which satisfied all requirements of the statute of frauds. Bartelo, a wealthy individual who had won a major lottery prize three years ago, planned to pay all cash for the property. The parties closed on February 15, with Sophia conveying the ten-acre tract to Bartelo by warranty deed in exchange for Bartelo's full payment of the price.

(a) Prior to signing the earnest money contract, while the parties were negotiating, Sophia disclosed to Bartelo the following facts: the 40-acre parcel was subject to a mortgage loan, with an amount due of approximately $148,000; the mortgage had a maturity date of September 1 of the following year, when the debt was payable in full; Sophia was not able to obtain a release of the mortgage to clear title because she did not have the right to prepay the mortgage debt and the mortgagee was not willing to accept prepayment. The contract provided: "Title shall be good and marketable, free of all liens except the existing mortgage on the property, which Seller promises to pay in full upon maturity. Seller also promises to obtain a release of mortgage and record same no later than 20 days after maturity date." The deed does not mention the mortgage, and no other document executed at closing mentions the mortgage. Sophia fails to pay the mortgage debt the following September. Bartelo discovers this and complains. Is Bartelo entitled to sue Sophia for breach of the promise made in the earnest money contract, or is Bartelo limited to whatever rights he may have under the warranty deed?

(b) In March, Bartelo's finances have taken a turn for the worse. He wants to borrow money, using his new property as collateral, but he is unable to get a suitable mortgage loan due to the existing mortgage owed by Sophia. Bartelo hires an attorney, who advises him that his warranty deed includes a covenant that there are no liens on the property, and that the mortgage violates that covenant. The attorney sends Sophia a letter, demanding that she pay off the mortgage within five days and stating that she will be responsible for damages incurred by Bartelo if she fails to do so. If Sophia does not or cannot comply, should Bartelo have a cause of action for breach of the covenant in the warranty deed?

(c) Sophia had a residence on the 30 acres that she was retaining, and she did not want the conveyed property to be used for commercial purposes. During negotiations, Bartelo agreed to this limitation, and the earnest money contract provided: "No trade or business of any kind shall be conducted on the property." The warranty deed delivered at closing did not contain this or any other restriction. Two years later, Bartelo opens a commercial nursery on the ten-acre parcel. Should Sophia have the right to force him to stop this use?

(d) In (c), suppose that Bartelo had sold the parcel to Eve. Eve opened the nursery, and she was unaware of the restriction in the earnest money contract. Should Sophia have the right to close Eve's nursery?

(e) The ten-acre parcel had a portable storage building, which Sophia wanted to keep. She and Bartelo agreed that she could remove it, and the earnest money contract provided: "Seller has the right to remove the portable storage building from the property." Sophia did not do so prior to the closing. On March 1, she hired a crew to relocate the building to her property. Before they began work, Bartelo intercepted them. He insists that the building belongs to him because Sophia did not remove it prior to closing. What result?

(f) Suppose the portable storage building was dilapidated. Bartelo considered it an eyesore. He had bargained for the earnest money contract to provide: "Seller will remove the portable storage building from the property." Again, Sophia did not do so before the closing. Can Bartelo insist that Sophia comply with her promise after the closing?

(g) In the situations above, if you represented Sophia or Bartelo what might you do in the contract or at closing to avoid or reduce the risk of messy arguments about the application of the doctrine of merger?

C. ESCROWS

The term *escrow* is sometimes confusing to laypersons because of the different ways it is used in real estate transactions. It may refer to a means of collecting funds for the payment of taxes and insurance; a method to handle the real estate closing; or a technique to resolve a closing contingency or problem. Each of these three common uses of escrow serves a distinct purpose.

The first type of escrow, the *loan escrow*, is used by lenders to collect and hold money from the debtor for paying annual real property taxes and fire and hazard insurance premiums. Lenders desire loan escrows for two reasons. First, with the escrow the lender does not have to worry about a default by the borrower in paying taxes, which could lead to a tax lien or tax sale that jeopardizes the lender's security. Similarly, for hazard insurance, the lender wants to control the payment of insurance premiums so it is certain that the property remains properly insured. In the event of a casualty, the lender will insist that the insurance proceeds be used either to restore the improvements or to pay all or part of the mortgage loan. Second, the lender typically holds escrow funds in a non-interest-paying account.

The second form of escrow, an *escrow closing*, means that the parties have appointed an escrow agent to conduct the closing. The escrow is usually documented by a written escrow agreement, which is signed by the buyer, the seller, and an escrow agent, and spells out the duties of all three parties.

The escrow agent administers the contract of purchase and sale and has fiduciary duties to both the buyer and the seller.

The third type of escrow, a *contingency escrow,* is a process used to resolve a problem that arises at or before closing. Often the problem concerns the physical condition of the property being purchased. When the problem consists of an unperformed obligation of the seller, the escrow usually consists of withholding part of the purchase price from the seller pending correction of the problem.

MILLER v. CRAIG
Court of Appeals of Arizona, Division 1, 1976
27 Ariz. App. 789, 558 P.2d 984

NELSON, Judge. This action was brought by the plaintiffs, George W. Miller and his wife, Johanna Miller (appellants here), to recover $5,000 in earnest money deposited in escrow with the defendant, Harry E. Craig (appellee here). The Millers' claim was based on alternate theories of conversion and breach of fiduciary duty. On appeal they seek reversal of a summary judgment granted in favor of Craig and allege error in the trial court's failure to grant their own motion for summary judgment. For the reasons stated below we find that the judgment in favor of the defendant, Craig, must be reversed and that the cause be remanded for entry of judgment in favor of the plaintiffs, Millers. . . .

In 1970 the Millers entered into an agreement with Mary E. Crouse[1] to sell their interest in a tavern located in the City of Phoenix. Pursuant to that agreement Craig, an attorney at law, was retained to draft the documents necessary to complete the sale and to act as the parties' escrow agent.

Prior to closing, a dispute arose between the parties. Ms. Crouse filed suit seeking rescission of the sales contract and recovery of $5,000, the amount deposited by her with Craig as earnest money. Millers counterclaimed for specific performance of the contract and for damages. The trial court resolved the controversy in favor of Crouse and judgment was entered entitling her to "recover of the defendants (the Millers) the sum of FIVE THOUSAND ($5,000) DOLLARS. . ."

Thereafter, Crouse, through her attorney, presented defendant Craig with a copy of the judgment and demanded return of the $5,000 deposit. Craig, without notifying the Millers or attempting to ascertain whether they would seek review of the judgment, disbursed the money to Crouse.[3] The judgment in favor of Crouse was subsequently reversed and judgment was

1. Ms. Crouse is not a party to this action.

3. Judgment in favor of Crouse was entered and filed November 24, 1971. In a letter dated November 29, 1971, containing a copy of the November 24 judgment, Crouse through her attorney demanded that defendant Craig return the $5,000 held by him as escrow agent. In response to the demand, the defendant, on November 30, 1971 and December 17, 1971,

entered for the Millers in the amount of the escrow deposit, as directed by the court in Miller v. Crouse, [19 Ariz. App. 268, 506 P.2d 659 (1973)].

After several unsuccessful attempts to recover the deposit from Craig, Millers initiated the present action. The parties filed cross-motions for summary judgment. Craig's motion was granted and judgment dismissing Millers' cause with prejudice was entered.

Two questions are presented for our consideration. First, whether Craig's transfer of the $5,000 to Crouse was a breach of his fiduciary duty as escrow agent. Second, if it was a breach, whether he is excused from the consequences thereof by reason of the following clause contained in the escrow agreement: "We, and each of us, agree that the said Harry E. Craig acting in the beforementioned capacity shall not become liable to either or both of us for anything whatsoever so long as said Agent acts with reasonable prudence in connection with his position, ..."

We answer the first question in the affirmative, the second in the negative. . . .

. . . With respect to those who have retained him, an escrow agent is a trustee and can properly execute his duties only as they are set out by the terms of the escrow agreement. Malta v. Phoenix Title & Trust Co., 76 Ariz. 116, 259 P.2d 554 (1953); Buffington v. Title Insurance Co. of Minnesota, [26 Ariz. App. 97, 546 P.2d 366 (1976)]. Deviation from those terms without the mutual consent of the parties concerned will subject the agent to liability for damages caused by his departure. Tucson Title Insurance Co. v. D'Ascoli, [94 Ariz. 230, 383 P.2d 119 (1963)]; Brean v. North Campbell Professional Building, 26 Ariz. App. 381, 548 P.2d 1193 (1976).

In the present case the sales contract, incorporated by reference in the escrow agreement, provided that the $5,000 earnest money was part of the purchase price and that the sale was to be completed upon transfer of Millers' Number 7 beer and wine license. Alternatively, the contract provided that the Millers might retain as liquidated damages the sum paid into escrow by Crouse should she fail to comply with the terms of the agreement. The contract contained no other provision authorizing disbursement of funds. It is clear, therefore, that Craig, by transferring the $5,000 without first securing plaintiff's consent, deviated from and exceeded his authority under the escrow agreement.

Craig contends the transfer was pursuant to a judgment on which he properly relied and therefore his conduct cannot be construed as a breach of duty. We disagree. The judgment in favor of Crouse dealt not with a specific res, the earnest money deposit, but merely entitled her to recover $5,000 from the Millers. It did not authorize a disbursement of funds held in escrow.

At the time of the Crouse demand, Craig should have inquired of the Millers regarding their intentions relative to an appeal. If they were not

---

forwarded checks totaling $5,000 to Crouse's attorney. Denial of plaintiffs' motion to amend the November 24 judgment or for a new trial was entered January 7, 1972. Plaintiffs' notice of appeal to Division I of the Court of Appeals was filed February 4, 1972.

going to appeal he should have sought their permission to return the funds to Crouse. If they intended to appeal, as subsequent events indicated was their intention, he should have notified Crouse that he would retain the funds in escrow pending the outcome of the appeal or pending execution. If none of these arrangements were satisfactory to either or both parties, Craig should have sought relief in the trial court, either in the pending action, or by interpleader. *See generally* Rule 22(a), Rules of Civil Procedure, 16 A.R.S.; 28 Am. Jur. 2d *Escrow* §40 (1966).

Finally, Craig argues that even if a fiduciary obligation was breached, it was done so in a "reasonable manner," exempting him from liability under the terms of the escrow agreement, *supra*, by which he is to be held harmless for acts done with "reasonable prudence." We find this contention absolutely without merit. As stated above, the duties of an escrow agent are defined in the escrow agreement and will be strictly construed. Any deviation therefrom without the requisite authority is per se unreasonable and cannot be done with "reasonable prudence." *Cf.* Tucson Title Insurance Co. v. D'Ascoli, *supra*; Malta v. Phoenix Title & Trust Co., *supra*. . . .

. . . Craig was fiducially responsible to both parties and it was incumbent upon him to determine whether *in fact* the controversy had been finally resolved so that he could properly disburse the money. Having failed in that duty, he is liable for his unauthorized disbursement.

The judgment of the Superior Court is reversed. The cause is remanded with directions to enter judgment for the Millers.

Problem 6E

Go back to the *Lanza* case and assume that the buyers saw the water in the basement during the final walk-through prior to closing. (In the actual case, the buyers discovered the wet basement after they took possession, using it as an excuse not to make good on a postdated $1,000 check to the seller.) Imagine yourself as the attorney in this situation, representing both parties without the ethical violations confronting Mr. Lanza. Unlike him, you made proper disclosure to all parties and acted appropriately in all respects. Assume that the parties are still willing to close, provided the water problem can be overcome. How might you use a contingency escrow to respond to the situation? Your assignment is to draft a viable contingency escrow agreement, using a $1,000 hold-back from seller's proceeds and including provisions to protect yourself as the escrow agent. Recall that the *Lanza* court suggested that preparing and recording a short-term mortgage might be an appropriate way to handle this type of situation. Compared to the mortgage, what are the advantages and disadvantages of the contingency escrow agreement that you are drafting?

7 Contract Remedies

The remedies for breach or default under a real estate contract are similar to the remedies provided by basic contract law, and both the parties may turn to a variety of remedies. The primary categories of remedies for the breach of real estate contracts are damages, forfeiture of the buyer's part payments (sometimes analyzed as liquidated damages), equitable remedies, and tort remedies related to the contract. In addition, in this chapter we also explore some related concepts, such as slander of title and the filing of a lis pendens. Keep in mind that other types of legal actions, beyond those discussed herein, may be appropriate in given situations. Because real estate transactions involve a variety of human relationships and can become complex, at times the lawyer should consider additional remedies. For instance, you may wish to prevent someone from proceeding under a contract by seeking an injunction to prohibit her from taking any further action. At times, when rights under a contract are in dispute, a party's best course of action may be to seek a declaratory judgment that determines the parties' respective rights. There may be a need for an ejectment action to recover possession of property from a wrongdoer or for a quiet title action to resolve a title dispute. There can even be situations, in the process of doing a transaction, where tempers flare up, leading to tortious or criminal behavior such as assault, trespass to land, or even outright physical violence. In these cases, a lawyer will pursue appropriate remedies and actions depending on the nature of the specific problem that arises.

A. DAMAGES AND FORFEITURE OF PAYMENTS

Damages to compensate a party include recovery for loss of expectation value on the transaction, out-of-pocket expenses, and lost profits, among other things. These damage remedies are all designed to make the injured party whole in an economic sense. The loss to the injured party is considered fungible in that an award of money is deemed capable of providing appropriate relief for the loss. Though often left unsaid, the concept of fungibility is the cornerstone of this category of remedy, because it allows us to equate the loss of rights under the contract with an award of cash as damages. In a sense, money is used as a mediating device to make the injured party whole, either by replacing the monetary objective of the contract with a cash award or by giving the injured party the monetary resources deemed sufficient to go back out into the marketplace to find a suitable replacement for the thing (the real estate) that was the object of the original contract.

Fungibility plays another important role in determining loss-of-bargain damages. The general measure of damages is the difference between the contract price and the fair market value of the property at the time of the breach, not at the time set for performance or some other date. The reference to fair market value implies fungibility because it supposes that we can find independent and objective criteria of value by looking at other comparable opportunities that are available in the market. Things that are fungible have a ready market for sale and resale. Value is set by the prices that willing buyers and sellers voluntarily pay or take for these items in an open market of exchange. The more fungible and more competitive the market is, the more objective and reliable the value of a thing will be. This is because a competitive market is assumed to leave the seller powerless in the sense that every seller takes her terms from the market. If a seller, offering a similar product, charges more or sells on less favorable terms than other sellers in the market, her sales will rapidly diminish as buyers move their purchases to other sellers. Thus, sellers in a competitive market must either take their terms from the market (respond to the demands of buyers) or adequately distinguish their products. The idea that buyers will simply ignore a seller who seeks to do business at too high a price or on unfavorable terms implies two additional assumptions of competitive markets. First, information is assumed to be generally well known and easily available to all market participants; second, buyers and sellers are free to move and shift their resources as they shop for the best deals. These market assumptions are important for purposes of remedies because the less true they are in any given context, the more likely it is that money damages will not provide the injured party with satisfactory compensation. In such situations, we tend to prefer other types of remedies.

For real estate contracts, sellers usually prefer to avoid the complexities of collecting damages based on loss of the expectation interest. Instead, sellers rely on a clause in the contract stating that if the buyer defaults, the seller has the right to terminate the contract and retain the earnest money or deposit already paid by the buyer. The amount of earnest money is highly negotiable both for residential and commercial transactions, and in most communities there is no standard amount. A typical range for earnest money is between 3 and 10 percent of the purchase price. The seller is allowed to retain the buyer's payment, without having to prove actual damages, under one of two theories. Either forfeiture of the deposit is rationalized as valid as a consequence of the buyer's default, or the clause is considered to be a valid attempt by the parties to liquidate damages.

Liquidated damages are damages that the parties to a contract agree to and quantify in advance of any breach. For real estate contracts, liquidated damages are very commonly used as a remedy for the seller. Either or both parties can agree to pay liquidated damages, and occasionally a seller will promise to pay liquidated damages if she breaches the contract. Not every liquidated damages clause is enforceable. Courts supervise their use to make sure they are consistent with the objectives stated earlier. The amount of liquidated damages must appear to be reasonable in light of all the circumstances. A court will refuse to enforce unreasonably large liquidated damages. Moreover, the actual damages from a potential breach must be difficult to predict at the time of contracting. For real estate contracts, it usually is difficult or impossible to determine actual damages in advance for either party.

UZAN v. 845 UN LIMITED PARTNERSHIP
Supreme Court, Appellate Division, First Department, 2004
10 App. Div. 3d 230, 778 N.Y.S.2d 171

MAZZARELLI, J. This appeal presents the issue of whether plaintiffs, who defaulted on the purchase of four luxury condominium units, have forfeited their 25% down payments as a matter of law. Because the governing purchase agreements were a product of lengthy negotiation between parties of equal bargaining power, all represented by counsel, there was no evidence of overreaching, and upon consideration of the fact that a 25% down payment is common usage in the new construction luxury condominium market in New York City, we hold that upon their default and failure to cure, plaintiffs forfeited all rights to their deposits. . . .

FACTS

In October 1998, Defendant 845 UN Limited Partnership (sponsor or 845 UN) began to sell apartments at The Trump World Tower (Trump World), a luxury condominium building to be constructed at 845 United Nations Plaza. Donald Trump is the managing general partner of the sponsor. Plaintiffs Cem Uzan and Hakan Uzan, two brothers, are Turkish billionaires who sought to purchase multiple units in the building.

In April 1999, plaintiffs and an associate executed seven purchase agreements for apartments in Trump World. Only four of those units (the penthouse units) are the subject of this lawsuit and appeal. As relevant, Cem Uzan defaulted on contracts to buy two penthouse units on the 90th floor of the building, and Hakan defaulted on contracts to purchase two other penthouse units on the 89th floor.[2]

2. The transactions for three of the seven total units closed in July of 2001. Antonio Betancourt, an associate of the Uzans, purchased two units on the 59th floor of the building, and plaintiff Cem Uzan purchased a unit on the 80th floor.

The Trump World Tower from the East River

The building had not been constructed when plaintiffs executed their purchase agreements. In paragraph 17.4 of those contracts, the sponsor projected that the first closing in the building would occur on or about April 1, 2001, nearly two years after the signing of the agreements. . . .

NEGOTIATIONS PRECEDING EXECUTION OF THE PURCHASE AGREEMENTS

Plaintiffs were represented by experienced local counsel during the two month long negotiation for the purchase of the apartments. There were numerous telephone conversations between counsel, and at least four extensively marked up copies of draft purchase agreements were exchanged. In consideration for plaintiffs' purchase of multiple units, the sponsor reduced the aggregate purchase price of the penthouse units by more than $7 million from the list price in the offering plan for a total cost of approximately $32 million. Plaintiffs also negotiated a number of revisions to the standard purchase agreement, including extensions of time for payment of the down payment. As amended, each purchase agreement obligated plaintiffs to make a 25% down payment: 10% at contract, an additional 7½% down payment twelve months later, and a final 7½% down payment 18 months after the execution of the contract. . . .

The executed purchase agreements provide, at paragraph 12(b), that:

> [u]pon the occurrence of an Event of Default . . . [i]f Sponsor elects to cancel . . . [and i]f the default is not cured within . . . thirty (30) days, then this Agreement shall be deemed canceled, and Sponsor shall have the right to

retain, as and for liquidated damages, the Down payment and any interest earned on the Down payment. . . .

DEFAULT, FAILURE TO CURE, AND THIS ACTION

On September 11, 2001, terrorists attacked New York City by flying two planes into the World Trade Center, the city's two tallest buildings, murdering thousands of people. Plaintiffs, asserting concerns of future terrorist attacks, failed to appear at the October 19, 2001 closing, resulting in their default. By letter dated October 19, 2001, plaintiffs' counsel stated:

> [W]e believe that our clients are entitled to rescind their Purchase Agreements in view of the terrorist attack which occurred on September 11 and has not abated. In particular, our clients are concerned that the top floors in a "trophy" building, described as the tallest residential building in the world, will be an attractive terrorist target. The situation is further aggravated by the fact that the building bears the name of Donald Trump, perhaps the most widely known symbol of American capitalism. Finally, the United Nations complex brings even more attention to this location.

That day 845 UN sent plaintiffs default letters, notifying them that they had 30 days to cure. On November 19, 2001, upon expiration of the cure period, the sponsor terminated the four purchase agreements.

Plaintiffs then brought this action. They alleged that Donald Trump had prior special knowledge that certain tall buildings, such as Trump World, were potential targets for terrorists. Plaintiffs also alleged that Trump World did not have adequate protection for the residents of the upper floors of the building. . . .

THE ROLE OF THE 25% DOWN PAYMENT

In his affidavit in support of the cross motion, Donald Trump stated that he sought 25% down payments from pre-construction purchasers at the Trump World Tower because of the substantial length of time between contract signing and closing, during which period the sponsor had to keep the units off the market, and because of the obvious associated risks. Trump also affirmed that down payments in the range of 20% to 25% are standard practice in the new construction luxury condominium submarket in New York City. He cited three projects where he was the developer, The Trump Palace, 610 Park Avenue and Trump International Hotel and Tower, all of which had similar down payment provisions. Trump also noted that:

> [i]n new construction condominium projects, purchasers often speculate on the market by putting down initial down payments of 10% and 15% and watching how the market moves. If the market value increases, they will then make the second down payment. If the market prices drop, they may then walk away from their down payment. . . .

Defendant also presented a compilation of sixteen recent condominium offering plans, all of which required down payments of either 20% or 25% of the purchase price for the unit. . . .

THE ORDER APPEALED

After hearing oral argument on the motion, the IAS court granted defendant partial summary judgment, finding that plaintiffs forfeited the portion of their down payment amounting to 10% of the purchase price, pursuant to Maxton Builders, Inc. v. Lo Galbo, 68 N.Y.2d 373, 509 N.Y.S.2d 507, 502 N.E.2d 184. The court held that the remainder of the down payment was subject to a liquidated damages analysis to determine whether it bore a reasonable relation to the sponsor's actual or probable loss. Defendant appeals from that portion of the order which denied it full relief.

DISCUSSION

More than a century ago, the Court of Appeals, in Lawrence v. Miller, 86 N.Y. 131 (1881), held that a vendee who defaults on a real estate contract without lawful excuse cannot recover his or her down payment. It reaffirmed this holding in *Maxton, supra,* again in 1986. The facts of *Lawrence* are common to real estate transactions, and parallel those presented here. In that case, plaintiff made a $2000 down payment on the purchase of certain real estate, and then defaulted. The seller refused to extend plaintiff's time to perform the contract, retained the down payment, and ultimately sold the property to another purchaser. In plaintiff's subsequent action for a refund of the down payment, the Court of Appeals affirmed a judgment dismissing the complaint, stating:

> To allow a recovery of this money would be to sustain an action by a party on his own breach of his own contract, which the law does not allow. When we once declare in this case that the vendor has done all that the law asks of him, we also declare that the vendee has not so done on his part. And then to maintain this action would be to declare that a party may violate his agreement, and make an infraction of it by himself a cause of action. That would be ill doctrine.

Lawrence, 86 N.Y. 131, 140.

For over a century, courts have consistently upheld what was called the *Lawrence* rule and recognized a distinction between real estate deposits and general liquidated damages clauses.[3] Liquidated damages clauses have traditionally been subject to judicial oversight to confirm that the stipulated damages bear a reasonable proportion to the probable loss caused by the breach. By contrast, real estate down payments have been subject to limited supervision. They have only been refunded upon a showing of disparity of

3. A liquidated damage clause is a contractual provision by which the parties stipulate to a fixed sum to be paid in the event of a breach.

bargaining power between the parties, duress, fraud, illegality or mutual mistake. *See* Cipriano v. Glen Cove Lodge # 1458, 1 N.Y.3d 53, 769 N.Y.S.2d 168, 801 N.E.2d 388.

In *Maxton,* plaintiff had contracted to sell defendants a house, and accepted a check for a 10% down payment. When defendants canceled the contract and placed a stop payment on the check, plaintiff sued for the down payment, citing the *Lawrence* rule. Defendants argued that plaintiff's recovery should be limited to its actual damages. In ruling for the vendor, the Court of Appeals identified two legal principles as flowing from *Lawrence.* First, that the vendor was entitled to retain the down payment in a real estate contract, without reference to his actual damages. Second, the "parent" rule, upon which the first rule was based, that one who breaches a contract may not recover the value of his part performance.

The Court noted that the parent rule had been substantially undermined in the 100 years since *Lawrence.* Many courts had rejected the parent rule because of criticism that it produced a forfeiture "and the amount of the forfeiture increases as performance proceeds, so that the penalty grows larger as the breach grows smaller." *Maxton,* 68 N.Y.2d 373, 379, 509 N.Y.S.2d 507, 502 N.E.2d 184.

The Court also noted that since *Lawrence,* the rule of allowing recovery of down payments of not more than 10% in real estate contracts continues to be followed by a "majority of jurisdictions," including in New York. . . .

After acknowledging that "[R]eal estate contracts are probably the best examples of arms length transactions," the Court broadly concluded:

> Except in cases where there is a real risk of overreaching, there should be no need for the courts to relieve the parties of the consequences of their contract. *If the parties are dissatisfied with the rule of (Lawrence), the time to say so is at the bargaining table.*

Maxton, 68 N.Y.2d 373, 382, 509 N.Y.S.2d 507, 502 N.E.2d 184 (emphasis supplied).

Applying the reasoning of these cases to the facts of the instant matter, it is clear that plaintiffs are not entitled to a return of any portion of their down payment. Here the 25% down payment was a specifically negotiated element of the contracts. . . .

Finally, there was no evidence of a disparity of bargaining power, or of duress, fraud, illegality or mutual mistake by the parties in drafting the down payment clause of the purchase agreements. . . .

Accordingly, the order of the Supreme Court, New York County (Alice Schlesinger, J.), entered July 21, 2003, which, to the extent appealed from, denied defendant 845 UN Limited Partnership's motion for summary judgment, should be reversed. . . . The Clerk is directed to enter judgment in favor of defendant appellant dismissing the complaint as against it.

Problem 7A

Debbie agrees to buy a home from Ed for $250,000. Debbie agrees to deposit $10,000 on signing the contract, to be held in escrow by Ed's broker, Brenda, pending closing, at which time the amount will be credited against the purchase price. The contract contains a clause stating:

> Liquidated Damages. The parties hereto agree that actual damages from a breach will be difficult to calculate and they hereby agree that the contract deposit amount shall serve as the agreed-to damages in the event of Buyer's default and in such event shall be forfeited to Seller.

The contract is signed and Debbie makes her deposit. During the executory contract period housing values drop dramatically and Debbie decides she is ready for a lifestyle change. Debbie breaches the contract by refusing to close on the deal.

(a) Debbie argues that the cases are full of comments that "the law abhors a forfeiture" and therefore this clause is unenforceable as written. Should her position prevail, or should a court uphold the provision?

(b) Should it make any difference if Debbie's breach is willful, as in she just changes her mind, or unintentional, as in she unexpectedly loses her job?

(c) Suppose that the clause is enforceable and Ed gets to keep the liquidated damages, but argues that he has additional damages of $5,000 because he had to resell at $235,000. Ed argues that the keeping of Debbie's deposit was merely a statement of a partial remedy which did not by its language eliminate any other remedy for damages or for equitable relief. In other words, it was not by its terms the sole and exclusive remedy between the parties. Should Ed be able to get more?

(d) What if Debbie could show that, in fact, Ed was able to resell the home very quickly for $245,000? She insists, therefore, that she should get back half of her deposit. In support, she argues that the facts reveal it is not difficult to determine damages for a residential contract, so Ed is just trying to invoke a penalty against her. Should she win?

(e) What if Ed asks Brenda, his broker, for Debbie's deposit after Debbie breaches, at a time when no litigation has been filed? How should Brenda respond? If Ed gets to keep the deposit, will he have to share it with Brenda? Can Brenda get all or part of her commission in such a situation?

B. EQUITABLE REMEDIES

There are four major equitable remedies that courts frequently award to protect parties to real estate contracts: specific performance, reformation, rescission, and equitable liens.

1. *Specific performance.* Perhaps the most important of the equitable remedies is specific performance. Under the traditional view of mutuality of remedy, both the buyer and the seller are generally entitled to specific performance. Some recent judicial trends have limited the blanket acceptance of the traditional conception of mutuality of remedy and have instead looked at the actual expectations of the parties and the nature of the breach to determine the appropriate remedy. Following the new trend, for example, a seller could not obtain a right of specific performance merely because the buyer would be in a position to invoke such a remedy. The seller would need to make out a case for specific performance on her own behalf, not simply by asserting the *doctrine of mutuality.*

Central to the remedy of specific performance is the requirement that the party seeking the remedy must be *ready, willing,* and *able* to perform. This means that the plaintiff must have satisfied all contract conditions and requirements that were her obligations before she can demand performance from the other side. Furthermore, she must stand ready, willing, and able to perform throughout the proceeding.

Sometimes a party seeks the remedy of specific performance when there are minor breaches in the contract, such as slight title defects, shortages in area, or defects in the property's physical condition. If the defect is minor, and therefore does not materially affect the buyer's intended use, the buyer might simply waive the nonconformity and proceed with the closing of the deal. However, if the problem is more than negligible, the buyer will want to pay less than the contract price and will ask for specific performance with an abatement of price to reflect the loss of value from the problem. Conversely, if the buyer balks at the minor defect or flaw, it may be the seller who wants to force the buyer to close on the contract under the original terms with the price abatement applied. Using the discretion of equity, a number of courts have granted specific performance coupled with price abatement when an improvement on the property is damaged by fire or when some other imperfection is noted.

2. *Reformation.* If the language of a written contract has an error or mistake, one of the parties may seek a correction through reformation. Typically, reformation is granted only if the plaintiff can establish a mutual mistake. When a mistake is mutual, the language of the contract fails to reflect the parties' actual intent. For example, a drafting error that results in an incorrect statement of the price or description of the property is subject to correction by reformation.

3. *Rescission.* Contracts often include conditions that give parties an express right to terminate, or rescind, the contract. When an express right is lacking, a court of equity may grant rescission based upon grounds such as fraud, misrepresentation, or mutual mistake of fact. Like other equitable remedies, the granting of rescission is subject to the court's discretion. Normally, rescission is granted only if the problem is sufficiently material so that continuation of the contract is not appropriate or feasible.

4. *Equitable liens.* By operation of law a seller obtains a *vendor's lien* on the title to the real property to secure the unpaid purchase price. Prior to closing, the vendor's lien attaches to the buyer's equitable title, which the buyer has as a consequence of the doctrine of equitable conversion. After closing, if the seller has not received full payment, the lien attaches to the title conveyed by the deed. The buyer has a reciprocal right, known as a *vendee's lien* to secure the return of the down payment or the payment of reliance damages in the event the sale does not close.

COX v. RKA CORPORATION

Supreme Court of New Jersey, 2000
164 N.J. 487, 753 A.2d 1112

VERNIEROV, J. Plaintiffs instituted this action to compel specific performance of a building contract involving construction of a new home. Their complaint, as amended, also seeks to void defendant's mortgage interest in the same parcel or, alternatively, to impress a superior lien on the property for the money that they had advanced toward the purchase price. As contract purchasers of real property, plaintiffs acquired a vendees' lien on the property. We must determine the extent to which that unrecorded vendees' lien should be granted priority over defendant's recorded mortgage that was given to finance the home construction.

We hold that the priority of an unrecorded vendee's lien does not extend to those payments voluntarily made by the vendee after the lender properly records its mortgage. However, because the issue is essentially one of first impression in New Jersey, we decline to apply our holding to the present dispute. In view of the uncertainty of the law at the time of these transactions, we conclude that plaintiffs' vendees' lien should be given priority as against defendant's mortgage interest for the full amount of their initial deposit, and all sums later advanced toward the contract price.

I

Harry and Betty Ann Cox executed a standard-form contract with RKA Corporation (RKA) for the purchase of real estate located in Pennsauken, New Jersey (the property). Under the contract, RKA was to construct a new home for plaintiffs on the property. The purchase price was $106,880. Plaintiffs paid an initial deposit of $12,000 to RKA on August 25, 1994, the date they signed the contract. The contract specified that the balance of the purchase price would be due "at settlement." . . .

Unbeknownst to plaintiffs, RKA then sought a construction loan from Roebling Savings and Loan Association (Roebling) in the amount of $80,250. When it applied for the construction loan, RKA supplied Roebling with a copy of the contract entered into with plaintiffs. The fact that the property was under contract or "pre-sold" to plaintiffs was a factor considered by Roebling in granting the loan. . . .

On October 21, 1994, RKA settled the construction loan with Roebling, which took back a mortgage on the property as security for the loan. . . .

Following the recording of Roebling's mortgage, plaintiffs made a series of payments to RKA towards the balance of the purchase price: $2,267 on January 3, 1995; $2,000 on March 15, 1995; $3,000 on June 15, 1995; $2,000 on July 28, 1995; and $61,958.53 on August 3, 1995. None of the payments was due on those dates. As noted, the contract did not require any payment beyond the initial deposit until the date of settlement. In total, plaintiffs paid RKA $83,225.53 prior to the settlement date (the $12,000 deposit and $71,225.53 in additional advances). Plaintiffs and RKA never closed title.

On or about November 28, 1995, the Coxes commenced this action for specific performance against RKA. RKA defaulted on the construction loan from Roebling, and the lender took steps to foreclose its mortgage. . . .

A default judgment was entered against RKA and Richard Niel in the amount of $83,225.53 for breach of contract and $249,676.59 for treble damages under the Consumer Fraud Act, N.J.S.A. 56:8-19. In respect of Roebling's mortgage, the trial court concluded, after a bench trial, that Roebling had taken its mortgage with knowledge of plaintiffs' interest in the property. Specifically, the court determined that plaintiffs' equitable interest, including the $12,000 deposit and all monies paid to RKA, constituted a lien superior to Roebling's recorded mortgage. . . .

II

The resolution of this dispute turns on the interplay among certain equitable principles and the policy undergirding New Jersey's recording statutes, N.J.S.A. 46:15-1 to 46:26-1. We begin with the equitable principles, the most important of which concerns the common-law concept of the vendee's lien.

New Jersey has recognized and enforced the notion of a vendee's lien at least as far back as 1830. Copper v. Wells, 1 N.J. Eq. 10 (Ch. 1830) (finding complainant's claim for permanent and valuable improvements made to land following agreement of sale is a lien in equity on property).

> Our courts, in affirming the existence and validity of vendees' liens, generally refer to . . . the trust relationship which arises between the parties upon the execution of a contract of sale of realty. When such contract is entered into, in the eyes of equity the contract is regarded for most purposes as though specifically executed and the original estate of each of the parties is regarded as "converted." The vendee becomes the equitable owner of the land and the vendor of the purchase money, and the vendor is considered the trustee of his estate in the land for the vendee. When the vendee pays a portion of the purchase money, the vendor becomes a trustee for him and the vendee

> acquires a lien just as if the vendor had executed a mortgage to him of his estate to the extent of the payment received.

Mihranian, Inc. v. Padula, 134 N.J. Super. 557, 563-64, 342 A.2d 523 (App. Div. 1975) (citations omitted), *aff'd*, 70 N.J. 252, 359 A.2d 473 (1976). . . .

Against that common-law backdrop, the Legislature has enacted New Jersey's recording statutes. . . .

By those enactments, New Jersey is considered a "race-notice" jurisdiction, which means that as between two competing parties the interest of the party who first records the instrument will prevail so long as that party had no actual knowledge of the other party's previously-acquired interest. Palamarg Realty Co. v. Rehac, 80 N.J. 446, 454, 404 A.2d 21 (1979). As a corollary to that rule, parties are generally charged with constructive notice of instruments that are properly recorded. . . .

III

With those principles and statutes in mind, we must now determine whether and to what extent plaintiffs may recover their expended funds. That plaintiffs are entitled to a vendees' lien for monies paid to RKA is plain. Plaintiffs' payments, seemingly made in good faith, entitle them to be equitably vested with a ratable portion of the estate. *Mihranian, supra*, 134 N.J. Super. at 564, 342 A.2d 523. Our law is clear and settled on that point.

What is not so clear is how to determine the priority or value of plaintiffs' lien *vis-a-vis* Roebling's recorded mortgage. Jurisdictions are not uniform in their approach to that question and we have found no reported New Jersey case addressing the issue precisely. . . .

In the present case . . . Roebling had actual notice of the $12,000 deposit paid by the Coxes toward the purchase price when it granted RKA its construction loan and recorded its mortgage. RKA supplied Roebling with the contract between itself and the Coxes that stated the deposit amount paid by the Coxes and the amount due at closing. Based on those facts, we conclude that plaintiffs' vendees' lien in the amount of the $12,000 deposit should have priority over Roebling's later-recorded mortgage interest. Prior case law and basic fairness compel that equitable result.

In respect of the advances voluntarily made by the Coxes subsequent to Roebling's mortgage interest, the record indicates that Roebling had neither actual nor constructive notice of those intended payments at the time the lender recorded its mortgage. Stated differently, the known equity of plaintiffs chargeable to Roebling was the amount stated in the contract, namely the $12,000. The lender knew of no other payments or advances to RKA intended by plaintiffs as none was required by the parties' agreement.

Conversely, the Coxes had constructive notice of Roebling's mortgage interest prior to making their advances to RKA because Roebling properly recorded the mortgage instrument. . . .

Some jurisdictions have held that the vendee may recover his or her deposit monies whenever "the subsequent lender knows a contract has been executed, whether or not it is aware of the terms of the contract, the vendee's identity, or the precise amount of any down payment made." 2 Grant S. Nelson & Dale A. Whitman, Real Estate Finance Law §13.3, at 286 n. 18 (3d ed. 1993) (citing Wayne Bldg. & Loan Co. v. Yarborough, 11 Ohio St. 2d 195, 228 N.E.2d 841 (1967); Palmer v. Crews Lumber Co., 510 P.2d 269 (Okla. 1973); South Carolina Fed. Sav. Bank v. San-A Bel Corp., 307 S.C. 76, 413 S.E.2d 852 (1992)). By extension, it is possible to argue that a vendee should recover all payments, even those made voluntarily in addition to the deposit, so long as the lender has knowledge of the underlying contract.

We disagree with that approach. We would not subordinate the lender's otherwise valid lien because of idiosyncratic actions taken by a vendee after the lender has recorded its mortgage. By the same token, we believe it would be inequitable to place a lender under an obligation to seek out and determine whether a purchaser intends to expend sums not provided for in the contract. . . .

VI

We affirm the judgment of the Appellate Division to the extent that it grants priority to the Coxes' vendees' lien as against Roebling's mortgage interest, for the amount of their initial deposit and all sums later advanced toward the purchase price of the property. In all subsequent matters, whose operative facts arise after the date of this opinion, we will apply a rule of law consistent with our holding here.

Stein, J., concurring in part and dissenting in part. . . . I disagree with today's ruling, pursuant to which contract purchasers who make non-obligatory payments to their builder subsequent to the builder's obtaining a construction loan secured by a recorded mortgage have a lien inferior to that of the mortgagee even if the mortgagee had knowledge of the contract.

I concur with the balance of the Court's holding to the effect that a vendee's lien generally is superior to that of a mortgagee with notice of the Vendee's interest, and that today's holding should be prospective — thereby entitling the Coxes to recoup the monies they have expended. I believe, however, that the Court has unduly emphasized the role of New Jersey's recording statutes in this case; has diminished the significance of common-law equitable principles; and has overlooked the significance of generally accepted real estate practices, including the routine and standard practice of obtaining a subordination of the vendee's lien in situations where third parties, with notice of the vendee's prior claim, become the vendor's buyers or creditors. . . .

Problem 7B

Hoda contracts to buy a house from James for $89,000. Hoda agrees that she will put down $9,000 and pay the remaining amount in four equal installments annually over the next four years. Hoda pays her down payment of $9,000 on January 1 and prepares to take possession of the property on January 10. James does not deliver possession of the property on January 10.

(a) Obviously, Hoda may have a contract action for breach. Does she also have a lien right that would allow her to enforce the return of her deposit by way of a lien claim against the property and a foreclosure right if necessary to effectuate and realize on her lien?

(b) Assume instead that Hoda takes possession on January 1 and fails to make the $9,000 payment by January 30. Should James have any lien rights against Hoda? What might be the extent of such a lien right?

(c) Should it make any difference in either of these situations if the contract said that "as to all obligations and undertakings of each party under this contract for purchase and sale, time is of the essence"?

(d) Should such lien rights be limited to the money paid or owed for real property interests only, or should they extend to amounts related to personal property included in a particular real estate sale?

(e) Suppose Hoda takes possession of the property, James gives her a deed, and she fails to make one or more of her payments. During this time, she sells the property to Rosa, a bona fide purchaser (BFP) who pays value in the belief that Hoda owns the property free and clear. James then comes along later and asserts a vendor's lien against Rosa. Who should prevail? Is the equitable vendee's/vendor's lien a secret lien that works to the detriment of others? What if Rosa got a mortgage loan from Big Bank in order to buy the home from Hoda and Big Bank is also a BFP with respect to its making of the loan? Should Big Bank's mortgage be inferior to that of the unrecorded equitable lien of James?

C. SLANDER OF TITLE AND LIS PENDENS

The tort action called *slander of title* is designed to protect the value of property. Changes in, or the perception of changes in, this bundle of rights have an effect on the property's value. Therefore, a property owner has an interest in protecting the legitimate nature of a property's title and its related reputation. If anyone maligns or disparages the reputation of the property, the owner can take steps to protect its reputation and value in a manner similar to that offered to defend her own good name—that is, the law recognizes a cause of action for slander of title that is similar to a slander action between individuals.

A *lis pendens* is a method of asserting a potential claim or conflicting interest against title to real estate when litigation is filed and pending. The lis pendens is a notice filed in the public records for real estate that gives notice that a legal action is currently pending, the outcome of which may have an impact on the status of title of the specifically described property. By definition, the lis pendens is designed to put a cloud on the owner's title (giving it an unmarketable title) and thereby make it difficult or impossible to transfer or otherwise deal with the property. It also serves the purpose of giving notice to any potential BFPs, thereby destroying their ability to take without knowledge of the pending dispute.

PALMER v. ZAKLAMA

Court of Appeal, Fifth District, California, 2003
109 Cal. App. 4th 1367, 1 Cal. Rptr. 3d 116

BUCKLEY, J. Jerry Palmer and Mark Yarber (Palmer and Yarber) bought a house in January of 1993 at a sheriff's sale in Bakersfield. The house was sold to satisfy a $9,000 judgment against the previous owners, Esmat and Selvia Zaklama (the Zaklamas), who by then were living in New Jersey. . . .

In 1984, the Zaklamas, who are both physicians, bought a house on Panorama Drive in Bakersfield for $147,500 (the Panorama house). They gave the seller, a Mr. Gannon, a down payment and a note for the balance of the purchase price, $105,000, payable at 11 percent interest. The note was secured by a deed of trust on the house.

The Zaklamas lived in the Panorama house until December of 1989, when they moved to Los Angeles briefly, and then to New Jersey. Before they left Bakersfield, the Zaklamas hired Thomas Sykora, who worked for a company called Responsive Property Management (RPM), to rent and take care of the house for them in their absence.

Sykora paid to have various repairs made to the house over the next few years, and billed the Zaklamas for these expenses. The Zaklamas refused to pay them. So, in 1992, when their outstanding balance was some $9,000, RPM sued the Zaklamas and obtained a judgment for this amount (the collection action). RPM then levied a writ of execution against the Panorama house, and a sheriff's sale was set for January of 1993.

Yarber saw a legal notice of the sale in the local newspaper, and mentioned it to his friend Palmer. The two men had talked about doing some real estate deals together and, after some investigation, decided the Panorama house would be a good place to start. They went to the sale and bought the house for $10,000. Yarber estimated its value at the time was between $210,000 and $240,000.

Palmer and Yarber cleaned up the house (which was still occupied by a renter) and listed it for sale shortly after they bought it. A prospective buyer offered them $200,000, and they made a counteroffer of $210,000. About then, however, Esmat Zaklama learned of the sheriff's sale (he would later claim he had not received notice) and he contacted a lawyer. In February of 1993, the lawyer recorded a lis pendens on the Zaklamas' behalf, giving notice an appeal was pending in the collection action. As a consequence, Palmer and Yarber were unable to proceed with the house sale.

The lis pendens also prevented Palmer and Yarber from borrowing money, at the then available rate of 8 percent, to pay off the 11 percent loan from Gannon. When the lis pendens finally was withdrawn, and Palmer and Yarber were able to get a loan in December of 1995, the interest rate had gone up to 9.6 or 9.7 percent. Moreover, the amount due Gannon had increased from about $70,000 at the time of the sheriff's sale, to approximately $115,000. The difference represented the expenses Gannon had incurred over the years attempting to collect delinquent house payments from the Zaklamas (including the costs of initiating foreclosure proceedings).

In April of 1993, the Zaklamas filed a petition for chapter 11 bankruptcy in New Jersey (the bankruptcy action). They also filed what they termed a "civil rights" suit in federal court in Fresno (the federal or civil rights action) against Palmer and Yarber, and seemingly everyone else having had anything to do with the sale of the Panorama house. The bankruptcy action raised the possibility, Esmat testified, that the sheriff's sale would be set aside as a preferential transfer. The civil rights action, he explained, sought to set aside the sale on the theory that Palmer and Yarber "were in cahoots" with Sykora, RPM, and the sheriff to acquire title to the Panorama house. Thus, the Zaklamas recorded notices of pending action in regard to these two cases as well, on the premise they would, if successful, affect the title to, or the right to possession of, the Panorama house.

In June of 1993, after the Zaklamas had filed the bankruptcy and federal actions, they met with Palmer and Yarber at a meeting arranged by Gannon (the former owner who still held a note on the house) in an effort to reach a settlement. According to Esmat, he offered Palmer and Yarber $20,000 if they would give him back the house, but they refused. According to Yarber, however, Esmat offered them nothing but freedom from further lawsuits, and said they should chalk up the $10,000 they would lose to a "learning experience."

Indeed, the collection, bankruptcy, and civil rights actions were not the end of the litigation by the Zaklamas against Palmer and Yarber. The tenant in the Panorama house, Pearl Minor, was refusing to pay rent to Palmer and Yarber. They got an eviction order and writ of possession, which they then attempted to serve. But when they arrived at the house, the Zaklamas had locked themselves inside with their children, Esmat's brother Shukry Messiah (who had replaced Minor as the tenant), and their mother. They refused to come out, or to unlock the door, despite repeated requests. Palmer and Yarber called the police. The Zaklama family was no more cooperative with the law, who eventually climbed into the house through an unlocked window and arrested them. The Zaklamas later sued the police, and many others (including Palmer and Yarber), for false arrest. . . .

The lis pendens relating to the bankruptcy action was terminated after the action was dismissed in March of 1995. The lis pendens relating to the civil rights action was expunged in July of that year. And Esmat withdrew the lis pendens relating to the appeal of the collection action in September.

In December of 1995 . . . Palmer and Yarber refinanced the house and paid off the balance of the Gannon loan, plus Gannon's expenses and accrued interest, a total of $115,000. The house was valued then, for purposes of the loan, at $177,000. They finally sold it in March or April of 1997 for $155,000. Yarber would attribute the loss in value from $210,000 in 1993 to $155,000 in 1997 to a downturn in the local housing market. In this same period, according to Yarber, they spent nearly $45,000 for repairs to the house. All told, Yarber estimated he and Palmer made $243 on the sale of the Panorama house.

Palmer and Yarber sued the Zaklamas on the theories of malicious prosecution, abuse of process, and slander of title to recover the losses they claimed to have suffered during the three or four year period the lis pendens prevented them selling or refinancing the Panorama house. They asserted the lis pendens, and the underlying legal actions, were meritless proceedings undertaken solely to coerce them into giving back the house, and on this basis they sought punitive damages as well. The Zaklamas, of course, denied these assertions and claimed in their defense that they had relied in all such matters on the advice of their attorneys. They also asserted their recordation of the lis pendens was privileged.

[Based on special verdicts of the jury, the trial court awarded Palmer and Yarber $235,463 in compensatory damages, plus punitive damages, against the Zaklamas.]

II. Discussion

. . . The essential premise of Palmer and Yarber's complaint was that the three actions underlying the lis pendens were brought for an improper purpose and/or were not the type of proceedings for which it was appropriate to record a notice of lis pendens. The initial question then, assuming this premise is correct, is: What cause or causes of action lie for wrongful recordation of a lis pendens? . . .

At common law, a purchaser or encumbrancer of real property acquired an interest subject to the outcome of any pending litigation affecting title to the property, even if the purchaser or encumbrancer had no notice of the litigation. Richardson v. White (1861) 18 Cal. 102, 106. . . .

California first adopted a statutory lis pendens procedure in 1851, which provided that a party to an action affecting real property could record a notice of lis pendens in the county where the property was located such that a subsequent purchaser or encumbrancer would be charged with constructive notice of the action from the time the recording was made. Sampson v. Ohleyer (1863) 22 Cal. 200, 210. The statutory procedure, and the amendments that followed, were intended to restrict rather than enlarge the common law doctrine of notice, and to curb abuses of the procedure. . . .

The Legislature amended the lis pendens statutes in 1968 to add [provisions that] established a procedure by which a property owner could expunge a lis pendens under certain circumstances. . . .

In 1992, following the efforts of a special committee of the Real Property Law Section of the California State Bar, the Legislature substantially revised the lis pendens statutes. . . .

The 1992 revisions were intended, among other things [to] expand the grounds for expungement. . . .

Also in 1992, the same year it revised the lis pendens statutes, the Legislature amended section 47 of the Civil Code to [limit] in the case of lis pendens the absolute privilege accorded "publications" made in the course of judicial proceedings. The recordation of a lis pendens is a republication of the pleadings in the underlying action and so is subject to the absolute privilege in Civil Code section 47. Albertson v. Raboff (1956) 46 Cal. 2d 375, 379, 295 P.2d 405. . . .

Albertson's holding that the recordation of a notice of lis pendens is absolutely privileged has been "partially abrogated" by the 1992 amendment. . . . Civil Code section 47 now provides in pertinent part:

> A privileged publication or broadcast is one made:
>
> (b) In any . . . (2) judicial proceeding, . . . except as follows: . . .
>
> (4) A recorded lis pendens is not a privileged publication unless it identifies an action previously filed with a court of competent jurisdiction which affects the title or right of possession of real property, as authorized or required by law.

Therefore, if the pleading filed by the claimant in the underlying action does not allege a real property claim, or the alleged claim lacks evidentiary merit, the lis pendens, in addition to being subject to expungement, is not privileged. It follows the lis pendens in that situation may be the basis for an action for slander of title. . . .

The Zaklamas, in reliance on *Albertson*, contend the complaint failed to state facts sufficient to constitute a cause of action for slander of title because the recordation of a lis pendens is absolutely privileged. However, as we have explained, the privilege does not attach unless the underlying action properly alleges a real property claim. Civ.Code, §47, subd. (b)(4). Moreover, it was the Zaklamas' burden in this case to show that the collection and bankruptcy actions were such claims. This they failed to do. Indeed, the Zaklamas' attorney effectively conceded the collections action was not one in which it was appropriate to record a lis pendens. *See, e.g.*, Allied Eastern Financial v. Goheen Enterprises (1968) 265 Cal. App. 2d 131, 133, 134, 71 Cal. Rptr. 126 (action for money damages alone will not support a lis pendens). And there is no evidence the trustee in the bankruptcy action actually attempted to set aside the sheriff's sale as a preferential transfer.

This same analysis also disposes of the Zaklamas' claim [that] a lis pendens, inasmuch as it simply puts the world on notice of a pending action, is not a false publication. It is false, however, if it asserts the action may affect the title to or possession of real property, when in fact it will not. . . .

[The court concluded that the defendants were not liable for abuse of process because recordation of a lis pendens is not "process," but it affirmed the judgment on the basis of slander of title and malicious prosecution.]

Problem 7C

John is driving to work early one morning when he runs into Daisy. Daisy is riding her bike to campus when she is hit by John. Daisy suffers broken bones and some serious injuries that cause pain and require medical treatment. Daisy hires a lawyer from an advertisement she sees on television one day while she is at home recovering from her injuries and watching a morning talk show. Daisy's lawyer thinks that she should be able to get about $300,000 from John, and she has discovered that John owns some investment real estate that could be made available as an asset to satisfy any judgment award that Daisy wins. Daisy's attorney files her lawsuit and simultaneously files a lis pendens against John's investment real estate.

(a) Should Daisy be able to file a lis pendens in this situation?

(b) Should John be able to sue for slander of title? If so, should Daisy or Daisy's attorney, or both, be liable?

Problem 7D

John owns property over which Daisy rides her bike. Daisy has ridden on a dirt "bike path" across John's property almost every day for the past ten years. One day, Daisy rides up to John's property and discovers that his land has been completely fenced and the path is blocked. Daisy contacts her lawyer and on the lawyer's advice, she commences a lawsuit asserting a right to continue to use the bike path to cross John's property. She simultaneously files a lis pendens in the public records for real estate recordings.

(a) Should Daisy be able to file a lis pendens?

(b) Should John be able to sue for slander of title?

D. TORT REMEDIES RELATED TO THE CONTRACT

Although contract damages are generally only compensatory in nature, in the right situation a party to a real estate transaction can obtain tort damages. These damages can emerge from the direct contract relationship between a buyer and a seller, or they can relate to the undertakings and contractual relationships entered into with third parties involved in the real estate transaction.

SEXTON v. ST. CLAIR FEDERAL SAVINGS BANK

Supreme Court of Alabama, 1995
653 So. 2d 959

Kennedy, Justice. The plaintiffs, William Jack Sexton and Marsha C. Sexton, sued St. Clair Federal Savings Bank ("St. Clair"), alleging breach of contract and breach of fiduciary duty. The Sextons appeal from a partial summary judgment 1) in favor of St. Clair on the Sextons' fiduciary relationship claim and 2) holding that the Sextons could not recover certain damages on their breach of contract claim.

This case arose out of a loan agreement between the Sextons and St. Clair, through which the Sextons borrowed approximately $160,000 from St. Clair to build a residence. The loan was secured by a construction mortgage. The loan agreement provided that St. Clair was to disburse the loan proceeds in increments approximating the stage of construction of the residence.

Several weeks after construction had started, St. Clair notified the Sextons that the stage of construction did not justify the amount of proceeds that had been drawn by the Sextons' builder. St. Clair advised the Sextons that, given the situation, it would not permit any more draws on the loan proceeds at that time. According to the Sextons, they learned that all but $17,000 of the loan proceeds had been disbursed by St. Clair and that approximately $93,000 of the monies disbursed had not been used by their builder on the construction of the residence.

The Sextons were unable to complete the construction, and they ceased making the required payments on the construction loan. St. Clair sued, seeking an order of foreclosure, the sale of the uncompleted residence to satisfy the indebtedness on the loan, and any deficiency that might exist after the sale. The Sextons counterclaimed, alleging that St. Clair had failed to monitor construction and to disburse the loan proceeds in proportion to the stage of construction consistent with the loan agreement. They alleged that St. Clair had thereby breached the loan agreement and had breached a fiduciary duty to them. In addition to punitive damages, the Sextons sought compensatory damages for what they claimed were their "direct, consequential, and incidental losses, including an amount for their mental anguish, emotional suffering, annoyance [and] inconvenience," and they sought to recover purported lost profits from their sale of investment property. They alleged that they sold that investment in an effort to raise money to complete the construction. . . .

As to the first issue raised by the Sextons—whether they can recover mental anguish-type damages—the trial court stated that in limited circumstances damages for mental anguish can properly be awarded on a breach of contract claim. The trial court correctly stated:

> Damages cannot be received for mental anguish arising from a breach of contract. There are exceptions to that general rule and they are as follows: "[W]here the contractual duty or obligation is so coupled with matters of mental concern or solicitude, or with the feelings of the party to whom the duty is owed, that a breach of that duty will necessarily or reasonably result in mental anguish or suffering, it is just that damages therefore be taken into consideration and awarded. . . . Another exception is where the breach of the contract is tortious, or attended with personal injury, damages for mental anguish may be awarded."

C.R. 211, *quoting* B & M Homes, Inc. v. Hogan, 376 So. 2d 667, 671 (Ala. 1979) (as *B & M Homes* quoted earlier cases). The court . . . concluded that, based on undisputed material facts, as a matter of law "the case . . . does not fall into those narrow exceptions." . . .

The Sextons argue that the trial court erred in so holding, and they emphasize the special nature of the breach of a contractual provision involving one's residence, as it relates to the applicability of the exception based on a "contractual duty" that is "coupled with matters of mental concern or solicitude." . . .

In the *B & M Homes* case, the plaintiffs sued a home builder, who had agreed to construct their new residence, but who did not do so in a workmanlike manner. The finished structure had "major defects." The plaintiffs sued on contract theories, and demanded damages for mental anguish. This Court applied the exception, stating: "It was reasonably foreseeable . . . that faulty construction of [the plaintiffs'] house would cause them severe mental anguish. The largest single investment the average American family will make is the purchase of a home. The purchase of a home by an individual or [a] family places the purchaser in debt for a period ranging from twenty (20) to thirty (30) years." *Id.*

The contract provision alleged to have been breached in this case deals with the Sextons' residence. We observe, also, that this provision was apparently aimed at preventing the very kind of situation that the plaintiffs allege occurred here: the squandering of the means to build that residence, the construction loan proceeds. That provision states: "[T]he bank is authorized to disburse funds under its control [from the] construction loan account, together with the net proceeds of the loan, only in proportion to its Inspector's Report of Progress or by Architect's or Superintendent's Certificate accompanied by a proper affidavit from the contractor." A St. Clair employee testified that it is within the bank's "normal process" for bank personnel to discuss the "monitoring procedures" with construction loan borrowers, and he agreed that this was done "in part[,] in order so that the [construction loan borrower] will have some confidence in entering into [a construction loan] agreement — so that they will know that they are having some type of protection." C.R. 275-76. Consistent with this testimony, William Jack Sexton testified that a bank employee had gone "over the loan papers" with him and that the employee had "pointed out that the bank would monitor [disbursements]." According to Sexton, the employee told him "that the wording [of the loan agreement] was that it should not — the funds wouldn't be used for any other expenditures other than for our own home — personal home."

St. Clair argues that the contract allegedly breached contemplated matters regarding an anticipated residence, rather than a residence occupied by the plaintiffs.[2] St. Clair says that therefore this case is not generally "characteristic of the cases that fit the exception to the general rule," which, it says, involves situations in which the contract relates to a current residence.

We agree that the exception based on a "contractual duty" that is "coupled with matters of mental concern or solicitude" has been applied in situations involving contracts relating to a plaintiff's current residence. *See, e.g.,* Orkin Exterminating Co. v. Donavan, 519 So. 2d 1330 (Ala. 1988). However, the contract at issue in the *B & M Homes* case, where the Court held that the exception applied, related to construction of a future residence. Similarly, in Lawler Mobile Homes, Inc. v. Tarver, 492 So. 2d 297 (Ala. 1986), where the Court held that the exception applied, the contract related to the sale and delivery of a mobile home, the plaintiffs' future residence. Like the plaintiffs in this case, the plaintiffs in *Lawler Mobile Homes* were living elsewhere at the time of the contract, and the contract in *Lawler Mobile Homes* did not relate to the residence in which they were residing at the time of contract. . . .

Applying the reasoning of those cases to the situation here, we hold that a reasonable construction lender could easily foresee that a borrower could undergo extreme mental anguish if that lender breached a provision such as the one these plaintiffs allege was breached. Here, the provision alleged to have been breached, although it appears as part of a contract to lend money, unquestionably relates to the construction of the Sextons' residence. Clearly, the contractual duty created by that provision — to monitor the construction of the Sextons' residence and the disbursements related to that construction — "is so coupled with matters of mental concern or solicitude, or with the feelings of the part[ies] to whom [that] duty is owed, that a breach will necessarily or reasonably result in mental anguish or suffering." *B & M Homes,* 376 So. 2d at 671 (quoting earlier cases). . . .

Affirmed in part; reversed in part; and remanded.

2. St. Clair also emphasizes that "the Sextons never had to fear being cast out on the street, being battered by the outside elements or having to find temporary substitute shelter." Such a point would be relevant on the question of the degree of the Sextons' alleged mental anguish, a question not before us.

Problem 7E

Jane contracts to buy a home from Bruce for $200,000. Bruce is developing a number of lots along a streetfront area. The home will have well water, and Bruce agrees to drill and connect the water supply to the home. Bruce ends up going down 185 feet and tapping into the water table. Jane closes on the home and moves into the property with her two children. The water is a problem from the beginning; it appears cloudy and tastes bad. Jane is told to let the water stand in a jug in the refrigerator overnight and that it will taste, look, and smell fine in the morning. She tries this and it seems to work. A few weeks later she sees a television news show about contaminated water that can cause cancer or other health problems. In particular, the show warns of potential problems for children from well water with high concentrations of certain minerals. Jane becomes concerned about her water. She has tests done, which find high levels of iron, sulphur, and calcium in her water. She is nervous about her children and loses sleep and gets headaches worrying about her water. She misses work several times. She asks Bruce to fix the well water supply, but he says there is nothing wrong with it. Bruce says he grew up in the area on well water, his house was only three lots down from hers, and he had no concerns about the quality of his well water. Jane hires a company to install water purifiers and softeners that cost $3,000. Still, Jane worries about her children's health, so she starts buying springwater from the store. She keeps receipts to show that she is spending $12 per week on springwater.

Jane discovers that the county can hook her up to a city water supply from a line that passes along a street about one-third of a mile from her home. The cost of bringing the line to her house will be $8,500. The county says that if Bruce had set this up at the time he was building Jane's home, the hookup could have been done for about $2,000, because they would have laid the line along ditches dug for other utilities. The county also says that Bruce was informed of this before he started any construction and before he contracted with Jane. Bruce opted to work with well water because he had a well-digging business and could supply water to the home by this method for less than $1,200.

Although excessive minerals in well water can cause problems for some people, there is no clear evidence that the well water at Jane's house is in fact causing any current physical harm to her or her children.

(a) What type of contract damages might Jane be able to get? (Assume that she has been buying springwater for 30 weeks at the time she brings this suit.)

(b) Should Jane be able to recover tort damages in connection with her contract problems? What issues should be addressed in such a case, and how might one go about setting the amount of recovery?

8
Allocating Title Risk

A. TITLE UNDER THE REAL ESTATE CONTRACT

Title to the property is an important concern in every sale of real estate. Uncertainty as to title constitutes a major form of historical risk. The risk of title error is historical in the sense that reaching a judgment about title involves the evaluation of evidence about the past. One of the primary reasons the real estate contract has an executory period is for the parties to handle title matters. Most parties do not obtain a title search prior to contracting; instead, they sign a contract on the assumption that most title issues will be manageable. All contracts deal with title by either an express term or an implied term.

In contracting about title, the starting point is the norm that the buyer has the right to *marketable title.* Some courts say the buyer has the right to *merchantable title,* a term that is synonymous with marketable title. The right to marketable title is an implied term of the contract, based on the parties' probable expectations. Marketable title disputes arise in many different contexts. Courts have used the term to address the merits of purchasers' objections to all of the following matters: defects in the record chain of title, outstanding possessory rights, future interests, mortgages, liens, easements, real covenants and equitable servitudes, zoning ordinances and other land use regulations, eminent domain, adverse possession claims, boundary disputes, encroachment of improvements, and access to land.

The marketable title provision operates to allocate risk between the parties. By entering into the contract, the seller impliedly promises that his title is marketable. This means that he has taken on the risk that a defect may be discovered that makes title unmarketable. If this happens, the seller has failed in his obligation under the contract and is responsible for damages.

In addition to being an implied promise, marketable title is an implied condition. The buyer's obligations to pay the purchase price and close the transaction are conditioned on title being marketable. If this condition fails, the buyer has no further obligation and does not have to go forward.

The seller's title must be marketable only at the closing, not earlier. Moreover, when the land is subject to a mortgage or other lien, the seller may use the purchase price to satisfy that encumbrance.

Most written contracts, however, are not silent on the issue of title. Many contracts have an express promise by the seller of marketable title; instead of changing the implied term, the parties simply recognize it. Often contracts use equivalent terms—requirements that title be "good," "perfect," "satisfactory," "clear," or "with no defects" generally are treated as synonyms for "marketable title." Sometimes the contract language sets forth procedures for the title search, including time parameters for the buyer to make title objections.

On the other hand, many contracts define the quality of title that the seller must furnish and the buyer must accept. The parties specify what the seller's obligations are and what is acceptable to the buyer. This is sometimes referred to as *contract title.* Contract title may be more lenient than marketable title, or it may be more strict.

Two common types of contract title are *insurable title* and *record title.* When the buyer plans to obtain a title insurance policy, the contract often describes the type of policy that will be satisfactory to the buyer. The contract may provide that a title insurance company's willingness to issue that policy fully satisfies the seller's title obligations. In effect, the parties replace the courts, as the arbiter of marketability, with the insurance company.

Record title requires proof of the status of title, gathered solely from deeds and other instruments that are recorded in the public records for recording interests in real property. This means that the seller's title cannot depend on an unrecorded instrument, such as a deed that hasn't been recorded, a will that hasn't been probated, or a claim based on adverse possession.

A marketable title is not necessarily a *record* title. After a contract is signed, the title search sometimes reveals that the seller lacks record title to some or all of the real property but has evidence of title by adverse possession. When the parties have failed expressly to allocate the risk of adverse possession title, courts must come up with an implied rule for them. There is a split of authority on the question of whether title by adverse possession is marketable when the seller has not successfully litigated the adverse possession claim, but has strong evidence of the underlying elements. One position, followed by the courts in California and some other states, is that marketable title must be based on the records. If title depends on possible testimony of witnesses who might be called in an adverse possession case, this raises a reasonable doubt as a matter of law. Under this approach, the duty is on the seller to disclose, prior to contracting, the fact that he is relying on adverse possession to shore up his title. This approach, however, goes beyond a requirement that the seller disclose a known fact. Some sellers cannot disclose their plan to rely on adverse possession because they are ignorant of the state of their title.

The alternative judicial position, followed by New York and other states, is that title by adverse possession is marketable, provided that the seller can clearly establish the requisite elements. It is thus a question of fact whether such a title is marketable. The rationale for this view is that many titles are not perfectly shown by the public records but are subject to flaws that pose only a very remote risk of loss. This rule, in contrast to its opposite, can be seen as putting a disclosure duty on the buyer. The seller need not disclose reliance on the law of adverse possession; rather, the buyer who wants a clear title of record, not depending at all on the statute of limitations, must expressly bargain for such a term.

Problem 8A

(a) Sara contracts to sell Simpleacre to Baker. The contract says nothing about the quality of title Baker is to receive. A title search reveals that in a deed recorded in 1930, a prior owner of the land conveyed the land "so long as liquor is not sold on the premises." Is title marketable? Does Sara's present use of Simpleacre matter? Does Baker's intended use of Simpleacre matter?

(b) Would it make a difference if in the contract Sara promised to deliver "a fee simple title of record"?

(c) What if the contract has a condition that "title must be satisfactory to Buyer's attorney"? Does this allow Baker to terminate even if the risk of loss from the anti-liquor provision is remote?

1. Encumbrances and Encroachments

An *encumbrance* is a nonpossessory right or interest in the property held by a third party that reduces the property's market value, restricts its use, or imposes an obligation on the property owner. Encumbrances include easements, real covenants, equitable servitudes, marital property rights, mortgage liens, tax liens, and other liens and charges. An encumbrance does not negate the present existence of the seller's estate itself. For example, a defect in the nature of an outstanding cotenant's interest is not an encumbrance; it means the seller does not own 100 percent of the fee simple absolute estate. Courts generally define *marketable title* as an estate that is totally free from encumbrances. Yet there are a good number of cases holding that a particular encumbrance does not impair marketability. In many states, the law is not settled in this area. The result often turns upon the specific details of the parties' transaction. The cases generally fall into the following five groups, which sometimes overlap.

An *encroachment* is an unauthorized extension of an improvement across a boundary line. This constitutes a trespass by the improver. Three types of encroachments are of concern to a purchaser. The improvements on the property under contract may encroach on neighboring tracts or on a street, or neighboring improvements may encroach on the property. Often the term *encroachment* is also used to describe a different locational problem. Improvements may be wholly located on the property in question, but they may improperly extend upon an easement, a setback area established by restrictive covenants or zoning, or other restricted space. All three types of encroachments generally render title unmarketable. When the seller's improvements encroach on the neighbor's land or a protected area, the purchaser may be required to remove the improvement or pay for damages. When the neighbor's improvements encroach, the purchaser may have lost title to the area covered by the encroachment under the law of adverse possession or by virtue of principles of equity.

STALEY v. STEPHENS

Court of Appeals of Indiana, First District, 1980
404 N.E.2d 633

ROBERTSON, Presiding Judge. Paul R. and Suzanne B. Staley (Sellers) commenced an action against Paul L. and Carolyn A. Stephens (Buyers) as a result of Buyers' refusal to complete the purchase of Sellers' property. In their answer, Buyers counterclaimed for damages predicated upon Sellers' failure to tender marketable title. At the close of Sellers' evidence, Buyers moved for judgment on the evidence. . . . The trial court granted the motion and found for the Buyers on Sellers' complaint, and additionally, found against the Buyers on their counterclaim. We affirm in part and reverse in part.

There are in essence two issues with which this court must deal. The first concerns the question of how a slight infringement on a side line set back requirement effects marketable title as a matter of law. Secondly, we must address the trial court's denial of Buyers' counterclaim before Buyers had the opportunity to present any evidence on their claim.

. . . [T]he parties contracted for the purchase of a home, and Buyers tendered to the real estate agent $1,000 as earnest money.[1] The Buyers were to receive, at the closing, an abstract of title disclosing marketable title to the real estate. At the time of the original subdivision, the tract was divided into ten lots. A restrictive covenant of this original subdivision required a ten foot side line set back. At a later date, Lot #10 of the original subdivision was further subdivided, and at the time of re-platting, the side line set back requirements of the Town of New Haven were incorporated by reference into this further subdivision. At that time, the New Haven zoning ordinance

1. During the pendency of this action, the earnest money was delivered to the court, which held the funds pending disposition of the cause.

required a side yard set back line of 8.5 feet. Sellers' property was located in this second subdivision.

A survey was made of the property as called for by the purchase agreement, and revealed that a portion of Sellers' house was only 8.4 feet from the side line, in violation of the New Haven zoning ordinance. It further provided, in the restrictive covenants of this subdivision, that any lot owner could enforce at law or equity any attempt to violate or any violation of the covenants by either injunctive relief or by the recovery of damages.

Upon notification of this defect, Buyers requested that Sellers obtain waivers from the other landowners waiving this side line set back violation. Sellers refused to do this, whereupon Buyers determined that the title was not acceptable and refused to complete the purchase.

The parties stipulated quite a number of the facts, and among the stipulations was that the Allen County Bar Association had adopted a standard of marketability which indicated that violation of side line set back requirements contained in restrictive covenants should be waived as to residential lots if the improvements in question were completed and in place for at least two years prior to the date of the examination of the title. This standard of marketability, however, was not agreed to by the parties, even though the house was built in 1970.

We first note that the "two year statute of limitations" as adopted by the Allen County Bar Association has no legal effect, unless a contract is specifically referenced to that period, and merely serves as a guide to the parties and the Bar Association itself. The applicable statute of limitations as passed by the General Assembly calls for a twenty (20) year period within which actions must be brought upon contracts in writing other than those for the payment of money. Ind. Code 34-1-2-2.

. . . Kenefick v. Schumaker, (1917) 64 Ind. App. 552, 116 N.E. 319, provides the basis for what little modern law there is on the subject of marketable title. In *Kenefick*, the court, after reviewing the standard espoused by commentators and applied in other jurisdictions, determined that the controlling test and more reasonable rule is that a title "which has no defects of a serious nature, and none which affect the possessory title of the owner, ought to be adjudged marketable." 64 Ind. App. at 565, 116 N.E. at 323. . . . What we are faced with in this case is a violation of between one-tenth of a foot and one foot six-tenths depending upon which restrictive covenant would be found controlling. The question that must be addressed is whether a title is marketable as a matter of law, notwithstanding a clear violation of a restrictive covenant.

A court of equity will not compel a purchaser to accept a title which is so doubtful that it may expose him to litigation, though the court may believe it to be good. Smith v. Turner, (1875) 50 Ind. 367. . . .

When viewed in this regard, it is evident that although the title defect is small, it is nonetheless a cloud on the title that may expose Buyers to the possibility of litigation due to the remedies available to other landowners in the subdivision. Even though a damage recovery may be nominal, Buyers would still incur the cost of defending against any litigation. Absent waivers from all landowners holding Buyers harmless, the possibility of litigation on the matter will not end until the running of the twenty year statute of limitations. Consequently, with the admitted cloud on the title, we are not prepared to say that the title was marketable as a matter of law. Therefore, . . . the trial court did not err in granting Buyers' motion for judgment on the evidence as to Sellers' complaint.

The second issue with which we must deal concerns the trial court's ruling on Buyers' counterclaim prior to the presentation of any evidence by the Buyers. . . .

. . . We fail to perceive how a motion for judgment on the evidence can be granted as to the counterclaim, when Buyers, who had the burden of proof, were not able to present any evidence as to their claim. . . .

Judgment affirmed in part; reversed in part.

Problem 8B

(a) Stanford contracts to sell his home to Belinda, promising to convey "good title to the property free of all liens and encumbrances." The title search reveals that the driveway leading to Stanford's garage straddles the boundary line. The neighboring lot is presently vacant, but the neighbor and Stanford each have express recorded easements to use the entire driveway. Does Belinda have a valid objection to title? To make a valid objection, must she prove that the easement for the common driveway reduces the value of Stanford's property? Suppose that Stanford can prove that it has no effect on value whatsoever, what result?

(b) Belinda, your client, wants out of her contract. She confides that the common driveway doesn't trouble her in the least—she wants out because her brother-in-law has convinced her that she is paying way too much for the property. What advice do you give her? Will you write a letter to Stanford's attorney that terminates the contract? What should the letter say?

2. *Effect of Public Regulation on Title*

Zoning and other forms of land use regulation often have a critical impact on property value. When the parties have failed expressly to allocate the risks associated with zoning and other types of public land use regulations, disappointed buyers have sometimes sought judicial protection by arguing that title is unmarketable. For this reason, in many states there is often some confusion about the relationship between zoning and title or marketable title. One view treats title narrowly, looking only at evidence bearing on fee simple ownership of an estate and the existence of encumbrances consisting only of servitudes and liens. Other courts have taken a broader view of marketable title, using this concept to protect buyers whose expectations concerning property use and value are frustrated when certain zoning problems are encountered. This approach ignores traditional conceptions of what the term *title* means in property law, but achieves an outcome that may be defensible for reasons of policy.

VOORHEESVILLE ROD & GUN CLUB v. E.W. TOMPKINS COMPANY

Court of Appeals of New York, 1993
82 N.Y.2d 564, 626 N.E.2d 917, 606 N.Y.S.2d 132

HANCOCK, Judge. The first issue in this case is whether the subdivision regulations of the Village of Voorheesville apply to a conveyance of a portion of a parcel of land where it is intended by the parties to the transaction that the lands shall remain undeveloped. If the regulations apply, then the primary issue is whether defendant seller's failure to seek subdivision approval before the transfer renders the title unmarketable. We conclude that the Village's subdivision regulations apply to this sale of property. But we further hold that defendant's refusal to seek the subdivision approval here does not cause the title to be unmarketable. Because no provision in the contract requires defendant to obtain subdivision approval and the only basis for plaintiff's specific performance claim is its failed assertion of unmarketable title, we reverse, deny plaintiff's summary judgment motion for specific performance, and dismiss the complaint.

I

On January 15, 1986, plaintiff Voorheesville Rod & Gun Club, Inc., signed a standard preprinted contract with defendant E.W. Tompkins Company, Inc., to purchase a portion of defendant's property located in the Village of Voorheesville, Albany County, for $38,000. The contract specified that the property would be conveyed by warranty deed subject to all covenants, conditions, restrictions and easements of record, and also to zoning and environmental protection laws, "provided that this does not render the title to the premises unmarketable." The property to be conveyed consisted of 24.534 acres of undeveloped land used for recreational purposes. The parties agree that plaintiff buyer did not intend to change the existing condition or use of the property after the purchase.

On August 23, 1986, prior to the revised closing date, plaintiff's attorney sent defendant's attorney a copy of the Village of Voorheesville's subdivision regulations and requested that defendant comply with them. Defendant did not seek subdivision approval. Defendant sent plaintiff a time-of-the-essence notice, demanded a closing on August 29, 1986, and notified plaintiff that if it did not close, that would be considered an anticipatory breach of contract. When plaintiff failed to close, defendant canceled the contract and returned plaintiff's $5,000 deposit. On September 4th, plaintiff informed defendant that the cancellation was unacceptable because defendant's failure to obtain subdivision approval had rendered the title unmarketable and, for that reason, plaintiff's financing bank was unwilling to close. Plaintiff then sought the requisite approval from the Village of Voorheesville Planning Commission. The Commission denied the application, stating that the subdivision regulations required that the application be submitted "by the [property] owner or an agent of the owner."

Plaintiff commenced this action on September 12, 1986, for specific performance or damages for breach of contract and then moved for partial summary judgment seeking specific performance. Supreme Court ordered that the contract be specifically performed by defendant and directed that defendant apply to the Village for subdivision approval and close on the subject property within a reasonable time after approval. . . .

The Appellate Division affirmed. . . .

II

The preliminary issue is whether the Village's subdivision regulations apply at all under the circumstances presented. If they do not, that is the end of the matter and we do not reach the separate question of whether defendant's refusal to obtain subdivision approval rendered the title to the property unmarketable. Thus, we must first interpret the Village's Land Subdivision Regulations, which provide in pertinent part:

> Article II: *Definitions* . . .
> *Subdivision:* means the division of any parcel of land into two or more lots, blocks, or sites, with or without streets or highways and includes re-subdivision. . . .
>
> Article III: *Procedure in Filing Subdivision Applications*
> Whenever any subdivision of land is proposed to be made, and before any contract for the sale of, or any offer to sell any lots in such subdivision or any part thereof is made, and before any permit for the erection of a structure in such proposed subdivision shall be granted, the subdivider or his duly authorized agent shall apply in writing for approval of such proposed subdivision.

Defendant maintains that, pursuant to article III, subdivision approval is required only in instances where building or development is contemplated; and because no development of the subject property was intended, the regulations do not apply in this case. This claim is not persuasive. It is undisputed that defendant was selling only a portion of its property; therefore, the subject property transfer constituted a subdivision within the meaning of article II of the regulations. . . . Clearly, the stated policy of the regulations is that subdivision approval should be acquired for any proposed subdivision, not just those to be immediately developed.

III

Given that the subdivision regulations apply, we turn to the main issue: whether lack of subdivision approval constitutes a cloud on the title which renders the title unmarketable. It is undisputed that the contract is silent as to the specific issue of subdivision approval. Thus nothing in the contract imposes upon defendant the affirmative obligation of obtaining subdivision approval.[2] Rather, paragraph 4 of the contract, entitled "Existing Conditions," provides that the property would be conveyed by warranty deed

> subject to all covenants, conditions, restrictions and easements of record. *Subject also to zoning and environmental protection laws;* any existing tenancies; . . . and any state of facts which an inspection and/or accurate survey may show, *provided that this does not render the title to the premises unmarketable* (emphasis added).

As stated, plaintiff was to purchase the property subject to zoning laws, which are closely related to subdivision regulations (*see generally* Matter of Golden v. Planning Bd., 30 N.Y.2d 359, 372, 334 N.Y.S.2d 138, 285 N.E.2d 291; 2 Anderson, *New York Zoning Law and Practice* §21.02 (3d ed.)). This requirement conforms to the well-settled rule that "where a person agrees to purchase real estate, which, at the time, is restricted by laws or ordinances, he will be deemed to have entered into the contract subject to the same [and] [h]e cannot thereafter be heard to object to taking the title because of such restrictions" (Lincoln Trust Co. v. Williams Bldg. Corp., 229 N.Y. 313, 318, 128 N.E. 209; *see* Pamerqua Realty Corp. v. Dollar Serv. Corp., 93 A.D.2d 249, 251, 461 N.Y.S.2d 393; 3 Warren's Weed, *New York Real Property, Marketability of Title*, §8.07 (4th ed.); Annotation, *Zoning or Other Public Restrictions on the Use of Property as Affecting Rights and Remedies of Parties to Contract for the Sale Thereof*, §§3, 5[b], 39 A.L.R.3d 362, 370, 376).

The only limitation that the contract places upon plaintiff's duty to purchase the property subject to zoning laws is when the application of such laws would render title to the property unmarketable. It was not necessary for the contract to specify that a marketable title was required because, in the absence of a stipulation to the contrary, it is presumed that a marketable title is to be conveyed. . . .

. . . [M]arketability of title is concerned with impairments on title to a property, i.e., the right to unencumbered ownership and possession, not with legal public regulation of the use of the property (*see* Lincoln Trust

2. To the extent that plaintiff now claims—distinct from its argument that lack of subdivision approval renders the title unmarketable—that defendant has an implied good-faith contractual duty to obtain subdivision approval as a precondition of performing the contract, this issue was not raised by plaintiff in its summary judgment motion papers and thus is not preserved for our review.

We also note that this is not a case where the seller is seeking specific performance of a contract to compel a buyer to purchase property lacking subdivision approval or where a municipality is trying to block such a conveyance, and we do not address such situations here.

Co. v. Williams Bldg. Corp., 229 N.Y. 313, 318, 128 N.E. 209; 5A Warren's Weed, [*New York Real Property, Marketability of Title* §1.01 (4th ed.)]; *compare* 3 Warren's Weed, §§1.01, 2.01, *with* §8.07). Accordingly, a zoning ordinance, existing at the time of the contract, which regulates only the use of the property, generally is not an encumbrance making the title unmarketable (*see, Lincoln Trust, supra,* at 318, 128 N.E. 209; Anderson v. Steinway & Sons, 178 App. Div. 507, 513, 165 N.Y.S. 608, *affd.* 221 N.Y. 639, 117 N.E. 575; Pamerqua Realty Corp. v. Dollar Serv. Corp., 93 A.D.2d 249, 251, 461 N.Y.S.2d 393, *supra;* 3 Warren's Weed, *op. cit., Marketability of Title,* §8.07; 1 Rasch, *New York Law and Practice of Real Property* §22.61 (2d ed.)).

Where, however, a contract expressly provides that the seller warrants and represents that, upon purchase, the property will not be in violation of any zoning ordinance, the purchaser "is entitled to demand that the vendor rectify the same or return any moneys paid on account" (*Pamerqua Realty Corp.*, 93 A.D.2d 249, 251, 461 N.Y.S.2d 393, *supra; see* Artstrong Homes v. Vasa, 23 Misc. 2d 608, 201 N.Y.S.2d 138 (Meyer, J.); 3 Warren's Weed, *op. cit., Marketability of Title,* §8.07; 1 Rasch, *op. cit.*, §22.61). Contrary to plaintiff's claim, the present case does not fall within this exception to the general rule. Defendant did not warrant or represent that it would obtain subdivision approval; rather, plaintiff agreed to purchase the property subject to the zoning laws. In effect, plaintiff is attempting to add a term to the contract after the deal has been made. . . .

We recognize, as noted by the courts below, the increasing sophistication of municipalities regarding subdivision regulation and their ability to prevent the purchaser from developing property as allowed by the zoning laws until the requisite subdivision approval is obtained [citations omitted]. The solution for avoiding such problems, however, is not for the courts to expand the conditions which render title unmarketable, thereby altering the concept of marketability of title, but for the parties to real estate contracts to include specific provisions dealing with the duty to obtain subdivision approval.

Accordingly, the judgment appealed from and the order of the Appellate Division brought up for review should be reversed, with costs, plaintiff's motion for partial summary judgment should be denied, and defendant's cross motion for summary judgment dismissing the complaint should be granted.

Problem 8C

Susan and Ben contract to buy a three-bedroom house with no garage. The title search reveals neighborhood restrictive covenants that require a 20-foot setback from the side property lines. The zoning ordinance requires only 10-foot setback lines. A survey indicates that the house is 20.2 feet from one sideline and 30.8 feet from the other sideline. Nevertheless, Susan and Ben notify the seller that they are terminating the contract, stating that the restrictive covenants render title unmarketable. They claim they planned to add a garage to the house, and the 20-foot setback does not allow sufficient room. What result if:

(a) The contract requires the seller to convey "good and clear record title"?

(b) The contract says nothing at all about title?

(c) The contract requires the seller to submit to the buyer a "title report satisfactory to the buyer's attorney"?

3. *Buyer's Remedies for Title Defects*

Under contract law generally, when one party breaches, the other party is entitled to collect damages for loss of expectation, provided they are proven. If the breach is material, the reason for the breach does not matter. For real estate contracts, the general rule applies, but with a major caveat. When the buyer seeks damages because the seller is unable to convey marketable title, many states follow the "English rule" announced in Flureau v. Thornhill, 96 Eng. Rep. 635 (C.P. 1776), which does not allow expectation damages. In contrast, other states have adopted the "American rule," which awards expectation damages under the normal rules of contract law.

Chesapeake Builders, Inc. v. Lee, 254 Va. 294, 492 S.E.2d 141 (1997), considered a purchaser's right to recover damages as a result of a seller's failure to perform on a contract to deliver title to property covered by the real estate contract. In *Chesapeake,* the seller did not have title to one of multiple lots included in the contract for the sale of property. As a consequence, the purchaser sought damages to recover for the loss of his bargain and for specific performance. In considering the appropriate remedy, the court stated the following:

> Absent a contrary contractual provision, a purchaser of real estate may not recover damages for breach of contract beyond the return of the purchase money actually paid, with interest, unless the purchaser proves that: (1) the seller acted in bad faith in contracting to convey title at such time; (2) on or before the time fixed for the completion of the contract, the seller voluntarily rendered himself unable to complete the conveyance; or (3) the seller was able to make the conveyance contracted for and neglected or refused to do so.
>
> . . .
>
> Generally, when there is a deficiency in title, quantity, or quality of an estate, the purchaser has the option to require the seller to convey such part as the seller is able, with an abatement of the purchase price for any deficiency.

Problem 8D

Andy contracts to buy a two-year-old house from Sara for $90,000. Neighborhood covenants and a zoning ordinance both require that all parts of the house be set back at least ten feet from the side boundary lines. A survey discloses that the eaves of the house are only eight feet from a side boundary line.

(a) Andy decides that the risk posed by the encroachment is remote and he notifies Sara that "I elect to waive the title defect." Meanwhile, Sara decides that she prefers not to sell the house to Andy for $90,000. She responds, "Title is not marketable and for that reason the contract is terminated." She tenders Andy his earnest money. Can Andy refuse and get specific performance?

(b) Andy decides that the risk posed by the encroachment is significant, but he still wants the house. He notifies Sara that he wants a price abatement equal to the cost of remodeling the roof to cause the eaves not to encroach. He has an estimate from a home improvement contractor to do the job for $3,200. Sara objects. What result?

(c) What result in (a) and (b) if the parties signed a contract of sale stating: "If Purchaser furnishes Seller with a written statement of objections to title, and Seller fails to satisfy any valid objections within a reasonable time, then, at the option of Purchaser, upon written notice to Seller, this contract may be cancelled and shall be null and void"?

B. DEED COVENANTS OF TITLE

A *deed* is an instrument that conveys an interest in real estate. Deeds tend to be more standardized than contracts of sale. Printed forms are very often used, not only for residential sales but also for commercial transactions. Deed forms vary substantially from state to state. In many states, a statute specifies a deed form that may be used, with many printed forms following the statutory suggestions.

1. *Warranty Deeds and Quitclaim Deeds*

Among the most important provisions of a deed are its covenants of title, or warranties of title. Their function is to allocate between the parties the risk of problems related to the quality of title that arise at any time after delivery of the deed. The parties should be certain that the deed they use accurately reflects their expectations about title and what should happen if, after closing, a title problem of some sort is discovered.

At common law, no title covenants are implied; they must be express. The buyer, as grantee, must be sure that the deed spells out whatever guarantees of title the seller has undertaken as an express or implied part of their contractual arrangements. This principle is still the baseline American rule, unless changed by statute. In most states today, however, use of a certain phrase or a statutory deed form creates implied title covenants, which the statute specifies. These statutes vary widely from state to state, which is one reason why a lawyer licensed and knowledgeable about local real estate practice should draft or review the parties' deed.

Most deeds have general warranties of title. This means that the grantor's promises as to title are "general" in the sense that they cover the entire chain of title up to the time of delivery. With a *general warranty deed,* there are no time restrictions as to the title defects that are subject to the warranties. This gives the grantee the maximum amount of protection, with the grantor taking on all the title risk.

A *special warranty deed* offers less protection to the grantee than a general warranty deed. Unlike the general warranty deed, in which the grantor assumes all the title risk, the special warranty deed reflects a sharing of title risk between the parties. The warranties under a special warranty deed are limited to title matters arising while the grantor owned the property. All the grantor is promising is that since the moment he acquired title, he has not done anything to dilute or impair that title. In some states, the term *limited warranty deed* is used instead of *special warranty deed.*

A *quitclaim deed* is a deed that has no covenants of title. In contrast to the general warranty deed and the special warranty deed, the grantee bears *all* risk associated with quality of title. If it turns out that the property is subject to liens, encumbrances, or other title defects, the grantor is not liable. Indeed, if the grantor did not own the property at all and a third party has paramount title, the grantor is not responsible — the grantee bears the entire loss.

In thinking about deed covenants, we should consider the prevalence of title insurance in modern real estate transactions. During the past several decades, the institution of title insurance has made deed warranties of title significantly less important than they were years ago. When title insurance is used, the insurance company as third party is being compensated to undertake the risk of title defects. When the buyer obtains a good title insurance policy, the nature and strength of the deed warranties of title are not as great a concern.

EGLI v. TROY

Supreme Court of Iowa, 1999
602 N.W.2d 329

LARSON, Justice. When these plaintiffs, the Eglis, discovered a home being built on land they thought was theirs, they brought an action against the parties building the house, the Troys, as well as other adjoining neighbors, the Ransons, who the Eglis claim were also asserting dominion over some of the Egli land. The Eglis' action was brought under Iowa Code chapter 650 (1995) to establish ownership of the land by acquiescence.

The Troys and Ransons brought in their seller, Rosemary Greve, on a third-party petition asserting breach of a special warranty deed given to the Ransons (who later conveyed part of it to the Troys). The district court, Robert J. Curnan, Judge, entered summary judgment against the Troys and Ransons on their third-party claim against Mrs. Greve. Later, the court [received evidence and] ruled in favor of the Eglis on their claim that the property in question was bounded by a fence line. This is so, according to the court, because the fence line had been established for over ten years and the adjoining owners had acquiesced in the fence as a boundary. We affirm the acquiescence ruling but reverse the summary judgment in favor of the third-party defendant. . . .

The Eglis claim they own [two triangular parcels of land in Dubuque County] because they and their predecessors on the east side of the fence have treated the fence as the boundary, and the Troys, Ransons, and their predecessors on the west side of the fence have acquiesced in that boundary line for over ten years. . . .

When the Ransons purchased their property from Elmer and Rosemary Greve in 1988, part of it was purchased for cash, with a warranty deed, and the balance was purchased on an installment contract. The contract was paid off in 1996. In the meantime, Elmer Greve had died. When the Ransons paid off the contract, a court officer's deed was given to convey Elmer's share of the land to the Ransons. Rosemary Greve conveyed her interest by the special warranty deed now at issue. The deed provided in part:

> Grantors do Hereby Covenant with Grantees and successors in interest to Warrant and Defend the real estate against the lawful claims of all persons claiming by, through or under them, except as may be above stated.

The Ransons, relying on the covenants of this deed, seek protection in the event they lose on the Eglis' claim of title by acquiescence. The district court granted Greve's motion for summary judgment, ruling that Greve could not be held liable under any covenants of the deed because the suit by the Eglis was not a claim by "persons claiming by, through or under" her. . . .

We have not previously considered special warranty deeds under similar circumstances. . . . The Arkansas Supreme Court has stated a special warranty deed "simply warrants the title against all defects therein done *or suffered by* the grantor." Reeves v. Wisconsin & Arkansas Lumber Co., 184 Ark. 254, 42 S.W.2d 11, 12 (1931) (emphasis added).

The issue before us is whether a grantor who has allegedly acquiesced in the establishment of an encumbrance on real estate is responsible for a claim "by, through or under" the vendor, as these third-party petitioners claim. We believe the warranty in this case covers claims permitted by the vendor as well as those affirmatively created by her. If that were not so, encumbrances such as mechanics' liens, which are imposed by others, would be excluded from the warranty. We do not believe that would be a reasonable interpretation of the warranting language.

The third-party defendant, Greve, . . . argues principally that, even assuming acquiescence can give rise to a claim covered by the warranty, any title acquired by her neighbors across the fence through acquiescence occurred long before she and her husband acquired title in 1964. Therefore, according to her, any acquiescence in the boundary line during the time the Greves owned the property would be irrelevant.

The acquiescence, if any, cannot be pinpointed in terms of time. In fact, the district court, in denying the Eglis' motion for summary judgment (in which they attempted to fix a pre-1964 acquiescence as a matter of law) stated, "the court cannot find as a matter of law that the boundaries were established by acquiescence prior to the Greves' 1964 purchase of the . . . property." . . .

. . . A genuine issue of material fact was generated as to whether the Greves were responsible for any part of the ten-year period of acquiescence. It was therefore error for the court to grant summary judgment in favor of Greve. We reverse and remand for further proceedings on the third-party petition. . . .

2. *Types of Covenants*

The law of deeds recognizes six widely recognized covenants of title, each of which may be made general or special by incorporating the proper language for a general warranty or special warranty. Although the parties to a warranty deed are free to tailor their own covenants of title, expressing them as they please, in most transactions a combination of the six standard covenants suffices.

Three of the covenants of title are classified as *present covenants,* which means that the covenant speaks only to the state of affairs at the moment the deed is delivered. If a present covenant is breached, it is breached upon delivery. Thus, the statute of limitations generally begins to run at deed delivery. Present covenants do not run with the land; a grantee may sue only his immediate grantor on a present covenant, even though the statute of limitations has not expired on a covenant in a prior warranty deed in the chain of title. The following are present covenants.

Seisin. Under the covenant of seisin, the grantor promises he is seized of the estate the deed purports to convey. Historically, a person with seisin was in actual possession, claiming a freehold estate. Today, most courts view the covenant of seisin as a promise of good title to the estate.

Right to Convey. Under the covenant of right to convey, the grantor promises that he has the legal right to convey the estate the deed purports to convey.

Covenant against Encumbrances. Under the covenant against encumbrances, the grantor promises that there are no encumbrances on the land. It is generally accepted that the buyer's knowledge of encumbrances at the time of delivery of the deed does not preclude recovery against the grantor under this covenant. However, when the encumbrance is visible, many courts find an implied exception from the covenant against encumbrances.

The next three covenants of title are called *future covenants.* They protect the grantee from certain specified events that may occur after the deed is delivered in the future. Future covenants, in contrast to present covenants, run with the land, meaning that they protect successors in interest to the property. The present owner may sue not only his immediate grantor on a future covenant but also any remote grantor in the chain of title on future covenants contained in the remote grantor's warranty deed.

Covenant of Quiet Enjoyment. Under the covenant of quiet enjoyment, the grantor promises that the grantee may possess and quietly enjoy the land. The covenant of quiet enjoyment is breached if the grantee is actually or constructively evicted from all or part of the land by the grantor, by someone claiming under the grantor, or by someone with paramount title.

Covenant of Warranty. Under the covenant of warranty, the grantor warrants the title to the grantee. Typically, the clause uses the terms "warrant and forever defend" the conveyed land. In most states, this covenant has the same scope as the covenant of quiet enjoyment; it is breached by an actual or constructive eviction of the grantee from all or part of the property. Upon breach, the grantor must pay damages for the grantee's loss of possession.

Covenant for Further Assurances. The remedy for breach of the first five covenants is damages, with most states limiting the grantor's liability to the purchase price received plus statutory interest. Under the covenant of further assurances, the grantor promises to give whatever "further assurances" may be required in the future to vest the grantee with the title the deed purports to convey. In appropriate cases, if the grantor refuses to give further assurances, thus breaching the covenant, the remedy of specific performance is available as an alternative to damages.

Problem 8E

Nicole sells her 640-acre ranch to Kristin, delivering at closing a general warranty deed that contains all six standard title covenants, with no express exceptions. Four months after closing, Kristin discovers two problems. At the time of the conveyance, real estate taxes for the prior year were due and unpaid. Also, a footpath across the ranch goes from a neighbor's parcel to a lake that borders the ranch. It turns out that the neighbor, Ned, has an easement to use the footpath. Kristin demands that Nicole pay the taxes, along with a penalty assessed for late payment; plus, she wants damages due to the effect of the easement on the ranch. Nicole refuses, saying Kristin should have inspected and checked out these problems prior to closing and that merger applies.

(a) Who should prevail? Should it matter whether either party knew prior to closing that: (1) taxes were unpaid; (2) there was a footpath across the ranch; or (3) Ned periodically used the footpath?

(b) The state in which the ranch is located has a two-year statute of limitations for bringing an action on a deed covenant. Assume that Kristin first learns of the footpath easement two and one-half years after the closing when Ned proves that he has an unrecorded grant of easement, signed by Nicole's predecessor in title. Kristin has not seen Ned walking the footpath because he has been in Africa on assignment for the past three years and has left his home vacant. How, if at all, does the passing of time affect your analysis of the situation?

(c) What difference, if any, might it make in (a) and (b) if the transfer from Nicole to Kristin was by special warranty deed rather than by a general warranty deed?

BOOKER T. WASHINGTON CONSTRUCTION & DESIGN COMPANY v. HUNTINGTON URBAN RENEWAL AUTHORITY

Supreme Court of Appeals of West Virginia, 1989
181 W. Va. 409, 383 S.E.2d 41

HURA sold 1st to BTWCD

NEELY, Justice. The City of Huntington sold a parcel of city land to the Huntington Urban Renewal Authority so the latter could redevelop the property for residential use under a federal low interest loan program. The City sold this land by a general warranty deed for one dollar. The Authority executed an agreement to sell the land to the plaintiff/appellee, the Booker T. Washington Building Construction & Design Company, so the latter could improve the property and sell it to a private homeowner. The construction company built a residence but was unable to sell the property to its prospective purchaser because a title search revealed that the Authority had only a life estate in the property. The construction company never acquired title to the property.

The City purchased the property in 1981 from several members of the Mickens family. However, the deed to the City did not include conveyance by persons who were remaindermen under the will of Clarence E. Mickens. On 6 April 1984, the Booker T. Washington Company filed this action in the Circuit Court of Cabell County alleging the City and the Authority breached the contract because the Authority could not convey good and marketable title to the property as required by the contract. The construction company alleged that it suffered lost profits, interest, litigation expenses and other consequential damages. The construction company also alleged a willful and wanton refusal by defendants to cure the defect in the title and sued the City and the Authority for punitive damages. The City was dismissed as a defendant because it was not a party to the contract. However, on 6 September 1984, the Authority sued the City as a third-party defendant, calling upon the City to defend the title and to indemnify the Authority for any damages awarded against it and for costs and legal expenses.

On 4 January 1986, the City filed an action to condemn the property. By an Amended Final Order entered on 7 October 1986, the Circuit Court of Cabell County declared fee simple title to be vested in the City.[3] The City then argued that because it eventually passed good title through its condemnation action, it should be dismissed as a defendant. The Circuit Court of Cabell County agreed and granted summary judgment in favor of the City, dismissing it from the suit.[4] The Authority appeals, assigning as error the circuit court's order granting summary judgment.

The City argues that the filing of the lawsuit by the Booker T. Washington Company was not a sufficient ouster to violate the general warranty covenant. . . .

The requirement that there be an eviction or equivalent disturbance of the enjoyment of the property as a necessary element for a breach of the covenant distinguishes this covenant from the express covenant of seisin. . . . The Authority argues that the lawsuit by the Booker T. Washington Company constituted a constructive eviction while the City argues that no constructive eviction took place. . . .

In the case now before us, the Booker T. Washington Company sued the Authority for a breach of contract based on the Authority's inability to convey a marketable title. The Authority then filed its third-party action against the City for a breach of the general warranty covenant contained in the deed from the City to the Authority. There is one old case from another jurisdiction where the grantor purported to convey a fee but had only title to a life estate and the court held that the covenant of quiet enjoyment was not broken until the life estate expires and the covenantee is evicted. *Maupin* [*on Marketable Title*] at 379, n.22. However, that decision is not binding authority for us, and we believe such a holding to be untenable in this day of frequent land transactions. Certainly today, . . . the right to enjoy one's property necessarily includes the right to sell the property.

. . . Therefore, we hold that when the grantee of real property under a fee simple, general warranty deed contracts to sell the fee to a purchaser and, in fact, the grantee has only a life estate, if the purchaser sues the grantee for

3. Although there was no conveyance by the City to the Authority after the property was condemned, when a vendor acquires title after a conveyance by general warranty deed, the subsequently acquired title inures to the benefit of the purchaser as if it had passed by the original deed. Clark v. Lambert, 55 W. Va. 512, 47 S.E. 312 (1904); Yock v. Mann, 47 W. Va. 187, 49 S.E. 1019 (1905).

4. The court also granted summary judgment in favor of the fourth-party defendant, the law firm that prepared the Abstract of Title for the City.

an inability to convey marketable title, the covenant of general warranty in the deed to the grantee is broken, and the covenantor, upon proper notice, is obligated to defend the title or be answerable to the grantee in damages.

However, two inter-related questions remain: What action was the City bound to take in defending the title?; and, What is the City's potential liability for damages? The Booker T. Washington Company has sought damages from the Authority not for the value of the remainder estate, but consequential damages including lost profits and the value of improvements apparently resulting from the Authority's alleged breach of contract. The City eventually passed good title to the Authority at the successful conclusion of its condemnation action. What further liability, if any, does the City have to the Authority?

The general rule regarding the measure of damages in an action for breach of the covenant of general warranty was stated in Moreland v. Metz, 24 W. Va. 119 (1884):

> If a covenant of warranty is broken in Virginia or West Virginia, the measure of damages, when the land is entirely lost to the vendee, is the purchase money with interest from the date of the actual eviction, the costs incurred in defending the title and such damages as the vendee may have paid or may be shown to be clearly liable to pay the person who evicted him. But if the actual value of the land at the time of the sale be proven to be greater than the purchase-money with interest, & c., perhaps this actual value might be recovered in lieu of the usual measure of recovery. [Citations omitted.]

Damages Rule

Id. at 137–38.[10] If the purchaser suffers only a partial eviction, the measure of damages is the portion of the purchase money that represents the relative value of the land (or interest) lost compared to the value of the whole land (or interest). Butcher v. Peterson, 26 W. Va. 447 at 455 (1885). . . .

In the case sub judice, the City did eventually correct the deficiency in the title through its condemnation action and passed fee simple title to the Authority. The general warranty covenant given the Authority by the City does not mean that the City must completely indemnify the Authority. The action against the Authority by Booker T. Washington Company is based on a breach of contract to which the City is not a party, and the plaintiff is claiming several types of consequential and punitive damages. Although these damages might stem from the inability of the Authority to convey marketable title, they are not damages that can be awarded the Authority against the City for a breach of the latter's general warranty. The damages for

10. The minority rule, followed by some of the New England states, is that the measure of damages for a breach of general warranty is the value of the land at the time of eviction, including the value of any improvements made before the eviction. 24 W. Va. at 138-39; [6A] *Powell* [*on Real Property*] at 81A-148; Maupin, *supra* at 424-27.

which the City might be liable under its general warranty of title are limited to the value of the remainder estate at the time of conveyance as determined from the actual value of the fee simple estate (the consideration paid is prima facie but not conclusive evidence of the actual value of the fee) and the costs and reasonable attorneys' fees expended by the Authority to determine the actual state of the title to the land.

Because the City was successful in condemning the land and eventually passed fee simple title, the City thereby mitigated its damages. However, because the City was put on notice (by being named a party defendant) that the title was allegedly defective, it should have initiated the condemnation action (or taken other ameliorative action) immediately rather than waiting more than a year and a half before doing so. Therefore, should the Booker T. Washington Company recover damages from the Authority, the City will be liable to the Authority for interest on the value of the remainder estate from the date an answer was due on the plaintiff's original complaint until the final order in the condemnation action. In addition, the City will also be liable to the Authority for costs and reasonable attorneys' fees incurred by the Authority not to defend the breach of contract action, but to determine that the title to the property was defective. . . .

. . . If the Authority had desired to protect itself against the eventuality of a lawsuit and recovery against it by the construction company, it should have purchased title insurance before buying the property from the City. Commercial parties should know enough to purchase title insurance, particularly when planning to improve property. The concept of a general warranty deed is in many ways obsolete today, when title insurance can be purchased at a modest price with an almost absolute guarantee against title defects because title insurance lawyers seldom make mistakes.

Accordingly, the Circuit Court of Cabell County's award of summary judgment to the City of Huntington is reversed and the case is remanded for further proceedings consistent with this opinion.

Problem 8F

In 2003, Alice sells Orangeacre to Brian for $60,000 using a general warranty deed with all six covenants of title. In 2005, Brian sells Orangeacre to Chris for $70,000 using a special warranty deed with all six covenants of title. In 2006, Chris sells Orangeacre to Donna for $80,000 using a quitclaim deed. In 2007, Nasty, a neighbor, relocates his fence, moving it ten feet past the boundary line described in the deeds to Orangeacre. It turns out that Nasty has had paramount title to the ten-foot strip since 2001. Does Donna have a cause of action against any of the prior owners for loss of the ten-foot strip? If so, is there a limit to the amount of damages she may recover?

MAGUN v. BOMBACI

Superior Court of Connecticut, Judicial District of New Haven, 1985
40 Conn. Supp. 269, 492 A.2d 235

HIGGINS, Judge. The plaintiffs purchased the subject real estate, with dwelling house and improvements located thereon, by general warranty deed from the defendants on August 4, 1978. Among other provisions, the deed provided "... *with the buildings and all other improvements thereon*. . . ." (Emphasis added.) The premises were conveyed free and clear of all encumbrances, except as mentioned in the deed. The deed contained no reference to the location of the driveway and/or sewer lines, or any other improvement.

From the evidence, it is established that part of the driveway and portions of the sewer lateral line were, in fact, located on property adjacent to the subject premises. This is the condition that existed when the defendants purchased the property in 1973 from the Stone Construction Company and when they sold the property to the plaintiffs in 1978. The evidence does not establish that the defendants had any definitive information concerning the driveway and sewer line problems until after they sold the property to the plaintiffs.

The plaintiffs base their claim for damages on the theory in law that this factual situation raises a breach of the covenant against encumbrances.

An encumbrance includes every right to or interest in land which may subsist in third persons to the diminution of the value of the land, but consistent with the passing of the fee. Aczas v. Stuart Heights, Inc., 154 Conn. 54, 60, 221 A.2d 589 (1966). It must be a lawful claim or demand enforceable against the grantee. Straite v. Smith, 95 Conn. 470, 472, 111 A. 799 (1920). The location of the driveway and sewer lines partially on the property belonging to another does not constitute an encumbrance against the fee herein conveyed.

The habendum clause in the deed granted to the plaintiffs "the above . . . bargained premises with the appurtenances thereof. . . ." The plaintiff claims that sewer and driveway that encroach or are located on another's property are so related to the reasonable use of the bargained for property that they constitute appurtenances thereof. In effect, the plaintiffs claim that the defendants' lack of ownership of a portion of these alleged appurtenances constitutes an encumbrance on the property conveyed.

For something to pass appurtenant to land, two conditions must be satisfied: it must be something (1) which the grantor has the power to convey, and (2) which is reasonably necessary to the enjoyment of the thing granted. Gager v. Carlson, 146 Conn. 288, 292–93, 150 A.2d 302 (1959); Whittelsey v. Porter, 82 Conn. 95, 101, 72 A. 593 (1909). Although the evidence would satisfy the second prong of this test, the defendants in no way had any power to convey that part of the driveway and sewer line located on property of another.

It is evident that this situation has resulted from misapprehension of the parties as to what the actual factual situation was. The complaint in no sense raises any question of fraud or misrepresentation, nor, indeed, does the evidence tend to sustain any such theory of recovery.

The court recognizes that there are cases that appear to hold that the encroachment of a building on the purchaser's land upon adjacent property does constitute a violation of the covenant against encumbrances. Jones v. Carlson, 17 Conn. Sup. 109 (1950); Gamorsil Realty Corporation v. Graef, 128 Misc. 596, 597, 220 N.Y.S. 221 (1926); Fehlhaber v. Fehlhaber, 80 Misc. 149, 150, 140 N.Y.S. 973 (1913). It appears, however, that the result in Burke v. Nichols, 41 N.Y. 670, 1 Abb. App. 260 (N.Y. 1866), is more nearly in conformity with Connecticut precedent as spelled out in *Whittelsey*. In that case, the house on the conveyed property encroached on adjoining land. The purchaser claimed that this encroachment constituted a breach of the covenants of the deed. That court disagreed and held that the rule was that land does not pass as an appurtenant to land. Since the adjoining land was not conveyed or described by the deed, the plaintiff had no claim against the defendant by reason of the failure of title to that portion of the house and fence that stood thereon. The court noted that no action could have been maintained for the breach of any of the covenants of the deed.

This court opines that this may be the core reason why many wise purchasers require a survey to establish the location of the improvements on land sought for purchase.

Accordingly, this court concludes that the evidence fails to establish a cause of action upon which relief can be granted. Judgment is hereby rendered in favor of the named defendants.

Problem 8G

Two years ago Jack and Diane Wood bought a single-family home, located on Lot 3, from Tom and Sue Tanner. Interest rates have fallen and the Woods plan to refinance their home mortgage loan. At their rear, the Woods' lot borders Lot 17, which is owned by Paul and Paula Pound. Last week, the Woods ordered a new survey of Lot 3, which disclosed that the Pounds' fence encroaches on their backyard by approximately ten inches for the entire 80-foot length of the rear boundary line. The Woods' new lender refuses to close the mortgage loan unless the matter of the fence encroachment is cleared up. The Woods ask the Pounds to move the fence to where it belongs, but they refuse, claiming they have acquired title to the strip by adverse possession.

Research indicates that James and Sara Coleman, predecessors in title to Lot 17, bought that lot 13 years ago from Dandy Developer. A year later, they hired a contractor to build the fence. Two years ago, they conveyed Lot 17 to the Pounds. Fifteen years ago, Dandy Developer conveyed Lot 3 with a completed house to Susan Block. Ten years ago, Block conveyed to the Tanners. All the deeds in the chain of title for both lots, back to Dandy Developer, are general warranty deeds, each containing all six standard covenants. Do the Woods have a cause of action against any of their grantors, immediate or remote? Do the Pounds have a cause of action against any of their grantors? The jurisdiction has a 3-year statute of limitations for contract claims and a 10-year statute of limitations for recovering possession of land.

9

Land Descriptions

A. TYPES OF DESCRIPTIONS

Both real estate contracts and deeds must contain a description of the land. This is also true for other instruments that involve real property, such as mortgages, leases, covenants, and easements. The land description, often called the *legal description,* is a crucial part of the transaction. One of the requirements imposed by the statute of frauds is a written description; it is not sufficient that the parties orally agree to the location and size of the parcel.

There are three methods of land description in widespread use today. The oldest method is the *metes and bounds description,* which describes every boundary line of the parcel. It tells the reader how to draw a square, rectangle, or other geometric shape on the face of the earth. The description starts at a point of beginning, which is usually a corner of the parcel adjoining a public road. Each boundary line is defined by length and "course" (direction given by reference to a compass). See Figure 9-1. Surveyors indicate the course by divergence from the north-south line. In most communities today, surveyors use true north-south, rather than magnetic north-south.

All boundaries do not have to be straight lines. Many parcels adjoin bodies of water, where the boundary is defined by some aspect of the water's edge, which is irregular. On dry land, surveyors draw curved boundary lines, defining the curve by reference to an imaginary circle, which is specified by arc, chord, and radius. For an example, see the survey at page 218.

The second method of legal description is the *Government Survey System.* Developed by Thomas Jefferson for the Northwest Territories in 1785, the system divides land into townships and sections, using a system of square and rectangular grids. The federal government subsequently extended the scheme to much of the midwestern and western parts of the United States. The starting point for every government survey description is the intersection of a principal meridian (P.M.), a line of longitude which runs north-south, and a baseline (B.L.), a line of latitude which runs east-west.

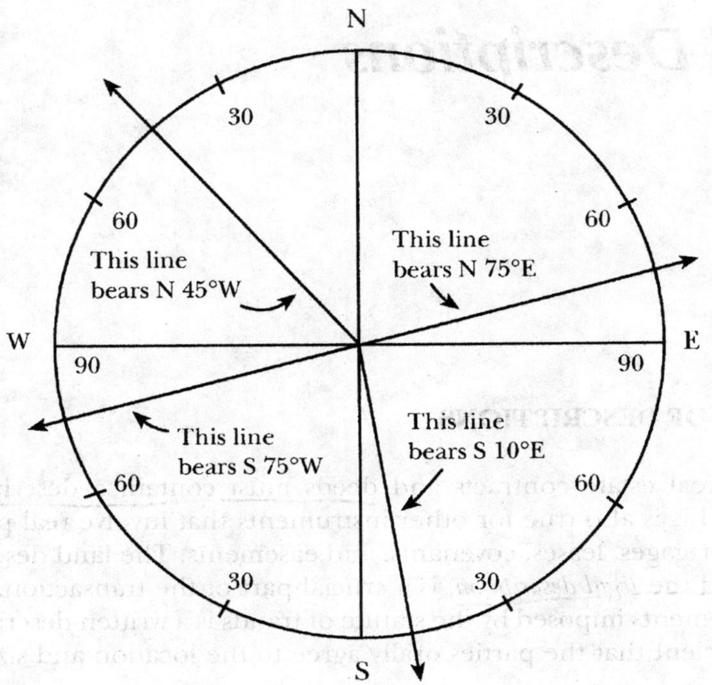

The circle has 360 degrees. Each degree contains 60 minutes, and each minute contains 60 seconds. All survey lines that are not due north, south, east, or west are described by the angle of divergence from the north-south axis.

Figure 9-1
Directions of Survey Lines

Each principal meridian and baseline is identified by a distinctive number or name. See Figure 9-2.

Under the government survey system, the basic units of area are *townships* and *sections.* Each township is a square with sides that are approximately six miles (we say "approximately" because small corrections are occasionally necessary to accommodate projection of the system on the globe). Each township is located by reference to the intersection of a principal residence and baseline.

Notice that the term *range* denotes distance east-west along the baseline, and *township* denotes distance north-south along the principal meridian. An unfortunate feature of the government survey system is its use of the word "township" with two meanings: a unit of area (36 square miles) and a unit of distance (6-mile north-south increments).

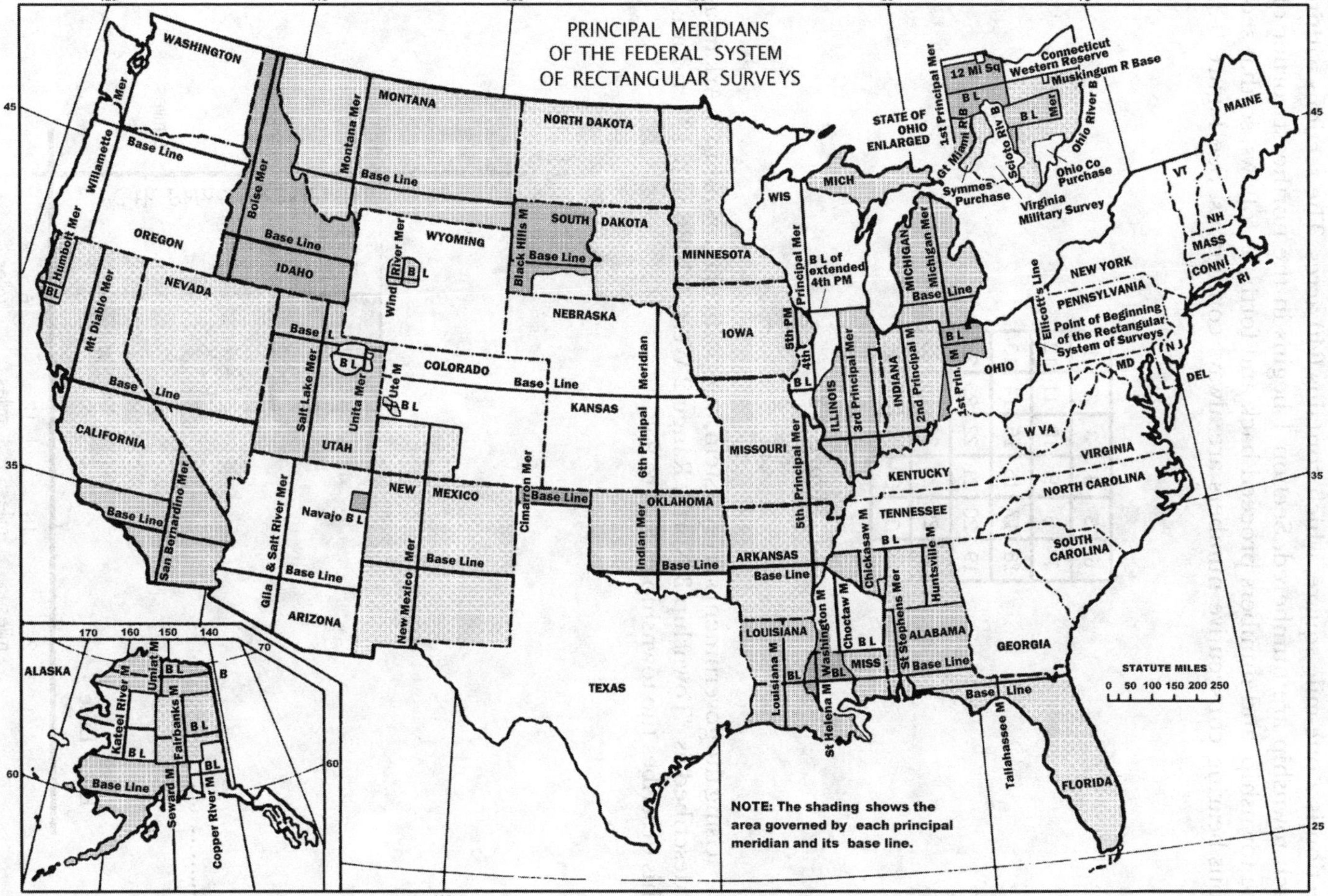
PRINCIPAL MERIDIANS
OF THE FEDERAL SYSTEM
OF RECTANGULAR SURVEYS
WASHINGTON
Willamette Mer
Base Line
OREGON
Humbolt Mer
BL
MONTANA
Montana Mer
Base Line
Boise Mer
Base Line
IDAHO
NORTH DAKOTA
SOUTH DAKOTA
Black Hills M
Base Line
WYOMING
Wind River Mer
B L
NEVADA
Mt Diablo Mer
Base Line
CALIFORNIA
San Bernardino Mer
Base Line
Salt Lake Mer
Uinta Mer
UTAH
Ute M
B L
COLORADO
NEBRASKA
KANSAS
Base Line
6th Prinipal Meridian
Cimarron Mer
Base Line
OKLAHOMA
Indian Mer
Base Line
Gila & Salt River Mer
Base Line
ARIZONA
Navajo B L
NEW MEXICO
New Mexico Mer
Base Line
TEXAS
MINNESOTA
IOWA
5th PM
4th
Principal Mer
B L of extended 4th PM
WIS
MISSOURI
5th Principal Mer
ARKANSAS
Base Line
LOUISIANA
Louisiana M
St Helena M
Washington M
MICH
MICHIGAN
Michigan Mer
Base Line
ILLINOIS
3rd Principal Mer
INDIANA
2nd Principal M
1st Prin. M
B L
OHIO
KENTUCKY
TENNESSEE
Chickasaw M
B L
Huntsville M
MISS
Choctaw M
St Stephens Mer
ALABAMA
Base Line
Tallahassee M
Base Line
FLORIDA
GEORGIA
SOUTH CAROLINA
NORTH CAROLINA
VIRGINIA
W VA
MD
DEL
N J
PENNSYLVANIA
NEW YORK
Ellicott's Line
Point of Beginning of the Rectangular System of Surveys
CONN
RI
MASS
NH
VT
MAINE
STATE OF OHIO ENLARGED
1st Principal Mer
12 Mi Sq
Connecticut Western Reserve
Muskingum R Base
Ohio River B
Gt Miami R B
Scioto Riv B
Symmes Purchase
Virginia Military Survey
Ohio Co Purchase
ALASKA
Kateel River M
Umiat M
Fairbanks M
Seward M
Copper River M
Base Line
STATUTE MILES
0 50 100 150 200 250
NOTE: The shading shows the area governed by each principal meridian and its base line.
Longitude West 95 from Greenwich

Figure 9-2

Each township is divided into 36 sections. This means that each section is a one-mile square, which contains 640 acres. The sections within each township are numbered. Section 1 begins in the northeast corner of the township, and numbers proceed back and forth, as follows, so that sections bearing consecutive numbers are always contiguous. See Figure 9-3.

6	5	4	3	2	1
7	8	9	10	11	12
18	17	16	15	14	13
19	20	21	22	23	24
30	29	28	27	26	25
31	32	33	34	35	36

Figure 9-3

Using the government survey system, one particular township in Arkansas is described as "Township 3 North, Range 2 West, 5th Principal Meridian." This describes the township in Figure 9-4.

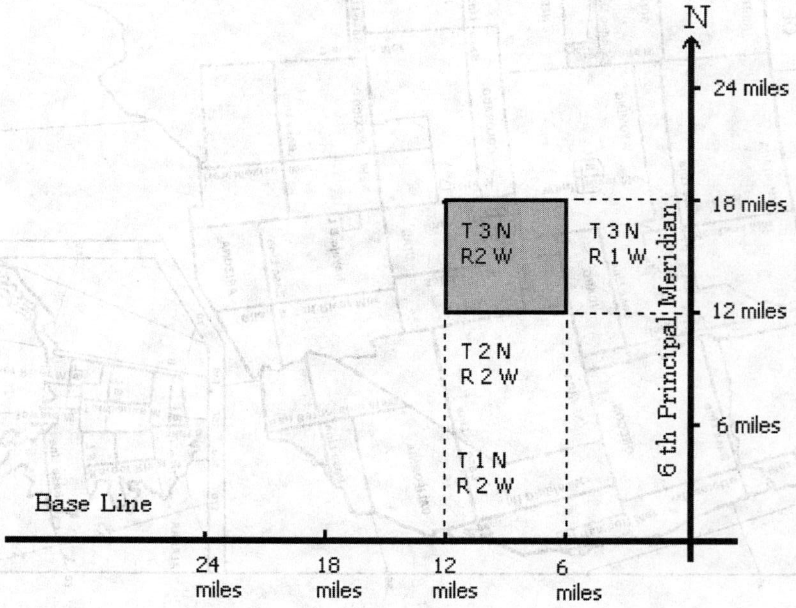

Figure 9-4

Farmland, ranchland, and other rural lands are commonly sold in full sections and subparts of sections. The subparts typically used are half sections, quarter sections, and smaller square and rectangular units. In the Arkansas township mentioned above, one may convey part of a particular section using the following description: "The southern half of the northeast quarter of Section 17, Township 3 North, Range 2 West, 5th Principal Meridian." Abbreviations are commonly used. Thus, this description may be written as: "S 1/2 NE 1/4, §17, T.3N., R.2W., 5th P.M." Look at Figure 9-5 to see if you can identify this land. It is customary to add the name of the county and state where the land is located, but legally this is not necessary. (Do you understand why?)

The third method of legal description is by reference to subdivision maps, or *plats,* which are filed as part of the public land records. Lots in the subdivision are then described by referring to the recorded plat. Much urban and suburban land, both residential and commercial, is described by this method.

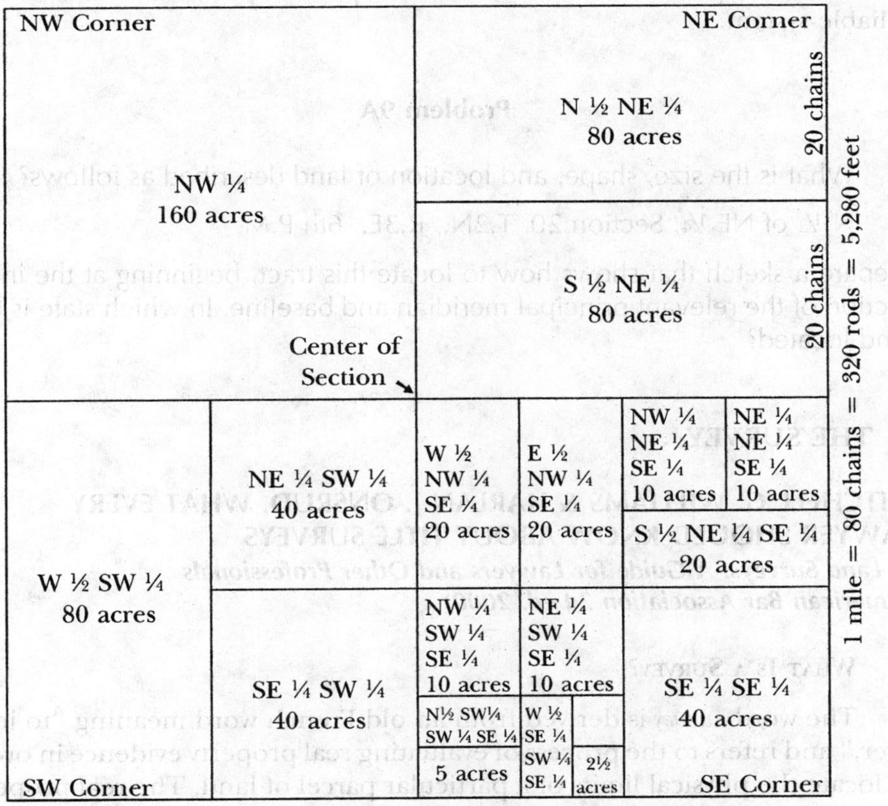

Figure 9-5
Section of Land (640 acres), Government Survey System

A good land description, it is often said, describes one and only one parcel of land. It permits the reader to find the described parcel, to the exclusion of all other parcels of land in the world. As a matter of logic, this means that all the boundary lines of the parcel must be capable of identification on the ground. One must be able to tell where one parcel stops and the neighboring parcels begin. The land near the boundary counts as part of the described land just as much as the land near the middle.

Boundaries must be identified to describe adequately a parcel of land. Thus, all good land descriptions are metes and bounds descriptions, either directly or because they are reducible to metes and bounds descriptions. Descriptions under the Government Survey System and by reference to subdivision plats, when properly crafted, work because they enable a reader to draw all the boundary lines. In each case, the reader must look not only at the deed but also at the Government Survey System reference points or the recorded subdivision plat; when this is done, the reader in effect has found a metes and bounds description for the subject parcel. The virtue of Government Survey descriptions and subdivision plat descriptions is efficiency. Both function as a type of shorthand as they incorporate by reference an external, reliable system.

Problem 9A

What is the size, shape, and location of land described as follows?

N ½ of NE ¼, Section 20, T.2N., R.3E., 6th P.M.

Prepare a sketch that shows how to locate this tract, beginning at the intersection of the relevant principal meridian and baseline. In which state is this land located?

B. THE SURVEY

MITCHELL G. WILLIAMS & HARLAN J. ONSRUD, WHAT EVERY LAWYER SHOULD KNOW ABOUT TITLE SURVEYS

in Land Surveys: A Guide for Lawyers and Other Professionals (American Bar Association 2d ed. 2000)

WHAT IS A SURVEY?

The word *survey* is derived from an old French word meaning "to look over," and refers to the process of evaluating real property evidence in order to locate the physical limits of a particular parcel of land. The real property evidence considered by the surveyor typically consists of physical field evidence, written record evidence, and field measurements. The surveyor, having made an evaluation of the evidence, forms an opinion as to where he believes a court of law would locate the boundary lines of the property. The typical modern day surveyor sees himself as an expert evaluator of evidence, and would expect to arrive at the same opinion of boundary location regardless of who commissioned the survey. The surveyor's opinion is founded on experience and applicable legal precedents; unlike the attorney, the surveyor does not see himself primarily as an advocate for his client. . . .

. . . The evaluation of land surveying evidence is not a "science" in the sense that there is one procedure to follow which will yield the "correct" result. Surveyors occasionally disagree on the proper location of a boundary line — not necessarily because one surveyor measures better than the other, but more commonly because each surveyor has weighed the evidence differently and has formed different opinions. Just as two lawyers may draw different conclusions from the same line of cases, surveyors may disagree about the appropriate location for a boundary. Being a professional opinion, a survey is subject to review by a court in the event that a boundary dispute reaches litigation. Because a survey is primarily a professional opinion, the attorney should remember that a survey and supporting documentation provided by one professional surveyor may be far superior or far inferior to that provided by another. Almost any field technician with basic training can make measurements with an acceptable degree of precision and replicability. In those instances in which locating the bounds of a land parcel requires an extensive amount of evidence evaluation, an individual with the requisite amount of education, knowledge, and experience should be employed to accomplish the survey with competence.

Why a Survey?

There are five fundamental reasons for requiring land surveys in real estate transactions:

1. The Existence of the Property

Nearly all titles to land in the United States depend on an original grant or patent and subsequent conveyance instruments. All of these instruments contain descriptions of the land conveyed. It is a fundamental principle that for a deed to be valid it must contain a sufficient description. Whether a metes and bounds description or a description by reference to a parcel on a map is sufficient to transfer the property often depends upon whether a knowledgeable surveyor can interpret the description to reasonably locate the property physically on the ground. In determining whether the land description is reasonably clear, the surveyor determines whether the land description forms a mathematically closed figure and whether the description reasonably conforms to the physical evidence on the earth's surface. The first is done by numeric calculation, the second by a physical measurement process in the field.

2. THE RELATIONSHIP OF THE PROPERTY TO ADJOINING PROPERTIES

Merely locating the lines described in a deed on the ground is not adequate to establish the physical limits of a property owner's interest. All parcels of land exist in relation to the parcels surrounding them. Surrounding parcels may include privately or publicly owned lands, rights-of-way, easements, roads, and water bodies. At some point in the past, all adjoining land parcels were held in common by a single grantor. Over time, parcels were partitioned off or subdivided to arrive at the current ownership configuration. As a general rule, the description in a senior deed or prior conveyance controls over any discrepancy in a later one. If the drafter made an error or created an ambiguity in describing a parcel being partitioned off from a larger parcel, or made an error in a later attempt to "correct" or refine an earlier description, the legal descriptions of adjoining parcels may be inconsistent. Their "common" boundary may in fact either overlap or not meet. Failure to discover overlaps may leave the holder of the junior deed owning much less property than the junior deed on its face would indicate. The presence of gaps or gores also poses problems when attempting to consolidate several adjacent parcels under a single owner for development purposes. When consolidation is attempted, one must definitively establish ownership to these leftover land strips. If a gore exists along a street line or right-of-way, it has the potential of creating a landlocked parcel.

3. THE RELATIONSHIP OF OCCUPIED LINES TO RECORD LINES

Not infrequently, the boundary lines of a parcel as physically occupied or possessed by its owner differ from the distances and direction or the monuments called for in the deed. Discrepancies between possession and the record deed lines may range from minor variations in fence line locations to substantial encroachments of multi-story buildings. A land survey should always show the occupied lines, the deed record lines, and the extent of any mismatch. Significant mismatches suggest potential claims of ownership by senior right or adverse possession, or a change in a boundary line by mutual agreement and acquiescence. To cut off any potential rights of another to a claim of adverse possession, the property owner may want to record an appropriate document confirming his claim of ownership or seek a change in possession to match the record lines.

4. THE LOCATION OF PHYSICAL IMPROVEMENTS

This reason for requiring a survey is related to the previous one, but deals with the relationship of all physical improvements on the parcel to the boundary lines of the parcel, not just those improvements near the exterior limits of the parcel. Features which surveyors are often requested to locate include fences, walls, driveways, pavements, buildings, structures, utilities, wells, and natural features such as streams and ponds. This information is necessary to determine the presence of features which may limit the value or use of the property and to determine conformity with local ordinances regarding minimum building setbacks. When most attorneys and lay persons think of a survey, this is the type of information they expect to see on the surveyor's final survey map.

5. UNRECORDED EASEMENTS AND OTHER FACTS NOT OF RECORD

There are numerous unrecorded rights that can affect title to land which may not show up in a title search but will become obvious upon an inspection of the property. The right of a neighbor to use utility lines, drainage ditches, sewer lines, and unrecorded travel easements across the property may have arisen by prescription or other methods of unwritten land transfer. A visual inspection of the property will usually give some physical indication as to whether such adverse rights may exist; e.g., the presence of manholes or vent pipes suggest[s] underground sewers or utilities. Typically, only a survey in which unrecorded physical features are referenced to the property lines will induce a title insurance company to remove its exception in regard to "any state of facts an accurate survey might show."

Types of Surveys

The above five reasons for obtaining a survey are fundamental in the case of a title survey or boundary survey. For construction or engineering surveys, the concerns are different, and a survey prepared for an architect or consulting engineer will normally have vastly different standards than a title survey. Therefore, an attorney who uses an engineering survey to advise a client about boundary and title questions flirts with malpractice. For example, a topographic survey usually indicates the contour, shape, and physical features of the ground within certain boundaries; absent some statement to the contrary, the preparer of such a survey does not concern himself with the question of the legal location of the boundary lines and adjoining lots. The topographic survey, like the "plot plan," is designed to aid an architect or engineer in the design and layout of a building, not to give a professional opinion on the location of the boundaries. Some attorneys believe that if they acquire an "as-built" survey, they have acquired the highest quality survey available. An "as-built" survey, however, is merely a detailed map of a building or other improvement and its relation, as built, to the plans it was built from. It may appear complex and comprehensive to lay persons, but its preparation probably addressed few or no boundary or title concerns. The purpose of an "as-built" survey is to determine if the completed project accords with previously approved plans and specifications.

The Presumed Priority of Conflicting Title Elements That Determine Boundary Location

A surveyor is guided by legal principles in his evaluation of the evidence for a boundary line location. One such principle is the presumed priority of conflicting title elements that determine boundary line location. A right of ownership can arise from two sources: by written means (such as a deed or written boundary line agreement) or by unwritten means (such as adverse possession). The resolution of conflicts between written and unwritten rights is one of the most difficult problems for both surveyors and lawyers. . . .

When such a conflict occurs, it is necessary to decide which terms were intended to control and which terms were informational. Which term is controlling is generally determined by its order of importance as determined by the courts. One summarized listing of a judge-made priority ranking among the terms of a deed is as follows:

1. Call for a survey
2. Call for monuments
   a. Natural
   b. Artificial
   c. Record boundaries (in the event of a gap)
3. Calls for Directions and Distances
4. Calls for Directions
5. Calls for Distance
6. Call for Coordinates
7. Call for Area

If the results obtained by adhering to the above ranking are clearly contrary to the overall intent expressed in the deed, however, the clearly stated contrary intent expressed in the deed will control.

The above priorities are based on assumptions about the relative certainty of each type of evidence. The presumption that directions should control when in conflict with distances is based on the assumption that angles and bearings can be determined more precisely than distances. In some jurisdictions, however, directions were historically observed with an imprecise magnetic compass and distances were measured with a precise steel tape; in these jurisdictions, courts held that distances should control over directions when in conflict. It makes sense that when the reasons for adhering to the presumed priority ranking no longer exist, the presumed ranking should fail and the best available evidence should prevail.

Sample Evaluation of a Property Line Fact Situation

In order to illustrate the land surveyor's use of the foregoing rankings in arriving at an opinion as to where property ownership lines are likely to lie, we present the following hypothetical facts. Alice owns the large parcel of land showing in Figure 1. The parcel was surveyed and corners monumented in 1932. There are no conflicts between Alice's lines and those of her neighbors. Alice sells a portion of her parcel to Betty in 1960. The land description in Betty's deed from Alice reads as follows:

> Beginning at the NW corner of Alice's property as marked by a 2" iron pipe; thence East along the centerline of White Road 400 feet to the center of the

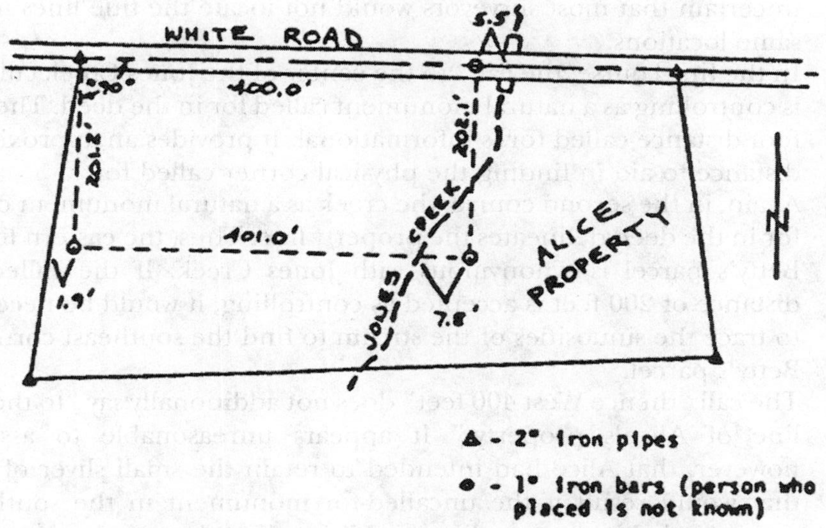

Figure 1

Jones Creek culvert; thence South 200 feet along Jones Creek; thence West 400 feet; thence North 200 feet to the point of beginning.

The field survey exposes the information shown in Figure 1. There is little or no possession evidence along Betty's lines other than the evidence shown: i.e., there are no fences, tree lines, hedges, or evidence of cultivation along her lines. There is absolutely no field or record evidence to suggest that Jones Creek has significantly changed its course since 1960.

How might a surveyor reasonably evaluate this evidence? One of the surveyor's obligations in accomplishing a land survey is to locate the title lines and then locate occupation lines in respect to those title lines. Under the fact situation presented, it is proper to consult only the terms of Betty's deed description in locating the title lines.

- The call for the 2-inch iron pipe is a call for an artificial monument, and if the surveyor can establish that the iron pipe actually found is the pipe called for in the deed, it fixes the location of the point of beginning. The found 1-inch diameter iron bars are not called for in the deed and, therefore, are not legally artificial monuments. There is nothing to suggest that they were set during a survey except that the bars are of a material and size typically used by surveyors in marking property corners and the bars are in the approximate locations where a current survey would place Betty's property corners. These uncalled-for monuments should be accepted as marking the southerly line of Betty's parcel only if the lines of this parcel are so uncertain that most surveyors would not locate the title lines in the same locations.

- In the first course, the call "to the center of the Jones Creek culvert" is controlling as a natural monument called for in the deed. The 400-foot distance called for is informational. It provides an approximate distance to aid in finding the physical corner called for.
- Again, in the second course, the creek as a natural monument called for in the deed delineates the property line. Thus, the eastern line of Betty's parcel is synonymous with Jones Creek. If the called for distance of 200 feet is accepted as controlling, it would be necessary to trace the sinuosities of the stream to find the southeast corner of Betty's parcel.
- The call "thence West 400 feet" does not additionally say "to the east line of Alice's property." It appears unreasonable to assume, however, that Alice had intended to retain the small sliver of land that would result if the uncalled-for monument in the southwest corner is held as controlling. Additionally, when measured along Betty's southerly line, the creek is less than 400 feet away from Alice's west property line. Therefore Betty's parcel appears to be defined on its west end by Alice's west property line.
- The only side of Betty's parcel yet to be located is the southerly boundary. When considering the overall written intentions of the parties to the deed, it appears that the parties intended to partition off a parcel in the northwest portion of Alice's property bounded by Jones Creek on the east, bounded by Alice's west line on the west, and having dimensions of approximately 400 feet by 200 feet.
- The sequence of the calls in a description is generally held by the courts to be immaterial. Therefore, reading the description backwards, one possible location for Betty's southwest corner is at a distance of 200 feet from the point of beginning along Alice's west property line. It would then appear reasonable to define the southerly line of Betty's parcel by a line extended from this monument and running easterly parallel to White Road. This would result in a configuration for the parcel in close agreement with the overall written intent of the parties.
- In the alternative, the court might find the southerly line of Betty's parcel to lie a perpendicular distance of 200 feet from and run parallel with the centerline of White Road. Because the grantor had the responsibility for making the description clear and failed to do so, any ambiguity in the description should be resolved in favor of the grantee. This configuration also closely agrees with the overall written intent of the parties. This is the solution that a large number of surveyors would probably reach.
- In some eastern states, particularly in rural areas, uncalled for monuments tend to carry substantial weight in the courts. In such

> jurisdictions, the court would probably strive to hold a straight line passing through the two 1-inch diameter bars as defining Betty's southerly property line. Due to the inconsistency in the dimensions between the monuments along the east and west bounds, however, it appears unlikely that a surveyor set the bars. They probably were set by a lay person to mark the approximate locations of the property corners and never intended to mark the precise actual locations of the corners. Under these facts, the 1" iron bars should not be held as marking the location of Betty's southerly line.

The primary purposes in presenting the preceding example are to illustrate the thought processes that a surveyor goes through in evaluating property line evidence and to stress that the location of property lines is more often a matter of legal opinion than scientific fact. . . .

Problem 9B

Study the survey set forth in Figure 9-6 (page 218) from the standpoint of a potential purchaser. How much does the survey tell you about the tract it describes? Review the five reasons listed by Williams and Onsrud for obtaining a survey. Does the survey satisfy all five criteria?

C. LEGAL ADEQUACY OF DESCRIPTION

Under the statute of frauds, all writings that affect title to land must contain a written description of the land. This is true not only for deeds but also for other instruments that usually are recorded — for example, easements, covenants, and mortgages — as well as instruments that usually are not recorded, such as leases and contracts of sale.

Most statutes of fraud in the United States are tailored on the English model, enacted in 1677. The English statute of frauds treated contracts and conveyances in separate sections, and this separation remains a feature of modern U.S. statutory law governing real estate transactions. With respect to contracts for the sale of interests in land, the statute of frauds for contracts requires a memorandum, which as one of its elements must include a written description of the land. With respect to conveyances, a separate statute specifies the formal requisites for deeds and other instruments of conveyance; again, one of the requisites is a written land description. In most states, neither the contract statute of frauds nor the conveyance statute of frauds provides any express standard for assessing the sufficiency of the land description. This responsibility devolves to the courts. In most states, the judicially enunciated standards and interpretational rules appear to be

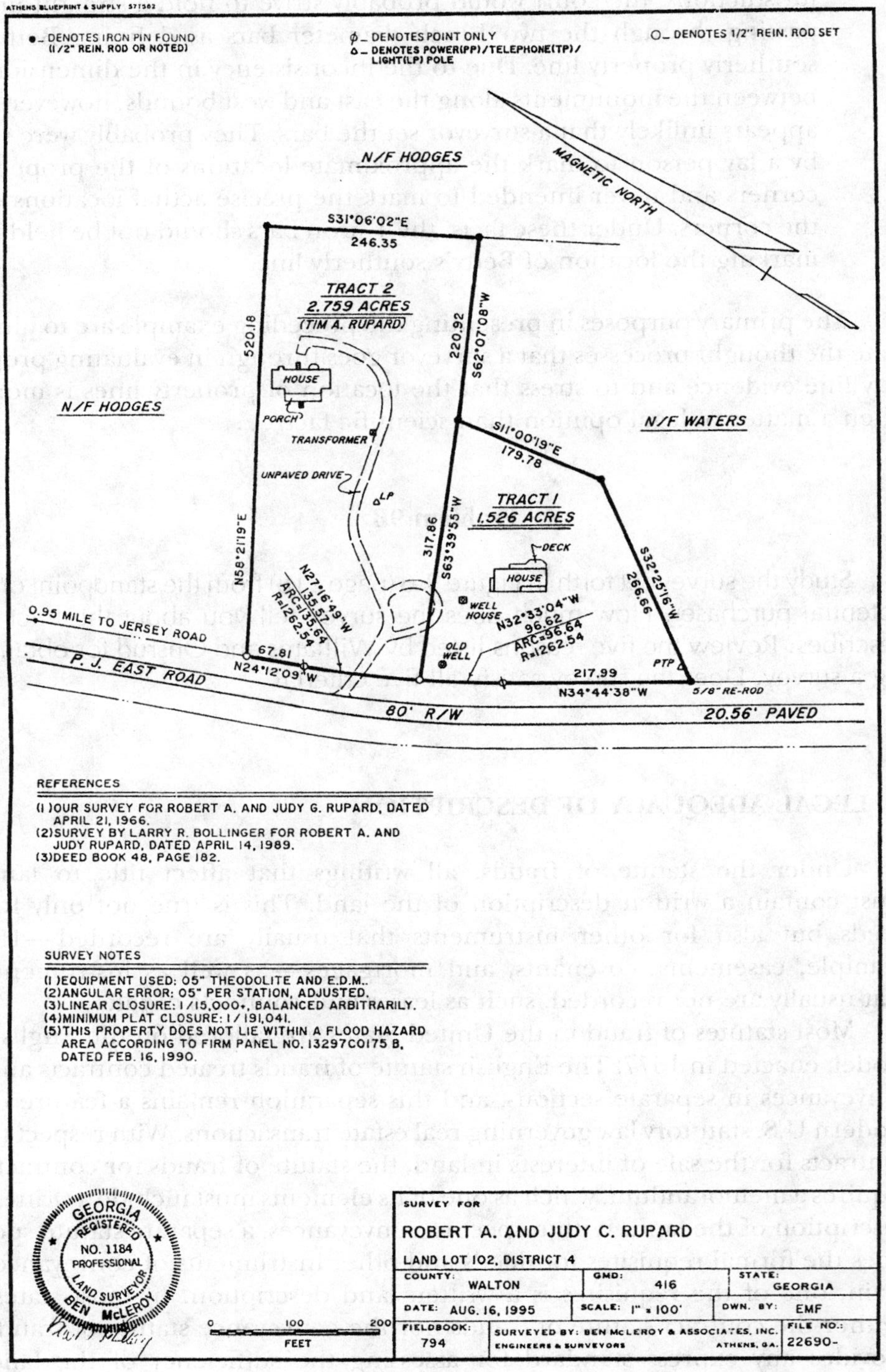
ATHENS BLUEPRINT & SUPPLY 577582
● – DENOTES IRON PIN FOUND (1/2" REIN. ROD OR NOTED)
ϕ – DENOTES POINT ONLY
δ – DENOTES POWER(PP)/TELEPHONE(TP)/LIGHT(LP) POLE
O – DENOTES 1/2" REIN. ROD SET
MAGNETIC NORTH
N/F HODGES
S31°06'02"E
246.35
TRACT 2
2.759 ACRES
(TIM A. RUPARD)
520.18
220.92
S62°07'08"W
HOUSE
PORCH
N/F HODGES
TRANSFORMER
N/F WATERS
S11°00'19"E
179.78
UNPAVED DRIVE
LP
TRACT 1
1.526 ACRES
317.86
S63°39'55"W
N58°21'19"E
DECK
HOUSE
S32°25'16"W
266.66
N27°16'49"W
135.57
ARC=135.64
R=1262.54
WELL HOUSE
N32°33'04"W
96.62
ARC=96.64
R=1262.54
0.95 MILE TO JERSEY ROAD
OLD WELL
67.81
N24°12'09"W
217.99
PTP
P. J. EAST ROAD
N34°44'38"W
5/8" RE-ROD
80' R/W
20.56' PAVED
REFERENCES
(1) OUR SURVEY FOR ROBERT A. AND JUDY G. RUPARD, DATED APRIL 21, 1966.
(2) SURVEY BY LARRY R. BOLLINGER FOR ROBERT A. AND JUDY RUPARD, DATED APRIL 14, 1989.
(3) DEED BOOK 48, PAGE 182.
SURVEY NOTES
(1) EQUIPMENT USED: 05" THEODOLITE AND E.D.M..
(2) ANGULAR ERROR: 05" PER STATION, ADJUSTED.
(3) LINEAR CLOSURE: 1/15,000+, BALANCED ARBITRARILY.
(4) MINIMUM PLAT CLOSURE: 1/191,041.
(5) THIS PROPERTY DOES NOT LIE WITHIN A FLOOD HAZARD AREA ACCORDING TO FIRM PANEL NO. 13297C0175 B, DATED FEB. 16, 1990.
GEORGIA REGISTERED NO. 1184 PROFESSIONAL LAND SURVEYOR BEN McLEROY
0 100 200
FEET
SURVEY FOR
ROBERT A. AND JUDY C. RUPARD
LAND LOT 102, DISTRICT 4
COUNTY: WALTON
GMD: 416
STATE: GEORGIA
DATE: AUG. 16, 1995
SCALE: 1" = 100'
DWN. BY: EMF
FIELDBOOK: 794
SURVEYED BY: BEN McLEROY & ASSOCIATES, INC. ENGINEERS & SURVEYORS ATHENS, GA.
FILE NO.: 22690-

Figure 9-6

the same, whether the description at issue is contained in a contract or a conveyance. A minority of states impose requirements on contract descriptions that are more lenient than those imposed on conveyances.

Compliance with the relevant statute of frauds is not the only concern for an attorney who deals with a land description to be used in a real estate transaction. A description may be good enough to comply with the statute but nevertheless cause problems. It may contain ambiguities or other flaws, it may be difficult to interpret, or its meaning may turn on extrinsic evidence that is either not readily accessible or is indeterminate. The problem, for example, may be only a simple error in the direction of line — the description reads "south 40° west 80 feet" when it must say "south 40° *east* 80 feet." Such an error, which may seem slight and hard to catch by proofreading, can have a drastic effect and make the description very different from what the parties intended. Whenever a description is less than totally clear, an owner may have to resort to costly and time-consuming litigation to obtain a definitive conclusion as to what the description really means. A good real estate attorney wants to avoid, not invite, judicial scrutiny of land descriptions. She aims not only to satisfy the minimum requirements of the statute of frauds but also to employ a land description that is as clear, definite, and easy to interpret as is reasonably possible.

ROBERT G. NATELSON, MODERN LAW OF DEEDS TO REAL PROPERTY

165-169 (1992)

The Sufficiency of the Description

The cases often contain language to the effect that a deed conveys nothing but what is described in the instrument, that a deed without an adequate legal description is void, and that a deed describing only part of the property intended to be conveyed passes only the portion described. These statements are misleading. If the deed is defective because the land description is insufficient, a proponent who can prove by clear and convincing evidence the content of the underlying contract can obtain a decree either reforming the deed or directing the grantor to issue a new one. In addition, the parties may cure initially defective descriptions by correction deed and, in the absence of prejudice to third parties, the courts recognize these as completing the original instrument.

The relationship between a land description and extrinsic evidence is the subject of several judicial maxims, including the following:

- In the absence of fraud or mistake, extrinsic evidence is not admissible to contradict clear language in the operative portions of a deed.
- Extrinsic evidence is not admissible to supply the deed with an adequate property description or enlarge the scope of the description.

- Extrinsic evidence is admissible to clarify an unclear document.
- Extrinsic evidence is admissible to apply the description to its subject matter.[10]

Despite the reference in these maxims to extrinsic evidence, the language used by most courts and commentators has focused primarily on the quality of the deed language without adequately considering the role of outside proof. . . . Courts and commentators have arrived at various "tests" of sufficiency that are deceptively self-contained. For example, Professor Brewster's test is whether the land description provides the *means* by which a competent surveyor could identify the limits of the property on the ground. This formulation has been followed by some cases. The Georgia courts hold that a deed description is sufficient if it provides the *key* by which the boundaries of the conveyed land may be identified with reasonable certainty. Other tribunals require a *nucleus of description*.

As a matter of practice, however, a valid legal description depends as much on the quality of the extrinsic evidence as on the content of the deed. . . . The language of the instrument, even if logically consistent, is undecipherable without *some* extrinsic proof.[16] Moreover, the quality of the extrinsic proof often determines whether the words in the instrument are adequate or inadequate.

Although it usually is held that the sufficiency of the deed's land description is a question of law for the court, it really is a question of fact, of evidence. And the courts have been flexible about the evidence they consider. They certainly do not limit their inquiry according to whether the evidence happens to be in the deed. In each case, the task is to reconstruct the scope of each litigant's consent and enforce any terms with respect to which their respective agreements overlap; and, in the absence of overlap, to craft a remedy that will either encourage productive bargaining or reflect the sort of bargain the parties themselves would have arrived at had they considered the matter initially. This process requires considering extrinsic evidence as well as the deed, in proportions that differ from case to case. Only if the deed has no description at all or the description is irresolvable nonsense[20] do the courts close the case without going beyond the instrument itself. In that event, the courts hold that no amount of parol [evidence] will save it. Yet even here a qualification is required, for the matter is closed

10. J. Brewster, *The Conveyance of Estates in Fee by Deed* 93 (1904); Brasher v. Tanner, 256 Ga. 812, 353 S.E.2d 478 (1987). Extrinsic evidence also is admissible to demonstrate that the description fails in fact to describe a parcel of land. *Id.*

16. For example, extrinsic evidence may demonstrate whether the word "north" means magnetic north or true north. Martin v. Tucker, 111 R.I. 192, 300 A.2d 480 (1973); Annot., 70 A.L.R.3d 1220 (1976).

20. J. Brewster, *The Conveyance of Estates in Fee by Deed* 92 (1904) provides an example from Gloss v. Furman, 164 Ill. 585, 45 N.E. 1019 (1897) ("The east vigintillionth of a vigintillionth of the east one-sixty-fourth inch of lot one . . . and the east vigintillionth of a vigintillionth of the east one-quarter inch of lot two . . ."). Yet even a property description that fails to close may be saved by admitting extrinsic evidence. United States v. La Rosa, 765 F.2d 693 (7th Cir. 1985).

only when the litigants are not the original parties to the deed and not privy to the underlying contract. If the litigants are the parties to the deed and have a valid underlying contract, a court of equity simply orders the grantor to execute a new deed.

1. Descriptions in Contracts of Sale

When the parties to a contract of sale describe the land by means other than a formal legal description, anything can happen in court. In this area generalizations are risky, but two different judicial attitudes are displayed that can be viewed as polar extremes. One view, properly debunked by Professor Natelson, strictly enforces the statute of frauds, requiring that the writing completely describe the tract by permitting the location of all boundaries, with no ambiguity and no need to look to extrinsic evidence. Under this view, all competent surveyors would arrive at the same outcome in applying the writing to the ground. At this end of the spectrum are decisions, reported in a number of states that invalidate descriptions that fail to specify the county and state where the tract is located. The opposite view cares more about enforcing the parties' bargain in fact than about compliance with legal formality. It posits that when the parties have some written description of the land, the contract should be enforced if the land can be identified with reasonable certainty by supplementing the writing with extrinsic evidence (including oral testimony). Extrinsic evidence that doesn't contradict the writing may be used liberally. Many states cannot neatly be labelled as following one extreme or the other. Rather, the case law of a given state often reflects both strands, with decisions that may be reconciled on their facts but are difficult to rationalize in terms of overall policy.

Problem 9C

Emma and Will are neighbors, Emma previously having purchased her tract from Will. Both Emma's and Will's tracts of land front on the north side of Highway 223 and have a common boundary of approximately 1,140 feet. Will agrees to sell additional land to Emma. They sign a contract describing the land to be conveyed as: "5 acres of land adjoining property owned by Emma located on north side of Highway 223. This 5 acres to be surveyed at earliest time possible at which time plat will be attached and serve as further description of property." Given this land description, should the agreement be enforceable against Will?

2. Descriptions in Deeds and Other Recorded Instruments

When land is described in a deed conveying fee title or in other recorded instruments, a prime characteristic of the writing is its permanence.

It becomes part of the chain of title for the property, to be retrieved and evaluated for many decades. This raises special concerns with respect to the quality of the land description, concerns that are not present in short-term contractual arrangements such as earnest money contracts, brokers' agreements, and many leases. For this reason, should the standards for validity and the introduction of extrinsic evidence be stricter for conveyances than for contracts? Or, instead, should the standards depend not on the type of instrument but on the presence of successors in interest? In other words, should a court be more willing to admit extrinsic evidence when the dispute is between the original parties who used the language, with no concerns for the expectations of third parties who may have relied on the written records?

We should also consider the fact that for recorded instruments, interpretation may occur many years after the writing was made, when the original parties are dead and gone. Proper interpretation may turn not only on the inferred intent of parties who cannot be consulted but also on community norms and customs from the historical period in question. Even when it is clear that the deed is legally sufficient, difficult issues of interpretation may arise. For example, an ancient deed that conveys rural land "up to the hills" might mean the boundary is located at the foot of the hills or at the crest. *See* Padilla v. City of Santa Fe, 753 P.2d 353 (N.M. 1988) (1930 deed written in Spanish referring to "las lomas" boundary goes to crest; insufficient evidence of custom that Spanish deeds of this era conveyed only to bottom of hills).

WALTERS v. TUCKER
Supreme Court of Missouri, 1955
281 S.W.2d 843

HOLLINGSWORTH, Judge. This is an action to quiet title to certain real estate situate in the City of Webster Groves, St. Louis County, Missouri. Plaintiff and defendants are the owners of adjoining residential properties fronting northward on Oak Street. Plaintiff's property, known as 450 Oak Street, lies to the west of defendants' property, known as 446 Oak Street. The controversy arises over their division line. Plaintiff contends that her lot is 50 feet in width, east and west. Defendants contend that plaintiff's lot is only approximately 42 feet in width, east and west. The trial court, sitting without a jury, found the issues in favor of defendants and rendered judgment accordingly, from which plaintiff has appealed.

The common source of title is Fred F. Wolf and Rose E. Wolf, husband and wife, who in 1922 acquired the whole of Lot 13 of West Helfenstein Park, as shown by plat thereof recorded in St. Louis County. In 1924, Mr. and Mrs. Wolf conveyed to Charles Arthur Forse and wife the following described portion of said Lot 13:

> The West 50 feet of Lot 13 of West Helfenstein Park, a Subdivision in United States Survey 1953, Twp. 45, Range 8 East, St. Louis County, Missouri,. . . .

Plaintiff, through mesne conveyances carrying a description like that above, is the last grantee of and successor in title to the aforesaid portion of Lot 13. Defendants, through mesne conveyances, are the last grantees of and successors in title to the remaining portion of Lot 13.

At the time of the above conveyance in 1924, there was and is now situate on the tract described therein a one-story frame dwelling house (450 Oak Street), which was then and continuously since has been occupied as a dwelling by the successive owners of said tract, or their tenants. In 1925, Mr. and Mrs. Wolf built a 1½-story stucco dwelling house on the portion of Lot 13 retained by them. This house (446 Oak Street) continuously since has been occupied as a dwelling by the successive owners of said portion of Lot 13, or their tenants.

Despite the apparent clarity of the description in plaintiff's deed, extrinsic evidence was heard for the purpose of enabling the trial court to interpret the true meaning of the description set forth therein. At the close of all the evidence the trial court found that the description did not clearly reveal whether the property conveyed "was to be fifty feet along the front line facing Oak Street or fifty feet measured Eastwardly at right angles from the West line of the property . . ."; that the "difference in method of ascertaining fifty feet would result in a difference to the parties of a strip the length of the lot and approximately eight feet in width"; that an ambiguity existed which justified the hearing of extrinsic evidence; and that the "West fifty feet should be measured on the front or street line facing Oak Street." The judgment rendered in conformity with the above finding had the effect of fixing the east-west width of plaintiff's tract at about 42 feet.

Plaintiff contends that the description in the deed is clear, definite and unambiguous, both on its face and when applied to the land; that the trial court erred in hearing and considering extrinsic evidence; and that its finding and judgment changes the clearly expressed meaning of the description and describes and substitutes a different tract from that acquired by her under her deed. Defendants do not contend that the description, on its face, is ambiguous, but do contend that when applied to the land it is subject to "dual interpretation"; that under the evidence the trial court did not err in finding it contained a latent ambiguity and that parol evidence was admissible to ascertain and determine its true meaning; and that the finding and judgment of the trial court properly construes and adjudges the true meaning of the description set forth in said deed.

Attached hereto is a reduced copy of an unchallenged survey of Lot 13, as made by plaintiff's witness, Robert J. Joyce, surveyor and graduate (1928) in civil engineering at Massachusetts Institute of Technology, for use in this litigation. Inasmuch as the two properties here in question front northward on Oak Street, the plat is made to be viewed from the bottom toward the top, which in this instance is from north to south [see Figure 9-7].

It is seen that Lot 13 extends generally north and south. It is bounded on the north by Oak Street (except that a small triangular lot from another

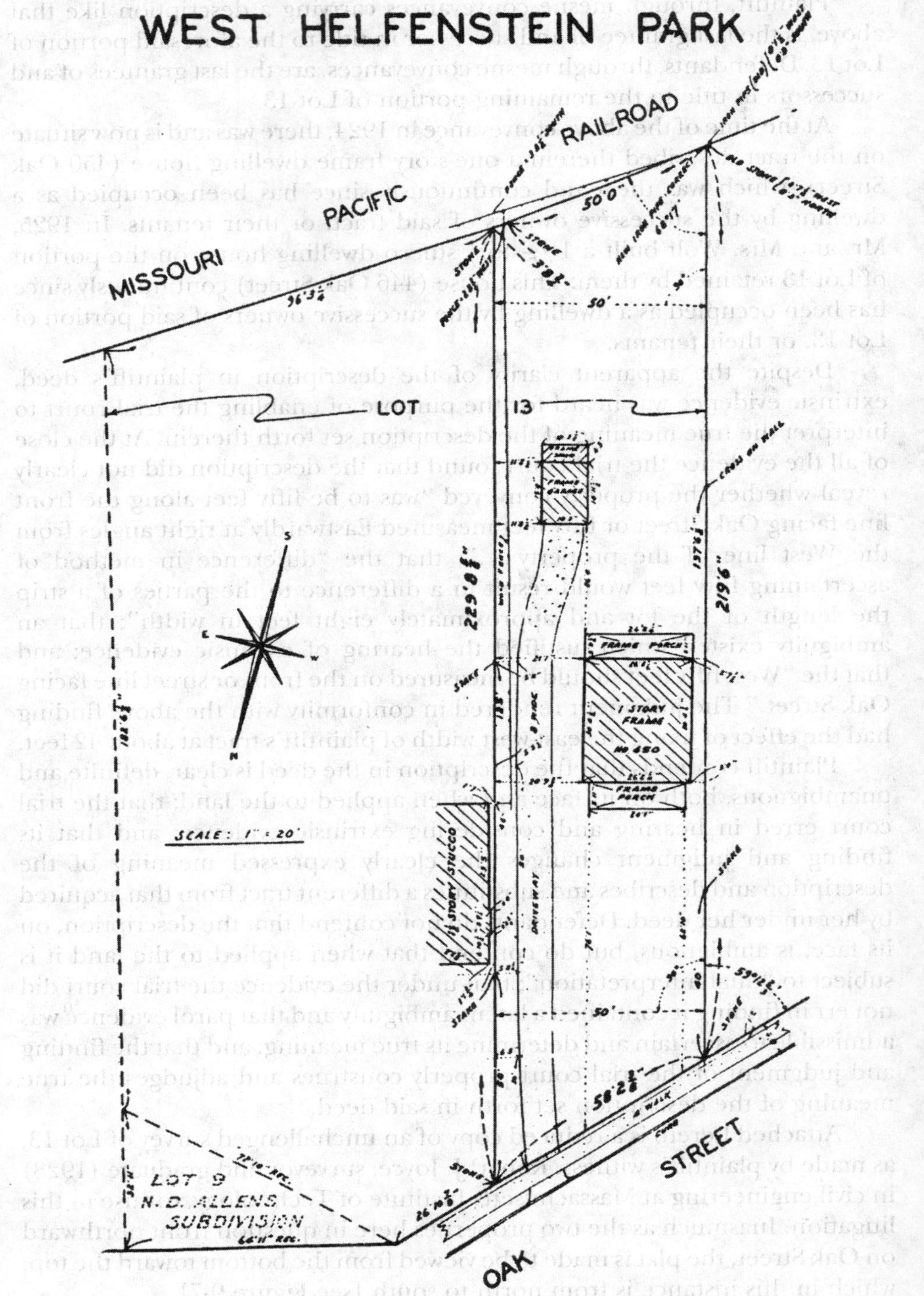
WEST HELFENSTEIN PARK
MISSOURI
PACIFIC
RAILROAD
LOT 13
1 STORY FRAME
NO. 450
FRAME PORCH
FRAME GARAGE
1½ STORY STUCCO
DRIVEWAY
SCALE: 1" = 20'
LOT 9
N. D. ALLENS
SUBDIVISION
OAK
STREET
229' 8⅝"
219' 6"
96' 3¾"
50' 0"
58' 2⅞"
50'
CROSS ON WALL
STONE
STAKE
WALK
CURB

Figure 9-7

subdivision cuts off its frontage thereon at the northeast corner). On the south it is bounded by the Missouri Pacific Railroad right of way. Both Oak Street and the railroad right of way extend in a general northeast-southwest direction, but at differing angles.

Joyce testified: The plat was a "survey of the West 50 feet of Lot 13 of West Helfenstein Park." In making the survey the west boundary line of Lot 13 was first established. Lines 50 feet in length (one near the north end and one near the south end of the lot, as shown by the plat) were run eastwardly at right angles to the west line of the lot, and then a line was run parallel to the west line and 50 feet, as above measured, from it, intersecting both the north and south boundaries of the lot. This line, which represented 50 feet in width of Lot 13, made a frontage of 58 feet, 2 3/8 inches, on Oak Street, and 53 feet, 8 3/4 inches, on the railroad right of way. The line, as thus measured, comes within 1 foot, 1 3/4 inches, of the west front corner of the stucco house (446 Oak Street), within 1 foot, 7 inches, of the west rear corner thereof, and within less than 1 foot of a chimney in the west wall.

The trial court refused to permit the witness to testify, but counsel for plaintiff offered to prove that, if permitted, witness would testify that the methods used by him in making the survey were in accordance with the practices and procedures followed in his profession in determining the boundaries of lots such as was described in the deed. The witness further testified that the method used by him was the only method by which a lot such as that described in the deeds in question could be measured having precisely and uniformly a width of 50 feet; and that a 50 foot strip is a strip with a uniform width of 50 feet.

Defendants also introduced in evidence a plat of Lot 13. It was prepared by Elbring Surveying Company for use in this litigation. August Elbring, a practicing surveyor and engineer for 34 years, testified in behalf of defendants:

> In view of the fact that the deed (to the west 50 feet of Lot 13) made reference to the western 53 feet, and in view of the fact that the line which would have been established construing the dimension to be 50 feet at right angles, coming within a foot or so of an existing building (the stucco house), we felt that the line was intended to have been placed using the frontage of 50 feet on Oak Street and thence running the line (southward) parallel to the western line of Lot 13.

The line so run, as being the east line of plaintiff's tract, was 8.01 feet west of the northwest corner of the stucco house and 8.32 feet west of its southwest corner. The Elbring plat does not show the actual width of plaintiff's tract as thus measured. But, concededly, there is no point on it where it approximates 50 feet in width; and, while it "fronts" 50 feet on Oak Street, its actual width is between 42 and 43 feet.

Both plats show a concrete driveway 8 feet in width extending from Oak Street to plaintiff's garage in the rear of her home, which, the testimony shows, was built by one of plaintiff's predecessors in title. The east line of plaintiff's tract, as measured by the Joyce (plaintiff's) survey, lies 6 or 7 feet east of the eastern edge of this driveway. Admittedly, the driveway is upon and an appurtenance of plaintiff's property. On the Elbring (defendants') plat, the east line of plaintiff's lot, as measured by Elbring, is shown to coincide with the east side of the driveway at Oak Street and to encroach upon it 1.25 feet for a distance of 30 or more feet as it extends between the houses. Thus, the area in dispute is essentially the area between the east edge of the driveway and the line fixed by the Joyce survey as the eastern line of plaintiff's tract.

Plaintiff adduced testimony to the effect that she and several of her predecessors in title had asserted claim to and had exercised physical dominion and control over all of the 50 feet in width of Lot 13, which included the concrete driveway and 6 or 7 feet to the east thereof. Defendants adduced testimony to the effect that they and their predecessors in title had asserted claim to and had exercised physical dominion and control over all of Lot 13 east of the driveway. The view we take of this case makes it unnecessary to set forth this testimony in detail. . . .

The law is clear that when there is no inconsistency on the face of a deed and, on application of the description to the ground, no inconsistency appears, parol evidence is not admissible to show that the parties intended to convey either more or less or different ground from that described. But where there are conflicting calls in a deed, or the description may be made to apply to two or more parcels, and there is nothing in the deed to show which is meant, then parol evidence is admissible to show the true meaning of the words used. . . .

No ambiguity or confusion arises when the description here in question is applied to Lot 13. The description, when applied to the ground, fits the land claimed by plaintiff and cannot be made to apply to any other tract. When the deed was made, Lot 13 was vacant land except for the frame dwelling at 450 Oak Street. The stucco house (446 Oak Street) was not built until the following year. Under no conceivable theory can the fact that defendants' predecessors in title (Mr. and Mrs. Wolf) thereafter built the stucco house within a few feet of the east line of the property described in the deed be construed as competent evidence of any ambiguity in the description. Neither could the fact, if it be a fact, that the Wolfs and their successors in title claimed title to and exercised dominion and control over a portion of the tract be construed as creating or revealing an ambiguity in the description.

Whether the above testimony and other testimony in the record constitute evidence of a mistake in the deed we do not here determine. Defendants have not sought reformation, and yet that is what the decree herein rendered undertakes to do. It seems apparent that the trial court considered the testimony and came to the conclusion that the parties to the deed did not intend a conveyance of the "West 50 feet of Lot 13," but rather a tract fronting 50 feet on Oak Street. And, the decree, on the theory of interpreting an ambiguity, undertakes to change (reform) the description so as to describe a lot approximately 42 feet in width instead of a lot 50 feet in width, as originally described. That, we are convinced, the courts cannot do.

The judgment is reversed and the cause remanded for further proceedings not inconsistent with the views expressed.

McGHEE v. YOUNG

District Court of Appeal of Florida, Fourth District, 1992
606 So. 2d 1215

POLEN, Judge. This appeal concerns a dispute between neighbors regarding the boundary line between their property. Appellants, the McGhees, own lot 2 of the Rustic Hills development in Martin County. The McGhees filed a complaint for ejectment against Evelyn Young, the owner of lot 1. Lot 1 adjoins lot 2, with the south boundary of lot 1 forming the north boundary of lot 2. In its final judgment the trial court determined that the legal boundary between lots 1 and 2 was a line that corresponded with the location of certain monuments found in the ground, and was approximately equidistant from each parties' home, rather than, as appellants now contend, the line that corresponded to the metes and bounds descriptions contained in the parties' deeds and the recorded plat of Rustic Hills, which line cuts through Young's home, garage, and septic tank drain field.

The parties are in agreement for the most part as to the facts of this case, with one significant exception. The parties agree that the deeds to their respective lots contain metes and bounds descriptions that correlate to the plat of survey of Rustic Hills. They agree that the original surveyor of the land placed 4" by 4" concrete monuments in the ground while taking metes and bounds measurements of the placement of these monuments. The parties' deeds contain these metes and bounds descriptions and reference the minor plat of Rustic Hills, although this plat was not filed until sometime after several lots in the subdivision, including these two, were conveyed from the developer.

Where the parties disagree is on the location of those original concrete monuments placed in the ground. There was substantial competent evidence to support the trial court's finding that the monuments were located along the line that became the fence line between the McGhees' lot 2 and Young's lot 1, the boundary which the trial court ultimately determined to be the legal boundary.

Having determined that the placement of the monuments in the ground differed from the metes and bounds descriptions contained in the deeds and depicted in the minor plat of Rustic Hills, the question became which should control, the monuments, or the descriptions as contained in the deeds and subsequently recorded in the plat? The trial court applied the reasoning contained in Tyson v. Edwards, 433 So. 2d 549 (Fla. 5th DCA), *petition for review denied*, 441 So. 2d 633 (Fla. 1983). . . .

In [*Tyson*] Judge Cowart noted the distinction between the role and practice of the surveyor and that of the lawyer, architect, or design engineer. The latter group is accustomed to reducing abstract ideas to paper and then relying upon the written document to achieve the original goal as written. In this case the written document is always considered authoritative and any deviation or discrepancy between this written document and what is actually done, is resolved in favor of "changing the physical to conform to the intention evidenced by the writing." *Id.* The surveyor, however, plays a different role and has a different practice with respect to his profession. While the original surveyor has a right or responsibility to establish new boundaries when he surveys previously unplatted land or subdivides a new tract, the sole duty of all subsequent or following surveyors is to locate the points and lines of the original survey by locating existing boundaries. *Id.* No following surveyor may establish a new corner or line, or correct erroneous surveys of earlier surveyors, when they track the original survey in locating existing boundaries. This is so because "man set monuments as landmarks before he invented paper and still today the true survey is what the original surveyor *did on the ground by way of fixing boundaries by setting monuments* and by running lines ('metes and bounds'), and the paper 'survey' or plat of survey is intended only as a map of what is on the ground." *Id.* (emphasis added). . . .

Applying *Tyson* to the instant case leads to the conclusion that the monuments, as located on the ground, control over the written descriptions of what the surveyor intended to do, that intention being evidenced in the deeds to the parcels as well as the later recorded minor plat of Rustic Hills. The correctness of this position is strengthened by a consideration of the ramifications of the alternative position. As Judge Cowart noted:

> Even if it were true [that application of this rule of law would require the "redrawing" of several lot lines], it is far better to redraw lines on a piece of paper to make them consistent with occupancy on the ground than to uproot and move all of the property owners who have in good faith erected homes, fences and other improvements in conformity with monuments on the ground, in order to make their actual occupancy and possession conform to what is erroneously shown on a piece of paper recorded in the courthouse.

Id. at 554 n.2. . . .

In summary, we conclude that the trial court correctly applied the principles recited in *Tyson* in determining that the monuments located on the ground between lot 1 and lot 2 should control as to the location of the legal boundary line. Although the McGhees argue that the trial court erred in finding that the monument located at point "L" was the *original* monument, the record contains substantial competent evidence to support the court's finding. The final judgment is affirmed.

SCHWARTZ, ALAN, R., Associate Judge, dissenting. In my judgment, this case is not governed by Tyson v. Edwards, 433 So. 2d 549 (Fla. 5th DCA 1983), *pet. for review denied*, 441 So. 2d 663 (Fla. 1983), but by Rivers v. Lozeau, 539 So. 2d 1147 (Fla. 5th DCA 1989), *review denied*, 545 So. 2d 1368 (Fla. 1989). I would reverse on the authority of that decision.

Problem 9D

Your new client Goldy has just arrived at your law office with a boundary line problem and a confession to make. She owns a house in the suburbs on a one-acre lot. The neighborhood is about 25 years old. Three years ago, Goldy added a redwood fence to the backyard. She did the work herself but made a mistake. When she started, she looked for monuments for the back corners of her lot, but couldn't find them, so she guessed at the corners. Well, she guessed wrong. After she completed the fence and started clearing brush and digging to make flower beds along the fence line, she found iron pins for both corners approximately one yard in from the fence corners. Goldy moved the iron pins, pounding them into the ground just outside the two fence corners. Now everything's fine, right? Last week, Goldy's backyard neighbor, Spanky, stopped by. Spanky is selling his house, and his buyer insisted on a new survey. The surveyor, according to Spanky, says the iron pins are in the wrong location and should be on the other side of the fence. Spanky asked Goldy who built her fence and whether she has any survey of her property. Goldy told Spanky she got a survey when she bought her house ten years ago, she hasn't had a surveyor on her lot since then, and she built the fence herself. This is all Goldy said to Spanky. Goldy believes either Spanky or his buyer will soon make trouble about the fence and boundary.

Goldy has told you her story. It's time for you to start talking. What's your advice and counsel for Goldy? Does it matter whether you are in Florida, where *McGhee* is precedent, or in a jurisdiction where a different rule applies or where the rule is unclear?

10
Public Records

The system of public records resolves competing claims to land. To understand the system, it is important to have a firm grasp of how the common-law system resolves competing claims. At common law, the basic rule is "first in time, first in right." At common law, there is one exception to letting time decide priorities — between a prior equitable claim and a subsequent legal claim held by a bona fide purchaser without notice of the prior claim, the subsequent purchaser wins. The rationale is that because both grantees have an equity but only one has legal title, the legal title should control to break the tie.

All states have recording acts. These acts vary considerably from state to state, but they have a number of common features. The acts set up a system that provides for the recording of instruments that affect title to land. A deed or other instrument must be acknowledged before it qualifies for recording. Most instruments are acknowledged before a notary public ("notarized"), but other public officials, such as judges, also may acknowledge a person's signature of an instrument.

The recording system has two basic functions, the first being *title assurance.* The point here is risk reduction. Buyers and other persons who deal with property don't want their expectations about the quality of title to be defeated. The recording system reduces risk by providing a method for determining who owns a tract of land.

The second basic function of the recording system is to establish priorities when there are successive transfers of interests. Often successive transfers do not directly conflict (as when A sells Blackacre twice), but it is necessary to rank them. *Priority* means the law determines who among various claimants has the superior, prior interest.

A. TITLE SEARCH PROCESS

1. Chain of Title Concept

Title search practices vary widely from state to state, and sometimes counties in the same state have different local practices. Notwithstanding local variations, the basic process for searching title has four common steps. First, the title examiner must discover the *chain of title*. Every parcel of land has a chain of title, the first link being the sovereign and the last link being the present owner. The best possible title search traces title back to the sovereign, reconstructing the entire chain of title. In most states, this is not done for most title searches. Custom, sometimes backed by state bar title standards or by legislation, dictates that the search typically goes back a set period, such as 50 or 60 years.

After the searcher has constructed the chain of title (at this stage, it's best to say the apparent chain of title), the second step is to look for *adverse recorded transfers* by the present owner and by all prior owners in the chain of title. To find these adverse transfers, the searcher checks the records of deeds and other instruments in the county where the land is located. An adverse transfer may upset the apparent chain of title by showing that a prior owner conveyed the land twice or that the apparent present owner has conveyed to someone else. Other adverse transfers do not jeopardize the conclusion that the apparent present owner actually owns the estate.

The third step is for the searcher to study full copies of all recorded instruments previously uncovered, both links in the chain of title and adverse transfers. Deeds in the chain may contain reservations, exceptions, real covenants, or other matters. Formalities of all recorded instruments, such as the parties' names, the land descriptions, and acknowledgments must be examined. The searcher may find that some of the adverse transfers do not presently affect title.

The fourth and last step is for the searcher to consult other records, in addition to recorded instruments, for adverse interests. These sources vary from state to state, but there are always other records that must be examined. Federal claims, such as tax liens and bankruptcy records, are kept completely outside of the state recording system. Many state-created claims against land are reflected in sets of records other than the land records; common examples are ad valorem taxes, lis pendens, judgment liens, and mechanics' liens.

2. *Index Systems*

With thousands and thousands of recorded instruments on file, even in modest-sized counties, an index system is essential to find the relevant documents for a title search. In most states, the index system uses only the names of the parties to the deeds and other instruments. Typically, the indexes are printed and separately bound for each calendar year or for sets of years. A searcher uses the name indexes (often called *"grantor-grantee"* indexes) to construct a chain of title for the land by working backward from the present owner. When the searcher finds a deed into the present owner, the searcher takes the name of the grantor in that deed (the immediately prior owner) and looks for that name in the grantee indexes to find how that owner acquired the property. After the searcher constructs a chain of title of sufficient length, he uses the grantor indexes to check for the presence of adverse record transfers by each owner.

The other index system is the *tract index*, which divides all the land in the county into parcels and organizes deeds and other instruments according to the parcel or parcels they affect. Tract indexes are much better and easier to use than name indexes. Most states, however, organize their public land records only by name indexes, which are often required by state statute. Only six states have tract indexes in all counties. Several states have tract indexes for selected counties, sometimes initiated as a pilot program.

3. Sample Search

Duncan Doubtful has contracted to sell a house and tract of land to Hope Goodtitle, and a title search is necessary to see whether title is marketable. A title search thus is assigned to an attorney or other title professional, whom we will call Sara Searchwell. To get started, Searchwell may ask Doubtful how he got the land and, if by deed, for a copy. If Doubtful has title insurance, Searchwell will want a copy of the policy. As it turns out, Doubtful is unhelpful — he is unavailable, uncooperative, or simply not the type of guy who keeps any important papers where he can find them. Thus, all Searchwell knows is that Doubtful claims to be the present owner and that the contract has a legal description of the land: "Lot 7, Block 3, Shaky Heights Subdivision, according to the plat recorded in Vol. 19, Page 45 of the Plat Records of Luck County, State of Orange."

Like most states, Orange has name indexes for its records. Searchwell begins to use them by looking for Doubtful in the grantee indexes. After looking through several volumes, beginning with the current year and working back, she finds a deed to Doubtful in 2000:

Date	*Grantees*	*Grantors*	*Type*	*Book*	*Brief legal*
. . .	. . .	. . .	. . .	. . .	. . .
5-14	Doty, Stan	Freeman, Amy	Deed	54-17	Ten Oaks Subd
9-23	Doubtful, Duncan	Cramer, Christine	Deed	54-5	Shaky Hts Subd
6-20	Douglas, Betty	Stamp, Scott	Mortg	55-3	Lexington Rd
. . .	. . .	. . .	. . .	. . .	. . .

She determines that Doubtful got his deed from a grantor named Christine Cramer. Now Searchwell must start looking for Cramer as a grantee prior to the conveyance to Doubtful — that is, Searchwell must make sure that

Cramer had title to the property prior to granting it to Doubtful. When she finds Cramer as a grantee, she will then learn of Cramer's grantor and that will be the next link to trace back in the chain of title. If the remainder of the search is this easy (which is unlikely), all links in the chain of title may be documented by recorded deeds. Often, however, an apparent gap surfaces. Searchwell quickly traces title back to Gregory Brown, who in 1980 deeded the lot to Christine Cramer, but she then encounters a problem going further back. She can't find any person named Brown as a grantee for this property in any of the grantee index books for this century. Searchwell doesn't give up, but she has to do some detective work. Maybe Brown acquired the land by inheritance or devise, evidenced by local probate court records. In most states, probate transfers of land are documented only in the probate court records, without cross-reference or other indication in the land records. Perhaps Brown acquired the land by a deed that he never recorded. It's possible that a judicial decree quieted title in Brown, with the decree not reflected by a recorded instrument. Brown, for example, may have prevailed in court on a claim of title by adverse possession. If Brown is alive and can be located, Searchwell might ask him how he got the land. If Sara is unable to construct a chain of title of sufficient length, the present owner's title will not be marketable.

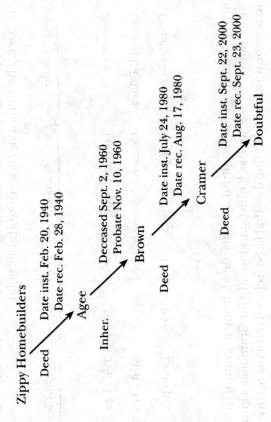

Searchwell does her work and finds probate court records showing that Brown inherited the land in 1960 from his aunt, Charlotte Agee. Returning to the recorder's office to plow through the grantee indexes for Agee, she finds a deed from Zippy Homebuilders Inc. to Agee in 1940. Searches in Orange usually go back only 50 years, so Searchwell stops here. Her chain of title is long enough to meet the local standard, without determining whether Zippy Homebuilders' title can be traced through the records back to the sovereign. The chain of title that Searchwell has put together looks like this:

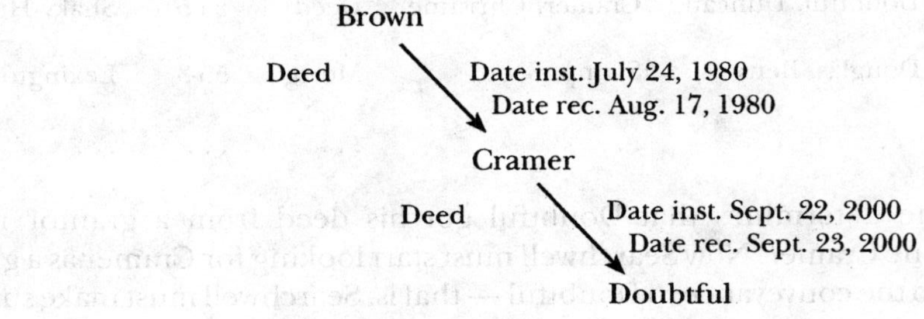

Now it's time for Searchwell to check for adverse record transfers. She uses the grantor indexes, beginning by looking under "Doubtful, Duncan" in the index volumes for 2000, when he acquired the property, through the present. She finds two entries, both mortgages: in 2000, to borrow money to buy the house, Doubtful granted a mortgage to Mean Mortgage Co., and in 2004 he granted a mortgage to Home Equity Loans of America. Searchwell then checks for any adverse transfers by Cramer, using the indexes for years 1980 through 2000, finding a mortgage given in 1980 when Cramer bought the house. Repeating the process for Brown for the years 1960 through 1980, she finds nothing. For Agee, she finds a mortgage granted in 1940, a utility easement granted in 1941, and a set of restrictive covenants, which she and other neighbors entered into in 1942. Searchwell finds releases, which are recorded, for the two older mortgages (Agee's and Cramer's). Searchwell studies all the recorded documents, including the subdivision plat, which is a key part of the present legal description and is referred to in all instruments in the chain of title. The plat was recorded in 1939, the year before Charlotte Agee bought the house from Zippy Homebuilders. The plat apparently was recorded when the neighborhood was first developed; very probably Agee was the first owner of the house, having bought it new from the developer. Searchwell finds all the instruments, including the plat, to be in order. There is no indication that the old easement and covenants have expired. Searchwell checks the other sets of records in Luck County that reveal liens and other encumbrances, finding that the taxes are paid currently and finding no evidence of other problems. Her title report, therefore, is:

> Duncan Doubtful has an estate in fee simple absolute, subject to (i) Easement from Charlotte Agee to Luck Power Co., dated May 4, 1941, recorded May 11, 1941, Vol. 45, Page 13, Deed Records, Luck County, Orange; (ii) Covenants dated Jan. 5, 1942, recorded March 23, 1942, Vol. 46, Page 32, Deed Records, Luck County, Orange; (iii) Mortgage from Duncan Doubtful to Mean Mortgage Co., dated Sept. 22, 2000, recorded Sept. 23, 2000, Vol. 132, Page 2, Deed Records, Luck County, Orange; (iv) Mortgage from Duncan Doubtful to Home Equity Loans of America, Inc., dated June 1, 2004, recorded June 4, 2004, Vol. 135, Page 340, Deed Records, Luck County, Orange.

Searchwell, as a prudent title examiner, is careful to disclose the scope of her search and, thus, the limits of her opinion. She has not inspected the property, and unrecorded interests that affect title may exist. She has not ordered or seen a survey, and her search is not designed to disclose the boundary and title problems that an accurate survey would show. She stopped her search in 1940, and there is the possibility that older interests, validly recorded, are presently outstanding.

If Searchwell has the opportunity to search title to Doubtful's property using a tract index, using either a private title plant or one of the few public tract index systems, the operation will be much faster and easier. With a properly maintained tract index, Searchwell looks up Shaky Heights

Subdivision, and under that heading finds Block 3, Lot 7. Each tract typically has its own page in the index; tracts with many recorded instruments have several index pages. The page for Block 3, Lot 7 is as shown in Figure 10-1.

Date filed	*Grantors*	*Grantees*	*Type*	*Book-Page*
5-13-39	Zippy Homebdrs		Plat	19-45
2-28-40	Zippy Homebdrs	Agee, Charlotte	Deed	40-325
2-28-40	Agee, Charlotte	Big Bank	Mortg	40-326
5-11-41	Agee, Charlotte	Luck Power Co	Easement	45-13
3-23-42	Agee, Charlotte	Shady Hts owners	Covts	46-32
11-5-51	Big Bank		Release	59-452
8-17-80	Brown, Gregory	Cramer, Christine	Deed	95-320
8-17-80	Cramer, Christine	Second Savings	Mortg	95-321
9-23-00	Cramer, Christine	Doubtful, Duncan	Deed	131-598
9-23-00	Second Savings		Release	132-1
9-23-00	Doubtful, Duncan	Mean Mortgage	Mortg	132-2
6-4-04	Doubtful, Duncan	Home Equity	Mortg	135-340

Figure 10-1
Shaky Heights Subdivision, Block 3, Lot 7
Plat Book Vol. 19, Page 45

Notice that everything Searchwell found and needed is referenced there, in one place, with the exception of the probate transfer from Agee to Brown. A tract index system, like name indexes, often fails to show probate transfers. Notice also that the tract index starts with the subdivision plat. If Searchwell wants to search further back, she needs to find out how the system is organized for pre-1939 records. Perhaps there is a tract index page for a larger parcel of land, which Zippy Homebuilders acquired and subdivided in the late 1930s. Perhaps the tract index system does not go back to a patent from the sovereign, and early name indexes must be consulted.

Searchwell obtained the same information for the buyer, Hope Goodtitle, whether she used name indexes or tract indexes. In our example, both systems worked satisfactorily, without flaws or errors. How is the title search used? Goodtitle will require that Doubtful obtain releases of his two mortgages at or before the closing. The lenders will agree to furnish those releases, of course, only if they are paid their existing loan balances at or before closing. Does Goodtitle have the right to object to the easement or the covenants? How would you find out? (If you do not remember how to attack this question, review Chapter 8.)

B. TYPES OF RECORDING ACTS

Recording statutes modify the common-law "first in time, first in right" rule. Subsequent takers of interests sometimes beat prior valid interests that are unrecorded. The statutes expand the common-law rule that a subsequent legal *bona fide purchaser* (BFP) cuts off a prior equity. There are three basic types of recording acts, which specify when the subsequent taker defeats the prior taker.

1. Race Statute

The key idea for the race statute is that "the first to record wins." The race statute (sometimes called a "pure race" statute) evokes the image of two competing grantees in a footrace to the recorder's office. The first grantee to record wins, regardless of whether he has notice of the other claimant and regardless of which interest is prior in time. Only three states — Delaware, Louisiana, and North Carolina — have a race statute as their general recording act. There is a split of authority as to whether the subsequent grantee must pay value to cut off a prior unrecorded interest. The North Carolina statute explicitly requires the payment of value, the Louisiana statute explicitly does not, and Delaware law is not clear. Several states use a race approach for certain specialized types of conveyances. Ohio, for example, has a pure race system for mortgages.

2. Notice Statute

The key idea for the notice statute is that "the last BFP wins." Under a notice statute, a subsequent purchaser who takes without notice of the prior unrecorded interest wins. If there are competing purchasers, each of whom claims to qualify as a BFP by paying value and taking without notice, the last BFP to take a conveyance wins. Notice is evaluated at the time the grantee pays value. There are three types of notice:

Actual Notice: The purchaser has actual knowledge of the prior interest.

Constructive Notice: The purchaser is deemed to have notice of all recorded interests, whether or not the grantee in fact searches title.

Inquiry Notice: If the purchaser has knowledge of facts suggesting that someone might have an unrecorded interest, the grantee has a duty to inquire and is charged with knowing whatever that inquiry would have revealed. The most important aspect of inquiry notice is a duty to inspect the land; the purchaser generally takes subject to the rights of parties in possession and other unrecorded interests that are visible from inspection.

3. Race-Notice Statute

The race-notice statute is a hybrid of the first two types of recording acts. The key idea is that among later competing claimants "the first BFP to record wins." The subsequent purchaser must both record before the holder of the prior-in-time interest records (as under a race statute) and take without notice of the prior interest (as under a notice statute). This means the BFP must do three things to prevail: pay value, without notice of the prior claim, and record first. Thus, the race-notice statute is less protective of BFPs than either a race statute or a notice statute. If there are competing purchasers, each of whom claims to qualify as a BFP, the first BFP to record his instrument wins. Almost all states have either a notice act or a race-notice act; these two types are about equally common.

4. Recordable Interests and Nonrecordable Interests

The recording act, no matter which type, only protects a BFP against an off-the-record interest that is capable of being recorded. If a prior-in-time claimant asserts a property right that he is not permitted to place on the record, the recording act has no application to that claimant's dispute with a subsequent purchaser. Instead, common law must resolve the dispute, and it generally applies the "first-in-time, first-in-right" baseline.

Recording acts define what instruments should be recorded. Their scope varies from state to state, but in every state there are some interests in land that are not required to be recorded. There are two types of nonrecordable interests: those that cannot be created by instrument, such as claims of adverse possession, prescriptive easements, and marital property rights; and instruments that are not eligible for recording. For example, in many states, short-term leases are not recordable. The consequence of having nonrecordable rights in land is that a purchaser is bound by them, even though their existence is not ascertainable by a search of the records. Often a prudent purchaser can detect these unrecorded interests by inspecting the land (for example, the adverse possessor may have remained in open, visible possession after expiration of the limitations period), but this is not always the case.

Problem 10A

A conveys Greenacre to B on April 1. B does not then record his deed. On April 5, A sells Greenacre to C, delivering a deed to Greenacre in exchange for C's payment of the purchase price. When C pays the purchase price, he knows that A conveyed Greenacre to B four days earlier. On April 6, C records his deed. On April 7, B records his deed.

(a) Who owns Greenacre under (1) a race statute, (2) a notice statute, or (3) a race-notice statute?

(b) Does it make a difference if the A-to-B transaction is a sale or a gift? (The term *conveys* does not tell us whether B paid anything.)

Problem 10B

A conveys Whiteacre to B on May 1. B does not record his deed and does not take possession of Whiteacre. On May 5, A sells Whiteacre to C, delivering a deed to Whiteacre in exchange for C's payment of the purchase price. When C pays the purchase price, he has no notice of A's prior conveyance to B. On May 6, B records his deed. On May 7, C records his deed.

(a) Who owns Whiteacre under (1) a race statute, (2) a notice statute, or (3) a race-notice statute?

(b) Suppose neither B nor C has recorded his deed, and it's now May 31. Who owns Whiteacre under each of the three types of statutes?

C. BONA FIDE PURCHASER STATUS

1. *Notice from Records*

A purchaser has constructive notice of any interest that is validly recorded. In most contexts, this straightforward proposition is easy to apply. The recorded instrument directly creates an estate or other interest in land, and any subsequent purchaser is therefore bound by it. Some records, however, refer to matters and transactions that are not themselves recorded, raising issues about the scope of constructive notice. A recorded deed may have a recital to a mortgage that is not recorded, or it may say that the grantor acquired the property from his mother by inheritance. A *lis pendens* that is recorded refers to ongoing litigation the outcome of which may affect title to real property; the pleadings and other filings can be located not in the real property records but at the office of the relevant court. Parties sometimes decide not to record an entire instrument but only a shorter memorandum; for instance, the parties to a commercial lease may record a Memorandum of Lease, which keeps the amount of rent and other details off record.

PELFRESNE v. VILLAGE OF WILLIAMS BAY

United States Court of Appeals, Seventh Circuit, 1990
917 F.2d 1017

POSNER, Circuit Judge. The district court dismissed Donald Pelfresne's suit against a municipality and a number of its officials and employees as barred by the Anti-Injunction Act, 28 U.S.C. §2283, and then refused to allow him to amend his complaint. The appeal presents interesting questions, rarely encountered in a federal court, of property law.

In November 1984 the Village of Williams Bay in Walworth County, Wisconsin brought suit in the Circuit Court of Walworth County against Michael Schiessle. The suit sought a court order to raze four single-family houses located on property owned by Schiessle in Williams Bay that were in disrepair and believed to be unsafe. The Village filed a notice of lis pendens (pending litigation) in the Walworth County registry of deeds.

The next month, December 1984, Schiessle conveyed the property to Lommen Eley and John Koch to hold in trust for him, whereupon the Village named Eley and Koch as additional defendants in its suit. The suit was dismissed in July of the following year (1985) on technical grounds and promptly refiled, but no new notice of lis pendens was filed. In February 1986 Eley and Koch conveyed the property to Anita Catania, but the conveyance was not recorded.

On June 25, 1986, judgment was entered for the Village in the refiled suit. The judgment ordered the buildings razed and also awarded the Village damages and costs totaling $629.42. The clerk of the circuit court, pursuant to statute, prepared the judgment docket card that appears at the end of this opinion. Wis. Stat. §806.10(1). The card notes the damages and costs but not the raze order.

In September 1987, months after the judgment in the circuit court action had become final upon the exhaustion of the defendants' appellate remedies, both the release of the notice of lis pendens in the first suit (the one that had been dismissed) and the deed to Catania were recorded in the Walworth County registry of deeds, along with another deed from Catania, this one made in either 1986 or 1987 (the record is unclear which) to Allen Veren. Schiessle continued as the beneficial owner.

The day after these instruments were recorded, Pelfresne bought the property for $60,000 and ten days later he brought this suit, basing federal jurisdiction on diversity of citizenship. (He is a citizen of Michigan, while all the defendants are citizens of Wisconsin.) The suit depicts him as a bona fide purchaser for value who under Wisconsin law was not bound by the raze order contained in the judgment that had been entered against Schiessle, Eley, and Koch in June 1986. . . .

. . . The Anti-Injunction Act forbids a federal court to enjoin state court proceedings and the prohibition has been interpreted to bar an injunction against the enforcement of a judgment obtained in such proceedings, even though such an injunction is directed not against the state court itself but against the victorious party in state court proceedings, who is trying to enforce the judgment he obtained. . . .

[The district judge dismissed the complaint under the Anti-Injunction Act]. . . .

However, a stranger to the state court litigation — hence one who cannot be regarded as a litigant in state court, disappointed or otherwise — is not barred. . . .

. . . Only a party, or, what amounts to the same thing in contemplation of the law, one who is in privity with a party, is barred by the Anti-Injunction Act. County of Imperial v. Munoz, 449 U.S. [54], 59, 60 n.3 [1980]; Hale v. Bimco Trading, Inc., 306 U.S. 375, 377-78 (1939).

The question of privity is central to this case. Pelfresne concedes that if the raze order issued by the Circuit Court of Walworth County is a lien on the property that he bought, then he is in privity with the defendants in the circuit court action. He further concedes that it is a lien on the property enforceable against him if he knew about the raze order when he bought the property, or if, though he did not know about it, he is treated by Wisconsin law as if he did: in legalese, if he had "constructive notice" of the order.

He may well have had actual notice. Schiessle has been the beneficial owner of the property throughout the elaborate series of transfers that preceded the sale to Pelfresne and that appear to have been motivated by a desire to escape the raze order, and Pelfresne is Schiessle's nephew. Either they are in cahoots or the uncle has tried to pull a fast one on his nephew; the fact that Pelfresne brought this suit to enjoin the raze order just ten days after he bought the property supports the former hypothesis. But there has been no finding of actual notice as yet, so we proceed to the question of constructive notice.

At first glance "constructive notice" may seem another of those unworthy legal fictions that contribute to the law's poor reputation among laymen. It means no notice, and its purpose and effect may therefore seem to be to pretend that a person who did not know something did know it. In fact, however, it is a mainstay of the system of protecting interests, both prior and subsequent, in land by means of a system of public records. One who records his interest in the proper records office is thereby protected against subsequent claimants and need not attempt to publicize that interest in any other way, and he is also protected against any prior claimants who by failing to record their interests had failed to provide notice in the prescribed manner.

But was the Village's raze order properly recorded? It was if it was within the "chain of title" of the property, a term that "includes instruments, actions and proceedings discoverable by reasonable search of the public records and indices affecting real estate in the offices of the register of deeds and in probate and of clerks of courts in the counties in which the real estate is located." Wis. Stat. §706.09(4). A purchaser of real estate has constructive notice of a prior interest if "there appears of record in the chain of title of the real estate affected . . . an instrument affording affirmative and express notice of such prior outstanding interest conforming to the requirements of definiteness of sub. (1)(b)." §706.09(2)(b). We go to subsection (1)(b) to discover those requirements and read there that "any conveyance, transaction or event not appearing of record in the chain" does not place a purchaser on constructive notice unless the conveyance, etc. "is identified by definite reference in an instrument of record in such chain" and that to be definite the reference must specify "the nature and scope of the prior outstanding interest created." In other words, even an instrument that appears in the chain of title will place a subsequent purchaser on notice of an interest created by that instrument only if it specifies the interest's nature and scope.

If the instrument in Pelfresne's chain of title is the judgment in the circuit court action, then since the judgment includes the raze order, the requirement of definite reference is satisfied and Pelfresne loses. That is what the district judge thought. If on the other hand the instrument is the judgment docket card, then Pelfresne's hand is greatly (though, as we shall see, not necessarily decisively) strengthened, for the card contains no definite reference — no reference, period — to the raze order.

To be in the chain of title, an instrument must, according to the passage from section 706.09(4) quoted earlier, be one "affecting real estate." So we must decide whether it is the judgment or the judgment docket that affects real estate, i.e., that creates a lien. We think it is the latter. Every judgment that is "properly docketed" creates, under Wisconsin law, a lien against real estate owned by the person or persons against whom the judgment is entered. Wis. Stat. §806.15(1). The Wisconsin courts take this specification literally: no docket, no lien. Wisconsin Mortgage & Security Co. v. Kriesel, 191 Wis. 602, 211 N.W. 795 (1927). "[P]roperly docketed" means written up on a judgment docket card that is entered, alphabetically by the name of the defendant, in the judgment docket, in effect an index of judgments. Wis. Stat. §806.10(1). The card in this case was filed in triplicate, one card under the name of each of the three defendants in the Village's suit, and the card mentions no raze order. The judgment entering that order therefore was not docketed; did not create a lien, other than for $629.42, the monetary part of the judgment, which was entered on the card; therefore did not (with the same qualification) affect real estate; therefore (again with the same qualification) was not in the chain of title of Pelfresne's predecessors in title. Burner v. Wille, 30 Wis. 2d 658, 141 N.W.2d 895 (1966).

This may seem a cruel blow to the interests of creditors. It is not. The Village, the judgment creditor, could have filed the judgment containing the raze order in the registry of deeds. "[E]very conveyance, and every other instrument which affects title to land in this state, shall be entitled to record in the office of the register of deeds of each county in which land affected thereby may lie." Wis. Stat. §706.05(1). "[I]nstrument which affects title to land" is broadly construed. It includes equitable as well as legal judgments. Cutler v. James, 64 Wis. 173, 24 N.W. 874 (1885). Although we can find no previous case involving raze orders, we think it must also include an equitable judgment that, in ordering the demolition of buildings, affected the defendants' title to the property that included those buildings. Surely the statutory term "land" includes the buildings on it, though this too is a question on which we find no cases.

The clincher is Wis. Stat. §66.05(8)(b), the statute under which the raze order was issued. It provides (in subsection (8)(b)(3)) that the order binds subsequent owners "if a lis pendens was filed before the change of ownership." This implies that a raze order creates an interest affecting land, and hence extinguishes the rights of subsequent purchasers, even if bona fide, provided it is properly recorded. No doubt this is why in its initial suit the Village filed a notice of lis pendens with the register of deeds. Once that suit was over, the notice was properly removed. The Village neglected to file a notice of lis pendens in the refiled suit; had it done so, then perhaps after it obtained the judgment it would, as it should, have replaced the notice of lis pendens with the judgment.

The fact that the docket card contains no space for an equitable judgment is telling. Such judgments, which affect the land directly, should be filed with the register of deeds. The clerk's docket is designed for money judgments, which merely by virtue of being entered and properly docketed become liens against any land that the defendant should happen to own; because of that automaticity, the filing of a mere money judgment in the registry of deeds would clog that registry with paper unnecessarily.

This may seem to conclude the case triumphantly for Pelfresne. Not so. Remember what section 706.09(2)(b) says: the purchaser takes subject to any interest of which he has "affirmative and express notice" from an instrument in the chain of title. The recording system is for the protection of purchasers (including creditors) who are "bona fide" in the sense not only of purity of heart but also of some minimum degree of carefulness. The docket card showing the money judgment against Pelfresne's predecessors was an instrument in the chain of title, and the language of "affirmative and express notice" has been held not to extinguish the traditional duty of "reasonable inquiry." Kordecki v. Rizzo, 106 Wis. 2d 713, 719-21, 317 N.W.2d 479, 483 (1982). Anyone searching title on Pelfresne's behalf would first have gone to the registry of deeds and there found, in the file for the property that Pelfresne wanted to buy, the identity of the previous owners, including Schiessle, the equitable or beneficial owner, and Eley and Koch, two in a string of holders of the legal title. The next step, a step required by the statutory definition of chain of title as including instruments recorded in the office of the clerk of the circuit court for the county in which the property is located, was to look up these names in the judgment docket card file of the clerk's office. There one would have found—and there Pelfresne's title searcher, who had already found the deed to Eley and Koch in the registry of deeds, did in fact find—the card for the Village's judgment. Although the judgment was for a small amount of money, the fact that it was entered jointly against three recent owners of the land that Pelfresne was buying should have set the alarm bells to ringing. Almost certainly it was a judgment arising out of their ownership.

The duty of reasonable inquiry is a function in part of the burden of inquiry. It would have been a matter of minutes for Pelfresne's title searcher to look up the judgment and find the raze order in it. Especially when we consider the personal relationship between Pelfresne and Schiessle, the indications that Pelfresne was on inquiry notice of the raze order are very strong, and that is notice enough as we have seen to put him in the chain of title from the defendants in the Village's suit. A finding of inquiry notice, however, like other assessments of reasonableness, is one of fact. . . . We shall therefore remand for a determination of whether Pelfresne was on inquiry notice. Also open on remand of course is whether he had actual notice.

Affirmed in part, reversed in part, and remanded.

	☐ Execution(s) Issued (see reverse) ☐ Foreign Judgment (see reverse)		☐ Satisfaction. Full or Partial Filed (see reverse) ☐ Release of Certain Real Estate Filed (see reverse)
JUDGMENT DEBTOR (Name & Address) ▶ Schiessle, Michael; 805 Northwest Highway, Parkridge, Illinois; ▶ *Lommen D. Eley; 127 North Deerborn Street, Suite 631; Chicago, Illinois and **John P. Koch; 127 North Deerborn Street,***			JUDGMENT CREDITOR (Name & Address) Village of Williams Bay P.O. Box 580, Williams Bay, Walworth County, Wisconsin
Occupation Schiessle; engaged in the profession of law; Eley, engaged in the practice of law; Koch engaged in the practice of law			Occupation engages in the operation of said village under Wisconsin Law
Case Number 85 CV 708			Attorney of Creditor Richard R. Grant of Consigny, Andrews, Hemming & Grant, S.C., Janesville, WI
Date of Judgment 6/25/86	Date Docketed 6/25/86	Time Docketed 4:00 p.m.	Other Judgment Debtors
Judgment Amount	Costs	Total Costs & Judgment $629.42	Remarks ***Suite 631; Chicago, Illinois Judgment docketed in 3 places

Problem 10C

Carla, the present owner of Pinkacre, has contracted to sell Pinkacre to David. Together, Carla and David hire a local attorney, Toby, to search title and handle the closing. Toby finds, as one link in the chain of title, a deed from Aaron, recorded in 1990, conveying Pinkacre to Byron "subject to a mortgage dated June 1, 1986, to Junior Morgan, securing a promissory note in amount of $20,000." Toby conducts a complete search, finding no recorded mortgage to Morgan and no other evidence of record concerning Morgan's note or mortgage. The subsequent deed from Byron to Carla does not mention the mortgage to Morgan. Carla says she has not paid the mortgage loan and knows nothing about it. Toby decides that title is marketable and closing takes place, with Carla conveying Pinkacre to David by warranty deed. One month later, Morgan returns from a long stay at the Gray Bar Hotel somewhere in the Caribbean and demands that David pay the promissory note. David refuses. Morgan threatens to foreclose. Does Morgan have the right to foreclose? Assume the debt evidenced by the promissory note is not time-barred and Morgan has a valid but unrecorded mortgage, executed by Aaron, which secures payment of the note.

2. *Defects in Recorded Instruments*

Occasionally an instrument is recorded although it does not meet the formal statutory requirements for recordation. When this happens, usually the defect relates to acknowledgment; all states limit recordation to documents that are properly acknowledged. Most courts, examining the language of their recording acts, have concluded that a defectively acknowledged deed does not impart constructive notice because it should not be there. This means that the grantee who claims under the defective instrument has some risk of losing to a subsequent BFP. A few states have reformed their recording statutes to eliminate this risk.

Recorded instruments may be defective for reasons other than improper acknowledgment. Deeds that are forged and deeds that were signed by the grantor but were not delivered to the grantee are deemed void, even though these defects are not ascertainable by looking at the deed itself. Labelling these deeds "void" means that the original owner can recover the land, even though the grantee under the void deed has sold the land to a BFP. In contrast, less serious defects are said to render a deed "voidable," but not void. For example, if a grantor is induced by fraud or misrepresentation to sign and deliver a deed, this makes the deed voidable, not void. This permits the grantor to recover the property as long as the grantee continues to own it, but protects a subsequent BFP who relies on the first grantee's apparent title. This distinction between void deeds and voidable deeds is closely analogous to the principles that apply to the bona fide purchase of personal property. *See* UCC §2-403.

METROPOLITAN NATIONAL BANK v. UNITED STATES

United States Court of Appeals, Fifth Circuit, 1990
901 F.2d 1297

E. Grady Jolly, Circuit Judge. The United States appeals from the district court's judgment holding that the United States' perfected tax lien, filed against three parcels of real property owned by the taxpayer, Weaver & Sons, Inc., was not entitled to priority over the interests claimed in the property by the appellees, Metropolitan National Bank (the "Bank"), James M. Oberlies, and Robert E. Ryan. 716 F. Supp. 946. We hold that the appellees were not entitled to priority under section 6323(a) of the Internal Revenue Code, and we therefore reverse the judgment of the district court and remand the case for further proceedings.

I

. . . On February 23, 1978, Weaver & Sons, Inc. (the "taxpayer"), by its president, S. Albert Weaver, executed a deed of trust in favor of First State Bank and Trust, the predecessor of appellee Metropolitan National Bank. The deed of trust recited that the taxpayer was indebted to the Bank in the amount of $400,000, and listed certain real property owned by the taxpayer located in Gulfport, Mississippi, as security for the indebtedness. The deed of trust designated Robert L. Taylor as trustee for the lender, and Robert L. Taylor, in his capacity as a notary public, acknowledged the signature of the grantor's president. The deed of trust was filed and recorded by the Chancery Clerk's office in Harrison County, Mississippi on February 24, 1978.

On February 23, March 2, March 9, March 16, and June 2, 1987, assessments were made against the taxpayer for unpaid federal withholding, Federal Insurance Contributions Act (FICA), and Federal Unemployment Tax Act (FUTA) taxes. Notices of the federal tax liens resulting from these assessments were enrolled with the Harrison County Chancery Clerk's office on May 7 and August 27, 1987. The unpaid balance of these assessments totaled $195,621.61, plus interest and statutory additions to tax.

The taxpayer defaulted in payment of its obligation to the Bank, and subsequently filed a Chapter 7 bankruptcy petition . . . on August 19, 1987. . . . [T]he Internal Revenue Service ("IRS") filed a proof of claim dated November 24, 1987. At the time the taxpayer defaulted, it owed $268,833.55 on the loan secured by the deed of trust.

On March 8, 1988, the taxpayer executed a corrected deed of trust in favor of the Bank's predecessor institution in the amount of $400,000, secured by the subject property. The corrected deed of trust was properly acknowledged and recorded in the Harrison County Chancery Clerk's office on March 9, 1988.

The bankruptcy court lifted the automatic stay, authorizing the Bank to repossess and foreclose upon the subject property. Notices of foreclosure were posted in the county courthouse, published in the local newspaper, and sent to the IRS by certified mail. A nonjudicial foreclosure sale was held on April 19, 1988, at which the Bank, for $103,600, and appellee Robert E. Ryan, for $31,000, each purchased a portion of the subject property. Thereafter, the Bank conveyed a portion of the property it had purchased in the foreclosure sale to appellee James M. Oberlies. The IRS took no action to stop the foreclosure, or to prevent the sale of the property to the Bank or to Ryan and Oberlies.

II

The appellees brought this action against the United States under 28 U.S.C. §2410, seeking to quiet title to the property. The United States counterclaimed, joining the taxpayer as an additional defendant, seeking to foreclose its federal tax liens against the subject property and to collect

$195,621.65, the outstanding tax liability of the taxpayer. On cross motions for summary judgment, the district court granted summary judgment in favor of the appellees. The district court held that the original deed of trust was improperly acknowledged and that, even though the deed of trust was recorded, because the defect in the acknowledgment was apparent on the face of the deed, the recordation of the deed did not provide constructive notice to subsequent creditors that the property was encumbered. Nevertheless, the court held that, even though the deed was improperly acknowledged and should not have been recorded, the deed "provided actual notice to anyone who cared to review the records of the Chancery Clerk." The district court did not hold, however, that agents of the United States had in fact reviewed the county records prior to filing the notices of federal tax liens against the taxpayer, or that the United States possessed any information sufficient to place it on "inquiry notice" of the deed. Finally, the district court concluded that the United States' tax lien was not entitled to priority over the Bank's interest because, under state law, the Bank held equitable title to the property by virtue of the original defective deed of trust, and the United States had actual notice of such equitable title. . . .

III

A

Under 26 U.S.C. §6321, the amount of a delinquent taxpayer's liability constitutes a lien in favor of the United States upon all of the taxpayer's property and rights to property, whether real or personal. The lien imposed by §6321 is effective from the date of assessment of the tax, and continues until the liability is satisfied or becomes unenforceable by reason of lapse of time. 26 U.S.C. §6322. . . .

. . . Section 6323 of the Internal Revenue Code, as amended by the Federal Tax Lien Act of 1966, governs the validity and priority of federal tax liens imposed by §6321 against "certain persons." The appellees rely on the special priority rules of subsection (a) of §6323, which provides, in pertinent part, that a federal tax lien shall not be valid against any "holder of a security interest" until notice of the tax lien has been filed. Thus, the respective priorities with respect to federal tax liens and competing claims that are protected under §6323(a) are dependent upon which claim is perfected "first in time." Both parties agree that, if the Bank was a "holder of a security interest" at the time the United States filed its federal tax liens, the appellees' interests are entitled to priority over the federal tax liens and that the tax liens were thus extinguished in the foreclosure sale.

The definition of "security interest" is found in 26 U.S.C. §6323(h)(1):

> The term "security interest" means any interest in property acquired by contract for the purpose of securing payment or performance of an obligation or indemnifying against loss or liability.

A security interest exists only when the lienholder satisfies two requirements:

> (A) if, at such time the property is in existence and the interest has become protected under local law against a subsequent judgment lien arising out of an unsecured obligation, and (B) to the extent that, at such time, the holder has parted with money or money's worth.

Because the subject property is in existence and the Bank parted with money in return for the deed of trust, the Bank's interest in the subject property by virtue of the original deed of trust is entitled to priority over the subsequently filed federal tax lien under §6323(a) if, as a result of filing the original deed of trust, the Bank is "protected under local law against a subsequent judgment lien arising out of an unsecured obligation." 26 U.S.C. §6323(h)(1). . . .

B

Because the corrected deed of trust was not filed until after the federal tax liens were filed, the issue before us is whether the Bank held an interest under the original deed of trust that was protected under Mississippi law against a subsequent judgment lien arising out of an unsecured obligation. . . .

. . . [O]ur examination of the relevant Mississippi cases and statutes convinces us that the Bank's interest under the original deed of trust would not have been entitled to protection against a subsequent judgment lien arising out of an unsecured obligation unless such a judgment lien creditor had actual notice or knowledge of the defectively acknowledged deed of trust.[1]

(1) Under Mississippi law, all deeds of trust are "void as to all creditors and subsequent purchasers for a valuable consideration without notice, unless they be acknowledged or proved and lodged with the clerk of the chancery court of the proper county, to be recorded. . . ." Miss. Code Ann. §89-5-3 (1972). . . .

1. Other courts have taken two different approaches in determining the kind of protection Congress contemplated that a security interest must have in order to be "protected under local law against a subsequent judgment lien." One line of cases applies the "subjective knowledge lien creditor test," and places the United States in the shoes of a subsequent judgment lien creditor. Under those cases, if the United States obtains actual or constructive knowledge of the competing nonfederal interest prior to filing its federal tax liens, and if, under local law a judgment lien creditor is protected only if he is without actual or constructive knowledge of a prior interest, the tax lien is not entitled to priority over the nonfederal interest. *See, e.g.*, United States v. Ed Lusk Constr. Co., 504 F.2d 328, 331 (10th Cir. 1974); United States v. Trigg, 465 F.2d 1264, 1268-69 (8th Cir. 1972), *cert. denied*, 410 U.S. 909 (1973). The other line of cases applies a "hypothetical judgment lien creditor test" that focuses on the protection state laws give to the security interest against other hypothetical lien creditors. Under that test, the question is whether the security interest is protected under local law against any hypothetical judgment lien creditor that might arise, whether or not the government has knowledge of the competing nonfederal interest. *See, e.g.*, Dragstrem v. Obermeyer, 549 F.2d 20, 25-27 (7th Cir. 1977). We do not need to decide which test should apply in this case. The district court applied the "subjective knowledge" test, and both parties have assumed the applicability of that test in their presentation of the case to this court.

A deed of trust is not eligible for recordation unless it is properly acknowledged, and an instrument that does not contain a proper acknowledgment does not impart constructive notice to creditors or bona fide purchasers, pursuant to Miss. Code Ann. §89-3-1 (1972):

> [A] written instrument of or concerning the sale of lands . . . shall not be admitted to record in the clerk's office unless the execution thereof be first acknowledged or proved, and the acknowledgment or proof duly certified by an officer competent to take the same in the manner directed by this chapter; and any such instrument which is admitted to record without such acknowledgment or proof shall not be notice to creditors or subsequent purchasers for valuable consideration.

It is undisputed, and the district court correctly held, that the original deed of trust dated February 23, 1978 was improperly acknowledged by the trustee named in the deed. *See* Holden v. Brimage, 72 Miss. 228, 229-30, 18 So. 383, 383 (1894) (an acknowledgment to a trust deed taken before an officer who is himself trustee therein, with power to sell to pay debts, is void and does not entitle the deed to be recorded). Under Mississippi law neither a grantee designated by a deed of trust, nor the trustee designated to act for the grantee, can properly acknowledge a deed of trust.

> Under Mississippi law, the taking of an acknowledgment is a judicial or quasi-judicial rather than a ministerial act, and . . . this act cannot be performed by a grantee in the deed, or by one who, though not a grantee, is the procuring cause of the conveyance or has a financial or beneficial interest in the transaction. . . . It would be against public policy to permit a grantee, mortgagee, or trustee, or other person beneficially interested in the transaction to take an acknowledgment to an instrument in which he is named as a party or has a beneficial interest. The object of the law is to prevent the perpetration of fraud, and the policy of the law seems to be that the officer taking the acknowledgment must not be in such relationship to the grantee that there shall exist any temptation for the officer to do aught but his duty impartially.

Mills v. Damson Oil Corp., 686 F.2d 1096, 1102-03 (5th Cir. 1982) (*quoting* 1 *Delvin on Real Estate and Deeds,* §477d (3d Ed. 1911)). The acknowledgment taken by the trustee in this case was thus void.[2] Jones v. Porter, 59 Miss. 628 (1882) (where the acknowledgment of a grantor was taken by the husband of the grantee, who was the procuring cause of the conveyance, the acknowledgment was void). Because the acknowledgment was void, the deed of trust was not eligible for recordation and, even though the deed was recorded, it nevertheless did not impart constructive notice to creditors

2. Although the acknowledgment was void, it does not follow that the deed itself was void. Pursuant to Miss. Code Ann. §89-5-3, a deed that is neither acknowledged nor recorded is "nevertheless valid and binding" as between the parties and their heirs, and as to all subsequent purchasers (and creditors) with notice or without valuable consideration.

under Miss. Code Ann. §89-3-1. *See also* Holden v. Brimage, 72 Miss. at 229-30, 18 So. at 383; Wasson v. Connor, 54 Miss. 351, 352-53 (1877) (where grantee acknowledged grantor's signature, "[t]he deed never having been legally acknowledged, [it] was, of course, improperly recorded, and it afforded notice to nobody").

In Mills v. Damson Oil Corp., this court [noted that most reported cases] concern patent defects, i.e., "defects which are apparent on the face of the acknowledgment." *Mills,* 686 F.2d at 1104. The defect in *Mills* was "entirely latent" because there was "nothing in the deed or its acknowledgment to indicate that the named grantee, Lurline Daws, and S. B. Daws, who took the acknowledgment, were related to each other, or, indeed, that either was married." *Id.* Because only one Mississippi case, Roebuck v. Bailey, 176 Miss. 234, 166 So. 358 (1936), discussed the effect of a latent defect in an acknowledgment on bona fide purchasers, and because in that case the Mississippi court recognized a potential distinction between latently and patently defective acknowledgments, this court certified the following question to the Mississippi Supreme Court:

> Whether a defectively acknowledged and recorded deed imparts constructive notice if the defect in the acknowledgment is entirely latent?

Mills, 686 F.2d at 1114. The Mississippi Supreme Court answered "yes." Mills v. Damson Oil Corp., 437 So. 2d 1005, 1006 (Miss. 1983).

Nothing in the Mississippi Supreme Court's answer to the certified question in *Mills* casts any doubt on the cases involving defectively acknowledged deeds in which the defects are patent. . . . The original deed of trust in this case names Robert L. Taylor as trustee, and Robert L. Taylor acknowledged the signature of the grantor. Thus, it is clear that the defect in the acknowledgment is patent, and the district court correctly held that the deed did not give constructive notice to subsequent bona fide purchasers and creditors. We therefore conclude that, under Mississippi law, the recordation of the defectively acknowledged deed of trust did not impart constructive notice, and thus did not protect the Bank's interest under the deed of trust against a subsequent judgment lien creditor in the absence of actual notice to such a subsequent judgment lien creditor.

(2) . . . Under Mississippi law, a prior deed, whether recorded or unrecorded, is good against a subsequent purchaser or creditor with actual notice of it. . . .

The appellees contend, and the district court held, that the United States had actual notice because the deed was recorded and could have been located had the United States searched the records. This argument confuses the concepts of actual notice and constructive notice. The mere recording of a deed does not provide *actual* notice to strangers to a transaction who are not in possession of facts that would place them on inquiry notice. Rather, the primary purpose of recording is to impart *constructive* notice.

The appellees contend, however, that the United States had a "duty to inquire" because its agents had knowledge of sufficient facts to place it upon inquiry notice to check the title to the subject property. . . .

In support of their position that the United States had a duty to inquire, the appellees argue, without any citation of authority, that the fact that the taxpayer had not paid its taxes should have provided notice to the United States that the title to any property owned by the taxpayer would be subject to other liens or problems. We disagree. The fact that the taxpayer was delinquent in its federal tax obligations created no inferences concerning the taxpayer's title to any particular property and falls short of the type of information necessary to place the United States on inquiry notice. We also reject the appellees' argument that the taxpayer's filing of a petition in bankruptcy should have led the United States to conduct an investigation that would have resulted in the discovery of the Bank's deed of trust. We need not consider whether the taxpayer's filing of its bankruptcy petition was sufficient to put the IRS on inquiry notice because the record contains absolutely no factual support for the appellees' argument. For example, the record does not indicate when the United States received notice of the filing of the bankruptcy petition, or whether it received such notice prior to the filing of its federal tax liens.

We conclude that the record does not support the district court's holding that the United States had actual notice of the defective deed of trust. The record contains no evidence indicating that the United States was aware of the deed of trust prior to the time it filed its federal tax liens, or that it possessed any knowledge of circumstances that would have put it on inquiry which, if pursued, would have led it to actual knowledge of the defective deed of trust. Although the district court's statement that the defective deed of trust could give actual notice "to anyone who cared to review the records of the Chancery Clerk" is correct as far as it goes, there is no evidence that any agent of the United States reviewed the records of the Harrison County Chancery Clerk, and, under the facts in the record, the United States did not have inquiry notice of the existence of the deed.

(3) The district court further held that the defectively acknowledged deed of trust gave the Bank "equitable title" sufficient to defeat the claims of "a subsequent purchaser or party coming after the document in question, who has notice of the questionable document." Even if we assume that the defectively acknowledged deed of trust gave the Bank "equitable title," the United States, as we have already noted, did not have notice of the defectively acknowledged deed of trust. . . .

C

The district court's holding that the federal tax lien was extinguished in the foreclosure sale of the property under the provisions of 26 U.S.C. §7425(b) is based on its erroneous conclusion that the tax liens were junior to the Bank's lien. . . . We therefore hold that the district court erred in concluding that the senior tax liens of the United States were discharged by the Bank's nonjudicial foreclosure sale.

For the foregoing reasons, the judgment of the district court is reversed, and the case is remanded to the district court for further proceedings.

Problem 10D

Caroline Messersmith and Frederick Messersmith owned land in Golden Valley as tenants in common. Caroline executed and delivered to Frederick a quitclaim deed to the property, which Frederick did not record. Five years later, on May 7, Caroline executed a mineral deed conveying to Herbert Smith an undivided one-half interest of all oil, gas, and other minerals in and under the property. Smith paid her $1,400. A notary public was not present when she signed the deed. Smith took the deed to a notary, who called Caroline over the telephone and then placed on the deed the usual notarial acknowledgment, including the notary's signature and seal. For a valid acknowledgment, state law requires that the grantor personally appear before the notary to acknowledge her execution of the deed.

On May 9 Smith executed a mineral deed conveying to Herbert E. B. Seale an undivided one-half interest of all oil, gas, and other minerals in and under the property. Seale paid value to Smith and had no actual notice of Frederick's quitclaim deed. Both the deeds to Smith and to Seale were recorded on May 26. Frederick recorded his deed on July 9 of the same year. Frederick brought an action to quiet title to all of the property. Seale claims title to one-half of the mineral estate. What result, and why, under a (1) race statute, (2) notice statute, and (3) race-notice statute?

3. Notice from Possession

In notice and race-notice states, a purchaser takes subject to rights of parties in possession and other unrecorded interests that are visible from an inspection of the property. Even though holders of these interests could have recorded and failed to do so, they are protected by their state's view of inquiry notice. Possession by someone other than the seller gives rise to a duty of inquiry. The rule envisions a dialogue between the purchaser and the possessor. The purchaser is bound by whatever rights would have been uncovered by diligent inquiry of the possessor.

There is one general exception to the duty to inquire of possessors. When possession is consistent with record title, there is no duty of inquiry. Thus, when there is a recorded lease, there is no duty to ask the tenant why he is there. In many states, there is also an exception to inquiry notice for possession by a grantor who recently deeded the property to the seller.

The rationale is that it is not unusual for a grantee to let the seller remain in possession for a reasonable period of time after the conveyance. When this exception applies, it protects the purchaser as BFP from the possessing grantor's claim either that he has unrecorded rights, such as a life estate, or the right to rescind the transfer for some reason such as fraud.

In re WEISMAN

United States Court of Appeals, Ninth Circuit, 1993
5 F.3d 417

REINHARDT, Circuit Judge. We are faced with the question whether under California law a husband's occupation of his family residence with his second wife can create a duty in a bona fide purchaser for value or a bankruptcy trustee to inquire as to whether his former wife still retains the ownership interest in that property that appears of record. Guided by reality, our answer is yes.

I. FACTUAL AND PROCEDURAL BACKGROUND

Debtor Sheila Weisman (formerly Sheila Peters) married defendant Marc Peters in 1963. They bought a house, which is the subject of the instant dispute, in Campbell, California in 1967. The couple lived in the Campbell residence until March 1985, when Sheila Peters moved out. The couple's marriage was dissolved that fall, but the judgment of dissolution was not recorded. Pursuant to their property settlement, Marc Peters had the right to purchase his former wife's interest in the house they had previously shared. He did so by refinancing and using the loan as the purchase price. However, the lender required Sheila Weisman, who had married debtor Marc Weisman in November 1985, to remain on the title to the property.

As a result of the refinancing transaction, title to the Campbell residence was transferred from Marc Peters and Sheila Peters, as community property, to Marc Peters and Sheila Weisman (a married woman), as tenants in common.[2] The deed reflecting the transfer was dated June 23, 1986, and was recorded July 2, 1986. Marc Weisman then executed a quit claim deed in favor of Sheila Weisman on June 24, 1986, which was also recorded on July 2, 1986. After receiving payment from Marc Peters for her interest in their former home, Sheila Weisman executed a quit claim deed in favor of him on June 25, 1986. The deed was delivered on August 27, 1986, but was not recorded until December 8, 1988. Marc Peters married Nianne Neergaard in August 1986 and the couple has lived in the Campbell residence since that time.

2. Although Sheila Weisman was remarried, her interest in the house was held as separate property.

In August 1988, Sheila Weisman and her second husband, Marc Weisman, filed a voluntary bankruptcy petition under Chapter 7 of the Bankruptcy Code (liquidation). A trustee, plaintiff Jerome Robertson, was appointed. After learning that Sheila Weisman was a record title holder to the Campbell residence, the trustee filed a complaint against Marc Peters for authorization to sell that property, as permitted by the Bankruptcy Code. After hearing oral argument, the bankruptcy court found for defendant Peters. The district court reversed the bankruptcy judge's finding as clearly erroneous and entered judgment for the trustee. Peters appealed. . . .

II. Analysis

The Bankruptcy Code, 11 U.S.C. section 544(a)(3), gives a bankruptcy trustee "strong arm powers" to avoid transfers of real property of the debtor that would be voidable under state law by a bona fide purchaser (BFP) of the property from the debtor. . . . Here, California law applies and will determine whether the trustee can set aside Sheila Weisman's (hereinafter "Weisman") unrecorded transfer of all of her interests in the house to Marc Peters (hereinafter "Peters").

California is a race-notice jurisdiction and requires every conveyance of real property to be recorded in order to be valid against a subsequent purchaser of the same property. Cal. Civil Code §1214. However, an unrecorded instrument is valid as between the parties thereto and those who have notice of it. Cal. Civil Code §1217. Although 11 U.S.C. section 544(a)(3) creates the legal fiction of a perfect BFP and explicitly renders the trustee's actual notice of prior grantees irrelevant, [*In re*] Professional Investment Properties, 955 F.2d [623,] 627 n.2 [9th Cir. 1992], we have held that constructive or inquiry notice obtained in accordance with California Civil Code section 19 can defeat a trustee's claim. [*In re*] Probasco, 839 F.2d [1352,] at 1354-56 [9th Cir. 1988].

The resolution of this case turns on California Civil Code section 19. It provides:

> Every person who has actual notice of circumstances sufficient to put a prudent man upon inquiry as to a particular fact, has constructive notice of the fact itself in all cases in which, by prosecuting such inquiry, he might have learned such fact.

In this context the question is whether a prudent purchaser, in light of the information reasonably available to him on the date the Weismans filed their bankruptcy petition, would have made an inquiry into the possibility that Peters owned his residence outright. A "prudent purchaser" describes someone who is shrewd in the management of practical affairs and whose conduct is marked by wisdom, judiciousness, or circumspection. *See Probasco*, 839 F.2d at 1356. Such a purchaser will be charged with knowledge of 1) the nature of the property; 2) its current use; 3) the identities of the persons occupying it; 4) the relationship among them; and, 5) the relationship between those in possession and the person whose purported interest in the property the purchaser intended to acquire. . . .

. . . If, under the circumstances, the trustee should have made an inquiry as to whether Weisman had transferred all of her interests in the Campbell residence to Peters, then . . . the trustee [is charged] with knowledge of the unrecorded deed that did just that. Such knowledge would prevent the trustee from prevailing in this strong arm action. *See Probasco*, 839 F.2d at 1354-56.

Resolution of the question whether the trustee was under a duty to make an inquiry depends in part on the interplay of several long established and related principles of California real estate law:

1. Open, notorious, exclusive, and visible possession of real property by one other than the vendor is notice sufficient to put a prospective purchaser on inquiry of any rights held by the occupant, unless there is no duty under the circumstances to make inquiry.
2. There is no duty to inquire upon a subsequent purchaser regarding any unknown claims or interests by a person in possession of real property where the occupant's possession is consistent with the record title.
3. Where possession is inconsistent with the record title and thereby creates a duty to inquire, a prospective purchaser is charged with constructive notice of all facts that would be revealed by a reasonably diligent inquiry, regardless of whether the purchaser has ever seen the property.

The essential dispute between the parties is whether Peters' and Neergaard's possession of the house was consistent or inconsistent with the record title in Peters' and Weisman's names. The trustee argues that the possession was consistent because, as a cotenant, Peters had the right to possess the whole of the property. The trustee maintains it was immaterial that Weisman lived elsewhere and that Neergaard resided on the property. Peters contends possession was inconsistent with title because of a combination of 1) the change in title from Marc Peters and Sheila Peters to Marc Peters and Sheila Weisman, a married woman, demonstrating that the couple had divorced and Sheila had remarried, and 2) the presence of Peters' second wife, Neergaard, on the property with him. Peters argues that knowledge of these facts would have caused a prudent purchaser to conduct an inquiry.

The trustee places great reliance on the case of Schumacher v. Truman, 134 Cal. 430, 66 P. 591 (1901), as did the district court. There, a husband and wife owned a parcel of real property. They entered into an unrecorded agreement giving the husband complete management and control over the property. Later the couple divorced and they took title as tenants in common. The husband then subleased his interest in the property to a tenant, who took up exclusive occupation of the property. The wife sold her interest in the property to a third party. The husband argued that anyone in the wife's chain of title took an interest in the property subject to the unrecorded agreement giving him exclusive management and control. The California Supreme Court disagreed and held that there was no constructive notice of the unrecorded agreement between the wife and husband. It reasoned that the exclusive possession by the husband's tenant was consistent with record title and, therefore, a prospective purchaser had no duty to make further inquiry. The tenant's possession was considered to be the equivalent of sole occupation by the ex-husband, and it could be presumed that sole possession by him was in the interest and benefit of the absent cotenant, his ex-wife. *Schumacher,* 134 Cal. at 433.

That same presumption is inapplicable here. Inquiry becomes a duty for a prospective purchaser of property when the visible state of affairs is inconsistent with the alleged rights of the person who has proposed to sell the property in question. . . . Here, the trustee is charged both with knowing that Neergaard resided on the property with Peters and that she was his second wife. He is also, of course, charged with knowledge of Weisman's remarriage because that information is on the recorded deed to the Campbell residence.

Peters and his second wife, Neergaard, occupied their family home for all the world to see. They did so as a married couple. Record title placed a one-half ownership interest in their home in the hands of Weisman, Peters' former wife, who herself had already remarried. Under the circumstances the bankruptcy court could reasonably find that Peters' and Neergaard's possession of their residence was sufficiently inconsistent with record title that a prudent purchaser would have inquired whether Peters had previously obtained *all* the ownership interests or whether Weisman still retained a 50 per cent interest in Peters' and Neergaard's house.

In determining inconsistency, we take a practical approach. The state of affairs at the Campbell residence would have made a prudent purchaser suspicious that Weisman, divorced and remarried, no longer actually owned any interest in the home occupied by her former husband and his new wife. Circumstances have changed since 1901. No longer are wives and former wives statutorily disabled from managing and controlling their property, *see, e.g.*, Kirchberg v. Feenstra, 450 U.S. 455, 457 & n.1 (1981), and certainly they are not ordinarily willing to allow a former husband to enjoy exclusive use of their property by living in it with a second wife. Nor are former husbands particularly anxious these days to have a former wife own half of the home in which they reside with her successor. As we approach the end of the century the nature of financial arrangements between divorced spouses is generally far different than it was when the century began.[11] In any event, the circumstances relating to Peters' home were such as to give rise to a duty to inquire on the part of a prudent purchaser.

A reasonable inquiry into the true ownership of the Campbell residence would have confirmed the suspicions that would have been aroused by a realistic analysis of the visible circumstances at the property. Inquiry would have revealed that Peters, in fact, had full title and that Weisman had no interest to sell. . . . [T]he trustee is charged with that knowledge and, therefore, does not qualify as a BFP able to set aside, under 11 U.S.C. section 544(a)(3), the unrecorded transaction whereby Weisman gave Peters complete ownership of the house in which he, but not she, continued to reside. Accordingly, the district court erred in reversing the bankruptcy court.

III. Conclusion

The bankruptcy court did not clearly err in finding that, given the discrepancies between Peters' and Neergaard's possession of their residence and record title, a prudent purchaser would have inquired of Peters as to whether his former wife continued to own an interest in her former home. Consequently, the judgment of the district court is reversed and the case remanded to the bankruptcy court for the entry of judgment in favor of Peters.

Problem 10E

Aunt Patty, now in her early 80s, agreed to sell her house to her nephew Snake at a very low price, provided that she could live there until she died. Snake had his lawyer draft a deed, which purported to convey a present fee simple absolute to Snake. Snake paid the money, Aunt Patty signed and delivered the deed, and Snake recorded the deed. Six months later, Snake's creditors force him into bankruptcy. The trustee claims a right to sell the house to satisfy Snake's claims, free and clear of Aunt Patty's rights. Aunt Patty has never moved out of the house. What result?

4. Shelter Rule

CHERGOSKY v. CROSSTOWN BELL, INC.

Supreme Court of Minnesota, 1990
463 N.W.2d 522

Keith, Justice. This case raises the question whether a person who assumed the obligations of an unrecorded contract for deed at the time

11. It was at the turn of the century that a three-judge panel of the California Supreme Court decided Schumacher v. Truman, the principal case relied upon by the trustee.

he acquired an interest in a piece of real property in Richfield, Minnesota, may assert priority over the unrecorded contract for deed after purchasing a mortgage on the property from a bona fide purchaser who recorded the mortgage before the contract for deed was recorded.

George and Dorothy Chergosky, appellants, brought this suit against Crosstown Bell, Inc. (Crosstown), and Alfred Teien for breach of a contract for deed agreement on the Richfield property. The Chergoskys also named Griffith and the law firm of Katz, Davis & Manka as parties to determine the priority of their interests in the property. On cross motions for summary judgment, the district court held that Crosstown breached the contract for deed. The district court found damages against Crosstown in the amount of $97,850.65 plus prejudgment interest and costs and disbursements, and pierced the corporate veil to hold Teien also personally liable. The district court further held that the Chergoskys' claim was superior to those of both Griffith and Katz, Davis & Manka.

Crosstown, Teien, and Griffith appealed from the summary judgment entered in favor of the Chergoskys. The court of appeals upheld the trial court's award of damages to the Chergoskys and the imposition of personal liability on Teien but reversed the trial court's ruling on the priority issue and held that Griffith's mortgage was superior to the Chergoskys' contract for deed because Griffith acquired the mortgage through a bona fide purchaser. Chergosky v. Crosstown Bell, Inc., 454 N.W.2d 654, 656-57 (Minn. App. 1990). We accepted the Chergoskys' petition for further review.

I

On November 4, 1971, Alfred and Donna Teien, the record owners of the property at 6244 Cedar Avenue in Richfield, leased the property as well as a building and garage to be constructed thereon to Northwestern Bell Telephone Company (Northwestern Bell) for a term of 20 years. The lease gave Northwestern Bell the option to purchase the property for $650,000 at the end of ten years. Alfred Teien later formed Crosstown Bell, Inc., a Minnesota corporation, of which Teien was the sole shareholder and officer. The Teiens transferred title to the Richfield property to Crosstown on April 27, 1972, and assigned the Northwestern Bell lease to Crosstown as well. Crosstown acquired permanent financing from Union Central Life Insurance Company, which took a first mortgage on the property that it recorded on September 12, 1972.

In 1977, in need of money, Alfred Teien contacted a friend, George Chergosky. Crosstown entered into a contract for deed conveying the vendee's interest in the Richfield property to George Chergosky and his wife Dorothy, made effective January 1, 1977. The purchase price of $550,000 included $50,000 up front and monthly payments of $5,504.89. The contract for deed gave Crosstown the option to repurchase the property from the Chergoskys, which would be required if Northwestern Bell exercised its purchase option. The Chergoskys did not record the contract for deed until August 19, 1985.

On December 7, 1978, Alfred and Donna Teien borrowed $120,000 from Summit State Bank of Bloomington (Summit), and as security Crosstown gave a mortgage on the Richfield property that Summit recorded on December 18, 1978. Summit did not have notice of the Chergoskys' contract for deed at the time it took the mortgage.

In June 1982, Northwestern Bell notified Crosstown of its intention to exercise its lease purchase option. Crosstown disputed the timeliness of the notice, and in January 1983, brought a declaratory judgment action alleging that Northwestern Bell had not exercised its purchase option in a timely manner.

While this litigation was pending, on March 31, 1983, Robert Griffith, a long-time friend of Teien, acquired a 70% undivided interest in the Richfield property in exchange for past and present loans he made to Teien personally and to Crosstown. At the time Griffith, Teien, and Crosstown entered into this contract Griffith clearly had notice of the Chergoskys' contract for deed.

On August 22, 1985, while the litigation with Northwestern Bell still was pending, Griffith purchased the $120,000 note as well as other notes with a face value of $370,000 for $350,000 from Metropolitan Bank, Summit's assignee. As part of this transaction, Griffith received an assignment of the $120,000 second mortgage on the Richfield property, which Griffith recorded in November 1985.

On October 18, 1985, the trial court ordered Crosstown to convey marketable title to the Richfield property to Northwestern Bell, and ordered Northwestern Bell to pay the option purchase price into the court. *See* Crosstown Bell, Inc. v. Northwestern Bell Tel. Co., 381 N.W.2d 911 (Minn. App. 1986) (affirming the trial court's order). The subject matter of this dispute is the funds which remain on deposit with the court after satisfaction of the first mortgage pursuant to court order.

II

As the holder of the second mortgage, Griffith claims priority over the Chergoskys to the remaining proceeds from the sale of the Richfield property because he acquired the mortgage through a bona fide purchaser who recorded its mortgage before the Chergoskys recorded their contract for deed. . . .

Under the Minnesota Recording Act, a bona fide purchaser who records first obtains rights to the property which are superior to a prior purchaser who failed to record. . . .

Generally, a bona fide purchaser of property which was subject to a prior outstanding unrecorded interest may pass title free of the unrecorded interest to a subsequent purchaser who otherwise would not qualify as a bona fide purchaser under the recording act. Henschke v. Christian, 228 Minn. 142, 147, 36 N.W.2d 547, 550 (1949). This bona fide purchaser filter rule protects the alienability of property. Without this rule the bona fide purchaser would be deprived of the full benefit of the purchase — the right to transfer good title to a subsequent purchaser. *See, e.g.*, 8 G. Thompson, *Commentaries on the Modern Law of Real Property* §4315, at 380 (1940 & photo. reprint 1963).

Summit paid valuable consideration for its mortgage, took the mortgage without notice of the Chergoskys' contract for deed, and recorded the mortgage before the Chergoskys recorded their contract for deed. As between the Chergoskys' contract for deed and the second mortgage in the hands of Summit, Summit has priority. Generally, the filter principle then would operate to pass Summit's superior interest to Metropolitan and then to Griffith.

III

We first must examine the nature of the March 31, 1983, contract between Griffith, Teien, and Crosstown, to determine whether Griffith's rights and obligations under that contract affect his ability to claim the priority of a bona fide purchaser even though he had actual knowledge of the contract for deed when he acquired the mortgage. . . .

When the intention of the parties to a contract is totally ascertainable from the writing, construction is for the court. . . .

. . . Read as a whole to harmonize the different parts of the instrument, the contract provides that Griffith assumes 70% of the obligations of the contract for deed but that Crosstown and Teien will be liable to Griffith for any amounts that he pays under the contract for deed. We thus conclude as a matter of law that Griffith assumed 70% of Crosstown's obligations under the contract for deed in the March 31, 1983 contract with Crosstown and Teien.

IV

The issue then becomes whether Griffith, who has assumed obligations to the Chergoskys based on the contract for deed, can rely on the bona fide purchaser filter principle to assert priority to the Richfield property over the Chergoskys. The bona fide purchaser filter principle is subject to a well-recognized exception, which prevents the grantor or former owner of the property, who held the property subject to a prior equity, from acquiring the rights of a bona fide purchaser. Walker v. Wilson, 469 So. 2d 580, 582 (Ala. 1985); Clark v. McNeal, 114 N.Y. 287, 295, 21 N.E. 405, 407 (1889).[4] Professor Cribbet wrote that this exception "prevents a holder of the title from

4. The Rhode Island Supreme Court applied this exception to the brother and wife of the original mortgagors who acquired a mortgage through a bona fide purchaser. Rogis v. Barnatowich, 36 R.I. 227, 89 A. 838 (1914). In *Rogis*, a church gave a first mortgage which was not recorded until after a second mortgage, given by the church and two of its members, was

using the [bona fide purchaser] as a 'filter' to cleanse his defective ownership." J. Cribbet, *Principles of the Law of Property* 287-88 (2d ed. 1975). . . . By asserting priority to the Richfield property, Griffith, in effect, is attempting to build title on his own default or at least on the default of Crosstown/Teien, with whom Griffith is closely associated and who, along with Griffith, is the co-owner of the vendor's interest in the property. *See* Conner v. How, 35 Minn. 518, 29 N.W. 314 (1886). In *How,* Mayo, who had purchased property and assumed the two mortgages on the property, defaulted on the first mortgage and then bought the property from the purchaser at the foreclosure sale. We held that Mayo remained liable on the second mortgage because he could not "build up a title upon his own default." *Id.* at 520, 29 N.W. at 316.

We agree with the trial court that the same principles apply in this case. Griffith was obligated to the Chergoskys under the contract for deed. Griffith, prior to his acquisition of the second mortgage, held his 70% interest in the Richfield property subject to the Chergoskys' contract for deed and with a personal obligation to the Chergoskys under the contract for deed. *See* Barry v. Jordan, 116 Minn. 34, 37, 133 N.W. 78, 79 (1911). Having assumed the obligations of the contract for deed, Griffith cannot rely on the bona fide purchaser filter rule to obtain an interest in the property which is superior to the Chergoskys.

The bona fide purchaser filter rule is essential to the sound functioning of the secondary mortgage market. We emphasize that it is the unique facts concerning the March 31, 1983 contract, in which Griffith assumed 70% of the vendor's obligations to the Chergoskys under the contract for deed, that place this case in the well-recognized but limited exception to the bona fide purchaser filter principle.

We reverse the court of appeals and reinstate the trial court's judgment in favor of the Chergoskys on the priority issue.

Problem 10F

(a) Oprah, in need of money to launch a TV show, borrowed $10,000 from Creditor, giving Creditor a mortgage on Newacre to secure the loan. Creditor did not record its mortgage, and Oprah remained in possession of Newacre. One year later, Oprah sold Newacre to Amy for $40,000, without informing her of the mortgage. Amy promptly recorded. Then Creditor recorded its mortgage. The following year, Amy contracts to sell Newacre to Bart for $50,000. Bart closes the purchase, paying the purchase price in full. Creditor has never been paid. Is Creditor's mortgage on Newacre valid as against Bart?

---

recorded. The court held that the brother and wife of these two members, who acquired the second mortgage from a bona fide purchaser, were not entitled to succeed to the rights of the bona fide purchaser. *Id.* at 231, 89 A. at 840.

(b) Assume the same transaction, except that one year after the sale from Amy to Bart, Bart contracts to sell Newacre to your client, Daffy, for $60,000. Your title search reveals Creditor's mortgage, as well as the chain of deeds from Oprah to Bart. Should you raise an objection to Bart's title?

5. *Payment of Value*

The second requirement for a grantee to qualify as a BFP, in addition to lack of notice of the prior interest, is payment of value. This is true under pure race statutes as well as under both types of notice-based statutes. Two sets of issues concerning value are raised; one concerns measurement, the other concerns timing.

The measurement issue relates to how much consideration is needed. The requirement of valuable consideration is intended to disqualify a donee who receives a gift, either by deed or as heir or devisee, but it is not always easy to distinguish purchasers and donees. Standard deed forms often recite that the grantee has paid "ten dollars and other good and valuable consideration," and such forms are often used for gifts. Nominal consideration, however, does not suffice to make a donee into a BFP. Nevertheless, the consideration doesn't have to be full market value, it just has to be substantial. Many courts treat a deed recital of the payment of consideration with some respect, saying it gives rise to a presumption that valuable consideration was given.

With regard to timing, the standard traditional doctrine is that the purchaser is not a BFP before he actually pays the consideration to the seller. This means that a binding promise to pay, although it may be consideration in the general contract-law sense, is not enough for the recording act. For example, when a purchaser signs an executory contract, paying the seller a normal amount of earnest money, the purchaser is not yet a BFP. Only at closing, when he pays the remainder of the purchase price, does he become a BFP. The significance of this rule is that the purchaser bears the risk that third parties might record their claims or otherwise give notice of their claims after the contract is signed but prior to closing.

Mortgagee as Purchaser. In all states, lenders as well as buyers qualify as BFPs. Some recording acts specifically state that mortgagees are entitled to defeat prior unrecorded interests. Other states with acts that refer only to "purchasers" have interpreted the term to include mortgagees. The money they lend to the mortgagor is valuable consideration, given in exchange for the mortgage. A mortgage given to secure antecedent debt raises special problems. If the mortgagee does not give new value when it takes the mortgage, in most states the mortgagee is not a purchaser. If the mortgagee gives new value by, for example, extending the term of the loan, it is a BFP who takes free of prior unrecorded interests of which it lacks notice.

Problem 10G

Eight months ago Larry rented his single-family house to Teresa and Thomas, pursuant to a written one-year lease. During lease negotiations, Teresa and Thomas asked for and got an option to purchase the house for $105,000 at the end of the lease term. The written lease, which the tenants promptly recorded, contains an integration clause and fails to mention the option. The purchase option is set forth in a side letter agreement, which was not acknowledged or recorded. The side letter is sufficient to satisfy the statute of frauds.

Two months ago, Larry agreed to sell the house to Pamela for $120,000 pursuant to an unacknowledged, unrecorded contract of sale. When Pamela inspected the house, Teresa and Thomas weren't there, although Larry told her that the furnishings in the house belonged to the tenants. Under the contract between Larry and Pamela, the one-year lease is a permitted encumbrance, and at closing Larry is to assign his interest in the lease to Pamela. Larry "forgot" to tell Pamela about the tenants' purchase option.

(a) Pamela closes the purchase without learning of the tenants' purchase option and records her deed. At the end of the one-year lease, the tenants notify Pamela that they are exercising their option to purchase for $105,000. What result?

(b) After signing the contract, Pamela decides to introduce herself to Teresa and Thomas — soon she'll be their new landlord. Early during their conversation, they mention their option and the likelihood that they'll exercise it. Pamela says she knows nothing about their option and plans not to honor it. What result? Does it matter what type of recording act the state has?

(c) Assume that Pamela never inspected or visited the house prior to signing the contract of sale with Larry. Does this change the analysis in (a) or (b)?

(d) Assume that Teresa and Thomas's lease is not recorded, but that Larry supplied Pamela with a copy of the lease (but not the side letter) while they were negotiating the contract of sale. Does this change the analysis in (a) or (b)?

D. SPECIAL PROBLEMS: INTERESTS THAT ARE HARD OR IMPOSSIBLE TO FIND

The prevalent use of name indexes to organize recorded instruments can make a deed or other instrument that is recorded difficult or even impossible for a searcher to find. There is something called a *wild deed,* which means an instrument is literally recorded and properly indexed, but it cannot be found by use of the name indexes because there is a missing link. Because the wild deed is completely impossible to find, courts have treated it as unrecorded despite the fact that it's physically recorded as well as name indexed.

The *late recorded deed* and the *early recorded deed* are like the wild deed, in that the name index system impairs the searcher's access to them. A deed or other instrument is late recorded when there is a substantial gap in time between delivery and recordation, and in the meantime the record owner has transferred ownership to someone else. The difficulty is that the searcher will stop looking in the grantor indexes for adverse transfers after the time the record owner transferred to someone else.

The early recorded deed is the flip side of the late recorded deed. A person transfers an interest in land he does not own and subsequently acquires an estate in that land. This is much like a familiar transaction in stock where a person "sells short," contracting to sell stock he does not own with the understanding that he will acquire it to make good on the undertaking. In the land context, when the grantor eventually gets title, the doctrine of estoppel by deed operates to transfer that title to the prior grantee. An explanation often given by courts is that, without estoppel, the grantor would have breached his deed warranties of title. The estoppel-by-deed rule prevents this breach by passing the appropriate title to the grantee. For this reason, a number of courts have refused to apply estoppel by deed in transactions involving early recorded quitclaim deeds.

Jurisdictions are about evenly split on whether late recorded deeds and early recorded deeds are treated as validly recorded, thus imparting constructive notice to subsequent purchasers. Unlike the wild deed, late and early recorded deeds can be found if the searcher does the extra work of checking index books for years before and after the dates each record owner acquired and parted with title.

A title search not only has to account for fee ownership, but it must also uncover any servitudes, such as *easements* and *restrictive covenants,* that bind the property. Most servitudes are created by express language, set forth in documents in the property's chain of title, and thus pose no special problems of searching. However, our system of land law permits the creation of several types of servitudes by implication, such as easements implied from prior existing use, easements by necessity, and reciprocal negative easements. Typically, such servitudes are created at the time land is sold in the process of subdivision, when the grantor retains neighboring land that is either burdened or benefited by the implied servitude. Although the implied servitude may serve the worthwhile purpose of effectuating the intent of the parties to the sale, when third parties subsequently come on the scene, these implied rights are hard to detect in the search process. Similar title search problems are raised by prescriptive easements, easements by estoppel (also called irrevocable licenses), and express restrictions that are imposed upon the grantor's retained land (here, the problem arises when the recording office fails to index the deed as affecting not only the conveyed parcel but also the retained parcel). For all of these types of servitudes, there are some cases that protect the purchaser as BFP and others that fail to do so on the theory that the purchaser had some type of constructive or inquiry notice.

Occasionally the recorder's office makes a mistake in the recording process. As a result, a subsequent purchaser may not be able to find a prior instrument that was filed for recording, or actually recorded. The question then becomes: Who bears the risk of losing his interest in the real property—the recording party or the subsequent purchaser who did not and perhaps could not find the prior instrument? In some states, when the error is attributable to a recording employee's negligence, a suit for damages is possible. Sometimes the public employee is bonded, but typically the bond is for a small amount. In other states, sovereign immunity bars such an action.

FIRST CITIZENS NATIONAL BANK v. SHERWOOD
Supreme Court of Pennsylvania, 2005
583 Pa. 466, 879 A.2d 178

CAPPY, Chief Justice. . . .

First Citizens National Bank ("First Citizens") bought a piece of real property, which had been owned by J. Joel Turrell as Trustee for Genevieve Van Noy ("Turrell"), by virtue of a Sheriff's Deed. Prior to the purchase, First Citizens searched the mortgage index and discovered no encumbrances. After the sale was completed, First Citizens learned that Turrell had executed a mortgage in favor of Arthur W. Sherwood ("Sherwood"). The Bradford County Recorder of Deeds had properly recorded the Sherwood Turrell mortgage. The mortgage was misindexed, however. Instead of being indexed under Turrell's name, it was indexed under Van Noy's name. Apparently, First Citizens had not cross checked the mortgage index under Van Noy's name as well as Turrell's and thus did not discover the mortgage.

Upon discovering the Sherwood Turrell mortgage, First Citizens filed an action to quiet title. The trial court granted summary judgment in favor of First Citizens. It held that when a lien had been improperly indexed, subsequent purchasers would not be deemed to have constructive notice of the lien. Accordingly, as the Sherwood Turrell mortgage had been improperly indexed, the trial court concluded that First Citizens would not be deemed to have constructive notice of it.

Sherwood appealed. The Superior Court, relying heavily on case law from other jurisdictions, reasoned that a subsequent purchaser shall not be deemed to have notice of a prior lien so long as a "diligent search" would not have uncovered the lien. First Citizens Nat'l Bank v. Sherwood, 817 A.2d 501, 504-05 (Pa. Super. Ct. 2003). The Superior Court held that the question of diligence is a factual one, dependent upon how accessible the records were at the time the search was conducted. Of import to the Superior Court was whether the particular county's records were computerized or not. As the trial court had not conducted a factual inquiry into how accessible Bradford County's records were, the Superior Court remanded this matter to the trial court for further proceedings. . . .

Our analysis focuses on two statutes. The first states that when a written agreement relating to real property is recorded, "[t]he legal effect of the recording of such agreements shall be to give constructive notice to subsequent purchasers. . . ." 21 P.S. §357. Section 357 goes on to state that "the rights of the subsequent purchasers . . . shall be limited thereby with the same force and effect as if said subsequent purchasers . . . had actually joined in the execution of the [mortgage] . . . ." The second statute applies in those instances when a mortgage is properly indexed, and provides that such proper indexing "shall be notice to all persons of recording of the same." 16 P.S. §9853. . . .

[W]e conclude that the language of 21 P.S. §357 is plain and unambiguous. Per §357, the legal effect of the recording of a written agreement such as a mortgage is to give subsequent purchasers constructive notice of the mortgage. There is no ambiguity in the statute. There is no scope for us to read into that statute an equitable exception whereby a subsequent purchaser may be excused from constructive notice when the mortgage was properly recorded but improperly indexed. In applying 21 P.S. §357 to the matter sub judice, First Citizens must be deemed to have constructive notice of the Sherwood Turrell mortgage as it is beyond cavil that the Sherwood Turrell mortgage was properly recorded.

First Citizens attempts to avoid this conclusion via two separate arguments. First, it argues that 16 P.S. §9853 supports its position that a subsequent purchaser has no notice of a mortgage where that mortgage is improperly indexed, regardless of whether the mortgage was properly recorded. As noted by First Citizens, §9853 states that a properly indexed mortgage shall be notice to all persons of the recording of the mortgage. First Citizens argues that if a proper indexing is notice to all persons, then the obverse is true: a subsequent purchaser presumptively has no notice where a mortgage is improperly indexed.

This argument fails. First, 16 P.S. §9853 does not create a negative inference—namely, §9853 does not stand for the proposition that a subsequent purchaser per se lacks notice where a mortgage is improperly indexed.

Furthermore, even if this were a logical interpretation of 16 P.S. §9853, First Citizens would still not be entitled to relief. This is because such an interpretation of 16 P.S. §9853 is squarely at odds with 21 P.S. §357's dictate that proper recordation of a mortgage constitutes constructive notice of the mortgage to subsequent purchasers. Accordingly, even if we were to adopt First Citizens' construction of 16 P.S. §9853, then we would have to find that 21 P.S. §357 and 16 P.S. §9853 are in conflict with each other. Were we to find that the two statutes were in conflict, 21 P.S. §357 would prevail in any contest between the two because it was the statute enacted later in time?[3]

Finally, we address a concept that runs through First Citizens' arguments to this court. This concept is that we should adopt First Citizens' position because it is sensible. In essence, First Citizens invites us to find in its favor because it is prudent to charge a subsequent purchaser with constructive notice only in those situations where the mortgage is both properly recorded and properly indexed.

We cannot accept this invitation. In addressing an issue of statutory construction, this court's power is limited. Where the Legislature has crafted a statute which is clear and is squarely on point, we may not decline to apply it simply because we find that there are better policy options. Nor may we decline to follow an unambiguous statute on the basis that other jurisdictions have charted a different course with regard to the same issue. . . .

In sum, we conclude that since the Sherwood Turrell mortgage was properly recorded, then per 21 P.S. §357 all subsequent purchasers are deemed to have constructive notice of it. Accordingly, the order of the Superior Court is reversed, and this matter is remanded to the trial court for proceedings consistent with this opinion.

Justice Eakin files a dissenting opinion in which Justice Saylor joins. . . .

The duty of indexing mortgages and deeds is placed on the Recorder of Deeds, but as between the parties, the mortgagee ultimately bears the risk of improper indexing. Section 9853 specifically addresses the subject of notice: "[t]he entry of recorded deeds and mortgages *in said indexes,* respectively, shall be notice to all persons of recording of the same." 16 P.S. §9853. Clearly, the absence of good indexing cannot be good notice. In order to protect its interest and place those who may later search on constructive notice, [citation omitted], the mortgagee must bear the burden of checking the proper indexes after recordation to insure that the Recorder of Deeds properly indexed and recorded the mortgage. This is a small burden indeed for the mortgagee — it is an impossible burden to place on the public. It is the mortgagee who asks for the mortgage in return for advancing money. It is the mortgagee that files the mortgage in order to protect its security interest. . . .

Reliance on 21 P.S. §357, a statute dealing with deeds, not mortgages and other impermanent transfers, is misplaced. Allowing improper indexing to serve as notice to the world is illogical, and the conclusion that 16 P.S. §9853 conflicts with §357's plain meaning is erroneous. In fact, the majority's abridged reading of §357 actually renders 16 P.S. §9853 meaningless.

3. 21 P.S. §357 was enacted into law in 1931; 16 P.S. §9853 was enacted in 1875.

If proper recordation alone gives the world constructive notice of a mortgage, then there is no need to index the mortgages at all—recordation without indexing must suffice. Surely the legislature did not intend this absurd result. . . .

Problem 10H

Thrifty Rentals, Inc., a Colorado corporation, deeds a tract of land with a small building, located on N. Pine St., to John Martz. Martz files the deed at the recorder's office, paying the recording fee. Two months later, Jake obtains a judgment lien against Thrifty Rentals, Inc., and properly records it. The recording act requires that the recorder's office maintain name indexes. It also stipulates that an instrument provides constructive notice to third parties from the date of its recordation. Is the judgment lien valid as against Martz if the recording officer made any of the following mistakes with respect to the deed from Thrifty to Martz, which remained uncorrected until after Jake's recording?

(a) She indexed the grantor's name as "Thrift Rentals, Inc."

(b) She indexed the grantor's name as "Shrifty Rentals, Inc."

(c) She indexed the grantee's name under "J" as "John, Martz" rather than "Martz, John."

(d) She indexed the names properly, but the column of the index that contains a short property description refers to "N. Martz St." when it should refer to "N. Pine St."

(e) Does it matter whether Jake has actually searched the records to determine whether Thrifty has record title to the land?

11
Title Products

The recording system is the backbone of title assurance. When someone searches title, it always involves searching the county land records. It also often involves inspecting the land (or hiring a surveyor to inspect the land) to look for unrecorded interests or other title-related problems. In the last chapter, we saw that searching titles requires the meticulous following of a number of steps, coupled with the application of legal knowledge. Local practices can vary considerably, and within local communities individual searchers often develop their own systems for collecting and organizing title data.

The title search process and the final product are two different things. The search process can result in several different types of final products, each giving a different set of rights to the purchaser. The three main products are: (1) title abstracts; (2) attorneys' title opinions or title certificates; and (3) title insurance policies.

A. TITLE ABSTRACTS

A *title abstract* is a written distillation of the record search process. It summarizes all recorded deeds and other recorded items in the chain of title, including encumbrances. A complete abstract takes the chain of title back to the sovereign, but today many searches (and thus many abstracts) go back only a customary period, such as 50 or 60 years. Typically, the person making an abstract studies each recorded document, putting pertinent information on blank abstract forms, which are either printed standardized forms or forms tailor-made by the abstractor.

After doing this research and note-taking, the abstractor prepares the finished product. Most abstracts are arranged chronologically, with a synopsis or summary of all items found, including those believed to have no present operative effect on title (for example, a mortgage lien for which there is a release or discharge of record). Generally, the abstract contains a certification that it contains all instruments of record that affect the land. The purpose of the abstract is to give the purchaser sufficient information to decide whether record title is acceptable. Most abstracts do not directly opine on the present state of title by saying, for example, that Jones has record title to a fee simple absolute subject to one lien and one restrictive covenant. Instead, interpretation of the abstracted instruments is left to the reader, who must review the entire abstract and infer the present condition of title.

In some localities, attorneys prepare abstracts, but in most states abstracts are made by nonlawyer professionals. In some states, title abstractors must be careful not to overstep their boundaries or they may find themselves liable for the unauthorized practice of law. The South Carolina Supreme Court held in *Ex Parte Watson*, 589 S.E. 2d 760, 762 (S.C. 2003):

> [W]hen nonlawyer title abstractors examine public records and then render an opinion as to the content of those records, they are engaged in the unauthorized practice of law. But if a licensed attorney reviews the title abstractor's report and vouches for its legal sufficiency by signing the report, title abstractors would not be engaged in the unauthorized practice of law.

Roughly half the states, most of them in the West, regulate the business of abstracting. Bonding of abstractors to cover liability for erroneous abstracts is typically required. Some states require licensing of abstractors, with the passage of an examination. In several states, an abstract company is required to have its own private title plant. *See, e.g.*, Okla. Stat. tit. 74, §227.10 to 227.30; Abstracts of Oklahoma v. Payne County Title Co., 825 P.2d 1334 (Okla. 1992) (abstract company must develop its own index; statute does not permit company to copy and use county indexes).

In general, a title abstractor is liable in negligence to her clients and to third parties who can be expected to rely on the abstractor's work product. In the case of First American Title Ins. Co. v. First Title Service Co., 457 So. 2d 467, 472 (Fla. 1984), the Florida Supreme Court recognized abstractor liability to third parties and tried to limit the scope of the liability:

> To hold an abstracter liable to every stranger to the contract of employment who might happen to come to see and rely on the abstract would be like holding a title insurer liable to anyone who knows of the issuance of an insurance policy but who has not paid a premium. For the reasons stated we decline to expose abstracters to liability to any person who foreseeably relies on a negligently prepared abstract to his detriment.
>
> While the policy arguments put forth by the petitioner . . . do not persuade us to adopt open-ended liability for negligence to any foreseeably relying persons, they do convince us that, when an abstract is prepared in the knowledge or under conditions in which an abstracter should reasonably expect that the employer is to provide it to third persons for purposes of inducing those persons to rely on the abstract as evidence of title, the abstracter's contractual duty to perform the service skillfully and diligently runs to the benefit of such known third parties. . . .

Problem 11A

In 1980, Poor Abstract Co. did an abstract on Blackacre for Alice, who in reliance on the abstract purchased Blackacre for $80,000. A single-family house is located on Blackacre. In 1990, Alice sold Blackacre to Baker for $130,000, conveying by quitclaim deed. In 2000, Baker sold to Carla for $150,000, conveying by general warranty deed. In 2007, Carla leased Blackacre to Thomas for 20 years, also granting Thomas an option to purchase Blackacre at any time during the lease term for $180,000. In the 1990 sale, Alice delivered the original 1980 abstract to Baker. In the 2000 sale, Baker promised he had marketable title, and as evidence gave Carla copies of the abstract and the 1990 deed. In the 2007 lease, Carla promised she had marketable title and gave copies of the abstract and the deeds to Thomas.

It turns out that Poor Abstract Co. did a poor job of searching title in 1980, missing a recorded covenant that restricts Blackacre to use for one single-family house only. There are presently a number of duplexes and townhouses in the neighborhood where Blackacre is located, and Thomas had planned to add more residential units to Blackacre.

(a) Does Thomas have a cause of action against Poor Abstract Co.? If so, what is the measure of damages?

(b) Assume that Thomas does not assert a cause of action against Poor Abstract Co., but instead recovers damages from Carla under the lease. Carla, in turn, successfully proceeds against Baker under the Baker-Carla deed. Does Baker have a cause of action against Poor Abstract Co.?

B. ATTORNEYS' TITLE OPINIONS AND CERTIFICATES

An attorney who writes a title opinion or title certificate is performing an important task and is held to a high standard of care. The client has hired the attorney based on the belief that she has the professional skills and judgment needed to protect the client's expectations concerning the real estate transaction.

A title opinion or certificate does not guarantee the client that title is in fact marketable. It only reflects the attorney's professional *opinion* that based on the evidence she has, it appears to be marketable. This means that when a title problem arises causing grief or loss to the client, the attorney is not necessarily liable just because the opinion has turned out to be wrong. Just as a physician does not guarantee that a certain operation or treatment will help a patient, a title attorney does not guarantee that title is perfect, with no chance of unpleasant surprises in the future. With our system of public records, coupled with the many types of off-record claims that may have validity, an attorney's undertaking to guarantee title would be foolhardy. All the title attorney promises, by implication if not expressly, is that she has done competent, professional work, complying with the norms established by and followed in the legal community where she practices. If there is a recorded interest that the attorney does not locate, or if she locates an instrument but reaches the conclusion that it does not affect or no longer affects the subject property, she is liable only if her failure to find or failure properly to evaluate is negligent. Attorneys aren't infallible, though perhaps too often they pretend to be. When an attorney makes a mistake in a title matter, the client may be able to prove that the mistake constitutes negligence or malpractice, but this depends on the circumstances.

NORTH BAY COUNCIL, INC., BOY SCOUTS v. BRUCKNER

Supreme Court of New Hampshire, 1989
131 N.H. 538, 563 A.2d 428

Souter, Justice. In this action for legal malpractice in failing to make adequate disclosure of a cloud on the title to real property, the plaintiff appeals a defendant's verdict rendered after jury trial in the Superior Court (Smith, J.). Because a verdict should have been directed for the plaintiff on the issue of liability, we reverse and remand for a new trial on damages.

The title problem underlying this action was first brought to the court's notice in North Bay Council, Inc. v. Grinnell, 123 N.H. 321, 461 A.2d 114 (1983), upon which we rely in part for an understanding of facts and procedural history. In 1951, William Morse Cole conveyed a tract of some 1200 acres in Orford and Piermont to Kaiora Camp, Inc. The recorded deed from Cole to the camp contained this paragraph:

> RESTRICTIONS: It is a condition of this conveyance that the Grantee herein and is (sic) successor shall not, for a period of TEN YEARS from the date of this deed, use the land and premises herein conveyed for any purpose other than agriculture, lumbering, and a SUMMER CAMP for children under secondary school age; and that any other Commercial Enterprise such as maintaining a Public House of entertainment and/or recreation, a Public Boat Livery or a Public Store, is excluded from the provileges (sic) under this conveyance; but the term Commercial Enterprise shall not be construed to include the building and rental or sale of a dwelling or dwellings for single-family use standing not less then (sic) two hundred feet from all other dwellings on said land; and further, the Grantee and its successors herein, shall not sell any part of the property herein conveyed until it shall have first offered it for purchase to the Grantor, his heirs or assigns, at the highest price at which they have received a Bona Fide Offer.

Cole died in 1961, and the following year Kaiora Camp agreed to sell the land for $125,000 to Bay Shore Council, Inc., Boy Scouts of America, the corporate predecessor in interest of the plaintiff, North Bay Council, Inc. . . . In anticipation of its purchase, the plaintiff acted through a Massachusetts lawyer associated with it as a director or trustee, Charles Demakis, who hired the defendant, Karl T. Bruckner, Esq., to provide an abstract of title and an opinion about its quality. The title examination disclosed Cole's restrictions set out above, but it revealed no indication that the property had been released from the restrictions, or that the restrictions had been waived by those entitled to their benefit, or that the obligation imposed by the right of first refusal had been satisfied by Kaiora Camp.

Because time was short, the defendant gave no written opinion prior to the closing, but he did communicate with Demakis over the telephone. The defendant testified that he apprised Demakis of the language creating the right of first refusal for the benefit of Cole, his heirs and assigns, and gave his opinion that the resulting restriction had expired by its own terms ten years after the date of Cole's deed. The plaintiff proceeded to accept conveyance of the land and thereafter received the title abstract certified by the defendant, which quoted the paragraph of restrictions in Cole's deed, together with the defendant's written opinion that the plaintiff then had "good" title to the tract, subject to several listed encumbrances not relevant here, but without mention of the first refusal.

Although Kaiora Camp paid no heed to Cole's restrictions when it conveyed the land to the plaintiff, the first refusal right attracted attention in 1979, when the plaintiff was negotiating a sale of the major part of the property to Webville Enterprises, Inc. . . . Webville's lawyer discovered the first refusal provision, which he viewed as creating a cloud on the plaintiff's title, and soon thereafter Cole's heirs, his two daughters, learned about it. The heirs declined at that time to purchase the tract, but after the plaintiff had begun action to quiet the title in North Bay Council, Inc. v. Grinnell *supra,* they claimed the right to purchase at the price the plaintiff had paid in 1962. North Bay Council, Inc. v. Grinnell, 123 N.H. at 323, 461 A.2d at 115.

In that earlier action, the superior court construed the first refusal right as enduring beyond ten years from the date of Cole's deed, but subject to the rule against perpetuities, so as to limit its enforceability to twenty-one years from Cole's death in 1961. North Bay Council, Inc. v. Grinnell, *supra* at 324, 461 A.2d at 116. The heirs nevertheless lost their bid to enforce the right at the 1962 price when the court found them chargeable with laches in asserting their claim, North Bay Council, Inc. v. Grinnell, 123 N.H. at 325, 461 A.2d at 117, and the appeal to this court was ostensibly limited to the application of the rule against perpetuities and the doctrine of laches, *id.* at 324, 461 A.2d at 116. Our affirmance of the superior court's judgment left the plaintiff in a position to sell the property and to begin this malpractice or negligence action against the defendant.

The plaintiff's declaration faults the defendant, not in examining the title or in abstracting the record, but in advising that the title was good, subject only to the exceptions not relevant here. The nub of the claim is negligence in failing to advise that the language creating the first refusal right constituted an objectionable cloud on Kaiora Camp's title.

As a consequence of its reliance on the title opinion, the plaintiff is said ultimately to have incurred damages resulting from delay in disposing of the property until the title could be cleared through the prior litigation. The case was tried to a jury, which returned a verdict for the defendant. . . .

A plaintiff is entitled to a directed verdict on liability only if no rational trier of fact viewing the evidence most favorably to the defendant could fail to find on undisputed facts that each element of liability has been proven. . . . The elements of liability in a legal malpractice action to which this rule may be applied require demonstration of a relationship, as of client and attorney, upon the latter of whom the law imposes a duty to exercise care, skill and knowledge in providing legal services to the client; a breach of that duty; and a connection of legally recognized causation between the breach and resulting harm to the client. . . .

The obligation of the lawyer giving an opinion on title to real estate reflects the normal concern of a client intending to buy land, who, in the absence of a different agreement with an intending seller, seeks ideally to acquire property free from third-party interests. Given the fact that no transaction in life can promise entire certainty of consequences, the buyer's actual objective is to limit the risk of harm from third-party claims to some practically achievable minimum. . . .

Accordingly, a lawyer evaluating title to real property for an intending buyer is bound by the standard of professional due care to disclose and explain the significance of any feature of the title, subject to discovery within the requisite scope of the lawyer's title examination, that would lead a reasonably prudent purchaser to refuse to take conveyance of the property, at least when paying full value for it. IV American Law of Property [§18.7 (1952)]. Under the standard of the prudent purchaser, features subject to such disclosure and advice include not only actual defects and encumbrances, but any apparent defects and encumbrances subject to reasonable objection as creating risks of adverse claims or losses that the prudent buyer would refuse to run, which are thus spoken of as clouds on the title. *See* Dowd v. Gagnon, 104 N.H. 360, 363, 187 A.2d 63, 65 (1962).

As the second element of its case on liability, therefore, the plaintiff had to demonstrate that a reasonably prudent buyer in 1962 would not have paid full value for property with a record title that included Cole's 1951 first refusal provision, in the absence of any indication of record that its terms had been released, waived or satisfied, and that the defendant failed to explain that, on the state of the entire record, the terms of the 1951 deed thus rendered the title unmarketable. The plaintiff had the burden, that is to say, to demonstrate the significance of the preemptive 1951 deed language; its inconsistency, standing alone, with marketability of title in 1962; and the defendant's failure to give adequate advice to this effect.

The first step in thus establishing breach of duty, to demonstrate the significance of Cole's restriction, presented a matter to be resolved by the court, under the rule that interpretation of the terms of a deed is an issue of law. Baker v. McCarthy, 122 N.H. 171, 174-75, 443 A.2d 138, 140 (1982). The trial court committed error, however, not only by leaving it to the jurors to place the final construction on Cole's language, but also by charging them that the specific issue of interpretation was whether the right of first refusal created in 1951 was enforceable at the time of Kaiora Camp's conveyance to the plaintiffs. As we have seen, a cloud is sufficient to render title unmarketable, and a cloud is defined by reference, not to the ultimate enforceability of a third party's demand, but to the reasonableness of a buyer's objection to a potential third-party claim. Buxton v. Glennon, 122 N.H. [674, 676, 448 A.2d 420, 421 (1982)]. Thus, the appropriate question was not whether Cole's heirs could have enforced the right of first refusal in 1962, but whether Cole's language, considered in light of the entire record title, raised a reasonable question about the plaintiff's ability to convey free of preemptive third-party rights. Another way to phrase the appropriate question would have been to ask whether the first refusal provision could reasonably be read to provide a colorable basis for a third-party claim that, if pressed, would cause damage to the buyer, whatever its ultimate resolution might be.

When the question about the meaning of the 1951 language is posed this way, the deed restriction does not present a difficult problem of interpretation. The paragraph headed "Restrictions" contains four clauses separated by semi-colons. The terms of the first restrict the uses of the land to agriculture, lumbering and a children's summer camp, for a period ten years from the date of the deed. The second and third clauses forbid any other commercial uses of the land except as sites for single-family houses at least two hundred feet apart. The fourth clause creates the right of first refusal. The plaintiff argues that if the ten-year limitation contained in the first clause also applied to the second and third, the latter two would be redundant, since there would be no need to forbid a commercial use such as running a public house if the only permissible uses were agriculture, lumbering and camping for children. On this reasoning, therefore, the ten-year limitation applies to the first clause in which it is contained, but not to the second or third, with the result that the land was open to commercial residential development after ten years. Finally, if there is thus good reason to infer that the time limitation has no application to the second and third clauses, then the contextual basis to hold the limitation applicable to the fourth clause creating the right of first refusal must at best be doubtful. (And the doubt would not disappear even upon realizing that Cole's wife joined in his deed in order to give Kaiora Camp a ten-year right of first refusal over certain other land that she owned.)

What is significant is not whether this analysis would ultimately have been held to be right or wrong (even though it is consistent with the results reached by the superior court when it construed the fourth clause in the earlier litigation). What is important is that the analysis rests on a textual basis placing it within the realm of reasonable argument that there was no express limit of time within which Cole or his heirs were entitled to first refusal.

. . . A gambler might have bought from the camp under these circumstances, but the evidence indicated that no prudent purchaser would have done so, let alone for full value, subject to the risk that some time in the future Cole or his heirs could demand conveyance of the property to them at the price paid by the plaintiff to the camp. No contrary opinion was presented to the jurors, who could not reasonably have found otherwise.

The third step in considering breach of duty is to inquire whether the defendant did whatever was reasonably necessary to apprise the plaintiff of the title's unmarketability, and on this question we perceive no conflict in evidence for the jury to resolve. The title opinion rendered after the closing and supposedly confirming the defendant's prior advice made no reference whatever to the provision in question or to the absence of any recorded indication of release, waiver or compliance, or to the risk of at least a colorable third-party claim inherent in this state of the title. Moreover, the defendant's own account of his conversation with Demakis before the closing indicates that at best he mentioned the 1951 language and advised that the period of its enforceability had expired. No one could have found that he had advised of the risk created by the provision. . . .

The remaining element of liability required proof that the failure to give adequate advice was a cause of the litigation and delay that the plaintiff claims as the source of monetary damages. . . . Because the object of hiring a title attorney to advise about risks inherent in the title is to enable a buyer to act prudently either in declining to take title subject to those risks, or at least in assessing the risks intelligently if the buyer should decide to take title anyway, proof of the causal link between negligent title advice and subsequent damage required evidence of the buyer's reliance upon the advice. . . .

In this case, the burden to prove reliance is not subject to complication by claims of comparative or contributory negligence, and there is no evidence that the damages flowed from any title defect other than the cloud that the defendant failed to identify as such. Hence it is fair to say here that causation may be established by proof that the plaintiff completed the purchase in sole reliance on the defendant's opinion that the title was free from the cloud under consideration, and that the subsequent delay and litigation were within the risk of harm that the defendant's opinion failed to disclose. On neither point was there any evidence on which the jury could reasonably have found in the defendant's favor. . . .

. . . As we observed before, the risk was that the individuals arguably entitled to exercise the right of first refusal in 1962 would claim that they had not received the offer to which they had been entitled and would demand the conveyance that they could then have obtained, or its economic equivalent. That, of course, is exactly what Cole's heirs subsequently demanded and would have received, but for the successful defense of laches sustained by this court in the prior appeal. No reasonable juror could have reached any other conclusion. . . .

Reversed and remanded.

Problem 11B

In 1957, Connerly, the owner of Blackacre, forfeited Blackacre to the state for failure to pay taxes, but continued to live there. In 1964, the state conveyed the property to Pritchard. In 1967, Pritchard quitclaimed the property to Connerly's daughter, Josie, who maintained a residence on the land after her father's death in 1963. The quitclaim deed contained a clause reserving all mineral rights to Pritchard. Eight months ago, Josie contracted to sell Blackacre (all minerals as well as surface) to Hurst for $300,000. Hurst's attorney, I. M. Cautious, discovered the chain of title described here and told Hurst that title wasn't marketable.

(a) Josie refused to refund Hurst's $15,000 earnest money payment because her attorney disagreed with Cautious, arguing that Josie acquired good, marketable title to the minerals by adverse possession. Hurst hired a trial lawyer to bring action against Josie to recover the earnest money but lost because the trial court found title to be marketable. Is Cautious liable to Hurst?

(b) When Cautious claimed Josie's title wasn't marketable, Josie voluntarily refunded the earnest money, with both parties agreeing to terminate the contract. Three months later, Josie sold Blackacre to Big Mineral Co. for $350,000. Big Mineral quickly brought an action to quiet title against Pritchard, winning on summary judgment. Big Mineral has begun to develop Blackacre for mineral production; its present estimated value is $600,000. Is Cautious liable to Hurst?

C. TITLE INSURANCE

Unlike so much of our property law inherited from England, title insurance is an American invention, with its roots in Philadelphia during the 1870s. Title insurance is a form of title assurance that serves as an alternative to an abstract of title or a lawyer's opinion. Gradually, title insurance has captured a greater and greater share of the title assurance market. Since the 1960s, this growth has accelerated and has become national rather than regional, the primary cause being movement of capital. Real estate finance markets became national, and interstate purchasers of mortgage loans demanded a national product for title assurance. Out-of-state lenders and institutional buyers of mortgages were (and are) not willing to rely on the opinions of local title attorneys with whom they are not familiar. Title insurance provides a vehicle for stating an opinion of title within the context of an insurance policy. The policy is written consonant with a set of underwriting standards and issued by a corporation that is regulated and required to have reserve assets. It is easier to learn about a few regulated title insurance companies than it is to learn about numerous individual attorneys. This is one of the commercial appeals of title insurance.

It is standardized, the players are generally well known, and they are regulated with information available concerning asset reserves and loss records. Though all of this makes title insurance highly marketable in an integrated economy, it is still important to know something about the skill of the people working for the title company who make the determinations as to status of title. A client, after all, is more interested in getting an accurate statement of title than she is in knowing that there are assets to reach in the event that litigation is needed over a disputed title problem.

Title insurance has two main functions: the insurer searches the records and discloses its findings, and it insures undisclosed risks. These are the two reasons why purchasers and mortgagees buy title insurance. The first function, search and disclose, is also fulfilled by title abstracts and attorneys' title opinions. The insured purchaser or lender pays to acquire valuable information in order to reduce historical risk. The insured wants to know that she is getting good record title and wants to know what encumbrances, if any, burden that title.

The second function, insurance of undisclosed risk, represents risk spreading, the classic function of all types of insurance products. A title abstract or an attorney's title opinion may be wrong, even though the abstractor or attorney was careful. When an erroneous abstract or opinion causes loss to a purchaser, the abstractor or attorney is liable only if the purchaser can prove malpractice. This is the critical difference between these products and title insurance. The insurer has absolute liability for insured defects. A title insurance company pays claims for losses stemming from insured risks, regardless of whether it was at fault (negligent) in searching title.

In modern transactions, approximately 25 percent of closings involve a title-related issue or problem; consequently, informed purchasers and lenders have a strong preference for title insurance. The distinction between the legal standard of liability, fault-based for abstracts and title opinions versus no-fault for title insurance, is critical. When a purchaser or lender suffers a loss because title turns out not to be as expected, she wants to be paid without having to prove negligence or malpractice, which, even in a simple case, may be hard to do. In addition, wholly apart from the liability standard, there are compelling institutional reasons for favoring title insurance. An insurance company is required to meet state-prescribed solvency standards, and it is used to paying claims when they are found to be covered risks. Abstractors and attorneys, when found liable for defective title work, will not always be solvent. Most, but not all, abstractors are bonded; most, but not all, attorneys carry malpractice insurance in some amount. It doesn't make sense to use or rely on an attorney's malpractice carrier when there is the practical alternative of a solvent, regulated insurance company.

For these reasons, a real estate attorney should almost always use title insurance, rather than a title abstract or a title opinion. This is true regardless of the type of transaction—whether the client is a homebuyer, a purchaser of commercial property, a developer, or a lender; and whether the client's investment is small, such as a modest house or condominium, or large. In fact, given the changing nature of the housing and mortgage markets, a strong case can be made that a lawyer who fails to obtain title insurance for a homebuyer or lender is guilty of malpractice. *See* Robin Paul Malloy & Mark Klapow, *Attorney Malpractice for Failure to Require Fee Owner's Title Insurance in a Residential Real Estate Transaction,* 74 St. John's L. Rev. 407 (2000); Robin Paul Malloy, *Using Title Insurance to Avoid Malpractice and Protect Clients in a Changing Marketplace,* 11 The Digest 51 (2003). This argument recognizes that real estate markets are no longer local or even regional. Integrated financial and sales markets have made real estate markets national, and in some respects (by way of secondary mortgage market activities) international in scope. As a result, the standard of professional conduct has been elevated and title insurance has become the expected norm.

It is also important to remember that a title insurance policy is no substitute for continuing to seek the best possible warranty deed from the seller. A title policy provides insurance coverage for matters covered by the policy. In some situations, however, a title issue may not come within the policy and in this situation a buyer would then look to a cause of action on the deed warranties.

1. The Commitment and the Policy

In a typical transaction with title insurance, there are two primary documents of legal significance: the title insurance commitment and the policy. Suppose a buyer has contracted to buy a tract of land, with title insurance to be obtained. Prior to closing, while the contract is executory, the buyer (or someone else) contacts a title insurer and orders a *title insurance commitment,* also often called a *title insurance binder* or *preliminary title report.* Only after doing a title search will the company issue a commitment or binder. If it has a title plant for the county where the land lies, it searches "in house"; otherwise, it contracts out, ordering a title search from a local abstractor or local attorney.

Upon completing the title search, the company issues its written commitment. The commitment is the company's promise to issue a policy, on a designated standard form, provided that it receives the insurance premium and that certain other specified conditions are met. A title policy is only issued after closing.

Insurance policies issued today are standardized. The vast majority of policies are on forms promulgated by a trade organization called the American Land Title Association (ALTA). In Texas, the state board of insurance has promulgated its own forms, and in California, the forms of the California Land Title Association (CLTA) are sometimes used. A title policy can insure a variety of real property interests, not only fee simple estates but also interests such as leaseholds and life estates. As mentioned earlier, both buyers and lenders often obtain title insurance. Different policy forms are used; the buyer obtains an Owner's Policy, the lender a Loan Policy or a Mortgagee Policy.

To determine whether a particular title problem is insured, you must study the policy of title insurance carefully. Policies are laid out in several different parts, which must be read in combination. The key parts are (1) the insuring provisions, (2) the conditions and stipulations, (3) the exclusions from coverage, (4) the exceptions from coverage (typically listed on Schedule B), and (5) the endorsements, if any.

The most common and significant exclusions and exceptions, usually expressed in standardized language, are:

1. Survey exception. There is no coverage for matters an accurate survey would show, such as encroachments, boundary line disputes, or shortages in area.
2. Zoning and building laws.
3. Rights of parties in possession not shown by the public records.
4. Rights or claims of which the insured has knowledge prior to issuance of the policy.
5. Taxes or assessments for the current year, which are not yet due and payable, and taxes or assessments that are not shown as existing liens by the public records.
6. Liens for work performed on the property and materials incorporated into the property (mechanics' and materialmen's liens).

All policies have some title risks that are not insured. With respect to the scope of coverage, the company and the insured have opposing interests. The company wants to minimize the risk of claims that must be paid, and the insured wants maximum protection. The scope of coverage is negotiable and, especially in commercial transactions, is often negotiated by the company and the insured purchaser or lender. For most policies, the exclusions and exceptions are the key determinant of coverage. As a general rule of thumb, if a title matter affects the insured land and the policy does not exclude it from coverage, then it is an insured risk. The insuring provisions, as well as the conditions and stipulations, are boilerplate that is seldom touched. Broad exclusions and exceptions minimize coverage; narrow exclusions and exceptions expand coverage.

The primary benefit of title insurance coverage is that the insured can recover if there is an actual loss as a result of someone else asserting a claim or interest that turns out to be superior to the stated interest of the insured. Title insurance also covers the insured for actual loss resulting from a document that is improperly signed, sealed, acknowledged, or delivered; or if there is fraud, forgery, incapacity, or impersonation involved in the transaction.

The insured is also covered against improper filing of documents, meaning that the title company will generally take on the responsibility to record all closing documents. Any errors made in the title search or loss as a result of a wild deed or other undiscoverable title defect would also be covered unless otherwise eliminated from coverage. Many policies also protect a legal right of access to and from the property. It is important to note, however, that legal access and physical access may not be the same thing. For example, land with a legal right of access may be submerged under flood waters for nine months of the year and yet remain legally accessible. The other major benefit to title insurance is that the policy also covers attorneys' fees, in that the title company will defend against claims. This can be valuable if the title company is willing to pursue a matter, but the policy gives the company the alternative of simply paying a claim up to the full amount of the coverage. Obviously, the company will assess the cost of litigation against the cost of paying the submitted claim and other potential claims on similarly situated properties, which they might have to address.

When both a lender and an owner policy are issued, the title insurance liability exposure is not cumulative. The lender is paid to the amount of the outstanding debt and then the owner is paid. Together, the title insurance company is only liable up to the full amount of the stated title insurance coverage.

Problem 11C

Last year, Bucky Buyer purchased Blackacre from Susie Seller for $200,000. Pursuant to the contract of purchase, Susie paid for an owner's policy of title insurance that names Bucky as the insured. Blackacre consists of a subdivision lot and a single-family house. Both Bucky's deed and the insurance policy describe the insured property as "Lot 14, Block 2, Happytown Subdivision, according to the plat thereof recorded in Plat Book 489, Page 24, Records of Franco County." The policy insures a fee simple absolute estate in Blackacre without the addition of any special endorsements or specific exceptions. The policy contains the same set of general exceptions as set out in the above text. Read these exceptions carefully. Which of the following problems are insured risks?

(a) Ten years ago, Susie's predecessor in title, Nathan Norton, granted a water pipeline easement to a neighbor, Starr Tompkins. Tompkins promptly recorded the easement, but the recorder's office misindexed it under "Tomkins, Starr" in the grantee index.

(b) Same facts as in (a), except the misindexing error is in the grantor index—the grantor is indexed as "Morton, Nathan" instead of "Norton, Nathan."

(c) Does it matter in (a) or (b) whether the easement holder has constructed a water pipeline across Blackacre? Assume the pipeline is

(i) completely underground or (ii) is visible at the surface, near a boundary, where it crosses a creek.

(d) Real estate taxes for the year before Susie sold Blackacre to Bucky were never paid. This fact is reflected by records in the tax commissioner's office. The city hasn't taken any steps to enforce payment.

(e) Blackacre is all of subdivision lot 14 except for the "west 50 feet," which was previously conveyed to another person. Bucky has learned that the lot is smaller than he expected. He thought the 50 feet should be measured along the street, which does not run precisely east-west. The matter was litigated, with the court holding for the neighbor, against Bucky.

(f) Bucky learns Blackacre is subject to a negative reciprocal easement, which prevents him from adding a gasoline station to part of the property.

(g) The house on Blackacre is dilapidated, with a number of substantial violations of the building code. Last year, the city brought suit against Susie, seeking a raze order because Susie repeatedly refused demands that she make repairs. The city promptly filed a lis pendens at the recorder's office. Assume the lis pendens was filed (i) three days before the policy was issued; (ii) one week after the policy was issued.

VESTIN MORTGAGE, INC. v. FIRST AMERICAN TITLE INSURANCE COMPANY

Supreme Court of Utah, 2006
139 P.3d 1055

WILKINS, Associate Chief Justice. Vestin Mortgage, Inc. (Vestin) sought to recover under two policies of title insurance issued by First American Title Insurance Company (First American). The claim arises from the adoption of a special improvement district (SID) by the municipality in which the real property lies. First American said the notice of intent to create the SID recorded by the municipality was not a defect in title covered by the policies and moved to dismiss Vestin's complaint. The district court agreed and granted the motion. Vestin appealed to the court of appeals, which affirmed. Vestin now challenges the decision of the court of appeals on certiorari. We affirm.

BACKGROUND

Vestin, or its predecessor, made two loans to The Ranches, L.C., each secured by trust deeds on real property located in Eagle Mountain, Utah. In connection with the loans, First American issued two title insurance policies that insured Vestin's interest under the trust deeds.

Between the dates of the two loans, Eagle Mountain adopted a resolution declaring its intention to create a SID, adopted a resolution creating the SID, and recorded a "Notice of Intention" with the county recorder's office in Utah County, in accordance with Utah Code section 17A-3-307.

The notice disclosed that the town council had adopted a resolution declaring the council's intention to create the SID, the project's total anticipated cost, and the council's intention to assess real property within the boundaries of the SID to pay for the improvements. The notice also included a copy of the ordinance that was adopted creating the SID. The property securing the Vestin loans lies within the SID.

Some months after the title policies were issued, Eagle Mountain adopted the "Assessment Ordinance" which levied the assessment on real property within the SID. This ordinance included a provision which indicated, for the first time, that if the property were sold, the property's share of the assessment would be accelerated and due in full upon the sale instead of being payable in small annual amounts over an extended period of time.

About two years after the second policy was issued by First American, The Ranches defaulted on the two loans and Vestin took title to the property pursuant to its trust deeds through a nonjudicial foreclosure. Vestin then entered into a contract to sell the property, and in conjunction with this potential sale, Vestin received an updated title report regarding the property. Vestin alleges that it is at this time that it first learned of the assessment levied against the property by the SID and that the assessment became immediately due and payable upon the sale of the property. After Vestin disclosed this information to the buyer, the buyer refused to proceed with the sale of the property. Vestin filed a claim with First American in which Vestin contended that the policies insured against the assessment. First American denied the claim. . . .

Analysis

. . . .

We begin our analysis by looking at the plain language of the policies, paying particular attention to the insuring clauses as did the court of appeals. There are three insuring clauses within the policies that are relevant to Vestin's claim. These are the policy jacket cover, F.A. Form 31, and CLTA Form 104. We will review them in turn.

I. The Policy Jacket Cover

The policy jacket cover states that First American "insures . . . against loss or damage . . . sustained or incurred by the insured by reason of" and then goes on to list nine insurable events or conditions. The condition at issue here is number two, addressing "[a]ny defect in or lien or encumbrance on the title." Vestin argues that the creation of the SID and the filing of the Notice of Intention did in fact create a defect in the title. First American, on the other hand, argues that neither the creation of the SID nor the filing of the Notice of Intention created a defect. Instead, the actual levying of the assessment created the defect in the title, and the assessment was actually levied by the city of Eagle Mountain after the policies had been issued and thus falls outside the coverage of the policies.

Unlike other insurance contracts, title insurance does not insure against future events. Thus, in order for a defect, lien, or encumbrance to fall within the insurance policy's coverage, it must have been in existence as of the effective date of the policy. At a minimum, an existing assessment that has been recorded would be considered a defect in the title and would be covered unless it had been otherwise exempted or excluded. The more difficult question, and the one before us now, is whether the recorded notice of the possibility of a future assessment also rises to the level of a defect, lien, or encumbrance. We conclude that it does not.

Neither the creation of the SID nor the filing of the Notice of Intention creates a lien on real property that affects the title. Utah Code section 17A-3-323 (2005) provides that an assessment becomes a lien on the property assessed on the day the ordinance levying the assessment becomes effective. In Vestin's case, the effective date of the ordinance that levied the assessment was after the date on which the policies were issued by First American. No lien could have attached as a result of this SID at the time First American provided the policies.

Additionally, neither the creation of the SID nor the Notice of Intention is an encumbrance on the property. No claim or liability attached to the title or property arises by virtue of the creation of the SID or Notice of Intention. Likewise, no defect in the title is occasioned by the creation of the SID or the Notice of Intention. . . .

It is important to remember that the "defect," "lien," or "encumbrance" mentioned in the policy jacket cover had to be *in* or *on* the *title*. The SID and Notice of Intention simply had no effect in or on the title. The policies unambiguously applied only to actual assessments and did not include an obligation to disclose the SID or Notice of Intention.

II. F.A. FORM 31 AND CLTA FORM 104

We also look to the other two insuring clauses for any obligation to provide notice of the creation of a SID and possible assessment. The first, F.A. Form 31, provides in part that First American will insure

> against loss which the Insured shall sustain by reason of any of the following matters:
>
> (1) Any incorrectness in the assurance which the Company hereby gives:
>
> (a) That there are no covenants, conditions, or restrictions under which the lien of the mortgage referred to in Schedule A can be cut off, subordinated, or otherwise impaired.

In addition, the CLTA Form 104, as it appears in the policy at issue, states that First American will insure

> against loss or damage which such insured shall sustain by reason of any of the following . . .

5. The existence of any subsisting tax or assessment lien which is prior to the insured mortgage except: NONE

6. The existence of other matters affecting the validity or priority of the lien of the insured mortgage, other than those shown in the policy except: NONE

Neither of these forms obligated First American to disclose information regarding the SID or the possibility of a future assessment. We find no ambiguity in this regard in either of these two forms. The forms, at their core, insure the mortgage liens that Vestin held in the property. Specifically, the forms insure against loss or damage that Vestin would sustain due to the *mortgage* being "cut off, subordinated, or otherwise impaired," the loss of priority, and "other matters affecting the validity" of the mortgage lien.

Neither the creation of the SID nor the Notice of Intention affected the priority or validity of the mortgage lien, nor was the mortgage lien "cut off, subordinated, or otherwise impaired." Once The Ranches defaulted on the loans, Vestin was able to exercise its rights under the trust deeds without any consequence arising from the SID and to take ownership through a nonjudicial foreclosure. Nothing in the Notice of Intention or in the SID affected the mortgage lien or affected the title Vestin acquired. Only the actual assessment ordinance has affected Vestin in any way, and only as to the ability to sell the property, not as to the validity of title. Vestin still holds a valid title to the property. . . .

III. THE EXCLUSION AND EXCEPTION SECTIONS OF THE POLICIES

Vestin also seeks to extend coverage through the exclusions and exemptions that are enumerated in the policies, in particular through the governmental police power exception. As the court of appeals concluded, "Because the existence of the SID and the notice of Eagle Mountain's intention to levy assessments do not affect Vestin's title and, therefore, are not covered by the policies, the exclusions to the policies and the recorded police power exception to those exclusions are not applicable." We agree. If there is *no* coverage, then an exception that prevents application of an exclusion from coverage has no application. . . .

Problem 11D

Last year, Bucky Buyer purchased Blackacre from Susie Seller for $340,000. Pursuant to the contract of purchase, Susie paid for an owner's policy of title insurance which names Bucky as the insured. The policy insures a fee simple absolute estate in Blackacre without the addition of any special endorsements or specific exceptions. The policy contains standard insuring clauses and general exceptions. Which of the following problems are insured risks?

(a) Prior to closing, Bucky's inspection of Blackacre revealed that the furnace needed major repairs. Susie agreed that under the contract of sale, she was responsible for the repairs. Rather than delay closing, Bucky agreed that $300 of his purchase price should be put in escrow, with Susie's attorney, to secure her obligation to fix the furnace. The repairs turned out to cost $586, which Bucky paid. Bucky has obtained the escrow proceeds, but despite numerous demands Susie has failed to pay him the difference.

(b) Blackacre contains a restaurant building. Bucky learns that the building is located only 8.5 feet from the side boundary line, in violation of the zoning ordinance, which requires a 10-foot setback.

(c) At the time Susie sold Blackacre to Bucky, she also owned other contiguous land. Blackacre is undeveloped, and Bucky has no present plans to develop the property. However, under the county subdivision regulations, subdivision approval was required prior to the sale to Bucky, and that approval was never sought. The county is demanding that Bucky apply for subdivision approval. Review Voorheesville Rod & Gun Club v. E.W. Tompkins Co., *supra* p. 187.

(d) Bucky learns that Blackacre is subject to zoning that prevents him from building a gasoline station on part of Blackacre.

(e) Blackacre fronts on a public highway, with pavement that is 30 feet wide. Bucky begins to build a convenience store near the highway, but learns that his building encroaches upon the highway right-of-way, which is 50 feet wide.

(f) Blackacre fronts on a public highway, which has been there for a long time. Bucky orders a survey and learns that the highway encroaches upon Blackacre by an average of three feet.

2. *Title Insurance and the Contract of Purchase*

In many contracts to buy land, the purchaser intends to obtain title insurance as the primary or sole method of title protection. Typically, the purchaser has made this decision before entering into the contract of purchase, and therefore the contract expressly refers to title insurance. For example:

> Seller at Seller's expense shall furnish an Owner's Policy of Title Insurance issued by ____________ in the amount of the purchase price and dated at or after closing. The Policy shall guarantee Buyer's title to be good and indefeasible in accordance with the standard form of policy used by said company.

HARVEY v. J & H HOLDINGS, INC.

District Court of Appeal of Florida, Second District, 1975
310 So. 2d 371

BOARDMAN, Judge. Appellants/defendants, Vernon D. Harvey and Alice E. Harvey (sellers), timely appeal an adverse final summary judgment entered by the trial court in favor of the appellee/plaintiff, J & H Holdings, Inc. (buyer), in which the sellers were ordered to pay the sum of $6,325.32, plus court cost.

This controversy initially arose out of a real estate transaction entered into between the sellers and the buyer. The precise question presented to us is whether the sellers complied with their covenant respecting the character of the title they agreed to convey. . . .

The sellers entered into a written sales agreement with the buyer to convey a certain parcel of land, consisting of approximately 10 acres situate in Sarasota County. The agreement, in pertinent part, provided:

> . . . Sellers . . . convey title to the premises to the buyer, by a good and sufficient warranty deed, warranting title to be free and clear of all liens and encumbrances, except the water easement set forth above, restrictions and conditions of record. . . .

It was agreed between the parties that the title search would be made by Lawyers Title Insurance Corporation (title insurer). The transaction was subsequently closed without incident. The buyer took title and possession of the property. Neither the sellers nor the buyer was represented by an attorney at the closing. As was agreed, title insurer issued an owners' title insurance policy to the buyer and prepared the warranty deed conveying the property. At the request of the sellers the title insurer issued a mortgagees' insurance policy in the amount of the purchase money mortgage.

After the buyer took possession, it learned that the sellers had granted an easement over this property to an abutting property owner. The easement was duly recorded among the public records of Sarasota County, for a period of about ten years prior to the date of closing. No reference or exception was made of the existence of the easement either in the owners' title insurance policy or the warranty deed signed by the sellers.

The buyer then sued the title insurer in a separate action for money damages for its negligence in failing to advise the buyer of the record easement. The result of which action was that final judgment was entered by the trial court, after jury verdict, against the title insurer in favor of the buyer in the amount of $7,825.23, which sum included $5,350 as damages to the property by virtue of the easement, $975.23 court costs, and $1,500 as attorney's fee.

There is no dispute that under the provisions of the owners' title insurance policy the title insurer had the right of subrogation and thus became subrogated to the rights of its insured, the buyer. In said action the trial court entered partial summary judgment in behalf of the buyer ruling that the easement constituted a legal encumbrance and a defect on the title. Title insurer satisfied the judgment. The instant action was instituted by the buyer for the use and benefit of the title insurer against the sellers for reimbursement of the money it had paid to the buyer.

The main thrust of the sellers' argument is that the title insurer, having issued the title insurance policy and prepared the warranty deed, is estopped from recovery against the sellers because of its own negligence. We cannot agree that the sellers can successfully rely on the theory of estoppel, under the facts presented, to bar recovery by the title insurer. The sellers urge that they are free from liability as to title insurer by having been issued a mortgagee insurance policy. This position is not tenable for the record shows that one of the mortgagee policy provisions clearly states that it did not insure against any loss by reason of defects or encumbrances created by or known to the sellers. There is no question that the sellers should have had knowledge of the easement. The record shows it was the sellers who granted the easement to Stanley E. Harvey and Ruth Harvey, husband and wife, presumably persons related to the sellers. Further, and more significantly, the said easement granted not only the permanent right of ingress and egress over the purchased lands, but also gave the grantees the right to dig soil and to widen an existing canal. . . . We can find absolutely nothing in the record to indicate that the encumbrance, *i.e.*, easement, *supra*, should be excluded from the operation of the covenant of the sellers to convey title by general warranty deed free and clear of all encumbrances. The sellers simply did not convey title to the property as they had agreed to do. . . .

Accordingly, we affirm.

Problem 11E

Lamar contracts to buy a 12-year-old apartment complex from Candi. Paragraph 3 of the contract states: "Seller shall deliver, at closing, a general warranty deed conveying said property, subject to (1) covenants, restrictions, utility agreements, and easements of record, if any, now in force, provided same are not now violated; and (2) any state of facts an accurate survey may show, provided same does not render title unmarketable." Paragraph 7 of the contract states: "Seller shall order and obtain, at Seller's expense, and Purchaser shall accept, a title insured by a reputable title insurance company selected by Seller." Candi picks Reputable Title Insurance Co., which searches and prepares a title insurance commitment.

(a) Reputable finds and lists, as a special exception, a restrictive covenant recorded in 1985 that restricts occupancy of the apartment units to "adults only," purportedly for the benefit of a neighboring retirement community. The Fair Housing Act, since its amendment in 1988, prohibits discrimination against families with children in the rental and sale of housing. A number of families with children presently live in Candi's apartment complex. Lamar objects to the special exception for the 1985 covenant, but Reputable refuses to remove it. Can Lamar terminate the contract? If so, may Lamar obtain expectancy damages?

(b) Reputable finds and lists, as a matter that requires curative action prior to closing, a problem in the chain of title. Twenty-two years ago, before the apartments were built, Thomas, who then owned the land, died and was survived by his wife. She promptly conveyed the property, by properly recorded warranty deed. There are no probate court records showing a transfer, by will or intestate succession, to his wife. The chain of title since that deed, which eventually leads to Candi, is fine. Candi's attorney persuades Reputable that the risk of missing heirs or devisees showing up is remote, and thus curative action is not necessary. Therefore, Reputable issues a new commitment, deleting any requirement concerning, or reference to, Thomas or his estate. At closing, Lamar's attorney asks if the Thomas probate matter has been cleaned up. He is not satisfied by the answer that "it hasn't, but Reputable is issuing a clean policy." He claims title is not marketable, and he and his client, Lamar, leave the closing. Is he correct? Is title marketable?

(c) Suppose you represent the prospective buyer of an apartment complex, and the seller submits for your review a draft contract, with Paragraphs 3 and 7 as quoted at the beginning of this problem. Are they acceptable to you? Are there any changes you want to propose?

3. *Ethical Problems: Conflicts and Confidentiality*

The business of insuring titles is the practice of law, and not surprisingly attorneys are heavily involved in the title insurance industry. Title companies are often owned and managed by attorneys, and companies often hire attorneys as employees to work "in house." Usually, no special ethical problems are raised in connection with this practice — the company attorney has duties to only one client.

Real estate attorneys who are not insurance company employees often participate in providing title insurance. There are a number of different arrangements in use. The attorney or her law firm may be an agent for a title insurance company, with an underwriting agreement giving the agent a percentage of the insurance premium in exchange for services such as the agent's title search, issuance of commitment, and supervision of the closing. Alternatively, the attorney or firm may own a corporation that functions as an agent. Instead of an agent with broad powers and responsibilities, the attorney may do title work as "examining counsel," submitting an abstract or a certificate to the insurer and receiving a share of the premium as compensation. Another relationship is that of closing attorney, where the insurance company pays the attorney to attend the closing and handle all the closing items necessary for the policy to be written, including receipt of the premium. Closing attorneys usually are paid a flat fee rather than a percentage of the premium. In some states, like Florida, the real estate attorneys operate their own title insurance fund so that members can directly compete with other commercial insurance companies. In many cases, the lawyers involved in title insurance work are recognized or rewarded for having a good record or few errors or claims.

Ethical problems often result when attorneys represent persons other than or in addition to the insurance company. Imagine that your law firm is an agent for a title insurance company. If you have a client buying property and she needs title insurance, which insurer would you like your client to use? Thus, it is not surprising that in many transactions, an attorney who represents a buyer or lender has an economic interest in the title insurance used in the same transaction. Most, but not all, of the ethical problem areas involve multiple representation, or the appearance of multiple representation, and related issues of disclosure and informed consent.

Problem 11F

Laurie represents a residential developer, Daffy, who is buying 80 acres of undeveloped land. Daffy told Laurie that the seller told him that, six months ago, he granted a 40-foot-wide utility easement to Great Power Co. running along one of the tract's boundaries. Daffy and the seller agreed to a lower purchase price because of the easement. Laurie orders a title insurance commitment from an insurer with whom she and her firm have no affiliation. The title insurance commitment does not refer to Great Power Co.'s easement.

(a) What action, if any, should Laurie take at the present time?

(b) Assume that Laurie personally searches the land records for the past year, and finds the Great Power Co. easement recorded in the proper office. A local attorney — one of Laurie's friends — is agent for the insurer and, in his search, evidently missed the easement. What should Laurie do? What are her ethical obligations to her client? To the insurance company? To her friend?

Problem 11G

Laurie represents a residential developer, Daffy, who is buying 80 acres of undeveloped land. She is also an agent for Reputable Title Insurance Co., and she acts in that capacity in connection with Daffy's purchase. Both Daffy and Reputable are aware of her multiple representation. Laurie has a new associate at her firm search title to the tract. That search finds title to be marketable, and Reputable issues a clean owner's policy. One month later, Daffy comes to see Laurie, telling her about a problem with someone called Great Power Co., whose workers are starting to clear vegetation from a strip of the property.

The Great Power Co. claims it has a 40-foot-wide utility easement running along one of the tract's boundaries, granted by Daffy's seller seven months ago. Daffy admits to Laurie that the seller told him about the easement prior to the signing of the contract of sale, and Daffy figured it wouldn't reduce the land value all that much.

Laurie rechecks the records, and finds that Great Power's easement was properly recorded prior to the signing of the contract of sale between Daffy and his seller. The new associate just plain missed it. What should Laurie do? What are her ethical duties to each client?

12

Improving the Efficiency of the Title System

The recording system, despite its faults, is a mainstay of American land law, destined to remain in place for the foreseeable future. Proposals for structural reform, such as the Torrens registration system discussed below, have generally failed. Instead, successful reforms have conceded the present structure of the recording system, seeking incremental improvements by ameliorating some of the system's worst features.

The weaknesses of the recording system fall into two general categories. First, stale recorded interests accumulate over time. The system makes it easy and inexpensive to record virtually any type of instrument. This is a virtue in that it encourages all owners to use the system, thereby getting protection and furnishing information that will be valuable to subsequent purchasers, but in the long run it is also a vice that impedes efficiency. Stale interests of record, often decades old, cloud titles.

The old interests usually are economically devalued. They were valuable to their holders when initially created and recorded, but as time passes, their value wanes. Often the only remaining value of old interests is as an impediment to title — they have blockage value only. Because the present possessor lacks marketable title to the old clog, the owner (or apparent owner) of the old interest can block a transaction, insisting on compensation before signing a quitclaim deed or release.

An additional problem with stale interests is that their owners become hard to identify. For example, it may be difficult or impossible to find the present owners — heirs or successors — of old undivided interests, old rights of entry for breach of conditions, and old covenants related to land use.

The second major group of recording system weaknesses comprises the off-the-record risks. Deeds and other instruments may be void or voidable for reasons such as nondelivery, incapacity, fraud, and adverse possession.

Attempts made over the years to improve the functioning of the recording system consist of changes in title practices and statutory reforms. With respect to title practices, title standards and the evolution of title insurance have improved operation of the system. The law of adverse possession strengthens titles to land by barring potential claims of persons who are not in possession of a parcel after a specified period of time has elapsed, provided that certain conditions are met. Title standards, along with statutory reforms (*e.g.*, title curative acts, marketable title acts, and Torrens statutes), are examined in this chapter.

A. TITLE STANDARDS

KRAETTLI Q. EPPERSON & KEVIN A. SULLIVAN, TITLE EXAMINATION STANDARDS: A STATUS REPORT
4 Probate & Property 16 (Sept/Oct 1990)

The American system of conveying real property relies in large part not only on the recording system but also on the title examiner's standards for reviewing and then either approving or disapproving the quality of title as reflected in the record. Such standards arise from several sources, depending on the local community and state's practices. . . .

Beginnings of Standards

In the absence of any officially recognized community or statewide standards, each examiner must individually interpret the applicable law and relevant facts according to the examiner's understanding of the risks involved. This decision-making is sometimes distorted by the knowledge that another examiner—one who is perhaps "overly meticulous"—probably will be rechecking the title and the original examiner's work at a later date when another conveyance or loan is made. . . .

To avoid the tendency toward rejecting almost every title (since there is seldom a perfect title), state bar organizations in about one-half of the states have adopted statewide standards, with several counties and cities adopting local standards as well. It is assumed that in states without statewide standards the standards vary from examiner to examiner or are dictated by the willingness of local title insurers to insure a particular title.

Connecticut was the first state to adopt statewide standards, which were approved by its state bar association in 1938. Nebraska followed suit in 1939. Each set of statewide standards is adopted by each state's bar association, although Nebraska has followed the unique practice of having its standards adopted by the state legislature. Since 1938, 27 states have adopted standards, although seven of these 27 states have allowed their standards to fall into disuse.

When title examination standards are drafted, it is usually from the standpoint of an examiner looking at an existing record, rather than from the perspective of a lawyer who is in the midst of preparing the necessary documents or pleadings. An examiner who is limited to the current record is often forced to forget about what might be done if he or she "had it to do over again" instead of having to decide, "is it good enough as is?"

The issues typically faced by an examiner fall into three categories:

1. Issues on which there is no disagreement within the bar on the status of title because the law is both clear and well-known;
2. Issues on which competent lawyers seriously disagree; or
3. Issues on which competent lawyers agree but on which novice examiners might be ignorant and on which overly meticulous examiners might disagree with the majority of examiners.

A set of standards can be the most efficient and effective if it addresses only the issues in category 3. A set of standards is unnecessary for the issues in category 1 and is subject to serious challenge if it ventures into topics falling under category 2. However, standards are often adopted to cover matters included under category 1 because those standards serve the useful educational purpose of discussing the law, from the unique viewpoint of a title examiner, even if restating a statute or case law. . . .

After statewide standards were adopted in 23 states, the University of Michigan Law School and the Section undertook a joint effort to draft model standards. This project resulted in a set of model title standards by Lewis M. Simes and Clarence B. Taylor (*1960 Model Title Standards Report*). This set, which included 101 separate standards, contained 22 chapters covering such topics as the abstract, the examiner, name variances, marital interests, conveyances by and to trustees and mechanics liens.

This earlier report was based on a review of all existing statewide standards and was predicated on the well-founded conclusion that many factors affecting the marketability of title either cannot be determined from the record (such as proof of delivery, the competence of the grantor or the absence of forgery and fraud) or are only technical in nature and do not expose the examiner's client to any real risk of a third party challenge to the marketability of title (such as abbreviations of names).

New ABA Title Standards Project

"That it is desirable for state bar associations to adopt title standards . . . has rarely been questioned in recent years," the *1960 Model Title Standards Report* stated. . . .

Several recent trends and events suggest it is time to revisit the status of title examination standards in America, including the following:

- The growing number of transactions involving multiple parcels of real property located in more than one state;
- The growing number of nationwide real property issues that lend themselves to a nationwide rather than a state-by-state approach

(e.g., Federal Savings and Loan Insurance Corporation (FSLIC), Federal Depositors Insurance Corporation (FDIC) and the Resolution Trust Corporation (RTC) conveyances, governmental forfeiture procedures and environmental liens); and

- The adoption in 1987 by the title insurance industry of the following definition for unmarketability of the title: "an alleged or apparent matter affecting the title to the land, not excluded or excepted from coverage, which would entitle a purchaser of the estate or interest described in Schedule A or the insured mortgage to be released from the obligation to purchase by virtue of a contractual condition requiring the delivery of marketable title." . . .

To expand on and update the standards found in the 1960 Model Title Standards Report, the [State Customs and Practices] Subcommittee [of the Conveyancing Committee of the Real Property, Probate and Trust Law Section of the ABA] is initiating efforts to promote and coordinate drafting model title standards for newly developing areas of the law. These areas include dealing with (a) titles going through the FDIC, the FSLIC and the RTC in their various capacities; (b) governmental forfeitures, especially drug-enforcement related actions; and (c) environmental liens. This activity will be coordinated with the major title insurance companies, which are already dealing with these new problems on a daily basis, and with appropriate federal agencies. . . .

LEWIS M. SIMES & CLARENCE B. TAYLOR, MODEL TITLE STANDARDS
(1960)

STANDARD 2.1. EXAMINING ATTORNEY'S ATTITUDE.

The purpose of the examination of title and of objections, if any, shall be to secure for the examiner's client a title which is in fact marketable and which is shown by the record to be marketable, subject to no other encumbrances than those expressly provided for by the client's contract. Objections and requirements should be made only when the irregularities or defects reasonably can be expected to expose the purchaser or lender to the hazard of adverse claims or litigation.

Comment: Title Standards are primarily intended to eliminate technical objections which do not impair marketability and some common objections which are based upon misapprehension of the law. The examining attorney, by way of a test, may ask himself after examining the title, what defects and irregularities he has discovered by his examination, and as to each such irregularity or defect, who, if anyone, can take advantage of it as against the purported owner, and to what end. . . .

STANDARD 3.1. PERIOD OF SEARCH.

[In this standard, it is assumed that record titles in the jurisdiction are so long that it is unreasonably burdensome to trace title back to the government, or that if land titles do not originate with the United States or with the state, it is impracticable to trace titles back to their origin. Of course, if the Model Marketable Title Act, or similar legislation, were in force, then the length of search, for most purposes, would be determined by such legislation. This standard is not as satisfactory as a marketable title act, since defects in title prior to the period of search as stated in the title standard constitute a risk which a vendee must assume. Whereas, if a marketable title act is in force, defects in title prior to the period of the act are extinguished.]

A record title covering a period of fifty years or more is marketable: provided that the basis thereof is a warranty deed, one or more quitclaim deeds supported by a reasonable record proof that they convey the full title, a patent from the United States, or a conveyance from the state, a probate proceeding in which the property is reasonably identifiable, a warranty mortgage deed if subsequently regularly foreclosed, or any other instrument which shows of record reasonable probability of title and possession thereunder; provided further that the period actually searched does not refer to or indicate prior instruments or defects in title, in which case such prior instruments may be used in turn as a start, and that the period actually searched discloses instruments which confirm and carry forward the title so established.

Comment: In applying this standard, it is necessary to trace the record title back to a "root" or "start," which may be, and generally is, more than fifty years back. Any defects in the record title subsequent to the date of recording of the "root" or "start" must be considered by the examiner. . . .

STANDARD 5.1. RULE OF IDEM SONANS.

Differently spelled names are presumed to be the same when they sound alike, or when their sounds cannot be distinguished easily, or when common usage by corruption or abbreviation has made their pronunciation identical. . . .

STANDARD 5.2. USE OR NON-USE OF MIDDLE NAMES OR INITIALS.

The use in one instrument and non-use in another of a middle name or initial ordinarily does not create a question of identity affecting title, unless the examiner is otherwise put on inquiry.

STANDARD 5.3. ABBREVIATIONS.

All customary and generally accepted abbreviations of first and middle names should be recognized as the equivalent thereof. . . .

Standard 5.5. Effect of Suffix.

Although identity of name raises the presumption of identity of person, the addition of a suffix such as "Jr." or "II" to the name of a subsequent grantor may rebut the presumption of identity with the prior grantee.

Comment: Ordinarily it is said that the suffix is no part of the name. Thus, where the grantee in one instrument is "John Lawrence, M.D." and the grantor in the next instrument is merely "John Lawrence," it would be presumed that they are the same person. But if the grantee in one instrument is "John Lawrence, Sr." and the grantor in the next instrument is "John Lawrence, Jr.," the presumption that they are the same person would be rebutted. Or, if the grantee in one instrument is "John Lawrence," and, in another instrument, the grantor is "John Lawrence, Jr.," and it appears that there are both a father and a son of the name of John Lawrence, the presumption of identity is rebutted.

B. TITLE CURATIVE ACTS

One consequence of the high volume of instruments presented for recording in many localities is that inevitably some contain various sorts of defects. The acknowledgment may be missing or defective, the grantee may have failed to pay the recording fee or a transfer tax, the instrument may lack a seal, or delivery may be suspect. Some of these defects may be observable from a close inspection of the instrument. Other defects are off-the-record in the sense that the instrument looks fine and only an investigation into the circumstances of the underlying transaction can reveal the problem. Many of these defects are violations of the statutory requirements for recording — the instrument, which is in fact recorded, was not entitled to be recorded, but it slipped into the system anyway.

Defective instruments of record pose two types of risk for parties dealing with the system. First, a party to the defectively documented transaction may have the right to attack the transaction, seeking rescission or some other remedy that affects title to the land. This risk goes to the core of marketable title. A careful, conservative title searcher who finds a technical defect will often raise an objection, even if the risk of loss is unlikely. Second, the defective instrument's recordation status is doubtful. When the defect, such as improper acknowledgment, is of the nature that the instrument was not entitled to be recorded, many courts hold that the instrument does not impart constructive notice. *See Metropolitan National Bank*, reproduced at p. 245. This presents a risk for the grantee under the instrument, as well as subsequent grantees whose chain of title includes the defective instrument. A BFP who lacks actual notice of the instrument has the ability to obtain superior rights to the property.

In response to the problems stemming from defective instruments of record, many states have passed title curative acts, which provide that instruments bearing certain defects are conclusively presumed valid after the passage of a specified number of years after recordation. The acts' features, including the time periods, differ markedly from state to state.

With curative legislation, more titles are marketable because searchers may safely disregard evidence of old defects. This increases the efficiency of the title assurance system, without imposing any significant costs—it is extremely rare that shoring up the record title by eliminating old formal defects cuts off substantive rights of claimants to the land.

Problem 12A

A title search for a client, Gomer, who is interested in buying an 82-acre farm, reveals the following information:

(1) A deed in the chain of title, recorded eight years ago, appears to be properly executed and to be acknowledged by a notary, but the space in the acknowledgment form where the date of acknowledgment is to be inserted was left blank.

(2) A deed in the chain of title, recorded 22 years ago, purports to convey a fee simple estate from John Wallace to Susan Dollar; however, the deed is executed only by the grantee, Susan Dollar, with the acknowledgment likewise reciting execution by Susan Dollar.

(3) The immediately prior deed in the chain of title, recorded 27 years ago, purports to convey a fee simple estate from Donald Mitchem to John Wallis, Jr. The title searcher, having asked the present record owner and several neighbors about the Wallace (Wallis) family, has been unable to establish whether John Wallace and John Wallis, Jr. are the same person.

(a) Is title to the farm marketable if the state:

(i) has no relevant title standards or legislation?

(ii) has adopted the Model Title Standards reproduced earlier in this chapter?

(iii) has adopted a title curative act, which provides: "When any instrument shall have been recorded . . . and the instrument contains any of the following defects: . . . (5) the instrument is not acknowledged; . . . (7) any defect in the execution, acknowledgment, recording or certificate of recording the same; such instrument shall, from and after the expiration of five (5) years from the filing thereof for record, be valid as though such instrument had, in the first instance, been in all respects duly executed [and] acknowledged. . . ." Okla. Stat., Title 16, §27a.

(b) Suppose that you are Gomer's attorney. Gomer tells you he really wants to buy the farm and doesn't want to make title objections just for the sake of making title objections. If title is really okay, he wants you to proceed to closing. Does this client information affect your evaluation of title? How do you advise Gomer?

(c) Suppose that you are Gomer's attorney. Gomer tells you he has cold feet and now realizes that in the signed contract, he agreed to pay way too much for this lousy farm. Does this client information affect your evaluation of title? How do you advise Gomer?

C. MARKETABLE TITLE ACTS

Eighteen states presently have marketable title acts. The primary goals of this remedial legislation are to limit the period of time covered by title searches and to render more titles marketable by eliminating stale interests. A period of 40 years is most common, but some states specify 30 or 50 years. The marketable title act operates to extinguish interests and defects that are older than the "root of title," which is the most recent deed or other instrument in the record chain of title that is more than 30 (or 40 or 50) years old. Without marketable title legislation, in states where searches customarily go back only an agreed-upon number of years, there is the risk of older, undiscovered, interests that are still valid. For example, a nineteenth-century deed may have conveyed a defeasible fee simple, with the future interest still outstanding. Thus, it is a calculated risk not to trace title back to the sovereign. This risk may be justified, given the real-world probability that ancient rights, not appearing of record during the past 40 years, either do not exist or will never be asserted. A marketable title act seeks to reduce the risk even further by cutting off ancient claims that do not appear of record during the specified period.

The aim of marketable title legislation is to render unnecessary searches of records prior to the root of title. An interest created prior to the root of title no longer affects title unless it is referred to in a post-root instrument, or re-recorded, or reflected by possession after the root of title. Unfortunately, all marketable title acts have exceptions, which substantially undercut the fundamental goal. Many older interests are sheltered by exceptions, the most common ones being: (1) interests of the United States government; (2) interests of state and local governments; (3) utility and railroad easements; (4) mineral rights; and (5) visible easements. As a practical matter, the list of exceptions means that the searcher who stops at the root of title is actually taking a significant risk of missing an interest that is still valid.

Consider how market title acts compare to a related problem under the Uniform Commercial Code (UCC). Under the UCC, security interests in goods and other personal property are perfected by the filing of financing statements. UCC §9-515 handles the problem of stale security interests by making a financing statement effective for a period of five years from the date of filing. A secured party who wants continued protection must file a continuation statement. Can a plan like the Article 9 system work for real estate?

Many states have specialized statutes that address particular types of old recorded interests. These have a narrower focus than marketable title legislation, which attempts to clear all types of old interests, save those given statutory exceptions. The most common statutes treat mortgages, mineral rights, and future interests that follow defeasible fee simples (rights of entry, possibilities of reverter, and executory interests).

A number of states have specialized statutes, more limited in scope than marketable title acts, which address the problem of outstanding mineral interests that cloud title. Regular adverse possession statutes have little impact with respect to minerals because possession of the land surface is typically not viewed as adverse to the rights of the mineral owner. These specialized acts, often called mineral lapse acts or dormant mineral interest acts, apply when mineral rights are severed from the surface estate and the mineral interest owner does not explore or produce for a long period of time, such as 20 years. Such acts function by transferring the mineral rights to the surface owner, thus making the surface owner's title fully marketable. Ancient mortgage statutes address the problem of a very old recorded mortgage for which there is no recorded release of lien. Generally, a period of 30 or 40 years applies, measured from the date of final maturity stated in the mortgage or, if the mortgage does not specify such a date, from the date of execution. Some states impose time limitations on the exercise of rights of entry and possibilities of reverter. One type of statute prohibits such interests from remaining in effect for more than a stated number of years, typically 30 or 40. The period begins running when the future interest is created and runs regardless of whether a breach of the limitation or condition has occurred.

SUNSHINE VISTAS HOMEOWNERS ASSOCIATION v. CARUANA
Supreme Court of Florida, 1993
623 So. 2d 490

SHAW, Justice. We review Sunshine Vistas Homeowners Assn. v. Caruana, 597 So. 2d 809, 811 (Fla. 3d DCA 1992), in which the district court certified the following question:

> Whether the Florida Marketable Record Title Act has the effect of extinguishing a plat restriction which was created prior to the root of title[1] where the

1. "'Root of title' means any title transaction purporting to create or transfer the estate claimed by any person and which is the last title transaction to have been recorded at least 30 years prior to the time when marketability is being determined. The effective date of the root of title is the date on which it was recorded." §712.01(2), Fla. Stat. (1989). "The document with which an abstract of title properly commences." *Black's Law Dictionary* 1330 (6th ed. 1990).

muniments of title[2] in the chain of title describe the property by its legal description which makes reference to the plat and the muniments of title state that the conveyance is given subject to covenants and restrictions of record?

. . . Townsend Construction Corporation (Townsend) bought a parcel of property in the Sunshine Vistas subdivision of Coconut Grove in 1990 and, with Caruana, began constructing a building thereon. The Sunshine Vistas subdivision plat, filed in 1925, contains a setback restriction which the Sunshine Vistas Homeowners' Association (Homeowners) seek to enforce through a declaratory judgment action.

The Marketable Record Titles to Real Property Act (act) is intended to simplify and facilitate land title transactions. . . . The act provides that a person "vested with any estate in land of record for 30 years or more" has "a marketable record title . . . free and clear of all claims" except claims preserved by section 712.03. Section 712.02, Fla. Stat. (1989). Townsend and Caruana argue that the act extinguishes the setback restriction because it is not specifically identified in the muniments of title beginning with the root of title. Homeowners argue that the muniments make the specific identification that section 712.03 requires and thus the restriction is preserved. The trial court granted and the district court affirmed summary judgment in favor of Townsend and Caruana.

We quash the result below and answer the question in the negative. Section 712.03 provides:

> Exceptions to marketability. — Such marketable record title shall not affect or extinguish the following rights:
>
> (1) Estates or interests, easements and use restrictions disclosed by and defects inherent in the muniments of title on which said estate is based beginning with the root of title; provided, however, that a general reference in any of such muniments to easements, use restrictions or other interests created prior to the root of title shall not be sufficient to preserve them unless specific identification by *reference* to book and page of record or by *name of recorded plat be made therein* to a recorded title transaction which imposed, transferred or continued such easement, use restrictions or other interests. . . .

(Emphasis added.) Thus, a thirty-one-year-old restriction is preserved if the root of title or a subsequent muniment contains a "specific identification" to a recorded title transaction that imposed, transferred, or continued the restriction. *Id.* The "specific identification" to the title transaction can be made in one of two ways: (1) by reference to the book and page in the public

2. "Muniments of title" is defined thus: "Documentary evidence of title. The instruments of writing and written evidences which the owner of lands, possessions, or inheritances has, by which [one] is entitled to defend the title. . . ." *Black's Law Dictionary* 1019 (6th ed. 1990).

records where the title transaction that imposed the restriction can be found, or (2) by reference to the name of a recorded plat that imposed the restriction. *Id.*

Townsend's root of title is a 1951 deed conveying the property from Mr. and Mrs. Heurer to Mr. Pasco. It describes the property conveyed as follows:

> Lots sixteen (16) and seventeen (17), in block five (5), of SUNSHINE VISTAS, according to the plat thereof recorded in Plat Book 16, at page 29, of the Public Records of Dade County, Florida. This conveyance is given subject to covenants and restrictions of record and subject to taxes for 1951 and subsequent years.

The 1977 muniment, a deed from Mr. Pasco to Mr. Block, thus describes the property conveyed:

> Lots 16 and 17 in Block 5 of SUNSHINE VISTAS, according to the Plat thereof, as recorded in Plat Book 16 at Page 29, of the Public Records of Dade County, Florida. SUBJECT TO: limitations, restrictions and easements of record, if any, applicable zoning ordinances and regulations and taxes for the year 1978 and subsequent years.

The 1990 muniment, a deed from Mr. and Mrs. Block to Townsend Construction Corporation, describes the property conveyed:

> Lots 16 and 17 in Block 5 of SUNSHINE VISTAS, according to the Plat thereof, as recorded in Plat Book 16 at Page 29, of the Public Records of Dade County, Florida.

Each of these muniments makes reference to SUNSHINE VISTAS—the name of the recorded plat that imposed the restriction. The use restriction at issue here thus is preserved by these muniments. We therefore disagree with the courts below that the setback restriction is extinguished by the act. To so hold effectively reads out of section 712.03(1) the words: "unless specific identification by reference to . . . name of recorded plat be made therein"; we lack the power to delete words from the statute.[3] . . .

We accordingly quash the decision below, answer the question in the negative, and remand for consistent proceedings.

3. Indeed, one scholar takes the position that restrictive covenants in recorded plats are preserved by the "inherent in the muniments" language of the Model Marketable Title Act, on which Florida's act is based. *See* Walter E. Barnett, *Marketable Title Acts—Panacea or Pandemonium?*, 53 Cornell L. Rev. 45, 74-75 (1967) (discussing "accidental" preservation of restrictive covenants when plat is identified in describing the land conveyed); *see also* David P. Catsman, *Function of a Marketable Title Act*, 34 Fla. B.J. 139 (1960) (discussing the drafting of Florida's act).

Problem 12B

Bruno, a real estate attorney, has an angry client, Sam Strip. Bruno represented Strip in connection with his purchase, for $680,000, of a 4.2-acre tract of undeveloped land situated on the outskirts of Megapolis, in the path of suburban growth. The land is zoned light commercial, and Strip plans to build a strip shopping center. The transaction closed nine months ago, and Bruno personally conducted the title search. Most attorneys in Megapolis search titles back for a 50-year period. Bruno found title to be clear and marketable, searching back to a "root of title" consisting of a warranty deed recorded 57 years ago that conveyed a 185-acre tract that included Strip's 4.2-acre tract. Prior to closing, Bruno orally told Strip that title was good. Also prior to closing, Bruno advised Strip that he could purchase an owner's policy of title insurance for $2,800, but Bruno pointed out he would have to buy title insurance in the near future to satisfy the project lenders and he could save money by not purchasing a policy now. Strip made what he thought was an easy decision to save money, since his lawyer was not insisting that he buy title insurance.

Now Strip, wanting to break ground on the shopping center, has a major-league problem. Sixty-one years ago, the then-owner of the property conveyed a pipeline easement to Napper Natural Gas Company, and this easement cuts right across the 4.2-acre tract. The easement is properly recorded and an underground pipeline is in place, but at the present time no evidence of the pipeline is visible at the surface of the 4.2-acre tract. The center cannot be developed unless the gas company can be persuaded to relocate its easement. Strip claims Bruno is responsible for his title problem and needs to solve it or pay damages. Is Bruno liable if:

(a) Megapolis is in a state with no relevant title standards or legislation?

(b) Megapolis is in a state with the Model Title Standards (reproduced earlier in this chapter)?

(c) Megapolis is in a state with the Model Title Standards, plus the state legislature has enacted the following statute: "*Abstracts; Effect of Title Standards.* In the compilation or examination of an abstract of title to real estate, it shall not be considered negligence for a registered abstracter or an attorney to follow the Title Standards promulgated by the Nebraska State Bar Association." Neb. Rev. St. §76-557.

(d) Megapolis is in Florida, with the Marketable Record Title Act described in *Sunshine Vistas*?

D. TORRENS SYSTEM: TITLE REGISTRATION

The reforms to the title assurance system discussed in this chapter are all alike in that they keep the basic elements of the recording system intact.

Parties are encouraged to record instruments, which then serve as evidence of title that is available for inspection by other interested parties. Recording officers do not issue opinions as to title or as to the nature, legitimacy, or effect of any of the records.

In contrast, the Torrens system of title registration does not seek to reform or improve the operation of the recording system. Instead, it aims to be a complete replacement. For each registered parcel of land, the government issues a certificate of title that is intended to be conclusive. The principle is the same as for title to automobiles; under modern certificate of title acts, the government-issued certificate is proof of title, subject to any liens noted thereon. Compared to the system used for automobiles, the Torrens title system for land is necessarily much more complex, because of the many different types of interests in land recognized by our legal system, but the principle is the same. A Torrens certificate is much more than evidence of title, it *is* title—just as in the real estate game Monopoly, in which you own Boardwalk if you hold the one and only Boardwalk title deed, and otherwise you don't. In this sense, a Torrens certificate fits the image that many laypersons have of deeds to land—that for each parcel there is only one, and if it's not a forgery, it's by definition good.

JOHN L. McCORMACK, TORRENS AND RECORDING: LAND TITLE ASSURANCE IN THE COMPUTER AGE

18 Wm. Mitchell L. Rev. 61 (1992)

The weaknesses of the recording systems used in the United States are well known. Over the years, commentators have proposed replacing recording systems with the Torrens system of land title registration. Some proponents of Torrens point to the apparent success of registration systems in foreign countries, particularly Canada and the United Kingdom, as proof that title registration could work in the United States. . . .

While title registration has been used in continental Europe since the early Middle Ages, modern European title registration systems were not established until the 1800s. During the 1800s, England considered adopting a recording system but instead adopted a registration system in 1862. To a limited extent, England used some antecedents of the American recording system, but a comprehensive land title records system did not exist in England until this century. After substantial modifications and a number of false starts, registration was finally implemented throughout England and Wales after enactment of the Land Registration Act of 1925.[34] In the late 1850s, Sir Robert Richard Torrens invented and implemented the Torrens system of title registration in Australia.

34. Land Registration Act, 1925, 15 & 16 Geo. 5, ch. 21 (Eng.). The English program of compulsory registration is approaching completion of the mammoth task of registering every parcel in England and Wales [citations omitted].

Sir Robert based his system on the English method of registering ships. Each ship was assigned a page in the registry where the name and description of the ship appeared, along with the name of the owner and a statement of the liens and encumbrances against it. The owner received a duplicate of the page as a certificate of title and proof of ownership. Upon sale of the ship, the instrument of transfer and the certificate were sent to the registry office and a new page was prepared to show the transfer of ownership.

Sir Robert reasoned that a similar system could be used to register ownership of real estate and drafted legislation to accomplish that result. He promised that the new system would have four "grand characteristics": certainty, economy, simplicity and facility. . . .

Torrens is one of five general types of title registration systems used in the world and is the only type used in the United States. In 1895, Illinois became the first American state to enact Torrens legislation.[39] Within a few decades, Torrens was adopted by nineteen other states. Since then, the legislation has lapsed or has been repealed in nine of them. The Torrens system is used to a substantial extent today in only five states: Hawaii, Illinois, Massachusetts, Minnesota and Ohio. . . .

A. THE TORRENS SYSTEM IN OPERATION: MIRROR, CURTAIN, AND INDEMNITY

The Torrens system of title registration has three major components: 1) the register of titles, 2) the document vault, and 3) the assurance or indemnity fund. The basic goal is to make the governmentally maintained record a conclusive statement of ownership and the condition of title. This conclusive statement is intended to function as a "mirror" of the true state of the title and as a "curtain" between the present and the past which should make it unnecessary to conduct the kind of historical searches performed in recording systems. . . .

The assurance or indemnity fund is the third important component of the system. Upon initial registration or at some time thereafter, the owner or other party may be required to make a contribution to this fund. The fund is available to compensate those who suffer losses because of errors of the Torrens office personnel and to pay those who wrongfully lose interests in real estate because of the operation of the system.

Confidence in the Torrens system in California was shaken in 1937 when the entire state assurance fund was wiped out by a single claim. Repeal of the California Torrens Act followed in 1955. In Illinois and Massachusetts, local

39. The system was approved by the voters in Cook County on November 5, 1895. The statute was held unconstitutional in the following year. People *ex rel.* Kern v. Chase, 46 N.E. 454 (Ill. 1896). A second act was adopted and approved by the voters in 1897. This statute was held constitutional. People *ex rel.* Deneen v. Simon, 52 N.E. 910 (Ill. 1898). The Torrens office in Cook County opened on March 1, 1899, and has been in continuous operation ever since. In January 1991, legislation was signed which abolished Torrens in Illinois, effective January 1, 1992. 1990 Ill. Legis. Serv. 2959 (West); *see also* David Heckelman, *Bill Abolishes Torrens Title Registration,* Chi. L. Bull., Jan. 15, 1991, at 1.

funds are backed up by the assets and credit of the state or local government. In Hawaii and Minnesota, special state funds supply the back-up. . . .

D. TORRENS IN OPERATION: SECURITY OF TITLE

Initially, Torrens appears to have an appealing simplicity compared to recording. Instead of having to search for and examine the entire recorded legal history of a parcel, it seems that the title examiner under Torrens simply has to examine the original certificate of title which "conclusively establishes the legal status of the parcel's title, subject to some limited exceptions."[109] These so-called "limited" exceptions are usually referred to as "off-certificate risks" or "overriding interests." They make the Torrens register substantially less conclusive than it is sometimes perceived to be. Except where a party loses an interest in land to a good faith purchaser from a party to fraud, generally, those suffering losses from off-certificate risks are not entitled to indemnification from the assurance fund unless the registrar's actions constituted misconduct.

In no title registration system is the register absolutely conclusive.[112] Exceptions to conclusiveness found in Torrens systems are both statutory and judge-made[113] and fall into eight categories:[114]

1. *Caveats:* notices on certificates of possible claims or interests which are not technically registered;
2. *Governmental Interests:* a) rights under federal law in nations with federal systems of government, b) liens or equivalent interests which secure payment of taxes, c) governmental lands for uses such as streets and highways;
3. *Private special interest exceptions:* a) mechanics liens, b) judgment creditor or execution liens;
4. *Possessory interests:* a) short term leases usually where the lessee is in possession, b) easements by implication, c) other private easements, although these are rare;
5. *Equity:* equitable title, due process, and fairness claims or interests: a) rights to appeal or contest initial registrations, b) exceptions in

109. [Barry] Goldner, [Comment, *The Torrens System of Title Registration: A New Proposal for Effective Implementation,* 29 UCLA L. Rev. 661], 678-79 [(1982)].

112. The English title registration statute permits a broad range of overriding interests: legal easements, rights relating to adverse possession and "rights of every person in actual occupation of the land or in receipt of the rents and profits thereof, save where enquiry is made of such person and the rights are not disclosed." Additionally, the administrator has authority to change the record by "rectifying" it [citations omitted].

113. The existence of some of these excepted claims or interests can, in some instances, be discovered through other records in the registration office (and elsewhere) and through physical inspection of the property.

114. At least some strong or pervasive influences or policies are involved because these exceptions are not peculiar to title registration. Some are found in recording systems and marketable title acts as well. Carol M. Rose, *Crystals and Mud in Property Law,* 40 Stan. L. Rev. 577, 589 n.70 (1988).

certain cases of fraud, c) exceptions to protect the relatively weak or disadvantaged such as contract vendees or the uninformed, d) equitable title interests;

6. *Error exceptions:* Exceptions due to errors in administration of the system;
7. *Encroachments:* a) encroachments by structures on the property onto adjacent property or over a building line, b) encroachments by structures on adjacent property onto the subject property or over building lines; and
8. *Non-title related restrictions on ownership or use:* a) planning laws, b) zoning ordinances or statutes, c) building or housing codes, d) environmental laws or regulation, e) lack of access to the property.

. . . Even with the exceptions discussed, the typical register is probably more reliable and, thus, promotes security of titles more than the record in the typical recording system. In other words, the Torrens system does provide a better mirror of the title than does the recording system. It also provides better, though no means perfect, protection against non-record interests. Nonetheless, the belief that registration systems may be capable of eliminating the roles of title insurance companies or attorneys in modern conveyancing is probably overly optimistic. The prudent purchaser of a registered interest will still need professional title services. The exceptions to the conclusiveness of the register may make title insurance advisable in many cases.[154]

E. USER DIFFICULTIES WITH TORRENS

Initially, Torrens appears to be more user friendly than recording. It is obviously less burdensome for the user to examine the original certificate of title in the register than it is to wade through an often complicated recorded chain of title. While title examiners may find a registration system less painful and arduous, the parties initiating registration may have a quite different experience. The rigidity and inflexibility of a Torrens office can be frustrating and time-consuming.

Under recording, users ordinarily evaluate title data whenever they deem it necessary. These evaluations do not absolutely control whether data is added to the record. The recorder's acceptance of data for recording does not subject government to potential liability from an erroneous evaluation because the recorder usually makes no evaluations. In contrast, title registration operates as a piecemeal, continuing, quiet title action, albeit without all of the due process requirements applicable to initial registration. Government makes the evaluations one at a time, and they usually are conclusive. The act of acceptance includes a governmental judgment that the

154. The Torrens assurance fund usually does not provide compensation for losses caused by off-certificate risks. . . .

instrument was effective to create, transfer, modify or cancel the interest referred to therein. Consequently, the government may be liable for erroneous or wrongful evaluations. Under these circumstances, it is not surprising that registrars are frequently quite careful about accepting instruments for registration. . .

Instruments are examined when they are presented for registration. If the examiner believes the instrument is irregular or defective in some respect, the examiner will refuse registration.[159] For example, at some offices, the examiner may refuse registration if the signature appears to be forged. Registration of a forged instrument may cause the true owner to lose title to the land. To satisfy the registrar, a proceeding subsequent to registration may be necessary or, at a minimum, the transferring owner may have to appear in the Torrens office to acknowledge the authenticity of the signature and to prove identity.[161] . . .

. . . The high cost of initial registration and the opposition from the title assurance industry may have contributed to the failure of Torrens in the United States. However, the high public cost and burden of continuing administration of Torrens has been the most significant contributing cause of its failure. For users, Torrens is actually or potentially a more efficient, less costly system of land title assurance and transfer than recording. Arguably, title risks are or can be made to be so much less under Torrens compared to recording that title insurance may be unnecessary. But it is clear that Torrens or any other true registration system is more costly and difficult for government to administer than recording. This higher cost is inherent in title registration systems because much of the date [sic] consolidation, evaluation and management done by private parties under recording is done by government employees or their agents under registration. This aspect of title registration cannot be reduced to insignificance by reforms or improvements of title registration procedures except by a radical and probably unacceptable simplification of a jurisdiction's real property law or a limitation of registrable interests to a very few types.

159. This examination process, of course, has the advantage of detecting potential defects before they are entered into the record. A similar method of quality control exists in the Scottish recording system. There, the recorder (called the "Keeper of the Public Register") examines the instruments presented for recordation [citation omitted].

Under this process of examination, mistakes are caught, not buried, as is the case under the American recording system. This feature of the Torrens system may not be worth the cost to government and the cost and aggravation to the users of the system. Adjournment of real estate closings and repeated trips to the government office until the bureaucrats are satisfied are real costs, although difficult to measure. Few real defects are caught. The Registrar's objections often appear to be bureaucratic nitpicking. . . .

161. The author once represented a person who owned a Torrens registered condominium unit. He wanted to convey the unit to his fiancé and himself in joint tenancy. The Cook County Registrar refused to accept the deed which was prepared to accomplish that result because the Torrens office workers suspected that the signature might have been forged. The client was accordingly required to appear in person with two pieces of identification to prove his identity and acknowledge the execution of the deed.

Since local governments had a first-hand appreciation of the administrative difficulties and costs involved with Torrens, it is not surprising that some of the most effective opposition to title registration came from local governments responsible for its implementation and not, contrary to conventional wisdom, from the title assurance industry.[220] The worst enemies of Torrens included administrators charged with implementing it who were generally ill-equipped and disinclined to do so. Informed government administrators are not likely to welcome with enthusiasm a system that is more difficult and costly for them to administer. Informed local legislators and administrators normally will not support replacing a system that generates profits with one that may require a subsidy. . . .

IV. Computerized Recording

A. Registration and Recording: Land Title Assurance for the Computer Age

A world-wide movement is advancing toward computerized land title record systems. American title insurance companies have been developing computerized land title record systems since the 1960s. American local governments have been implementing unofficial computerized land title record systems since the late 1970s. In Australia, computerization of a Torrens system began in 1969. By 1982, computerization of the Austrian title registration system was well underway. In 1984, Ontario, Canada, authorized an official computerized recording and title registration system. This movement will accelerate as less expensive, more powerful and more user-friendly computer technology develops. Inevitably, computer systems will replace manual records, especially in populous jurisdictions with frequent land transfers and large amounts of data to manage.

B. Basic Components

A computerized land title assurance system, whether recording or registration, should have two basic components. First, it should contain a database with information on ownership and title, consisting primarily of the

220. The Cook County Recorder/Registrar led a successful effort to eliminate her Torrens system, the oldest and one of the largest in numbers of titles registered in the United States. No credible evidence exists that the title industry was behind this effort to abolish Torrens. The industry certainly had little or no financial interest in the outcome because it was insuring over 90% of Torrens transactions in Cook County at the time the effort to eliminate Torrens was initiated. . . .

The failure of Torrens in Cook County, after 90 years of implementation, was mainly caused by incompetent, unsatisfactory administration. The demise of Torrens in southern California in 1955, after 40 years of implementation, appears to have been due to grossly incompetent management [citations omitted]. . . .

In some states, Torrens acts were repealed, not at the urging of the title industry, but at the request of local recorders who found the existence of little used registration statutes to be a nuisance. . . .

facts pertaining to past title transactions and past legal evaluations of these facts. Second, it should contain maps showing the units of ownership in the system with permanent identifying symbols assigned to each unit. The database should be organized into computer records for each ownership unit in the system shown on the map. This proposed system is essentially a computerized version of the Austrian, German and Swiss title registration systems. The Chicago Title Insurance Company uses a similar plan for its computerized title plant in Cook County, Illinois. It also is the basic system currently being implemented in Ontario, Canada, for its title registration system.

Data pertaining to each title would be stored in a computer record permanently identified by a number, called a land parcel identifier. Individuals who are parties to documents can be identified by name and birth date;[223] other entities can be identified by name and taxpayer identification numbers. Photographic, electronically stored copies of title transaction documents would be retrievable upon command. . . .

Identifying land titles and parcels by permanent land parcel identifiers is not as simple as identifying humans with permanent numbers such as social security numbers. Humans cannot be subdivided or consolidated. The development of a workable system of permanent land parcel identifiers is not a simple undertaking, as dimensions of parcels may change through subdivisions, consolidations, and other accretions and deletions. A good system of permanent identification numbers also requires accurate and current maps showing the parcels identified. . . .

C. Registration or Recording?

Computerization has fundamentally changed the debate between the Torrens and recording systems. Computerization of recording can eliminate redundancies and eliminate many other deficiencies of the recording system by providing rapid access to relevant data and eliminating redundancies. Further, remote terminal access to computerized public records will remove most of the incentive for title companies and examiners to maintain private records. By contrast, Torrens already has good data management and retrieval characteristics, even without computerization.

The most difficult and important policy question faced by architects of computerized land title assurance systems is whether they should be purely recording systems or at least partially title registration systems. Persons considering this question should keep in mind that the vital distinction between the two systems lies in "the affirmations made by the state about the ownership of interests and the effect of documents." Fully computerized recording and title registration systems should be very similar both in physical characteristics and in the manner by which data are stored, managed and

233. Federal privacy legislation may preclude use of social security numbers and, in any event, persons may refuse to disclose them. Birth dates, however, are matters of public record in the United States.

retrieved. The basic issue is the extent to which the government will affirm the legal effect of information retrieved from the systems. . . .

For countries such as the United States, which have entrenched recording systems and little experience with title registration, recording has many attractive features unrelated to its inherent merit. A reformed, computerized recording system would be far easier to implement than a computerized registration system. . . .

The most obvious inherent advantage of recording is that it is less costly and less difficult for government to administer. Staffing a recorder's office is relatively easy because little expertise in real estate law is required. In contrast, at least some employees in a title registration office must have substantial expertise. Furthermore, because recording places relatively few demands on government resources, it is more responsive to sudden increases in the volume of data input than is title registration. Also, few resources are actually expended to close transactions in recording because government does not substantively review documents before recording. Moreover, no time is wasted because of adjourned closings due to governmental objections.

The advantages, however, bring on their own disadvantages. Lack of examination means that the recording system provides no formal control on the quality of data input. Title insurance companies, lenders, escrow agents or lawyers representing parties may indirectly contribute such control. Also, a non-binding quality check for errors at the point of data input, which is similar to procedures used in registration offices, might be a cost-effective way of promoting security of titles and efficiency. This quality check would avoid creating the inflexibility caused by a binding, conclusive approval procedure. Conveyancing on state-prescribed forms whenever possible would elevate the quality of data input and promote economy and efficiency. . . .

Problem 12C

Your client, Speedy Builders, is negotiating the purchase of an undeveloped 65-acre tract of land from Reo Realty, Inc. Speedy plans to develop a residential subdivision on the land. You prepared and submitted to Reo Realty a first draft of a contract of purchase, which specifies the agreed-upon contract price of $3.1 million. The title provision in the contract (which you drafted) calls for the seller to purchase an owners policy of title insurance for the buyer. Reo Realty has asked that you delete this provision, claiming that the land is registered under the state's Torrens system and that it has a "clean" certificate of title. According to Reo Realty, Speedy does not need title insurance. What is your response? Does it matter which of the states with Torrens systems the land is in?

13
Housing Products

To understand the lawyer's role in real estate transactions, we must have some basic knowledge about the housing products that are on the market today. In this chapter, we focus on ownership products because rental properties present themselves as commercial undertakings for most real estate lawyers. Also, residential landlord and tenant issues generally are discussed in appropriate detail in the basic course on property law.

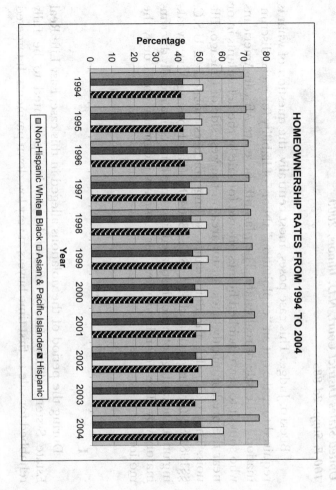

In the United States during the twentieth century, the proportion of American families who owned homes rose gradually. Since the Second World War, when the national rate of home ownership stood at 43.6 percent, opportunities for ownership have greatly expanded. Nevertheless, the market for real estate investment is not open to everyone. The goal of the private marketplace should be to enhance opportunity for all people and to

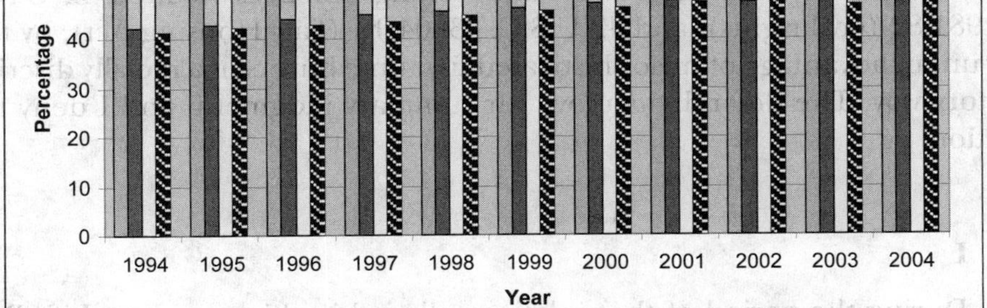

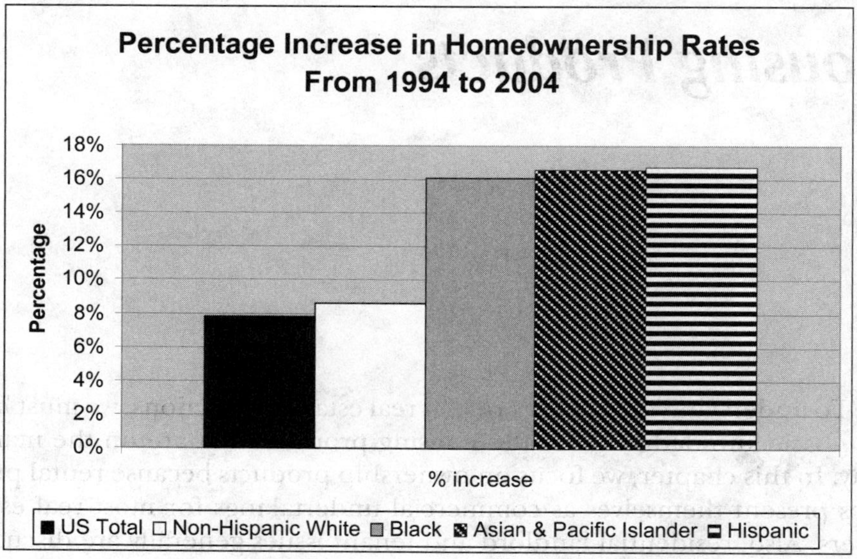

continue to expand the types of products that are available. Homeownership rates vary by a number of characteristics. Above are two diagrams that show differences in home ownership rates by race as reported by the U.S. Census.

HONORABLE v. EASY LIFE REAL ESTATE SYSTEM

United States District Court, N.D. Illinois, 2000
100 F. Supp. 2d 885

Bucklo, Judge. This case poses, most centrally, the question of what is required to make out an "exploitation" theory of liability for racial discrimination in the sale of real estate. The plaintiffs here are African-Americans who sought to buy rehabbed homes offered for sale by the defendants in or near the predominantly black Austin area on the west side of Chicago, Illinois. They claim that the defendants' selling practices violated 42 U.S.C. §§1981-82 (civil rights), and 42 U.S.C. §3604(b) (Fair Housing Act), by taking unfair advantage of unsophisticated first time buyers in a racially discriminatory way. The defendants move for summary judgment, and I deny the motion.

I

During the period of the violations alleged in this case, Easy Life Real Estate System ("Easy Life") offered homes it represented to be fully rehabbed for sale to first time buyers at very low down payments. It targeted the 95% African-American community of Austin on the West side of Chicago, arranging for Federal Housing Administration ("FHA") insured loans from certain lenders. Easy Life's agents told Ruby Honorable that one home in Austin, which she eventually bought, was "the only one" she qualified for. They falsely told Shirley and Stekeena Rollins that an Austin house Easy Life was selling was really in adjacent Oak Park, and then, when that deception was discovered, that it was too late to back out of the deal, although it was not. Easy Life's agents did not allow negotiation on the price of homes. They gave the buyers the funds for their down payments, making it appear that the money was a gift from a relative. They paid off Ms. Honorable's outstanding debts. Easy Life encouraged plaintiffs to bring in family members as co-signers, and had buyers sign blank pieces of paper where an explanation for credit delinquency could be filled in later. Easy Life prevented or discouraged plaintiffs from inspecting the homes, which were very shabbily done and not properly rehabbed.

II

A

In these circumstances, the plaintiffs argue that Easy Life and the other defendants (1) exploited unsophisticated buyers in a dual, racially segregated housing market by taking wrongful advantage of a situation created by socio-economic forces tainted by racial discrimination. In doing these things, according to the plaintiffs, the defendants also (2) intentionally discriminated against African-American home buyers by deliberately targeting them with predatory sales practices, committing "reverse redlining." The Fair Housing Act also allows for (3) disparate impact liability, but that is not at issue here. The defendants ask for summary judgment because the law requires that for exploitation theory liability, they must be shown to have "market power," enough influence to shape the market, but their expert testimony shows that the defendants did not have market power in the relevant market.

Under the "exploitation" theory, as the Seventh Circuit explains it, the plaintiffs argue that:

> As a result of racial discrimination there existed two housing markets . . . , one for whites and another for blacks, with the supply of housing available in the black market far less than the demand. Defendants entered the black market selling homes for prices far in excess of their fair market value and far in excess of prices which whites pay for comparable homes in the white market and on more onerous terms than whites similarly situated would encounter. . . .

Clark v. Universal Builders, 501 F.2d 324, 328 (7th Cir. 1974) (*Clark I*). To establish "exploitation" liability, the plaintiffs must show that (1) as a result of racial segregation, dual housing markets exist, and (2) defendant sellers took advantage of this situation by demanding prices and terms unreasonably in excess of prices and terms available to white citizens for comparable housing. Clark v. Universal Builders, Inc., 706 F.2d 204, 206 (7th Cir. 1983) (*Clark II*). Here (1) is not in dispute. Rather, the defendants argue that (2) is not true, that they could not have done what the plaintiffs allege because they lacked market power. . . .

B

The plaintiffs do not argue that the defendants colluded with anyone else to raise prices in the relevant market. They rather argue that there was a mechanism other than possession of market power through which the defendants charged African-American home buyers housing prices unreasonably in excess of what white buyers were charged. The plaintiffs say that this case "involves much more than . . . excess pricing"; it also involves "a pattern of deception and misrepresentation targeted at first time home buyers in the overwhelmingly minority Austin community." In particular, the evidence in the record shows that the defendants "were deliberately depriving buyers of truthful information necessary to take meaningful advantage of competitive alternatives" by "grooming buyers who were totally dependant on Easy Life."

According to the plaintiffs, then, the defendants were able to exploit African-Americans by carving out a noncompetitive enclave in the market. Whether or not the defendants had market power in the relevant market, they were able to retain their market share and persist in these practices while charging above-market prices by, in effect, taking the unsophisticated, first-time minority buyers who had the misfortune to fall into their clutches out of the competitive market by deceptively making these buyers wholly dependent upon them for the mechanics and wherewithal of home-buying, controlling their access to potential properties, loans, down payments, attorneys, and all their information. Their theory tracks the analysis of Professor Hanson and Douglas Kysar, who argue that "market outcomes frequently will be heavily influenced, if not determined, by the ability of one actor to control the format of information, the presentation of choices, and, in general, the setting within which market transactions occur," allowing some to "exploit those tendencies for gain." Jon G. Hanson & Douglas A. Kysar, *Taking Behavioralism Seriously: The Problem of Market Manipulation*, 74 N.Y.U. L. Rev. 630, 635 (1999). . . .

This is a novel, innovative and serious argument. Courts have been reluctant to assume consumers are too ignorant and benighted to fend for themselves merely because they are poor. . . . However, this is not a case where a court makes unwarranted presumptions that people lack the information, confidence, and experience to be "normal" consumers. Here the plaintiffs themselves argue that they were thus limited. . . .

More deeply, the economic theories that imply that market prices are efficient, thus beneficial for consumers, presuppose that consumers are informed, markets are competitive, and the costs of making transactions are not excessively burdensome. To produce theoretical equilibrium, neoclassical economics in fact assumes *perfect* information, *perfect* competition, and *no* transaction costs, among other idealizations. But these assumptions must be relaxed, and perhaps, ultimately replaced, if economic theory is to have any application to what happens in actual markets. . . .

Housing markets in particular, even in the ordinary case, may well be several steps removed from the standard assumptions because of the special characteristics of the product and the complexity of the transaction. . . .

When this situation is combined with evidence of racially discriminatory market manipulation by control of information and all aspects of the transaction in a context where the homebuyers are arguably especially vulnerable to manipulation, the plaintiffs have come forward with evidence that the business practices of the defendants might well have distorted the markets enough to enable them to stay in business while charging above market rates to their selected clientele. . . .

C

I here consider whether the defendants could prevail on their chosen terms. Did Easy Life have market power in the relevant market anyway? The defendants argue that for market power, Easy Life, as a matter of law, must have had at least a 35% market share in the relevant market, referring to the Federal Trade Commission's Horizontal Merger Guidelines, which state that firms with a market share below 35% are presumed to be unable to exercise market dominance. *See also* Valley Liquors, Inc. v. Renfield Importers, Ltd., 678 F.2d 742 (7th Cir. 1982) (*Valley I*) (antitrust), and 822 F.2d 656 (7th Cir. 1987) (*Valley II*) (same).

The plaintiffs respond that antitrust standards do not apply in a discrimination context. . . .

But the defendants are correct that, in the absence of some other mechanism, which, in this subsection, I assume for the sake of argument is lacking, the defendants would not have the "capability," required . . . to affect prices without market power. The antitrust standard for market share is not addressed to narrow antitrust concerns of efficiency as opposed to nondiscrimination, but to what courts have held to be required by economic theory to affect price in an otherwise competitive market. If the defendants cannot affect price, they cannot exploit minorities by discriminatory pricing. . . . This does not go to whether the defendants committed illegal discrimination under some other theory than the exploitation theory. . . .

III

Even if I were to accept the defendants' arguments about market power, there is an alternative reason why summary judgment cannot be granted. The defendants' motion is directed solely to the exploitation theory. It does not address the plaintiffs' intentional discrimination claims about "reverse redlining." Redlining is the practice of denying the extension of credit to specific geographic areas due to the income, race, or ethnicity of its residents. Reverse redlining is the practice of extending credit on unfair terms to those same communities. *See* S. Rep. No. 103-169, at 21 (1993), reprinted in 1994 U.S.C.C.A.N. 1881, 1905; *see also* Reverse Redlining: Problems in Home Equity Lending, before the Senate Committee on Banking, Housing, and Urban Affairs, 103rd Cong. 243-471 (1993).

These sort of practices come within the ambit of the Fair Housing Act; *see* NAACP v. American Family Mut. Ins. Co., 978 F.2d 287, 301 (7th Cir. 1992) (discriminatory denials of insurance and discriminatory pricing), which is to be read broadly. Courts have construed the statute to cover "mortgage 'redlining,' insurance redlining, racial steering, exclusionary zoning decisions, and other actions by individuals or governmental units which directly affect the availability of housing to minorities." Southend [Neighborhood Improvement Assoc. v. County of St. Clair], 743 F.2d [1207,] 1209-10 & n.3 [(7th Cir.1984)] (citing cases). The law is "violated by discriminatory actions, or certain actions with discriminatory effects, that affect the availability of housing." *Id.* at 1210. If so, the law would also prohibit reverse redlining. Although sections 1981 and 1982 are narrower, *id.*, they may be construed to prohibit some or all of the practices of which the plaintiffs produce evidence here; the defendants have at least waived the right to argue the contrary here by failing to do it.

.... Therefore I deny the defendants' motion for summary judgment.

Problem 13A

Emilio, a young attorney, has just graduated from law school and passed the bar exam. He takes a job with a large law firm in a major urban area. He has always dreamed of owning his own home. He wants to buy a one bedroom condominium home in a nice neighborhood. A real estate broker tells him that affordability is one of the biggest problems with getting into a first home. The real estate broker also informs Emilio that such homes in his city will cost about $250,000. Emilio has saved $25,000 to put down on a home purchase, and he has no college loans or other outstanding debt. Thus, he feels he is in a really good position to buy. He plans to borrow $225,000 and, with interest rates at 10 percent for a 30-year fixed rate mortgage, he is told that the monthly mortgage payment of principal and interest will be $1,974.56. The real estate broker also tells him that lenders in his town use a standard 28 percent rule to determine income qualification for a loan. The agent explains that this means that Emilio's monthly debt service on a mortgage cannot exceed 28 percent of his gross monthly income. How much income will Emilio need to qualify for the loan that he needs?

A. THE SINGLE-FAMILY HOME

Probably the most highly desired type of home in America is the single-family detached house. This is a mainstay of the home ownership market. The typical single-family detached home is placed on a lot with buffer space between it, the road, and neighboring houses.

One of the significant changes in the single-family detached housing market is the rise of the Planned Unit Development (PUD) and other planned communities. Presently, a great deal of newly constructed housing is built in planned communities. Most such developments are carefully controlled by restrictions placed on the entire property by the developer, who then divides it into lots for individual housing units. The numerous restrictions go far beyond the typical general zoning requirements, covering a full array of relationships between the properties and owners in a community. In the traditional subdivision, the property restrictions are usually thought of as private matters and are placed against each lot within the subdivision for the benefit of all the lots. These private subdivision arrangements are governed by the general rules of basic property law related to covenants and servitudes. In contrast, the restrictions, plans, and map of a PUD or its equivalent usually go through a review and approval process conducted by the local government. The review is designed to make sure that the planned community meets the minimal standards for density, safety, and other areas of concern established by the local government. Usually the standards also provide for a process of homeowner participation in future decisions related to the property.

One of the key reasons for the growth and appeal of planned subdivisions and PUDs is that they allow a developer better to target a particular market for home sales. By establishing blanket restrictions affecting an entire community, these forms of individual housing can promote a certain "lifestyle" for each family within the development. The idea is that people no longer want to just buy a home, they want to buy a lifestyle. Thus, you can find PUDs with houses built around a golf course, a marina, or equestrian activities; some even have accommodations for private airplanes owned by each homeowner, with roadways and runways that interconnect.

In most planned communities with a significant number of restrictions, the developer creates a homeowners association (HOA) to implement and enforce the various rules and regulations. The HOA is typically organized as a nonprofit corporation. Every unit and every owner in the community is made a part of the HOA. Usually each unit is given one vote, and then the owners elect board members and officers to carry out the rules and mandates of the association. The HOA often enacts rules and regulations governing property use that supplement the recorded covenants and servitudes.

The HOA enforces the governing rules and can do so by bringing legal actions against violators. It can usually seek injunctive relief in court against potential and ongoing violations, and it can also take affirmative steps on its own. An injunction might be sought to prevent construction of an impermissible improvement on a lot, and affirmative action might be taken to hire someone to mow the lawn at a home where the yard has not been kept in proper order. The HOA also has the power to charge for actions taken and can place a lien against the property of a person who fails to pay. This lien can be foreclosed and thus is a powerful weapon for enforcement. In many respects, the HOA acts like a small city government. It polices the rules, reviews architectural plans, and collects fees that enable it to operate. Every unit is assessed a fee in the form of monthly or annual assessments or dues. Like a tax, these fees are almost always secured by a lien provided for in the recorded covenants.

Although many single-family detached homes are not in planned subdivisions or PUDs, clearly the trend in recent years is to place more and more restrictions on single-family housing.

EVERGREEN HIGHLANDS ASSOCIATION v. WEST

Supreme Court of Colorado, 2003
73 P.3d 1

RICE, Judge. . . .

Petitioner Evergreen Highlands Association, a Colorado non-profit corporation ("Association"), is the homeowner association for Evergreen Highlands Subdivision-Unit 4 ("Evergreen Highlands") in Jefferson County. The subdivision consists of sixty-three lots, associated roads, and a 22.3 acre park area which is open to use by all residents of the subdivision. The Association holds title to and maintains the park area, which contains hiking and equestrian trails, a barn and stables, a ball field, a fishing pond, and tennis courts. The park area is almost completely surrounded by private homeowners' lots, with no fence or other boundary separating the park area from the homes. Respondent Robert A. West owns one of the lots bordering directly on the park area, and has used the facilities there to play tennis, fish, and walk his dog.

Evergreen Highlands Subdivision was created and its plat filed in 1972. The plat indicated that the park area was to be conveyed to the homeowners association. Protective covenants for Evergreen Highlands were also filed in 1972, but did not require lot owners to be members of or pay dues to the Association. The Association, however, was incorporated in 1973 for the purposes of maintaining the common area and facilities, enforcing the covenants, paying taxes on the common area, and determining annual fees. The developer conveyed the park area to the Association in 1976. Between the years of 1976 and 1995, when the modification of the covenants at issue in this case occurred, the Association relied on voluntary assessments from lot owners to pay for maintenance of and improvements to the park area. Such expenses included property taxes, insurance for the park area and its structures, weed spraying, tennis court resurfacing, and barn and stable maintenance.

Article 13 of the original Evergreen Highlands covenants provides that a majority of lot owners may agree to modify the covenants, stating in relevant part as follows:

> The owners of seventy-five percent of the lots which are subject to these covenants may release all or part of the land so restricted from any one or more of said restrictions, *or may change or modify any one or more of said restrictions*, by executing and acknowledging an appropriate agreement or agreements in writing for such purposes and filing the same in the Office of the County Clerk and Recorder of Jefferson County, Colorado.

Protective Covenants for Evergreen Highlands—Unit 4, art. 13 (Nov. 6, 1972) (emphasis added) (hereinafter "modification clause"). In 1995, pursuant to the modification clause, at least seventy-five percent of Evergreen Highlands' lot owners voted to add a new Article 16 to the covenants. This article required all lot owners to be members of and pay assessments to the Association, and permitted the Association to impose liens on the property of any owners who failed to pay their assessment. Assessments were set at fifty dollars per year per lot.

Respondent purchased his lot in 1986 when membership in the Association and payment of assessments was voluntary, a fact that Respondent contends positively influenced his decision to purchase in Evergreen Highlands. Respondent was not among the majority of homeowners who approved the 1995 amendment to the covenants, and he subsequently refused to pay his lot assessment. When the Association threatened to record a lien against his property, Respondent filed this lawsuit challenging the validity of the 1995 amendment. The Association counterclaimed for a declaratory judgment that it had the implied power to collect assessments from all lot owners in the subdivision, and accordingly sought damages from West for breach of the implied contract. The district court ruled in favor of the Association on the ground that the amendment was valid and binding; therefore, it never reached the merits of the Association's counterclaims.

The court of appeals reversed, finding that the terms "change or modify" as set forth in the modification clause of the covenants did not allow for the addition of a wholly new covenant, but only for modifications to the existing covenants. The court examined two divergent lines of cases from other states and concluded that the particular language used in Evergreen Highlands' modification clause supported the more restrictive interpretation, based on the principle that courts should resolve any ambiguities in covenant language in favor of the free and unrestricted use of property. West v. Evergreen Highlands Ass'n, 55 P.3d 151, 154 (Colo. App. 2001). The court of appeals did not address the issue of whether the Association had the implied power to collect assessments from lot owners, and therefore whether Respondent was in breach of an implied contract. We granted certiorari and now reverse and remand. . . .

A. Modification Clause of the Evergreen Highlands Covenants

The Association argues that the court of appeals erred when it held that the language of the Evergreen Highlands' modification clause only provided for "changes to the existing covenants, not the creation and addition of new covenants that have no relation to the existing covenants." West v. Evergreen Highlands Ass'n, 55 P.3d 151, 154 (Colo. App. 2001). Specifically, the Association argues that the word "change" is broad enough to encompass not only the modification of existing covenants, but the addition of new covenants as well. Based on our analysis of the language used in the Evergreen Highlands' modification clause, as well as the prevailing case law from other states, we agree.

1. The *Lakeland* Line of Cases

The court of appeals adopted the line of cases following Lakeland Property Owners Association v. Larson, 121 Ill. App. 3d 805, 459 N.E.2d 1164 (Ill. App. Ct. 1984). That case involved a situation nearly identical to the present one, in which a majority of lot owners voted to add a new covenant creating mandatory assessments and vesting the homeowner association with the power to impose liens for non-payment. Interpreting very similar covenant modification language (allowing a majority of the property owners to "change the said covenants in whole or in part," *id.* at 1167), the court disallowed the adoption of the new covenant. It held that "the provision . . . clearly directs itself to changes of existing covenants, not the adding of new covenants which have no relation to existing ones." *Id.* at 1169. The *Lakeland* reasoning has been adopted by other states.

In Caughlin Ranch Homeowners Association v. Caughlin Club, 109 Nev. 264, 849 P.2d 310 (Nev. 1993), a subdivision's original covenants imposed assessments only on residential parcels, although the modification clause provided for amendment of the rates. A year after the covenants were filed, a commercial club was developed and began operations on the property. Some six years later, after control of the homeowners association had passed from the developer to the lot owners, the homeowners association amended the covenants to levy assessments against the commercial parcel. Basing its reasoning on *Lakeland,* the Nevada Supreme Court disallowed the amendment, holding that the covenant modification clause allowing "amendments" referred only to "amendments of existing covenants as opposed to the creation of new covenants unrelated to the original covenants." *Id.* at 312.

In Boyles v. Hausmann, 246 Neb. 181, 517 N.W.2d 610, 613 (Neb. 1994), the modification clause allowed the majority of the homeowners to "change [the covenants] in whole or in part." The plaintiffs' lot was allegedly rendered unbuildable when the requisite majority of the homeowners association amended an existing covenant to increase the setback requirements. The *Boyles* court disallowed the additional covenant because, even though the restriction was appended onto an existing covenant, it was "new and different." *Id.* at 616.

Finally, in Meresse v. Stelma, 100 Wn. App. 857, 999 P.2d 1267 (Wash. Ct. App. 2000), the covenants for a six-lot subdivision allowed a majority of the lot owners "to change or alter them [the covenants] in full or in part." *Id.* at 1269. Five of the lot owners voted to alter the covenants to increase the access road easement, thereby stripping the sixth lot owner of a portion of his property. The court disallowed the amendment, holding that the amendatory language of the covenants "does not place a purchaser or owner on notice that he or she might be burdened, without assent, by road relocation at the majority's whim." *Id.* at 1273-74.

2. THE *ZITO* LINE OF CASES

Despite the fact that the *Lakeland* reasoning has been followed by other courts as recently as 2000, the same court that decided *Lakeland* issued a contrary opinion in 1992 with little explanation. In Zito v. Gerken, 225 Ill. App. 3d 79, 587 N.E.2d 1048 (Ill. App. Ct. 1992), existing subdivision covenants granted the homeowners association the authority to modify the covenants, although the exact language of the modification clause is not provided. The homeowners association adopted mandatory assessments and disgruntled homeowners sued. This time, however, the Illinois Appellate Court held in favor of the homeowners association, holding that: "[a] restrictive covenant which has been modified, altered or amended will be enforced if it is clear, unambiguous and reasonable"; "the 1987 amendment does not seek to change the character of [the subdivision] or to impose unreasonable burdens upon any lot owners"; and "the terms and conditions of the 1987 amendment impose a minimal collective burden upon the residents." *Id.* at 1050.

In Sunday Canyon Property Owners Association v. Annett, 978 S.W.2d 654 (Tex. Ct. App. 1998), the modification language allowed the covenants, upon a majority vote of the lot owners, to be "waived, abandoned, terminated, modified, altered or changed." *Id.* at 656. Based on this language, the court allowed the requisite majority to adopt an amendment creating a homeowners association levying mandatory lot assessments. . . .

Finally, in Windemere Homeowners Association, Inc. v. McCue, 1999 MT 292, 990 P.2d 769, 297 Mont. 77 (Mont. 1999), a majority of homeowners voted to amend the covenants to create a homeowners association authorized to levy the costs of road maintenance against property owners. Basing his argument on *Lakeland, Caughlin,* and *Boyles,* plaintiff homeowner challenged the amendment as an impermissible new covenant. The court, however, held that the modification clause in these covenants was "markedly different" than those in *Lakeland* and its progeny. . . . Consequently, the court held that this amendatory language was "broad enough" to justify the amendment. *Id.*

3. APPLICATION TO THE EVERGREEN HIGHLANDS COVENANTS

As this summary of cases from other jurisdictions illustrates, there exists a split in the law with respect to this issue. Respondent contends that these cases can be distinguished by how narrowly or broadly the particular modification clause is written, and argues that the amendatory language in Evergreen Highlands' covenants is much more akin to the narrow language found in the *Lakeland* line of cases than the more expansive language found in the *Zito* line of cases. He therefore argues that the *Lakeland* reasoning should prevail here.

There is little substance to the distinction between the "broad" or "narrow" amendatory language upon which Respondent relies. The covenant modification language in *Lakeland* and *Boyles* allowed a majority of lot owners to "change" the covenants, 459 N.E.2d at 1167, 517 N.W.2d at 613, and in *Meresse* to "change or alter" the covenants. 999 P.2d at 1269. The amendatory language in *Sunday Canyon* and in *Windemere*, however, provided that the covenants could be "waived, abandoned, terminated, modified, altered or changed." 978 S.W.2d at 656; 990 P.2d at 772. In the latter cases, the first three words — "waived, abandoned, and terminated" — all deal with ending a covenant, not adding a new one, and are therefore inapplicable here. The last three words — "modified, altered, or changed" — are the same as those in the *Lakeland* line of cases, with the addition of "altered," which is simply a synonym for "change" and "modify." Thus, distinguishing these cases from one another based on the breadth of the language used is an artificial, and ultimately unpersuasive, distinction.

Moreover, from a linguistic standpoint, the *Lakeland* conclusion that "change or modify" can only apply to the alteration of existing covenants, and not the addition of new and different ones, is not well-founded. Webster defines "change" as "to make different." *Webster's Third New International Dictionary* 373 (1986); *see also* Ticor Title Ins. Co. v. Rancho Santa Fe Ass'n, 177 Cal. App. 3d 726, 223 Cal.Rptr. 175, 179 (Cal. Ct. App. 1986) ("the words 'changed' and 'modified' include any alteration whether involving an increase or decrease."). Applying this definition to the language at issue, covenants could certainly be changed or made different either by the addition, subtraction, or modification of a term. Confining the meaning of the term "change" only to the modification of existing covenants, then, seems illogically narrow.

For these reasons, we find the court of appeals' reliance on a linguistic analysis to distinguish covenant modification language unsatisfactory. We instead conclude that the different outcomes in the *Lakeland* and *Zito* lines of cases are based on the differing factual scenarios and severity of consequences that the cases present. In those cases where courts disallowed the amendment of covenants, the impact upon the objecting lot owner was generally far more substantial and unforeseeable than the amendment at issue here. *See, e.g., Caughlin Ranch,* 109 Nev. 264, 849 P.2d 310 (covenants previously imposing assessments only on private lots amended to assess the sole commercial parcel in the subdivision at a substantially higher rate); *Boyles,* 246 Neb. 181, 517 N.W.2d 610 (changed setback requirement rendered plaintiff's lot unbuildable); *Meresse,* 100 Wn. App. 857, 999 P.2d 1267 (increased access road easement deprived plaintiff of a portion of his private lot).

In contrast, *Zito, Windemere,* and *Sunday Canyon,* like this case, all specifically considered — and allowed — the amendment of covenants in order to impose mandatory assessments on lot owners for the purpose of maintaining common elements of a subdivision. We accordingly find the *Zito* line of cases more applicable to the situation here. This interpretation also avoids the absurd result that could follow from application of the *Lakeland* reasoning; Evergreen Highlands would be unable to adopt a mandatory-assessment covenant when its original covenants were silent on the subject, yet could adopt such a covenant if its original covenants had expressly prohibited a mandatory-assessment covenant.

Moreover, the amendment at issue in this case was changed according to the modification clause of the original Evergreen Highlands covenants, and it is undisputed that Respondent was on actual notice of that clause when he purchased his lot in 1986. In addition, we note that, at fifty dollars per year, the mandatory assessment imposed on Respondent is neither unreasonable nor burdensome. To the contrary, the existence of a well-maintained park area immediately adjacent to Respondent's lot undoubtedly enhances Respondent's property value.

We conclude that the modification clause of the Evergreen Highlands covenants is expansive enough in its scope to allow for the adoption of a new covenant, and hold that the 1995 amendment to the Evergreen Highlands covenants, passed by the requisite majority of lot owners, is valid and binding on all lot owners in Evergreen Highlands.

B. The Implied Power of Homeowners Associations to Impose Mandatory Dues on Lot Owners for the Maintenance of Common Areas

The Association additionally argues that, even in the absence of an express covenant imposing mandatory assessments, it has the implied power to collect assessments from its members. To this end, the Association brought a counterclaim against West for breach of an implied contract obligating him to pay a proportionate share for repair, upkeep, and maintenance of the common area. The Association now argues that, based on West's breach of the implied contract, it is entitled as a matter of law to collect the unpaid assessments from Respondent.

We agree. Our review of case law from other states, the Restatement of Property (Servitudes), and the declarations for Evergreen Highlands in effect when West purchased his property, as supported by our understanding of the purpose of the Colorado Common Interest Ownership Act ("CCIOA"), [10 C.R.S. §§38-33.3-101 to 38-33.3-304 (2002)], convinces us that such an implied power exists in these circumstances. We therefore hold that Evergreen Highlands is a common interest community by implication, and that the Association has the implied power to levy assessments against lot owners to provide for maintenance of and improvements to common areas of the subdivision.

This being a question of first impression in Colorado, we first examine case law from other jurisdictions and find it largely in concurrence with our holding. When faced with this issue, a substantial number of states have arrived at the conclusion that homeowner associations have the implied power to levy dues or assessments even in the absence of express authority. *See, e.g.*, Spinnler Point Colony Ass'n, Inc. v. Nash, 689 A.2d 1026, 1028-29 (Pa. Commw. Ct. 1997) (holding that where ownership in a residential community allows owners to utilize common areas, "there is an implied agreement to accept the proportionate costs for maintaining and repairing these facilities.") . . .

Reflecting this considerable body of law, the newest version of the Restatement of Property (Servitudes) provides that "a common-interest community has the power to raise the funds reasonably necessary to carry out its functions by levying assessments against the individually owned property in the community. . . ." Restatement (Third) of Property: Servitudes §6.5(1)(a) (2000). . . .

We find the Restatement and case law from other states persuasive in analyzing the issue before us today. . . .

At the time Respondent purchased his lot in 1986, the Evergreen Highlands' declarations made clear that a homeowners association existed, it owned and maintained the park area, and it had the power to impose annual membership or use fees on lot owners. These declarations were sufficient to create a common interest community by implication. As explained by the Restatement:

> An implied obligation may . . . be found where the declaration expressly creates an association for the purpose of managing common property or enforcing use restrictions and design controls, but fails to include a mechanism for providing the funds necessary to carry out its functions. When such an implied obligation is established, the lots are a common-interest community . . .

Restatement (Third) of Property: Servitudes §6.2 cmt. a (2000); *see also id.* at illus. 2 (citing an example virtually identical to that of Evergreen Highlands and finding it a common interest community by judicial decree).

We accordingly adopt the position taken by the Restatement and many other states, and hold that the declarations for Evergreen Highlands were sufficient to create a common interest community by implication. The Association therefore has the implicit power to levy assessments against lot owners for the purpose of maintaining the common area of the subdivision. Respondent, as a lot owner, has an implied duty to pay his proportionate share of the cost of maintaining and operating the common area. We therefore remand the case to the court of appeals with orders to return it to the trial court to calculate Petitioner's damages in a manner consistent with this opinion. . . .

Problem 13B

Pass Christian Harbour Estates is a PUD community of 30 single-family detached homes built around a sailing club. Each lot in the subdivision has its own dock, and all lot owners are members of the homeowners association (the "Association") that governs the community as well as members of the sailing club (the "Club"). The Club sponsors sailing races and offers sailing lessons and other activities. The PUD rules describe in detail the docking rules and regulations for all sailboats. The developer quickly sells all 30 units to sailing enthusiasts. Several years go by, and one of the owners sells his home to Ted and Jane. When Ted and Jane move in they are very excited about the area and are looking forward to the fun of boating. After they get settled on the property, Ted and Jane bring in their boats for docking. One is a 30-foot sailboat and the other is a speedboat racer with a 400-horsepower engine. The Association sends a notice to Ted and Jane that the PUD is for sailing only and that the motorboat cannot be docked or used within the PUD. Ted and Jane reject the Association's notice and respond that they are entitled to use their dock and boating privileges as they see fit. They also point out that although the rules and regulations are very specific about the size, type, nature, and use of sailboats, there is no express limitation in any of the rules or regulations with respect to the exclusion of motorboats.

(a) Should Ted and Jane be able to keep and use the motorboat as they see fit?

(b) Ted and Jane argue that the rules and regulations, if there are any that prevent motorboats, apply only to the original owners and do not bind subsequent purchasers. Should this argument be successful?

(c) What if the Association holds a general meeting with notice to everyone to discuss the matter? According to the Association rules, a 60 percent majority vote of all lot owners is needed to amend the rules and regulations. At the meeting many people speak, and evidence is presented as to the noise, water pollution, and increased wake effects motorboats will bring. Then a vote is taken, with 80 percent of the owners voting to prohibit and exclude all motorboats from the PUD. Ted and Jane go to court to get an injunction to prevent the enforcement of the new rule on the grounds that it should not apply to them because it was enacted after they purchased their lot. Should they be successful?

(d) Pete, the lawyer for Ted and Jane, assisted them with their purchase and with the closing on their property. Pete is also an owner of a lot in the same PUD. Pete has not done any additional legal work for Ted and Jane since the closing on the property. After the closing and shortly before the dispute concerning the motorboat, Pete was elected President of the Association and Club. When the dispute arises, Pete, on behalf of the Association and Club, brings suit against Ted and Jane seeking an injunction on use of the motorboat and damages for costs alleged to have been caused by Ted and Jane in operating a motorboat within the property boundaries. Do you think that Pete should have concerns about his ethical conduct? If so, what might they be? What if Pete were not the Association president, but was a party to the suit against Ted and Jane merely as a result of being a property owner and thus an Association and Club member, the suit being on behalf of all members? What if Pete is called as a witness in litigation to describe the types of information given to Ted and Jane prior to closing so as to indicate their knowledge of the rules and regulations of the PUD?

B. CONDOMINIUMS

As a general definition, a *condominium* is a single unit in a multiunit project together with an undivided interest in common areas and facilities of the project. The owner of a condominium generally has fee simple title to the unit and owns a percentage share of the common property as a tenant in common with her neighbors. Literally, the term condominium comes from the concept of *codominion,* which means that there are shared or overlapping spheres of power, control, or ownership.

Property held as a condominium is a form of ownership, and it is not any particular architectural style. The condominium form of housing ownership has become a major component of America's total housing stock, particularly in states such as California, Florida, Hawaii, and New York. All states have statutes that govern the creation and operation of condominiums. Although most authorities believe a condominium may be created at common law, this has not proven workable due to a number of conceptual and procedural problems. The condominium statutes establish a specific set of ownership rights that are identified by reference to legal documents prepared in accordance with statutory requirements and filed with a government entity. Consequently, the first place to look when considering this form of property is at local state statutory law that enables the creation of this form of ownership. Once the state condominium statute is understood, case law must be consulted for purposes of interpretation and for examples of application in practice.

The primary legal document for a condominium project is the *Declaration of Condominium,* wherein a property owner declares the legally described property to be henceforth held in the condominium form. The declaration is filed in the local real property records so that all purchasers of condominiums will have actual or constructive notice of its contents. The declaration must spell out all the elements required to be addressed by the statutes and must clearly define by narrative reference, and usually by drawings, the identification of each ownership unit and all common property. The declaration must also address the rights and responsibilities of all unit owners regarding both the individual ownership property and the common property. Furthermore, the declaration establishes a condominium unit owners association, provides for rules and regulations to govern the orderly operation of the condominium, and authorizes assessments against each unit owner to pay for condominium expenses. With regard to assessments, the declaration usually provides rights and protections for lenders making mortgage loans to individual unit owners. In addition, there will usually be separate legal documents detailing the form and procedures governing the unit owners association.

The extent of the common property, usually called the *common elements*, is the distinguishing feature of the condominium form of ownership. A buyer's exclusive fee interest usually extends only to the interior space and surfaces of the unit. The common elements typically include the land, building systems, and project amenities. In a condominium development, there are likely to be both common elements and *limited common elements* associated with unit ownership. *Common elements* consist of all those portions of the condominium property that are not defined in the declaration as part of a unit. *Limited common elements* are those common elements defined in the declaration as being for the limited or exclusive use of a particular unit while not in themselves being part of the described unit. Examples include unit patios, balconies, window flower boxes, and parking spaces.

Some condominiums are set up so that the association is given a *right of first refusal* as to any unit that goes on the market for sale after the developer makes the initial sale (applies to the resale market). This right of first refusal gives the association some control over who can buy into the condominium. The right operates by giving the association the first option to purchase the unit on the same terms as are being extended to an arm's-length buyer who has executed an enforceable contract of purchase and sale.

In addition to the declaration of condominium, most condominiums are covered by a "blanket" set of rules and regulations enacted by the unit owners association. When a person challenges a condominium restriction, the standard of review applied by the court usually depends on the source of the restriction. The restrictions established in the declaration are given more deference than those passed by the association and its board. The items set forth in the declaration are generally considered to be covenants running with the land, thus binding current and future owners unless they violate a statute, public policy, or a constitutionally protected right. Items passed by the association and its board are of lesser status and are subjected to a stricter standard of review. They are enforced so long as they (1) comply with the procedures established for their promulgation, and (2) reasonably relate to the promotion of the health, happiness, and welfare of unit owners (including aesthetic considerations).

Problem 13C

Karin bought unit number six in the Lake Side Condominium. This is a condominium on the shores of a large freshwater lake and consists of ten units. Each unit is a separate single-family cottage. Each cottage is a two-story "Cape Cod" style structure with an attached one-story, two-car garage. About a year after Karin purchased her unit, she decided to construct an addition to her cottage over the garage that would bring the garage portion of the structure up to the second-floor roof line of the rest of the cottage. The association gave Karin notice to stop her construction because it violated the condominium restrictions set out in the declaration that defined each unit, and it violated the rules and regulations that required approval for any exterior alteration of a unit. Karin ignored the notice, stating only, "I can do what I want with my home." The second-floor room over the garage added 400 square feet of living space to Karin's home and increased its appraised value by $50,000. One month after the construction was finished, the association and two other unit owners brought an action against Karin for unlawfully taking or trespassing on property belonging to the other units. They asserted that the air space above the garage was a common element and consequently each unit owner owned an undivided 1⁄10 interest in that space.

(a) Suppose the association had acted earlier and had sought an injunction to prevent Karin from doing the construction. Should the court issue such an injunction? Should individual unit owners who are not joined by the association have the right to such an injunction?

(b) After Karin has completed the construction, should the court make her return the structure to its original form as a remedy? Should it make a difference if her violation is of a restriction in the declaration only or in the rules and regulations (outside of the declaration) only? Should it matter if her actions were intentional or not?

(c) Should air space be considered a common element? Should the action against Karin simply be for violating a prohibition, or should it be maintainable as an action for trespass and taking the property of others?

(d) In lieu of having Karin return the structure to its original form, is there any fair method of thinking about how damages might be computed to compensate the other unit owners for their loss of value?

(e) If Karin does not have to return the structure to its original form, does this mean that any other unit owner now has a basis for doing her own unapproved construction project?

CEDAR COVE EFFICIENCY CONDOMINIUM ASSOCIATION v. CEDAR COVE PROPERTIES

District Court of Appeal of Florida, First District, 1980
558 So. 2d 475

PER CURIAM. Appellant, a condominium association, challenges the trial court's final judgments denying those parts of claims for special assessments relating to repair costs of balcony and exterior closet doors.[1] It contends that under chapter 718, Florida Statutes, and the condominium documents it is well within its authority to specially assess the members of the association, including appellee,[2] for the cost of these repairs. We agree and reverse.

The association argues that the balconies are "limited common elements" and that the expense of repair and maintenance of all common elements are "common expenses" for which it may assess its members pro rata. Appellee contends that the balconies are included within the vertical boundaries of the condominium documents' definition of a "unit" and that under the Condominium Act, common elements are those portions of condominium property which are not included in the units. It points out that the condominium documents require the unit owner to maintain and repair all portions of a unit except those maintained by the association.

The pertinent portions of the Condominium Act and the condominium documents provide (emphasis added):

Chapter 718, Florida Statutes (1987)

718.103

(6) "Common elements" means the portions of the condominium property which are not included in the units.

(7) "Common expenses" means all expenses and assessments which are properly incurred by the association for the condominium. . . .

(16) "Limited common elements" means those common elements which are reserved for the use of a certain condominium unit or units to the exclusion of other units, as specified in the declaration of condominium. . . .

(23) "Unit" means a part of the condominium property which is subject to exclusive ownership. A unit may be in improvements[,] land, or land and improvements together, as specified in the declaration. . . .

718.113 . . .

Maintenance of the common elements is the responsibility of the association. The declaration may provide that limited common elements shall be maintained by those entitled to use the limited common elements. . . .

1. Case no. 89-392 involved expenses for initial balcony repairs at $1,000/voting unit and case no. 89-1472 involved further repairs to the balconies and the exterior closet doors at $1,200/voting unit with a total $2,500/voting unit assessment.

2. Appellee challenges assessments to its units located on the ground floor of the condominium.

Declaration of Condominium

[Definitions] . . .

(b) "Common Elements" shall be all parts of condominium property not included within the unit boundaries as described in Schedule "B."

(c) "Limited Common Elements" means those common elements which are reserved for the use and purpose of a certain condominium unit or units to the exclusion of other units as specified in Schedule "B."

(d) "Common Expenses" include (1) expenses of administration; expenses of maintenance, operation, repair, or replacement of the common elements, and of the portions of units to be maintained by the Association; (2) expenses declared common expenses by provisions of the Declaration or by the By-Laws; and (3) valid charges *against the condominium as a whole* such as ad valorem taxes for the year in which this Declaration is recorded. . . .

4.4 *Limitation upon Liability of the Association:* Notwithstanding the duty of the Association to maintain and repair parts of the condominium property, the Association shall not be liable to condominium unit owners for injury or damage, other than the cost of maintenance or repair, caused by any latent condition of the property to be maintained and repaired by the Association, *or caused by the elements or other owners or persons.* . . .

6.1 *Common Expense Fund:* . . . the Association shall estimate . . . charges . . . assessed to the owners (by) percentage attributable to each unit. If the estimated sum proves inadequate for *any* reason, . . . the Board may, at any time, levy a further assessment. . . . The common expense fund shall be assessed to cover the following: . . . (c) The expense of maintenance, operation, repair or replacement of the common elements including, *but not limited to,* preservation of landscaping, employment of personnel needed, preservation or repair of walls, drives, streets, and building *exteriors* as the board may, from time to time deem appropriate. . .

7.3 *Units; Association Responsibility:* the Association shall maintain and replace (1) All portions of a unit, *except interior surfaces,* contributing to the support of the building, which portions shall include but not be limited to the outside walls of the buildings. . . .

7.4 *Units; Owner Responsibility:* The responsibility of the unit owner shall be (1) To maintain, repair and replace at his expense all portions of his unit *except* the portions to be maintained, repaired and replaced by the Association. . . .

(3) Not to paint or otherwise decorate or change the appearance of any portion of the *exterior* of the building; . .

7.7 *Responsibility.* If the damage is only to those parts of one condominium unit for which the responsibility of maintenance and repair is that of the condominium unit owner, then the said owner shall be responsible for reconstruction and repair after casualty. *In all other instances, the responsibility of reconstruction and repair after casualty shall be that of the association.* . . .

7.9 *Assessments.* If the proceeds of insurance are not sufficient to defray the costs of reconstruction and repair by the Association, or if at any time during reconstruction and repair, or upon completion of reconstruction or repair, the funds for the payment of the costs of reconstruction or repair are insufficient, assessments shall be made against the condominium unit owners who owned the damaged condominium units, and against all condominium unit owners in the case of damage to the common elements, in sufficient amounts to provide funds for the payment of such costs. Such assessments against condominium unit owners for damage to condominium units shall be in proportion to the cost of reconstruction and repair of their respective units. Such assessments on account of damage in common elements shall be in proportion to the owners obligation of common expense. . . .

III. *Vertical Boundaries of Units:* The vertical boundaries of each unit *shall be the exterior of the outside walls* of the units. Where there may be attached to such outside walls a *balcony*, loggia, terrace, patio, a stairway, a stoop, landing steps, projecting cornices and copings, or other portion of the building, serving only the unit being bounded, *such boundary shall be deemed to include all of such structures and fixtures thereon.* However, as respects an interior wall, or walls between such units, including walls between balconies, the vertical boundaries of each unit shall be fixed at the center line of such walls between units, provided that such walls are not to be deemed party walls, but instead are part of the limited common elements as defined elsewhere in this Declaration, serving the only units affected. Every portion of a dwelling contributing to the support of an abutting unit shall be burdened with an easement of support for the benefit of such abutting unit. . . .

Articles of Incorporation . . .

ARTICLE III . . .

2. The Association shall have all the powers of a Condominium Association under and pursuant to Chapter 718, Florida Statutes, the condominium Act, and shall have all of the powers necessary to implement the purposes of the Association, including, but not limited to the following: . . .

c. To maintain, repair, replace and operate condominium property; specifically including all portions of the condominium property to which the Association has the right and power to maintain, repair, replace and operate in accordance with the Declaration of Condominium, the By-Laws, and Chapter 718 of the Florida Statutes, the Condominium Act. . . .

e. To reconstruct improvements on the condominium property after casualty or other loss, and the further improvement of the property. . . .

By-Laws . . .

6.5 *Special Assessments.* Special assessments, if required, shall be levied and paid in the same manner as heretofore provided for regular assessments. Special assessments can be of two kinds: (1) those chargeable to all members in the same proportions as regular assessments to meet shortages or emergencies, to construct, *reconstruct, repair,* or replace all or any part of the common elements (including fixtures and personal property related thereto) *and for other purposes as shall have been approved by the members at a duly convened meeting;* . . . .

In case number 89-392, the trial court found that the association had failed to establish its foreclosure claim. In denying the motion for new trial, the court referred to its opinion in case no. 89-1472, in which it found that the balconies were "limited common elements." The court construed the condominium documents, which contained no specific provision for "limited common element" maintenance responsibility, to provide that individual unit owners should maintain their own balconies. It based its conclusion upon the finding that ". . . balconies are included within the definition of what a unit is . . . ," upon the variation in balcony sizes between units, and upon the absence of ground floor unit balconies.

Competent substantial evidence supports the court's construction of "limited common elements" to include balconies and exterior closet doors, the simple maintenance of which may be the responsibility of individual unit owners. However, the court also found that the balconies and doors were included within the condominium documents' definition of a "unit." These two findings present an inherent conflict.

Our review of the condominium documents discloses no definition of a "unit." We assume that the trial court was referring to the schedule "B," part II description of the vertical boundaries of a "unit" as a "definition" of "unit." In our opinion, this description is not a definition, but rather a characterization of the area a unit purchaser is entitled to use.

Construing the statute and condominium documents as a whole, and considering the evidence presented, we find that the association is obligated to provide repair and maintenance as the board may deem appropriate. Section 4.4 of the declaration of condominium specifically provides that the association is liable for the maintenance or repair of damage caused by the elements or by other owners. The record indicates that repairs to balconies and exterior closet doors were in fact necessitated by the elements. Under Florida law, the association is authorized to do what is necessary to protect the structural integrity of the building, its aesthetics and its members from liability for unsafe, or decrepit building exterior conditions including balconies and exterior closet doors.

Appellee concedes the association's authorization to regulate and maintain the condominium's aesthetics, including the building exteriors, so long as it exercises good business judgment. The "business judgment rule" will protect a board of directors as long as the board has acted in a reasonable manner. Farrington v. Casa Solana Condo. Assn. Inc., 517 So. 2d 70 (Fla. 3d DCA 1987). "If, in the good business judgment of the association, such alteration or improvement is necessary or beneficial in the maintenance, repair, or replacement of the common elements, all unit owners should equally bear the cost as provided in the declaration, by-laws and statutes." Tiffany Plaza Condo. v. Spencer, 416 So. 2d 823, 826 (Fla. 2d DCA 1982).

Where the repairs have been found to be reasonable, courts have held that consent of the members is not required. *See Tiffany; Farrington.* Ground floor units derive several benefits from the association's exercise of its business judgment in repairing and maintaining the balconies and doors, including the promotion of market value and sales through pleasant and uniform aesthetics, and the avoidance of damages liability. The association's exercise of authority in this case is reasonable to accomplish such purposes and carries greater weight since it operated pursuant to almost unanimous consent not obtained from members in the cases cited above.

The Act's definition of "limited common elements" implies they are a subset of "common elements" and therefore a "common expense" properly within the scope of the association's authority. Sections 6.1 and 6.2 of the declaration of condominium authorize the association to levy an assessment to maintain and repair all unit exteriors and common elements. Even if the balconies and closet doors are not considered "common elements," it is difficult to refute their classification as part of the unit exterior. The balconies and doors fall within the scope of the association's broad authority to maintain condominium exteriors.

Section 7.3 authorizes the association to maintain and replace all portions of a unit including outside boundary walls of units. This authorization specifically includes the trial court's "description" of balconies and doors as included within the vertical boundaries of a "unit." Section 7.7 requires, as a prerequisite, a clear line of distinction between maintenance that is the responsibility of the unit owner and maintenance that is the responsibility of the association. Since it is not clear from the condominium documents whether or not a limited common element is the responsibility of the unit owner, we hold that maintenance and repair of the balconies and doors falls within the scope of "all other instances" and can only be construed as the association/board's responsibility.

Section 7.9 provides authority for the subject assessments only if the balconies and doors are considered common expenses. We find the "unit" interpretations fashioned below too restrictive of the condominium association's authority in the circumstances. Operation of incorporated condominium associations are commonly compared to the discretionary management function of a municipal corporation which also derives its powers, duties and existence from the state acting through its legislative body. Our interpretation reasonably extracts authorization of this discretionary management function from the Act and condominium documents construed as a whole.

The articles and the by-laws provide broad authority for the association to conduct reconstruction and repair operations for casualty or other loss and for other purposes approved by the members at a meeting. The weather damage, the repair of which was overwhelmingly approved by its members falls within the meaning of "other purposes." Therefore, it is well within the broad scope of authority granted the association to assess all unit owners for the subject repairs and improvements.

The express terms of the Condominium Act and the condominium documents grant broad authority to the association to regulate the use of the common elements and building exterior. *See* Juno By the Sea North Condo v. Manfredonia, 397 So. 2d 297, 304 (Fla. 4th DCA 1981).

The judgments below strictly construe the statutes and documents in a manner which does not provide buyers with the legislative interpretation polestar, "what the buyer sees is what the buyer gets." If a particular unit owner were to damage his own balcony or all balconies, it might be patently unfair, arbitrary and capricious for the association to assess all owners for the repair. But where, as here, the damage is due to the elements, it is prudent and reasonable for all association members to pay a proportionate share of the expenses of repair. It is clear that the intent of the condominium documents places repair and maintenance responsibility for all building exteriors upon the association and that the subject balconies and doors are included within this responsibility. The expenses incurred by the association, in reliance upon the near unanimous consent of its members to repair balconies and closet doors located on the condominium exteriors are valid and reasonable. We cannot say then, construing the statutes and condominium documents as a whole, that the association was without the authority to levy the subject assessments, nor that it acted unreasonably, arbitrarily or capriciously in protecting the condominium aesthetics and in protecting all members from possible damages liability.

Therefore, we REVERSE the trial court's denials of appellant's claims in foreclosure, and REMAND for proceedings consistent with this opinion.

Problem 13D

Olga is the owner of unit number 15 in a 25-unit condominium building. One day, Olga is visited by her friend Marina. Olga is busy in the kitchen preparing a late-night snack for them when she asks Marina to turn on the outside door light, the switch to this light being inside the unit on the wall near the entrance doorway. As Marina engages the light switch, a terrible spark is emitted, and she receives a severe electrical shock that burns the skin on her hand and arm. Marina is taken to the hospital and given medical treatment. She is required to have continuing treatment for a six-month period. During this time, she cannot use her hand and is unable to work at her job as a computer operator. The cause of the electrical mishap inside Olga's unit was determined to be a faulty wiring problem in the electrical junction box located in the hallway ceiling outside her unit. Marina hires a lawyer whose television advertisement she saw one morning while watching one of those great real-life talk shows. The lawyer has Marina sue Olga and the Condominium Association for $250,000.

(a) Should Olga be fully responsible for Marina's damages?

(b) Should the $250,000 be a liability of the association allocated to each unit owner in the same manner as any other fee or assessment?

(c) Should each unit owner be jointly and severally liable for the full amount even if it is determined that the association should pay for Marina's damages?

(d) What should be done in the condominium documentation to address such problems, and what should you look for in reviewing condominium documents with these concerns in mind?

C. COOPERATIVE HOUSING

Cooperative housing is another form of joint ownership in which a unit owner has exclusive use of a dwelling together with rights to shared or common areas. In a cooperative, title to all of the real estate is held by a nonprofit corporation, with each shareholder having the right to a dwelling unit pursuant to a long-term lease from the corporation. In some ways, a housing cooperative is similar to a condominium. For either form to work, project documents must clearly designate the ownership interests and use rights. A cooperative has a unit owners association and rules and restrictions much like those used in other forms of shared housing. Just as for condominiums, the cooperative unit owners are given voting rights and are assessed fees and charges based on allocations set forth in the organizing documentation. Like the condominium, the cooperative form of ownership can be applied to a variety of real estate activities, but it is almost always used in a multiunit housing building. Most cooperatives are located in urban areas, and although units in fashionable cooperative buildings can be very expensive, they also tend to be substantially cheaper (10 to 20 percent) than comparable units in condominium projects. In other words, the cooperative form of ownership is discounted relative to similar properties under alternative legal regimes.

The cooperative is distinguishable from the condominium and other forms of real property ownership in its use of a corporation as the vehicle for arranging joint ownership. In this regard, there are two legal approaches to the way in which an interest in a cooperative unit is categorized. In all cases, the purchase of a unit in a cooperative involves the acquisition of a stock certificate in the cooperative entity. This is treated as a personal property interest. Stock ownership carries a right to a lease for a particular unit in the cooperative. In many jurisdictions, the cooperative is, therefore, viewed as having both a personal property (stock certificate) and a real property (lease) component. In such a jurisdiction, each part of the transaction must comply with the appropriate rules related to either real property or personal property. In some jurisdictions, however, the cooperative form of ownership is considered to be a transaction involving the stock. The lease is considered to be ancillary, and, as a result, the entire interest is governed by the rules applicable to the stock as personal property.

The continuing viability of the cooperative housing market is driven mostly by a desire on the part of some homeowners to exercise a great deal of control over who will be their neighbors. Courts readily uphold express limitations on cooperative unit owners' transfers of ownership as long as those limits do not impose an unreasonable restraint on alienation, with *unreasonable* being understood within the unique context of the cooperative form of ownership.

Buying into a cooperative requires the approval of the cooperative board (sometimes referred to as an *absolute right of approval*). This is a pure approval process with an "in" or "out" vote, unlike the condominium right of first refusal. The current owners are given a great deal of discretion with respect to whom they approve or do not approve to be fellow stockholders and unit owners. This is because the owners are all shareholders in a corporate entity that has the building as it primary asset, and the mortgage financing used to construct the building as its primary debt. Shareholders acquire rights to a lease of a unit in the building and share joint and several liability on the debts of the corporation. Thus, the cooperative owners do not just live in close proximity and share ownership of common elements, they are financially responsible for a shared debt. This factor has traditionally allowed cooperative boards to reject ownership applications without giving a reason for denial. When reasons are given for a denial, they have typically been upheld by the courts so long as the reason does not violate an antidiscrimination statute. Thus, a board cannot deny an applicant for the stated reason that the applicant is black, Jewish, Catholic, or Moslem. Discrimination based on race, ethnicity, or religious affiliation is illegal. However, a board can find a lot of sustainable reasons to turn down such applicants, even if it results in a building that is continually occupied only by white Protestants.

Some real-world examples of excluding people from housing cooperatives may help to demonstrate the strong demand for the right to discriminate with respect to future owners. Many people do not get approved. Some famous people who have been rejected by cooperatives are Cher, Barbara Streisand, Gloria Vanderbilt, and Richard Nixon. Gloria Vanderbilt was once rejected for the stated reason that the board was concerned about her financial ability to pay (the fact that the board did not like her male companion went unstated), and former President Nixon had the honor of being rejected by two different cooperatives in New York City. But you do not have to be famous to be considered undesirable for some cooperatives. You can be rejected for having poor taste in clothing or a pet that is not pleasing to the eye, for being overweight, or for having an occupation and a lifestyle that simply do not fit in well with the image of the cooperative. Lawyers are often unwelcome because they are assumed to be litigious. Political figures and movie stars are seen as attracting too much attention. Not surprisingly, minorities also seem to have difficulty getting approved by cooperative boards. The typical review process for approval to purchase involves a written application form with income disclosure information followed by a possible telephone interview and almost always a personal interview with board members. The board can disapprove an applicant at any point in the process.

40 WEST 67th STREET v. PULLMAN
Court of Appeals of New York, 2003
100 N.Y.2d 147, 790 N.E.2d 1174, 760 N.Y.S.2d 745

ROSENBLATT, J. In Matter of Levandusky v. One Fifth Ave. Apt. Corp. (75 N.Y.2d 530, 554 N.Y.S.2d 807, 553 N.E.2d 1317 [1990]) we held that the business judgment rule is the proper standard of judicial review when evaluating decisions made by residential cooperative corporations. In the case before us, defendant [David Pullman] is a shareholder-tenant in the plaintiff cooperative building. The relationship between defendant and the cooperative, including the conditions under which a shareholder's tenancy may be terminated, is governed by the shareholder's lease agreement. The cooperative terminated defendant's tenancy in accordance with a provision in the lease that authorized it to do so based on a tenant's "objectionable" conduct.

Defendant has challenged the cooperative's action and asserts, in essence, that his tenancy may not be terminated by the court based on a review of the facts under the standard articulated in *Levandusky.* He argues that termination may rest only upon a court's independent evaluation of the reasonableness of the cooperative's action. We disagree. In reviewing the cooperative's actions, the business judgment standard governs a cooperative's decision to terminate a tenancy in accordance with the terms of the parties' agreement.

I

Plaintiff cooperative owns the building located at 40 West 67th Street in Manhattan, which contains 38 apartments. In 1998, defendant bought into the cooperative and acquired 80 shares of stock appurtenant to his proprietary lease for apartment 7B.

Soon after moving in, defendant engaged in a course of behavior that, in the view of the cooperative, began as demanding, grew increasingly disruptive and ultimately became intolerable. After several points of friction between defendant and the cooperative, defendant started complaining about his elderly upstairs neighbors, a retired college professor and his wife who had occupied apartment 8B for over two decades. In a stream of vituperative letters to the cooperative — 16 letters in the month of October 1999 alone — he accused the couple of playing their television set and stereo at high volumes late into the night, and claimed they were running a loud and illegal bookbinding business in their apartment. Defendant further charged that the couple stored toxic chemicals in their apartment for use in their "dangerous and illegal" business. Upon investigation, the cooperative's Board determined that the couple did not possess a television set or stereo and that there was no evidence of a bookbinding business or any other commercial enterprise in their apartment.

Hostilities escalated, resulting in a physical altercation between defendant and the retired professor. Following the altercation, defendant distributed flyers to the cooperative residents in which he referred to the professor, by name, as a potential "psychopath in our midst" and accused him of cutting defendant's telephone lines. In another flyer, defendant described the professor's wife and the wife of the Board president as having close "intimate personal relations." Defendant also claimed that the previous occupants of his apartment revealed that the upstairs couple have "historically made excessive noise." The former occupants, however, submitted an affidavit that denied making any complaints about noise from the upstairs apartment and proclaimed that defendant's assertions to the contrary were "completely false."

Furthermore, defendant made alterations to his apartment without Board approval, had construction work performed on the weekend in violation of house rules, and would not respond to Board requests to correct these conditions or to allow a mutual inspection of his apartment and the upstairs apartment belonging to the elderly couple. Finally, defendant commenced four lawsuits against the upstairs couple, the president of the cooperative and the cooperative management, and tried to commence three more.

In reaction to defendant's behavior, the cooperative called a special meeting pursuant to article III (First) (f) of the lease agreement, which provides for termination of the tenancy if the cooperative by a two-thirds vote determines that "because of objectionable conduct on the part of the Lessee[,] the tenancy of the Lessee is undesirable."[3] The cooperative informed the shareholders that the purpose of the meeting was to determine whether defendant "engaged in repeated actions inimical to cooperative living and objectionable to the Corporation and its stockholders that make his continued tenancy undesirable."

Timely notice of the meeting was sent to all shareholders in the cooperative, including defendant. At the ensuing meeting, held in June 2000, owners of more than 75% of the outstanding shares in the cooperative were present. Defendant chose not attend. By a vote of 2,048 shares to 0, the shareholders in attendance passed a resolution declaring defendant's conduct "objectionable" and directing the Board to terminate his proprietary lease and cancel his shares. The resolution contained the findings upon which the shareholders concluded that defendant's behavior was inimical to cooperative living. Pursuant to the resolution, the Board sent defendant a notice of termination requiring him to vacate his apartment

3. The full provision authorizes termination "if at any time the Lessor shall determine, upon the affirmative vote of the holders of record of at least two-thirds of that part of its capital stock which is then owned by Lessees under proprietary leases then in force, at a meeting of such stockholders duly called to take action on the subject, that because of objectionable conduct on the part of the Lessee, or of a person dwelling in or visiting the apartment, the tenancy of the Lessee is undesirable."

by August 31, 2000. Ignoring the notice, defendant remained in the apartment, prompting the cooperative to bring this suit for possession and ejectment, a declaratory judgment cancelling defendant's stock, and a money judgment for use and occupancy, along with attorneys' fees and costs.

Supreme Court denied the cooperative's motion for summary judgment and dismissed its cause of action that premised ejectment solely on the shareholders' vote and the notice of termination. The court declined to apply the business judgment rule to sustain the shareholders' vote and the Board's issuance of the notice of termination. Instead, the court . . . held that to terminate a tenancy, a cooperative must prove its claim of objectionable conduct by competent evidence to the satisfaction of the court.

Disagreeing with Supreme Court, a divided Appellate Division granted the cooperative summary judgment on its causes of action for ejectment and the cancellation of defendant's stock. . . . We agree with the Appellate Division majority that the business judgment rule applies and therefore affirm.

II. The *Levandusky* Business Judgment Rule

The heart of this dispute is the parties' disagreement over the proper standard of review to be applied when a cooperative exercises its agreed-upon right to terminate a tenancy based on a shareholder-tenant's objectionable conduct. In the agreement establishing the rights and duties of the parties, the cooperative reserved to itself the authority to determine whether a member's conduct was objectionable and to terminate the tenancy on that basis. . . .

Levandusky established a standard of review analogous to the corporate business judgment rule for a shareholder-tenant challenge to a decision of a residential cooperative corporation. The business judgment rule is a common-law doctrine by which courts exercise restraint and defer to good faith decisions made by boards of directors in business settings . . . In *Levandusky,* the cooperative board issued a stop work order for a shareholder-tenant's renovations that violated the proprietary lease. The shareholder-tenant brought [an action] to set aside the stop work order. The Court upheld the Board's action, and concluded that the business judgment rule "best balances the individual and collective interests at stake" in the residential cooperative setting. *Levandusky,* 75 N.Y.2d at 537.

In the context of cooperative dwellings, the business judgment rule provides that a court should defer to a cooperative board's determination "[s]o long as the board acts for the purposes of the cooperative, within the scope of its authority and in good faith," *id.* at 538. In adopting this rule, we recognized that a cooperative board's broad powers could lead to abuse through arbitrary or malicious decisionmaking, unlawful discrimination or the like. However, we also aimed to avoid impairing "the purposes for which the residential community and its governing structure were formed: protection of the interest of the entire community of residents in an environment managed by the board for the common benefit," *id.* at 537. The Court concluded that the business judgment rule best balances these competing interests and also noted that the limited judicial review afforded by the rule protects the cooperative's decisions against "undue court involvement and judicial second-guessing," *id.* at 540. . . .

[T]he procedural vehicle driving this case is [Real Prop. Actions & Proceedings] RPAPL §711(1), which requires "competent evidence" to show that a tenant is objectionable. Thus, in this context, the competent evidence that is the basis for the shareholder vote will be reviewed under the business judgment rule, which means courts will normally defer to that vote and the shareholders' stated findings as competent evidence that the tenant is indeed objectionable under the statute. . . .

Despite this deferential standard, there are instances when courts should undertake review of board decisions. To trigger further judicial scrutiny, an aggrieved shareholder-tenant must make a showing that the board acted (1) outside the scope of its authority, (2) in a way that did not legitimately further the corporate purpose or (3) in bad faith.

III

A. THE COOPERATIVE'S SCOPE OF AUTHORITY

Pursuant to its bylaws, the cooperative was authorized (through its Board) to adopt a form of proprietary lease to be used for all shareholder-tenants. Based on this authorization, defendant and other members of the cooperative voluntarily entered into lease agreements containing the termination provision before us. The cooperative does not contend that it has the power to terminate the lease absent the termination provision. Indeed, it recognizes, correctly, that if there were no such provision, termination could proceed only pursuant to RPAPL §711 (1).

The cooperative unfailingly followed the procedures contained in the lease when acting to terminate defendant's tenancy. In accordance with the bylaws, the Board called a special meeting, and notified all shareholder-tenants of its time, place and purpose. Defendant thus had notice and the opportunity to be heard. In accordance with the agreement, the cooperative acted on a supermajority vote after properly fashioning the issue and the question to be addressed by resolution. The resolution specified the basis for the action, setting forth a list of specific findings as to defendant's objectionable behavior. By not appearing or presenting evidence personally or by counsel, defendant failed to challenge the findings and has not otherwise satisfied us that the Board has in any way acted ultra vires. In all, defendant has failed to demonstrate that the cooperative acted outside the scope of its authority in terminating the tenancy.

B. FURTHERING THE CORPORATE PURPOSE

Levandusky also recognizes that the business judgment rule prohibits judicial inquiry into Board actions that, presupposing good faith, are taken in legitimate furtherance of corporate purposes. Specifically, there must be a legitimate relationship between the Board's action and the welfare of the cooperative. Here, by the unanimous vote of everyone present at the meeting, the cooperative resoundingly expressed its collective will, directing the Board to terminate defendant's tenancy after finding that his behavior was more than its shareholders could bear. The Board was under a fiduciary duty to further the collective interests of the cooperative. By terminating the tenancy, the Board's action thus bore an obvious and legitimate relation to the cooperative's avowed ends.

C. GOOD FAITH, IN THE EXERCISE OF HONEST JUDGMENT

Finally, defendant has not shown the slightest indication of any bad faith, arbitrariness, favoritism, discrimination or malice on the cooperative's part, and the record reveals none. . . .

Levandusky cautions that the broad powers of cooperative governance carry the potential for abuse when a board singles out a person for harmful treatment or engages in unlawful discrimination, vendetta, arbitrary decisionmaking or favoritism. We reaffirm that admonition and stress that those types of abuses are incompatible with good faith and the exercise of honest judgment. . . .

The very concept of cooperative living entails a voluntary, shared control over rules, maintenance and the composition of the community. Indeed, as we observed in *Levandusky*, a shareholder-tenant voluntarily agrees to submit to the authority of a cooperative board, and consequently the board "may significantly restrict the bundle of rights a property owner normally enjoys." 75 N.Y.2d at 536. . . .

Order affirmed, with costs.

Problem 13E

Dorothy May intends to purchase a unit in a wonderful new building in her city. It has everything she is looking for, including security and service personnel. She is contracting to buy unit 26 for $350,000. The building is a cooperative. Dorothy comes to your law office to discuss representation in her transaction. At your initial meeting, Dorothy explains that she knows a little about real estate because her sister used to be a part-time salesperson about ten years ago. Dorothy tells you that she knows there are three important types of deeds used in conveyancing of real property: the general warranty deed, the special warranty deed, and the quitclaim deed. What she wants to know from you is your advice on which deed would give her, as buyer, the best protection in her transaction. What would you tell her?

Problem 13F

You are an associate in a law firm that represents a number of shared housing developments. In this capacity, your firm provides legal counsel to a number of cooperative boards. You have been assigned by the partner in charge to be responsible for the Ocean Breeze Cooperative. In that capacity, you are visited by Dr. Sue Westminster, the president of the board. She comes to you with a problem. A fellow doctor named Bill Wu is seeking to be approved to buy into the Ocean Breeze. Sue tells you it is a sticky and very confidential problem because Dr. Wu is Chinese and she does not think he will fit in. Sue says, "The Ocean Breeze is very comfortable because the 20 units in the building are occupied by people who are very similar . . . share the same values . . . you know, go to the same church and have a common ancestral history to be proud of. Some members of the cooperative have voiced strong objection to letting in any Chinese . . . but it's not personal and it certainly is not just because he is Chinese . . . these members would feel the same about Hispanics, blacks, and even Sicilians."

Having said this, Sue wants to know how she can best state a reason for denying Dr. Wu's application while being sure to avoid any personal liability as well as any liability for the cooperative. She says that she knows this sort of thing is done all the time, and she just wants you to make sure she proceeds in a way that will be legally defensible. She also states, "I am certain that you are quite a clever young lawyer or else your partner would never have assigned us to you. . . . Several of our cooperative members, myself included, do a lot of private investing and pay large amounts in legal fees to your firm every year. And, by the way, did you know that Debbie, one of your partners in the litigation department, is one of our cooperative members?" With that Dr. Westminster departs your office, leaving instructions that you communicate with her by 10:00 A.M. the next morning concerning the necessary wording for the rejection letter to Dr. Wu.

In this situation, what do you think your legal and ethical obligations should be to the client, the firm, the bar, and the courts? How will you resolve this, and what practical dynamics will have to be confronted? How can you best deal with these conflicts and with your own personal ethical obligation and duty?

D. TIME-SHARE HOUSING

Time-share housing takes the condominium concept one step further by dividing a unit's air space into blocks of time. The purchaser of a time-share gets the right to occupy a unit for a designated period of time (usually one or two weeks) each year. Most time-share properties are marketed as vacation alternatives. These units are offered as a way to own your vacation home instead of paying for a hotel room or renting a suite. You can thereby enjoy the benefits of equity appreciation, assuming that the value of the property does in fact increase over time.

Time-shares are not a major part of the housing market, but when taken together with the other types of properties discussed in this chapter they help to illustrate some of the many approaches available for structuring real estate development, ownership, and use. Legally, time-shares are like condominium units in that they involve use rights to a unit together with shared or common elements and expenses. The developer has several choices for structuring a time-share project. Each structure gives the buyer a different legal interest or "bundle of rights." The most basic choice is whether the buyer will have a real property interest or a personal property interest.

There are two ways the buyer can get a fee simple interest. The seller may convey undivided interests in the fee to all the buyers of time-share units as tenants in common, with a recorded instrument setting forth their rights to possess their designated intervals. Alternatively, the seller can convey a separate and distinct "interval estate" that includes as part of its definition the agreed-upon time parameters. Either type of fee interest is transferable by deed. In many time-share developments, the buyer doesn't get a fee interest. The buyer may receive the right to use the unit for a recurring annual period for a fixed term such as 30 or 40 years. Then the developer or some other entity retains the reversion in fee. At the end of the fixed period, all the time-share interests terminate. The buyer's interest may be characterized as either a lease or a contractual license. If it is a license, then it constitutes personal property and not an interest in real estate.

Another approach is to form a recreation or resort club, selling memberships in a club entity that entitle you to specific use privileges. The use privileges can be to a specific unit or to a designated class of units during your time interval. Some arrangements involve buying points in the entity, and the more points you buy the more use options you get. The particular structure of the ownership interest must be detailed in the documents creating the time-share property, and these documents must be carefully reviewed in order to establish the proper steps for transfer and the rights and limitations of ownership. As with other forms of communal ownership interests, there will be rules and regulations as well as some sort of owners association or management group. There will also be fees and assessments against owners to pay the expenses of upkeep on the property.

Almost all time-share properties include the option to participate in an exchange program that allows unit buyers to swap their use rights with people in other distant locations so that they need not always go to the same place on their vacation. This exchange feature probably accounts for the fact that the majority of unit owners in most time-shares live within a few hours' driving time from the location of the time-share property.

ROYAL ALOHA PARTNERS v. REAL ESTATE DIVISION

Court of Appeals of Oregon, 1982
59 Or. App. 564, 651 P.2d 1350

Joseph, Chief Judge. The issue in this proceeding under ORS 183.400 is whether the Real Estate Division has the statutory authority to make rules concerning the sale of "right to use" memberships in condominium time-sharing plans. Petitioner Royal Aloha Partners (Aloha) is involved in the acquisition of condominiums to be used by members of the Royal Aloha Vacation Club (Club). Petitioner Products Management intends to conduct similar activity.

Aloha acquires interests in condominium units in various vacation spots around the world. It then conveys them to Club for use by its members. Title to the property remains with Club, and members purchase only the right to use the condominium units for vacations. A member's "right to use" time-sharing interest carries with it no fee interest in the unit, in contrast to a time-sharing ownership interest, which combines fee ownership with the right to possession and occupancy of a unit on a time-sharing basis with other fee owners.

The Division promulgated rules purporting to cover both kinds of time-sharing interests. OAR 863-30-050(15) defines "time-sharing plan" as

> . . . any arrangement, plan, scheme or device, excluding exchange programs, whether *by membership*, agreement, share, tenancy in common, sale, lease, deed, rental agreement, license, *right to use agreement* or otherwise, whereby a purchaser in exchange for consideration, receives a right to use accommodations and facilities for a period of time less than a full year during any given year, but not necessarily for consecutive years and which extends for a period of more than 3 years. "Time sharing plan" includes but is not limited to:
>
> (a) "Time share estates," as defined by subsection (23) of ORS 94.004, making up all or a portion of a time sharing plan offered to prospective purchasers in Oregon.
>
> (b) "Interests in subdivided lands," as defined in subsections (4) and (9) of ORS 92.305, making up all or a portion of a time sharing plan offered to prospective purchasers in Oregon (whether or not the interests are created or located within a city or county that has a comprehensive plan and implementing ordinances that have been acknowledged under ORS 197.251), including but not limited to, any interests . . . offered in a time sharing plan involving, in whole or in part, condominium accommodations and facilities that are not "time share estates" as defined in subsection (23) of ORS 94.004. (Emphasis supplied.)

The Division claims to derive its authority to regulate the sale of "right to use" interests from the Condominium Act, ORS ch. 94. . . .

Inclusion of specific matter in a statute usually implies a legislative intent to exclude related matters not mentioned. Gantenbein v. PERB,

33 Or. App. 309, 319, 576 P.2d 1257, 1258, *rev. den.* 282 Or. 537 (1978). Because the statute expressly provides that *fee* time-sharing interests are within its coverage, and in the absence of anything in the legislative history suggesting that that can mean anything but what it says, we conclude that the legislature did not intend to include *non-fee* time-sharing interests.

The clear implication of the statute is that the kinds of "interests or estates" specifically set out are the only ones covered by the statute. . . .

Neither the Subdivision Control Law nor the Condominium Act authorizes the regulation of sales of "right to use" time-share interests. Therefore, OAR 863-30-050 to 863-30-080, insofar as they purport to regulate such interests, are invalid.

Problem 13G

Jason buys a one-week time interval at a time-share located in a famous ski resort. One of the things that Jason finds attractive about the property is that there is an exchange program available that he can participate in if he would like to swap his unit use rights with those of people located in some 50 other properties in countries all over the world. After Jason has owned his unit for three years, he decides he wants to try a swap. Upon inquiry, he is told that the exchange program is no longer available because the company that ran it went out of business. Should Jason be able to get out of his unit (get his money back, all or some)? Should it make any difference if the exchange company was a separate corporation but one also formed and operated by the developer that did the time-share project? Should it make any difference if the exchange program ended shortly after the time-share project was sold out by the developer?

E. HOUSING ACCESSIBILITY

Housing products must comply with regulations respecting accessibility to persons with disabilities. The following case provides an example.

UNITED STATES v. EDWARD ROSE & SONS

United States Court of Appeals, Sixth Circuit, 2004
384 F.3d 258

SILER, Circuit Judge. This housing discrimination case turns on what doors must be accessible to the handicapped. At issue are two sets of apartment complexes, designed with an inaccessible front door, but an accessible back patio door. The district court granted the U.S. Justice Department ("government") a preliminary injunction halting the construction and occupancy of the buildings. The main defendant, the builder and owner, Edward Rose & Sons ("Rose"), appeals, arguing that court erred (1) by misconstruing the requirements of the Fair Housing Act, 42 U.S.C. §3601 *et seq.* ("FHA"), and (2) by incorrectly weighing the relative preliminary injunction interests and harms. We affirm the district court's grant of the preliminary injunction.

I. Factual and Procedural Background

Defendant Rose constructed and owns the nineteen apartment buildings, located in Michigan and Ohio, at issue. These buildings are at various stages of construction, but all have the same basic design. The ground floor apartments at issue have two exterior entrances—a front door and rear patio door. The front door is closer to the parking lot, but is handicapped inaccessible because it can only be reached by descending stairs. At the bottom of the stairs is a landing shared by two front doors leading into two different apartments. The rear patio entrance is accessible, but is located farther from the parking lot.

The government alleged that the apartments violated the disability portions of the FHA. The district court granted a preliminary injunction, adopting the government's position that the front door was the "primary entrance" used by the public and guests, and as such, it was a "public" or "common area" that the FHA mandates be accessible. *See* 42 U.S.C. §3604(f)(3)(C)(i). In reaching this conclusion, the court relied on the Housing and Urban Development ("HUD") regulations, guidelines, and design manual. The preliminary injunction halts construction on the "covered dwellings" and restrains the defendants from occupying "covered dwellings" not yet leased. In this case, "covered dwellings" means simply the ground floor. *See* 42 U.S.C. §3604(f)(7) (stating if building has no elevator, only the ground floor is a covered dwelling subject to the FHA). Rose appeals. . . .

The government asserts that because the landing at the bottom of the stairs is a "common area," §3604(f)(3)(C)(i) mandates that the landing must be accessible. The landing in front of the entrances is not accessible because it can only be reached by the stairs. The government argues that this entrance is the "primary" door because it is in the front and closest to the parking lot. As such, it is the entrance most visitors will use, and thus the space or landing in front of the door is a public or common area. Additionally, the stair landing is shared by two entrances to two different apartment units, and thus a common area used by two tenants. . . .

We find that, in this particular case, the stair landing in front of the entrance is a common area that the statute mandates be accessible. The fact that two apartment units share the stair landing makes the space a common area. The plain meaning of "common use" unambiguously covers the entrance under dispute. At the time of the statute's enactment, dictionaries generally defined "common" as belonging to or shared by two or more individuals. *See The Oxford English Dictionary* 565 (J.A. Simpson & E.S.C. Weiner eds., Clarendon Press 2d ed. 1989) (defining common as "belonging equally to more than one" and "possessed or shared alike by both or all."). . . .

Our ruling is narrow; we simply hold in this case that because the two apartments share the stair landing, the stair landing qualifies as a "common area" that must be accessible. We express no opinion on what the FHA would require if the stairs only led to one apartment unit entrance . . .

In sum, we find that the stair landing qualifies as a "common area" that the FHA mandates be accessible. Thus, the government's likelihood of success on the merits is strong. . . .

Affirmed.

14

Possession and Use of Mortgaged Property

By the fourteenth century, the English mortgage had assumed a settled form that has endured as part of the common law. The mortgagor conveyed title to the lender, with the lender holding a freehold estate. The lender, holding the historic relic called *seisin,* got all the incidents of title, the most important being the right to immediate possession. The borrower's only property right in the land was a future interest—title returned to the borrower upon timely repayment of the debt.

At first, the lender's estate and the borrower's right of redemption were cast in the form of a defeasible conveyance. The limitation or condition was that the mortgagor pay the debt by the specified due date, often called *law day.* If payment was timely made, the mortgagor then had the right to resume possession immediately. If not, then the mortgage terms provided for the mortgagee to keep title to the land. An alternate form was also used in English mortgage practice and, over time, became more popular than the defeasible conveyance. Lenders, in an effort to gain more control over the termination of their rights in the land, bargained for fee simple absolute title, making a promise to reconvey to the mortgagor in the event he timely paid the debt. Under this device, payment or tender of payment by the mortgagor would not automatically strip the mortgagee of his right to possession. Instead, it required the affirmative act of the lender in executing a conveyance back to the borrower.

This regime, grounded on freedom of contract between lender and borrower, allocated virtually all of the transactional risk to the borrower. Naturally, hardship sometimes resulted. In equity, the Chancellor began to intervene to protect deserving mortgagors from the harshness of the common law. Time was not of the essence in equity, despite the parties' agreement, because the lender could be made whole by payment of the debt with accrued interest. The debtor's right to pay late, as recognized by the Chancellor, became known as the *equity of redemption.* Over time, the muscle of equity became routine, thereby expanding equity's jurisdiction over mortgages as the common-law courts' jurisdiction shrank. Early in the seventeenth century, all mortgagors who had failed to pay their debt by law day, when they pled a present willingness and ability to pay, merited an equity of redemption, regardless of the reasons for nonpayment.

As a corollary to the newly found equity of redemption, the Chancellor refused to permit waivers, striking down devices that were said to "clog" the mortgagor's redemption right. As the Chancellor realized, lenders, then as today, generally control loan terms and loan documents. Thus, if borrowers could waive their redemption rights, lenders would routinely extract such waivers. The rule against clogging the equity of redemption developed in a series of cases involving lenders' crafty drafting attempts. It applied to all clauses set forth in the mortgage or in contemporaneous agreements that sought to nullify or restrict the borrower's right. For example, a side agreement in which the mortgagor agreed not to assert redemption rights later than one month after default in payment of the debt was an invalid clog.

During the pivotal seventeenth century, when equity transformed English mortgage law, the parties' allocation of possessory rights also changed. At the beginning of the century, the norm was still possession by the mortgagee from the time of the mortgage conveyance, but by the 1660s mortgagor possession until default had become the general practice.

The invention of the equity of redemption put mortgagees in a tenuous and uncertain position. The pendulum had swung, with a pro-mortgagor regime replacing the earlier pro-mortgagee regime. After default by the mortgagor, even if the mortgagee was in possession of the mortgaged land, the mortgagee was subject to the risk that at some point in the future, the mortgagor would file a bill in equity asserting his equity of redemption. To eliminate this title risk, mortgagees sought redress in equity. In the cases developing the equity of redemption, borrowers were plaintiffs. During the seventeenth century lenders became plaintiffs, filing bills alleging a mortgage default and asking for a decree ordering the borrower to pay by a fixed date or be forever barred from exercising the equity of redemption. The Chancellor responded favorably, setting a fixed date that he determined to be reasonable under the facts and circumstances. Such an action became known as *foreclosure*. It foreclosed, or barred, the mortgagor's redemption right. The procedure did not involve a sale of the land; if the mortgagor failed to redeem by the judicially set date, the mortgagee's title became absolute, at which point the mortgagee could elect to keep the land or sell it. Today, this type of decree is known as *strict foreclosure*. Presently in the United States only a few jurisdictions use strict foreclosure on a widespread basis. Instead, modern foreclosure procedure requires a public sale of the land, with the sales proceeds applied to the debt.

Modern United States mortgage law has as its mainstays the borrower's equity of redemption and the lender's right to foreclose on the property, relying heavily on traditional English mortgage law. There is not, however, unanimity as to the nature of the mortgagee's property rights in the land prior to foreclosure. In the United States, there are presently three different theories. A number of states, most of them in the East, cling to the English common-law tradition, holding that the mortgage instrument conveys fee title to the mortgagee.

A majority of states, often but not always due to statute, reject the title theory and hold that the mortgagee prior to foreclosure has only a *lien*. Under this approach, the mortgagor keeps legal and equitable title to the estate after signing the mortgage, and the mortgagee's property rights are limited to the right to foreclose after default. Essentially, the lender has a future interest that enables it to sell the property, contingent on loan default and the prosecution of foreclosure.

For many issues of mortgage law, it often does not matter what mortgage theory the state follows. It is principally important in analyzing the right of the mortgagee to obtain possession prior to the completion of foreclosure. The title theory dictates a baseline rule that the mortgagee has the right to possession, even prior to default. However, the parties can change the principle that the right to possession follows legal title by contract.

Several states — Ohio and Pennsylvania are prime examples — follow what is called an *intermediate theory* or *hybrid theory* of mortgages. These states split the difference between the title theory and lien theory, holding that the mortgagor retains title unless and until he defaults, and upon default the mortgagee automatically gets title. Compared to the title theory, the intermediate theory has the virtue of explaining why the mortgagor has the right to possession after signing the mortgage. Compared to the lien theory, the intermediate theory is pro-creditor in that it validates the position of a mortgagee who claims the right to take possession of the property upon a default prior to foreclosure. This may be significant because in many states foreclosure is not speedy; it may take months from the commencement of foreclosure to its completion.

In principle, the three mortgage theories should affect, in addition to analysis of possession, the allocation of other rights and duties between mortgagor and mortgagee and with respect to third parties. Whichever one has title should have all the incidents of title. At traditional English common law, courts followed the logic of the title theory rigorously, parcelling out rights such as inheritance and marital property based on the conception that the mortgagee has title and the mortgagor has a mere personal right of redemption. In the United States, however, courts have cared much less for doctrinal neatness. In all title-theory states, the mortgagor is generally treated as the substantial owner of the property both with respect to rights (such as the right to sell, the right to develop, the right to recover for injury to property) and with respect to duties (such as the duty to pay real estate taxes and the duty to maintain the property in accordance with laws and in a reasonably safe condition).

There are, however, several areas besides possession in which the state's mortgage theory matters. First, much commercial property that is mortgaged produces income in the form of rents paid by tenants to the borrower-landlords. Loan documentation typically includes the borrower-landlord's collateral assignment of rents to the mortgagee, either as a provision of the mortgage or as a separate assignment instrument. In a title-theory state or intermediate-theory state, such an assignment may be unnecessary because a mortgagee who is entitled to possession is automatically entitled to a security interest in the rents. Rents and profits are considered to be an incident of possession. Thus, the underlying title theory may protect a lender who, due to accident or some other reason, fails to obtain an express assignment of rents. Lien-theory states that follow the logic of their theory, refusing to let the parties contract around the theory, should refuse to recognize the efficacy of an assignment of rents prior to foreclosure. In essence, the lender receives the fruits of possession if he can collect rents before completing foreclosure. However, almost all lien-theory states give some effect to rent assignments, although typically they are more stingy than title-theory states. Commonly, in lien-theory states the mortgagee who holds an express assignment is often said to have only an "inchoate lien" on rents, which requires that the mortgagee take specific steps to collect rents. Usually this means the mortgagee must obtain actual or constructive possession of the property by bringing a foreclosure action, obtaining a court-appointed receiver, or some similar legal proceeding. In contrast, title-theory states, where the mortgagee already has title to the property, require less for the mortgagee to collect rents. Typically, it suffices to send a simple notice to the tenant requesting that future rents be paid directly to the mortgagee.

Second, in some title-theory states, a mortgagee who has not taken possession is personally liable on covenants made by the mortgagor that run with the land due to privity of estate. The most important application of this principle is in cases holding that when a commercial tenant mortgages its leasehold, the leasehold mortgagee becomes liable to the landlord for rent and other covenants.

Third, environmental liabilities of owners of contaminated land may extend to mortgagees who have title by virtue of the title theory of mortgages. Most of the concern has centered around the federal "Superfund" statute, also known as CERCLA, 42 U.S.C. §§9601-9675. Under CERCLA, owners and operators of properties containing hazardous waste have statutory liability for the costs of cleanup. CERCLA, however, contains an exemption for a "person, who, without participating in the management of a facility, holds indicia of ownership primarily to protect his security interest in the . . . facility." *Id.* §9601(20)A. This exemption was apparently designed to protect title-theory lenders who hold "indicia of ownership," provided they refrain from participating in management decisions, and lenders who acquire ownership or possession as a result of foreclosure. CERCLA is not the only environmental law that raises issues concerning the treatment of mortgage lenders who hold title. Potential lender liability exists under other federal and state environmental statutes, many of which lack express provisions governing lender liability.

A. POSSESSION BY MORTGAGOR: DOCTRINE OF WASTE

Whenever real property is owned by more than one person, there is the potential for the doctrine of *waste* to come into play. The basic principle is that the owner who is in possession owes the other owners the duty not to damage or destroy the property. This duty not to commit waste applies to cotenants. The doctrine of waste also applies to protect the owners of future interests, such as reversions and remainders that will or may become possessory after a life estate expires. Moreover, a tenant under a lease arrangement owes the landlord the duty not to commit acts of waste, whether the property is commercial, residential, or unimproved.

From your beginning course in property, you may recall that the modern law of waste seeks to achieve a balance between the rights of the possessor and the rights of the other owners. The basic goal is to preserve the economic value of the property for the nonpossessing owners. Thus, a life tenant ordinarily cannot remove a house or cut valuable timber, and a cotenant cannot begin mining operations without reaching agreement with the other owners. Yet the possessor is entitled to make reasonable use of the property, and often reasonable use requires the making of some changes to the property.

In mortgage law, the doctrine of waste plays the same role of adjusting and shaping the legal relationships of multiple owners as it does in other contexts. Whether the mortgagee's interest is conceptualized as title or a lien, it is important to recognize that it is property, and therefore whenever land is mortgaged it is subject to multiple ownership by the mortgagor and mortgagee together. We can think of the mortgagee's property right as a type of future interest. If the mortgagor fails to repay the debt or perform his other obligations, the mortgagee has the right to look to the security — in other words, to obtain the property to satisfy the default. The law of waste performs the vital role of protecting the economic value of the mortgagee's right to security. Therefore, not only are there acts the mortgagor must refrain from doing, such as tearing down a valuable building, but the law of waste also imposes affirmative duties on the mortgagor. The labels *voluntary waste* and *permissive waste* often used by courts reflect this dual nature of waste.

BELL v. FIRST COLUMBUS NATIONAL BANK
Supreme Court of Mississippi, 1986
493 So. 2d 964

ROBERTSON, Justice, for the Court. This action arises upon two homeowners' covenant to their mortgagee that they would keep their mortgaged home in reasonable repair and commit no waste thereon. No doubt because of evidence that five days preforeclosure, homeowners stripped the home, a jury found for the mortgagee and assessed modest punitive damages as well. . . .

In the year 1973 John H. Bell, Sr. and Sharon B. Bell, husband and wife, owned a residence in Columbus, Mississippi, known as Lot No. 54, Pleasant Ridge Estate, Third Extension, Lowndes County, Mississippi. The Bells were the Defendants below and are the Appellants here. On May 11, 1973, the Bells executed a deed of trust conveying the above described lot and all improvements thereon to W.H. Jolly, Jr., Trustee, for the use and benefit of First Federal Savings & Loan Association of Columbus. . . .

Thereafter, the Bells engaged in several business ventures and maintained a banking relationship with the First Columbus National Bank, Plaintiff below and Appellee here. As security for various loans made by the bank, the Bells, on May 24, 1974, July 1, 1980, and June 7, 1981, executed and delivered to the bank second deeds of trust covering their residence. As a result of business failures, the indebtednesses owing both to First Federal and the bank fell into arrears.

On July 7, 1983, the Bells filed their voluntary petition in bankruptcy . . . . On November 3, 1983, the Bankruptcy Court entered its order granting the Bells their discharge in bankruptcy. During the course of the bankruptcy proceedings, of course, no effort was made by the bankruptcy trustee to take possession of the Bells' residence. As property subject to a perfected security interest held both by First Federal and the bank, the residence never became a part of the bankruptcy estate.

In due course thereafter, First Federal Savings & Loan commenced foreclosure proceedings with respect to its 1973 deed of trust. On February 12, 1984, five days before the scheduled foreclosure sale, the Bells held a garage sale. An advertisement published in the want ad columns of the Columbus newspaper read as follows:

> Sunday, Feb. 12—12:00 Noon to 6:00 p.m. Indoors. Custom Drapes, linens, housewares, adult and children's clothes and shoes, carpet scraps, light fixture & much, much more. 703 19th Avenue North.

A neighbor, Ann Fussell, attended the sale with her daughter and observed carpet rolled up in one room and the padding. Sharon Bell told Fussell that the carpet was for sale and made the statement, "We're selling just about everything—anything you want to buy." Fussell took some shutter doors for the kitchen or bath down to her house, but when she determined they would not fit, she brought them back. She observed one light fixture being taken down and sold in the dining area; she also observed someone purchase a roll of carpet.

The foreclosure sale occurred on February 17, 1984, at which time the bank purchased the property which, of course, necessitated the bank paying off the indebtedness owed to First Federal. Several days later Robert E. Lamar, a vice president at the bank, inspected the premises and found that the carpet, electrical fixtures, and ceiling fans had been removed, wall covering in every room, with the exception of two bathrooms, had been torn and damaged, and in two bedrooms, the closet doors and jams had been removed. In the kitchen, built in appliances and several cabinet units had been removed, base and wall cabinets had been removed which housed an oven, cook top and vent-a-hood, and a dishwasher had been removed from a cabinet next to the sink. Also the intercom system and speakers had been removed from the wall. The removal of these fixtures as well as other damage to the house reduced its fair market value, necessitated repairs and replacements, and has led to this lawsuit.

On April 17, 1984, First Columbus National Bank filed its complaint in the Circuit Court of Lowndes County, Mississippi, naming John H. Bell, Sr. and Sharon B. Bell as defendants. The bank asserted their deeds of trust and specifically claimed reliance upon a covenant in each such deed of trust to the effect that the Bells bound themselves

> to keep the improvements thereon [upon the property conveyed in trust] in reasonable repair and not permit waste of said property;. . . .

The bank alleged that it was forced to repair the house and replace the missing fixtures before it could be sold and that it incurred repair and replacement expenses in the amount of $5,350 for which amount it sought recovery from the Bells. The bank further alleged that the Bells had damaged the property wilfully and wantonly and demanded $5,000 in punitive damages.

On May 14, 1985, this matter came on for trial before the Circuit Court of Lowndes County sitting with a jury, and on that same day the jury returned a verdict in favor of the bank and against the Bells in the amount of $5,350 in actual damages and $1,500 in punitive damages. . . .

The Bells make two points here. First, they argue that the bank's claim has been discharged in bankruptcy.

To be sure, a bankruptcy adjudication bars a secured creditor's suit on the underlying debt. The right of the secured creditor to foreclosure upon its collateral, however, remains unimpaired. [Citations omitted.] These general statements do not carry us far, because here we confront a claim of post-bankruptcy violation of a pre-bankruptcy contractual obligation. . . .

The record reflects that on May 20, 1985, following the jury's verdict final judgment was entered in favor of the bank and against the Bells. Three days later the Bells filed their motion for judgment notwithstanding the verdict and, for the first time, formally asserted the bankruptcy discharge as a defense to the bank's action. This plea came too late. Assuming arguendo that the bank's claim on the covenant was one dischargeable in bankruptcy, *see* 11 U.S.C. §365, the Bells lost their right, if any, to invoke the shield of their discharge by failure timely to assert it affirmatively.

Second, we find unpersuasive the argument that the bank lost the benefit of the reasonable repair and no waste covenants by purchasing the property at foreclosure. . . .

Here the bank was within its every right to proceed against the Bells for recovery of losses the bank had sustained as a proximate result of the Bells' breach of their covenants of reasonable repair and no waste. Those obligations were not extinguished in the foreclosure sale nor was the bank's right to enforce them waived or in other ways lost. There was substantial credible evidence adduced at trial to the effect that the Bells did in fact commit waste upon the property and failed to have it in reasonable repair. . . .

The Bells next argue that the Circuit Court erroneously allowed the bank's witness to use replacement cost as a measure of the bank's damages. Such an approach, we are told, put the bank in a better position than it would have occupied had the breach of covenant not occurred. The bank's damages witness gave an estimate of what it would cost to repair damage to the house and replace the items removed, while the Bells offered testimony to the effect that the items removed were a number of years old and that their usable life expectancy was near an end. The Bells argue that the bank's damages, if any, should be determined by reference to the value of what was taken — used-depreciated items — rather than reasonable replacement cost for new materials. As the Bells put it, is the bank "entitled to the value of new fixtures, when most of the old ones were in excess of eleven years old"? . . .

In the case at bar, the diminution in value before and after the damage to the property may have been greater than the cost of repair. At least one bank witness testified to an adjusted damages figure of $7,000. Notwithstanding, we find that the bank has elected to proceed upon a reasonable cost of replacement and repair theory. It being as a practical matter impossible to obtain depreciated fixtures, the bank reasonably had no choice to purchase and install new items, the reasonable aggregate cost of which was $5,350. The bank chose its remedy; there is no unjust enrichment to it under these circumstances. . . .

Finally, the Bells mount a challenge to the jury's assessment of $1,500 in punitive damages against them. Before punitive damages may be assessed against a party, there must be substantial evidence either (1) that he acted with malice or (2) that he acted with gross negligence or reckless disregard for the rights of others. Aetna Casualty & Surety Co. v. Day, 487 So. 2d 830, 832 (Miss. 1986); Weems v. American Security Insurance Company, 486 So. 2d 1222, 1226 (Miss. 1986). The evidence regarding the Bells' deliberate stripping of the house five days before foreclosure is more than sufficient to present a jury issue and render the verdict beyond our authority to disturb. Bankers Life and Casualty Co. v. Crenshaw, 483 So. 2d 254 (Miss. 1985).

Affirmed.

Problem 14A

Six years ago, Harry Homeowner bought his home for $100,000, financed with a mortgage loan for $90,000 from Big Bank. Harry has always made his monthly payments on time. Presently, the loan has a principal balance of $85,672. Last month, Harry held a garage sale, at which he sold all five ceiling fans from rooms in the house, the dishwasher, and the garage door opener, reaping a total of $255. All these items were part of the house when he bought it. Harry does not plan to replace them.

(a) Does Big Bank have a cause of action against Harry? If so, what should be its remedy?

(b) What result if (1) Harry's mortgage provides that "the mortgagor shall keep the property in reasonable repair and commit no waste thereon;" or alternatively if (2) Harry's mortgage says nothing about repairs, replacements, or waste.

(c) Assume that Harry decides to remodel his home. He knocks down several interior walls and makes a unique living space. He hires professionals to do a first-class job. When the project is finished it looks great. The new layout of the home has changed a three-bedroom home into a one-bedroom "bachelor pad." Even though the work is first-class, Harry's broker friend advises that it will be a lot more difficult to sell the house now because it will appeal to only a very few people, perhaps no one but Harry. Harry tells his friend not to worry because he plans to stay in the house for a long time. Does Big Bank have a cause of action against Harry? Will it have a cause of action if Harry defaults and it becomes difficult to sell the home or it has to be sold at a very low price?

B. POSSESSION BY MORTGAGEE

Mortgagee in possession is a term applied to a lender that takes physical control of a debtor's property prior to foreclosure. Generally, the reason the lender takes possession of mortgaged property is to preserve and protect its asset value. Such a lender is not considered to be the owner of the property simply as a result of taking possession, even in a state that follows the title theory or intermediate theory of mortgage law. For this reason, the mortgagee in possession has a special duty to the mortgagor to act prudently in taking care of the property, and must make a full accounting of rents and profits derived from the property.

MYERS-MACOMBER ENGINEERS v. M.L.W. CONSTRUCTION CORPORATION

Superior Court of Pennsylvania, 1979
271 Pa. Super. 484, 414 A.2d 357

WIEAND, Judge. Does a mortgagee who goes into possession of an incomplete condominium development upon default in the terms of a mortgage by the mortgagor owe a duty to use undistributed mortgage funds to satisfy the mortgagor's unpaid debts? The lower court held that a mortgagee in possession becomes a quasi trustee with a responsibility to satisfy outstanding, job related claims against the mortgagor. We disagree and reverse.

M.L.W. Construction Corporation was the owner and developer of a series of condominiums on a nineteen acre tract in East Pennsboro Township, Cumberland County. HNC Mortgage and Realty Investors agreed to lend construction money in the amount of $5,850,000, which sum was secured by a construction mortgage. After $2,900,000 had been advanced, the developer defaulted. HNC thereupon exercised the right given by the terms of the mortgage to assume control of the project as a mortgagee in possession. Subsequently, HNC foreclosed on its mortgage and purchased the incomplete development at sheriff's sale. The project was completed by a contractor employed by HNC.

The appellee, Myers-Macomber Engineers, had performed site-preparation work pursuant to a contract with M.L.W., for which it is owed an unpaid balance of $11,298.98. In this action of assumpsit appellee alleged that M.L.W. had breached its contract to pay for services rendered. M.L.W. did not contest the claim. In a separate count against HNC, appellee contended that the lender was liable for the value of engineering services on theories of unjust enrichment. The trial court submitted this issue to a jury, which returned a verdict in favor of appellee and against HNC for $11,000. Motions for new trial and judgment n.o.v. were denied, and judgment was entered on the verdict. HNC appealed.

"Mortgagee in possession" is a term applied to the special status of a mortgagee who has obtained possession of property from the mortgagor with the consent of the latter. *See generally* 55 Am. Jur. 2d *Mortgages* §§184, 185, 193-196; Osborne, *Mortgages* §§160-176 (2d ed., 1970). Such consent is usually contained, as here, in the mortgage agreement. This remedy avoids the drastic step of foreclosure, while enabling the mortgagee to protect and preserve its security interest. The mortgagee does not thereby limit its right to foreclose, and, upon foreclosure, the mortgagee may purchase the property at sheriff's sale. Girard Trust Company v. Dempsey, 129 Pa. Super. 471, 476, 196 A. 593, 595 (1938). Frequently, foreclosure becomes necessary despite the salvage efforts of a mortgagee in possession. If the mortgagor should avoid foreclosure by paying off the mortgage debt while the mortgagee is in control of the property, however, the mortgagee must surrender possession to the mortgagor. . . .

When a mortgagee goes into possession, he does not become the owner of the real estate. . . . As a mortgagee in possession, his duty is to comport with the same standard of conduct as a prudent owner, i.e., he must manage the property in a reasonably prudent and careful manner so as to keep it in a good state of preservation and productivity. Landau v. Western Pennsylvania National Bank, 445 Pa. 217, 282 A.2d 335 (1971); Integrity Trust Co. v. St. Rita Building & Loan Assn., 317 Pa. 518, 177 A. 5 (1935). *See also* Osborne,

Mortgages §168 (2d ed., 1970). The mortgagee in possession has a duty to collect the rents and profits which accrue during his occupancy and apply them to the mortgage debt. Provident Trust Co. of Philadelphia v. Judicial Building & Loan Asso., *supra.* Moreover, the mortgagor is entitled to an accounting from his mortgagee who has taken possession. Landau v. Western Pennsylvania National Bank, *supra*; Winthrop v. Arthur W. Binns, Inc., 160 Pa. Super. 214, 50 A.2d 718 (1947).

The fiduciary duty of a mortgagee in possession, however, is owed only to the mortgagor. Thus, the mortgagee cannot be required to account to a second mortgagee for income received while the mortgagee was in possession, McNicholas' Appeal, [9 A.2d 200 (1939)]; or to a creditor of the mortgagor, Supreme Council of the Royal Arcanum v. Susque Frozen Foods, 44 Northumberland L.J. 13 (1972). Similarly, a mortgagee in possession is not liable to a purchaser at sheriff's sale for taxes owed on the property. Fassitt v. North Tioga Building & Loan Asso., 133 Pa. Super. 146, 2 A.2d 499 (1938).

It follows that in the absence of a valid agreement by which the mortgagee has assumed or guaranteed payment of the mortgagor's debts, the mortgagee cannot be required to pay unsecured claims held by creditors of the mortgagor. Such creditors must look to the mortgagor upon whose credit they relied.

Appellee argues that the mortgagee will be unjustly enriched if it is permitted to retain the benefit of appellee's engineering work. Reliance is placed on the principle that when a person receives a benefit from another, and it would be unconscionable for the recipient to retain that benefit, the doctrine of unjust enrichment requires the recipient to make restitution. . . .

In the instant case, appellant was not enriched unjustly. When appellant took possession of the condominium project it had already advanced to the developer the sum of $2,900,000. Included in the monies advanced was the entire amount budgeted for site preparation. Thus, it was not unjust that it received the benefit of such engineering work when it was compelled by the developer's default to take possession of the incomplete building project. Moreover, it does not appear that the mortgagee, after purchasing the real estate at sheriff's sale and employing its own contractor to complete the project, was able to dispose of the completed project at a profit.

The legislature in Pennsylvania has by statute provided the mechanics' lien as a means by which a contractor or subcontractor can obtain security for work done. Other security can be acquired by contract. If the right to file a mechanics' lien has been waived, if a contractor chooses to rely upon the personal credit of the party with whom he contracts, a court should not rewrite the contract of the parties or legislate a right to receive payment from a mortgagee who has been compelled to go into possession to preserve its security. Such a rule would do much to impair the availability of capital upon which the building industry so greatly depends. In any event, if additional remedy is needed, it should come from the legislature and should not be decreed by judicial fiat. East Penn Contracting Corp. v. Merchants

National Bank of Allentown, 37 Leh. L.J. 268 (1977), *aff'd*, 254 Pa. Super. 613, 387 A.2d 114 (1978).

Reversed and remanded for the entry of judgment n.o.v. in favor of appellant.

Problem 14B

Best Bank, your client, is a mortgagee that has just taken possession of an office building that has 40,000 square feet of space. Cook, the owner who defaulted, finished construction six months ago. Half the building is occupied by tenants, the other half is unrented. "For Rent" signs, put up by Cook, are in front of the building. Newspaper ads run by Cook have expired, and Best cannot find any real estate broker's agreements, signed by Cook, covering the property. Best did find, however, in the building manager's office an unpaid electric bill for $2,458 for the month ending four days prior to Best's entry into possession.

(a) Does Best have a duty to try to rent the unoccupied space? What measures, if any, should Best take?

(b) Does Best have a duty to pay the electric bill?

C. RECEIVERS

When the borrower defaults, the mortgagee has several remedies it may pursue prior to foreclosure. Two choices discussed earlier are taking possession directly (the mortgagee in possession) and invoking an assignment of rents. A third possible remedy is to obtain a court-appointed receiver, who will take possession and operate the property. Generally, receivership is used for income-producing or commercial properties, but it may be useful for owner-occupied housing if waste is threatened and foreclosure is likely to proceed slowly. Receivership is available in all states as an incident to an action for foreclosure. Receivership is an equitable remedy, and this means that courts usually look at a number of factors to decide whether to appoint a receiver. The standards for appointments vary from state to state, sometimes because of state statutes. In some states, therefore, it is easier than in others to get a receiver appointed. Most courts require that the mortgagee prove not only a material default by the borrower but also that a receiver is necessary to prevent further injury to the mortgagee. Typical facts include waste or the threat of waste committed by the borrower, inadequate security compared to the amount of the debt, and the borrower's insolvency or weak financial position.

Mortgage instruments often have a receivership clause, which typically authorizes the mortgagee to obtain the appointment of a receiver if the borrower defaults. Judicial attitudes toward such clauses diverge. Some courts pay substantial deference to them on the basis of freedom of contract. Other courts ignore them, reasoning that the remedy of appointing a receiver is inherently equitable in nature, and thus contractual provisions usurp the judicial function and are unenforceable. Some courts appear to adopt a middle ground, looking at a number of factors to determine whether a receiver should be appointed and treating the presence of a contract provision as one factor that is material but not controlling.

CHASE MANHATTAN BANK v. TURABO SHOPPING CENTER, INC.
United States Court of Appeals, First Circuit, 1982
683 F.2d 25

BOWNES, Circuit Judge. Turabo Shopping Center, Inc. (Turabo) appeals an order of the district court appointing a receiver to manage, operate, and control a shopping center owned and run by Turabo during the pendency of a mortgage foreclosure action on the center brought by Turabo's creditor and mortgagee, The Chase Manhattan Bank, N.A. (Chase). This is an appealable interlocutory order, 28 U.S.C. §1292(a) (2).

Turabo owns and operates the shopping center, the Plaza del Carmen Shopping Center, in Caguas, Puerto Rico. In the mid-1970's, Turabo obtained interim construction financing from Chase in order to build the center and mortgaged the shopping center to Chase. Chase loaned Turabo a total of $6,799,800, all of which, according to Chase, is still owing. The amount of interest now owing is disputed, Chase claiming that it is just over $3,000,000 and Turabo contending that it is closer to $2,300,000. Turabo was expected to obtain permanent financing elsewhere and to pay off Chase, but that has not come to pass. Under the terms of the mortgage agreement, Chase is now to be repaid by the assignment of rents due Turabo from tenants in the shopping center, and Chase has received some—but, Chase claims, not all—of the rents to which it is entitled. Adrian Perez-Agudo, president of Turabo, and Maria Eugenia Gonzalez de Perez are guarantors of Turabo's loan and codefendants in this foreclosure action, although only Turabo has appealed the order.

In April, 1981, Chase filed suit to foreclose on the mortgage and, approximately a month later, moved for the appointment of a receiver. After a hearing, the district court granted the motion and appointed a still-unnamed receiver with wide powers to supervise operation of the shopping center. The district court based its order on alternative grounds: first, that the twenty-first clause of the mortgage agreement entitled Chase to have a receiver appointed, and, second, that even in the absence of that clause, equity favored the appointment. . . .

The law governing the appointment of receivers in federal courts has not been reduced to a convenient formula. We have observed that

> to warrant the appointment of a receiver to manage and operate [mortgaged property pending foreclosure], as well as only to collect [its] rents and profits, there must be at the least a "sufficient showing" of something more than the inadequacy of the security and the doubtful financial standing of the debtor.

Garden Homes, Inc. v. United States, [200 F.2d 299, 301 (1st Cir. 1952)]. We did not determine what that "something more" was, but other courts have looked to such factors as

> fraudulent conduct on the part of the defendant; imminent danger that property would be lost, concealed, injured, diminished in value, or squandered; the inadequacy of the available legal remedies; the probability that harm to plaintiff by denial of the appointment would be greater than the injury to the parties opposing appointment; and the plaintiff's probable success in the action and the possibility of irreparable injury to his interests in the property.

CFTC v. Comvest Trading Corp., [481 F. Supp. 438, 441 (D. Mass. 1979)] (footnotes (citing cases) omitted). Also relevant are the probability that appointment of a receiver will protect the interests of the party seeking appointment and the nature of the receiver's duties. . . .

We believe that the district court was well within its discretion in appointing a receiver; indeed, the evidence compelled such an order. In addition to the fact that the value of the shopping center is probably inadequate to cover amounts still owed to Chase by Turabo, three pieces of essentially uncontradicted evidence showed unfair and arguably fraudulent dealing on Turabo's part and the likelihood of continuing injury to Chase's interest in the shopping center. First, Turabo's general laxity in rent collection from shopping center tenants was especially marked in its treatment of three tenant companies run by the sister of Perez-Agudo, Turabo's president. Those companies paid no rent for a considerable period of time.[1] Second, Turabo, not having paid its lawyer and agent for obtaining tenants, allowed the lawyer to set up a restaurant[2] in the shopping center without charging rent and without signing a rental contract. The admitted reason for the absence of a contract was to prevent Chase from making a claim to rental payments from the restaurant. Finally, Perez-Agudo withheld approximately $100,000 in rent assigned to Chase in order, among other purposes, to retain attorneys to defend Turabo in the mortgage foreclosure action and to obtain an appraisal of the shopping center to be used in the foreclosure litigation.

1. The district court was within its discretion in concluding that Chase had not agreed to forebear collection of some rents because of flood damage to the three tenants.

2. This lawyer, Ema Sara Portela, acted through a number of corporate entities, but the district court did not treat them as distinct, and Turabo has not argued to the contrary.

Because we uphold the appointment of the receiver on equitable grounds, we have no occasion to consider the effect of the twenty-first clause of the mortgage agreement.[3]

The order of the district court is affirmed.

Problem 14C

Gary owns an office building that he bought two years ago for $130,000. He paid $20,000 in cash, giving the seller, Sam, a promissory note for $110,000, secured by a purchase-money mortgage on the property. For 20 months, Gary timely made monthly payments of principal and interest, but he failed to make the last two payments, which were due May 1st and June 1st. On June 20th, Sam accelerated the maturity of the debt and filed an action to foreclose his mortgage. It is now June 25th and Sam has filed a motion for the appointment of a receiver. The debt, including accrued interest, is now $105,500. Should the court grant Sam's motion if:

(a) The present fair market value of the property has risen in a strong market and is between $140,000 and $145,000?

(b) The property has declined in value due to a weak market for office space rentals and has a present fair market value between $105,000 and $110,000?

(c) The property has declined in value as a result of physical deterioration caused by Gary's failure to make needed repairs, and it has a present fair market value between $110,000 and $115,000?

(d) Should it matter, in any of the situations in (a) through (c), whether Gary is solvent or insolvent?

(e) Should it matter, in any of the situations in (a) through (c), whether the mortgage contains a receivership clause providing:

> In the event of any default under the promissory note secured hereby or under the terms of this mortgage, the holder of this mortgage, in any action to foreclose it, shall be entitled to the appointment of a receiver, without regard to waste, adequacy of the security, or solvency of the mortgagor.

(f) Should it matter, in any of the situations in (a) through (c), whether the mortgage contains an assignment of rents?

(g) Should it matter, in any of the situations in (a) through (c), whether the state follows the title theory, intermediate theory, or lien theory of mortgages?

3. Chief Judge Coffin, while concurring in this opinion, would prefer to place primary emphasis on this clause, its validity never having been put in issue below. The court's recitation of the equitable grounds, in his view, makes crystal clear that whether or not such a contract clause is sufficient, without more, to justify appointment of a receiver, the "more" exists here in abundance.

15

Residential Mortgage Markets and Products

In Chapter 14, we sketched the history of mortgage law, concentrating on a few basic principles that govern the traditional as well as the contemporary relationships between mortgagor and mortgagee. With this as background, we now explore the current situation in residential mortgage law by putting it into the market context. Large, growing financial markets support mortgage lending activities, and the dynamics of these markets shape the opportunities and the risks of real estate acquisition and investing. First, we consider access to credit for persons who want to enter the market to get home mortgage loans. Second, we present a simple framework for understanding the primary mortgage market. Third, we look at how the secondary mortgage market operates and how it creates expanded access to investment capital. Fourth and finally, we examine the basic mortgage products that are exchanged in the markets and thus are available to borrowers.

A. ACCESS TO MORTGAGE MARKETS

Access to mortgages is rationed by lenders. This sometimes raises issues of law and policy because some applicants are able to get mortgages, others are not, and others who are evaluated as presenting higher-than-normal risk are offered less advantageous terms.

To understand access issues, we must think of mortgage lending as a business. For lenders, extending credit is an investment opportunity. Whereas a homeowner looks at the mortgage as a necessary living expense, the lender looks at it as a financial investment. Lenders make financial capital available for real estate activities because they find such activities to be rewarding in terms of economic profit. Making a loan represents an investment of capital upon which a profitable return must be earned. A lender thinks of any particular loan as just one of many possible investment options for its money. In this sense, the lender is much like any one of us when we take our hard-earned savings and contemplate such options as depositing them in a savings account, a money market fund or a retirement account, or using them to buy stocks or bonds. When we think about these options, we consider the risk and the return on how we invest our money. A lender views real estate funding in a similar way. A lender has control over large amounts of capital and must make decisions on how best to invest that money to get a good return within an acceptable range of risk.

Access to credit is important for anyone who seeks to purchase property. As a general rule, standard industry criteria are followed by lenders in deciding who can borrow money and how much they can get. The lender is interested in two key factors concerning the debtor or borrower. The lender cares about the *willingness* and the *ability* of the debtor to repay the loan. These two factors are different because a person may be able to pay back a loan and yet refuse to do so as a result of a dispute with the bank or with the seller of the property, or because property values have dropped dramatically and the debtor becomes unwilling to pay any more to protect the declining asset, or perhaps for some totally unrelated reason. Similarly, a person may be more than willing to repay a loan and yet be unable to as the result of losing a job or some other hardship.

A lender must assess both of these factors very carefully. A borrower's income and outstanding debts are considered, along with employment history, credit history, and savings or net worth. Often there is a personal interview of the borrowing applicant by the lender's loan officer. All this information is evaluated in order to make an informed decision with respect to the potential borrower's ability and willingness to pay back the loan. Some of the factors used in the evaluation are more objective than others. Generally speaking, the factors related to ability to pay are more objective than those related to willingness to pay. Central to the determination of ability to pay is an evaluation of the income and other outstanding debt obligations of the borrower. With respect to income, most lenders follow a 28 percent rule, indicating that a debtor should not qualify for a loan requiring monthly mortgage payments exceeding 28 percent of gross monthly income. In addition, most lenders also use a 36 percent rule, indicating that a debtor should not have total debt payments (mortgage payments plus all other debt obligations) exceeding 36 percent of gross income. These two numerical guidelines are widely followed, though some variation may be made for particular borrowers or for high-cost housing markets. To the extent that a local variation from these norms is used to calculate ability to pay, it is likely that most lenders in the given area would employ the same variation, perhaps using a 30 percent rule instead of the 28 percent rule in an expensive urban market. The advantage to a simple numerical test is that it is fairly easy to calculate and leaves little room for discretion.

In contrast to a simple test for ability to pay, a much more subjective inquiry is made to determine willingness to pay. Credit and employment history must be evaluated, and any past credit problems or payment disputes with other parties must be cleared up to the satisfaction of the lender.

Borrowers apply to individual lending institutions for loans, and lenders evaluate the applications to determine the loans that will be funded. Information on mortgage lending reflects different rates of success in the loan application process for different groups of borrowers. Mortgage information is kept by lenders and required to be reported annually under the Home Mortgage Disclosure Act of 1975, 12 U.S.C. §§2801-2810. The Federal Financial Institutions Examination Council publishes reports based on the information. According to information published for the year 2004, one can observe different loan approval rates for different groups of applicants.

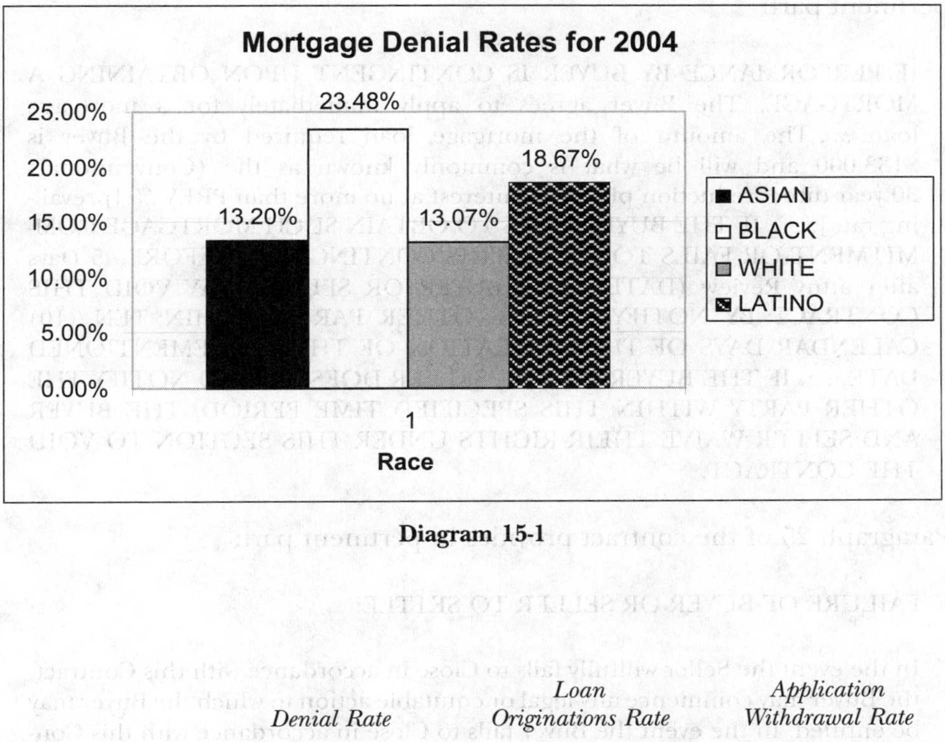

Diagram 15-1

	Denial Rate	*Loan Originations Rate*	*Application Withdrawal Rate*
ASIAN	13.20%	65.37%	8.89%
BLACK	23.48%	52.83%	9.19%
WHITE	13.07%	69.58%	7.40%
LATINO	18.67%	60.16%	8.96%

Diagram 15-2

MALUS v. HAGER

Superior Court of New Jersey, Appellate Division, 1998
312 N.J. Super. 483, 712 A.2d 238

WEFING, J.A.D. Defendants Kenneth and Jean Hager appeal from the trial court's grant of summary judgment in favor of plaintiffs Richard and Rosemarie Malus. We reverse.

The parties executed a contract dated March 3, 1996 under which plaintiffs agreed to purchase the Hagers' home in Tinton Falls, New Jersey for $140,000. Their contract contained a clause for attorney review; both parties were represented by counsel. Plaintiffs paid a deposit of $7,000, held in the trust account of Hagers' attorney. Paragraph C (iii) of the contract reads in pertinent part:

> IF PERFORMANCE BY BUYER IS CONTINGENT UPON OBTAINING A MORTGAGE. The Buyer agrees to apply immediately for a mortgage loan. . . . The amount of the mortgage loan required by the Buyer is $133,000 and will be what is commonly known as the (Conventional) 30 year direct reduction plan with interest at no more than PREV % [prevailing rate]. . . . IF THE BUYER FAILS TO OBTAIN SUCH MORTGAGE COMMITMENT OR FAILS TO WAIVE THIS CONTINGENCY BEFORE 45 Days after attny Review (DATE), THE BUYER OR SELLER MAY VOID THIS CONTRACT BY NOTIFYING THE OTHER PARTY WITHIN TEN (10) CALENDAR DAYS OF THE EXPIRATION OF THE AFOREMENTIONED DATE. . . . IF THE BUYER OR THE SELLER DOES NOT SO NOTIFY THE OTHER PARTY WITHIN THIS SPECIFIED TIME PERIOD, THE BUYER AND SELLER WAIVE THEIR RIGHTS UNDER THIS SECTION TO VOID THE CONTRACT.

Paragraph 25 of the contract provides in pertinent part:

> FAILURE OF BUYER OR SELLER TO SETTLE:
>
> In the event the Seller willfully fails to Close in accordance with this Contract, the Buyer may commence any legal or equitable action to which the Buyer may be entitled. In the event the Buyer fails to Close in accordance with this Contract, the payments made on account, at the Seller's option, shall be paid to the Seller as liquidated damages, or the Seller may commence any legal or equitable action to which the Seller is entitled, applying to such action the monies paid by the Buyer on account of the purchase price. Liquidated damages means the Seller will keep the money paid on account and not commence any legal action for the Buyer's failure to Close. . . .

Plaintiffs applied for a mortgage loan in accordance with paragraph C(iii) and, within the forty-five day period, obtained a commitment from Chase Manhattan bank for a mortgage loan.

The closing was scheduled to take place on July 15, 1996. On July 11, 1996, plaintiff Richard Malus was terminated, not for cause, from his employment. On July 12, 1996, defendants, unaware of this development and expecting the closing to take place on July 15, moved out of the home at Tinton Falls and placed certain of their belongings in storage until they were able to complete their own relocation.

Under the terms of Chase Manhattan's mortgage commitment, it retained the right to cancel the commitment letter "[i]f prior to funding, your financial condition or employment status adversely changes. . . ." In light of Mr. Malus's loss of employment, Chase exercised its rights under that reservation and declined to fund the mortgage.

Mr. and Mrs. Malus sought return of their $7,000 deposit. When Mr. and Mrs. Hager declined, this lawsuit resulted.

The trial court granted summary judgment to the plaintiffs on the basis of Northeast Custom Homes, Inc. v. Howell, 230 N.J. Super. 296, 553 A.2d 387 (Law Div. 1988). Plaintiff in that case was a custom builder and it prepared a contract defendants executed on January 24, 1987 for the purchase of a home then under construction for $857,486. Defendants were not informed of a right to have the contract reviewed by an attorney but were, after the contract was executed, referred to an attorney to assist in preparation for the closing. Defendants gave a deposit of $85,748. The contract stated it was "contingent upon buyer obtaining a conventional mortgage . . . within 45 days. . . ." Defendants obtained a timely mortgage commitment but Mr. Howell was terminated from his job approximately two weeks after the commitment was issued. His employer had advanced the deposit money and demanded its repayment. The lender then withdrew its commitment, based upon the change in his employment status. Northeast later sold the property for $835,000, a loss slightly in excess of $20,000. The parties commenced litigation over entitlement to the $85,748 deposit the Howells had previously made. The trial court in that case concluded that the Howells were entitled to the return of the deposit. In doing so, it construed "the mortgage contingency clause to mean that not only the mortgage commitment but also the availability at closing of the mortgage proceeds together constitute the condition precedent to the purchasers' obligation to perform." 230 N.J. Super. at 304.

We disagree with that construction for its result is to place the parties in an intolerable state of limbo until the closing is finally consummated. Contracts such as these set firm deadlines for the occurrence of specified events in order that the parties are able to plan and to act with confidence that after a certain point there is an enforceable agreement. Confusion and uncertainty can only result from extending, as a matter of law, the mortgage contingency clause to the date of closing.

. . . We note that in this case, although the Hagers were later able to resell their home at the same contract price, that closing did not occur until approximately four months after the initial, scheduled date. The Hagers were responsible for the mortgage, taxes and maintenance on the premises in the interim and also incurred additional moving and storage fees.

If the parties wish to provide in their contract for an eventuality such as this, they are free to do so. We decline, however, to impose the risk of an otherwise firm deal unravelling upon an unknowing and blameless seller, leaving him with no ability to recoup his increased expenses.

We are satisfied that the matter is controlled by Paragraph 25 of the parties' contract. The Maluses having failed to close on this transaction, the Hagers were entitled to retain the deposit.

The judgment of June 4, 1997 is reversed and the matter is remanded for entry of judgment in favor of defendants.

UNITED COMPANIES LENDING CORPORATION v. SARGEANT

United States District Court, Massachusetts, 1998
20 F. Supp. 2d 192

YOUNG, District Judge. This case comes before the Court as a case stated. That is, the parties have stipulated to all material facts and it remains for this Court to review the record, draw such inferences as are reasonable and, applying the governing law, enter such judgment as may be appropriate. . . .

I. BACKGROUND

United Companies Lending Corporation ("United") makes, sells, and services refinancing, first lien residential mortgage loans which are used primarily for debt consolidation, home improvement, or major household purchases. United is licensed to do business in Massachusetts as a mortgage lender. United operates in the subprime market making loans to consumers who have a higher credit risk than borrowers in the prime market.

Subprime loans are more costly to the lender to originate, sell, and service than traditional "A credit" loans. In the subprime market, the lenders evaluate the credit-worthiness of a borrower "by establishing various risk classifications with associated pricing parameters." Joint [Statement of Undisputed Facts] ("Joint Stmt.") ¶3. There is no standard set of credit risk assessment criteria as exists in the prime market. The subprime market typically takes into consideration a potential borrower's 1) credit history; 2) the household debt-to-income ratio if the loan is approved; and 3) the combined loan-to-value ratio for home equity loan and other mortgage debt on the property. "Standards vary, however, within the subprime market, and different lenders may assign different weights for each of these factors, for a given credit grade. (One firm's 'B' loans may look like another firm's 'C' loans.)". Joint Stmt. ¶4.

Subprime loans have higher securitization costs associated with the sale of these loans on the private secondary market compared to loans in the prime market because they are "non-conforming" loans. United loans are also sold "with recourse" in the event of a default by the borrower. As a result of these terms, the risk to the lender on a subprime loan is substantially higher than on a prime loan. "Due to the higher risks and costs associated with subprime loans, the total cost of such loans to the borrower — as reflected in the Annual Percentage Rate ("APR") — is generally higher than the cost of loans by traditional lenders such as banks. Such costs typically include interest, origination fees or 'points' and other fees associated with the closing of the loan." Joint Stmt. ¶9.

Daisy Sargeant ("Sargeant") is the owner of a New England triple-decker in Dorchester, Massachusetts. She resides on the second floor and rents out the first floor and third floor apartments for $600 per month each. Desiring to make improvements to the interior and the exterior of the house, she responded to an advertisement in the Boston Herald regarding the availability of loans. She contacted the toll-free number in the advertisement and received a mortgage application. The advertisement was placed by a California-based mortgage broker, John P. McIntyre ("McIntyre"). McIntyre referred Sargeant's name to David Richard ("Richard"), a United mortgage loan originator located at the Warwick, Rhode Island office. Richard contacted Sargeant. Richard is the United agent with whom Sargeant dealt in obtaining the mortgage loan at issue.

On August 9, 1995, Sargeant completed the loan application and executed disclosure documents related to the loan. Sargeant was classified as a "C" borrower by United. On August 23, 1995, United approved Sargeant's loan. A title search disclosed an undischarged mortgage on the property, however, as well as unpaid real estate taxes. United states that McIntyre negotiated with the lien holder who agreed to accept $5000 as payment in full. United reapproved the loan, and the closing was held in Warwick, Rhode Island, on September 29, 1995. Sargeant thus obtained a loan from United for $134,700. The mortgage had an adjustable interest rate with an initial rate of interest of 10.99%. The loan provided that the rate could be adjusted upward one percent every six months with a maximum interest rate of 16.99%. The initial annual percentage rate charged on the mortgage was 13.556%. The loan proceeds were disbursed as follows: $15,681 was applied to the home improvements upon their completion; $4,910 was applied to pay off credit card debt; and $93,000 was applied to two prior mortgages on her residence.[1] According to the settlement statement, Sargeant was assessed a brokerage fee payable to United in the sum of $13,461.40. United claims that this entry is incorrect and that the $13,461.40 was paid to United as an origination fee or "points." Sargeant was also charged a broker's fee in the amount of $4,150 made payable to McIntyre.

1. One of the mortgages totaled $88,000 to AFSCI and the other totaled $5,000 to Foremost Servicing Company, Inc. Sargeant claims that she was not making any payments in connection with the $5,000 mortgage and alleges that she did not have any obligation to do so.

Her total closing costs and fees equaled $23,029.87. Her initial mortgage payments were $1,281. Her previous mortgage payments were $956 per month.

Sargeant fell behind in the repayment of her loan and United initiated foreclosure proceedings against her. Sargeant then filed a consumer complaint with the Consumer Protection and Antitrust Division of the Massachusetts Attorney General's Office.

After the filing of this Complaint, the Attorney General, on behalf of the Commonwealth of Massachusetts, commenced an action against United in the Massachusetts Superior Court sitting in and for the county of Suffolk seeking, inter alia, to enjoin United 1) from making any mortgage loans in violation of Mass. Gen. Laws ch. 184, §17D and the Mortgage Brokers and Mortgage Lenders Regulations of the Attorney General, 904 C.M.R. §8.00 et seq., and 2) from making any mortgage loans in violation of Mass. Gen. Laws ch. 183, §63. A preliminary injunction issued in that case on January 24, 1997, prohibiting United from taking any further action in foreclosing on Sargeant's property and requiring it to notify the Commonwealth thirty days prior to a foreclosure sale on any other residential property. *See* Commonwealth of Massachusetts v. United Cos. Lending Corp., Civil Action No. 96-7070-F.

At this point, United went forum shopping. *Cf.* Coady v. Ashcraft & Gerel, 996 F. Supp. 95, 98-99 (D. Mass. 1998). It commenced this defendant class action suit against Daisy Sargeant and all persons similarly situated, seeking a declaratory judgment that 940 C.M.R. §8.06(6) is void and unenforceable, that the mortgage loan origination fee or points charged to Sargeant were lawful and proper, and that a judgment of default against Sargeant on the mortgage note was therefore appropriate. Sargeant counterclaimed, asking for a declaration that the mortgage transaction was an unfair or deceptive act because it was unconscionable pursuant to 940 CMR §8.06(6), and that rescission of the mortgage loan is therefore permissible. . . .

II. Discussion

Pursuant to his authority under the Massachusetts General Laws, the Attorney General has the authority to make rules and regulations interpreting what acts or practices by mortgage lenders and brokers are unfair or deceptive and, therefore, illegal under Mass. Gen. Laws ch. 93A, §2(a). *See* Mass. Gen. Laws ch. 93A, §2(c). "Such rules and regulations shall not be inconsistent with the rules, regulations and decisions of the Federal Trade Commission and the federal courts interpreting the provisions of 15 U.S.C. 45(a)(1)." *Id.* Whether the Attorney General has acted within the confines of such authority in the promulgation of a regulation thus requires this Court to make two sequential assessments. First, is the regulation consistent with the decisions of the Federal Trade Commission and the federal courts interpreting 15 U.S.C. 45(a)(1)? If so, is the Regulation arbitrary, capricious, or manifestly contrary to the state statute?

Here, the Attorney General has promulgated regulations governing the activities of mortgage brokers and mortgage lenders which apply to "any mortgage lender or broker advertising or doing business within Massachusetts, regardless of whether or not the lender or broker maintains an office in Massachusetts." 940 C.M.R. 8.02. Regulation 8.06(6) ("the Regulation"), which became effective August 1, 1992, states that:

> It is an unfair or deceptive practice for a mortgage broker or lender to procure or negotiate for a borrower a mortgage loan with rates or terms which *significantly deviate from industry-wide standards or which are otherwise unconscionable.* (emphasis added).

This is the regulation that United challenges in this case.

A. CONSISTENCY WITH LEGISLATIVE INTENT

. . . .

The Regulation, consistent with the Attorney General's rule-making authority, provides a basis for interpreting whether the charging of points is an unfair or deceptive practice.

The fact that the charging of points is permissible where there is disclosure, without requiring the direct correlation between the amount charged and the services rendered, does not imply that such points may be charged without limit or that the charging of certain points does not constitute an unfair act. The Attorney General's regulations may proscribe even good faith business practices that could be unfair or deceptive. . . .

B. CONSISTENCY WITH APPLICABLE FEDERAL LAW

Having concluded that the Regulation is in force, the Court must now consider whether it is void. United argues that the Regulation is void because the definition of unfair or deceptive practice as defined by the Regulation is inconsistent with the rules, regulations, and decisions of the Federal Trade Commission and the federal courts interpreting the provisions of 15 U.S.C. 45(a)(1).

In 1964, the Federal Trade Commission issued a policy statement articulating a three-prong test for whether a practice is unfair or deceptive. . . . The three-prong . . . test considers whether a practice 1) causes substantial injury to consumers, 2) violates established public policy, or 3) is immoral, unethical, oppressive, or unscrupulous.

In December, 1980, in response to congressional inquiry concerning the scope of the Federal Trade Commission's unfairness jurisdiction under 15 U.S.C. §45(a)(1), the Commissioners submitted to Congress a policy statement on the definition of consumer unfairness in order "to provide a greater sense of certainty about what the Commission would regard as an unfair act or practice under [15 U.S.C. §45(a)(1)]." Letter from the Federal Trade Commission to the Honorable Wendell H. Ford and the Honorable

John C. Danforth (Dec. 17, 1980) reprinted in H.R.Rep. No. 156, Pt. 1, 98th Cong. 34 (1983) ("Policy Statement").

. . . First, [the Policy Statement] gives greater clarification to the consumer injury portion of the test. Consumer injury is substantial when 1) the harm is neither trivial nor merely speculative and, generally, involves monetary harm; 2) the injury is not outweighed by countervailing consumer or competitive benefits of the practice; 3) the injury is not reasonably avoidable by a consumer.

The second part of the . . . test—violation of an established public policy—is reaffirmed in the Policy Statement. . . . The subsequent articulation of the FTC unfairness test indicates that the public policy prong is supplemental to the consumer injury prong and not independent of it. *See* Federal Trade Commission, Credit Practices Rule Statement of Basis and Purpose and Regulatory Analysis, 49 Fed. Reg. 7740, 7743 (1984) ("Credit Practices Statement"). "Consumer injury is the central element of any inquiry regarding unfairness." *Id.*

The third prong of the . . . test—unethical or unscrupulous conduct—is abandoned in the Policy Statement as the Commissioners deemed this prong to be duplicative. "Conduct that is truly unethical or unscrupulous will almost always injure consumers or violate public policy as well. The Commission has therefore never relied on the third element . . . as an independent basis for finding of unfairness, and it will act in the future only on the basis of the first two." Policy Stmt. at 40.

In this case, the consumer injury at issue is a monetary harm. The Attorney General's Regulation attempts to prevent the charging of excessive origination fees or points in residential mortgage loan transactions which increase the debt obligation of the consumer and the potential for default. United argues that a limitation on the permissible origination fee or points charged would cause United either to charge a higher interest rate, thus increasing the cost of the loan to the consumer, or to withdraw from the Massachusetts mortgage market altogether, with the consequence that consumers like Sargeant could not obtain the loans and necessary credit to "get back on their feet." United argues that this cost outweighs the benefits of the Regulation and that the Regulation is thus inconsistent with the applicable Federal law. This Court disagrees.

Evidence in the record indicates that in 1995, the period when the loan transaction took place, the majority of subprime lenders did not charge ten points on loans but rather charged five points or less. . . . Although points may be necessary to raise the loan yield in order to obtain a return that is competitive with other types of loans, a two-fold increase above the average points charged by subprime market lenders is not necessary to achieve this objective, especially when the mortgage loan is an adjustable rate mortgage as opposed to a fixed mortgage.

United avers that market forces will ensure fairness in mortgage broker and lending practices . . . .

The economic circumstances surrounding the enactment of the Regulation establish the fallacy of this argument. With the abandonment of the inner-city neighborhoods by mainstream lending institutions during the 1970s and 1980s, the deregulation of the banking industry, the appreciation of real estate values in Massachusetts, and the rise of secondary mortgage market, the groundwork was laid for the lending practices that fueled the home improvement and second mortgage lending scams of the 1980s and early 1990s. . . . The new credit device was not without flaws, as the increase in home equity financing was paralleled by an increase in foreclosures. [Julia Patterson Forrester, *Mortgaging the American Dream: A Critical Evaluation of the Federal Government's Promotion of Home Equity Financing*,] 69 Tul. L. Rev. 373, 381-82 & n.38 (1994). Some of these foreclosures were precipitated by the unscrupulous behavior of unregulated mortgage brokers and lenders who engaged in predatory lending practices that included offering high-rate and high-fee loans to borrowers who lacked access to mainstream banks because of redlining practices, had marginal credit histories, and had limited financial sophistication.

> The targets of predatory lenders are usually people who have substantial equity in their homes due to rising real estate values or due to the reduction of purchase money debt, but who are short on cash because of their low or fixed incomes. They may need money to make home repairs or improvements, to pay for necessities such as medical care, or to consolidate household debts. These homeowners generally do not obtain home equity loans primarily for their tax advantages but because borrowing against their homes is the only way that they can obtain the credit they need to make home repairs or to survive periods of economic distress. Those most often affected are minorities, the elderly, and the inner-city and rural poor.

Id. at 387-89. . . .

Redlining and reverse redlining[5] by banks, savings and loans, finance companies, and second mortgage companies impede the self-correcting elements of the market, rendering it unable to prevent consumer injury. This market failure prevents the borrower from taking action reasonably to avoid the financial pitfalls created by predatory lending. Mortgage lending practices in Massachusetts during the eighties and early nineties represented an instance of market failure. Government intervention to address this failing was appropriate. . . .

5. Redlining is the practice of denying the extension of credit to specific geographic areas due to the income, race, or ethnicity of its residents. The term was derived from the actual practice of drawing a red line around certain areas in which credit would be denied. Reverse redlining is the practice of extending credit on unfair terms to those same communities. *See* S. Rep. No. 103-169, at 21 (1993), reprinted in 1994 U.S.C.C.A.N. 1881, 1905; *see also* Reverse Redlining: Problems in Home Equity Lending Before the Senate Committee on Banking, Housing, and Urban Affairs, 103rd Cong. 243-471 (1993).

Mortgage scams and predatory lending are most common in those states lacking sufficient legal and regulatory structures. . . .

The failure of the mortgage lending market to self-correct means injury to the borrower was not reasonably avoidable. . . . [W]here there is market failure, negotiability is a blunt instrument. This truth is at the core of both regulatory and legislative action to regulate the mortgage broker and lending industry. As the consumer injury caused by reverse redlining and predatory lending is substantial, is not outweighed by countervailing benefits, and is not reasonably avoidable by the borrower, a determination that such conduct is unfair is consistent with the rules, regulations, and interpretations of the Federal Trade Commission. . . .

This Court concludes that the Regulation is not inconsistent with the pronouncement of the Federal Trade Commission or federal courts' construing of 15 U.S.C. §45(a)(1). . . .

D. ARBITRARY AND CAPRICIOUS APPLICATION OF THE REGULATION

United argues that the Attorney General inappropriately applies the Regulation by focusing on the points charged and not the cost of the entire transaction to the consumer. United asserts that the number of points charged was necessary in order for the annual percentage rate to be 13.556%. . . . Any rate or term in a mortgage loan that substantially deviates from industry-wide standard or is otherwise unconscionable violates the Regulation. . . .

CONCLUSION

1. For the reasons stated herein, this Court declares that the Regulation is valid and enforceable.

2. The origination fee charged by United constituted an unfair and deceptive trade practice as the points charged substantially deviated from industry-wide practice in Massachusetts. Therefore, Sargeant is entitled to actual damages of $13,461.40 plus interest. McIntyre was not entitled to a brokerage fee as he failed to provide Sargeant with the requisite disclosure. Such failure to disclose constitutes an unfair and deceptive trade practice in violation of Mass. Gen. Laws ch. 93A, §2(a) and a violation of the disclosure requirements of Mass. Gen. Laws ch. 183, §63. Therefore, Sargeant is entitled to actual damages of $4,150 plus interest. Sargeant is also entitled to reasonable attorney's fees in prosecuting to her Chapter 93A claims. . . .

Problem 15A

Your bank client comes to you for advice. The client is concerned about a potential law suit that it has heard people talking about in the community. The bank officer has heard that the bank may be sued on behalf of low-income borrowers because it tends to make few loans to borrowers who want to buy low cost housing. The banker explains that it costs as much for the bank to make a small loan as it does to make a big loan. The labor time, overhead, and expense is basically the same on all loans. At the same time, the bank earns money by charging fees and points and this income is much more profitable on the big loans. As a result, the bank tries to make big loans and avoid small ones. The bank also pays its loan officers a percentage commission on all loan applications that get approved for funding. Since the loan officers work on commission, they prefer the opportunity for originating big loans. The result is that less than 2 percent of the loans originated by the bank are for a dollar amount less than $200,000.

Your client seeks advice on the potential problems that might be raised by this situation. The client also wants to know if it will be appropriate to make more low cost housing loans, provided that the bank can charge the borrower a higher interest rate or more fees, so as to enhance the profitability of the small loans. The client explains that while small loans produce an accounting profit, they really do not produce an economic profit unless the bank can charge these borrowers more for a loan.

B. PRIMARY MORTGAGE MARKETS

The mortgage market is comprised of four general segments or sectors: (1) saving by households and others, (2) lending by organizations and institutions, (3) borrowing by households and others, and (4) selling mortgages and notes through the secondary market. In this section, we focus on the relationship among these segments, particularly the first three segments, which constitute the primary mortgage market. The primary mortgage market is the market for originating loans with individual borrowers. A more complete discussion of segment four, the secondary mortgage market, is taken up in the next section of this chapter. Understanding the basic market relationships is essential to a real estate and mortgage law practice. Diagram 15-3 illustrates the relationships among these market segments and also refers to alternative capital markets, which are explained in the following text.

In Diagram 15-3, the intermediaries are the financial institutions and lenders that make funds available for real estate activities. These intermediaries generally include banks, savings and loans, mortgage companies, insurance companies, and pension funds. Each of these intermediaries takes in assets from savers. Banks and financial institutions use deposit accounts, certificates of deposit, and other investment vehicles to attract savings and investment assets. Having attracted these assets, the intermediaries look for ways to profit from their holding of the resources, and one way they do this is by making loans to real estate borrowers. These loans are seen as investments because they will be paid back with an interest return. Thus, the intermediary is a market facilitator who takes in large sums of money that are then used for lending purposes. This is an important and cost-effective way of putting savers and borrowers together.

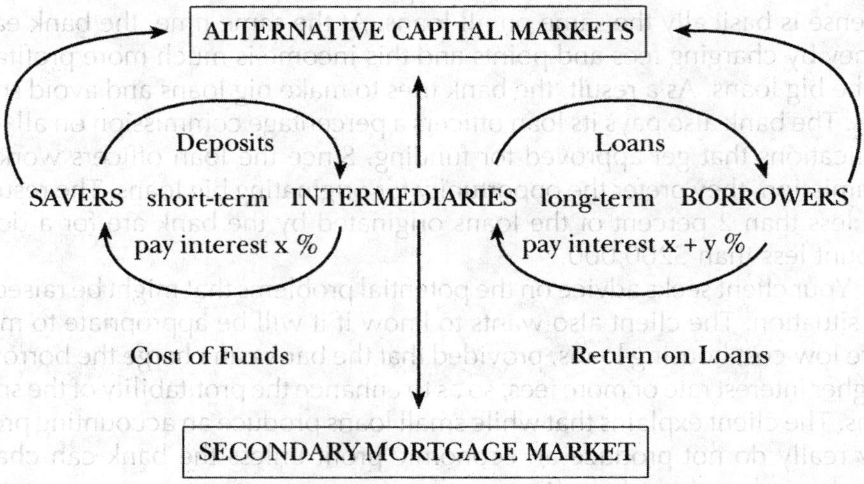

Diagram 15-3

Savers are looking at a variety of ways in which they can save money and earn a return on their investment. They may consider deposits to checking, savings, or money market accounts. They may look at certificates of deposit, commercial paper, time instruments, stocks, bonds, whole life insurance, or special retirement accounts. In each instance, the saver is considering the return that will be provided for saving in a particular investment form. Some forms of saving will be more risky than others, such as the difference between an insured bank deposit account and a stock investment in a start-up technology company. The saver will compare risk and return between these options and make a selection knowing that the greatest returns are likely to be found in the riskiest investments.

The main point here, however, is that savings fluctuate over the short run, and the ability to attract savers rests on a need continually to offer competitive returns to the people who invest. Cost of funds to intermediaries, therefore, are short-term market sensitive.

Borrowers in our diagram include property buyers, including homebuyers and real estate developers. Although there are many other types of borrowing in our economy, we are concerned with borrowing directed at real estate activities.

Unlike savings, the lending side of our diagram is usually a long-term activity. For example, people deposit and spend their paychecks weekly or monthly, but they borrow for 3 to 5 years to purchase an automobile or for 15 to 30 years when they borrow to buy a home. This means that with respect to real estate activities, the intermediaries have a time horizon imbalance, because their cost of funds is affected by short-term swings in the market while their returns are structured to long-term obligations. The lending side of the equation for a lender involves not only risk of default by the borrower but also long-term uncertainty about inflation and money markets. Pegging the interest rate on a long-term fixed rate loan can be difficult, and if the lender sets the rate too low at the outset, it may end up losing a lot of money.

C. SECONDARY MORTGAGE MARKETS

1. Reduced Risk, Enhanced Liquidity

Secondary mortgage activity has reduced lender risk and enhanced liquidity. The secondary mortgage market created an easy way in which lenders could diversify their investment portfolios by making it easy for a New York lender to buy California mortgages or securities backed by such mortgages. In this way lenders became better able to smooth out their profit expectation by creating investment "baskets" with "eggs" gathered from many different markets. The use of mortgage-backed and mortgage-related securities also made the lender's portfolio more liquid because these securities were in a form that could be readily sold in an open market. The market for such security devices is far more liquid than the market for thousands of individual residential mortgages.

A further benefit of enhanced diversity and liquidity from the secondary mortgage market is the ability to move capital to areas of expanding real estate activity. For instance, people in the Northeast might be saving more money with lending institutions than is needed to supply local borrowing needs for real estate activities. At the same time, there may be a boom in building activity in the Southeast and not enough local savings to fund all the potentially desirable projects. The secondary mortgage market facilitates the easy flow of capital between regions and thus helps move funds to the areas of highest demand at lower cost than was possible prior to the development of this market.

A second benefit of the secondary mortgage market has been added uniformity of mortgage forms and law among the various states. The need to standardize mortgages for ease of investment opportunity has simplified the practice of residential real estate law and in some ways has helped make the real estate market move in the direction of other commercial markets. The reduced complexity opens the door to more transactions at lower costs and creates ownership and investment opportunities for an expanding number of individuals and groups.

The third key implication of the secondary mortgage market is that it has changed the structure of lending activity. Most lenders now sell the majority of their loans to investors in the secondary mortgage market. This, in turn, has several implications. First, the lenders must view their secondary mortgage market investors as their key customer base. Thus, they must make their mortgage terms and options respond to what investors would like to buy rather than to the needs or desires of particular local home loan applicants.

This change in the structure of the lending practice has had a great impact on how lenders make their profits. Rather than holding loans and profiting by collecting interest based on the loan terms, lenders have increasingly concentrated on upfront fee-generating activities. Now, many lenders think in terms of processing loan applications and loan originations for a fee. They pocket the fee and sell the loan using the incoming funds from the sale as the source of additional capital for further lending. In this way the lending business becomes a highly service-oriented process in which profit is made on churning paper and money between borrowers and secondary market investors. In short, the lenders have positioned themselves out of being the end investor in the loan and instead now make substantial money by being intermediaries to a market that was virtually nonexistent prior to 1970.

The diagram of the secondary mortgage market in Diagram 15-4 may help make our discussion a little more understandable.

In the secondary market, the prices paid by investors for mortgages are highly sensitive to market conditions and may fluctuate weekly or even daily. Mortgages are generally sold at a discount from "par," with par meaning full face value on the loan. The discount rate is established by the participants in the secondary mortgage market as sellers and investors make exchanges. If a mortgage is to be purchased at par, rather than at a discount, the buyer will generally charge a fee. Thus, a loan can be sold at less than face value (at a discount) or, in the alternative, at par with a fee paid to the buyer. For example, a large investor might purchase mortgages at par provided a 1/2 percent fee is paid against the face value of the loans, or it might purchase the mortgages at a 1/2 percent discount from par.

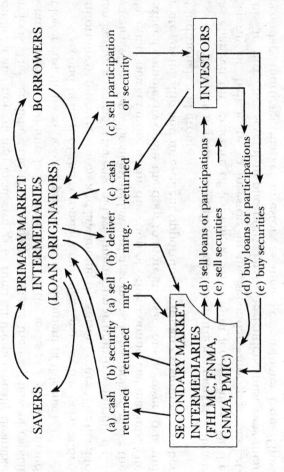

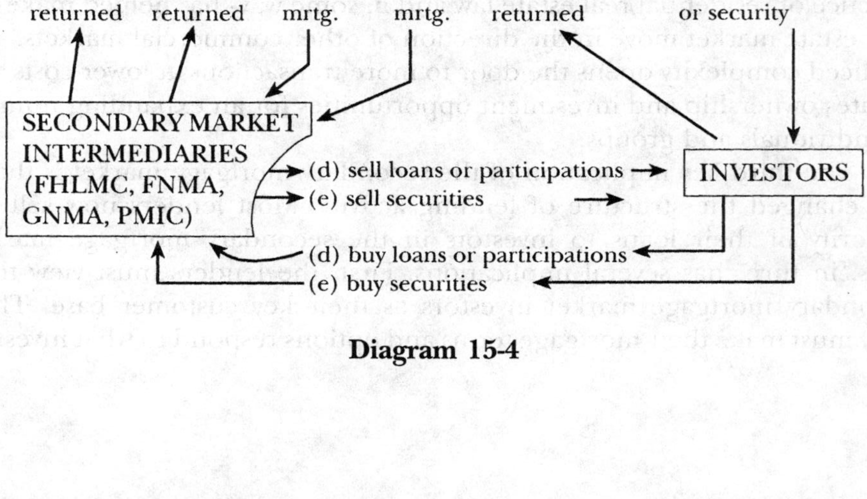

Diagram 15-4

The discount rates used in the secondary market are related to the borrower's payment of "points," which are fees collected by lenders in the primary mortgage market to cover a number of their expenses and to generate profit. Points are discussed in more detail in the next section of this chapter. When a lender quotes the points or fees to prospective borrowers, it takes into account the present discount rates and fees for selling mortgages at par in the secondary market. Thus, if it anticipates selling to the investor at par with a 1/2 percent fee, it adds this charge to its quote: the borrower in effect pays the secondary mortgage market fee, and the lender makes a profit by serving as intermediary.

One significant risk of mortgage-related securities is the prospect of a dramatic fall in market interest rates. The price paid by the investor is based on the expected stream of income that will be generated by the flow of monthly mortgage payments. To calculate the return, it is necessary to estimate the life of the loans in the pool or, in other words, to predict how long the mortgages will remain outstanding. If interest rates drop dramatically, as they did in the early 1990s to 20-year lows, many people will pay off their higher-rate mortgages by refinancing at the current lower rates. This rush to make early payoffs means that mortgages get paid off quicker than expected, and investors in mortgage-related securities may find that the income stream supporting their investment is far less than originally expected. In a similar way, a major recession that puts many borrowers into default may jeopardize the expected income stream supporting a mortgage-related security.

D. MORTGAGE PRODUCTS

Now that you have a general understanding of what the mortgage markets look like and how the money gets there, we will examine a number of mortgage products that are commonly offered in the residential real estate market. Before looking at specific types of mortgages, however, we will first consider three related topics: the concept of *points*; the *APR, or annual percentage rate*; and the matter of *mortgage insurance.*

1. Points and Annual Percentage Rate (APR)

Institutional lenders that make home mortgage loans usually require the borrower to pay upfront fees called *points.* Instead of the term *points,* in the formal paperwork lenders typically identify these fees using more official names such as "loan processing fee," "loan discount," or "loan origination fee," but they all mean the same thing. Points are charged in addition to the interest on the loan and any other specific charges for such things as an application fee, credit check, survey, or title examination. One point is equal to 1 percent of the loan amount. A point is also referred to as 100 *basis points.* Thus, one point charged for a $100,000 loan is $1,000, and if instead the lender charged 50 basis points, that would be the same as ½ point or $500.

The borrower must pay the specified points before the loan is funded, so lenders collect them at or before the loan closing. They may be paid in one of two ways. Most commonly, the lender discounts the points by subtracting them from the face amount of the loan and disbursing funds equal to the difference. Alternatively, some lenders require that the borrower use out-of-pocket cash to pay the points. Only in the rare instance when the lender requires the borrower to pay points on a certain date before the loan closing does it matter which way they are collected. The attorney or closing officer, however, should confirm how the points are to be assessed so that she can advise the borrower how much cash she must bring to the closing.

The *APR*, or *annual percentage rate*, is a calculation of the cost of a loan using a federal formula set forth in the Real Estate Settlement Procedures Act (RESPA), 12 U.S.C. §§2601-2617, enacted in 1974. All the points and other expenses the lender requires the borrower to pay are treated as if they were interest, and the lender must add them to the stated interest to compute the "real" rate of interest or cost of the loan. Under RESPA, prior to closing the lender must disclose to the borrower the APR in addition to the quoted rate of interest that will appear in the promissory note. A primary purpose of the federal regulation is to foster competition by getting all lenders to use the same method and report the APR using the same format. Thus, borrowers receive standardized information about the cost of possible loans so that they can comparison shop.

KANE v. EQUITY ONE, INC.

United States District Court, Eastern District of Pennsylvania, 2003
2003 U.S. Dist. LEXIS 23810

SCHILLER, J. Plaintiff Mary Kane brought this action alleging violations of the federal Truth-In-Lending Act ("TILA"), 15 U.S.C. §§1601-1693, by Equity One, Inc. ("Equity One") and Sovereign Bank, ("Sovereign"), and violation of state laws relating to lender liability by Equity One and Michael J. Frankenfield d/b/a Tri-State Financial Services ("Tri-State"). Presently before this Court are Defendant Equity One's and Defendant Sovereign's motions to dismiss. . . .

I. BACKGROUND

This case concerns residential mortgage loan financing provided to Plaintiff Mary Kane on June 8, 2000. Plaintiff alleges that a broker from Tri-State solicited her to refinance a wrap-around mortgage that included both her own home and the home of her son, Derrick Kane. According to Plaintiff, she went to the offices of Equity One to sign the loan documents with the expectation that the transaction would be structured as one loan. Despite her expectations and without explanation, the transaction was split into two separate loan documents with separate Federal Truth-in-Lending Disclosure Statements and Settlement Statements. The larger of the two loans was for $48,805 at an annual percentage rate ("APR") of 11.489 percent and a term of 15 years. The second loan was for $9,710 at an APR of 14.257 percent and a term of 10 years. Additionally, Plaintiff alleges that the smaller loan included a charge of $1415.55 for a gas bill despite the fact that Equity One also assessed this charge in a separate loan that was extended to Mr. Derrick Kane, Plaintiff's son, on the same date. Approximately one month after the loans were extended, Equity One sold both loans to Sovereign Bank. Thereafter, on March 24, 2003, Plaintiff's counsel contacted both Equity One and Sovereign asserting Plaintiff's right to rescind the loan pursuant to TILA. To date, Sovereign has not responded to Plaintiff's request for rescission. . . .

A. CLAIMS AGAINST DEFENDANT EQUITY ONE

1. TILA

Plaintiff alleges that Equity One violated TILA by structuring her mortgage refinancing as two separate loan transactions instead of as one closed-end transaction in accordance with her expectations. Defendant Equity One responds that TILA permits lenders to structure a transaction as two separate loans with separate disclosures. Equity One's contentions are correct provided that the borrower expected that the transaction would be structured in that manner. However, a lender may violate TILA if a borrower expected to receive a single loan executed in one transaction and nonetheless received two separate loans. *See* Hemauer v. ITT Fin. Servs., 751 F. Supp. 1241, 1243-44 (W.D. Ky. 1990) (finding lender violated TILA by executing two loans for one transaction on same day despite fact that borrowers only made one request for loan).

Although the Third Circuit has not yet encountered a case alleging "loan splitting" under TILA, other courts have found that such practices violate TILA's mandate that the lender provide a single, comprehensible disclosure of the cost of credit. 12 C.F.R. §226.17(a) (2003) (requiring that lenders group all disclosures for single transaction in one writing). . . . These courts describe "loan splitting" as "a situation where the debtor wants, requests and expects to get a single loan consummated in a single transaction, but the lender instead documents and makes disclosures for the loan as if it were two separate transactions." . . .

. . . At this stage of the proceedings, this allegation is sufficient to make out a case of loan splitting . . . I accordingly deny the motion to dismiss Plaintiff's TILA claims against Equity One.

2. Home Ownership and Equal Protection Act

In 1994, TILA was augmented by the Home Ownership and Equity Protection Act ("HOEPA"), which requires additional disclosures for certain high-cost loans. Pub. L. No. 103-325, tit. I, §151, 108 Stat. 2190 (1994) (amending 15 U.S.C. §1601-02, 1604, 1610, 1639-41, 1648). HOEPA applies to consumer credit transactions that are secured by the consumer's principal dwelling, other than a residential mortgage transaction, a reverse mortgage transaction, or a transaction under an open-end credit plan, if:

> (A) the annual percentage rate at consummation of the transaction will exceed by more than 10 percentage points the yield on Treasury securities having comparable periods of maturity on the fifteenth day of the month immediately preceding the month in which the application for the extension of credit is received by the creditor; or
>
> (B) the total points and fees payable by the consumer at or before closing will exceed the greater of-
>
> (i) 8 percent of the total loan amount; or
>
> (ii) $ 400.

15 U.S.C. §1602(aa) (2003).

Plaintiff contends that if the two loans had in fact been executed as one loan, with the same percentage of equity and with the gas bill included as a finance charge, then the single hypothetical consolidated loan would violate HOEPA. Therefore, Plaintiff suggests, Equity One violated HOEPA by failing to provide the required disclosures for this high-cost loan transaction. . . . Although Plaintiff has not identified, and the Court has not uncovered, any case law applying HOEPA in the context of a loan-splitting allegation in which the two loans, if combined, would be covered by the HOEPA provisions, this Court cannot dismiss Plaintiff's novel claim as a matter of law at this time. . . .

B. CLAIMS AGAINST ASSIGNEE DEFENDANT SOVEREIGN

Plaintiff asserts that Sovereign, as the assignee of both loans, is liable for TILA violations in the original credit transaction and for failing to rescind the transaction. As fully discussed below, I find that Plaintiff has not alleged a set of facts that would subject Sovereign as an assignee to liability for TILA violations in the original loan transaction. Sovereign is, however, subject to Plaintiff's claim for rescission.

1. Assignee Liability under TILA's General Provisions

Plaintiff alleges in her Amended Complaint that, by virtue of the fact that there were two separate loans, Sovereign "knew or should have known that this was unusual or irregular and that misrepresentations were likely to have been made in the course of the transaction." Furthermore, Plaintiff states that, through inspection of the loan documents, "Sovereign did or should have noticed the questionable nature of the charges referenced herein and should have been alerted to the fact that it was likely that TILA violations pervaded this transaction." Specifically, the "questionable charge" Plaintiff refers to is the alleged double payment of the gas bill.

TILA imposes assignee liability in consumer credit transactions secured by real property only if the violation is "apparent on the face of the disclosure statement." 15 U.S.C. §1641(e)(1)(A) (2003). Section 1641(e) further explains that a violation is apparent on the face of the disclosure statement if:

> (A) the disclosure can be determined to be incomplete or inaccurate by a comparison among the disclosure statement, any itemization of the amount financed, the note, or any other disclosure of disbursement; or
>
> (B) the disclosure statement does not use the terms or format required to be used by this subchapter.

15 U.S.C. §1641(e)(2)(A), (B) (2003).

Plaintiff's allegations fail to state a claim of assignee liability under TILA for two reasons. First, TILA's assignee liability provision expressly limits liability to violations apparent on the face of the assigned documents. Plaintiff fails to allege any violations apparent on the face of the assigned loan documents. . . .

Second, the Third Circuit has held that TILA's assignee liability provisions do not impose any duty of additional inquiry on assignees. Ramadan v. Chase Manhattan Corp., 229 F.3d 194, 198 (3d Cir. 2000). . . .

In sum, the gravamen of Plaintiff's Amended Complaint — that Equity One violated TILA by structuring the transaction as two separate loans despite Plaintiff's belief that only one loan would be extended — is predicated on the borrower's subjective expectation and therefore is not apparent in the documents describing the transaction that was executed. Thus, even taking her allegations as true, Plaintiff has failed to state a claim of assignee liability under TILA.

2. Assignee Liability under HOEPA Provisions

Under TILA, HOEPA loan assignees are subjected to a broader standard of liability than assignees of non-HOEPA loans. *See* Cooper v. First Gov't Mortg. and Investors Corp., 238 F. Supp. 2d 50, 55 (D.D.C. 2002). The provision for assignee liability for HOEPA loans provides as follows:

> Any person who purchases or is otherwise assigned a [HOEPA] mortgage . . . shall be subject to all claims and defenses with respect to that mortgage that the consumer could assert against the creditor of the mortgage, unless the purchaser or assignee demonstrates, by a preponderance of the evidence, that a reasonable person exercising ordinary due diligence, could not determine, based on the documentation required by this subchapter, the itemization of

> the amount financed, and other disclosure of disbursements that the mortgage was a mortgage [subject to HOEPA].

15 U.S.C. §1641(d)(1) (2003).

. . . Although Plaintiff's contention raises factual issues that compel this Court to deny Equity One's motion to dismiss the HOEPA claims asserted against it at this time, Plaintiff's allegations are clearly not sufficient to state a claim of assignee liability against Sovereign. As discussed above, Plaintiff's loan documents only contained one assessment of the gas bill charge. Thus, there is no way that Sovereign could have determined, based solely on the documentation of the loan, the itemization of the amount financed and other disclosure of disbursements that this loan was a HOEPA loan.

3. Rescission by [*sic*] Assignee

Plaintiff seeks rescission of the loan as well as $2,000 in statutory damages and an award of attorney's fees and costs for Sovereign's refusal to respond to Plaintiff's notice of rescission. Under TILA, a borrower who has a right to rescind against the original lender also has the right to rescind against any assignee. 15 U.S.C. §1641(c) (2003). When a lender takes a security interest in a borrower's principal dwelling in exchange for credit, TILA permits the borrower to rescind the transaction until three business days after the consummation of the transaction or the delivery of the material disclosures required by the statute, whichever is later. 15 U.S.C. §1635(a) (2003). If the lender does not give the required disclosures, the borrower's right to rescind expires three years after the consummation of the transaction or upon the sale of the property, whichever is first. 15 U.S.C. §1635(f) (2003). Failure to disclose the proper finance charge, amount financed, APR, total payments, or payment schedule constitutes a material violation which entitles the borrower to rescind the loan. 15 U.S.C. §1635(a); 12 C.F.R. §226.23(a)(3); *see* Brodo v. Bankers Trust Co., 847 F. Supp. 353, 356 (E.D. Pa. 1994). Within twenty days of receiving notice of the borrower's intent to rescind, the lender, or subsequent assignee, must "return . . . any money or property given as earnest money, downpayment, or otherwise, and [must] take any action necessary or appropriate to reflect the termination of any security interest created under the transaction." 15 U.S.C. §1635(b). Violation of the obligations under this section constitutes a separate TILA violation. 15 U.S.C. §1635(g).

While Plaintiff may assert a valid claim for rescission against Sovereign if she can prove a material violation of TILA's requirements by the original lender, the language of the statute does not permit an award of statutory damages or attorney's fees against an assignee for failure to respond to a valid rescission notice. *See Brodo*, 847 F. Supp. at 359 ("Congress did not wish to impose liability for damages and attorney's fees on an assignee who was not responsible for and who had no notice of TILA disclosure violations at the time of an assignment.") Although *§1641(c)* provides that a material violation by a creditor creates a right to rescind against the creditor's assignee, TILA's civil liability provision only permits "creditors" to be held liable for a monetary penalty or award of attorney's fees for a TILA violation. 15 U.S.C. §1640(a); *Brodo*, 847 F. Supp. at 359. Neither *§1641(c)* nor any other provision of the TILA provides for a statutory penalty or award of attorney's fees against an assignee for failure to respond to a valid rescission notice. *See Brodo*, 847 F. Supp. at 359. In the absence of such authority, this Court must dismiss Plaintiff's claim against Sovereign for statutory damages and attorneys fees. Plaintiff may proceed, however, with her claim for rescission against Sovereign.

Therefore, Plaintiff has failed to state a claim for assignee liability under the general provisions of TILA or under HOEPA. Plaintiff's claim for statutory damages, attorney's fees and costs against Sovereign is dismissed. Plaintiff may proceed against Sovereign only for rescission. . . .

For the foregoing reasons, I deny Defendant Equity One's motion to dismiss and grant in part and deny in part Sovereign's motion to dismiss. . . .

2. Mortgage Insurance

Mortgage insurance protects a residential lender against risk of loss in the event a borrower defaults and the property is sold through foreclosure for a price less than the outstanding debt. Mortgage insurance should not be confused with title insurance or casualty insurance, nor should it be confused with "mortgage insurance" that pays off your loan balance if you die. The death benefit form of mortgage insurance is typically offered by a loan officer when making the loan or by an independent salesperson who obtains the borrower's name and address from the mortgage instrument when it is recorded after the loan closing. This type of mortgage insurance is really a form of term life insurance, and loan officers and other salespeople frequently receive commissions for selling it to borrowers.

Generally, lenders will require mortgage insurance for any loan that exceeds 80 percent of the appraised value of the property. Mortgage insurance is designed to protect the lender from a decline in property value. It is also a way of hedging against the inaccuracy of property appraisals when loans are made for a large percentage of their estimated value. For loans that are less than 80 percent of the appraised value of the property, lenders do not normally require mortgage insurance. The 20 percent or greater equity cushion is typically considered sufficient for purposes of protecting a lender from most reasonably predictable declines in a property's value.

There are two major forms of mortgage insurance that a real estate attorney is likely to encounter. The first is mortgage insurance offered by the public sector, including FHA (Federal Housing Administration) and VA (Veterans Administration) insurance. The FHA insures loans made to homebuyers for reasonably priced homes; there are purchase price caps for eligibility related to median home prices in an area. The FHA has specific underwriting guidelines that must be followed to qualify for its insurance program. Assuming the guidelines are followed, borrowers are generally allowed to take out a loan for as much as 95 percent of the purchase price. There are also some special government programs and variations that allow a borrower to borrow as much as 98 percent of the purchase price. The borrower pays the cost of FHA mortgage insurance at closing as a one-time fee. If the mortgage is paid off in the first several years, the borrower can usually get a predetermined percentage of the prepaid insurance fee refunded. FHA insurance is 100 percent insurance. This means that it covers the lender for the full amount of the loan. The VA plan is similar, with the program enabling veterans to obtain 100 percent financing, backed by a VA guaranty that the lender will be fully paid in the event of foreclosure. Both the FHA and VA plans enable home purchases with higher loan-to-value ratios than are generally available for conventional loans, which means that particularly high risks are covered by these plans.

The second type of insurance is private mortgage insurance (PMI), which lenders require for conventional loans that exceed 80 percent of the appraised value of the property. The borrower generally pays for PMI on a monthly basis at a set premium, which is added to the monthly sum for principal, interest, and escrow charges for items such as real estate taxes and casualty insurance. Once the outstanding mortgage debt on the property falls below 80 percent of the appraised value (equity now exceeds 20 percent), the borrower has the right to have the PMI discontinued, thereby reducing the amount of the monthly check sent to the lender. PMI does not provide 100 percent insurance coverage for the lender. Typically, PMI will cover 20 to 25 percent of the value of the property. Thus, if a property should for some reason drop in value by 40 percent, the insurer covers only part of the loss, with the lender absorbing the excess. It is usually the lender's obligation first to bring legal action against a defaulting borrower and to pursue other remedies for the collection of unpaid loan amounts. After taking these measures, the lender may make a claim on the insurance for any shortfall. In some situations, however, the lender may be able to assign the matter to the insurer at various points in the process after a default. In such a situation, the insurer would take on more of the risk and cost of dealing with the borrower and the property. The specific rights and obligations of lender and insurer are contained in the insurance documents.

The ultimate consequence and value of mortgage insurance are that it expands the pool of potential homebuyers by reducing the need for substantial savings to be used as a down payment.

Problem 15B

(a) Janis contacts her local bank concerning a possible home mortgage loan. She is told that she can get a $200,000 loan at 9 percent plus 3 points. Explain to Janis what the 3 points are, why they are charged, and how much money is involved.

(b) Janis is told that 25 basis points of her 3 points are needed for secondary mortgage market purposes. Explain to Janis what this might mean and how much money is involved.

(c) Janis agrees to take the above quoted loan at 9 percent interest and 3 points. When she gets to the closing of her loan she is handed a piece of paper that says her APR on the loan is 10.47 percent. Janis is upset and wants to know why the bank is changing the deal from the 9 percent loan she agreed to take. Give Janis a simple explanation of what is going on and why the two rates are different, and tell her the interest rate she will actually be paying on the money borrowed according to her promissory note and mortgage. Janis also wants to know which interest rate she should use to figure her income tax mortgage deduction for mortgage interest. What will you tell her?

(d) In looking over her closing statement for this loan, Janis sees a borrower expense labeled as "PMI $42 per month." Janis turns to you as her lawyer and asks you what this is all about. Explain the item to your client.

(e) At the closing, Janis is ready to execute her mortgage when the bank hands her a document to sign which is labeled "Deed of Trust." Janis notices for the first time that some company called First Guarantee Title Co. is a party to her loan, and its name is shown in the deed of trust as the "trustee." Janis is confused because, up until this point, she has referred to mortgage financing throughout the entire transaction. Explain the situation to Janis.

3. The Fixed Rate Mortgage

Since the 1930s, the fixed rate mortgage (FRM) has served as the benchmark for housing finance. Still very popular today, the FRM offers a fixed rate of interest on the borrowed money that never changes over the life of the loan. Most FRMs are for a term of 30 years, but 25-year terms are also occasionally used. Shorter-term FRMs, sometimes referred to as "quick pay" mortgages, are commonly offered for 15-year terms. Whichever loan term is used, all monthly payments are equal in amount, and each payment consists of two parts, an interest charge for the prior month and an amount applied to reduce the principal. This is called *amortization,* meaning the borrower is paying money according to a schedule to reduce the loan balance. The FRM is said to be "self-amortizing" because if the loan goes to full term the last monthly payment will reduce the loan amount to exactly zero. Interest is "front-end loaded" in the sense that the early payments are virtually all interest with very little allocated to the reduction of principal. Each month slightly less interest is paid, with a tiny increase in principal repayment. Near the end of the loan term, most of the monthly payment goes to reduce principal rather than to pay interest. For example, consider a $200,000 fixed rate loan at 7 percent interest. On a 30-year term, the payment on such a loan will be $1,330.60 every month for the full term of the mortgage. For the first monthly payment, $1,166.67 is interest and the remaining $163.93 is principal. For the second payment, $1,165.71 is interest and $164.89 is principal. For the 360th and final payment of the 30-year term, $7.72 is interest and $1,322.88 is principal. The graph in Diagram 15-5 shows the amortization of this 30-year loan.

Although this process may seem complicated, lenders use standard amortization formulas that they must make available to the borrower. Traditionally, they used amortization tables from books, but now computer software generates amortization schedules based on the original loan amount, the rate, and the length of the term. The reason that lenders front-end load a loan is simple. Each month they want to be sure they collect all the interest they earn on the outstanding balance, and since the balance is large at first and gradually declines, they must take more interest out of the earlier payments. Borrowers may be dismayed that their early payments do so little to reduce their debt, but there is one upside. During the early years, the borrower gets a larger interest deduction for income tax purposes, with this tax benefit diminishing as the loan term progresses. Because of the time

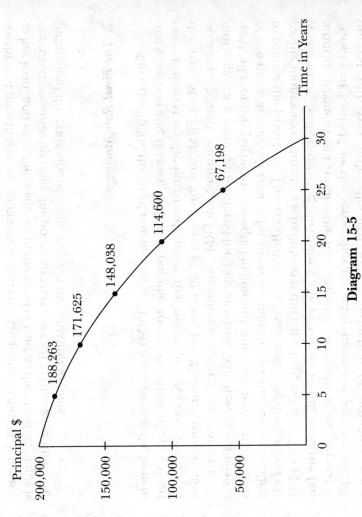

Diagram 15-5

value of money, the deductions are worth more to the borrower in the early years than if they were deferred.

The borrower's selection of the length of the term involves trade-offs. Of course, the shorter the loan term, the larger the monthly payment for the same amount borrowed. However, the shorter the term, the less the total interest paid because the borrower has not used the lender's money for as long a period of time. The difference in total cost is dramatic. Returning to our $200,000 FRM at 7 percent, in addition to paying back the original $200,000 borrowed, the borrower will also pay $279,018 in interest over the life of the loan. In contrast, consider the cost of the same loan on a 15-year term. The monthly payment would be $1,798 and it would take 15 years to fully amortize the loan. In addition to paying back the original principal amount of the loan, the borrower will pay a total of $123,579 in interest. The 30-year term mortgage ends up costing much more than twice that of the 15-year loan. Whether the borrower qualifies for the 15-year loan typically depends on her ability to pay the additional $467 per month under the lending guidelines of 28 percent and 36 percent discussed in the first part of this chapter. If a borrower can afford the higher monthly payment and wants to pay off more quickly, the 15-year mortgage can save her over $155,000. From the lender's point of view both loans are designed to be equally profitable. The reason for offering choices is to expand the market for loans by appealing to the investment and payment desires of different potential customers.

4. *The No-Point Mortgage and the Buy-Down Mortgage*

The no-point mortgage and the buy-down mortgage work in similar ways. Each of them can be offered with just about any form of mortgage. With the no-point mortgage, the borrower gets the loan at the stated interest rate without being charged any points at the closing. The buy-down loan involves an offer to provide financing at a below-market rate of interest. The central concept for both vehicles is that the borrower is offered a choice, but the choice is not free; the choice presented merely rearranges the manner in which the lender receives its profit.

As a marketing gimmick, the trade-off between points and the mortgage interest rate can be effective. Some borrowers will lack cash and will choose a higher rate of interest rather than pay points. Others will be told that under the 28 percent and 36 percent rules they do not qualify for a loan at a particular rate, but if they have cash to pay points they can qualify for and obtain a loan with a lower rate of interest and a lower monthly payment. Those more fortunate borrowers who have both sufficient savings to pay lots of points and enough income to choose the option of a no-point mortgage will not all attach the same utility to the choices. Some borrowers will want to pay points with cash and then enjoy the prospect of a lower monthly payment. Other borrowers will not want to take money out of savings, and they will accept the higher monthly payments as they go along. Some borrowers in this group may also be seeking to borrow the maximum amount permitted, perhaps at a 95 percent loan-to-value ratio, and paying points at closing would in effect reduce the amount of money that they are really borrowing.

In selecting a trade-off between interest rate and points, the borrower's expectations about how long she will own the property is an important consideration. A no-point or very low point mortgage benefits people who sell within a short period of time, such as four or five years. This is because of the way the mortgage is structured. The lender's calculation of the trade-off between points and the interest rate is not based on the mortgage going to full term, but is based on a much shorter payback time. For a mortgage that bears several points, it takes about four to five years for the borrower to recover the value of the points in the form of lower monthly payments. With a no-point mortgage that stays in place beyond four or five years, the higher monthly payments will soon surpass the value of the points that were saved. Consequently, a no-point mortgage with a higher interest rate is cheaper for a buyer who expects to be in the home for only a couple of years. Conversely, for a buyer expecting to stay longer than five years, it is generally cheaper to pay points and get a lower interest rate.

The buy-down mortgage requires that a fee be paid to a lender in exchange for offering a mortgage loan at a below-market rate of interest. Like the no-point mortgage, it reflects a trade-off of interest rate and upfront payments. This fee can consist of a high number of points charged for a specific loan interest rate, or it can be packaged in a less visible way. The basic idea, however, is that this loan is called a buy-down mortgage precisely because a price has to be paid to obtain (buy) the lower rate of interest.

5. *Adjustable Rate Mortgages*

Adjustable rate mortgages (ARMs) are mortgages in which the interest rate changes during the term of the loan. ARMs are most popular when market interest rates are considered to be relatively high. Borrowers take ARMs during such time periods because they hope that rates will go down soon and that they will enjoy a future drop in the interest charged on the loan. If FRMs are priced very low, many people will take the opportunity to lock in to a lifetime of stable payments at what they hope will prove to be a desirably low interest rate. ARMs, in contrast, appeal to borrowers because they start with a lower interest rate than comparable FRMs. This can make them more affordable at the outset because the debtor's income requirements can be measured against the ARM's initial lower monthly mortgage payments. Consequently, some people use the ARM as a way to get into a property and worry about the problem of upward rate adjustments later. Lenders, however, should give some thought to a debtor's future ability to pay, because they do not want to be stuck foreclosing on the property in a year or two when the debtor is unable to pay a greatly increased mortgage bill. To evaluate any particular ARM, there are three main components to consider: the index, the adjustment period, and the caps.

Index. The *index* is the reference source used for making interest rate adjustments throughout the life of the loan. The interest rate on the outstanding principal balance will float or adjust on a regular basis in response to upward and downward movements in the index. The index must be clearly understood and expressed in the promissory note and in other loan documents. Examples of typical indexes for ARMs are: (1) the weighted average cost of funds to lending institutions as published by the federal government, (2) the Federal Housing Authority's average national mortgage rate determined from its field office reports, (3) the quoted rates for a specific category of U.S. Treasury Bills, and (4) the London Interbank Offered Rate (Libor). It is interesting that some U.S. home mortgage lenders desire the Libor rate, which as its name implies relates to European financial markets as quoted in London. Some lenders like to link part of their loan portfolio to Libor rates because they feel it gives them a bit of a hedge against what is happening in American financial markets.

For many ARMs, the adjusted interest rate includes a spread added to the current index rate. Thus, the loan documents may specify that the interest rate will be the rate for one-year U.S. Treasury Bills plus 3 percent or the Libor rate plus 2.75 percent. Not all lenders use the same spread, and it is critical for the borrower to focus on the spread as much as the index itself. Also, the initial rate for an ARM is a fixed quote given by the lender, and it does not depend on what the index plus spread happens to be at or before loan closing. To market ARMs, most lenders quote an attractive, low interest rate that in effect functions as a "teaser" designed to lure borrowers. In other words, were the index plus spread used at closing, the initial rate might be 1½ or 2 percent higher.

Adjustment Period. In addition to selecting the index, the parties must agree on the frequency of the adjustments. Each time they refer to the index to change the mortgage interest rate, they will also need to change prospectively the borrower's monthly payments. At each change, a new amortization is made, taking account of the present principal balance, the new rate, and how many years of the term still remain.

Caps. Most ARMs have "caps" that limit how much the interest rate can move at an adjustment period. A typical cap might provide that the interest rate adjustment at the end of any adjustment period (assume 12 months) shall not exceed 2 percent in either direction no matter what happens to the index. There may also be a lifetime cap that sets the maximum limit for an interest rate adjustment during the life of the loan.

Convertibles. In the residential mortgage market, a hybrid mortgage called a *convertible* is sometimes used. This loan starts out as an ARM, but at a stated date in the future, usually after several years, it converts to a FRM at the then-prevailing FRM interest rate. Sometimes the conversion provision operates automatically, but often the borrower has the option to decide whether to invoke the conversion. The convertible mortgage can be a good choice if interest rates are high at the time the buyer takes out a home loan but rates are expected to drop in the next few years. With this conversion option, a borrower can take advantage of a drop in interest rates without all the costs associated with refinancing an existing loan. This, however, presumes that the fixed rate will be favorable at the time the conversion takes place.

6. Balloon Mortgage

The balloon mortgage features regular monthly payments but has a much larger final payment due at the end of the term. Typically, the lender uses a long-term amortization schedule to calculate monthly payments but specifies a maturity date that is much sooner. The balloon loan, therefore, is not self-amortizing. The borrower has promised to make a big cash payment at the specified maturity date, which is called the *balloon payment.* This mortgage got its name from the image of someone blowing up a balloon. If the borrower cannot come up with the cash to make the payment, arrange for new financing, or sell the property, the entire transaction might "explode" against the borrower, who could lose the property through foreclosure.

Balloon mortgages are used for several reasons. Sometimes they are used as *bridge loans* for borrowers who want short-term financing pending the funding of a long-term loan. In the residential setting, bridge loans are commonly used to finance a home purchase when the borrower is trying to sell her old home but has not yet succeeded. As a buyer, she may not qualify for a standard mortgage loan while she still has the outstanding debt on the old home. As a way of getting the new home now, such a buyer might seek a short-term bridge loan to cover her for six months or a year pending the sale and payoff of the loan on the first house.

Second, the balloon loan is popular when current market interest rates are very high. The borrower gets this short-term mortgage in the hope that the market will dramatically drop by the time the balloon payment comes due. Third, home sellers who agree to help finance their buyers frequently offer balloon mortgages. This often happens when market interest rates are high and sellers are finding it hard to sell their homes. In such a setting, the seller usually does not want to wait 20 or 30 years to be paid in full. The parties agree to a balloon loan so the buyer can get into the house, with everyone hoping that the market will change before the term expires.

7. Other Mortgages

In addition to the mortgages already mentioned, there are several others that one might encounter. Under a *level payment adjustable rate mortgage*

(LPARM), the interest rate is adjusted throughout the life of the loan but the monthly payment remains the same. It is a loan in which the borrower wants the stability of a known monthly payment, and the lender wants to shift the risk of rising interest rates to the borrower. As to the adjustment features of this mortgage, one must consider the same components discussed earlier for all ARMs. The difference with the LPARM is that, because of the commitment to level payments, the loan cannot be neatly amortized to zero over a fixed term of years. Instead, one of two things must happen: either the loan term is lengthened or shortened, or a balloon payment will be due at maturity. To the extent that the loan is not self-amortizing and the underlying debt increases, this is a loan with *negative amortization.*

The *shared appreciation mortgage* (SAM) is one in which a lender gives a debtor a favorable interest rate on a loan in exchange for a percentage interest in the equity appreciation of the property. A lender might, for example, take a 30 percent interest in the equity appreciation of the property, to be determined by appraisal and payable at some fixed point in time, such as at the earlier of when the mortgage is repaid or 10 years. A lender would make such a deal only if it expects property values to rise. If the equity payment is due when the borrower sells, then it can be subtracted from the seller's cash proceeds. If the amount is due when no sale has taken place, then the borrower must either come up with cash or refinance the equity component. The obvious difficulty with a SAM is that the borrower and the lender may disagree about the fair market value of the home. Thus, there has to be a clearly described process for fixing the value. There is also a potential problem when an owner makes improvements to the property after the loan is made. Will it be possible, for instance, to separate out the equity appreciation in the original property value as opposed to the appreciation attributable to the later improvements? From a tax perspective, will the amount paid as an equity appreciation fee be treated as interest? If so, when and how might it be deductible? Finally, is the lender a joint owner of the property for purposes of any contract, tort, or environmental liability that might arise in the future? One can readily see that although the SAM offers a borrower a way to get a mortgage at a below-market rate by giving the lender the promise of future money, it does raise many potential points of conflict between borrower and lender.

The *reverse annuity mortgage* (RAM) is a mortgage marketed to senior citizens who own their homes as a major source of wealth subject to little or no mortgage debt. For this group of elderly people, the RAM is designed as a way to provide a supplement to their retirement income while allowing them to remain in their homes. The concept behind the RAM is to pay the homeowner the value of her home over time with monthly annuity payments. The RAM reverses the typical mortgage structure. Instead of a borrower making monthly payments to the lender until the loan is paid in full, the RAM has the lender make payments to the debtor until the limit of a pre-established credit line is reached. The credit line is typically around 75 to 80 percent of the equity value of the home. The annuity may be either for the remainder of the borrower's lifetime or for a fixed term, such as 15 years. If a lifetime annuity is used, the size of the monthly payment to the homeowner is based on actuarial tables of life expectancy. The lender expects to be paid in full at the end of the process, which for a lifetime annuity occurs at the owner's death or, if sooner, the sale of the property by the owner. If a fixed term annuity is used, obvious problems arise when the owner lives long beyond the specified period. At that point, she will no longer get the annuity payments that she grew accustomed to, and the lender will have its investment return delayed, and thus diminished, unless the loan documents call for payment of the debt at a stated time even if the debtor is still alive.

There are the *growing equity mortgage* (GEM) and the *graduated payment mortgage* (GPM), both of which work in a similar manner. Each offers an affordable monthly payment during the first few years but then makes up for this by dramatically increasing the monthly payments by steps in succeeding years in accordance with a prescribed formula (not an index). The idea behind these mortgages is that a person with the expectation of a rapidly rising income can get into a home now and make up the difference later as her income rises. Under the GEM there is also a pitch for "forced savings" as one's bigger monthly payments in succeeding years result in a quicker mortgage payoff, consequently enhancing the owner's equity value in the home. There are also variations in loans known as *stretch mortgages.* These loans basically couple an adjustable interest rate with *an adjustable term* that can be stretched to extend payment for *a longer number of years* than the original term. In this way, the borrower deals with the same payments of a constant amount but can have adjustments made to the number of payments that will be required to pay off the loan. For some borrowers with fixed or limited income potential, this is a better alternative for getting a cheap loan than an adjustable rate mortgage, where monthly payments may go up dramatically from year to year.

The *price level adjusted mortgage* (PLAM) is generally more often talked about in textbooks than used in real life. The basic concept of the PLAM is that it seeks to adjust the value of the outstanding debt to account for inflation. Advocates of the PLAM focus on the fact that lenders fear that when they lend money today, inflation may make it less valuable when paid back. If, for example, I borrow $100 from you today and pay you back at the end of the year when there has been 10 percent inflation, I am really paying back the equivalent of only $90. The problem becomes worse in countries where annual inflation rates of 50 percent, 100 percent, or more are not without precedent. To avoid the risk of losing their profit as well as their principal, under these circumstances lenders will charge very high interest rates, which may make borrowing unaffordable to most people. The PLAM seeks to remove the risk of inflation from the setting of mortgage rates so that interest rates will reflect the actual cost of money, which is generally estimated to be as low as 3 percent.

The *interest only mortgage.* As the name implies, this mortgage requires the borrower to pay interest only each month during the term of the loan. At the end of the term, or when the property is sold and the mortgage paid off, the borrower must pay back all of the principal plus any accumulated negative amortization that may be applicable under the terms of the mortgage. Some residential variations allow for interest only payments for a stated number of years; such as for 3 to 10 years. At the end of the interest only term, monthly payments increase substantially to cover full payments of interest and principal, and to make up for the early years of no repayment of principle. This can be a popular mortgage option in very high cost areas with expected high rates of future equity appreciation. The borrower gets the property with a monthly payment within her reach and hopes that equity appreciation will be significant enough to generate a return at the end of the loan.

Piggyback mortgage loans are an alternative used in a few situations to get around PMI (private mortgage insurance). The piggyback loan involves making an 80 percent mortgage loan available to a borrower who really needs to borrow more than that amount to get in the home. The 80 percent loan is made not requiring PMI, and simultaneously a home equity loan is funded for an additional amount needed by the borrower: 10-20 percent. Such loans are coming under regulatory scrutiny, but they indicate the ingenuity of mortgage forms in the current marketplace.

CROWLEY v. BANKING CENTER

Superior Court of Connecticut, Judicial District of Fairfield, 1994
1994 WL 685023

RUSH, Judge. The present action was instituted in February of 1987 and relates to a mortgage loan made by the defendant Bank to the plaintiff in January 1981. By mortgage documents dated January 30, 1981, the Bank loaned the plaintiff $112,000 for the purchase of residential property located in Westport, Connecticut. The mortgage note called for an interest rate of 13% per annum and was a variable or adjustable interest rate mortgage, adjustable yearly in accordance with the terms contained in Mortgage Rider Agreement (the "Agreement"). The plaintiff claims that the defendant Bank did not adjust the interest rate in accordance with the Bank's "market rate" as required by the Agreement.

In pertinent part, the Agreement provides as follows:

CHANGE IN INTEREST RATE

The yearly changes: By signing below, I agree that you can change the interest rate for the Note each year. Here's how you'll do that: Each year on the 1st day of the calendar month just before the anniversary date of the Note, you'll look to see what your "market rate" for variable rate mortgage loans are.

> (Your market rate is the interest rate you'll charge for new variable rate mortgage loans having the same loan to value ratio that this loan did when you made it.) If your "market rate" is different from the existing rate for the note, you'll increase or decrease the interest rate for the Note to your "market rate."
>
> When a Change takes effect: Any change in the interest rate for the Note will take effect on the first day of the month following an anniversary date.
>
> Increases are limited during 1st 5 years: For the first 5 years of this loan you'll make no single increase that's greater than 1 percentage point, regardless of what your "market rate" is. But this will be true only so long as the existing rate for the Note is the same or more than the original rate for the Note.
>
> When increases during the 1st 5 years not limited: If the existing rate is less than the original interest rate then you'll increase the interest rate for the Note as follows: First, if the difference between the existing rate and the original interest rate for the loan is less than 1 percentage point you'll increase the interest rate for the Note either 1 percentage point or to your "market rate" whichever results in the smallest increase. Second, if the difference between the existing rate and the original interest rate for the Note is greater than 1 percentage point you'll increase the interest rate for the Note to the original rate or your "market rate" which ever results in the smallest increase.

Currently, most adjustable rate mortgage loans are adjusted with reference to an "external index" such as the prime rate or 6 month treasury bill index. The loan to the plaintiff, however, was adjustable, under the Agreement, in accordance with the market rate of the defendant Bank, i.e., an "internal index." The parties are in agreement that the plaintiff was entitled to have the interest rate of his loan adjusted in accordance with the "market rate" being charged by the defendant Bank. The phrase "market rate" appears in the above quoted provisions of the Agreement and in similar language contained in the Truth in Lending Disclosure Statement but does not appear in any other place in the loan documents.

Some years after the mortgage loan to the plaintiff, the defendant Bank began offering borrowers on adjustable rate mortgages an option of paying a lower interest rate on a loan for the first year by paying "points" at the inception of the loan. A "point" is one percent of the amount of the loan. For example, in 1984, on a particular class of adjustable rate mortgages, the Bank offered borrowers the following options:

Interest Rate on Note	*Points*
13.25%	0
11.75%	1½
10.75%	2½
9.75%	3½

Thus a borrower in the foregoing example could pay interest on a loan for the first year at the rate of 13.25% and pay no points, or, the borrower could, if desired, pay interest for the first year at the rate of 9.75% provided the borrower paid $3\frac{1}{2}$% of the amount borrowed at the initiation of the loan. The lower interest rates on the note upon the payment of various points has been termed the "bought down" rate or the "buy down" rate. The amounts paid by a borrower and received by the Bank over the one year period were approximately the same whether points were paid or not.

The plaintiff eventually paid off the mortgage and claims that he was entitled, during the period that the mortgage was outstanding, to have his interest rate adjusted in accordance with the lowest rate offered by the bank for adjustable rate mortgages without reference to the payment of any points. Thus the plaintiff claims that if the Bank offered adjustable rate mortgages similar to his for a "bought down" rate, he was entitled to be charged that "bought down" rate without having to pay any points and without reference to the fact that "bought down" rate was achieved by other borrowers only by the payment of points. Thus the plaintiff therefore claims that he was entitled to have his adjustable rate mortgage adjusted in accordance with the following percentages for the following years as opposed to the interest rate actually charged by the bank loans.

Review Date	*Interest Rate Charged by Bank on Plaintiff's Loan*	*Plaintiff's Claim of Appropriate Interest Rate*
12/1/84	12.875%	9.75%
12/1/85	11%	8.25%
12/1/86	8.75%	6.75%
12/1/87	9.75%	7.62%
12/1/88	11.50%	8.50%

The plaintiff's sole claim is that he is entitled, under the Agreement, to the "bought down" rate without the necessity of paying any points to achieve that rate. The plaintiff does not claim that the Bank miscalculated the rates, that the rates were unfair or unreasonable, or that rates were not competitive. The defendant Bank, on the other hand, asserts that the appropriate market rate is the rate charged for borrowers who do not pay any points in as much as the plaintiff would not be paying any points at each yearly adjustment. . . .

In the present case, the plaintiff does not claim that the rates charged to him were unfair except insofar as he claims the contract language requires a different interpretation. The plaintiff makes no claim that the rates actually charged to him were not competitive or that they were unreasonable. The testimony of the defendant's experts which the Court credits, indicated that the adjustment of rates by the defendant was fair, reasonable, and in accordance with industry practice.

When the plaintiff initially took out the loan he was concerned that his mortgage loan would be adjusted so that the interest rate charged would always be competitive, and he was prepared to take the risk presented by the use of an "internal index." The rates actually charged by the defendant Bank fulfilled the reasonable expectations of the plaintiff at the time the agreements were executed. . . .

On the basis of the facts submitted, there was ample evidence to justify the verdict of the jury in favor of the defendant Bank. The jury could well conclude, as does the court, that the reasonable expectations of the plaintiff were fulfilled and that the position advocated by the defendant Bank was the only reasonable interpretation of the agreement.

Problem 15C

Earl has a SAM against his home in favor of Big Bank. Earl purchased the home with the SAM six years ago. At the time, he paid $200,000 and borrowed $180,000 from Big Bank. The SAM gives Big Bank a one-third interest in all equity appreciation on the property during the first ten years of the mortgage. This amount is to be paid at the earlier of the sale or other disposition of the property or on the tenth anniversary date of the loan.

(a) At the end of year six, Earl transfers the property to his sister at a contract price of $100,000. Assuming no default on any mortgage payments, is there anything that Big Bank will want to do, or will be able to do, about this situation?

(b) Now assume that at the end of year six Earl transfers it by contract to Dotty, a person new to the area. Dotty pays $230,000 for the property. Big Bank seeks $10,000 as its one-third interest in the equity appreciation of the home. Earl says that the house went up in value only because he finished off the basement himself and because of extensive gardening and landscaping additions that he added. Earl says none of the $30,000 is due to an equity appreciation in the original home value. What should Big Bank's response be, and what result should occur in such a situation?

(c) Assume that Earl does not sell the property and the tenth anniversary of the loan is reached. Big Bank wants to collect on its share of the equity appreciation. Big Bank sends an appraiser to establish the price of the property. The appraiser sets the value at $260,000. Big Bank claims a payment of $20,000 under the SAM. Earl counters with evidence of his real property tax assessment, which shows that his county assesses the value of his home at its original $200,000 amount. What should be the outcome? How can the parties prevent disputes later on? Draft a provision that will give Big Bank what it wants in a fair and reasonable manner. Also draft a disclosure statement that will explain your SAM language to Earl so that he has a full and fair disclosure in accordance with the Truth in Lending Act.

(d) Assume that when Earl originally wanted to purchase his hom[e] could not qualify for any mortgage from an institutional lender. You [have] known Earl for a long time, and over the years you have done a variety of legal work for him. As Earl's lawyer you agree to help Earl out and offer to lend him the money, which you will finance as a personal investment, securing the repayment of the loan with a mortgage. Will there be any problems with your doing this under a SAM, an ARM, or any other type of financing arrangement? What ethical issues are raised by this situation, and can they be dealt with while still allowing you to make the loan?

Problem 15D

Debba is a developer of single-family homes. She has a development of 100 homes that she has built and is marketing to first-time buyers. The homes are nice, but they are small and priced on the low end of the market. She is having a difficult time getting buyers for her homes. Debba comes up with a marketing plan that she hopes will stimulate sales to her potential customers, whom she believes are likely to be couples just starting a family or thinking about this. Her plan is to offer buyers a free, 18-year tax-free municipal bond that will equal the original value of the home they purchase at the time of its maturity. The pitch is that the young couple not only gets a house but also a valuable investment bond that will be available for college expenses or other purposes at a time in the future when they need it. Debba's promotional materials declare that she offers young couples "both a home at a great price and security for the future at no extra charge." She likes to say, "It's almost like getting something for nothing." You are the lawyer for a young couple considering buying a home from Debba. Do your best to explain how this deal works. Are they really getting something for nothing? If not, how is the deal structured? What are the implications of such an arrangement in terms of other related costs?

8. *Purchase Money Mortgage*

The *purchase money mortgage* (PMM) is any mortgage in which credit is extended to enable the debtor to buy or acquire the property on which the mortgage is placed. Generally, people in real estate refer to a PMM only when the seller is the one providing financing to the buyer. Actually, however, a third-party lender can also be said to extend PMM financing if it is used to acquire the property that is put up as collateral for the loan. In this respect, the PMM in real property is the same concept as the purchase money security interest (PMSI) under Article 9 of the UCC (*see* §9-107). Although PMMs are very common, not all extensions of mortgage credit are purchase money transactions. For instance, RAMs or home equity loans are not PMMs. Likewise, people sometimes grant a mortgage on their property in order to finance other purchases or activities.

The PMM is unlike the PMSI under UCC Article 9 in that it may or may not have a special priority status. Under real property law, the priority of a claim against real estate is governed by the recording statutes and related legal principles. In some states this means that a PMM will generally be given whatever priority it has with respect to other creditor claims based on when it was recorded in the public records. Some other states, however, will grant a special priority to a PMM that is made contemporaneously with any third-party financing, even if recorded later. This is different from the PMSI under Article 9, which provides a uniform system for PMSI lenders to obtain a super priority over the competing claims of secured creditors that are prior in time. In the real property context, priority for a later creditor, even if a PMM creditor, can generally be earned only by getting the party with the earlier priority to agree to a subordination of her claim.

ALH HOLDING COMPANY v. BANK OF TELLURIDE

Supreme Court of Colorado, 2000
18 P.3d 742

Justice Coats delivered the Opinion of the Court. . . .

. . . The Petitioner, ALH Holding Company, sold real property to Linda Crocker and Robert Hackley (the "buyers") for $165,000. In connection with the sale, the buyers borrowed $110,000 from ALH in exchange for a promissory note secured with a vendor's purchase money deed of trust in favor of ALH. The buyers also borrowed $55,000 from the Respondent, the Bank of Telluride, and similarly signed a promissory note secured with a purchase money deed of trust in favor of the Bank. Both ALH and the Bank knew, before the closing, that the other would be loaning money to the purchaser and that both loans would be secured by deeds of trust conveying interests in the same property. Telluride Mountain Title Company closed the transaction for both parties on June 29, 1993, and on the following day recorded the deeds of trust. The deed of trust in favor of the Bank was recorded before that of ALH.

After the buyers defaulted on both notes, the Bank initiated a public trustee's foreclosure sale of its interest in the property, characterizing its own deed of trust as a superior lien to that of ALH. ALH brought an action against the Bank, seeking a preliminary injunction and a declaratory judgment resolving the respective priorities of the two deeds of trust. The parties stipulated to certain facts and moved for a determination of the question of priority as between the two deeds of trust pursuant to C.R.C.P. 56(h). The district court concluded that as a matter of Colorado law, a vendor's purchase money deed of trust takes priority over a third-party's purchase money deed of trust, and it entered judgment in favor of ALH.

With one member dissenting, a panel of the court of appeals reversed. . . .

This court granted ALH's petition for a writ of certiorari to consider whether the court of appeals properly applied the state's recording statute and if not to indicate the principles upon which the priority of interests should be determined.

II

Recording statutes in this country have long operated to alter the priority of various property rights on the basis of notice, recording, or some combination of the two. Colorado has had a recording statute since 1861. *See* §9, Colo. G.L., p. 65 (1861). The statute has undergone numerous revisions from its original form and is currently codified at section 38-35-109(1) of the Colorado Revised Statutes. At the time applicable to the events in this case, the recording statute included the following language:

> All deeds, powers of attorney, agreements, or other instruments in writing conveying, encumbering, or affecting the title to real property, certificates, and certified copies of orders, judgments, and decrees of courts of record may be recorded in the office of the county clerk and recorder of the county where such real property is situated. No such unrecorded instrument or document shall be valid as against any class of persons with any kind of rights who first records, except between the parties thereto and such as have notice thereof.

This is a race-notice recording statute.

Where a security agreement, or mortgage, is executed between a purchaser and a vendor as part of the same transaction in which the purchaser acquires title to the property, the execution of the deed and the mortgage are considered simultaneous acts. Chambers v. Nation, 178 Colo. 124, 129, 497 P.2d 5, 7 (1972); Bank of Denver v. Legler, 142 Colo. 333, 336, 350 P.2d 1059, 1061 (1960). As a matter of law, such a purchaser never has an unencumbered title to property in which he can assign further rights. *See Chambers,* 178 Colo. at 129, 497 P.2d at 7; *Legler,* 142 Colo. at 336, 350 P.2d at 1061. Therefore, even a third party who loans money to the purchaser that is applied to the purchase, and who takes back a mortgage on the purchased property, cannot acquire rights to the property from the purchaser unencumbered by the vendor's mortgage, regardless of the order in which the documents are signed. *Legler,* 142 Colo. at 336, 350 P.2d at 1061.

By acquiring its rights to the property in the same transaction, with full knowledge that the loan of the vendor, ALH, would be secured by a deed of trust, the Bank necessarily had notice of ALH's unrecorded instrument within the meaning of the recording statute. Whether or not the Bank's deed of trust was actually signed before that of ALH at the closing, the Bank's deed of trust could not have the legal effect of acquiring rights to the property before the execution of ALH's instruments, of which the Bank was aware. The statute, therefore, could not resolve the question of priorities in favor of the Bank. . . .

III

When the priority of rights in real property is not dictated by the operation of the recording statute, the rule in Colorado has long been that security interests, or mortgages, given in exchange for money applied to the purchase of the property have priority over all other liens [citations omitted]. The rationale for the rule derives, here again, from the fact that execution of the deed and mortgage are considered simultaneous acts, such that the title never rests in the buyer unencumbered by the mortgage. As between the owner of property who never parts with the title except in exchange for a mortgage from the purchaser and a third party who lends money to the purchaser for part of the purchase price and accepts a mortgage on the property in return, the same logic demands that the vendor's mortgage have priority. . . .

Although Colorado has never expressly adopted the Restatement (Third) of Property §7.2, the . . . cases, which support the priority of a vendor purchase money mortgage over third-party purchase money mortgages, are consistent with the Restatement . . . . As the Comments to the Restatement explain:

> [T]he equities favor the vendor. Not only does the vendor part with specific real estate rather than money, but the vendor would never relinquish it at all except on the understanding that the vendor will be able to use it to satisfy the obligation to pay the price. This is the case even though the vendor may know that the mortgagor is going to finance the transaction in part by borrowing from a third party and giving a mortgage to secure that obligation. In the final analysis, the law is more sympathetic to the vendor's hazard of losing real estate previously owned than to the third party lender's risk of being unable to collect from an interest in real estate that never previously belonged to it.

Id., cmt. 6.

Furthermore, nothing in these cases suggests that the parties cannot avoid the effect of the priority afforded vendor purchase money deeds of trust by subordinating the vendor's lien to that of the third-party lender by agreement. . . .

IV

Although the Bank's deed of trust was recorded before that of ALH, the Bank was not entitled to the benefits of the recording statute because it had notice of ALH's unrecorded instrument prior to acquiring rights of its own in the property. Furthermore, in the absence of a statutory determination of the relative priorities of the two deeds of trust, or any agreement of the parties resolving the matter, the deed of trust of ALH, the vendor, has priority over the deed of trust of the Bank concerning the same real property. The judgment of the court of appeals is therefore reversed, and the case is remanded.

16

Mortgage Obligations

The purpose of any mortgage is to secure the payment or performance of some obligation owed to the mortgagee. Usually, the obligation is a debt and, although there is no legal requirement that the debt be reflected by a writing, there almost always is a writing. When the parties have gone to the trouble of signing a mortgage, it would be remarkable if they neglected to commit the debtor's promise to pay to a written form. Most often the debt is evidenced by a promissory note, which is an instrument separate and apart from the mortgage. Two federal entities, the Federal National Mortgage Association (FNMA) and the Federal Home Loan Mortgage Corporation (FHLMC), both of which are active in the secondary mortgage market, have promulgated mortgage instruments, which have uniform clauses for use in all 50 states. The FNMA/FHLMC instruments, including their promissory note forms, are very widely used in residential lending.

A. PAYMENT OF THE DEBT

1. Usury

Usury laws limit the amount of interest a lender may charge on a loan. They generally apply to mortgage loans to the same extent as they do unsecured loans and loans secured by assets other than real property. Most usury laws are state laws, set forth either in state constitutions or in statutes. Traditional usury laws impose simple, fixed limits. A number of states have general ceilings of 10 percent or 12 percent per annum that apply to certain categories of loans. State usury laws vary considerably with respect to the maximum legal rate; the types of lenders, borrowers, and loan transactions that are covered; and the penalties imposed on lenders for usury violations.

Most usury violations involve loan transactions that are more complex than the standard mortgage loan in which the parties simply execute a fixed interest rate loan that directly, on its face, exceeds the stated legal maximum. For example, loans with variable or adjustable interest rates often present usury problems. If an adjustment makes the interest rate exceed the maximum for a certain time period, some courts look at the entire loan term, spreading the interest over that period to see whether there is a violation. Other courts, however, hold that variable interest may not be spread over the term of the entire loan. There is a usury violation if for any period the lender bargains for too much interest. Lenders who are aware of the usury risks of variable rate loans are able to solve the problem by structuring the loan properly. The loan documents may add a "cap" to the interest rate clause, providing that notwithstanding the prime rate, the interest payable on the loan would never exceed 12 percent per annum. This would protect a lender even in a jurisdiction that rejects the spreading principle.

How interest is compounded on a loan may also raise usury problems. The maximum usury rates are generally interpreted as "simple interest" with interest compounded annually. Thus, with a 10 percent limit, a $10,000 loan outstanding for one year cannot yield any more than "simple interest" of $1,000. If the lender compounds interest more frequently, there is usury even though the stated interest rate is only 10 percent. For example, if interest is compounded monthly on the $10,000 loan, the total interest due at the end of one year will be $1047.12. Similarly, interest is usually paid in arrears, after it is earned, and if the loan documents provide for the borrower to prepay some amount of interest in advance, this may trigger a usury violation.

Hidden interest is another area where lenders sometimes get into trouble with the usury laws. Lenders often charge borrowers fees and amounts that are not denominated as interest, but legally they may constitute interest if they are paid for the use of the loan money. For example, points paid by the borrower to get the loan are generally considered interest, whether they are described as loan origination fees, processing fees, or discount points. This type of disguised interest is spread over the term of the loan to determine whether its use violates the usury laws. Borrower payments for other items, such as loan application fees or the lender's attorneys' fees, may or may not constitute hidden interest.

Lenders need to take great care not to violate state usury laws, because the penalties are often severe. At a minimum, the lender forfeits the interest that is in excess of the maximum rate permitted by the usury statute. This remedy does not have a great deal of bite in it, as the loan is simply recast to allow the lender to receive the maximum amount he could have bargained for lawfully. In many states, though, harsher penalties apply to discourage usury. The lender may have to pay statutory damages that are double or triple the amount of excess interest. In some states, no interest may be collected on the loan, leaving the lender with only the right to receive the loan principal; in a few states, such as New York, the lender also loses his right to continue to collect principal.

When property is sold, often the buyer gets financing from the seller rather than from a third-party lender. Such instances of purchase-money financing may raise questions of usury when the seller bargains for a high price for the credit she extends. In most states a purchase-money loan is not subject to the usury laws and is thus legal per se. An exemption commonly called the *time-price* or *credit-sale doctrine* immunizes the seller's purchase-money financing from attack based on usury, regardless of how much the buyer pays. The explanation given by courts is that the parties' agreement about how and when the purchase price is to be paid does not involve a loan under the usury statute. The purchase and sale transaction is not separable into two distinct components of cash price and financing terms. The seller can quote a cash price and a credit price, and the difference between the two is not considered interest for purposes of usury. The difference, known as the *time-price differential*, can be anything the parties agree to. Moreover, in most states that apply the time-price doctrine, it doesn't matter how the parties refer to price and interest in their transaction.

The topic of usury, traditionally the domain of the states, is now a blend of state and federal law. To protect the national markets for home mortgage lending, Congress intervened by passing the Depository Institutions Deregulation and Monetary Control Act of 1980, 12 U.S.C. §1735f-7. The Act preempts state interest-rate limits on almost all loans secured by first liens on residential real property made after March 31, 1980. Preemption means that there is no maximum rate that the lender may charge; the Act does not specify a federal usury limit.

Congress, not wanting to intrude unduly on state autonomy, gave the states the power to override preemption by passing superseding legislation. To do so, a state had to adopt a law prior to April 1, 1983, explicitly stating that the state did not want the federal Act to apply. Most states did not override federal preemption, but during the three-year window 15 states and Puerto Rico chose to reinstate their own usury laws. Most of these states with overriding legislation presently set no usury limit on first-lien residential loans, but they have preserved their authority to regulate by future enactment if they so choose.

SEIDEL v. 18 EAST 17th STREET OWNERS, INC.

Court of Appeals of New York, 1992
79 N.Y.2d 735, 598 N.E.2d 7, 586 N.Y.S.2d 240

KAYE, Judge. In this mortgage foreclosure action, plaintiff-lenders seek to preclude a defense of usury, on the ground that the defense was waived by defendant-borrowers, that they are estopped from raising the defense, or that it is otherwise unavailable to them. We reject the lenders' arguments, and dismiss their action to enforce a concededly usurious loan.

I

In October 1982, Southside Development Co., a partnership, borrowed $150,000 from Eta Herbst (plaintiffs' decedent), to help finance its purchase of an eight-story loft building in Manhattan, which it planned to convert to cooperative ownership. In exchange for the loan, Southside executed in Herbst's favor a $225,000 bond bearing 8% interest, secured by a second mortgage on the building. The bond was to mature in 37 months, with quarterly interest-only payments due in the interim. Under the parties' written agreement, $150,000 was to be prepaid to Herbst when title passed to the cooperative corporation. In addition, Herbst was given an option to exchange the remaining $75,000 due on the bond for the shares and proprietary lease to a floor of the building. The same arrangement was made with Ellen Raacke, who is not a party to this litigation.

In late 1985, Southside conveyed the building to the cooperative, 18 East 17th Street Owners, Inc. (Owners). In mid-August 1986, Owners made a principal payment of $75,000 and, by separate check, a payment of interest then due. A few days later, Herbst, having previously exercised her option for a floor of the building, resold her shares in the cooperative to a third party for $237,000. Herbst died on August 31, 1986.

Plaintiffs — the executors of Herbst's estate — commenced this action to foreclose on the mortgage after their demands for the $75,000 due on the bond, and accrued interest, went unheeded. Owners moved to dismiss the complaint and cancel the bond and mortgage, asserting that the transaction was usurious. In response, plaintiffs contended that Owners could not assert the usury defense because (i) Owners was a stranger to the original transaction and could not, as a grantee taking subject to an existing mortgage, claim usury in that mortgage; (ii) Southside, by conveying the building subject to a mortgage, waived the defense, which could not thereafter be raised by anyone; and (iii) the doctrine of estoppel in pais applied, based on the conduct of a Southside partner and Owners principal (Maurice Reichman), who allegedly was also Herbst's attorney.

Supreme Court computed the actual interest rate of the loan to be 28.6%, and the lenders do not dispute that figure, or that the loan is usurious. However, Supreme Court found triable issues of fact as to whether Owners could assert the usury defense. Although the deed conveying the property from Southside to Owners did not explicitly mention the mortgage, the court observed that the cooperative offering plan documents acknowledged the mortgage, and thus there was a factual issue as to whether the conveyance was "subject to" the mortgage. In the court's view, this same factual issue had to be resolved before a determination could be made as to Southside's waiver of usury. Finally, on the estoppel claim, the court found issues of fact regarding Reichman's conduct and Herbst's reliance.

On defendants' appeal, the Appellate Division — over a two-Justice dissent — affirmed for the reasons stated by Supreme Court, and identified two additional issues for trial. 175 A.D.2d 770, 573 N.Y.S.2d 612. The Appellate Division opined that the transaction could be viewed as a joint venture, thus unregulated by usury laws, and that defendants' more favorable treatment of Raacke raised issues of good faith and fair dealing implicit in all contracts. The Appellate Division certified to this Court the question whether its order was correct, which we answer in the negative.

II

Statutes prohibiting usurious loans were enacted in 15th century England, became part of New York's colonial history, and have remained since (*see,* 1960 Report of N.Y. Law Rev. Commn., 1960 Legis. Doc. No. 65, at 75-80; Curtiss v. Teller, 157 App. Div. 804, 143 N.Y.S. 188, *aff'd.,* 217 N.Y. 649, 112 N.E. 1056). Their purpose is "to protect desperately poor people from the consequences of their own desperation." (Schneider v. Phelps, 41 N.Y.2d 238, 243, 391 N.Y.S.2d 568, 359 N.E.2d 1361.)

In its present form, the usury statute provides: "No person or corporation shall, directly or indirectly, charge, take or receive any money, [goods or things in action] on the loan or forbearance of any money . . . at a rate exceeding" 16% per annum (General Obligations Law §5-501[2]; Banking Law §14-a[1]). When "any bond, bill, note, assurance, pledge, conveyance, contract, security or any evidence of debt, has been taken or received in violation" of the usury laws, "the court shall declare the same to be void, and enjoin any prosecution thereon, and order the same to be surrendered and cancelled." (General Obligations Law §5-511[2].)

The consequences to the lender of a usurious transaction can be harsh: the borrower is relieved of all further payment—not only interest but also outstanding principal, and any mortgages securing payment are cancelled. In effect, the borrower can simply keep the borrowed funds and walk away from the agreement. Moreover, the borrower can recover any interest payments made in excess of the legal rate (General Obligations Law §5-513). New York usury laws historically have been severe in comparison to the majority of States (1960 Report of N.Y. Law Rev. Commn., 1960 Legis. Doc. No. 65, at 77), reflecting the view of our Legislature that the prescribed consequences are necessary to deter the evils of usury.

Statutory and judicial exceptions may in some circumstances mitigate the harshness. Corporations—generally the antithesis of the "desperately poor people" referred to in Schneider v. Phelps (*supra*)—are ordinarily barred from asserting a usury defense (General Obligations Law §5-521[1]).[2] Banks forfeit interest but not principal (General Obligations Law §5-511[1]). Moreover, the defense may be waived; it may be unavailable to certain persons not party to the original transaction; and a borrower may

2. Although Owners is a corporation, Supreme Court held that a corporation succeeding to the rights of a party that could have asserted a usury defense likewise may assert the defense, citing Merchants Exch. Natl. Bank v. Commercial Warehouse Co., 49 N.Y. 635, and thus Owners' corporate status was not in itself a bar to the defense. On this appeal, plaintiffs do not contest that holding, and we therefore do not pass on the issue. We note that in any event a corporation may raise the defense when the interest rate is criminally usurious (General Obligations Law §521[3]), i.e., greater than 25% per annum (Penal Law §190.40), and that the rate in this case was found to be 28.6%.

be estopped from asserting it. This appeal concerns the last three exceptions to a defense of usury.

STANDING AND WAIVER OF USURY

This Court has stated that "the mortgagor may . . . waive the usury and elect to affirm the mortgage by selling and conveying his property subject to the lien and payment of such mortgage, and the purchaser, in that case, takes the equity of redemption merely and cannot question the validity of the mortgage on [the] ground of usury." (Hartley v. Harrison, 24 N.Y. 170, 172.) . . .

Whatever application these exceptions might have when an independent third party obtains property subject to a mortgage in an arm's length transaction, we conclude that they are inapplicable in this case. The conveyance of the encumbered property from Southside to Owners was contemplated in the agreement between Herbst and Southside, and indeed was the very purpose of the loan. Moreover, Southside's partners were the officers and principals of Owners. Significantly, Owners' acquisition of the building was merely a function of the building's conversion to cooperative ownership, not a result of a sale to an independent third party.

Thus, even if the property was transferred "subject to" the mortgage, on these facts no inference of waiver can be drawn from Southside's conveyance to Owners, nor can it be said that Owners is a true stranger to this transaction. . . .

ESTOPPEL IN PAIS

We next consider plaintiff's estoppel in pais claim. In Payne v. Burnham, 62 N.Y. 69, a usury case, the Court noted that as a general rule, " 'a party will be concluded [sic] from denying his own acts or admissions which were expressly designed to influence the contract of another, and did so influence it, and when such denial will operate to the injury of the latter.' " (*Id.*, at 73.)

In usury cases, we have applied the doctrine where the mortgagor executes an estoppel certificate (a statement that there are no setoffs or defenses to the mortgage, *see, e.g.*, Real Property Law §258, Schedule M, §7) and a third party, relying on the representations, obtains the mortgage (*see*, Hammelburger v. Foursome Inn Corp., 54 N.Y.2d 580). . .

In this case, plaintiffs urge a different theory of estoppel in pais, based not on an estoppel certificate but on the borrower's conduct. Plaintiffs allege that Reichman, a principal of Southside and Owners, was also Herbst's attorney; that Reichman suggested the interest rate and drafted the documents; and that Herbst relied on his representations that the transaction was legal.

The Appellate Divisions, and the majority of States to consider the issue, have recognized that a borrower may be estopped from interposing a usury defense when, through a special relationship with the lender, the borrower induces reliance on the legality of the transaction. . . . Otherwise, a borrower could void the transaction, keep the principal, and "achieve a total windfall, at the expense of an innocent person, through his own subterfuge and inequitable deception" (Angelo v. Brenner, 90 A.D.2d 131, 133, 457 N.Y.S.2d 630 [3d Dept.]).

Even assuming plaintiffs' factual allegations are true, however, their claim must fail. "An indispensable requisite of an estoppel in pais, is that the conduct or representation was intended to, and did, in fact, influence the other party *to [her] injury*." (Payne v. Burnham, 62 N.Y. at 73, *supra*; emphasis added.) Herbst suffered no cognizable injury that should be remedied by equity. To the contrary, for her initial outlay of $150,000, she realized at least $312,000 (defendants claim significantly more) within four years. Any reliance on Reichman was to her benefit, not detriment.

Indeed, given this concededly usurious loan, Herbst's estate would be entitled, at most, to recovery of the amount advanced, with legal interest (*see*, Hammelburger v. Foursome Inn Corp., 54 N.Y.2d at 588, 446 N.Y.S.2d 917, 431 N.E.2d 278, *supra*; Claflin v. Boorum, 122 N.Y. at 389, 25 N.E. 360, *supra*; Payne v. Burnham, 62 N.Y. at 74, *supra*). There is no dispute, however, that the estate already received more than those amounts (even excluding Herbst's profit on the option) and that this action is for usurious interest—the difference between the amount loaned and the face amount of the bond. Equity is not available to effectuate such recovery.

III

Finally, we consider whether the transaction may be construed as a joint venture, and whether implied covenants of good faith and fair dealing are relevant in this case. These issues were first raised by the Appellate Division itself and are not strenuously pressed by plaintiffs on this appeal.

Usury laws apply only to loans or forbearances, not investments (General Obligations Law §5-501[1], [2]). If the transaction is not a loan, "there can be no usury, however unconscionable the contract may be." (Orvis v. Curtiss, 157 N.Y. 657, 661, 52 N.E. 690.) We disagree with the Appellate Division's suggestion that Herbst could be considered a joint venturer of Southside or Owners.

The parties' agreement refers to Herbst as a "Lender" and a "loan" of $150,000. Southside executed a bond and a mortgage, traditional loan instruments. The mere presence of a unilateral option in favor of Herbst—in lieu of $75,000 of the bond face amount—did not transform the lender into a joint venturer. . . . This arrangement, in form and substance, plainly was a loan.

We also disagree with the Appellate Division's suggestion that defendants could be required to comply with an illegal agreement based on principles of good faith and fair dealing. Apparently, defendants paid Raacke in accordance with the terms of her usurious loan agreement. That defendants chose not to assert a usury defense against Raacke, however, does not preclude them from raising the defense against plaintiffs. Indeed, to follow out plaintiffs' argument, implied covenants of good faith and fair dealing would require every borrower to comply with an agreement to pay usurious interest. The usury laws take precedence over any such implied covenants.[3]

Accordingly, the order of the Appellate Division should be reversed, with costs, defendants' motions to dismiss the complaint granted, defendant Owners' motion granted to have the bond and mortgage surrendered and the lis pendens cancelled, and the certified question answered in the negative.

How did the *Seidel* court calculate the interest rate on the loan made to Southside to be 28.6 percent? This is due to the effect of the large discount— Southside received \$150,000 but obligated itself to repay \$225,000 after 3 years plus quarterly interest at 8 percent calculated on the face amount of the bond (\$225,000). The effective annual rate for the quarterly interest was 12 percent (8% × \$225,000/150,000). When the bond matured after 3 years, payment of the extra \$75,000 was interest; 16.6 percent on an annual basis (25,000/150,000). Add both types of interest together: 12% + 16.6% = 28.6%. And Herbst's deal was even better than this. This usury calculation ignores Herbst's option to swap \$75,000 of principal for one floor in the building, which turned out to be a profitable exchange.

2. *Late Payment*

Lenders of course want their borrowers to pay their installment payments on time. To encourage prompt payment and penalize tardiness, many lenders include loan provisions that impose extra costs on borrowers who pay late. Most residential mortgage loans expressly provide for a late charge if the borrower fails to pay an installment after a specified grace period. There are several different ways late payments may be calculated. The most common type of late charge assessed today is a percentage of the unpaid installment; for example, for a default in making a \$500 payment that is due every month, a \$30 fee (which is 6 percent of the payment) might be imposed. Other variations lenders have employed include: (1) setting a fixed charge for all borrowers, such as \$25, based on administrative expenses such as sending out late notices; (2) assessing a higher interest rate on the unpaid installment after default; and (3) assessing a higher interest rate on the entire principal balance after default. Borrowers have sometimes challenged the legality of various late-charge provisions, claiming that they amount to an

3. Defendants contend, as a factual matter, that there is no issue of unequal treatment because both lenders received the identical amount—\$312,000 plus interest—although by different means. In that we hold, as a matter of law, that implied covenants are not material in the usury context, we need not consider defendants' argument.

unlawful penalty. Courts have generally analyzed late charges under the law of liquidated damages, which permits parties to contract for the payment of a fixed amount to be paid upon a breach, provided that actual damages are difficult or impracticable to calculate and the liquidated sum is a reasonable estimate of actual harm. The leading case in this area is Garrett v. Coast & Southern Federal Savings & Loan Ass'n, 511 P.2d 1197 (Cal. 1973), a class action that invalidated the following late charge provision (type (3) above):

> The undersigned further agrees that in the event that payment of either principal or interest on this note becomes in default, the holder may, without notice, charge additional interest at the rate of two (2%) per cent per annum on the unpaid principal balance of this note from the date unpaid interest started to accrue until the close of the business day upon which payment curing the default is received.

The court observed:

> We are compelled to conclude that a charge for the late payment of a loan installment which is measured against the unpaid balance of the loan must be deemed to be punitive in character. It is an attempt to coerce timely payment by a forfeiture which is not reasonably calculated to merely compensate the injured lender. We conclude, accordingly, that because the parties failed to make a reasonable endeavor to estimate a fair compensation for a loss which would be sustained on the default of an installment payment, the provision for late charges is void.

The court, however, was careful to note that the principal vice was the lack of proportionality between the late charge and the amount of the unpaid installment. To guide lenders in their drafting of other clauses, it stated that a late charge should be upheld "where it is established that the measure of actual damages would be a comparatively small amount and that it would be economically impracticable in each instance of a default to require a lender to prove to the satisfaction of the borrower the actual damages by accounting procedures."

For residential loans but not commercial loans, state and federal regulations commonly apply to regulate late charges. To protect borrowers from lenders who might try to assess high charges, many states have statutes that regulate late charges for residential mortgages. *E.g.*, Cal. Civ. Code §2954.4 (late payment charge limited to greater of $5 or 6 percent of late installment; 10-day grace period); N.Y. Real Prop. Law §254-b (charge limited to 2 percent of late installment; 15-day grace period); Wis. Stat. Ann. §138.052(6) (charge limited to 5 percent of late installment; 15-day grace period).

At the federal level, residential mortgage lenders are subject to various regulations concerning late charges. Fannie Mae (FNMA), for conventional mortgages (not federally insured or guaranteed), requires after 15 days a late charge equal to 4 percent of the late installment or such lesser amount permitted by state law. Freddie Mac (FHLMC) authorizes but does not require a 5-percent late charge after 15 days. FHA and VA mortgage loans bear late charges of 4 percent of the unpaid installment after 15 days. 24 C.F.R. §203.25; 38 C.F.R. §36.4212(d). The Office of Thrift Supervision (OTS), which regulates all federally chartered thrift institutions, authorizes its institutions to impose late charges on residential borrowers. Its regulations generally preempt inconsistent state laws. 12 C.F.R. §545.2. The OTS regulation does not set a maximum charge, but it resembles some state statutes in its combination of disclosure principles and other substantive rules.

3. *Prepayment*

Prepayment means the borrower pays part or all of the principal before the due date specified in the promissory note. Prepayment may take place for an installment note or for a note with a single maturity date on which all of the principal plus accrued interest is due at one time. Prepayment may be total or partial. With total prepayment, the borrower pays the entire loan balance, with accrued interest, to the date of prepayment. The promissory note, being totally satisfied, is cancelled, and the lender releases the mortgage. Partial prepayment means the borrower pays some but not all of the principal before it matures. This commonly happens for installment notes, when the borrower elects to pay one or more installments before they are due.

Prepayment may be voluntary, when the borrower decides to make a payment before the time specified in the note. Alternatively, prepayment may be compelled by the lender and thus involuntary from the borrower's point of view. This might happen if the borrower defaults and the lender has the right to accelerate the maturity of the date or if the borrower sells the property and the mortgage contains a "due-on-sale" clause.

The economic effect of prepayment depends on the interest rate provisions of the promissory note and how they compare to market rates of interest at the time of prepayment. Almost always, when the borrower desires to prepay the note, totally or partially, the reason is because the interest rate is too high (from the borrower's viewpoint). Prepayment is attractive to the borrower because interest ceases to accrue on the prepaid principal; the borrower will not have to pay the interest on the loan that the lender would have continued to earn.

Notice that the borrower and the lender have diametrically opposed positions with respect to any potential prepayment, just as they do with respect to the setting of the interest rate generally. If the interest rate is high compared to the prevailing market, the borrower wants to prepay, and the lender wants to continue to receive its bargained-for rate (no prepayment). If the interest rate is low, the borrower does not want to prepay, and the lender would be delighted if for some reason the borrower decided to prepay or if the lender were able to cause the borrower to pay early (for example, if the lender were able to accelerate the maturity).

When may the borrower prepay a loan? This depends on the terms of the promissory note. Many notes have an express provision on the subject, either permitting prepayment at the borrower's option or restricting prepayment. Restrictions often consist of a complete prohibition on prepayment or the imposition of a charge to be paid by the borrower if the borrower prepays. Typically the charge is called a *prepayment penalty* or a *prepayment premium* (the later being the better word choice since it avoids the term "penalty") and is calculated as a percentage of the amount of principal being prepaid or as advance interest on the prepayment for a certain number of months. Sometimes the prepayment clause prohibits or restricts partial prepayment but permits total prepayment, the rationale being that partial prepayments create extra administrative expense for the lender because the lender must recalculate amortization for the remainder of the loan term.

WESTMARK COMMERCIAL MORTGAGE FUND IV v. TEENFORM ASSOCIATES, L.P.

Superior Court of New Jersey, Appellate Division, 2003
362 N.J. Super. 336, 827 A.2d 1154

WEFING, J.A.D. . . .

On July 28, 1999 defendants executed a promissory note to plaintiff for the sum of $3,145,000. The note carried an interest rate of eight percent and called for equal monthly payments of $23,076.90 for a period of five years, at which point the balance was due in full. To secure their obligation, defendants granted plaintiff mortgages on three parcels of commercial property . . .

Less than a year later, defendants fell behind in their payments. Plaintiff filed a complaint in foreclosure in July 2000. . . . In November 2000, plaintiff was granted partial summary judgment and the matter was forwarded to the Office of Foreclosure, where plaintiff sought entry of final judgment. Defendants disputed the amounts due under the note and mortgages and the matter was returned to the Chancery Division for a hearing. Following that hearing, the Chancery Division concluded that the amounts sought, totaling in excess of $200,000, were reasonable and were due and owing. A Final Judgment of Foreclosure was entered thereafter, from which defendants have appealed.

The matters in dispute fall into four categories: late fees, default interest, prepayment fees and attorneys fees. The July 28 note provided for all four items. Defendants contend that the amounts allowed in each category are unreasonable and unwarranted. For the reasons stated in this opinion, we disagree.

I

Paragraph 5 of the July 28, 1999 note provides as follows:

> 5. If any installment under this Note shall not be received by Holder on the date due, Holder may at its option impose a late charge of six percent (6%) of the overdue amount. Considering all of the circumstances on the date of this Note, such late charge represents a fair and reasonable estimate of the costs that will be sustained by Holder due to the failure of Borrower to make a timely payment. The parties further agree that proof of actual damages would be costly or inconvenient. Such late charge shall be paid without prejudice to the right of Holder to collect any other amounts due or to declare a default under this Note or the other Loan Documents or to exercise any other rights and remedies of Holder. If the late charge provided for herein exceeds the maximum late charge provided by applicable law, such late charge shall be automatically reduced to the maximum late charge permitted by applicable law.

Defendants contend this paragraph is invalid, under the settled principle stated in Westmount Country Club v. Kameny, 82 N.J. Super. 200, 205, 197 A.2d 379 (App. Div. 1964), that "[p]arties to a contract may not fix a penalty for its breach. . . . such a contract is unlawful."

Our analysis of the question presented must perforce begin with the Supreme Court's recent opinion in MetLife v. Washington Avenue Associates, L.P., 159 N.J. 484, 732 A.2d 493 (1999). That also was a foreclosure action involving commercial property. The Note in question in that case called for the debtor to pay a late fee of five percent of any delinquent payments. The debtor challenged that as unreasonable. The Supreme Court, however, disagreed.

The Court noted that liquidated damages clauses in a commercial context between sophisticated parties are presumptively reasonable. *Id.* at 496, 732 A.2d 493. The Court held that the burden of establishing a particular clause as unreasonable rests upon the party challenging it as such. *Ibid.* . . . [T]he Court concluded that late fees based upon a percentage of the delinquent installment are generally allowed and that five percent was not an unusually large or unreasonable fee in commercial transactions. . . .

. . . We recognize that the late fee in question here is six percent, as opposed to the five percent deemed reasonable in *MetLife.* In light of the defendants' total failure of proof, however, we have no basis to conclude that an increase of one percentage point is sufficient to overcome the presumption of reasonableness and, thus, affirm the decision of the Chancery Division judge that six percent was reasonable in the context of this case.

There is an additional aspect to defendants' challenge to the award of late fees. They cite Crest Savings & Loan Ass'n v. Mason, 243 N.J. Super. 646, 649, 581 A.2d 120 (Ch. Div. 1990), for the proposition that a lender cannot collect late charges "for nonpayments of installments claimed to be due after the filing of the complaint." We have no quarrel with the principle, but it is inapplicable. This complaint was filed in July 2000 and we have no indication in this record of any late fees charged for any period after that date.

II

Paragraph 6 of the note provides as follows:

> 6. If the unpaid balance hereof is not received by Holder on the Maturity Date, or on the Acceleration Date (defined below) such amount shall bear interest at the Note Rate plus two (2%) per annum (the "Default Rate") from such date until paid in full. Considering all of the circumstances on the date of this Note, such interest represents a fair and reasonable estimate of the costs and expenses that will result from the loss of use of the money due. The parties further agree that proof of actual damages would be costly or inconvenient. Interest at the Default Rate shall be paid without prejudice to the right of Holder to collect any other amounts due or to declare a default under this Note or the other Loan Documents or to exercise any other rights or remedies of Holder.

Defendants challenge this clause on default interest on the same basis that they challenged the clause on late fees. We apply the same analysis that we did to the question of the reasonableness of the late fees and reach the same conclusion. . . .

Here, the note called for an increase of two percentage points in the interest rate upon default, raising it from eight percent to ten percent. Based upon the result reached in *MetLife* and defendants' total failure to present any proof to the contrary, the Chancery Division judge correctly determined the ten percent default interest rate to be reasonable.

III

We turn now to the question of the prepayment premium. . . . Paragraph 8 of the July 28, 1999 note provided for a prepayment premium and specified the method of its calculation. The paragraph included the following language, which was set off from the balance of the text by being placed in all capital letters:

> BORROWER ACKNOWLEDGES AND AGREES THAT SUCH PREPAYMENT PREMIUM REPRESENTS A REASONABLE AND FAIR ESTIMATE OF COMPENSATION FOR THE LOSS THAT HOLDER MAY SUSTAIN FROM THE PREPAYMENT OF THIS NOTE. BY INITIALING BELOW, BORROWER ACKNOWLEDGES AND AGREES THAT IT HAS NO RIGHT TO PREPAY THIS NOTE IN WHOLE OR IN PART WITHOUT THE PREPAYMENT PREMIUM EXCEPT AS SPECIFICALLY PROVIDED HEREINAFTER, AND BORROWER SPECIFICALLY ACKNOWLEDGES AND AGREES THAT IT SHALL BE LIABLE FOR THE PREPAYMENT PREMIUM ON ANY

> ACCELERATION OF THIS NOTE IN ACCORDANCE WITH ITS TERMS AT ANY TIME.
>
> IN THE EVENT OF AN ACCELERATION, THE PREPAYMENT PREMIUM SHALL BE DETERMINED BY HOLDER AS OF THE DATE A NOTICE OF DEFAULT AND ACCELERATION IS SENT BY HOLDER, AND SHALL BE DUE AND PAYABLE AS OF THE DATE ON WHICH A NOTICE OF DEFAULT AND ACCELERATION IS SENT BY HOLDER. THE BORROWER NO LONGER HAS THE LEGAL RIGHT UNDER APPLICABLE LAW TO REINSTATE THE NOTE BY PAYMENT OF DELINQUENT INSTALLMENTS. FURTHERMORE, BY INITIALING BELOW, BORROWER WAIVES ANY RIGHTS IT MAY HAVE UNDER APPLICABLE LAW TO OBJECT TO OR AVOID PAYMENT OF THE PREPAYMENT PREMIUM, AND BORROWER EXPRESSLY ACKNOWLEDGES AND AGREES THAT HOLDER HAS MADE OR ACQUIRED THE LOAN EVIDENCED BY THIS NOTE IN RELIANCE ON SUCH AGREEMENTS AND WAIVER BY BORROWER, THAT HOLDER WOULD NOT HAVE MADE OR ACQUIRED THIS LOAN WITHOUT SUCH AGREEMENTS AND WAIVER BY BORROWER, AND THAT HOLDER HAS GIVEN INDIVIDUAL WEIGHT TO SUCH AGREEMENTS AND WAIVER BY BORROWER IN ENTERING INTO OR ACQUIRING THIS NOTE AND THE OTHER LOAN DOCUMENTS.

Immediately following those two paragraphs was a space for the borrower's initials, which was completed, signaling agreement to those terms.

A borrower does not have the right, under New Jersey law, to prepay a commercial loan, unless the documents afford that right. Norwest Bank Minnesota v. Blair Road Associates, 252 F. Supp. 2d 86, 97 (D.N.J. 2003). "Since a lender has the right not to have the loan prepaid but rely on collecting the interest contracted for, the lender is entitled to charge a penalty to the borrower for the privilege of prepayment." *Ibid.*

Prepayment premiums are designed to protect a lender against potential losses it may incur if a loan is paid earlier than contracted for. United States v. Harris, 246 F.3d 566, 573, (6th Cir. 2001). "The primary purpose of these clauses is to protect the mortgagee against the loss of a favorable interest yield. . . . Prepayment may also result in further losses, such as the administrative and legal costs of making a new loan . . . and in some cases additional tax liability." Restatement (Third) of Property: Mortgages §6.2 comment a (1997).

> Essentially, prepayment fees are nothing more than liquidated damages clauses. The lender has committed itself to leave its funds outstanding for a fixed period at a given interest yield, and to suffer the market rate risk inherent in this position. If rates rise after the loan has been made, the value of the loan to the lender will fall accordingly. This risk is inherent in the role of a fixed-interest lender, and it is only partially mitigated by the inclusion of a due-on-sale clause. In return for absorbing the risk of rising rates, the lender wants "call protection": some assurance that if market rates fall, the borrower will

> not merely prepay the loan and refinance at a lower rate. From the lender's viewpoint, a prepayment is a derogation of the right to earn the agreed yield for the full term even if extrinsic rates drop. In other words, the borrower breaches its obligation to keep the loan in effect for its full term.

Whitman, *Mortgage Prepayment Clause: An Economic and Legal Analysis,* 40 U.C.L.A. L. Rev. 851, 871-72 (1993).

A lender's right to demand a prepayment premium is not unlimited. A prepayment premium cannot be charged, for instance, if the prepayment is the result of the property having been taken by eminent domain. Jala Corp. v. Berkeley Savings & Loan Ass'n, 104 N.J. Super. 394, 250 A.2d 150 (App. Div. 1969). In addition, a prepayment premium cannot be charged if the prepayment results from destruction of the property by casualty such as fire and insurance proceeds are used to pay the loan. *Id.* at 400, 250 A.2d 150 (*citing* Chestnut Corp. v. Bankers Bond & Mortgage Co., 395 Pa. 153, 149 A.2d 48 (1959)).

Courts across the country have divided on the question whether a prepayment premium may be properly imposed, however, when the prepayment is the result of the lender's accelerating the debt.

One of the leading authorities on the question is *In re* LHD Realty Corp., 726 F.2d 327 (7th Cir. 1984). The court in that case refused to allow a prepayment premium after the note had been accelerated. The court explained that, by definition, acceleration "advances the maturity date of the debt so that payment thereafter is not prepayment but instead is payment made after maturity." *Id.* at 330-31. In setting forth its reasoning, the court stated:

> [t]he point is, we think, that a lender may abandon or waive its claim to interest payable over a period of years and to what amounts to insurance against a decline in interest rates. Thus, the lender, by its acts, may establish that it prefers accelerated payment to the opportunity to earn interest over a period of years. It is not appropriate, under these circumstances, for the lender to receive a prepayment premium in lieu of the interest foregone since it has voluntarily waived the unpaid interest in the expectation of accelerated payment of the remaining principal.

Id. at 331. . . .

Other courts have held to the contrary. [citations omitted]

The Restatement (Third) of Property, *supra,* aligns itself with those authorities which permit collection of a prepayment premium in the event of acceleration. It notes the following:

> [I]f the borrower fully understood and had the opportunity to bargain over the clause, either with the assistance of counsel or by virtue of the borrower's own experience and expertise, the clause will ordinarily be enforced. . . .
>
> Controversy has sometimes arisen concerning the collectability of a prepayment fee when the prepayment results from the mortgagee's acceleration

> of the secured debt on account of the mortgagor's default. Such prepayments have occasionally been described as "involuntary." In the first instance, the question is simply whether the relevant clause in the mortgage or the debt instrument purports to cover this sort of prepayment. If it clearly does so, there is no general reason courts should refuse to enforce it. The payment may be "involuntary" in the sense that the mortgagor would prefer that the debt not be accelerated, but it is still the mortgagor's action in defaulting that triggers the acceleration. The mortgagee obviously has no duty to refrain from accelerating a defaulted loan, and the acceleration gives rise to a payment that may impose costs and risks on the mortgagee identical to those flowing from a voluntary prepayment. Indeed, the mortgagee can fairly assert that the risk of a prepayment resulting from default and acceleration is well within the range of risks which the mortgagee has agreed to absorb in return for the fee. Of course, in a particular instance a court might find a demand for a prepayment fee on an accelerated debt to be unconscionable or to violate the duty of good faith and fair dealing.

Restatement (Third), *supra*, §6.2 comment c. . . .

We are satisfied that in the context of the present action, the position adopted by the *Restatement* . . . is correct. While there is a certain ineluctable logic to the statement that payment after acceleration cannot be considered prepayment, we can perceive no reason why the debtor should be relieved of the terms of the contract freely entered into. The terms were clear and unambiguous, the parties clearly experienced and sophisticated in loan transactions of this type. The certainty of the remedy provided by the clause undoubtedly affected the pricing of the loan. If we were to deem the clause unenforceable, we would be providing defendants with a better contract than they were able to negotiate for themselves; we decline to do so. . . .

Nor do we consider it necessary in the context of this case for the chancery judge to have conducted a hearing to determine whether the borrowers were versed in such complex transactions. . . .

The enforceability of such a prepayment premium clause should be measured in the same manner as those providing for late fees and default interest — reasonableness. And, as with those clauses, defendants presented no evidence of unreasonableness or sharp practices at the hearing the chancery judge afforded them. We affirm the determination that the prepayment premium at issue here was a reasonable charge.

IV

We turn now to the final matter, the award of attorneys fees. The chancery judge awarded a total fee of $45,153.46. Defendants contend that the amount awarded exceeds the permissible limit under R. 4:42-9(a)(4) and that a hearing should have been held to determine the reasonableness of the fee request.

The award of attorneys fees is governed by R. 4:42-9. The eight subsections of the rule deal separately with the instances in which a court may award counsel fees. Under subsection (a)(4), a court may award a counsel fee in a foreclosure action and the rule specifies the manner in which the fee is to be calculated:

> on all sums adjudged to be paid the plaintiff amounting to $5,000 or less, at the rate of 3.5%, provided, however, that in any action a minimum fee of $75 shall be allowed; upon the excess over $5,000 and up to $10,000 at the rate of 1.5%; and upon the excess over $10,000 at the rate of 1%, provided that the allowance shall not exceed $7,500. If, however, application of the formula prescribed by this rule results in a sum in excess of $7,500, the court may award an additional fee not greater than the amount of such excess on application supported by affidavit of services. In no case shall the fee allowance exceed the limitations of this rule.

Defendants complain that the amount awarded does not comport with that percentage scale. Defendants also complain that plaintiff's counsel did not file an appropriate affidavit of services as required for a fee in excess of $7,500. Defendants overlook the fact, however, that plaintiff's counsel had already submitted an affidavit of services to the Office of Foreclosure when it requested entry of judgment. In light of the familiarity of the chancery judge with this matter, we see no practical benefit to returning the matter to the judge for a further affidavit and consideration. . . .

The order under review is affirmed. . . .

Problem 16A

You represent a lender who is planning to make a commercial loan on a small shopping center, payable in monthly installments at 8.75 percent per annum. Your client wants to charge a higher interest rate after material default by the borrower. The promissory note form that your client has used for other transactions reads:

> Should Payor default in the payment of any installment of principal or interest, such installment shall bear interest at the rate of 12 percent per annum from the date unpaid interest started to accrue until the close of the business day upon which payment curing the default is received. The entire principal balance shall bear interest at the last hereinabove stated rate after maturity, whether by acceleration or in due course.

Your client wants your advice with respect to this clause. What changes, if any, do you recommend? Your client also wants to know whether it's permissible to charge a late fee in addition to raising the interest rate after default.

B. NONDEBT OBLIGATIONS

The vast majority of mortgages granted in the United States secure payment of debts. A common legal definition of the term *debt* is an obligation to pay a fixed amount of money. Most, but not all, debts secured by mortgages arise from loan transactions. Recall that some courts, in the context of usury under the time-price doctrine, do not consider credit extended by the seller to be a loan. A mortgage may also be granted to secure a debt that is not founded on agreement. For example, A sues her neighbor B for nuisance and obtains a judgment for damages, which B cannot immediately satisfy. B grants A a mortgage on his property to secure the judgment debt, payable in accordance with an accompanying promissory note, in exchange for A's agreement to forbear from other efforts to collect the debt.

In most mortgage debt transactions, the mortgagor, in addition to promising to pay the debt, makes other promises. For example, the mortgagor covenants to pay real property taxes, to insure the improvements, not to commit waste, and not to sell or transfer the mortgaged property without the mortgagee's consent. In a construction mortgage, the mortgagor promises to complete the building being financed by the lender. These obligations are not themselves debts, as they are either nonmonetary or are not fixed in amount, but they are collateral to the debt held by the mortgagee. They are designed to preserve the value of the mortgagee's security while the debt remains unpaid. Once the debt is paid, these nondebt obligations vanish.

Occasionally mortgages are granted to secure obligations other than debts. When there is no debt owed either by the mortgagor or a third party but there is another secured obligation, such a mortgage may be valid. A simple rule might be to permit such a mortgage in all cases, provided that the underlying obligation is valid—that is, legally enforceable under contract law principles and other relevant rules. However, most courts require that the obligation have an ascertainable monetary value.

PAWTUCKET INSTITUTION FOR SAVINGS v. GAGNON
Supreme Court of Rhode Island, 1984
475 A.2d 1028

WEISBERGER, Justice. This is a civil action in interpleader brought by Pawtucket Institution for Savings (Pawtucket) to determine which creditors of R. & R. Construction Company (R. & R.) are entitled to the surplus remaining in Pawtucket's possession subsequent to a foreclosure sale of property belonging to R. & R. The decision of the trial justice awarded the entire surplus to the second mortgagee, appellee Lawrence E. Gagnon (Gagnon). The appellant, F. D. McKendall Lumber Company (McKendall), the third mortgagee, now appeals from the judgment of the Superior Court and contends that the second mortgage was invalid, therefore entitling it to the surplus. . . .

Pawtucket was the holder of a first mortgage on property located on Sweet Avenue in Pawtucket, Rhode Island dated January 24, 1966 of which R. & R. was the mortgagor. Upon default by R. & R., Pawtucket foreclosed on said property. At the public auction held on October 26, 1967, Gagnon, the second mortgagee of record, purchased the real estate for the sum of $81,000. After payment of the balance due on its note and expenses, Pawtucket deposited the surplus sum of $10,153.95 in the registry of the Superior Court. A complaint for interpleader joining as defendants the junior mortgagees, attaching creditors, mechanics lienors, and the United States as holder of a tax lien, was then filed by Pawtucket for the court's determination in respect to distribution of the surplus proceeds derived from the sale.

. . . Gagnon . . . entered into a written contract with R. & R. which provided that R. & R. would build a nine-unit apartment house at 155 Sweet Avenue, Pawtucket, Rhode Island, upon the agreement that Gagnon pay $82,000 for the building upon completion. Pursuant to the contract, Gagnon advanced the sum of $25,000 to R. & R. Subsequently, R. & R. executed and delivered a mortgage deed on the property to Gagnon to secure R. & R.'s obligations under the contract. The mortgage was recorded on September 7, 1966. It is undisputed that R. & R. did not complete the construction of the apartment building.

. . . McKendall . . . held a mortgage on the Sweet Avenue property in the face amount of $28,000, of which a remaining $16,236.40 was then due. The mortgage was recorded after Gagnon's mortgage on January 12, 1967. McKendall contends that Gagnon's mortgage, although prior in time of recording, is invalid and void in that it is not predicated upon any promissory note; it lacks consideration; was given to secure an obligation not legally enforceable by mortgage; and its terms are uncertain, vague, and fail to set forth clearly the obligation of R. & R., which is purportedly secured by the giving of said mortgage. Upon the trial justice's holding that the second mortgage to Gagnon was valid and enforceable, judgment was entered for Gagnon for the balance of funds held in the court registry. The issue presented before us is whether the obligation described in the Gagnon mortgage is capable of reduction to a definitely ascertainable amount so as to render the mortgage valid.

In the case at bar, the mortgage deed to Gagnon states: "This mortgage is given for the specific purpose of securing performance of a construction agreement between the mortgagor [R. & R.] and the mortgagee [Gagnon] relating to the erection of an apartment house on the within described premises, which, according to the terms of said agreement, are to be sold and conveyed by the mortgagor to the mortgagee upon completion of construction." Further, the deed purports "to secure the payment of TEN (10.00) DOLLARS and other valuable considerations with interest . . . as provided in a certain negotiable promissory note of even date herewith."

A mortgage is defined as "security for the performance of an act by some person." Osborne, *Handbook on the Law of Mortgages* §102 at 156 (2d ed. 1970). The Supreme Court of the United States long ago, speaking through Chief Justice Marshall, recognized that mortgagees were not precluded from successfully claiming under their mortgage because of a variance between the obligation described and the truly existing obligation so long as such obligation was actual and fair. Shirras v. Caig, 11 U.S. (7 Cranch) 34, 51 (1812).

This court has previously recognized that a legal mortgage is an executed conveyance requiring the same consideration as any other executed transfer of property. However, there must be an underlying obligation which the mortgage secures. Turner v. Domestic Investment & Loan Corp., 119 R.I. 29, 34, 375 A.2d 956, 959 (1977). . . . In the case at bar the mortgage deed . . . secures the performance of the obligations arising under the construction agreement referred to in the mortgage document.

According to the majority view the amount of the debt need not be stated precisely provided there exists sufficient description to make identification reasonably possible. "[T]he claim must be described and defined with such accuracy as to make identification reasonably possible and certain. . . . [I]n all jurisdictions the mortgage will operate as security for only those obligations which are covered by the agreement of the parties and identified by it." Osborne, §108 at 170. The construction agreement is identified in the mortgage, and thus the mortgage operates as security for this obligation. There exists a sufficient description of the debt to render identification reasonably possible. At the point of foreclosure, the mortgage secured Gagnon for $25,000 in payments made under the contract to R. & R. together with R. & R.'s obligation to complete the building. Therefore, we conclude that the amount secured by the mortgage is reasonably ascertainable and hence sufficient in form and content to constitute a valid mortgage.

The functional purpose of a mortgage is to serve as security for an obligation which is usually set forth in an instrument separate from the mortgage deed and customarily merely referred to by recitals in the mortgage. This practice underlies the rule that in the event of any discrepancy between the terms of the mortgage and those contained in the separate instrument of indebtedness in respect to any material element of the secured claim (e.g., amount, maturity, etc.), the mortgage recital must yield. Osborne, §108 at 171. In the instant action, there exists a conflict between the statements in the mortgage deed and those in the obligation referred to in said deed. Thus, the recital concerning the existence of a promissory note set forth in the mortgage deed must give way to the terms of the construction agreement referred to in which no promissory note is mentioned.[1]

1. It is undisputed that there was no promissory note. The reference to such note is part of a standard-form deed from which the printed recitation of the existence of a promissory note was not stricken.

The absence of the promissory note fails to negate the existence of the obligation between the parties set out in the construction agreement. A mortgage is valid without any note or bond, so long as it secures an existing debt. 2 Jones, *Law of Mortgages,* §436 at 558 (8th ed. 1928). Therefore, we hold that the validity of the mortgage is not affected by the absence of a promissory note.

With respect to the issue of whether Gagnon sustained his burden of proof with regard to his claim to the foreclosure surplus, it is our opinion that sufficient evidence was presented to support Gagnon's claim to the funds deposited in the registry. . . . Gagnon introduced into evidence an itemization of expenses required to finish the apartment building as proof of the costs of completing the work. At the trial below, McKendall failed to object to such evidence or to introduce rebuttal evidence on the issue of costs; and therefore, such costs shall be deemed prima facie the amount Gagnon was entitled to recover. These costs far exceed the amount of the surplus proceeds of the mortgage sale deposited into the registry of the court. The trial justice found, after considering all of the evidence both documentary and oral: "[T]here is no question in the Court's mind that Gagnon more than amply proved his damages and his entitlement to the sums now in the Registry of the Court. Even after these sums are paid to him, Gagnon is still out of pocket many thousands of dollars." . . .

Therefore, for the reasons stated, McKendall's appeal is denied and dismissed, the judgment below is affirmed, and the papers in the case may be remanded to the Superior Court.

Problem 16B

Nancy and Otis own neighboring rural parcels with a common boundary of 500 feet. They both would like to have a line of eucalyptus trees planted on the boundary, for which they will split the cost. Both neighbors are busy and are not sure which one will be able to get around to the project first. Because they want a written agreement now, they sign a "Reciprocal Easement and Mortgage Agreement," wherein each agrees that if the other does the landscaping work, (s)he will reimburse the other for half the cost. Each neighbor also grants to the other a mortgage on his (her) parcel to secure that obligation to pay half of the landscaping project costs. Are these mortgages valid?

C. ASSUMPTIONS AND TAKING SUBJECT TO MORTGAGE OBLIGATIONS

Mortgaged real property is often bought and sold, and when it is, two things can happen to the debt secured by the mortgage. The first alternative is that the mortgagor might pay off the debt. This is necessary for the seller to convey marketable title. For a sale transaction, usually the seller uses part of the purchase price paid at closing to pay the debt in full, with the lender executing a release of mortgage.

The other option is for the sale to close with the existing debt remaining in place. In this event, the mortgage survives the transfer, provided it is properly recorded. If the mortgage is unrecorded, but the transferee does not qualify as a bona fide purchaser, the mortgage still survives the transfer. When the debt and the mortgage continue, there are three different ways the parties may handle the debt. First, the buyer may *assume* the mortgage debt, in which case the buyer promises the seller that the buyer will pay all of the debt in accordance with its terms. The buyer may also *take subject to* the mortgage debt. This means that the buyer does not promise to pay the debt but agrees that the mortgage is permitted as an exception to good title and that the seller is not responsible for paying the debt.

With a loan assumption, the buyer, having expressly promised to pay the debt, is personally liable if she fails to do so. In contrast, a buyer who takes subject to has no personal liability if she fails to pay the debt. This is a form of *nonrecourse* financing. The buyer who takes "subject to" usually pays the debt because, if she doesn't pay, she risks losing the property to the mortgagee, who may choose to foreclose. Her advantage, compared to the assuming buyer, is that she does not have the risk of a personal judgment for all or part of the loan balance.

When the mortgage debt survives the closing, the third possibility is that the mortgagor/seller is still required to pay it. The mortgage is an encumbrance to title, which is to be removed when the seller pays off the debt. Obviously, such a transaction poses risk for the buyer because of the possibility that the seller will default by not making timely payments. This type of arrangement is commonly coupled with a form of seller financing called a *wrap-around mortgage loan.* With a wrap-around loan, the buyer gives the seller a promissory note, secured by a second mortgage on the property, and the seller uses installment payments made by the buyer to pay the mortgagee under the prior loan. Wrap-around mortgages are discussed further in Chapter 19.

The Assumption Triangle: Grantor's and Grantee's Position. The assumption of a mortgage loan results in a set of rights and obligations involving three parties: the mortgagor-grantor, the assuming grantee, and the mortgagee. The grantee is primarily liable to pay the debt; this is the meaning of the assumption agreement between the grantor and the grantee. Although many laypersons think the grantor is out of the picture legally after a loan assumption closes, this is not so. The grantor remains personally liable as the maker of the promissory note until the loan is paid in full, unless the mortgagee releases the grantor from liability. After the transfer, the grantor's liability becomes *secondary* because the grantee is *primarily* liable. The grantor thus is a surety with respect to the debt, and the principles of the law of suretyship generally apply to govern the relationship between the grantor and the grantee. For the grantor to be released from liability on the mortgage debt, she must obtain a written release from the mortgagee. The legal relationships among the three parties may be visualized as a triangle:

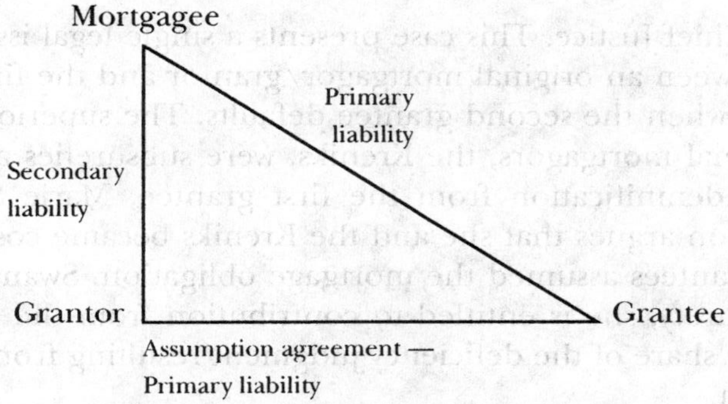

The Assumption Triangle: Mortgagee's Positions. In all states, the assuming grantee is personally liable to pay the debt to the mortgagee. In some cases of loan assumptions, an assumption agreement is entered into between the grantee and the mortgagee. Then the grantee's personal liability stems from straightforward enforcement of this agreement. But in many loan assumptions, there is no contract between the grantee and the mortgagee; indeed, often there is no contact whatsoever between them. Even so, the assuming grantee is personally liable to the mortgagee. Courts have employed two rationales, the first of which is that the mortgagee is considered a third-party beneficiary of the assumption agreement between the grantor and the grantee. The second rationale is that the mortgagee has derivative rights against the assuming grantee: by subrogation it steps into the grantor's shoes and enforces the grantee's promise to the grantor to assume the debt. Courts have often used suretyship principles to explain the basis for subrogation. The grantee is the principal obligor, the grantor is the surety, and the mortgagee is enforcing her right against the surety by taking the promise made by the grantee to the grantor-surety.

Problem 16C

Sara owes Lucy $100,000, secured by a mortgage on Blackacre. The loan is payable in monthly installments of principal and interest, with 64 installments remaining to be paid. On June 5th, Sara sells Blackacre to Bertis for $110,000, with Bertis making a down payment of $10,000.

(a) If Bertis has assumed the mortgage debt, who should pay the installment owed to Lucy on July 1st? If instead Bertis has taken subject to the mortgage debt, who should pay the July 1st installment?

(b) If Bertis has assumed the mortgage debt and no one pays the July 1st installment, does Lucy have a cause of action against Sara? Against Bertis? What if instead Bertis took subject to the mortgage debt?

SWANSON v. KRENIK

Supreme Court of Alaska, 1994
868 P.2d 297

MOORE, Chief Justice. This case presents a single legal issue regarding the rights between an original mortgagor/grantor and the first grantee of real property when the second grantee defaults. The superior court ruled that the original mortgagors, the Kreniks, were subsureties and therefore entitled to indemnification from the first grantee, Marie Swanson. On appeal, Swanson argues that she and the Kreniks became cosureties when the second grantees assumed the mortgage obligation. Swanson contends that, as a cosurety, she is entitled to contribution from the Kreniks for a proportionate share of the deficiency judgment resulting from the default.

We affirm.

I

. . . In 1977 Thomas Krenik and Leila Krenik executed a promissory note secured by a deed of trust on their property in favor of the Alaska Federal Savings and Loan Association of Juneau (Alaska Federal).

In 1981 the Kreniks conveyed the property to Keith Swanson and Marie Swanson, who assumed the Alaska Federal note and deed of trust. Alaska Federal consented to this assumption without releasing the Kreniks. The Swansons also executed a second deed of trust in favor of the Kreniks.

In August 1983, Marie Swanson[1] conveyed the property to Ray Rush and Howard Luther, Jr. With the consent of all parties, Rush and Luther assumed the Alaska Federal note and deed of trust as well as the second deed of trust. Rush and Luther executed a third deed of trust in favor of Swanson.

In 1986 Rush and Luther defaulted on the Alaska Federal obligation. In 1988 Alaska Federal filed suit against the Kreniks, Swanson, and Rush and Luther, seeking judicial foreclosure. Both Rush and Luther filed for bankruptcy in 1989. Swanson then filed a cross-claim against the Kreniks, alleging that she and the Kreniks were "joint co-debtors" and therefore jointly liable for any deficiency judgment. In turn, the Kreniks filed a cross-claim against Swanson, seeking entry of judgment against her based on the 1981 assumption agreement.

Superior Court Judge Brian Shortell granted Alaska Federal's motion for summary judgment in its foreclosure action on the first deed of trust. The court issued a decree of foreclosure and sale of real property and entered final judgment.

In the following months, both Swanson and the Kreniks moved for summary judgment on their respective cross-claims. Swanson argued that she and the Kreniks became cosureties when Rush and Luther assumed the

1. Keith Swanson died in March 1983.

mortgage debt. The Kreniks maintained that Swanson had no right of contribution from them and that Swanson had a duty to indemnify them for any amounts they were forced to pay Alaska Federal.[2] The court ruled in favor of the Kreniks.

After the foreclosure sale, the court issued a deficiency judgment to Alaska Federal against both Swanson and the Kreniks for a sum of $1,173,992. Swanson paid the judgment. This appeal followed. . . .

III

As both parties in this case recognize, when an original mortgagor transfers mortgaged land to a grantee who assumes the mortgage, the assuming grantee becomes the principal mortgage obligor and the mortgagor becomes a surety. Restatement of Security §83(c) and cmt. e (1941); *see also* First Interstate Bank v. Nelco Enters., 64 Wash. App. 158, 822 P.2d 1260, 1263 (1992); Cely v. DeConcini, McDonald, Brammer, Yetwin & Lacy, P.C., 166 Ariz. 500, 803 P.2d 911, 912 n.3 (App. 1990); Moss v. McDonald, 772 P.2d 626, 627 (Colo. App. 1988); Grant S. Nelson & Dale A. Whitman, *Real Estate Finance Law* §5.10, at 283-84 (1985).

The parties agree that in 1981 the Swansons expressly assumed the Kreniks' mortgage obligation under the Alaska Federal note and deed of trust. The assumption agreement states in part that the Swansons "assume and agree to pay the [Kreniks'] indebtedness evidenced by the Note and Deed of Trust, and to perform all of the obligations provided therein." In 1981, therefore, the Swansons became the principal obligors on the debt. The Kreniks, who were not released from their obligation to Alaska Federal, became sureties. In the event of a default by the Swansons, Alaska Federal retained its right of recourse against both the Swansons and the Kreniks for any amount outstanding on the loan. If the Kreniks satisfied any amount due, their status as sureties would entitle them to indemnification from the Swansons. *See First Interstate Bank,* 822 P.2d at 1263 (if the surety discharges the mortgage debt, it is entitled to indemnification from the assuming grantee). Conversely, the Swansons would not be entitled to indemnification or contribution from the Kreniks for any deficiency satisfied by the Swansons.

Swanson's contention is that, upon Rush and Luther's assumption of the deed of trust in 1983, she and the Kreniks became cosureties. Her claim is based largely on Paragraph 10 of the 1983 Rush and Luther assumption agreement, which states:

> Rush and Luther, [the Kreniks] and Marie O. Swanson, whether principal, surety, grantor, endorser or other party hereto, *agree to be jointly and severally bound* . . . and expressly agree that the Note or any payment thereunder may

2. The Kreniks also sought summary judgment against Swanson based on the second deed of trust.

> be extended from time to time and consent to the acceptance of further security including other types of security all without in any way affecting the liability of said parties.

(Emphasis added). Swanson argues that this paragraph demonstrates the Kreniks' express consent to become joint debtors with her on the Alaska Federal deed of trust.

Swanson misinterprets this provision. Indeed, the fact that Paragraph 10 also binds Rush and Luther as jointly and severally liable with Swanson and the Kreniks would defeat Swanson's interpretation of the clause. We conclude that the language of Paragraph 10 establishes the Kreniks' agreement to be jointly and severally bound with all assuming grantees *as to the mortgagee,* Alaska Federal, in the case of a default on the loan. It does not, however, establish any relationship or hierarchy among the successive grantors regarding contribution or indemnity.

The relationship between Swanson and the Kreniks is clarified in Paragraph 13 of the 1983 Rush and Luther assumption agreement, which states:

> [The Kreniks] and Marie O. Swanson agree that their present liability under the Note and Deed of Trust *shall not be impaired, prejudiced or affected in any way whatsoever by this Agreement* or by sale or conveyance of said premises, or by the assumption by Rush and Luther of the Note and Deed of Trust or by any subsequent change in the terms, time, manner or method of payment of said indebtedness, or any part thereof contracted by [Alaska Federal] and Rush and Luther or the transferees of Rush and Luther, whether or not such changes or transfers have been consented to by [the Kreniks] and Marie O. Swanson.

(Emphasis added).

The unambiguous terms of this provision indicate that the 1983 assumption agreement did not alter Swanson's obligations to the Kreniks under the previous assumption agreement. Accordingly, Swanson and the Kreniks did not become cosureties in 1983 as Swanson maintains. As between themselves, they remained principal obligor and surety, respectively. Therefore, with respect to Rush and Luther, who became the principal obligors, Swanson and the Kreniks became surety and subsurety, respectively. In this relationship, the Kreniks' liability on the deed of trust remains one step removed from that of Swanson, as it was under their original agreement. Therefore, Swanson is liable for the deficiency resulting from Rush and Luther's default on the deed of trust, and she is not entitled to contribution from the Kreniks. We find that, absent some express agreement to the contrary, a second grantee's purchase of property and assumption of a mortgage obligation does not modify the surety-principal obligor relationship created between the mortgagor and the first grantee in their previous transaction. . . .

Commentators have similarly observed that, where there is a series of conveyances accompanied by a chain of assumptions, "the liability for the mortgage debt is cast upon the grantees in the inverse order of assumption." Milton R. Friedman, *Discharge of Personal Liability on Mortgage Debts in New York,* 52 Yale L.J. 771, 774 n.13 (1943); *see also* Frederic P. Storke & Don W. Sears, *Transfer of Mortgaged Property,* 38 Cornell L.Q. 185, 198 (1953) (in an assumption chain, any grantee is a surety for subsequent grantees and a principal for earlier grantees.) . . .

Lastly, we are unpersuaded by Swanson's argument that the equities of this case mandate a finding of cosuretyship. *See* Restatement of Security §146(c) (1941) ("A surety is a subsurety if he has so stipulated . . . except to the extent that his stipulation will inequitably increase the obligation of another surety."). In our view, the equities in the present situation fall on the side of the Kreniks. As original mortgagors, they had no real influence over their grantee's decision to convey the property to a second grantee, or over the selection of that grantee. They did not stand to directly benefit from the transfer. Their only real involvement in the transaction consisted of a reacknowledgement of their underlying obligation to Alaska Federal, so that the transfer could be accomplished. While it is unfortunate that Swanson is faced with a substantial obligation in this case, it would seem patently unfair to actually enlarge the Kreniks' original liability under the 1981 assumption agreement simply because Swanson transferred the property to a second grantee. . . .

The decision of the superior court is affirmed.

D. MODIFICATION AND EXTENSION OF MORTGAGE DEBT

Mortgage debt is often long-term, remaining in effect for many years and repayable in monthly installments or at other periodic intervals. Due to its long-term nature, when market conditions change, the borrower and lender often find it makes sense to renegotiate the transaction and change one or more of the loan features. This raises no special problems when the original mortgagor still owns the property and that person and the mortgagee recast their transaction, but great legal complexity can arise when the mortgagor has conveyed the property to a third person who has assumed or taken subject to the debt. What typically happens is that the mortgagee and grantee modify or extend the debt without including the mortgagor-grantor in the agreement. If, after the extension or modification, the grantee for some reason defaults, the issue is whether the mortgagor is still personally liable on the debt, or whether the unconsented-to extension or modification has discharged the mortgagor's liability.

Analysis of the mortgagor's liability is complicated by several variables. As a starting point, if the grantee assumed the debt, the law of suretyship controls. Under suretyship principles, the general rule is that any extension

What
= Surety

of the maturity date for payment of the debt discharges the surety, unless the surety agrees to that extension. The rationale is that the extension adds to the surety's risk. The surety agreed to undertake the risk of secondary liability for a particular, limited time period, and to extend the risk for a longer period of time increases that risk. The same discharge rule applies for modifications other than extensions that increase the surety's risk. For example, an increase in the interest rate discharges the surety because it increases the amount of debt and makes it more likely that the grantee will default, because the grantee must come up with more money to pay the mortgagee.

The standard suretyship principles clearly apply to all assumptions of debts that are not evidenced by negotiable instruments. When, as is often the case, the mortgage note is a negotiable instrument, different rules may come into play. Prior to 1990, §3-606 of the Uniform Commercial Code (UCC) governed extensions and releases granted by the note holder. Although the language of §3-606 is not crystal clear, most courts interpreted it as codifying basic common-law suretyship principles, including the rule that an extension made without the mortgagor's consent results in a total discharge, regardless of whether the mortgagor actually suffers loss.

The 1990 Official Text of Article 3 completely dropped §3-606, without providing any other language to govern the rights of makers of negotiable mortgage notes after a transfer of the mortgaged property. A new §3-605 deals with extensions and modifications that affect indorsers and accommodation parties, but not makers themselves. A few states still have the pre-1990 version of Article 3, and in those states the UCC still covers disputes regarding extensions when the note is negotiable. In states with the new Article 3, the issue now turns on common-law suretyship principles, whether or not the note is a negotiable instrument.

FIRST FEDERAL SAVINGS & LOAN ASSOCIATION v. ARENA
Court of Appeals of Indiana, Fourth District, 1980
406 N.E.2d 1279

CHIPMAN, Judge. First Federal Savings and Loan Association of Gary, (First Federal), appeals from a grant of summary judgment in favor of Michael and Grace Arena, (Arenas), in a foreclosure action brought by First Federal against the Arenas and their grantee, Sanford G. Richardson, as well as various lienholders. . . .

FACTS

On May 26, 1965, the Arenas executed a note, mortgage, and supplemental agreement with First Federal. The note provided for a loan of $32,000 at an interest rate of 5¾, and the mortgage securing this note provided for advances of up to $6,400. March 11, 1966, the Arenas were granted an advance of $5,100, and in consideration, they executed a modification and extension agreement which provided they would owe a new balance of $36,664.81, and the interest rate would be increased to 6%. A separate note, mortgage, and supplemental agreement were also executed by the Arenas in relation to this advance.

March 10, 1969, the Arenas conveyed the real estate which was the subject of both the May 26, 1965, and March 11, 1966, mortgages to Sanford G. Richardson by warranty deed subject to the two mortgages to First Federal.[1] The same day, without notice to or the consent of the Arenas, Mr. Richardson and First Federal entered into a modification and extension agreement, under the terms of which Richardson assumed both of the mortgages in question, and the time for payment was extended to twenty years; there was also a change in the interest rate from 6% to 7¼%. Thus, this agreement, signed only by Richardson and First Federal, was designed to be a modification of First Federal's earlier agreement with the Arenas by extending the time of payment and modifying the terms of payment to which the Arenas and First Federal had agreed.

After June 27, 1975, Richardson failed to make the payments due under the March 10, 1969, modification and extension agreement. As a result, a default on the mortgages and notes occurred and a suit in foreclosure was filed on behalf of First Federal against the Arenas, Richardson, and several lienholders. . . .

Decision

. . . By reason of an expressed provision to that effect in the supplemental agreements between the Arenas and First Federal, the Arenas were not released from liability upon extension of the mortgage in the agreement between Mr. Richardson and First Federal; however, this agreement not only extended the time for payment, but it also modified the terms of payment by increasing the interest rate. It is our opinion the trial court properly found the Arenas had not consented to such a change in interest rates and, therefore, were released from liability.[3] Arenas' grantee and First

1. Although the grantee's preliminary offer to purchase provided Mr. Richardson would "assume" the existing mortgages on the property, the warranty deed evidencing the consummated contract recited the conveyance was "subject to" the Arena's mortgages to First Federal. Based upon the general rule that any inconsistencies between the terms in the preliminary contract and the deed are to be settled by the deed alone, since all prior negotiations are considered merged in that instrument, Wayne International Building & Loan Assn. v. Beckner, (1922) 1919 Ind. 664, 134 N.E. 273; Guckenberger v. Shank, (1941) 110 Ind. App. 442, 37 N.E.2d 708, along with the fact none of the parties argued there was any mistake in drawing the deed or that they intended to make it read other than as in fact it was written, we have concluded, for purposes of this opinion the conveyance was "subject to" the mortgage.

3. If the full amount due on foreclosure did not exceed the value of the property at the time of execution of the Modification and Extension Agreement, it was proper for the trial

Federal could not modify the original mortgagors' agreement without the mortgagors' consent.

The focal point in this controversy is the meaning to be accorded a reservation of rights clause which appeared in the supplemental agreement executed by the Arenas when they obtained the initial mortgage and later secured the advance. The agreement provided:

> THE UNDERSIGNED, Michael Arena and Grace Arena, Husband and Wife, . . . , hereinafter referred to as the Mortgagor, hereby executes and delivers to FIRST FEDERAL SAVINGS AND LOAN ASSOCIATION OF GARY, . . . , hereinafter referred to as the Mortgagee, this Supplemental Agreement, pursuant to a Mortgage executed and delivered concurrently herewith, and this Supplemental Agreement is expressly made a part of said Mortgage, ...
>
> THE MORTGAGOR COVENANTS:
>
> 6. That in the event the ownership of said property or any part thereof becomes vested in a person other than the Mortgagor, the Mortgagee may, without notice to the Mortgagor, deal with such successor or successors in interest with reference to this mortgage and the debt hereby secured in the same manner as with the Mortgagor, and may forbear to sue or may extend time for payment of the debt, secured hereby, without discharging or in any way affecting the liability of the Mortgagor hereunder or upon the debt hereby secured.

First Federal asserts the reservation of rights language set out above permitted it, in dealing with Richardson, to increase the interest rate and extend the time of payment without first obtaining the Arenas' consent while still retaining their liability. Appellant takes the position that the portion of paragraph six providing for no discharge modified forbearing to sue and extending time for payment as well as dealing in the same manner as with the mortgagor; therefore, since the interest rate was increased when the Arenas were given their additional advance, according to First Federal, raising the

---

court to completely discharge the Arenas. Mutual Ben. Life Ins. Co. v. Lindley, (1932) 97 Ind. App. 575, 183 N.E. 127; Stevens, *Extension Agreements in the "Subject-To" Mortgage Situation,* 15 U. Cin. L. Rev. 58 (1941). As a corollary, if the value of the land at the time of this agreement was less than the amount of the mortgage on the property, the Arenas should have remained liable to the extent of the difference.

Although it was improper for the trial court to hold there was a complete discharge without also holding the value of the land at the time of the March 10, 1969, agreement fully supported the mortgage loan, First Federal never raised any error regarding the extent to which the Arenas were discharged; consequently, we can only assume the amount due on foreclosure on March 10, 1969, would have been less than the value of the property at that time.

We note, since Mr. Richards offered to purchase the real estate in question for $37,000, and the aggregate balance remaining unpaid when Mr. Richardson and First Federal executed the Modification and Extension Agreement was $33,393.83, it appears the value of the land, in fact, did exceed the amount due, and thus, a complete discharge would have been proper.

interest rate in its agreement with Richardson would merely be dealing with him in the same manner as it had dealt with the Arenas and, consequently, should not result in a discharge.

The Arenas, on the other hand, contend the reservation of rights clause in the Supplemental Agreement made no reference to the alteration or modification of the interest rate but rather, referred only to an extension of the time for payment or the decision to forbear to sue. . . .

When the Arenas conveyed the real estate to Richardson subject to the existing mortgages to First Federal, the land became as to said parties, the primary source of funds for payment of the debt. Mutual Ben. Life Ins. Co. v. Lindley, (1932) 97 Ind. App. 575, 183 N.E. 127. No technical relation of principal and surety arose between the Arenas and their grantee from this conveyance, but an equity did arise which bears a close resemblance to the equitable rights of a surety. As a result, the Arenas assumed a position analogous to that of a surety, and the grantee became the principal debtor to the extent of the value of the land conveyed. Mutual Ben. Life Ins. Co. v. Lindley, *supra*; Warm, *Some Aspects of the Rights and Liabilities of Mortgagee, Mortgagor and Grantee*, 10 Temple L.Q. 116 (1936).

While a mortgagor in such a situation may consent in advance to future modifications or agree his liability will not be discharged by subsequent agreements between his grantee and the mortgagee, such clauses are to be strictly construed against the mortgagee, *see* Friedman, *Discharge of Personal Liability on Mortgage Debts in New York*, 52 Yale L.J. 771, 788 (1943), since it would be unjust to subject the mortgagor to a new risk or material change to which he has not consented. . . .

While it is true paragraph six indicated First Federal could deal with successors in interest to the mortgage in the same manner as with the mortgagor, this provision did not say First Federal could do so with impunity. We agree with the trial court that the portion of this paragraph providing for no discharge only modified forbearing to sue or extending the time for payment. . . . At the risk of being redundant, we again note, paragraph six stated in part:

> 6. (T)he Mortgagee may, without notice to the Mortgagor, deal with . . . successors in interest with reference to this mortgage and the debt hereby secured in the same manner as with the Mortgagor, *and*. . . . (our emphasis)

The punctuation used clearly sets this portion of paragraph six apart from the remainder of the paragraph which then goes on to provide the mortgagee

> may forbear to sue or may extend time for payment of the debt, . . . , without discharging or in any way affecting the liability of the Mortgagor hereunder or upon the debt hereby secured.

In order to give the reservation of rights clause the expanded application urged by First Federal so that it also applied to dealing in the same manner as with the mortgagor, it would be necessary to ignore the punctuation used and the maxim that such clauses should be strictly construed against the mortgagee. Further, such a construction would change the reservation of rights provision from applying in two definite situations to an open-ended invitation to argue there was no discharge because the mortgagee either could have or in fact had dealt with the mortgagor in the same manner; the possible activities which arguably could then come within this clause's application would be indefinite. . . .

Judgment affirmed.

Problem 16D

Ferguson, the maker of a $500,000 mortgage note held by Lark, sells the mortgaged property for $520,000 to Jennifer, who assumes the note. Jennifer then sells for $490,000 to Kellogg, who assumes the note, and Kellogg in turn sells to Lotto, who takes subject to the mortgage debt. The note has a present balance of $480,000 and is payable in installments. The property has declined in value and is now worth, depending on appraisers' opinions, between $430,000 and $450,000. What effect is there on Ferguson's and Jennifer's liability under the following circumstances?

(a) Lotto wants to make a smaller monthly payment and extend the loan term. Lark agrees, and Lark and Lotto sign a written extension agreement. Prior to extension, the loan had a monthly payment of $15,200 and final maturity in five years. Now it has a monthly payment of $11,500 and matures in eight years.

(b) Instead, the extension agreement increases the interest rate from 7 to 8 percent, along with the extension from five to eight years.

(c) Instead, the extension agreement keeps the loan term the same but increases the interest rate from 7 to 8 percent. Lotto agreed to this because he had defaulted, and this change was the only way Lark would agree to waive his right to foreclose.

(d) Instead, there is no agreement between Lark and Lotto, but Lark accepts a prepayment of $30,000 tendered by Lotto.

(e) Instead of an extension agreement, Lark and Lotto reduce the remaining loan term from five years to four years, thereby increasing the monthly payment to $17,800.

E. RESTRICTIONS ON TRANSFER BY MORTGAGOR

The general rule is that the mortgagor's interest in the property is freely alienable. This is true regardless of which theory of mortgage law (title, lien, or intermediate) the state follows (see Chapter 14). In a lien-theory state, the mortgagor who makes a conveyance transfers title; in a title-theory state, although the mortgagor cannot transfer "title," the mortgagor's equity of redemption, which amounts to "equitable title," is freely alienable.

This mortgage rule follows an underlying policy in favor of free transferability, which is basic to many areas of property law. In the mortgage context, the policy favoring free alienability is not so strong that it cannot be curtailed by the parties' contract. Certain restraints on alienation, voluntarily agreed to by mortgagor and mortgagee, are legally enforceable. The most common type of restraint is the *due-on-sale clause*, which provides that if the borrower sells the property without the lender's approval, the entire principal balance of the loan immediately becomes due and payable. Lenders developed the due-on-sale clause primarily to preserve their security by regulating ownership and occupancy of the mortgaged property. Later in the 1960s, lenders began using the clause to stop the financing of sales by loan assumption when interest rates were rising. Prior to 1982, state law governed the enforceability of due-on-sale clauses for both types of situations, except for loans made by federally chartered institutions that were subject to Federal Home Loan Bank Board regulations.

In 1982, Congress passed the Garn-St. Germain Depository Institutions Act, 12 U.S.C. §1701j-3, to preempt state laws that protected mortgagors from lender enforcement of due-on-sale clauses. The Garn-St. Germain Act in essence federalizes the automatic enforcement theory of due-on-sale clauses adopted by some states prior to the Act. In so doing, it resolved an intense economic, political, and legal debate that pitted borrowers and buyers against lenders. Under the Act, as a general rule lenders may enforce due-on-sale clauses in accordance with their express terms. Passed in 1982, the Act responded to the same economic pressures associated with high inflation and rising interest rates that led to the 1980 federal preemption of state usury laws.

In principle, the Act is supposed to benefit not only lenders but also borrowers by making mortgage loan credit available at a lower cost and on a uniform, national basis. Residential lenders claimed that they would have to raise loan rates on new loans if they were unable to use due-on-sale clauses to retire unprofitable old loans. Most mortgagors move and repay mortgage loans long before the scheduled maturity of 30 years.

What is a due-on-sale clause for purposes of the legislation? The Act defines the term as "a contract provision which authorizes a lender, at its option, to declare due and payable sums secured by the lender's security instrument if all or any part of the property, or an interest therein, securing the real property loan is sold or transferred without the lender's prior written consent." *Id.* §1701j-3(a)(1).

In one respect, the Act protects residential borrowers by barring a lender's use of the due-on-sale clause for certain transfers, which are sometimes called "nonsubstantive transfers":

> (d) *Exemption of specified transfers or dispositions.* With respect to a real property loan secured by a lien on residential real property containing less

> than five dwelling units, including a lien on the stock allocated to a dwelling unit in a cooperative housing corporation, or on a residential manufactured home, a lender may not exercise its option pursuant to a due-on-sale clause upon—
>
> (1) the creation of a lien or other encumbrance subordinate to the lender's security instrument which does not relate to a transfer of rights of occupancy in the property;
>
> (2) the creation of a purchase money security interest for household appliances;
>
> (3) a transfer by devise, descent, or operation of law on the death of a joint tenant or tenant by the entirety;
>
> (4) the granting of a leasehold interest of three years or less not containing an option to purchase;
>
> (5) a transfer to a relative resulting from the death of a borrower;
>
> (6) a transfer where the spouse or children of the borrower become an owner of the property;
>
> (7) a transfer resulting from a decree of a dissolution of marriage, legal separation agreement, or from an incidental property settlement agreement, by which the spouse of the borrower becomes an owner of the property;
>
> (8) a transfer into an inter vivos trust in which the borrower is and remains a beneficiary and which does not relate to a transfer of rights of occupancy in the property; or
>
> (9) any other transfer or disposition described in regulations prescribed by the Federal Home Loan Bank Board.

12 U.S.C. §1701j-3(d). Prior to the Act, in many states the right of the lender to accelerate for transfers of these types was unclear. In some of the states that followed the automatic enforcement theory for due-on-sale clauses, it seems that acceleration would have been permitted. The Act preempts state law permitting such acceleration.

Problem 16E

Jane Homeseller wants to sell her house to John Homebuyer for $110,000. Her loan from Third Savings, which she took out when she bought the house 3 years ago, bears interest at 7.5 percent, has a present balance of $85,000, and is amortized over 30 years. Current residential interest rates for 30-year fixed rate loans are around 11 percent. John has an excellent credit rating; in fact, his salary is higher than Jane's. Jane and John agree that as part of the purchase price John will assume Jane's loan. Because the mortgage has a standard due-on-sale clause, they ask Third Savings to consent to the sale. Third Savings refuses to consent unless John agrees to an increase in the interest rate to 10.25 percent and also agrees to pay an assumption fee of $200. Does Third Savings have a right to impose these conditions? What if it required a rate increase to 11 percent? To 11.5 percent?

F. DEFAULT CLAUSES

Default and alleged default constitute the prime battleground of lenders and borrowers. From the lender's point of view, a loan that is in material default is a problem going to the essence of its expectations. At the outset of the transaction, the lender considered credit risk, evaluating the borrower's ability to pay and his evident willingness to pay.

When a loan default issue arises, it's important to realize that stress levels on both sides are very often high. And, when the borrower's default appears serious, the lender has to decide what measures to take and when.

In a mortgage loan with standard documentation, the promissory note and the mortgage are the places where *default* is defined. In more complex loans, other documents may also apply. The mortgage may refer to other documents, such as a loan agreement or an assignment of leases, to specify other events of default. The first step in analyzing a default scenario is straightforward. Has a default occurred and can the lender prove it? This depends primarily on the parties' express agreement. (Why primarily? Why not absolutely?) Analysis of every dispute about default must begin with a very careful reading of the documents. Sometimes the answer is clear, but other times the parties' language must be interpreted in light of the events that have transpired.

Problem 16F

Here are two clauses taken from a uniform Security Instrument promulgated jointly by two federal entities, the Federal National Mortgage Association (FNMA) and the Federal Home Loan Mortgage Corporation (FHLMC):

> 6. Occupancy, Preservation, Maintenance and Protection of the Property; Borrower's Loan Application; Leaseholds. Borrower shall occupy, establish, and use the Property as Borrower's principal residence within sixty days after the execution of this Security Instrument and shall continue to occupy the Property as Borrower's principal residence for at least one year after the date of occupancy, unless Lender otherwise agrees in writing, which consent shall not be unreasonably withheld, or unless extenuating circumstances exist which are beyond Borrower's control. Borrower shall not destroy, damage or impair the Property, allow the Property to deteriorate, or commit waste on the Property. Borrower shall be in default if any forfeiture action or proceeding, whether civil or criminal, is begun that in Lender's good faith judgment could result in forfeiture of the Property or otherwise materially impair the lien created by this Security Instrument or Lender's security interest. Borrower may cure such a default and reinstate, as provided in paragraph 18, by causing the action or proceeding to be dismissed with a ruling that, in Lender's good faith determination, precludes forfeiture of the Borrower's interest in the Property or other material impairment of the lien created by this Security Instrument or Lender's

security interest. Borrower shall also be in default if Borrower, during the loan application process, gave materially false or inaccurate information or statements to Lender (or failed to provide Lender with any material information) in connection with the loan evidenced by the Note, including, but not limited to, representations concerning Borrower's occupancy of the Property as a principal residence. If this Security Instrument is on a leasehold, Borrower shall comply with all the provisions of the lease. If Borrower acquires fee title to the Property, the leasehold and the fee title shall not merge unless Lender agrees to the merger in writing.

7. Protection of Lender's Rights in the Property. If Borrower fails to perform the covenants and agreements contained in this Security Instrument, or there is a legal proceeding that may significantly affect Lender's rights in the Property (such as a proceeding in bankruptcy, probate, for condemnation or forfeiture or to enforce laws or regulations), then Lender may do and pay for whatever is necessary to protect the value of the Property and Lender's rights in the Property. Lender's actions may include paying any sums secured by a lien which has priority over this Security Instrument, appearing in court, paying reasonable attorneys' fees and entering on the Property to make repairs. Although Lender may take action under this paragraph 7, Lender does not have to do so.

Any amounts disbursed by Lender under this paragraph 7 shall become additional debt of Borrower secured by this Security Instrument. Unless Borrower and Lender agree to other terms of payment, these amounts shall bear interest from the date of disbursement at the Note rate and shall be payable, with interest, upon notice from Lender to Borrower requesting payment.

Which of the following events constitutes a default? Does Lender have to take any action first to make the action an act of default? Which of the following events do you expect may be especially difficult for the lender to prove in court? For now, ignore various affirmative defenses and claims that the borrower may make to the effect that the parties' language should not be applied literally, as it is written.

(a) Borrower moved into the house the day the loan closed. Borrower has worked for General Computer Company for five years. One week before loan closing, she applied for a promotion in the company, which she just learned about. It would be a big step up and would require moving to the West Coast. Four months after loan closing, Borrower gets good news: "I got the promotion!" She promptly moves and rents the house, signing a one-year lease.

(b) Borrower, a *Home Improvement* kind of guy, added a solarium to the house. So far, only one major mistake has surfaced. The zoning administrator has discovered that the solarium encroaches by four feet on the side setback line and is threatening to sue Borrower unless he removes the encroachment promptly. Mr. Home Improvement, tired of work, refuses, thinking this is no big deal.

(c) Borrower, an arsonist, burns his house to the ground.

(d) Husband and wife are Borrower, and husband has just gotten arrested for selling illegal drugs on the property. The federal government has brought a complaint seeking civil forfeiture of the property. Does it matter whether another provision of the security instrument contains Borrower's express promise not to use the property for illegal purposes? Would it make a difference if only wife was Borrower, but the government nevertheless brought a forfeiture action?

(e) Borrower just received a certified copy of a complaint, naming him as defendant. His neighbor, who owns the house in back of Borrower's, is asserting ownership by adverse possession of a 15-foot strip of Borrower's lot.

G. ACCELERATION

Acceleration is the process by which the lender, after default by the borrower, makes the entire debt due and payable. The due date for future installment payments or a balloon payment is moved up or "accelerated." In a sense, acceleration is the flip side of prepayment. When a borrower prepays, he is deciding that the debt should be paid now rather than in the future in accordance with the schedule of payments agreed to by the parties. When a lender accelerates, he is deciding that—because of the event of default—the debt should be paid in full now.

From the lender's perspective, acceleration is a key step in the foreclosure process. The lender's goal in foreclosure is to sell the mortgaged property and use the sales proceeds to repay the entire debt or as much of the debt as it can. Although it is possible in most jurisdictions to foreclose on an installment loan without acceleration, it is messy and usually not a good idea.

It is important to realize that virtually all loan documents explicitly address the issue of acceleration. Typically, the acceleration clause is contained in the promissory note. Acceleration or some aspect of acceleration is sometimes covered in the mortgage instrument as well. What happens if the loan documents lack an acceleration clause? Might the lender accelerate the debt on the theory of anticipatory repudiation? The traditional answer, applied by almost all courts, is that maturity of future installments cannot be accelerated. The mortgagee pays dearly for the error; it must either attempt to collect the installments as they fall due or wait until final maturity of the debt.

There are two basic types of acceleration clauses. One provides that the entire debt shall be due and payable if a specified event happens, such as a certain type of default. The parties' language is such that acceleration happens automatically if the event occurs. No action by the lender is necessary. Automatic acceleration clauses are not commonly used today. In the past they were employed fairly often, but now most acceleration clauses give the lender the option to accelerate maturity of the debt. The lender has the choice; it may declare an acceleration, insisting that the borrower pay the debt in full, or it may forbear. If the basis of the lender's right to accelerate is a default by the borrower in paying one or more installments of money to the lender, rather than accelerate the lender may decide to try to collect just the arrears. Most lenders believe the optional acceleration clause is preferable to an automatic acceleration provision because it gives the lender more flexibility and control.

Much litigation between lenders and borrowers focuses on issues of acceleration. Borrowers frequently challenge a lender's claim of acceleration on procedural as well as substantive grounds. Procedural challenges focus on the process followed by the lender. If the documents have an optional acceleration clause, the lender must take some affirmative action that demonstrates its intent to accelerate. Otherwise, the loan is unaccelerated, a point of highly practical significance. Prior to the moment of acceleration, the borrower has the right to cure the default and, if he does so, the lender cannot accelerate.

What affirmative act of the lender qualifies legally to accelerate the loan? There is no simple answer. A single act may suffice, or several steps may be required, such as notice to the borrower of intent to accelerate followed by an act evidencing acceleration. In some cases, a lender may validly accelerate a loan with no notice to the borrower whatsoever. Different states have different requirements, some judicial, others statutory. Many but not all states have enacted statutes that protect mortgagors, either by requiring notice prior to acceleration or by permitting the mortgagor to pay arrearages after acceleration, thereby reinstating the installment loan. Some statutes protect only residential mortgagors, but other statutes protect all mortgagors. Some federally chartered institutions are subject to federal regulations that deal with acceleration. Moreover, acceleration clauses often specify what steps the lender may take to accelerate, and in many but not all circumstances the courts defer to the parties' agreement as to the procedural steps for acceleration. In many promissory notes, the borrower waives the right to receive notices and demands of various types. Though such waivers are generally effective, courts tend to scrutinize them carefully. They often say that a waiver must specifically identify the rights that are being surrendered. If the waiver is worded generally or is ambiguous, it is likely to be construed against the lender, in favor of the borrower.

Substantive challenges to acceleration focus on whether the lender had a legally sufficient reason to insist on acceleration. Can the lender prove the alleged default? Even if the lender follows all the proper procedural steps, if it had no substantive right to accelerate, obviously it loses. Often the dispute is more complex than the basically straightforward question of whether an event of default occurred. The borrower may have defaulted, but general legal principles such as waiver or estoppel may bar the lender from accelerating. The most frequent fact pattern that invokes waiver or estoppel involves the lender's acceptance of a number of late payments. This conduct may send a message that late payments are permissible and may be tendered in the future without the borrower fearing repercussions. In effect, the lender is estopped by her conduct from claiming that time is of the essence. The lender cannot just accelerate when the borrower, yet again, tenders the money late. To make timely payment of the essence again, the lender must notify the borrower that from now on payments must be made on time or else he will exercise his option to accelerate the loan.

In addition to using waiver and estoppel to protect borrowers, most courts, at least in some class of cases, will safeguard borrowers from the harsh consequences of acceleration by evaluating how serious the default happens to be. If the court perceives great hardship to a borrower, especially when the default appears inadvertent and there is little risk to the lender if the loan remains unaccelerated, the court is likely to deny the lender's acceleration demand. Judicial explanations are often along one or more of the following lines: the default is technical, not material or substantial; the event has not impaired the lender's security; or general principles of equity permit the court to intervene to protect the borrower from a penalty or a forfeiture.

Problem 16G

(a) Lender lends $100,000 to Borrower, repayable in equal monthly installments of $800 per month for 30 years. One year later, when the loan balance is $98,600, Borrower defaults by failing to make the monthly payments due on April 1 and May 1. On May 14, Borrower mails a check for $1,600 to Lender. On May 16, the check arrives in Lender's mailbox as part of the morning delivery. That afternoon, Lender's loan officer, unaware of Borrower's check, declares acceleration and posts a letter to Borrower informing Borrower of that unhappy fact. Is the loan validly accelerated?

(b) Assume the same transaction, except Borrower mails the check by putting a properly addressed, stamped envelope into a U.S. Post Office mailbox on the morning of May 16. It is delivered to Lender the afternoon of May 18, two days after Lender's loan officer declared acceleration. Is the loan validly accelerated if (i) Lender promptly returns Borrower's check to Borrower, or (ii) Lender cashes Borrower's check, giving Borrower a credit for the amount of the check against the entire loan balance?

17
Foreclosure

Foreclosure is the process, after default, by which the lender gets value from the collateral to repay part or all of the debt. In many states, the process consists of litigation and is called *judicial foreclosure*. In others, foreclosure is usually done privately, outside the courts, by the mortgagee or by a third party such as a trustee under a deed of trust. This process is called *power of sale foreclosure* or nonjudicial foreclosure. In both basic types, the property is sold, with the sales proceeds applied to repay the debt. Foreclosure, regardless of the process used, is the sine qua non of secured financing. If law did not provide a foreclosure process, every creditor would be a general unsecured creditor. Creditors could still reach the debtor's assets upon default, but doing so would require a proceeding under the standard judicial machinery for collection of judgments. This would involve bringing an action on the debt, reducing it to a monetary judgment, and then reaching the desired property by making use of local procedures for attachment liens, judgment liens, levies, and execution sales.

There are some other advantages for lenders, in addition to the possibility of foreclosure, stemming from standard mortgage clauses, many of which we have discussed in prior chapters. For example, the borrower's promise to pay taxes on the property, not to commit waste, and not to sell the property without the lender's consent (the due-on-sale clause) all provide some protection to the lender, even if the lender does not or cannot foreclose. The main reason, however, why the mortgage reduces risk is that if the borrower defaults by failing to pay the debt or by breaking other promises, the lender has the option to do more than bring an action for breach of promise or an action on the unpaid installments or the accelerated debt. The lender also has the option to foreclose.

When thinking about foreclosure, one critical distinction to keep in mind is the difference between an action on the debt and a foreclosure action. These are the mortgage lender's two basic options when the mortgagor is not voluntarily paying the debt. Sometimes the mortgage lender wants to pursue both options. They are not necessarily an either-or choice. Why might the mortgagee want a judgment on the debt, even though she is foreclosing? If the value of the property is less than the debt and the mortgagee realizes this, she expects that foreclosure will result in a *deficiency*. Therefore, along with foreclosure, the mortgagee wants a judgment equal to the shortfall — this is called a *deficiency judgment*. If there is any prospect that the judgment may be collectible, the deficiency judgment is worth having.

Today, in the United States generally, the mortgagee has the option of suing on the debt, foreclosing on the property, or doing both. If both are sought, they may be pursued simultaneously or consecutively. Unless there are statutory or contractual restrictions, the mortgagee is not required to sue on the debt and foreclose at the same point in time. With a judicial foreclosure action, if the mortgagee anticipates a deficiency, a single action can seek both a foreclosure decree and a deficiency judgment against the borrower. The foreclosure action is considered to be an action in equity, with the action on the debt considered to be at law, but this combination is permissible given the modern procedural unification of law and equity.

The opposite of a deficiency resulting from foreclosure is a *surplus*. When the mortgaged property is worth much more than the unpaid debt, there is surplus value that belongs to the property owner, the mortgagor. If the auction sale at foreclosure is at a price that exceeds the debt, including the expenses of foreclosure, there are surplus proceeds. These proceeds are paid to the mortgagor, provided there are no third parties who have asserted claims against the mortgagor in the foreclosure action. If there are third parties with valid claims, such as junior lienors or tenants whose leases are terminated, they are compensated out of the surplus. Even in this circumstance, however, the surplus is used for the mortgagor's benefit, as it extinguishes the mortgagor's debts owed to third parties.

A. TYPES OF FORECLOSURE

There is no single way for a mortgagee to foreclose on the mortgaged property. State law determines what foreclosure processes are available, and they vary substantially. All states have foreclosure statutes that define and govern foreclosure proceedings, which must be consulted. In addition, the parties' contract, as reflected in the mortgage instrument, often affects how the lender may foreclose. Most mortgages have a foreclosure clause, which covers such matters as notices to be given to the borrower prior to foreclosure, time periods that must expire before the lender takes certain steps to foreclose, and where and when a foreclosure sale may take place. Although foreclosure rules and procedures vary markedly from state to state, there are common elements. These common elements are best understood by focusing on the three basic types of foreclosure presently used in the

United States: strict foreclosure, judicial foreclosure with public sale of the property, and power of sale foreclosure (also called nonjudicial foreclosure).

1. *Strict Foreclosure*

English foreclosure is called "strict foreclosure." This is our American term for it; to the English it was just "foreclosure" with no ominous-sounding adjective. See Chapter 14 for a brief description of the historical steps in mortgage law leading up to strict foreclosure. Depending on your point of view (lender or borrower), the term "strict foreclosure" sounds either delightful or awful. The basic idea is that the Court of Chancery, at the instance of the mortgagee, "foreclosed" (barred) the mortgagor's equity of redemption by setting a final payment date. The judicial date was strictly enforced; hence "strict" foreclosure. If the mortgagor failed to pay by the judicially set date, the ballgame was over. With strict foreclosure, the mortgagee could just keep the property. After foreclosure, she could sell it, but she wasn't required to do so. If the mortgaged property was worth more than the debt, the mortgagee had no duty to account to the mortgagor for the surplus value. Today, England largely uses power of sale foreclosure, rather than historic strict foreclosure.

In the United States today, strict foreclosure is not in widespread use. Early on in our history, most communities came to believe that strict foreclosure was too harsh when the mortgagor had substantial equity in the property. Although in principle the court could alleviate harshness by setting a long time for final payment when the property was worth much more than the debt—for example, many months—judges usually did not do this, and often they did not even obtain evidence of property value.

2. *Judicial Foreclosure*

In judicial foreclosure, the mortgagee brings an action asking the court to issue an order calling for a sale of the mortgaged property. It resembles strict foreclosure in that both procedures are actions brought before a trial court, with a judge setting a date by which the mortgagor must pay or else lose the property. In both cases, the mortgagor loses her equity of redemption if she does not pay by the judicial deadline. The difference is what happens when the deadline arrives—that is, *how* the mortgagor loses the property. With strict foreclosure, the mortgagee just keeps the property, and if the mortgagee does not yet have possession, she is entitled to possession. With judicial foreclosure, a court-supervised public sale of the property occurs. Traditionally and still today, in many communities this is by public auction, outside on the courthouse steps. Usually a public officer such as the sheriff conducts the auction sale.

Judicial foreclosure developed in the United States to safeguard mortgagors from losses stemming from strict foreclosures. Judicial foreclosure is thought to be superior because the "market" decides how much the mortgaged property is worth. In principle, this protects the mortgagor with a large equity in the property because public bidding at the foreclosure sale is thought to provide the best opportunity for a sale that will yield a foreclosure surplus — the best chance that the price paid by the high bidder will exceed the mortgage debt. This assumption is based on the belief that an auction creates a market and that the price bid at an auction, therefore, reflects the fair market value of the property. From this perspective, it is assumed that the defaulting borrower has her best chance of getting a fair and full price for the property, which should present her best opportunity for receiving a foreclosure surplus. It should be noted that this "market" assumption is held in law even in situations where few or perhaps only one bidder is present at the foreclosure sale.

The procedural details of judicial foreclosure depend on state law, with a number of local differences, but there are some common key elements that revolve around the identification of which persons' rights are to be adjudicated. The lender, with her attorney's help, must decide whom to sue. Foreclosure is not an *in rem* proceeding. A foreclosure decree binds parties who are defendants with proper service of process. Thus, nonparties are generally not bound by the foreclosure decree or the foreclosure sale, and this is important if nonparties have property rights in the foreclosed-upon property.

To answer the question of whom the lender should include as defendants in the foreclosure action, we need to consider the status of title to the mortgaged property that should pass to the foreclosure purchaser. The central goal of foreclosure is to give the purchaser *the same title the mortgagor had at the moment the mortgage was granted*. This is the lender's prime objective with respect to title. How is this accomplished? Foreclosure has to terminate not only the mortgagor's equity of redemption but also all junior interests. All rights in the mortgaged property, other than the mortgage itself, are either prior to or junior to the mortgage. The foreclosure terminates the mortgage that is being foreclosed. Prior interests are not terminated or affected by the foreclosure; that, in essence, is what it means to be prior. Junior interests are supposed to be cut off. Junior interests may consist of the full range of rights in real property that are recognized in our legal system — for example, leases, easements, covenants, junior mortgages, and judgment liens.

In terms of foreclosure procedure, the persons who hold junior interests are *necessary parties*. They are necessary in the sense that they have to be joined as defendants to accomplish the goal of transferring title to the buyer in the condition it was in when the mortgage was granted.

Another key element in foreclosure practice is identification of *proper parties*. A proper party is a person who has rights or duties with respect to the property or the debt but who is not a necessary party — the central title goal can be accomplished without making the proper party a defendant. This person is a "proper" party in the sense that it is useful to ascertain or define her rights or duties as part of the foreclosure proceeding. Joinder may be desirable, but it is not essential as with a necessary party. The significance of labelling a person as a "proper party" is that she can be joined without her consent. The proper party can be forced in as an additional defendant. Proper parties include holders of prior interests in the property and persons who are liable on the debt but who do not presently have an ownership interest in the mortgaged property. Thus, if the foreclosing mortgagee plans to seek a deficiency judgment, a guarantor or surety for that debt is a proper party in the foreclosure action.

ENGLISH v. BANKERS TRUST COMPANY OF CALIFORNIA, N.A.

Court of Appeal of Florida, 4th District, 2005
895 So. 2d 1120

Stone, J. We affirm a summary judgment of foreclosure in favor of Bankers Trust. The trial court properly allowed Bankers Trust to join English in a re-foreclosure of a mortgage where it failed to join the true owner of the property, an indispensable party, in the first foreclosure.

There are no disputed issues of material fact. Bankers Trust first attempted to foreclose, in a separate case, in early 2002. It named only English, the original owner and mortgagor, as a defendant. That foreclosure resulted in a final judgment setting the debt at $73,839.75, and setting a foreclosure sale. Bankers Trust purchased the property at the foreclosure sale. Immediately thereafter, Bankers Trust learned of English's conveyance to Lesa Investments, and it brought a *de novo* foreclosure action naming both English and Lesa Investments. Another party, Van Zamft, was also added.

English does not deny the default in payment. Instead, she answers that, because there had been a prior foreclosure action and sale, she could not be joined in the re-foreclosure.

The trial court correctly concluded that the first action was void. Significantly, this is not a re-foreclosure to extinguish a junior lienor. Rather, this second action is an initial foreclosure as to the fee simple owner. Because Lesa Investments, the undisputed owner, was not a party to the first suit, the initial foreclosure judgment could not result in a valid sale, as the owner of the fee simple title was an indispensable party. Community Fed. Svgs. and Loan Ass'n v. Wright, 452 So. 2d 638, 640 (Fla. 4th DCA 1984).

If the initial sale were not void, then there would be merit in English's claim that res judicata precludes this second action as to a deficiency judgment. The first foreclosure sale, however, is void for failure to join the fee simple owner. . . .

We note that, more than a century ago, the Florida Supreme Court recognized that "a foreclosure proceeding resulting in a final decree and a sale of the mortgaged property, without the holder of the legal title being before the court will have no effect to transfer his title to the purchaser at said sale." Jordan v. Sayre, 24 Fla. 1, 3 So. 329, 330 (Fla. 1888). If the foreclosure proceeding has no effect to transfer title because the legal title holder has not been joined, it is simply another way of saying that the foreclosure proceeding is void.

Although English may have a point in arguing that it is redundant to name her in the re-foreclosure of the property, there is no authority to support her position that joining her in the second foreclosure is precluded. Rather, it is reasonable to conclude that if the first foreclosure sale was invalid, because the legal title holder was not a party, then a second foreclosure action is necessary to enforce the mortgagee's rights.

It also follows that English's claim that the doctrine of merger precludes Bankers Trust from seeking a deficiency judgment must fail. If the first foreclosure sale and all related proceedings cannot stand, then the deficiency judgment awarded to Bankers Trust was also void.

With respect to the amount due from English, however, any such deficiency, including pre-judgment interest, is due only until the time of the original foreclosure proceeding. In White v. Mid-State Federal Savings & Loan Ass'n, 530 So. 2d 959 (Fla. 5th DCA 1988), the court held that where the senior mortgagee becomes the owner of the foreclosed property but re-foreclosure is necessary, it is error to continue to award interest, real property taxes, insurance premiums, and expenses for the period following the first foreclosure. . . .

Therefore, we reverse as to the amount of deficiency and remand for further proceedings. In all other respects, we affirm.

Problem 17A

Burnsy defaulted on his home equity loan and Big Bad Lender promptly sued to foreclose, selling the home to Lucky at foreclosure auction sale for $44,000. The home equity debt, including interest and penalties plus the costs of foreclosure, totaled $24,000. Big Bad Lender properly joined all necessary parties in the foreclosure action. Lucky obtained possession of the property the day after the foreclosure sale. A title search disclosed the following interests in the property, in the following order of priority:

1. Utility easement granted to Bigtown Lighting and Power Co.
2. Mortgage loan to Last Federal Savings Bank. Balance due is presently $80,000.
3. Big Bad Lender's mortgage, securing the home equity loan.
4. Lien held by homeowner's association to secure payment of unpaid dues totalling $1,000.

5. Lease from Burnsy to Terri Tenant for 12 months, calling for monthly rent of $500. On the date of the foreclosure sale, four months remained in the lease term.

(a) In this situation, who is a necessary party? A proper party?

(b) When Lucky buys the property at the sale, does he take title free and clear of all these identified interests? If not, which survive and why?

(c) How should the officer in charge of the foreclosure distribute the surplus proceeds of $20,000? If instead there was a much smaller surplus—only $800—how should that be distributed?

3. *Power of Sale Foreclosure*

Foreclosure by power of sale, also called *nonjudicial foreclosure,* is in widespread use in a number of states. This type of foreclosure allows lenders to foreclose by selling the property without court involvement. All the steps in the foreclosure process, including the sale, are handled either by the lender or by a third party, such as the trustee under a deed of trust. The availability and validity of nonjudicial foreclosure depend on both the parties' agreement and the state foreclosure statutes. In any given transaction, nonjudicial foreclosure can be employed only if the mortgage instrument authorizes the procedure by granting a power of sale to the lender or to a third party such as a trustee. However, since mortgagees by and large control the drafting of loan documents, in states where nonjudicial foreclosure is common the proper clauses are virtually always included in the mortgage document.

State statutes govern nonjudicial foreclosure by specifying notice provisions, sales procedures, and other formalities the lender or her agent must observe. Such statutes, which the parties cannot contract around, are designed to protect mortgagors from the risks stemming from the fact that no disinterested third party such as a judge is supervising the foreclosure process. The lawyer who handles or facilitates a nonjudicial foreclosure must realize that the statutory requirements are not mere formalities. Punctilious observance is mandatory. A deviation from statutory requirements generally means that the foreclosure sale, even after completion, is subject to attack and invalidation. Any slipup means the lender or the foreclosure purchaser incurs great risk that, after completion of foreclosure, the mortgagor or a third party with an interest in the property will challenge the sale.

The goal of nonjudicial foreclosure is the same as judicial foreclosure: to sell the property and apply the net sales proceeds to the debt. The goal with respect to title is also the same: to transfer to the foreclosure buyer the title in the condition it was in when the mortgage was granted. The reason for the nonjudicial alternative is to save the lender the time and expense of going to court. Judicial foreclosure, for example, usually provides safeguards to the mortgagor and to third parties, such as the buyer at foreclosure and the owners of junior interests. Such parties generally have less protection, both procedural and substantive, in the private, nonjudicial, context. Junior interest holders are entitled to notice of a judicial foreclosure, for instance (they are necessary parties and if omitted are not bound by the foreclosure), but in many nonjudicial foreclosure states, they are not entitled to notice of the foreclosure unless they have obtained such a right by contracting with the mortgagee.

Compared to judicial foreclosure, power of sale foreclosure is cheap and fast, which is why many states have it. In principle, the savings should benefit not only lenders, who incur lower foreclosure costs, but also borrowers. Losses from loans should be less if lenders can force a foreclosure sale without incurring court costs and waiting months for completion of judicial proceedings. This means less risk to the lender, and in a competitive market this reduced risk should also reduce the lender's price. A borrower who agrees to grant the lender a power of sale should in return pay a lower interest rate or bargain for other economically advantageous terms.

Foreclosure, as indicated earlier, is the province of the states, and there is substantial variation in local laws and procedures. During the past few decades, the federal government has chosen to intervene in several areas of real estate finance to supply uniform national practices and legal rules. In prior chapters, we discuss creation of the secondary mortgage market and preemption of usury laws and due-on-sale limitations. Federal intervention has also begun, on a limited basis, in the area of foreclosure. In 1981, Congress passed the Multifamily Mortgage Foreclosure Act, 12 U.S.C. §§3701-3717, to authorize nonjudicial foreclosure of mortgages on multi family properties held by the Department of Housing and Urban Development (HUD). In 1994, the Single Family Mortgage Foreclosure Act, 12 U.S.C. §§3751-3768, extended the scheme to HUD's single-family mortgages. The acts provide for HUD to appoint a foreclosure commissioner to conduct the sale. Procedural rules, including notice requirements to borrowers and other interested parties, are supplied. The acts preempt state limits on the collection of deficiency judgments. The federal objective is to reduce the time and expense incurred by HUD when it uses state judicial foreclosure procedures, thus saving government resources by cutting the losses incurred due to mortgage default.

Problem 17B

Jack, an attorney named as trustee under a deed of trust, conducts a foreclosure sale. At the time, the debt is $105,000. Assume that all proper notices have been given but the following happens at the sale:

(a) The first Tuesday of the month is the only day of the month that foreclosure sales may occur. An ice storm Monday night closes many roads in and leading to the city. Many local businesses are closed, but Jack close to the courthouse. Jack and a lender's representative appear at house, and Jack conducts the sale with an audience of one, selling the to the lender for $90,000.

(b) Jack's watch is fast. The sale is advertised for 10:00 A.M., bu the sale at 9:52. The sale takes approximately two minutes, and he and the sole bidder, the lender, are gone at 9:59. How do we know this? Assume (i) the borrower, with a prospective bidder, shows up at 10:02 ("would have been there on time, but parking's awful") and is surprised to find no action. Or (ii) as part of a plan to detect and suppress crime, the city has installed surveillance cameras on the courthouse facade and the borrower obtained a copy of the videotape, which shows Jack jumped the gun. The borrower has no evidence of prospective bidders who planned to show up at 10:00.

(c) Jack's watch is slow, plus parking is awful. He and the lender's rep show up at 10:16 and hold the sale.

(d) Assume that the state statute governing power of sale foreclosures provides that the sale must be made between the hours of 10:00 A.M. and 4:00 P.M. on the first Tuesday of the month. The statute further requires that written notice of the date, time, and place of sale must be posted and sent by certified mail to the debtor. What do you think the notice should say with respect to the time of sale?

B. EQUITABLE SUBROGATION

EASTERN SAVINGS BANK v. PAPPAS

District of Columbia Court of Appeals, 2003
829 A.2d 953

SCHWELB, Associate Judge. Eastern Savings Bank (Eastern) brought this action for a declaratory judgment to determine the priority of secured interests in real property as between Eastern's Deed of Trust securing the payment of an indebtedness owed to Eastern by Vasiliki Pappas and a lien based on an earlier judgment against Vasiliki Pappas in favor of three judgment creditors. The trial court granted summary judgment in favor of the judgment creditors. On appeal, Eastern contends that its lien is entitled to priority over the creditors' lien pursuant to the doctrine of equitable subrogation. We agree, reverse, and remand.

I

In June 1980, Aphrodite Pappas, who was the owner of certain real property at 2507 33rd Street, N.W. in Washington, D.C., conveyed that property to Vasiliki Pappas in fee simple. Soon thereafter, Aphrodite Pappas died, leaving three children as heirs.[1] Vasiliki Pappas was named personal representative of Aphrodite Pappas' estate. In 1986, however, the Probate Court removed Vasiliki Pappas as personal representative on account of numerous improprieties on her part in exercising her fiduciary responsibilities. On April 18, 1990, Vasiliki Pappas executed a deed of trust on the 33rd Street property to secure a loan made to her by CitiBank Federal Savings Bank in the amount of $159,000 which was duly recorded.

In 1992, and again in 1996, the successor personal representative of Aphrodite Pappas' estate obtained judgments against Vasiliki Pappas in the Superior Court for breach of fiduciary duty. Each judgment was against Vasiliki Pappas personally, and not against her in her capacity as personal representative. These judgments were duly recorded in the land records, and they became effective as judgment liens against all real property titled in the name of Vasiliki Pappas. D.C. Code §15-102 (a) (2001).

Meanwhile, Vasiliki Pappas' financial difficulties continued, and by 1998, she was in serious default on the CitiBank Deed of Trust. CitiBank instituted foreclosure proceedings. On November 3, 1998, Vasiliki Pappas secured a loan from Eastern which had the effect of refinancing the earlier CitiBank loan, and she duly executed a promissory note in the amount of $168,000 payable to Eastern, $153,800 of which was used to discharge the earlier CitiBank loan. This note was secured by a new Deed of Trust of the same date.[2]

Certified Title Corporation (Certified) performed a title search on the property on behalf of Eastern in connection with the refinancing of the Vasiliki Pappas indebtedness. Certified discovered the first judgment, which had been secured by the Successor Representative of the Estate of Aphrodite Pappas against Vasiliki Pappas in the amount of $3,461.12. Certified mistakenly understood, and incorrectly represented to Eastern, that this judgment had been entered against Vasiliki Pappas solely in her capacity as the former Personal Representative of Aphrodite Pappas' estate. A duly recorded judgment against Vasiliki Pappas in the amount of $62,397.76, which had been entered by the Probate Division of the Superior Court in 1992, apparently was not discovered, or, at least, not related to Eastern, during the initial title search. The title examinations were performed by an independent abstractor retained by Certified, and Eastern did not receive any title documents which would have imparted actual knowledge of any judgment beyond the one for $3,461.12.[3] Soon after executing the promissory note and Deed of Trust in favor of Eastern, Vasiliki Pappas defaulted on

1. The three heirs, who later became the judgment creditors, were Achilles Pappas, Mary Pappas West, and the late Frances Papageorge.

2. The interest rate on CitiBank's promissory note was approximately 10.5%; the rate on Eastern's note was 14.25%. See note 13, *infra.* In other respects as well, the terms of Eastern's note were less favorable to the debtor than the terms of CitiBank's note.

3. There is thus no claim in this case that Eastern, as distinguished from Certified, had actual rather than constructive notice of any judgment in favor of the heirs against Pappas in her individual capacity.

the Eastern loan. As CitiBank had done following Vasiliki Pappas' earlier default, Eastern instituted foreclosure proceedings. In connection with these proceedings, counsel for Eastern caused the title to be examined, and Eastern then actually learned for the first time that the judgment in favor of the heirs was against Vasiliki Pappas individually, and not in her capacity as Personal Representative of Aphrodite Pappas' estate.[4] It was also at this time that Eastern learned the full amount of Vasiliki Pappas' total judgment debt.

In March 1999, sixteen years after the death of Aphrodite Pappas, the Probate Court ordered the distribution to the heirs of portions of the judgments secured by the Successor Personal Representative against Vasiliki Pappas. On December 19, 2000, Eastern brought suit against the heirs, claiming that its lien was superior to their judgment liens under the principle of equitable subrogation. Eastern and the judgment creditors filed cross-motions for summary judgment.

On December 30, 2001, in an eight-page order, the trial court granted the heirs' motion for summary judgment and denied Eastern's motion for the same relief. Citing, *inter alia,* Associates Fin. Servs. of Am. v. District of Columbia, 689 A.2d 1217 (D.C. 1997), the judge wrote that "the common law principle of 'first in time, first in right' governs competing creditors' claims against a property in the absence of an exception." She noted that the only statutory exception in the District is D.C. Code §15-104 (2001), which provides that the lien of a mortgage or deed of trust upon real property, given by the purchaser to secure the payment of the whole or any part of the purchase money, is superior to that of a previous judgment or decree against the purchaser.

The judge raised, but found it unnecessary to resolve, the issue whether this statutory exception should be extended by the court to a lender like Eastern, who provides refinancing to the borrower by paying off and retiring a prior indebtedness. Relying on *Associated Fin. Servs.*, 689 A.2d at 1222, and on Clay Properties v. Washington Post Co., 604 A.2d 890, 895 (D.C. 1992) (*en banc*), the judge determined that "a crucial question in deciding the competing interests of lienholders and creditors is notice." The judge went on to hold that because the judgments were recorded Eastern "was on inquiry notice of the judgment against Vasiliki Pappas," that Eastern "did not acquire creditor status for value without notice," and that "equity . . . does not justify moving Eastern to a position superior to the Pappas defendants." The judge therefore granted summary judgment to the heirs. This appeal followed.

4. Following the institution of the present action, Eastern learned that other judgments which had been entered against Vasiliki Pappas had been assigned to the heirs.

II

"Generally, priority of liens or security interests is determined according to the well-known principle of 'first in time, first in right.'" Malakoff v. Washington, 434 A.2d 432, 434 (D.C. 1981) (citations omitted). The question in this case is whether, and to what extent, this principle is affected by the doctrine of equitable subrogation.

In G.E. Capital Mortgage Servs., Inc. v. Levenson, 338 Md. 227, 657 A.2d 1170 (Md. 1995), the Maryland Court of Appeals explained that subrogation is "the substitution of one person to the position of another, an obligee, whose claim he has satisfied." . . .

> Where a lender has advanced money for the purpose of discharging a prior encumbrance in reliance upon obtaining security equivalent to the discharged lien, and his money is so used, the majority and preferable rule is that if he did so in ignorance of junior liens or other interests he will be subrogated to the prior lien. Although stressed in some cases as an objection to relief, neither negligence nor constructive notice should be material.

Id. at 1172, *quoting* G.E. Osborne, *Handbook on the Law of Mortgages* §282, at 570 (2d. ed. 1970).

In this jurisdiction, the doctrine of equitable subrogation was first applied to encumbrances on real property over a century ago. *See* Taylor v. MacGreal, 15 App. D.C. 32, 33 (1899). Thirty eight years later, in the leading case of Burgoon v. Lavezzo, 68 U.S. App. D.C. 20, 68 App. D.C. 20, 92 F.2d 726 (1937), the court applied the doctrine in a somewhat complex situation similar in principle to the one in the present case. The court held in *Burgoon* that where part of the purchase money for real property had been used to discharge an existing second mortgage, the purchaser was entitled to subrogation of that mortgage as against the holder of an existing third mortgage which was a matter of record and of which the purchaser had constructive but not actual notice. In reaching its decision, the court surveyed the authorities, already numerous in 1937, which had applied or refused to apply the doctrine of equitable subrogation where a lender or purchaser sought priority over intervening liens. Citing Hudson v. Dismukes, 77 Va. 242, 246-47 (1883), the court explained that subrogation "is the creature of equity, and is founded upon principles of natural justice . . . and is now applied in favor of all persons who are required to pay the debt of another to protect their own interests." 68 App. D.C. at 23, 92 F.2d at 729. The court in *Burgoon* was "unable to see how constructive notice to [the purchaser] of the [junior mortgagee's lien] could have anything to do with the right of the former to subrogation. . . . The question is: What is natural justice under the actual facts of the situation?" 68 App. D.C. at 24, 92 F.2d at 730 (*quoting* Prestridge v. Lazar, 132 Miss. 168, 95 So. 837, 838 (Miss. 1923)). . . .

Since the equitable doctrine of subrogation was ingrafted on the English equity jurisprudence from the civil law, it has been steadily growing in importance, and widening its sphere of application. It is a creation of equity, and is administered in the furtherance of justice. It is applied to give the party who actually pays the debt the full benefit and advantage of such payment. It has been long settled, and it is not controverted, that the doctrine applies where a junior incumbrancer discharges the prior incumbrance, and where the surety pays the debt of his principal, and in cases of like character. A just limitation of the application of the doctrine is that it does not apply to payments made by a mere volunteer or stranger. . . .

With respect to the issue here presented, the decision in *Burgoon* is also consistent with the Restatement (Third) of Property: Mortgages §7.6 cmt e. (1997):

> Perhaps the case occurring most frequently is that in which the payor is actually given a mortgage on the real estate, but in the absence of subrogation it would be subordinate to some intervening interest, such as a junior lien. Here subrogation is entirely appropriate, and by virtue of it the payor has the priority of the original mortgage that was discharged. This priority is often of critical importance, since it will place the payor's security in a position superior to intervening liens and other interests in the real estate. The holders of such intervening interests can hardly complain of this result, for it does not harm them; their position is not materially prejudiced, but is simply unchanged.
>
> Many judicial opinions dealing with a mortgagee who pays a preexisting mortgage focus on whether the payor had notice of the intervening interest at the time of the payment. Most of the cases disqualify the payor who has actual knowledge of the intervening interest, although they do not consider constructive notice from the public records to impair the payor's right of subrogation. Under this Restatement, however, subrogation can be granted even if the payor had actual knowledge of the intervening interest; the payor's notice, actual or constructive, is not necessarily relevant.[11]

The Restatement further states, and we agree, that "[s]ubrogation will be recognized only if it will not materially prejudice the holders of intervening interests." *Id.*

The heirs contend that they would be materially prejudiced if equitable subrogation were applied, because they had the right to expect, under the "first in time, first in right" rule, that their judgment liens would advance upon the satisfaction of CitiBank's lien and would therefore be superior to Eastern's lien, which was secured later in time. This contention was, however, explicitly rejected in *Burgoon*: "The junior lienor had a right to advance if the prior encumbrance was paid off by one not entitled to subrogation; *he had no such right if the prior lien was satisfied by one entitled to subrogation.*" 68 App. D.C. at 26; 92 F.2d at 732 (emphasis added). Moreover, the court emphasized, as

11. Because, albeit arguably on account of its own negligence or the negligence of Certified, Eastern did not have *actual* notice of the heirs' intervening liens, we need not decide whether to follow the majority rule (actual knowledge bars equitable subrogation) or the Restatement rule (it does not).

subsequently noted in the Restatement, that the intervening creditors suffer no prejudice if equitable subrogation is applied:

> The only advantage they have gained is through the money paid by [the purchaser], without any consideration whatever moving from them. They claim the benefit, solely through the mistake of [the purchaser]. The [junior lienor] does not pretend to have earned a farthing of their claim. They simply say, the cold blood of the law permits them to take . . . [the purchaser's] money.
>
> We think that to recognize equitable assignment does not impair any rights of the junior lienor worthy of equitable recognition against the position of one who in ignorance of the junior lien advances a part of purchase price to discharge a senior lien. For the only "rights" of the junior lienor that can be said to be actually impaired are gambling "rights" to profit by a purchaser's mistake.

68 App. D.C. at 26-28, 92 F.2d 732-33 (*quoting* Williams v. Libby, 118 Me. 80, 105 A. 855, 856-57 (Me. 1899)).

The heirs argue that the interest rate of Eastern's note is far higher than that of CitiBank's, that the terms of Eastern's loan are more exacting, and that the heirs are thereby prejudiced because any funds available to them will be incrementally depleted as a result of the refinancing. . . . Eastern concedes in its Reply Brief, and counsel repeatedly acknowledged during oral argument, that Eastern is subrogated only to the extent that it was required to pay CitiBank to satisfy Vasiliki Pappas' indebtedness to CitiBank.[13]

. . . For the reasons stated in detail in *Burgoon*, . . . and in the Restatement subrogation would work no injustice to the judgment-creditor heirs, who would retain the precise security interest that they possessed at the time Eastern redeemed the indebtedness to CitiBank. . . .

13. On remand, however, we explicitly leave open the question whether, and to what extent, Eastern is entitled to equitable subrogation for *interest* on the $153,800 it paid CitiBank to release CitiBank's Deed of Trust. Eastern argues that it is entitled to be subrogated for "$153,800 together with interest thereon at the rate provided in the Note secured by the CitiBank Deed of Trust from the date that indebtedness was paid." The heirs do not address this point; their entire argument is focused on the question whether Eastern is entitled to equitable subrogation at all.

This issue is not an easy one, and turns on the perspective from which it is viewed. The Restatement provides that a "payor is subrogated only to the extent that the funds disbursed are actually applied toward payment of the prior lien. There is no right of subrogation with respect to any excess funds." Restatement (Third) of Property, *supra*, §7.6 cmt. e. In this case, Eastern was required to pay only a total of $153,800 to secure from CitiBank a release of CitiBank's lien. If Eastern is held to be entitled, under principles of equitable subrogation, to interest at the rate provided in the CitiBank Note, its rights as a subrogee will exceed the amount which was "actually applied [by Eastern] toward payment of the prior lien."

On the other hand, the focus of the Restatement is on whether subrogation will prejudice intervening lien holders. *See id.* CitiBank's Note provided for interest, and the Note itself was in an amount in excess of the $153,800 now claimed by Eastern. The heirs are therefore arguably better off *vis-a-vis* Eastern than they were *vis-a-vis* CitiBank, and they would suffer no prejudice even if the court were to hold that Eastern is subrogated to the amount of $153,800 plus interest. . . .

For the foregoing reasons, the judgment of the trial court is reversed, and the case is remanded for further proceedings consistent with this opinion.

Problem 17C

In 2006, Able Insurance Co. refinanced a permanent loan on a small shopping center, lending $1,200,000 to Douglas Dowdy. The prior loan, made in 2001 for $1,000,000, had a balance due of $900,000 at the time of Able's refinancing. The refinancing involved payment of the old note in full, with a release of the 2001 deed of trust, and the execution and recording of Able's loan documents. In 2007, Douglas defaulted and Able foreclosed. Able hired Tom, a lawyer, to handle the power of sale foreclosure. Tom searched title and missed a mortgage for $100,000 from Douglas Dowdy to Easy Bank, which was made and recorded in 2004. Tom proceeded with the foreclosure, and at the sale Able purchased the property for $950,000. Does Easy Bank still have a mortgage, and if so, what is its priority if:

(a) Tom missed the mortgage because he did not do a careful title search.

(b) Tom missed the mortgage because it was incorrectly indexed under the name "Dowd, Douglas."

(c) Tom missed the mortgage because it was incorrectly indexed under the name "Gowdy, Douglas."

As between Able and Tom, if legal action is required against Easy Bank to clear title, who should bear this expense? If Tom had discovered the Easy Bank mortgage prior to conducting the foreclosure sale, what should he have done?

C. ECONOMICS OF FORECLOSURE: PROBLEM OF PRICE ADEQUACY

GREATER SOUTHWEST OFFICE PARK, LTD. v. TEXAS COMMERCE BANK NATIONAL ASSOCIATION

Court of Appeals of Texas, Houston (1st District), 1990
786 S.W.2d 386

WARREN, Justice. Greater Southwest Office Park, Ltd. ("Greater Southwest") appeals from the trial court's order granting summary judgment to Texas Commerce Bank National Association ("the Bank"), and dismissing Greater Southwest's cause of action with prejudice.

Greater Southwest was the maker of a promissory note, in the original principal amount of $5,000,000, payable to the Bank. The note was secured by a deed of trust and security agreement, executed by Greater Southwest for the benefit of the Bank. In November of 1987, the Bank declared a default and posted the real property, which was the subject of the deed of trust, for foreclosure. On December 1, 1987, the Bank purchased the land at a public foreclosure sale for the sum of $4,847,903.96, which was the amount of the outstanding debt plus the costs of the sale. The Bank did not sue Greater Southwest for a deficiency balance; therefore, the holdings made in this opinion are not intended to express our opinion in cases involving a deficiency suit when the debtor is claiming that the lender grossly underbid on the foreclosed realty.

On May 16, 1988, Greater Southwest filed its original petition claiming that: (1) the fair market value of the real property foreclosed on by the Bank was $10,529,000; (2) the Bank bid an unconscionably low price for the property at the foreclosure sale; (3) Greater Southwest and the Bank were in a "trust arrangement," giving rise to a duty to make an honest effort to secure a fair price for the collateral at the foreclosure sale; and (4) this conduct constituted constructive fraud, actual fraud, and an intentional tort. Greater Southwest prayed for compensatory damages in the amount of $5,682,000, and exemplary damages in the amount of not less than $10,000,000. . . .

Greater Southwest's entire cause of action rests on the premise that the Bank is liable to it in damages because it purchased the collateral at a foreclosure sale at a price that was less than fair or reasonable. Greater Southwest does not contend that the sale was irregular in any respect, nor does it seek to set aside the sale. . . .

Greater Southwest . . . relies on Lee v. Sabine Bank, 708 S.W.2d 582 (Tex. App. — Beaumont 1986, *writ ref'd n.r.e.*), and other cases involving the allowance of set-offs in suits for deficiencies, where it was alleged that the price bid by the lender was inadequate. In Lee v. Sabine Bank, Sabine Bank advanced Lee $500,000 to purchase a boat and for working capital; the bank retained a lien on the boat as security. With a balance of $404,000 still owing on the note, Lee defaulted. Sabine Bank purchased the boat at a judicial sale for $175,000, after crediting other pledged security and adding the expenses of sale and interest, leaving Lee with a balance of $226,064 owing under the terms of the note. Lee sued, seeking to prevent Sabine Bank from taking the other security pledged; Sabine Bank counterclaimed for the deficiency owed under the note. The trial court denied Lee's requested relief and awarded Sabine Bank judgment for its deficiency of $240,854. Lee claimed that the trial court erred by allowing him credit on the deficiency for the sales price bid by Sabine Bank, rather than the fair market value at the time of sale.

The court stated that "a lender who has secured collateral, whether personalty or realty is under a trust arrangement with the borrower, in the event of foreclosure, to make an honest effort to reduce the loan as much as possible by securing a fair price for the collateral." Lee v. Sabine Bank, 708 S.W.2d at 584. "[W]here there is a probable significant disparity between the sale price of the property and its fair market value, the borrower may contest the sale and present evidence contesting such." *Id.* at 585. It limited the rule to those cases where the lender or its surrogate was the purchaser at foreclosure. The court, however, affirmed the trial court because no evidence had been presented as to the market value of the ship at the time of the judicial sale.

First, we note that, because the *Sabine Bank* case did not concern realty, any comments by the court concerning the foreclosure of realty collateral is dicta. Second, we note that in our case, like *Sabine Bank*, no evidence was presented as to the fair market value of the collateral at the time of the foreclosure sale. . . .

We hold that: (1) in the absence of evidence of irregularity in the sale, causing the property to be sold for a grossly inadequate price, mere inadequacy of consideration is not grounds for setting aside a trustee's sale; (2) the rule applies whether the lender, its surrogate, or a third party is the buyer at the trustee's sale; and (3) the rule applies whether the borrower is seeking to set aside the trustee's sale or is suing for damages.

Because there was no irregularity alleged or shown in the trustee's sale, Greater Southwest's amended pleadings stated no cause of action against the Bank. Therefore, the trial court correctly dismissed the action. . . .

The allegations that Greater Southwest contends amount to constructive fraud and intentional tort are as follows:

(1) the Bank has a policy of bidding not less than 70% of the fair market value of the property on which it holds a first lien, but not more than the note balance owed;
(2) this scheme was intentional, willful, and without justification or excuse;
(3) a result of this policy is to not fairly compensate debtors;
(4) the Bank acted with gross indifference to its duty of honesty and fair dealing owed to Greater Southwest; and
(5) the Bank's conduct was deceptive, violative of confidences, and offends public policy.

The acts and attitudes of which Greater Southwest accuses the Bank do not amount to a breach of contract or a tort. In the absence of a forbidding statute, the presence of a policy or scheme to do an act which is otherwise lawful, does not make the act unlawful. If there is no duty on the Bank's part to bid a minimum amount at a trustee's sale, then its policy to bid 70% of the property's value, but no more than the amount owing, is not actionable. Further, we have found no Texas cases recognizing a "prima facie tort" (the infliction of an intentional harm by an act which is lawful, but results in special damage), nor have we been cited to any.

Greater Southwest's claim of a constructive fraud is based on its allegation that the Bank bid far less than the market value on the property in question and the following statement by Billy Goldberg in his affidavit:

> During the course of my business career, I have had a long business relationship with TCB. Either I or companies with which I was affiliated received and paid back millions of dollars in loans to TCB and its affiliates. During that time, TCB solicited by [sic] business and, through me, the

> business of Greater Southwest; and lead me to believe that I could trust them to be fair and honest in their conduct towards me and the companies with which I was affiliated. Because of this long relationship and the solicitation of my business, I came to trust and rely upon the conduct and representation of TCB's representatives.
>
> My relationship with TCB began in the middle 1970's, when I became friends with TCB's president, Bill Heiligbrodt. Either I, companies with which I was affiliated, or Greater Southwest then began a series of substantial loan [sic], most of which are now paid off, totaling several million dollars.

Constructive fraud is the breach of some legal or equitable duty which, irrespective of moral guilt, the law declares fraudulent because of its tendency to deceive others, to violate confidence, or to injure public interests. . . . The allegations contained in Goldberg's affidavit, if taken as true, are insufficient to create a trust or fiduciary relationship between Greater Southwest and the Bank.

In Texas, a special relationship does not normally exist between a borrower and a lender, and when one has been found, it has rested on extraneous facts and conduct, such as excessive lender control over, or influence in, the borrower's business activities. *See* State Natl. Bank v. Farah Mfg. Co., 678 S.W.2d 661 (Tex. App.—El Paso 1984, *writ dism'd by agr.*). Goldberg's mere subjective trust in the Bank, by itself, is not enough to transform the arms-length dealings of a debtor and creditor into a fiduciary relationship. Thigpen v. Locke, 363 S.W.2d 247 (Tex. 1962).

Each of appellant's points of error is overruled, and the judgment is affirmed.

D. STATUTORY MORTGAGOR PROTECTIONS

Many states have statutes designed to protect mortgagors in connection with the processes of foreclosure and debt collection. The most important devices—the one-action rule, limitations on deficiency judgments, and statutory redemption—are discussed in the following subsections.

1. *One-Action Rule*

California and a handful of other states have enacted a one-action rule, which limits the mortgagee to a single action that must include foreclosure and may include, if appropriate, a deficiency judgment. The one-action rule serves several purposes. First, there is an efficiency rationale in protecting the mortgagor from having to defend multiple actions that arise out of the same lending transaction. Additionally, this limit of one action helps to conserve judicial resources. The rule compels the mortgagee to satisfy the debt out of the mortgaged property first, before chasing other assets owned by the mortgagor. The mortgagee cannot bring a personal action on the debt; the mortgagee must first exhaust the security the parties agreed to for the debt before making other collection attempts.

2. Statutory Redemption

Foreclosure terminates the mortgagor's equity of redemption. This is the point of the foreclosure process. Up until the moment of the foreclosure sale, the equity of redemption means the mortgagor has the right to pay the debt and obtain a release of the mortgage. Depending on state law, the borrower may have an additional right called the right of *statutory redemption* that comes into play *after* the foreclosure sale. In a majority of states there are statutes creating postforeclosure redemption rights under certain circumstances. Historically, statutory redemption dates back to the nineteenth century when, during economic depressions when land values were falling, legislatures provided for redemption for a fixed period after execution sales of real estate. The statutes were primarily directed at protecting landowners from judgment liens, but often courts interpreted the statutes to protect owners from mortgage foreclosure sales as well. Legislatures frequently amended the legislation; for example, it was common to lengthen the redemption period during hard times and shorten it during business recoveries. The statutory details vary widely from state to state, and thus a lawyer who represents lender, borrower, or foreclosure purchaser must carefully study the relevant statutory framework. The primary principles are sketched here.

Existence of right to redeem. In some states, statutory redemption is available after both judicial and power of sale foreclosures. In others, it is available after one but not the other foreclosure process. Tennessee, for example, authorizes statutory redemption following judicial foreclosure but not foreclosure by power of sale. Obviously, this makes power of sale foreclosure even more popular among lenders in Tennessee. In a few states, a mortgagor is permitted to waive the right of statutory redemption, but in most states waivers are not permitted.

Time period. The statutes set a fixed time period after foreclosure for exercise of the right to redeem. Presently, the period ranges from a few months to 18 months. Sometimes the period varies according to the type of the mortgaged real estate. For example, longer redemption periods may be allowed for owner-occupied housing and farmland, and shorter periods may be available for abandoned property.

Redemption price. In almost all states, the redemption price is the foreclosure sales price plus interest and foreclosure costs. In most states, a statutory rate of interest is specified (often 8 or 10 percent), but in some states the redemption price bears interest at the rate specified in the mortgage debt instrument. A few states, instead of basing redemption on the foreclosure purchase price, require the redemptioner to pay the mortgage debt plus interest. Missouri follows this approach generally, and Alabama does so but only if the mortgagee is the purchaser at foreclosure. When there is a deficiency at foreclosure, this rule allows the purchaser to collect the amount of deficiency from the redemptioner.

Right to possession. In most states, the mortgagor has the right to possession during the statutory period. In effect, the foreclosure purchaser has bought a future interest—actually, a contingent future interest, given the possibility that redemption will occur. In a few states, the mortgagor must post bond to retain property, as a protection against waste. In a few states, the purchaser at the foreclosure sale is entitled to immediate possession, and if the redemption right is exercised, then possession reverts to the redemptioner.

Who can redeem. In some states, the redemption right is granted only to the mortgagor; in others, junior lienors are also entitled to statutory redemption. If a junior lienor redeems, in most states she gets title to the land—specifically, the same title the foreclosure purchaser had—just like a redeeming mortgagor. This contrasts with the junior lienor's right to redeem prior to foreclosure. There, the junior's redemption right is not to obtain title to the mortgaged property but to pay the senior debt, thereby acquiring that debt by subrogation.

Effect of redemption on liens. Generally, the mortgagor's redemption revives preforeclosure liens other than the lien foreclosed upon, the policy being not to let the mortgagor's default and foreclosure destroy the liens she created.

Compliance with statutory requirements. Many courts have ruled that substantial compliance with procedural requirements for redemption is sufficient. Minor flaws in following requirements will not disqualify mortgagors and lienors who act to redeem. Redemption statutes are liberally construed to protect mortgagors and lienors.

3. Limits on Deficiency Judgments

Many states have statutes, often dating from the Great Depression of the 1930s, that either prohibit mortgage lenders from obtaining deficiency judgments or impose other limitations. The statutes vary widely. Sometimes they apply only to particular types of transactions for which the borrower is thought to need or deserve protection—for example, home loans or farm loans. In addition, the statutory restriction may depend on the type of foreclosure process; the mortgagee may be barred from obtaining a deficiency judgment if she forecloses by power of sale rather than judicially. If she desires a deficiency judgment, judicial foreclosure, which presumably offers the borrower greater procedural and substantive safeguards, is required. In some states, such as California, a seller of real property who takes back a purchase-money mortgage cannot obtain a deficiency judgment.

Another approach is "fair value" legislation, which, instead of an outright ban on deficiency judgments, permits such a judgment only to the extent the debt exceeds the "fair value" of the foreclosed property. This disregards the actual foreclosure sales price paid if it is lower than fair value. Texas enacted such legislation one year after the *Greater Southwest Office Park* case. Tex. Prop. Code §51.003 (defendant is "entitled to an offset against the deficiency in the amount by which the fair market value . . . exceeds the sale price"). Fair-value laws are an indirect attempt to solve the problem of inadequate prices paid at foreclosure sales. A low price is still permitted, but it is not used to calculate the deficiency.

Antideficiency judgment acts that simply bar any deficiency judgment for a class of mortgage loans raise market concerns. Consider how they affect the market risk of owning real property. When a statute applies, it transfers the risk of market declines in real estate values from borrowers to lenders. For policy reasons, borrower waivers of statutory protection are generally invalid, so the law insists that the lender bear at least part of the risk. Why should lenders be forced to assume this risk? Do lenders have better information about market values and trends than borrowers? Is the concept of antideficiency judgment acts consistent with general notions of what it means to be the "owner" of land, where the owner has the potential benefit of appreciation along with the risk of falling value?

CODE OF GEORGIA
§44-14-161 (enacted 1935)

Sales made on foreclosure under power of sale — When deficiency judgment allowed; confirmation and approval; notice and hearing; resale.

(a) When any real estate is sold on foreclosure, without legal process, and under powers contained in security deeds, mortgages, or other lien contracts and at the sale the real estate does not bring the amount of the debt secured by the deed, mortgage, or contract, no action may be taken to obtain a deficiency judgment unless the person instituting the foreclosure proceedings shall, within 30 days after the sale, report the sale to the judge of the superior court of the county in which the land is located for confirmation and approval and shall obtain an order of confirmation and approval thereon.

(b) The court shall require evidence to show the true market value of the property sold under the powers and shall not confirm the sale unless it is satisfied that the property so sold brought its true market value on such foreclosure sale.

(c) The court shall direct that a notice of the hearing shall be given to the debtor at least five days prior thereto; and at the hearing the court shall also pass upon the legality of the notice, advertisement, and regularity of the sale. The court may order a resale of the property for good cause shown.

GUTHERIE v. FORD EQUIPMENT LEASING COMPANY

Court of Appeals of Georgia, 1992
206 Ga. App. 258, 424 S.E.2d 889

SOGNIER, Chief Judge. Ford Equipment Leasing Company conducted a nonjudicial foreclosure under a power of sale contained in a deed to secure debt executed by Thomas Gutherie to secure a loan made by Ford to Greensboro Lumber Company (GLC). Ford then instituted this confirmation proceeding. After a hearing, the superior court entered an order confirming the sale. Gutherie and GLC appeal.

The property at issue comprised a 300 acre farm and the residence and outbuildings of appellant Gutherie. At the time of the foreclosure sale, appellants were indebted to appellee in the amount of $1,078,587. Darryl Gossett was the high bidder at the December 1991 sale, acquiring the property for his bid of $200,000. The sale was made subject to other non-discharged debts and delinquent taxes totalling $261,297.

At the confirmation hearing, appellants did not challenge the validity of the notices and advertisements made by appellee, but instead contended that the sale did not bring the true market value of the property as required for confirmation under OCGA §44-14-161(b). Appellee's appraiser opined that the market value of the property was $919,450 if given two or more years to sell; however, he testified that he discounted this market value to $460,000 because he was instructed by appellee to calculate a "quick sale" value rather than a "market time sale" value. Appellants' two appraisers arrived at valuations of $950,000 and $985,000. While they agreed with appellee that a sale of such a property ordinarily would take six months to three years, they disagreed with the "quick sale" approach. One appraiser opined that while the rapid timing of the foreclosure sale might justify some discounting of the valuation, a 50 percent reduction was excessive, while the other appraiser stated that a quick sale value was not the same as true market value. The trial court found the total value bid at auction, $461,297, equalled the true market value and confirmed the sale.

. . . "True market value," which is used interchangeably with "fair market value," Aaron v. Life Ins. Co. of Ga., 138 Ga. App. 286(1), 226 S.E.2d 96 (1976), is "the price which (the property) will bring when it is offered for sale by one who desires, but is not obliged, to sell it, and is bought by one who wishes to buy, but is not under a necessity to do so." (Citations, punctuation, and emphasis omitted.) Wheeler v. Coastal Bank, 182 Ga. App. 112, 114, 354 S.E.2d 694 (1987). . . . The lender bears the burden of proving that the foreclosure sale brought at least the true market value of the property. *Id.* at 114, 354 S.E.2d 694.

The question presented . . . is whether a "quick sale value" may constitute competent evidence of the "true market value" of real property within the meaning of OCGA §44-14-161(b). Our courts have held that in determining true market value, a trial court may consider market conditions in general at the time of the sale under power and the effect of depressed market conditions on the value of a subject property. Gunnells v. Crump, 172 Ga. App. 607, 608, 323 S.E.2d 903 (1984); *see* Wall v. Federal Land Bank, 240 Ga. 236, 238, 240 S.E.2d 76 (1977). However, the parties have not cited, and our extensive research has not uncovered, any case that has condoned discounting the value of a foreclosed property on the basis that the sale was conducted in a shortened time frame. Accordingly, we will consider the view taken by our courts of the use of "quick sale" valuations in other contexts as well as authority in other jurisdictions.

In Parks v. Assoc. Commercial Corp., 181 Ga. App. 235-236, 237, 351 S.E.2d 661 (1986), this court addressed the use of a "quick sale value" in the context of repossession and disposal of secured collateral under the UCC. The record in *Parks* established that the price paid for the collateral at the public sale was equal to its "quick sale value" but substantially less than the price at which the collateral subsequently was resold. Considering this discrepancy together with evidence that the creditor had known prior to the sale that other prospective buyers were willing to pay more for the collateral than the bid-in price, we held that "these facts raise a serious question concerning whether the sale of the collateral was conducted in a commercially reasonable manner as required by OCGA §11-9-504(3)," and accordingly found the debtors had properly raised that ground as a defense. *Id.* at 237, 351 S.E.2d 661.

The definition of "fair market value" established by the Internal Revenue Service for use in valuation of real property for estate taxes is also instructive. "Fair market value" is defined as

> the price at which the property would change hands between a willing buyer and a willing seller, neither being under any compulsion to buy or to sell and both having reasonable knowledge of relevant facts. The fair market value of a particular item of property . . . is not to be determined by a forced sale price. Nor is the fair market value . . . to be determined by the sale price of the item in a market other than that in which such item is most commonly sold to the public. . . .

Treas. Reg. §20.2031-1(b). The first sentence of this definition is consistent with the willing buyer, willing seller definition used in Georgia. *See Wheeler, supra; see also* Wright v. MARTA, 248 Ga. 372, 375, 283 S.E.2d 466 (1981). Upon reviewing Georgia law on the computation of fair market value and considering the language and purpose of the confirmation statute, we are persuaded that the entirety of the IRS definition of fair market value is consistent with Georgia law and should be used to resolve the issue sub judice.

. . . [T]he General Assembly enacted OCGA §44-14-161 for the purpose of providing debtor relief by limiting and abating deficiency judgments. First Nat. Bank v. Kunes, 230 Ga. 888, 890, 199 S.E.2d 776 (1973). Accordingly, we hold that OCGA §44-14-161(b) must be read to require proof of true market value *under the usual market conditions* for sales of such property. Otherwise, the legislative purpose of OCGA §44-14-161 would be defeated. *See* OCGA §1-3-1(a) (in interpreting statutes, "courts shall look diligently for the intention of the General Assembly, keeping in view at all times the old law, the evil, and the remedy").

Applying this interpretation of OCGA §44-14-161(b) to the facts of the instant case, we conclude the trial court improperly considered evidence of the "quick sale" value of the subject property because such a valuation does not reflect the price that would be obtained in a sale under the usual market conditions. *Accord Parks, supra.* Use of the "quick sale" valuation in confirmation proceedings is inconsistent with the legislative purpose of OCGA §44-14-161(b) because it presumes that "true market value" may be construed to mean "market value under quick sale conditions." When the "quick sale" valuation is eliminated from the record, there remains no evidence to support the trial court's determination that the sale under power brought at least the true market value of the property. Consequently, the trial court erred by confirming the sale. *See Wheeler, supra* at 114-115, 354 S.E.2d 694.

Appellants have contended below and on appeal that the trial court should have denied confirmation and ordered a resale of the property pursuant to OCGA §44-14-161(c), which authorizes the court to order a resale "for good cause shown." Given that appellee did not prove that it sold the property for true market value but did obtain an appraisal (albeit a fatally flawed one) before the sale and did sell the property for an amount equal to that appraisal, a resale would be authorized. Adams v. Gwinnett Commercial Bank, 140 Ga. App. 233, 230 S.E.2d 324 (1976), *aff'd,* 238 Ga. 722, 235 S.E.2d 476 (1977); *see* Davie v. Sheffield, 123 Ga. App. 228, 180 S.E.2d 263 (1971) (resale may be had for mere inadequacy of price). Accordingly, we reverse the order of confirmation and remand this proceeding to the trial court for further proceedings consistent with this opinion. . . .

Problem 17D

During the boom years of Metropolis, apartment developers went crazy. Beginning three years ago, the rental market chilled considerably as a result of a combination of overbuilding and a weak economy. An apartment complex with 100 units, finished 2½ years ago at a cost of $2.3 million, has an occupancy rate of 52 percent. Lender, holding a $2.1 million debt, purchased it at a foreclosure sale for $1.3 million. Lender now seeks a deficiency judgment. Assume that the Georgia statute considered in *Gutherie* applies. Should Lender recover, and, if so, how much if the evidence shows:

(a) During the past year, seven other recently built Metropolis apartment complexes were sold at foreclosure, with the foreclosure prices ranging between 50 percent and 68 percent of construction cost.

(b) During the past year, nine recently built Metropolis apartment complexes were sold in voluntary sales that ranged between 78 percent and 93 percent of construction cost.

(c) Appraisers and economists basically agree that in two to three years, the rental market will absorb the oversupply of Metropolis apartment complexes, with average occupancy rates rising to the normal range of 92 to 98 percent, causing the market value of recently built, well-run, well-maintained complexes to eclipse their construction cost.

E. DEED IN LIEU OF FORECLOSURE

When, after default, a mortgage loan is in trouble, foreclosure is often unattractive to both the lender and the borrower. The borrower may concede the lender's allegation of material default and realize that she does not have a meritorious defense. Perhaps the borrower defaulted because of a loss in income or other financial setbacks so that she can no longer afford to own the property with the present amount of debt on it. Thus, she has no realistic chance of reinstating the loan or refinancing.

With a situation like this, it may be mutually advantageous to both parties for the borrower to transfer ownership to the lender. Such a transfer is documented by what is called a *deed in lieu of foreclosure.* The lender gets title right away and can keep or sell the property however it wishes — for example, by listing it with a broker — without following public foreclosure sale procedures. In exchange for the transfer, the borrower receives satisfaction of all or part of the debt. The borrower is relieved of responsibility for the property and avoids being the target of foreclosure, a process that for some borrowers is an emotional strain and an embarrassment, as well as a potential financial hurt. If the borrower is concerned about a potential deficiency judgment, agreeing to give a deed in lieu of foreclosure may avoid or reduce that risk because the borrower will not have extra liability for foreclosure costs. Essentially, the deed in lieu of foreclosure transaction is a negotiated sale of the property to the lender, where the lender pays the purchase price by cancellation of debt. The biggest risk to the borrower is underpricing the property. If the borrower has substantial equity, the transaction may be unwise, even though the lender cancels the entire debt. It replicates a decree in strict foreclosure, where the lender has no duty to account to the borrower for surplus value.

The transaction also poses significant risks to the lender. First, after consummation of the transaction, the mortgagor may try to set aside the deed in lieu of foreclosure, claiming that the deed clogs her equity of redemption. Had the lender taken a deed to the property from the mortgagor contemporaneously with the grant of the mortgage, such a deed would be clearly invalid under the clogging principle.

Second, some courts are willing to scrutinize a deed in lieu of foreclosure transaction on grounds of inadequacy of consideration or unconscionability. The fairness of the exchange may be called into question because of the extreme disparity of bargaining position, with a lender pressing hard to persuade a borrower in dire straits to capitulate.

Finally, the lender who contemplates acceptance of a deed in lieu of foreclosure has to consider the risks that third parties may have rights. There are two basic problems here. First of all, the lender has a title concern because a deed in lieu of foreclosure, unlike a properly conducted foreclosure, will not cut off junior interests that are subsequent to the mortgage. In addition to the title risk, there are other third-party risks if the mortgagor is or might be insolvent. Of course, given the default and the need to foreclose, insolvency is not at all unlikely. If the mortgagor files for bankruptcy or is pushed into bankruptcy within 90 days after the deed in lieu of foreclosure is given, the transfer may be set aside as a preference. Apart from bankruptcy, under the state law of fraudulent conveyances, there is the risk that other creditors of the mortgagor may attack the deed on the basis that it was given for less than market value.

18 Mortgage Substitutes

As we have seen in prior chapters, mortgage law contains significant protections for borrowers, many of which apply based on the parties' status regardless of their agreement in fact. For example, the mortgagor may not waive his equity of redemption when he enters into a loan transaction — this constitutes an impermissible "clogging" of the equity of redemption. And if the lender seeks to foreclose because of a default by the mortgagor, the lender must comply with statutory foreclosure procedures designed to protect both the mortgagor and holders of junior interests. The terms of the parties' loan documents are not permitted to override the anticlogging and foreclosure rules that seek to give the mortgagor sufficient time to save his rights in the property.

In essence, this means that the parties' status as mortgagor and mortgagee overrides their contract in fact in a number of respects. In particular, a mortgagee cannot bargain for greater rights with respect to the land that secures the debt than the basic rights stemming from the mortgage itself. "Once a mortgage, always a mortgage," courts have said. A prime example is the rule barring a mortgagee from taking, by collateral agreement, title to the land. If, along with a mortgage, a mortgagor signs and delivers a deed conveying the property to the mortgagee, authorizing the mortgagee to record the deed upon default, the deed is a nullity. The mortgagee hopes that this will avoid the need for costly and time-consuming foreclosure if the mortgagor defaults, but courts invariably dismiss such deeds as unlawful attempts to clog the mortgagor's equity of redemption.

A closely related concept comes into play when the parties, instead of trying to modify mortgage law or create their own mortgage law, try to avoid mortgage law altogether. For various reasons, people have often sought this outcome. A borrower may want to hide the fact that she needs money or is taking on debt. A lender may think mortgage law protects mortgagors too much. This party may prefer a substitute arrangement, and the other party who wants or needs credit may agree. Thus, parties will seek to avoid mortgage law by refraining from the use of standard mortgage loan documents like promissory notes, mortgages, and deeds of trust. Instead, they structure their transaction in some other way. As a starting point, it is important to realize that for centuries courts, both in England and the United States, have tried to understand the motivations of lenders who seek to escape mortgage law in order to gain legal advantages over borrowers. Courts have looked to substance over form, consistently ruling that if the parties' transaction basically is a loan, with real property as security if the borrower fails to repay, then mortgage law applies, regardless of how the parties label or characterize their deal. This is a "disguised mortgage"; at the lender's insistence, the parties have disguised their mortgage as something else, but the court has sharp eyesight. The label "equitable mortgage" is also used in this context, meaning that the transaction is not a formal, legal mortgage, but it is a function of equity jurisprudence to intervene and impose a duty on the holder of legal title to recognize an equity held by the grantor.

This chapter considers the principles that apply to a range of alternative arrangements involving land and deferred payments. These arrangements are referred to as *mortgage substitutes* because they perform economic functions similar to those of standard mortgage transactions. The label "mortgage substitute" does not mean that mortgage law must apply to the transaction — sometimes it does and sometimes it does not. Deciding when it will and when it should is complex, requiring the decisionmaker to weigh a number of variables concerning the parties' bargaining process, circumstances, and documents.

A. SALES AND DISGUISED MORTGAGES

The classic case of the disguised mortgage is the loan that masquerades as a straight-out sale, using a warranty deed to convey title to the buyer (lender). The deed is just a regular deed, the type commonly used in all sales transactions. It is called *absolute* because, unlike a mortgage, it says nothing at all about the grantor ever getting the property back or the grantee relinquishing his rights if the debt is paid. The lender orally promises to reconvey to the borrower if the borrower timely repays the debt. As long ago as 1470, English courts ruled that such transactions were really mortgages. Distinguishing sales from mortgages is not always easy, and many courts have struggled with this problem. Typically, it is the grantor under a warranty deed who claims the transaction really is a mortgage loan. The grantee's (lender's) payment (loan) is taken in exchange for the original conveyance, with the grantor (borrower) tendering repayment at a later date in exchange for a reconveyance of title. In the typical dispute, the grantee resists this argument and seeks to quiet title in itself. From the cases addressing this problem, no single test has emerged. Rather, courts have looked at many factors to decide whether the deed used by the parties was a mortgage.

In disputes of this sort, a key distinction to keep in mind is the difference between parol evidence and written evidence. If the grantor can produce written evidence of the debt or that he has a right to reacquire title, this strengthens his case. Many disputes revolve primarily around the interpretation of writings. For example, there may be an absolute deed and a promissory note, signed by the grantor and payable to the grantee. The primary issue will be how those two writings relate to each other: Are they independent transactions? Is the debt represented by the note outstanding, or has it been paid? Is the note secured or unsecured? Was the note cancelled in exchange for conveyance of title to the property?

In some disputes there is no written evidence of a debt, a mortgage, or a right of the grantor to reacquire the conveyed real estate. Such written proof, however, is not essential. Parol testimony is admissible, in spite of the statute of frauds. One justification is that the testimony "explains" rather than "contradicts" the deed. Alternatively, we may say the claim is essentially for reformation of the deed. Under a reformation action, a court can change an instrument based on parol testimony indicating that the parties made a mistake. Historically, in English law the rule permitting parol testimony that an absolute conveyance was intended to be defeasible predated the Statute of Frauds of 1677, and courts did not think the statute was intended to alter this long-established rule. Regardless of the rationale, it should be acknowledged that there is tension between the use of parol evidence to "impeach" an absolute deed and the policies underlying the statute of frauds. For this reason, many courts have tried to put such evidence on a leash. The burden of proof is on the party claiming that the deed is a mortgage. Moreover, it is often said that there is a presumption that an absolute deed is bona fide. To overcome this presumption, the proponent must prove a mortgage by clear and convincing evidence, a standard that is higher than a preponderance of the evidence.

Whether a particular transaction is a sale or a mortgage is a question of fact. The issue is one of intent, with both subjective and objective elements. To decipher intent, courts are willing to look at the totality of the circumstances surrounding the transaction.

Problem 18A

In 2001, Karen and her husband Mark Piper acquired a 40-acre parcel of property and were attempting to develop it as a subdivision of residential lots named Crystal Springs. In 2003, the Pipers began having difficulty meeting a mortgage obligation to Western Life Insurance Co. on the property. In June, Western obtained a foreclosure judgment against the property for $200,000. Carol and Jim Strong, who were neighbors and parcel owners in the subdivision, expressed an interest in helping the Pipers maintain ownership in order to preserve the Pipers' development plan. Together the Pipers and Strongs tried to convince Western to reinstate the mortgage with the loaning of the

Strongs' credit to the Pipers. Western, however, refused the proposed reinstatement.

To avoid the foreclosure sale, on October 1, 2003, the Pipers entered into an agreement with the Strongs whereby the Strongs paid the Pipers $200,000, the amount of the foreclosure judgment, which the Pipers turned over to Western to satisfy the judgment. In exchange for the payment, the Pipers executed a warranty deed on the property to the Strongs. In a separate agreement signed at the same time, the Strongs granted the Pipers a two-year option to repurchase the property. The documents were drafted by an attorney retained by the Strongs.

After a negotiated extension of one year, the option to repurchase expired in 2006. In 2007, the Pipers attempted to pay the Strongs the amount loaned, with interest, to regain possession of the property. The Strongs refused to accept payment or return the property. The Pipers filed suit, claiming the initial transaction was a mortgage, not a sale.

(a) Suppose the Pipers testify that despite what the documents indicate, they believe the money was a loan. The Strongs, on the other hand, testify there was no loan, merely an option for the Pipers to repurchase the land if they became financially able to do so. Based on this testimony and the preceding facts, should the trial court grant summary judgment? If so, for which party?

(b) Suppose appraisers testify at trial as to the property's fair market value. The Pipers' expert values the land at $340,000 as of October 1, 2003, and the Strongs' expert testifies: "The reasonable market value of the property on October 1, 2003, for a quick sale was $240,000 to $248,000." On cross-examination, the Pipers' expert concedes that her appraisal assumed a generous amount of time for marketing the property and that a quick sale, conducted under constraints like foreclosure sales, would in all probability not yield a price in excess of $250,000. Which side does this evidence on value favor? What if both sides agreed that the value on October 1 was $205,000? Was $500,000? Is it relevant whether after October the property value remained stable, declined, or rose sharply?

(c) Does it matter what the Pipers and Strongs agreed to as the option price? Suppose (i) the option price was the same as the purchase price, $200,000, *i.e.*, the Strongs would make no profit; (ii) the option price was $250,000 if the option was timely exercised at any time during the two-year period; (iii) the option price was equal to $200,000 plus interest at the rate of 14 percent per annum calculated from October 1, 2003, to the date of closing.

(d) You are the lawyer for the Pipers in this litigation. Do you have enough facts to persuasively argue that the transaction is an equitable mortgage? What other facts would you attempt to ascertain and why might they be relevant?

(e) You are the lawyer for the Strongs in this litigation. What additional facts do you hope to discover? Suppose instead that you are the lawyer who handled drafting the deed and option agreement for the Strongs in 2003. What, if anything, could you have done differently to reduce the risk of an equitable mortgage challenge?

(f) Suppose that, instead of the option agreement, along with the warranty deed on October 1, 2003, the Pipers and Strongs signed a purchase agreement, naming a price of $250,000, with both parties obligated to close on October 1, 2005. How does this change the arguments about whether the transaction is a sale or an equitable mortgage?

B. THE NEGATIVE PLEDGE

Recall that the basic point of a mortgage is that the lender knows that if the borrower fails to pay the debt, there is a specific asset set aside that the lender can reach. Through foreclosure, the lender can force a sale of the asset and apply the sales proceeds to the debt. This greatly reduces the risk of the loan to the lender. The lender has a property right in the asset — he has locked in his priority and has, for example, a first mortgage or a second mortgage. Perhaps there's another way for the lender to accomplish this objective. An unsecured loan is just about as good as a secured loan if the lender can be certain that, upon default, he can obtain a judgment lien and that his judgment lien will have first priority. How might the lender seek that certainty? This is the idea behind the *negative pledge* or *negative covenant.* The lender identifies a particular asset owned by the borrower, and the borrower promises not to convey or encumber that asset until the loan is repaid. This way, the lender is assured that, if there's a default, the lender can obtain a first-priority judgment lien on the asset.

TAHOE NATIONAL BANK v. PHILLIPS
Supreme Court of California, 1971
4 Cal. 3d 11, 480 P.2d 320, 92 Cal. Rptr. 704

TOBRINER, Justice. Defendant Beulah F. Phillips appeals from a judgment of the El Dorado County Superior Court that holds that an instrument entitled, "Assignment of Rents and Agreement Not to Sell or Encumber Real Property" (hereinafter referred to as "the assignment") was intended to be an equitable mortgage, and decrees its foreclosure.

We conclude that this judgment must be reversed. Plaintiff bank, which occupied the more powerful bargaining position and deliberately chose to use a standardized form providing for the assignment of rents and a covenant against conveyances, cannot be permitted to transform this assignment into a mortgage contrary to the reasonable expectation of its borrower. On examining the terms and purpose of the assignment, we conclude that it is not reasonably susceptible of construction as a mortgage at the instance of the bank, and thus that the trial court erred in invoking extrinsic evidence offered by the bank to prove it to be a mortgage.

Defendant and three co-venturers embarked on a real estate development in the Lake Tahoe area. About April 20, 1965, the venturers not only needed further capital but also owed plaintiff sums due on overdrafts on their accounts. Plaintiff agreed to lend $34,000 to defendant, who transferred the funds to the venture's account. In return, defendant gave plaintiff a single-payment promissory note, payable on demand or on May 20, 1965. At the same time plaintiff executed and delivered to defendant an instrument entitled: "Assignment of Rents and Agreement Not to Sell or Encumber Real Property."[2] This document provided that as security for the loan defendant assigned to plaintiff all rent due from the realty described therein and agreed not to encumber or convey that property. The bank was authorized to record the instrument and did so on May 27, 1965.

The real property described in the document was not the venture's apartment development, but defendant's residence, which she owned one-half in fee and one-half as trustee under the testamentary trust of her deceased husband. This property was unencumbered as of April 20, 1965. On December 6 of that year defendant recorded a declaration of homestead on the property.

Mr. Ross, president of plaintiff bank, testified that the venturers first requested an unsecured loan but that he refused to issue the loan without security and requested collateral; that defendant then offered her residence as collateral and showed him an FHA appraisal at $34,400. The venturers required the money within two hours, and, for reasons which are not entirely clear,[3] Mr. Ross determined that the bank could not conveniently prepare a trust deed within that time limit; consequently he selected instead a form for

2. The assignment reads as follows:

ASSIGNMENT OF RENTS AND AGREEMENT NOT TO SELL OR ENCUMBER REAL PROPERTY In consideration and as security for a loan made or purchased by TAHOE NATIONAL BANK (hereinafter called "Bank") which loan is evidenced (d) by a promissory note in favor of Beulah F. Phillips dated April 20, 1965, in the amount of Thirty Four Thousand and 00/100 ($34,000), the undersigned, and each of them, (hereinafter sometimes called "Borrower") hereby covenant and agree with Bank as follows: 1. The real property referred to herein is located in County of El Dorado, State of California, and is described as follows: "Lot 270, Tahoe Keys Unit No. 1, as said lot is shown on the Official Map of said Tahoe Keys Unit #1, filed in the office of the County Recorder of the County of El Dorado, State of California, on May 11, 1959, in Map Book C, Map No. 7." 2. Borrower hereby assigns to Bank all moneys due or to become due to Borrower as rental or otherwise for or on account of such real property, reserving unto Borrower the right to collect and retain any such moneys prior to Borrower's default under the terms of the loan described above; 3. Borrower will not create or permit any lien or encumbrance (other than those previously existing) to exist on said real property and will not transfer, sell, assign or in any manner dispose of said real property or any interest therein without the prior written consent of Bank; 4. Bank is hereby authorized and permitted to cause this instrument to be recorded at such time and in such places as Bank at its option may elect; 5. This agreement is expressly intended for the benefit and protection of Bank and all subsequent holders of the note described above. Borrower warrants and represents that Borrower owns the above-described real property. 6. This agreement shall remain in full force and effect until the loan described above shall have been paid in full or until twenty-one (21) years following the death of the last survivor of the undersigned, whichever first occurs. Dated: April 20, 1965 (s) Beulah F. Phillips.

3. Defendant's attorney inquired of Mr. Ross: "[W]ouldn't it have been just as easy to prepare a deed of trust on a form as an assignment of rents?" Mr. Ross answered: "No, it would not have been, simply because of the recording from the Tahoe Valley area into Placerville of

an assignment of rents and agreement against conveyances. The document was prepared by his secretary and executed by the parties.

Mr. Ross acknowledged that his bank and other banks make unsecured loans upon agreements by the debtor to maintain unencumbered assets of sufficient value in the county. He denied, however, that his purpose in having defendant sign the document in issue was merely to insure that she would have unencumbered assets reachable by the bank; he maintained that he took the document "knowing it was in actuality a mortgage instrument against that house in lieu of a deed of trust."

Mrs. Phillips testified that she did not intend to sign or believe that she was signing any security interest "like a mortgage or deed of trust." She added that since she owned half her interest as trustee she believed that she lacked authority to execute a mortgage or trust deed on the property.

Plaintiff brought suit against the venture on various notes and overdrafts and, in its fifth cause of action, asked foreclosure of the assignment as an equitable mortgage. The court entered judgment against the venturers, jointly and severally, for $92,386 plus costs, interest, and attorney's fees. It further found that the assignment was an equitable mortgage securing $34,000 of the debt, and decreed its foreclosure.

Mrs. Phillips alone appealed; her appeal challenges only that portion of the judgment finding the assignment to be an equitable mortgage and ordering foreclosure. . . .

Assignments similar to the present one are "used by many banks in conjunction with small, nominally unsecured loans such as home improvement loans." (California Real Estate Secured Transactions (Cont. Ed. Bar 1970) §2.37 (hereinafter cited as "CEB").)[6] They provide the lender with a measure of security, an assignment of rents and a contractual guarantee that property in which the debtor has an equity will remain unencumbered and unconveyed, and thus available for levy and execution should the creditor reduce his debt to judgment. Indeed, the plaintiff bank commonly makes loans upon the "security" of a promise by the debtor not to convey or

---

the deed of trust with an amendment or new title policy showing our position if there had been a proper first deed of trust of record."

This answer of Mr. Ross is inconsistent with his assertion that the assignment was intended to be a mortgage on defendant's property. If the bank requires the protection of a title policy before executing a trust deed, and prompt recording of the trust deed, logically the bank should impose the same conditions on execution of an instrument intended to serve the purpose of a trust deed.

6. A covenant against conveyances and encumbrances is sometimes referred to as a "negative pledge" agreement. (*See* G. Osborne, *Mortgages* (1951) §§43-44; Coogan, Kripke, and Weiss, *The Outer Fringes of Article 9: Subordination Agreements, Security Interests in Money and Deposits, Negative Pledge Clauses, and Participation Agreements* (1965) Harv. L. Rev. 229, 263-264; Comment (1965) 12 U.C.L.A. L. Rev. 954-962; *but see* CEB, §237.) As summarized in the article by Coogan, Kripke, and Weiss: "The case law in this area is rather thin and in general dates from the depression. It indicates that a purely negative covenant creates no security interest in the property described." (79 Harv. L. Rev. at p. 264; *see* G. Osborne, *supra,* at §44.) [Other citations omitted.]

hypothecate property, using for that purpose forms similar to that at issue here.

Thus we are not dealing with homemade security instruments in which the parties labor to produce a mortgage but fall short of the legal requirements and must be rescued by a court of equity. The form used was carefully drafted to produce a security interest with incidents differing from that of a mortgage.[8] As Justice Friedman pointed out in his dissenting opinion in the Court of Appeal [in this case]: "Here is a bank which prepared its own printed form, selected a particular one from its array of forms and handed it to the customer for signature. Doubtless the bank had printed forms of trust deed, perhaps even a few dusty, yellowed mortgages. Now the bank claims that by the printed form it selected, it intended to create the legal effect of a form it did not select." We conclude that the plaintiff, having selected a form for "assignment of rents and agreement not to sell or encumber real property," is bound by the terms of that agreement.

We turn now to the language of the assignment. Its title gives no hint of a power of foreclosure. It contains no language of hypothecation, no provisions imposing a lien or creating a mortgage, no discussion of foreclosure. . . .

Plaintiff points out that the assignment specifies that it was given "as security for a loan," and that the word "security" may signify a right of foreclosure (*see* Civ. Code, §2924; Coast Bank v. Minderhout [1964] 61 Cal. 2d 311, 314). That phrase, however, appears in the preamble which, read as a whole, states that "as security for a loan . . . the undersigned . . . hereby covenant and agree with Bank as follows." The natural interpretation of this language is that it is the six covenants of the borrower that "secures" that loan; that the word "security" in the preamble does not create additional rights and duties not specified in the covenants.

Plaintiff further contends that the term "security," and the provisions of the assignment describing the real property and permitting recordation, render the assignment ambiguous, thus requiring extrinsic evidence to determine whether it places a lien on defendant's property. . . .

8. *See* CEB, §2.37. Comment, *supra,* 12 U.C.L.A. L. Rev. 954, 962, 964, discusses the purpose of assignments such as that employed in the present case:

> [L]enders are willing in some instances to advance credit on the basis of a long pay-off period to a person who appears to have property which may be attached or secured in case the debtor becomes in financial difficulty. However, when the property is transferred, the credit picture immediately shifts and the lender wants to be in a position to accelerate maturity at once; he is no longer willing to take the risk over the long pay-off period—a risk he would gladly take if the property remained "locked with the debtor."

The comment adds:

> Even though the Financial Code prohibits savings banks and trust companies from securing their loans by taking second liens, lending institutions have made real estate loans to homeowners using the negative pledge agreement when the property specified in the agreement was already encumbered by a prior mortgage or trust deed on the theory that no security interest was created by the negative pledge agreement.

Since the alleged ambiguities appear in a standardized contract, drafted and selected by the bank, which occupies the superior bargaining position, those ambiguities must be interpreted against the bank. . . .

In the present case, we conclude that to permit a creditor to choose an allegedly ambiguous form of agreement, and then by extrinsic evidence seek to give it the effect of a different and unambiguous form, would be to disregard totally the rules respecting interpretation of adhesion contracts, and to create an extreme danger of over-reaching on the part of creditors with superior bargaining positions. The bank must bear the responsibility for the creation and use of the assignment it now claims is ambiguous; it is only "poetic justice" (CEB, §2.38) if such ambiguity is construed in favor of the borrower.[13] Legal alchemy cannot convert an assignment into an equitable mortgage, violating the customer's reasonable expectation and bestowing upon the bank the riches of an hypothecation of title.

We recognize that in Coast Bank v. Minderhout, *supra,* 61 Cal. 2d 311, we ordered foreclosure as an equitable mortgage of an instrument similar to the assignment in the present case, but we do not consider that case controlling. The agreement in *Coast Bank* contained an acceleration clause and stated that the loan was intended to improve the property described in the agreement—both characteristics indicative of a mortgage and both absent in the present assignment. Of greater significance is the differing context of *Coast Bank* and the present case. In *Coast Bank,* the borrower had breached a covenant prohibiting conveyance of the realty. Such a breach confronts the court with a difficult problem in fashioning a remedy. An award of damages would prove ineffective; "the maximum damages the bank could suffer from breach would be the amount of the debt, the same amount for which it could get a judgment on the note." (CEB, §2.38.) Specific performance of the covenant against conveyances might create an invalid restraint against alienation. (*See* Coast Bank v. Minderhout, *supra,* 61 Cal. 2d at p. 317.) . . .

In the present case defendant has performed all terms of the assignment,[14] with the result that defendant's interest in the realty, over the homestead exemption, is available to satisfy the bank's judgment on the note. If this security is not fully adequate, such is the result of the bank's choice of the governing instrument. . . .

Part 2 of the judgment against defendant Beulah Phillips is reversed.

13. Usually it will be the lender who chooses an ambiguous instrument, but Kogan v. Bergman (1966) 244 Cal. App. 2d 613, was that rare case in which the borrower drafted an ambiguous security device. The court gave the creditor an election to enforce the note as a secured or an unsecured note. (244 Cal. App. 2d at p. 261.)

14. The declaration of homestead by defendant did not breach her covenant against encumbering or conveying the property. "[A] homestead right is not an estate in the land, but a mere privilege of exemption from execution of such estate as the holder occupies." Arighi v. Rule & Sons, Inc. (1940) 41 Cal. App. 2d 852, 855. . . . The filing of a declaration of homestead creates no rights in third persons, and does not diminish the title of the declarant; it cannot be encompassed within the definition of an encumbrance.

Sullivan, Justice (dissenting). I dissent. . . .

In *Coast Bank* . . . this court unanimously held: "An agreement that particular property is security for a debt also gives rise to an equitable mortgage even though it does not constitute a legal mortgage." (Coast Bank v. Minderhout, *supra*, 61 Cal. 2d 311, 314.)

> Specific mention of a security interest is unnecessary if it otherwise appears that the parties intended to create such an interest. . . . [T]he question presented is not what meaning appears from the face of the instrument alone, but whether the pleaded meaning is one to which the instrument is reasonably susceptible. . . . The instrument restricts the rights of the Enrights [defendants] in dealing with their property for plaintiff's benefit; it describes itself as "For use with Property Improvement Loan," it specifically sets forth the property it covers, and it authorizes plaintiff to record it. These provisions afford some indication that the parties intended to create a security interest and are clearly sufficient to support the pleaded meaning.

(Coast Bank v. Minderhout, *Supra*, 61 Cal. 2d 311, 315.)

Of the four factors mentioned by the court in *Coast Bank* as indicating that the parties intended the instrument to create a security interest, only the second is absent in the case now before us. In addition, the Assignment contains an assignment of rents, a provision typically found in deeds of trust. . . .

The attempt by the majority to distinguish *Coast Bank* on its facts is equally unpersuasive. They first observe that in *Coast Bank* the agreement provided for an acceleration of the note in the event of a breach of the agreement. While it is true that the agreement in *Coast Bank* contained an acceleration clause whereas the Assignment before us does not, the court in *Coast Bank* did not find the acceleration clause to be a significant, much less essential, circumstance in concluding that the agreement created a lien on real property. . . .

Finally, we are urged to distinguish *Coast Bank* on the basis that the defendant in that case breached the agreement by conveying the property. However, in the instant case, defendant has also breached the Assignment by declaring a homestead on her property. A declaration of homestead is neither a conveyance nor an encumbrance for other purposes, but it does exempt the property from execution or forced sale. . . .

Problem 18B

Woody owns a small "strip" shopping center worth $3 million, encumbered by a mortgage loan with a present balance of $2 million held by Last Life Insurance Co. Your client, Crest Investors, wants to loan Woody $400,000 to be repaid in four annual installments of principal of $100,000 each, with interest also paid annually. Crest is unwilling to make an unsecured loan to

Woody, but Woody does not want to grant a second mortgage on the center. Crest is leaning toward the use of a negative pledge agreement and wants your advice. Is this a good idea? Can you assist Crest in structuring it properly? In particular, consider the following:

(a) Should Crest use all or part of the document signed in *Tahoe National Bank*, entitled "Assignment of Rents and Agreement Not to Sell or Encumber Real Property"? Do you recommend any additions or changes to that language?

(b) Crest has reliable written evidence that the balance due on the Last Life Mortgage loan does not exceed $2 million. Is there any need for you to study the Last Life mortgage instrument? Suppose the mortgage has a broadly worded due-on-sale clause.

(c) Should Crest record or not record the negative pledge agreement that you are drafting?

(d) Suppose litigation results over the negative pledge agreement that you are drafting. Who might be the plaintiff? Who might be the defendant or defendants? Will the court decide that the agreement is an equitable mortgage held by your client, Crest? Are you certain?

(e) Suppose that for some reason a court holds that the negative pledge agreement is not an equitable mortgage. Does this portend loss or disaster for Crest? Why or why not?

(f) How should this matter be resolved under California law? Now suppose you are in a state, like most states, that has no relevant case law. Does this bear on your advice to the client about whether to use a negative pledge? Assuming the decision is made to use a negative pledge agreement, will you draft differently for a California transaction than you will for a transaction governed by another state with no reported case law? Imagine that the shopping center is located in California, but Woody is a Utah resident and Crest Investors is located in and does business only in Utah. Which state's law will apply to the negative pledge agreement? Do the parties have the ability to choose?

C. INSTALLMENT LAND CONTRACTS

An installment land contract, also known as a *contract for deed*, is one type of arrangement for buying land. It is an executory contract under which the purchase price is payable in installments, usually monthly or annually, with the seller obligated to transfer title by deed when final payment is made. The buyer takes possession of the real estate at the outset of the transaction when the contract is signed, thus getting the use and enjoyment of the land before he completes the payments. Installment land contracts are used primarily in consumer transactions. The land may be improved — for example, with a single-family house — or unimproved, in which case the purchaser typically takes possession and builds a house or adds other improvements. There are two markets where installment land contracts are often employed, one involving merchant sellers and one involving nonmerchant sellers. Developers of vacation or resort property sometimes sell lots pursuant to installment land contracts. Occasionally new vacation homes are sold the same way. For a vacant lot, often the purchaser plans to wait before arranging for the construction of a vacation home, and in the meantime the installment land contract lets the purchaser select his lot and start making payments without the need for a substantial down payment. Individuals who own used homes or vacant lots also sometimes sell using installment land contracts. These sellers, who are not merchants, are providing a form of financing for buyers who probably cannot qualify for a standard mortgage loan because they are not able to make a substantial down payment or they have weak credit ratings. For this reason, the land contract is sometimes called the "poor man's mortgage," the connotation typically not being pejorative but instead supportive of a device that expands the availability of credit.

Installment land contracts are rarely used for transfers of commercial property or for transfers of undeveloped land that is slated for commercial development. It is also rare to find a residential developer who sells completed homes by means of land contracts. Instead, buyers of new housing obtain standard mortgage financing.

The most important thing to remember about the installment land contract is that it is an executory contract, and therefore the entire set of contract rules and remedies generally will apply. The main difference is the parties' time horizon. For a normal executory contract, sometimes called a "marketing contract," the period between contract signing and closing will be weeks or months. This period is determined by how long it takes the parties to prepare for closing and includes chores such as searching title and arranging financing. For an installment land contract the parties have agreed to postpone closing for a number of years, with the buyer in possession in the meantime. It is still an executory contract, but the period during which it remains executory is a long time, not a short time. Because contract law generally applies, we should keep in mind all the usual contract principles. For example, the contract must satisfy the statute of frauds or fall within one of the recognized exceptions. Risk of loss is on the buyer if there is no contract provision governing the matter, provided the jurisdiction follows the majority view of equitable conversion. If either party to the installment land contract breaches, the other party's remedial choices normally include expectancy damages, rescission, and specific performance.

The installment land contract has special features that distinguish it from short-term marketing contracts, and that is why we study it separately in this chapter. It is a long-term contract, pursuant to which the purchaser takes possession and often improves the property. The purchaser gradually pays the entire purchase price over time, which is unlike the short-term contract that calls for just one relatively small deposit prior to closing. Because of the long-term nature of the installment land contract and the payment schedule, the contract buyer builds up substantial equity in the property, which may be forfeited to the seller if the buyer breaches. A large volume of cases address the seller's remedies when the buyer defaults, with modern law generally evolving to protect the buyer from incurring a substantial loss of value.

Besides issues surrounding seller's remedies, the second primary area that merits special attention concerns the rights and duties of third parties. Because land contracts remain in effect for many years, transfers often take place. Third parties deal with the seller or the purchaser, acquiring interests through voluntary transfers (for example, sales and mortgages) as well as involuntary transfers (for example, foreclosures, judgment liens, and bankruptcies). Such transfers raise issues not only between transferor and transferee, but also with respect to the other party to the land contract.

In thinking about how the law should handle remedies and transfers, we should bear in mind how the parties structured their deal. The basic concept behind the installment land contract is that the seller does not part with title until all of the purchase price is paid. There is great similarity in function between an installment land contract and a purchase-money mortgage transaction, whereby the buyer gets a deed at closing and gives a mortgage back to the seller. The distinction, in principle, is that after taking possession, the contract buyer has only contract rights while the seller still has legal title, but the mortgagor buyer has legal title subject to the seller's mortgage.

Is this difference one of substance or is it merely one of form?

Problem 18C

Happy Acres Mobile Home Park sells lots in its mobile home park to purchasers using installment land contracts. Lots, which are improved with utility hookups and asphalt driveways, cost $16,000. Five years ago, Polly signed an installment land contract, providing for the $16,000 price to be paid in monthly installments of $171.94 per month for 15 years. The monthly payment includes interest at 10 percent per annum. Polly paid all monthly installments on time for 59 consecutive months, until this summer (her payments made total $10,144.46). She failed to make the payments due June 1 and July 1, and on July 6, Happy Acres sent her a notice of termination, which stated that Happy Acres was terminating the contract due to her default and that she should vacate possession of the lot and move her mobile home during the next 25 days. The contract states:

> If Buyer defaults in paying one or more monthly installments to Seller, then Seller shall have the right to terminate this contract by written notice to Buyer, in which event Seller shall have the immediate right to re-enter and

take possession of the premises. In the event Seller so terminates this contract, Seller shall be deemed relieved and discharged from any claims or obligations of any kind under this contract, and all payments made by Buyer shall be retained by Seller and shall be deemed rent for Buyer's use and occupancy of the premises up to the date of termination.

(a) Is Happy Acres' notice of termination valid? Does Happy Acres have the right to retain the payments it has received? Does it matter whether there is evidence of the rental value of the lot? Suppose that Happy Acres rents some of its unsold lots to tenants and that five years ago, when it sold to Polly, it charged $120 per month rent and it presently charges $160 per month rent.

(b) If a court denies Happy Acres the right to terminate the contract and retain all payments made to date, what alternative remedies should Happy Acres have?

(c) Should the parties' rights and remedies depend on the reason for Polly's default? For example, perhaps she lost her job or had unexpectedly high medical expenses; or alternatively she changed her lifestyle, deciding she preferred to spend her income on a new car and an expensive vacation and thus didn't have enough money left to continue paying Happy Acres.

(d) Polly bought her mobile home for $48,000 five years ago and it has a present fair market value of $34,000. It would cost $6,000 to move the mobile home to another site in the community. Should this affect the parties' rights and remedies? What if, instead of a mobile home, Polly had spent $64,000 for the construction of a prefabricated home placed on a slab foundation, and it wasn't economically feasible for the home to be moved?

(e) Suppose the facts show that Polly had not always paid on time until this summer, but she frequently made late payments in the past. About one-third of the time, she paid between the 5th and 25th of the month. Only twice did she pay later than the 25th. Once was 30 months ago, the other time 24 months ago. In both cases, Happy Acres phoned her on the first day of the following month and demanded payment, and both times she made a double payment on the next day for the last month and the current month. The contract does not provide for a late charge or penalty, and Happy Acres never tries to assess one. When Polly defaulted this time, Happy Acres called her on July 1, leaving an urgent message on her answering machine. Polly did not return the call prior to the July 6 notice of termination. How do these facts affect the analysis of the parties' rights?

YU v. PAPERCHASE PARTNERSHIP

Supreme Court of New Mexico, 1992

114 N.M. 635, 845 P.2d 158

MONTGOMERY, Justice. This is a "vendor and purchaser" case, involving the rights and liabilities, and other legal relations, between two of the parties interested in an installment land sale contract—the original vendor and a subvendee. The vendor is Paperchase Partnership ("Paperchase"); the subvendee is a married couple, Mr. and Mrs. Daniel T. Yu ("the Yus"). These parties, along with others interested in the contract, were before this Court on a previous occasion. In Paperchase Partnership v. Bruckner, 102 N.M. 221, 693 P.2d 587 (1985), we held that a subsequent contract between the original vendees, the Bruckners, and a later purchaser, as well as another contract between the later purchaser and the Yus, did not constitute "assignments" in violation of a clause in the original contract prohibiting assignment without the vendor's consent. The issue in the present case is whether the vendor (Paperchase) had the power to terminate the contract and forfeit the subvendee's (the Yus') interest when there was a default in the vendees' obligation to pay the real estate taxes on the property subject to the contract ("the Property") and the vendor did not notify the subvendee of the default or give it an opportunity to cure.

The trial court, in litigation instituted by the Yus to set aside the forfeiture, ruled that the vendor did not have such power under these circumstances and entered summary judgment in favor of the Yus. We agree with this ruling and affirm.

I

Paperchase sold the Property to the Bruckners for $180,000 in March 1977, using a standard-form real estate contract containing the following clause:

> It is mutually agreed that time is of the essence of this contract. Should the Purchaser fail to make any of the said payments [as required by the contract] . . . or fail or refuse to repay any sums advanced by the Owner . . . and continue in default for ten (10) [later amended to 15] days after written demand for such payments . . . has been mailed to the Purchaser . . . at 9108 Hannett N.E., Albuquerque, New Mexico, then the Owner may, at his option, either declare the whole amount remaining unpaid to be then due, and proceed to enforce the payment of the same; or he may terminate this contract and retain all sums theretofore paid hereunder as rental.

In 1979 the Bruckners sold the Property to A & O Investments for an undisclosed amount; in 1980 A & O Investments sold it to the Yus for $230,000; and in 1984 the Yus sold it to Maurice and Clara Strahl for $312,000. All of these sales were accomplished by standard-form real estate contracts, and each subpurchaser except the Strahls assumed the prior contracts and encumbrances.[1] Paperchase was not notified in writing of the

1. The Strahls took the property subject to the prior contracts and encumbrances. In the proceeding below, they disclaimed any interest in the Property, so their position in this litigation is not at issue and will not be considered in this opinion.

sales, nor was its consent obtained. In 1981, however, Daniel Yu telephoned Robert Buel, one of Paperchase's partners, and advised him that he had purchased the Property. After the Yus purchased the Property, they expended more than $200,000 in principal payments and improvements.

In April 1982, Paperchase sued the Bruckners, A & O Investments, and the Yus for a declaratory judgment that Paperchase could either accelerate the balance due on the contract or forfeit the purchasers' interest in the Property. This was the litigation resolved in Paperchase Partnership v. Bruckner. . . .

During the period May 1983 through November 1989, the original contract was in default on eleven different occasions. On each occasion, Paperchase sent a notice of default to the Bruckners' address as listed in the contract (the address on Hannett), not the address to which the Bruckners had moved in December 1977 and at which they had been served with process in April 1982. Paperchase did not send a notice of any of these defaults to either the Yus or the Strahls. Each notice to the Bruckners was returned unclaimed.

On November 3, 1989, Paperchase sent a notice of default to the Bruckners (at the address on Hannett) for failure to provide insurance on the property. On November 9, Mrs. Yu went to the offices of the escrow agent and discussed the insurance policy with someone on the escrow agent's staff. On the same day, Paperchase sent another default notice, to the same address on Hannett, notifying the Bruckners that they were in default for failing to pay the real estate taxes on the Property and that Paperchase had paid the taxes, demanding reimbursement within fifteen days, and threatening to terminate the contract and retain all sums previously paid if reimbursement was not made. No notice of default was sent to the Yus. On November 27, Paperchase elected to forfeit the purchasers' interest in the Property, and on the next day the escrow agent delivered a special warranty deed (restoring legal title in the vendor) and other escrowed documents to Paperchase. On November 29, the escrow agent wrote to the Yus and the Strahls, informing them of the forfeiture and, upon the Yus' inquiry, provided them with copies of the demand notices. At the time of the forfeiture, the unpaid balance on the Paperchase-Bruckner contract was $25,017.45. The estimated value of the Property ranged from less than $100,000 to more than $300,000. . . .

II

Paperchase relies for its position primarily on these statements in Campbell v. Kerr, 95 N.M. 73, 618 P.2d 1237 (1980):

> The Samuells-Kerr contract requires demand to be made at a specified address upon Kerr [the vendee]. This was done. *We know of no affirmative duty placed upon a vendor in this situation to attempt to find the vendee, or to contact*

> *subpurchasers*. . . . Stepnowski [successor to Samuells, the vendors] fulfilled his obligation under the contract to notify Kerr. If Kerr wished to insure notice, he should have notified his vendor or the escrow agent. Likewise, there is privity of estate, but not privity of contract between a vendor and subpurchasers. *Stepnowski had no legal duty to notify Campbell [a subvendee] of his demand upon Kerr.* A subpurchaser of land from a purchaser with notice of the terms of the contract between the original vendor and the purchaser takes the land subject to such terms. Campbell had notice of the terms of the Samuells-Kerr contract. She could have requested notice in the event of a demand from the vendor. She did not.

Id. at 79, 618 P.2d at 1243 (emphasis added; citations omitted). . . .

Paperchase strenuously argues that a ruling in the Yus' favor will require us to overrule *Campbell.* We think, however, that the broad statements in *Campbell* do not require this result and do not extend as far as Paperchase would like. . . .

[T]he sweeping statements in *Campbell* about the existence or nonexistence of a duty on the part of the vendor toward a subvendee are inapplicable in this case. On the surface it may appear that this case involves the question whether the vendor (Paperchase) was guilty of a breach of duty to notify the subvendee (the Yus) of the default under the contract and of the impending forfeiture. But the Yus are not suing Paperchase for damages for breach of a legal duty to themselves or even . . . for specific performance to enforce such a duty. Thus, on closer analysis one sees that what is really involved in this case is whether Paperchase can exercise its power under the contract to declare a forfeiture—whether . . . the vendor will be precluded from exercising its right to terminate the contract. To understand this line of analysis, it is necessary, or at least helpful, to indulge in a short digression into the so-called "Hohfeldian" approach to the rights and duties, and other legal relationships, between or among the parties to a transaction.

III

In 1913, Professor Wesley N. Hohfeld published in the Yale Law Journal his famous article, *Some Fundamental Legal Conceptions as Applied in Judicial Reasoning,* 23 Yale L.J. 16 (1913). The article provoked a firestorm of scholarly debate, which has continued to recent times,[3] concerning the nature of and distinctions among various legal concepts, and the terms used to denote them, relating generally to notions of legal "rights" and corresponding "duties." Hohfeldian analysis occasionally appears in judicial decisions (often in footnotes),[4] although for the most part—perhaps because the nuances of meaning and shades of distinction are just too elusive to be easily

3. *See generally* Joseph W. Singer, *The Legal Rights Debate in Analytical Jurisprudence from Bentham to Hohfeld,* 1982 Wis. L. Rev. 975. . . .

4. *See, e.g.,* Sims v. Century Kiest Apartments, 567 S.W.2d 526, 531-32 & n.2 (Tex. Civ. App. 1978) (distinguishing between a landlord's "power" to terminate a tenancy and his

grasped—reliance on Professor Hohfeld's terminology and conceptual relationships is not widespread in judicial opinions.

As Professor Hohfeld said,

> One of the greatest hindrances to the clear understanding, the incisive statement, and the true solution of legal problems frequently arises from the express or tacit assumption that all legal relations may be reduced to "rights" and "duties," and that these latter categories are therefore adequate for the purpose of analyzing even the most complex legal interests. . . .

Hohfeld, *supra*, at 28. To facilitate what he called a more "discriminating" analysis, Professor Hohfeld classified all fundamental legal relations into eight categories of "jural opposites" and "jural correlatives." He employed the following terms to denote these fundamental relations, and arranged them in the following two tables to display their interrelationships:

Jural Opposites

right	privilege	power	immunity
no-right	duty	disability	liability

Jural Correlatives

right	privilege	power	immunity
duty	no-right	liability	disability

Id. at 30.

The phrase "jural opposite," as Hohfeld used it, means that one of the eight terms (or "conceptions") entails the absence or "negation" of its opposite. Thus, the term "privilege" is the negation of the term "duty." *Id.* at 32-33. For example, one who has a privilege to enter upon another's land does not have a duty to remain off the land.

"The concept of 'correlatives' is harder to grasp." Singer, *supra* note 3, at 987. Two "[c]orrelatives express a single legal relation from the point of view of the two parties." *Id.* The familiar example of this relationship is the right-duty set of correlatives: If one party has a duty to perform an act, the other party has a correlative right that the act shall be performed. Hohfeld, *supra*, at 31-32.

"right" to do so, in deciding whether to recognize a cause of action for damages for retaliatory eviction); Fernandez v. Linea Aeropostal Venezolana, 156 F. Supp. 94, 97 (S.D.N.Y. 1957) (distinguishing between a "right" and a "power," which removes a previous "disability," to maintain a wrongful death action for a death occurring at sea); Zablocki v. Redhail, 434 U.S. 374, 392, 98 S. Ct. 673, 684, 54 L. Ed. 2d 618 (1978) (concurring opinion of Powell, J.) (distinguishing between "right" and "privilege" to marry for constitutional purposes); Gutierrez v. Vergari, 499 F. Supp. 1040, 1048 n.6 (S.D.N.Y. 1980) (distinguishing between rights and duties, on one hand, and powers and liabilities, on the other hand, for purposes of 42 U.S.C. §1983); Seattle Sch. Dist. No. 1 v. State, 90 Wash. 2d 476, 585 P.2d 71, 91 & n.10 (1978) (*en banc*) (holding that constitutionally imposed "duty" of state to provide for children's education entails children's correlative "right" to receive education).

In the context of the present case, and focusing on the legal conception or term applicable to Paperchase, it is relatively easy to see that the applicable concept is not "duty," but "disability." Hohfeld describes "legal power" as the opposite of "legal disability" and gives as the nearest synonym for a legal power the term legal "ability," the opposite of which is "inability" or "disability." *Id.* at 44-45. A legal "power" is described as the ability to alter a given legal relation. *Id.* at 44.

Thus, although many might say (loosely, as Hohfeld would have it) that Paperchase had the right to terminate its contract with the Bruckners upon their nonpayment of taxes, Hohfeld would (probably) have said that Paperchase had the power to do so, for no one was under a correlative duty to surrender title to the Property when the taxes were not paid. Rather, it is (probably) more accurate to say, in Hohfeldian terms, that Paperchase had the power to terminate the Bruckners' (and all subvendees') interest in the Property upon giving notice, making proper demand, and affording the requisite opportunity to cure the default.

The opposite of Paperchase's power part to terminate the vendees' (including the Yus') interest in the Property is a legal disability to terminate that interest in the event that certain conditions were not met. The question in this case is: Was one of those conditions the necessity to notify the Yus of the default in paying the taxes, when Paperchase had knowledge of the Yus' interest in the Property and could have (but did not) given them notice and an opportunity to cure the default? We shall return to this question in Part IV below.

The purpose of the foregoing excursion into Hohfeldian analysis is not to suggest that the solution to a legal problem appears, almost automatically, when one employs the right terminology. On the contrary, use of these terms, no matter how careful and discriminating one may be in their selection and application, probably does little more than describe the result of the court's analysis of the problem and the solution it reaches; the solution does not spring, magically, from the correct selection of the proper "jural conception." At the same time, Hohfeldian analysis has this one (perhaps among others) considerable virtue: It requires, or at least counsels, the legal advocate or jurist to be exceedingly careful ("discriminating," to use Hohfeld's word) in using terms like "right," "duty," "privilege," "liability," and the others. In the present case, Paperchase can be said to be guilty of using the term "duty" in a loose sense (understandably, in view of Campbell v. Kerr); but its (and *Campbell*'s) loose use of that term does not mean that Paperchase is, as it argues, entitled inexorably to prevail on this appeal.

IV

We return, then, to the question whether a vendor with knowledge of its subvendee's interest in the land, who does not give the subvendee notice of an impending forfeiture, has the legal ability — the power — to terminate the subvendee's interest. Stated otherwise, the question is whether the vendor in this situation is under a legal disability from terminating its subvendee's interest in the land. We have already seen that this Court in [Martinez v. Logsdon, 104 N.M. 479, 723 P.2d 248 (1986)] held that the vendor was precluded—*i.e.*, did not have the ability or the power—to terminate its subvendee's interest. Is this legal principle shared by the decisions of other courts around the country; and, if so, what is the underlying reason for the principle?

There are occasional statements consistent with *Campbell*, appearing in cases and in secondary authorities, that a subvendee is not entitled to notice of default when the original purchaser defaults on the contract with the vendor. *See, e.g.,* Porter v. Barrett, 233 Mich. 373, 206 N.W. 532, 533 (1925) ("Plaintiffs had no contract relations with defendant Robinson [a subvendee]. He was a stranger to them and their contract. Under such circumstances he was not entitled to notice of the forfeiture of a contract to which he was not a party."); Walter H. E. Jaeger, *Williston on Contracts* §927A, at 829-30 (3d ed. 1963) ("Where a purchaser enters into a subcontract and afterwards defaults on his obligations to the original vendor, the latter can foreclose [*i.e.,* forfeit] the contract without notice to the subpurchaser though the fact of the subpurchase is known."). It appears, however, that such statements are based on older authorities and may not take into consideration the numerous factors, many equitable in nature, through which the trend in the law has come to favor the rights of a subpurchaser where the subpurchaser has a significant equity in the property and the original vendor has notice or knowledge of the subpurchaser's interest. This trend is illustrated by the more modern case of Sofie v. Kane, 32 Wash. App. 889, 650 P.2d 1124 (1982), in which the court said: "In order to terminate or cancel their contract, both Kane and the Robins [the vendor and the vendee] were required to give notice to subsequent vendees of whom they had actual knowledge." *Id.* 650 P.2d at 1128 (*citing* Kendrick v. Davis, 75 Wash. 2d 456, 452 P.2d 222 (1969) (*en banc*), and Welling v. Mount Si Bowl, Inc., 79 Wash. 2d 485, 487 P.2d 620 (1971)). . . .

[E]quitable considerations . . . provide the key to an understanding of the reason for the rule we adopt today—that a vendor with knowledge of a subvendee's interest in property subject to a real estate contract, where the subvendee has a significant equity in the property subject to the contract, cannot declare a forfeiture of the subvendee's interest without giving the subvendee notice of default and an opportunity to cure. That reason is simply " 'the modern view that valuable contractual rights should not be surrendered or forfeitures suffered by a slight delay in performance unless such intention clearly appears from the contract or where specific enforcement [upon the seller] will work injustice after a delayed tender.' " Martinez v. Martinez, 101 N.M. 88, 91-92, 678 P.2d 1163, 1165-66 (1984) (*quoting* Katemis v. Westerlind, 120 Cal. App. 2d 537, 261 P.2d 553, 558 (1953) (alteration in original)). . . .

It is undisputed that Paperchase sold the property in 1977 for $180,000 and at the time of the default was owed about $25,000 on the contract. It is undisputed that the Yus bought the Property in 1980 for $230,000; that they made principal payments on their contract and improvements to the Property totalling approximately $200,000; and that they sold the Property in 1984 for $312,000. It is undisputed that Paperchase did not notify the Yus of the default in payment of taxes in November 1989, even though it had known of their interest since 1981 and had known their address since at least 1982. It is undisputed that the escrow agent (Paperchase's agent for this purpose, *see* In re Mancha, 35 B.R. 427, 429 (9th Cir. BAP 1983)), knew the Yus' address at the time of the default but did not provide them with a copy of the default notice until after the forfeiture had been effected and the escrowed documents had been returned to Paperchase. And finally, it is undisputed that Paperchase followed a systematic program of sending default notices to an address where it knew the notices would not reach anyone interested in the Property — not even the Bruckners, the purchasers under the original contract. So studied was Paperchase's adherence to the literal, but by then largely ineffectual, notice provision of the original contract that it says in its brief (in a remark that can only be described as revealing a penchant for understatement): "Moreover, the prior litigation could have only put the Yus on notice that Paperchase Partnership had a penchant for strictly enforcing the Paperchase Real Estate Contract." . . .

Frost, Justice (specially concurring). I concur in the foregoing opinion, except those portions which discuss and seemingly endorse Hohfeld's analysis of legal relationships. This discussion is unnecessary. A consideration of Mr. Hohfeld's analytical system should be left to law students and their professors where the views of Messrs. Austin, Bentham and John Stuart Mill could be given their due.

Problem 18D

Vanna owned an unencumbered fee simple estate in Gladacre. On February 5, 1998, Vanna, as vendor, executed an installment land contract with Brian and Betty Pride (husband and wife), as vendees. The purchase price under the land contract was $50,000, of which the Prides paid $3,000 down. The land contract obligated the Prides to pay the remaining $47,000 in equal monthly installments over 15 years.

Vanna had borrowed $5,000 on an unsecured basis from Second State Bank in 1997. On February 10, 1998, Vanna borrowed an additional $10,000 from Second State Bank and granted the bank a mortgage on Gladacre to secure this loan. At the same time Vanna granted Second State Bank a second mortgage (subordinate to the mortgage securing the $10,000 new loan) to secure repayment of the still outstanding $5,000 personal loan. Vanna did not tell the bank about the land contract with the Prides. On February 11, 1998, Second State Bank recorded both mortgages. On February 23, 1998, the Prides recorded their land contract. On April 1, 1998, Second State Bank assigned the second mortgage and the underlying $5,000 obligation to Also Financial Services, Inc., who recorded the assignment on April 3, 1998.

Vanna's financial situation took a severe turn for the worse. Both mortgage loans required monthly payments of principal and interest. Vanna failed to make the payments due June 1, 1998, for both loans, and has not made any payments since. On October 3, 1998, Second State Bank brought an action to foreclose its mortgage by judicial sale, serving process on Vanna, the Prides, and Also Financial Services. The foreclosure sale is scheduled for December 20, 1998. On November 10, 1998, Also Financial Services offered to pay to Second State Bank the amount of its first mortgage loan (now $9,980) in order to retire that mortgage obligation. Second State Bank refused, stating it would rather purchase the property itself at the foreclosure sale. Also Financial Services has filed a motion to enjoin Second State Bank's foreclosure and to compel the bank to accept payment.

On November 20, 1998, Also Financial Services filed its own foreclosure action, serving Vanna and the Prides. Also Financial Services alleges $5,120 is now due. The foreclosure sale for this action is scheduled for February 2, 1999. Gladacre has a present fair market value of $60,000 (free and clear of all liens). Vanna, being clearly insolvent, is judgment-proof. Gladacre is located in a state with a race-notice recording statute. The Prides, having become aware of all these facts, are concerned that their interest in Gladacre may be on shaky ground. You are the lawyer to whom they come. Should they worry? What can and should be done for the Prides? Without limiting the foregoing request for advice, please explain (1) whether Also Financial Services will succeed in paying off Second State Bank and if that will affect the Prides, and (2) whether the Prides should continue making monthly payments under the land contract to Vanna.

19
Junior Mortgages

We have already discussed junior mortgages in a number of places in this book. In this chapter, we focus on the market for junior mortgages, the special position of the junior mortgagee, and her legal relationships with the owner-mortgagor and the senior lienholder.

Junior mortgages can be used to *leverage* a property owner's investment. "Leverage" is not a complicated economic concept. All it means is that the owner or developer is obtaining funds from lenders or investors to do a real estate project or to finance a completed project. These funds may be from debt financing or from equity financing when the investor takes an interest in a capacity such as a partner, joint venturer, or shareholder in the project. In a "highly leveraged" deal, the developer is getting a lot of financing — debt or equity or both — and has little of her own money or capital invested or committed to the project. Leverage directly affects risk and return. The higher the leverage, the greater the potential return on the owner's out-of-pocket investment.

It is very common for real property owners who have an existing first mortgage, and who have equity in their property because its value exceeds the balance on the first mortgage, to decide they want to borrow additional funds. There are any number of reasons why they might want cash: their business may need capital for expansion or modernization; they may have debts to pay; they may need money for health care or to pay for their children's education; they may have the opportunity to purchase an investment that looks good to them; they might want to take a nice vacation. Although they might be able to get an unsecured loan for any of these purposes, they may find that lenders insist on collateral in the nature of a second lien on their property. Even if collateral is not required, in almost all cases the prospective borrowers will learn that the cost of the loan will be less if they agree to give security. As we have discussed before, this reduces the credit risk to the lender and enables the lender to offer a lower interest rate and more attractive terms than is possible for unsecured lending.

Be careful not to confuse the term "secondary financing" or "second mortgage" with the secondary mortgage market, which we studied in Chapter 15. These terms refer to completely different concepts. The secondary mortgage market involves the sale of primary mortgages from the originating lender to investors, and a very high percentage of those mortgages are first mortgages. It is true that second-lien residential mortgages (home improvement loans and home equity line-of-credit loans) are increasingly traded on the secondary mortgage market, but their priority has nothing to do with identifying the market in which they are traded. In contrast, the term *secondary financing* means there is already a first mortgage on the property, which has priority. It implies nothing about whether the lender might keep the loan or sell it to a new or "second" owner.

A junior mortgage is the primary type of secondary financing that is secured by property. A junior mortgage may be a second mortgage, third mortgage, or even fourth mortgage. In states where the principal security instrument is something other than a mortgage, the same ranking occurs, with the junior lenders generally using the same type of instrument as the first lenders. Thus, in California and Texas there are second and third deeds of trust, and in Georgia there are second and third security deeds. There is no legal or logical limit to how many mortgages may encumber a single piece of property, but for obvious practical reasons having to do with property value and transaction costs, one seldom encounters more than a handful of mortgages on one property in the real world. Note, however, that there can be many junior liens other than mortgages, and a troubled or delinquent property owner might incur a large number of mechanic's liens, judgment liens, and the like ranked against a single asset.

Other forms of secondary finance besides junior mortgages are used in real estate finance on occasion, but they are not common. For example, when a borrower owns rental property that is subject to a mortgage, a secondary lender may take a first assignment in one or more of the borrower's leases. Functionally in terms of risk, this is a second position because even though the lease is not part of the mortgagee's collateral, if that lease is junior to the mortgage, a properly conducted mortgage foreclosure will result in termination of that lease. Alternatively, when the borrower is an entity, a secondary lender may get a first lien on the ownership interests in the entity—for example, a pledge of corporate shares or a collateral assignment of partnership interests. Again, although the lender nominally has a first position, if the entity's only or principal asset of value is real estate subject to a first mortgage, the lender has the risk of being second in line. Another possibility is that the borrower will sign a negative pledge agreement covering the property that has equity. In each of the alternative types of secondary financing mentioned here, the secondary lender probably will have more risk than if she obtained a standard second mortgage. The main situation in which such an alternative might make sense for a particular deal is when there is an impediment to the owner's granting a second mortgage or to the lender's receiving a second mortgage. The first mortgage may prohibit second mortgages, or, if the lender is a financial institution, for regulatory reasons a second mortgage loan might be inappropriate or inadvisable.

In any case, it must be remembered that secondary financing is also an alternative to merely refinancing under a new first mortgage. That is, one might get a further advance under a first mortgage, roll the first mortgage over into a new larger first mortgage loan from the same lender, or simply pay off the first loan by borrowing from a new lender and taking on a larger debt. Generally, this route will not be taken if the current first loan has a favorable interest rate that would be upset on refinancing, or if no provision is made in the first mortgage for future advances. In addition, refinancing may have higher transaction costs than getting a second or junior loan, depending on the way in which a particular jurisdiction taxes mortgage lending and recording. Consequently, there may be sound business reasons for not simply replacing a current first loan with a new and bigger first loan.

In recent years, an increasing proportion of the market for homeowner second loans has consisted of home equity lines of credit. Home equity loans, secured by second mortgages, are amortized over a fixed term that is generally much shorter than the standard 30-year length of a first mortgage. Terms ranging from 5 to 15 years are typical, and homeowners on the average prepay home equity loans faster than first mortgage loans because the interest rates are higher. These secondary loans generally carry a higher rate of interest than a first mortgage because there is a greater risk that they will not get paid in full in the event of a mortgage foreclosure. This is because the earlier creditors will be paid first. A borrower who is approved for a home equity line of credit has the choice of how much actually to borrow, up to the maximum, at any time while the relationship continues.

Problem 19A

You are downtown relaxing late one evening after work at a sidewalk coffee bar having a cup of cappuccino with your friend Marcus, who is four years out of law school and has a good job as assistant district attorney. Marcus is a great litigator who really knows his criminal law and evidence, but he's sure you know much more about real estate and lending than he does. Marcus owns a riverfront condominium that has appreciated dramatically since he bought it right after graduation. He got in when the developer offered good discounts for preconstruction contracts while the units were being built. He bought for $150,000, with a $140,000 first mortgage, and he knows a present appraisal will value his unit at $240,000. His present loan balance is $137,000. Along with all the other junk mail, Marcus just received a letter from his bank saying he is preapproved for a home equity line of credit for up to 90 percent of the appraised value, less existing secured debts, and the letter promises there will be no closing costs if he acts within three weeks. The interest rate floats at 3 percent over prime, which is presently 6¾ percent. Marcus says this sounds pretty good to him. He has $30,000 left to pay in college and law school loans at a fixed rate of 10 percent. The old beater of a car he has been driving since the second year of law school is giving him fits, and he has his eye on a nice Mustang convertible that the car dealer can finance at 11½ percent. He also has credit card balances of about $7,000 and says the bank is gouging him at 18 percent on that. Marcus thinks maybe he should get the home equity loan, draw down about $60,000, and handle all three items. He wants to know what you think. Tell him all the pluses and minuses that you think he should consider before going forward.

A. PROTECTING THE JUNIOR MORTGAGE

1. Contract Terms and Practices That Reduce Risk

The primary risk to the junior mortgagee is that the senior debt holder will foreclose. As we saw in Chapter 17, if the senior mortgagee forecloses properly and the junior fails to act, the junior loses all of her property rights in the property that serves as the collateral for her loan. Now she is an unsecured creditor and is in a terrible position. Because the mortgagor has suffered a foreclosure on the property, the prospect that the mortgagor will voluntarily pay the junior debt in the near future is very remote. She therefore must hope that the mortgagor owns other assets—in addition to the foreclosed-upon property—that she can proceed against to satisfy the debt. This great risk of foreclosure under the senior mortgage is the reason why junior mortgages cost more than first mortgages. Risk and price are related, and the junior lender must charge a higher interest rate or take other measures to increase its yield (for example, by collecting upfront fees) to take account of her risky position. Thus, when the market interest rate for a particular type of first mortgage is 10 percent, if there is sufficient equity in the property to justify secondary financing, the rate for a second mortgage might be 12 or 13 percent.

In addition to pricing its mortgage loans differently to account for greater risk, junior lenders typically take other steps to protect their loans. A few of these additional steps include: verifying the outstanding loan amount of the senior loans and determining if the senior loans permit negative amortization or additional funding; inclusion of a cross default provision in the junior mortgage so that any default on the senior loan is an automatic default on the junior loan; a right to notice of any default on the senior loan; and a right to cure a default by the borrower on the junior loan.

2. Marshalling of Assets

Often a senior and junior mortgage cover precisely the same real property, but it is not at all unusual for there to be differences in the land, improvements, fixtures, and other types of collateral that are covered by competing mortgages and security documents. When secured creditors have liens that attach to different assets but there is some overlap, disputes over priorities often arise. The most common problem arises when the senior creditor seeks to foreclose and she has more assets as collateral than the junior creditor. When this happens, courts often apply the doctrine of *marshalling of assets.* This is a rule of equity that ranks or arranges the multiple assets in order, requiring that the senior creditor first proceed against the asset that is not subject to a junior lien. Some courts have applied marshalling only if a single debtor has created both debts. Thus, under this view, marshalling would not apply if a purchaser who assumes or takes subject to a mortgage granted by her seller later encumbers only part of the property covered by the first mortgage.

In re MARTIN
Supreme Court of Oklahoma, 1994
875 P.2d 417

SIMMS, Justice. This is a Certified Question of Law from the United States Bankruptcy Court for the Western District of Oklahoma based upon the following facts.

John R. Martin and Elsie B. Martin, debtors, filed a petition for relief under Chapter 13 of the United States Bankruptcy Code and subsequently converted the case to one under Chapter 12 of that code. Debtors own three parcels of property: (1) Lot 10, Block 10, Sights Acres Addition to the City of Clinton, Custer County, Oklahoma ("Homestead"); (2) Northwest Quarter of Section 36, Township 13 North, Range 18 W.I.M. ("Farm property"); and, (3) An undivided 100 acre mineral interest underlying the Northwest Quarter of Section 30, Township 12 North, Range 17 W.I.M. ("Minerals").

Debtors' bankruptcy schedules place the following values on the properties: (1) $53,250 on the homestead; (2) $45,600 on the farm property; and, $50,000 on the minerals. However, the secured creditor, Oklahoma Bank & Trust Company (Bank), disputes the values Debtors have placed on the properties, and a hearing on Bank's valuation motion is to be reset by the parties. Nevertheless, Debtors' indebtedness exceeds the value of the properties.

Debtors are indebted to the Small Business Administration ("SBA") in the amount of $44,057.65 with the debt secured by a first lien on the homestead and a second lien on the farm property. The indebtedness of Debtors of $40,510.26 to the State of Oklahoma/Commissioner of the Land Office ("CLO") is secured by a first lien on the farm property. Finally, Debtors are indebted to Bank in the amount of $151,346.94, and Bank is secured by a third lien on the farm property and first lien on the minerals.

Relying upon 42 O.S. 1991 §17 and 24 O.S. 1991 §4, Bank requested an order of marshalling of Debtors' assets. Bank urged the Bankruptcy Court to declare SBA's claim be satisfied out of the homestead property. With SBA's claim satisfied, Bank could then satisfy a part of its claim out of the excess value of the farm property after CLO's claim was satisfied. If the court excluded the homestead from marshalling, then CLO would have first priority to satisfy its claim against the farm property with SBA being entitled to the excess of that farm property. Bank's interest in including the homestead property in the marshalling of debtors' assets is quite clear.

Debtors objected to such marshalling, contending that Okla. Const. Art. XII, §2 and 31 O.S. 1991, §1, as well as public policy, prohibit Bank from compelling the satisfaction of SBA's claim from the homestead. Debtors further requested an order compelling the creditors to marshall their claims away from the homestead. The Chapter 12 Trustee aligned with Debtors in contending the homestead should be excluded from the marshalling of assets. . . .

Our inquiry must begin with the doctrine of marshalling of assets. This doctrine "rests upon the principle that a creditor having two funds to satisfy his debt may not, by his application of them to his demand, defeat another creditor, who may resort to only one of the funds." Meyer v. United States, 375 U.S. 233, 236, 84 S. Ct. 318, 321, 11 L. Ed. 2d 293 (1963). Thus, under marshalling, a senior lienholder must satisfy his claim by first resorting to property in which a junior lienholder has no interest. The doctrine is codified at 24 O.S.1991, §4 which provides:

> Where a creditor is entitled to restore [sic-"resort"] to each of several funds for the satisfaction of his claim, and another person has an interest in or is entitled as a creditor to resort to some but not all of them, the latter may require the former to seek satisfaction from those funds to which the latter has no such claim, so far as it can be done without impairing the right of the former to complete satisfaction, and without doing injustice to third persons.

The Bank also cites 42 O.S. 1991, §17 in support of its claim for marshalling. Section 17 reads:

> Where one has a lien upon several things, and other persons have subordinate liens upon or interests in, some but not all of the same things, the person having the prior lien, if he can do so without the risk of loss to himself, or injustice to other persons, must resort to the property in the following order, on the demand of any party interested: 1. To the things upon which he has an exclusive lien; 2. To the things which are subject to the fewest subordinate liens; 3. In like manner inversely to the number of subordinate liens upon the same thing; and, 4. When several things are within one of the foregoing classes, and subject to the same number of liens, resort must be had,— (a) To the things which have not been transferred since the prior lien was created; (b) To the things which have been so transferred without a valuable consideration; and, (c) To the things which have been so transferred for a valuable consideration.

Thus, Oklahoma statutory law contains provisions designed and intended to allow for the marshalling of assets in situations such as the one at bar where there are multiple properties and multiple creditors. However, the doctrine of marshalling of assets is not without exceptions. When our state constitution was drafted, its writers had the foresight to include a provision exempting homestead property from forced sale. Okla. Const. Art. XII, §2. Section 2 provides:

> The homestead of the family shall be, and is hereby protected from forced sale for the payment of debts, except for the purchase money therefor or a part of such purchase money, the taxes due thereon, or for work and material used in constructing improvements thereon; nor shall the owner, if married, sell the homestead without the consent of his or her spouse, given in such manner as may be prescribed by law; Provided, Nothing in this article shall prohibit any person from mortgaging his homestead, the spouse, if any, joining therein; nor prevent the sale thereof on foreclosure to satisfy any such mortgage.

Although this provision does not specifically state that a homestead may not be marshalled against, its intent is clear. Homestead property is exempt from any forced sale except in those specifically enumerated cases such as for the purchase money of the homestead or for taxes due thereon. Conspicuously absent from the authorized exceptions to this constitutional provision are instances of marshalling. Those enumerated exceptions are the only claims which regard the creditor's rights to the property as equal to or exceeding the rights of the debtor. . . .

In addition to the constitutional homestead exemption, statutory law contains a homestead exemption as well. . . .

The Oklahoma Legislature has made its intention quite clear in enacting this homestead exemption. The statutory homestead exemption, as well as the constitutional homestead exemption, prohibits homestead property from being forcibly sold for the payment of debts except under the specifically enumerated exceptions. Marshalling of assets is not one of those exceptions.

In addition, not only do the terms of the homestead exemption provisions make it clear that the homestead is excluded from marshalling, but the equitable nature of the doctrine of marshalling of assets also militates against allowing marshalling of homestead property. The doctrine was founded in equity and natural justice and is designed to promote fair dealing. . . .

In the majority of jurisdictions which have passed on the issue, it is held that the debtor has a right to compel the secured creditor to marshal away from the homestead. . . .

Debtors' protected equity in their homestead is superior to Bank's equity interest in marshalling. Application of the marshalling doctrine to allow Bank to force the sale of exempt property although it does not have a mortgage voluntarily given by Debtors or a claim for purchase money or taxes or improvements is in direct contravention of our constitution and statutes. The fact that this equitable doctrine has been codified by statute, 24 O.S. 1991, §4, *supra,* does not defeat or change its purpose. . . .

Thus, we join the majority of jurisdictions and adopt the exception holding that a debtor is entitled to exclude the homestead from marshalling of assets.

QUESTION ANSWERED.

HODGES, Chief Justice, with whom SUMMERS, Justice, joins, dissenting. . . .

As the majority recognizes, the purpose of [the two Oklahoma marshaling statutes] is to allow marshaling under the facts of this case. However, the majority suggests that these statutory provisions do not apply in this case because to do so would cause injustice to third persons, namely the debtor, which is prohibited by the provisions. This position is insupportable, especially where the debtor has voluntarily mortgaged the property and received purchase money. . . .

The majority also would find an exception implied in section 2 of article 12 of the Oklahoma Constitution and title 31 section 1 of the Oklahoma Statutes and an exception based on equity. I cannot agree that these two provisions on which the majority relies imply an exception and, even if an exception is implied, that such an implication should override explicit statutory mandates. Neither should equitable principles be applied to negate express legislative language. . . .

I would hold that the Oklahoma Constitution and the Oklahoma Statutes do not create or authorize an exception to the marshaling of assets when the debtor has voluntarily mortgaged the homestead property to secure payment of a debt and the Oklahoma marshaling statutes, Okla. Stat. tit. 42, §17 and tit. 24, §4 (1991), permit secured creditors to compel the marshaling of assets against homestead property which has been intentionally mortgaged.

Problem 19B

Kristina owns 38 acres of wooded rural property encumbered by a first mortgage with a balance of $38,000 owing to Rural State Bank. As a wedding present for her daughter, Regina, and the groom, Rick, Kristina marks off a lovely two-acre corner of the property with a pond and mountain view, where she has a cottage home built. She arranges financing with Jackson Finance, which agrees to take a mortgage for the $60,000 construction cost on the two acres. Construction is finished in time by the wedding date, the happy couple move in, and Jackson Finance ends up with a second mortgage on the two acres. Regina and Rick are tenants, with no written lease, and they pay Kristina rent equal to the monthly payments under the Jackson Finance loan. One year later, on the couple's anniversary, Kristina's generosity impels her to deed the two acres over to Regina and Rick. They agree to pay the Jackson Finance loan, and Kristina says she will handle all of the Rural State Bank loan.

(a) What sequence of events will it take for Rural State Bank or Jackson Finance to be required to marshall assets, as the doctrine is commonly applied? Should it matter that presently the two parcels are owned by different parties?

(b) Regina and Rick's house is their homestead under state law. Does this affect how marshalling of assets might apply as between Rural State Bank or Jackson Finance? Suppose Kristina has lived all along on her remaining 36 acres, and all this land qualifies as her homestead. Should this fact affect application of the marshalling principle?

(c) Regina and Rick default in making payments to Jackson Finance. There is no default under the Rural State Bank loan. Jackson Finance moves to foreclose, arguing that Kristina's 36 acres have a present value of $90,000 and under marshalling Rural State Bank's mortgage should be limited to that property so that Jackson can foreclose. Should the court find this argument persuasive?

(d) Kristina's careless driving results in a neighbor's wrongful death, and she suffers a tort judgment for $300,000, of which her car insurance pays only her policy limit of $100,000. The successful plaintiff obtains and files a judgment lien against all her real estate. Shortly thereafter, Kristina defaults on the Rural State Bank loan while Jackson Finance's loan is current. Rural forecloses, selling the entire 38 acres—including the children's house—for $88,000, which yields a surplus of $47,000 after paying Rural's debt and foreclosure costs. Who should get the surplus, Jackson Finance or the tort claimant? Or should they share the surplus in some proportion?

B. MORTGAGE SUBORDINATION

A particular piece of real property is often subject to more than one lien, and whenever this is the case it may become necessary to establish the priority of those liens. As a general principle, as we have seen earlier, priorities are ranked according to the idea of "first in time, first in right," subject to modification by state recording statutes. Sometimes specialized state statutes also affect priorities. For example, a mechanic's lien statute may give a worker or supplier of materials a special priority, and under Article 9 of the UCC the seller of a fixture who extends purchase-money credit is granted a prior status over some earlier mortgages or security interests.

When there are two or more mortgages on a property, it often happens that the general legal principles for priority are inappropriate or inadequate. The owner and the mortgagees may desire a different ranking than the general rules would produce based on the chronology of the parties' respective transactions. Even if there is no need to re-rank the priorities, there may be a need to make more definite the parties' respective rights and obligations with respect to certain matters. When either or both of these needs are present, the parties may use contract law to handle their concerns. The type of contract they sign may vary, but for real estate financings it is usually referred to as a *subordination agreement.* In contrast, for corporate finance and personal property financings, the arrangement is usually called an *intercreditor agreement.* The purpose of the agreement, whatever its name, is to establish or modify the relative rights of the creditors in their dealings with the borrower and the property that serves as collateral.

RANIER v. MOUNT STERLING NATIONAL BANK
Supreme Court of Kentucky, 1991
812 S.W.2d 154

SPAIN, Justice. This action arises out of the interpretation of a subordination agreement. In 1977, Phyllis Ranier loaned $200,000 to Algin and Doris Nolan and secured the promissory note with a first mortgage lien on their house and lot located in Montgomery County, Kentucky. In 1983, the Nolans applied for a home improvement loan with the Mount Sterling National Bank (Bank) to repair their home which was damaged by fire. Before approving the loan, the Bank required Mrs. Ranier to subordinate her lien on the Nolan property to the Bank's mortgage lien.

On February 28, 1983, Mrs. Ranier and the Bank executed a subordination agreement. The agreement, drafted by the Nolans' attorney, stated in pertinent part as follows:

> WHEREAS, Doris C. Nolan and Algin H. Nolan have entered into a loan agreement with the Mt. Sterling National Bank, Mt. Sterling, Kentucky, whereby they will borrow **the total sum of $125,000** from the Mt. Sterling National Bank, to be secured by a first real estate mortgage on the above described property in favor of the Mt. Sterling National Bank, and it is intended by the parties hereto that the above referenced real estate mortgage lien in favor of Thelma Phyllis Ranier . . . shall become a second and junior mortgage lien to the new first real estate mortgage lien in favor of Mt. Sterling National Bank. (Emphasis added.)

The Nolans then executed a six-month promissory note on March 8, 1983, in favor of the Bank in the amount of $125,000 and secured the note with a first mortgage lien on the Nolan property. The future advance clause of the mortgage stated that ". . . the total indebtedness at any one time outstanding shall not exceed the sum of . . . $125,000. . . ."

Without notice to Mrs. Ranier, the Bank, in July 1985, approved an additional loan to the Nolans in the amount of $75,000 to complete the repairs on their property. The Nolans signed a new promissory note in favor of the Bank in the amount of $200,000. The Nolans' original note in the amount of $125,000 was marked "renewed" by the Bank and returned to the Nolans. The note remained secured only to the extent of the Bank's first mortgage on the Nolan property. The record indicates that the note was renewed several times and a total sum of $95,269.04, including $17,182.82 in principal and $78,269.32 in interest, had been paid to the Bank. The Bank applied the principal and interest to the unsecured portion of the note.

The Nolans defaulted on their notes. A foreclosure action was instituted by the Bank and the Nolan property was sold by the Master Commissioner for $181,000. Both the Bank and Ranier moved for summary judgment on the issue of their respective priorities in the proceeds of the foreclosure sale. The trial court granted summary judgment in favor of the Bank on the issue of priority and awarded it the sum of $140,216.48, which included the original promissory note principal amount of $125,000, plus interest, court costs, and attorney's fees. Mrs. Ranier received the balance of $35,892.09.

Ranier appealed to the Court of Appeals which affirmed the decision of the trial court. . . .

The Court of Appeals held that . . . the terms of the subordination agreement governed the Bank's priority. The Court of Appeals and the trial court stated that the agreement did not contain any provision which prohibited the Bank from making additional loans to the Nolans nor any requirement that the payments made by the Nolans be applied to the original secured portion of the note.

We agree with the lower courts that the subordination agreement does not contain any provision which prohibited additional loans from the Bank to the Nolans, nor does it provide specifically that any payments received from the Nolans would be used first to reduce the original secured portion of the renewed promissory note. The Bank did not breach the subordination agreement when it renewed the note and approved an additional unsecured loan in the amount of $75,000 to complete the repairs on the Nolan residence. But we do believe that the Bank has breached its implied covenant of good faith and fair dealing when it failed to give notice to Mrs. Ranier of its subsequent loan to the Nolans and when it unilaterally applied the mortgage payments it received from the Nolans first to the unsecured portion of the new promissory note. . . .

Prior to the parties entering into the subordination agreement, Mrs. Ranier held a first mortgage position on the Nolan property. She was asked by the Bank and the Nolans to subordinate her advantageous security position in favor of the Bank so that the Bank would approve a $125,000 home improvement loan to the Nolans. Mrs. Ranier then acquiesced and entered into the subordination agreement in the good faith belief that her mortgage would be subordinated only to the extent of $125,000, on which the Nolans were making regular payments. The Bank then loaned the Nolans an additional $75,000. No notice was given to Mrs. Ranier, nor did she agree to further subordinate her mortgage to an additional $75,000. The renewed note in the amount of $200,000 was, in fact, two notes containing a $125,000 secured note and a $75,000 unsecured note. The Bank clearly benefited from the subordination agreement because it was able to obtain a first lien on the property and then it subverted the agreement by applying the payments it received from the Nolans, not to the $125,000 debt, but to the unsecured portion of the note. Mrs. Ranier has been relegated, to her detriment, to an inferior position in the proceeds of the foreclosure sale while the Bank has been allowed to collect on both its unsecured and secured notes, including interest, court costs, and attorney fees. We do not believe that the intent of Ranier when she entered into the agreement was to place her pre-existing first mortgage in the status of a second mortgage in perpetuity. Her intent clearly was that her mortgage be temporarily subordinated to the Bank's mortgage to the extent of $125,000. . . .

We recognize the rule that, as between the two of them, a creditor receiving payments from his debtor, without any direction as to their application, may apply them to any legal debt, secured or unsecured, which he holds against his debtor. Straub v. Chemical Bank, Ky. App., 608 S.W.2d 71 (1980). But where a third-party creditor executes a subordination agreement in favor of said creditor, the latter has an implied duty under equitable principles to apply the payment it receives from the debtor in a manner which does not prejudice the third-party creditor's subordinated security interest. . . .

The decisions of the Court of Appeals and Montgomery Circuit Court are reversed and the matter is remanded to the trial court. The proceeds of the foreclosure sale shall be distributed in accordance with this decision.

WINTERSHEIMER, Justice, dissenting. I respectfully dissent from the majority opinion because I do not believe the subordination agreement requires the interpretation placed on it by the majority and the doctrine of equitable subrogation is not applicable. . . .

The subordination agreement does not make any provision about the application of payments. There is no reference to any preexisting indebtedness, nor a limitation on the total indebtedness. . . .

I believe the circuit judge and the Court of Appeals have correctly analyzed the language of the subordination agreement, and I would not disturb their decision.

Problem 19C

Datlief owns a small grocery convenience store with four gasoline pumps where he pumps Big Star gas. He purchased the property a year ago with the help of his rich friend Alyssa, who invested $200,000 toward the $260,000 purchase price. Alyssa is to receive interest payable quarterly at the rate of 5 percent per annum plus 35 percent of the profits for the next 5 years. These terms are set forth in a promissory note signed by Datlief, secured by a mortgage on the store property.

Datlief wants to expand, and he draws up plans to add four more pumps, a car wash, and an addition that would add 600 square feet of space to the store, at a total cost of $150,000. Datlief goes to Last Bank to finance the expansion, and it agrees to finance $140,000, provided Alyssa subordinates her mortgage to the Bank's. Datlief approaches Alyssa and she agrees, signing a writing that states: "The undersigned hereby subordinates her title and lien created by that certain Mortgage dated January 21, 2006, which covers the real property described in Exhibit A attached hereto, to that certain Mortgage dated October 3, 2006, from Datlief to Last Bank and covering the same property." Both mortgages cover exactly the same parcel of land, "together with any and all improvements, fixtures, and appurtenances thereto."

(a) Datlief defaults under both loan transactions and Last Bank commences foreclosure proceedings. Alyssa claims the subordination is invalid and her mortgage lien is superior because:

1. The reference in the subordination agreement to the date of Alyssa's mortgage is incorrect; her mortgage was dated January 12, 2006, and was also recorded on January 12.
2. Exhibit A was never attached to the subordination agreement.
3. Alyssa did not receive any consideration whatsoever for signing the subordination agreement; the agreement does not even recite the receipt of Ten Dollars, One Dollar, a peppercorn, or anything at all.
4. The subordination agreement was never recorded in the real property records.
5. The subordination agreement was not signed by Last Bank, and indeed it does not have a signature block for it to sign. (Would it matter here if the form was prepared for both parties to sign, but Alyssa could show that Last Bank never signed it until after it began to foreclose?)

Please evaluate Alyssa's defenses. Are any of her defenses, singly or in combination, valid?

(b) The subordination agreement does not refer to the debt or promissory note held by either Alyssa or Last Bank. Should a reference to either or both be added? Would adding these details help Alyssa, Last Bank, or both parties? Suppose the agreement referred to "that certain Promissory Note made by Datlief dated October 3, 2006, in the amount of $140,000." Datlief defaults; Last Bank accelerates and forecloses; the property sells for $160,000. At the time of foreclosure, Last Bank is owed $138,000 in principal, $8,000 in accrued interest, and $6,000 in attorneys' fees. How much money should go to Datlief and how much to Alyssa?

(c) Datlief does not default under either loan transaction but he is unlucky. A tornado rips through town and destroys the roof and one wall of the store and the new car wash in its entirety. Datlief is no fool; he has "all peril" casualty insurance that will pay $80,000, which should be almost enough to repair and replace everything. Both Alyssa's and Last Bank's mortgages have a clause stating: "In the event of casualty to all or part of the mortgaged property, Mortgagee shall have the right to collect any and all casualty insurance proceeds to apply to the indebtedness secured hereby, or at Mortgagee's sole option Mortgagee may permit Borrower to use all or part of said proceeds to repair or rebuild said property." Both Alyssa and Last Bank claim the right to invoke this clause, to the exclusion of the other. What result and why? Suppose the clause is only in Alyssa's mortgage and not in Last Bank's, which is completely silent on the topic of insurance proceeds. Now what should happen? May whichever lender does not receive the insurance proceeds or the right to monitor their use declare a loan default and accelerate maturity of the loan?

(d) You are an associate at the law firm that represents Alyssa and you have been assigned to handle whatever must be done in connection with that nasty tornado that wrecked Datlief's property. Your best friend, Larry, is the loan officer at Last Bank. Larry is responsible for administering the commercial loans in the community where Datlief's store is located. Alyssa tells you that she and Datlief are named as insured persons under the casualty insurance policy and that Last Bank never got itself added to the policy. She says that Datlief has not told Last Bank about the tornado damage and plans not to. Alyssa thinks Datlief's repair plan is sound, the store has been profitable so far, and they are both concerned that Last Bank might see it differently and insist on keeping the proceeds. You are concerned that Last Bank has a legitimate interest in the transaction that should be protected, and you do not want to see Larry get in trouble at work—it's just so easy to lose a job nowadays. Tomorrow night, when you have dinner with Larry at a good restaurant, can you mention the tornado at Datlief's store? What if, instead of a direct reference, you just say, "Did that big storm earlier this month hit any of your loan properties?" Or "I know loan supervision is hard work. How often do you have to check your loan properties to make sure nothing is damaged or broken?"

(e) Suppose there is no tornado but the subordination went in the opposite direction—Last Bank's mortgage was expressly subordinated to Alyssa's, using the language set forth earlier. Both loans go into default, and Last Bank claims that the subordination is not valid to the extent of Alyssa's right to receive the 35 percent profit interest. (In other words, should a subordination using the language used in this fact pattern extend to a right to profits?) What result here?

C. WRAP-AROUND MORTGAGE

A wrap-around mortgage is a special type of junior mortgage in which the junior debt includes or "wraps" the senior debt. Both of the debts are installment obligations, and the borrower under the wrap-around mortgage pays the holder of the junior debt and mortgage, who in turn pays the holder of the senior debt. Typically, a wrap-around is used in one of two circumstances, either as a form of seller financing to enable a buyer to purchase a property or as a technique for refinancing a property. When parties use a wrap-around rather than ordinary junior financing, the most common reason is to preserve the economic value of an interest rate on the senior loan that is below the prevailing market rate at the time the wrap transaction is consummated. Tax planning is another reason why wraps are sometimes used for seller-financed deals. Income tax from the sale of property at a gain may be paid to the government over time, rather than all at once in the year of sale, if the seller chooses to use what is called the installment method of reporting gain. More favorable tax treatment is available to the seller if the deal is properly structured as a wrap-around rather than a straight sale in which the buyer assumes or takes subject to the seller's existing mortgage debt. The total amount of gain is the same either way, but there is more deferral of payment until later years.

A simple example of a wrap-around mortgage used to finance a purchase may help to illustrate the parties' positions and risks. Erin owns a duplex building and rents both dwellings to tenants. She has a mortgage loan held by Newtown Savings and Loan with a present balance of $90,000, payable in monthly installments of $950. These payments fully amortize the debt over the remaining term of 7 years. The interest rate is fixed at 7 percent, and the mortgage contains a standard due-on-sale clause. Jack wants to buy Erin's duplex for $150,000. He has $10,000 for a down payment, and the parties agree that Erin will finance the remaining $50,000 that Jack needs. The parties could structure the transaction with Jack giving Erin a $50,000 promissory note secured by an ordinary second mortgage on the duplex property, with Jack assuming Erin's existing loan, but this would require the consent of Newtown. Interest rates are much higher than 7 percent, and they feel certain that Newtown will either say no or demand either a high assumption fee or a higher interest rate. For this reason, they decide to use a wrap transaction. Jack gives Erin a promissory note for the stated principal amount of $140,000, bearing interest at 10 percent per annum, payable in monthly payments amortized over 15 years. This results in monthly payments of $1,504. To secure the note, Jack gives Erin a wrap-around mortgage that is recorded. Although the face amount of this mortgage includes (or "wraps") Newtown's debt, Newtown's mortgage is not terminated or released. It remains fully of record, with Erin's wrap-around mortgage being junior in position. Under the wrap-around documents, Erin is obligated to continue to make the monthly payments of $950 to Newtown. Thus, each month Erin nets $554, the difference between the payments on the wrap-around note and the wrapped note held by Newtown.

Wrap-around transactions are complicated compared to ordinary mortgage loans, and this complexity adds risk not only for the holder of the wrap-around obligation but also for the payor of that obligation.

Problem 19D

Veronica owns a 20-unit apartment building set on four acres of land subject to a mortgage loan with a balance of $1.4 million. Truman plans to buy the property from Veronica for $2.2 million. Veronica's lawyer says she wants to structure the sale as a wrap transaction. Truman says he is unfamiliar with this way of purchasing property and wants you to explain how it will work for this deal and what the risks and benefits are.

(a) Give Truman your thoughts. What documents will be necessary at closing to handle a wrap-around transaction for this deal? Also, in case Truman decides to go forward after hearing your advice, please prepare a list of what specific provisions you will want to see in the documentation to protect him and reduce his risks.

(b) An additional concern about the proposed wrap just surfaced. As a thorough and highly capable real estate attorney, you of course told Truman that you needed to obtain and study all the loan documents for Veronica's existing first mortgage loan as soon as possible. Truman had gotten copies from Veronica and just happened to have them in his case. You notice that the mortgage has a standard due-on-sale clause and prohibits the borrower from granting any junior or subordinate loan without the lender's consent. When you raise the issues with Truman, he says that he has already discussed it with Veronica and to go ahead with the sale and wrap without telling the first lender. Because the interest rate on the first loan is very attractive—3 percent below the present market—they feel certain they cannot get the lender's approval of the deal. Truman wants your advice. Can you help structure and implement the deal to make sure the lender will not learn about it, or at least to reduce the risk of discovery? Are there ethical limits to what you as a lawyer may do in this context? If you are able to assist them in arranging a secret deal, what if the lender finds out before the first mortgage is retired? Would discovery harm Veronica, Truman, or both? Should they expressly allocate this type of risk in writing?

20
Basic Commercial Real Estate

The commercial real estate market should not be thought of as completely different from the residential markets that we have already studied. In many ways, the commercial market is merely a more complex version of its residential counterpart. All of the same market context considerations discussed in Chapter 1 apply in both situations. The number of parties involved in the commercial transaction is likely to be greater, the amount of money at risk is usually higher, and the underlying legal issues are generally more difficult to address. Even so, the methods of thinking about residential transactions are equally useful when thinking about commercial ones. A good understanding of the residential real estate transaction will help you comprehend the dynamics of the commercial exchange. Likewise, as we learn more about the commercial exchange, we are better able to comprehend and appreciate the potential complexity of what is sometimes referred to as a "simple" residential transaction.

A. SELECTING A DEVELOPMENT ENTITY

Commercial real estate transactions typically involve a number of matters related to entity selection. The development process is a risky undertaking and involves transactions among a number of parties. Consequently, the developer is confronted with the question of how best to organize for conducting the business at hand. Few, if any, developers are likely to proceed with a project in their individual capacity. Instead, the typical developer will look for a vehicle or a means of conducting business that will limit personal liability. In considering the limits to liability, a developer generally is concerned with two key matters. First, the developer wants to limit her personal liability. This means that, as an individual, the developer does not want to risk her home, savings, or personally held investments. Second, the developer wants to protect as many business and corporate assets as possible. This is important when the developer has other businesses or other real estate holdings that are not held in her personal name but are held in some recognized business form, such as by a corporation or by a limited partnership, in which the developer has control or a substantial pecuniary interest.

A developer typically selects the corporate, limited partnership, or limited liability company (LLC) form of doing business. These vehicles allow developers to limit their liability to the capitalization of the entity itself. The corporate form can be useful when there are only a couple of shareholders who will put up the investment equity to get the project going. They can each be shareholders and control the company while limiting their financial exposure if the deal proves to be unsuccessful. Another popular choice for developers is the limited partnership. Typically, the general partner of the limited partnership is the developer and the limited partners are the investors. It is normal for the general partner in such an arrangement to also be a limited liability entity such as a corporation or a limited partnership. The limited partnership is therefore a nice vehicle for syndicating investment interests in the undertaking. The LLC provides certain tax benefits, but in general is structured like a partnership while providing the limited liability of a corporation. In most of these entities, the developer usually takes the responsibility for putting the deal together and managing its successful completion. For this the developer generally receives certain fees and financial interests, in addition to any other investment returns on the transaction.

If a developer is active in real estate markets, she is likely to create a new development entity for each new transaction in which she engages. By doing so, the developer protects her business assets and ensures that a default or bankruptcy on one particular project will not destroy other financially healthy activities of the overall enterprise. The developer must be careful properly to capitalize her development entity and to operate it as a separate company. If the entity is undercapitalized and not treated as a separate legal entity, the developer may become personally liable for the acts and omissions of the entity. This is the case, for example, when such circumstances give rise to "piercing the corporate veil" of an entity, thus exposing the principals to liability.

Problem 20A

Robin and Chris form a corporation for purposes of getting into the real estate development business. The corporation is called Roch, Inc., and Robin and Chris each have a 50 percent stake in the entity. Each shareholder contributes $10,000 cash to capitalize the company and gets 50 shares of stock in return. Roch, Inc. enters into an agreement with Small Bank whereby Small Bank agrees to extend $200,000 of financing to the company so that it can acquire a small office building that will be leased out to a law firm for use as the firm's law office. Small Bank is not one for a lot of paperwork, so it shakes hands on the deal with Robin and Chris and then gets Roch, Inc. to execute a simple note and mortgage. The note and mortgage are signed by Robin and Chris as president and vice president, respectively, of Roch, Inc. After Small Bank has loaned out the $200,000, its attorney discovers that Roch, Inc. was never properly formed as a legal entity. When informed of this, the bank inquires as to its ability to enforce the note and mortgage. The attorney for the bank asks you to give her advice. What kinds of issues would you discuss, and what types of questions would you want answered? What additional information would you want to know and why? What type of action should the bank take?

B. COMMERCIAL LENDING AND ARTICLE 9 OF THE UCC

A commercial real estate transaction involves financing issues that extend beyond the law of real property and of mortgages. A number of the issues that arise require an understanding of the Uniform Commercial Code (UCC). The UCC can apply to the use of a promissory note, which is an Article 3 instrument, and it can apply to methods of payment in a transaction that can be governed by Articles 3, 4, and 4A. In addition, Article 2 of the UCC, covering "goods," might apply when a sale of real property includes a transfer of appliances or other items of personal or movable property. Taking security for a loan can also raise UCC problems. In particular, some items of collateral cannot be secured by a real estate mortgage and require an Article 9 security interest. Similarly, Article 9 priority rules can come into play with respect to fixtures that can be secured under the law of the UCC and the law of real property mortgages.

In the commercial financing area we are especially concerned with the security given for the loan. We need to be sure that a lender has taken the correct steps to encumber the various property rights of the debtor that are offered as collateral for the loan. At the same time, the lender must be certain to follow all the appropriate steps necessary to perfect its security interest in the collateral so that it will establish a lien priority as against other competing claimants. Proper documentation and perfection are important in this process, to ensure that the lender has a right to proceed against the identified property in the event of default and also to protect its priority in situations where there may be more claims against the debtor/borrower's assets than can be satisfied by the collateral. The documentation requirements and the perfection and priority rules differ between real property mortgage law and the law under the UCC.

Under both real property law and the UCC, this documentation involves getting and perfecting a security interest in the collateral. With respect to real property, the proper documentation centers around the real estate mortgage, and perfection involves recording the mortgage in the local public records so as to establish the priority of the lender's lien. Under the UCC, the security interest is covered by Article 9 and requires a security agreement and perfection by either possession or filing of a financing statement in the appropriate state office. The method of perfection and the appropriate place to file under Article 9 vary depending on the type of collateral in question. Generally speaking, mortgage law applies to collateral consisting of real property and to things that are fixtures according to state law. Article 9, which is also adopted as state law, generally applies to personal property as well as to fixtures. Consequently, a lender will have to think of securing its transaction by categorizing items of collateral into one of three types: real property to be governed by a mortgage, fixtures to be governed by both mortgage law and Article 9 of the UCC, and any other type of property to be governed only by Article 9. There may actually be a fourth category of property to consider. This category would include such things as the specific items excluded from Article 9 under §9-109 and which are not either fixtures or real property. Intellectual property is an example. If a lender wants a developer to put up a patent, trademark, or copyright as partial collateral for a loan, it must follow federal statutes, which preempt Article 9, at least partially.

Problem 20B

Betty owns a certain piece of real property with a four-story office building located on it. The office building is about five years old and is fully leased. Veronica agrees to buy the property from Betty for $3 million. Veronica and Betty structure the deal as a transfer of the real property under a warranty deed, with the building and all improvements being transferred as personal property by bill of sale.

(a) Veronica has two lenders. She gets $500,000 from Big Bank, for which she signs a first mortgage on the land, and she gets $2.5 million from Commercial Credit Co., for which she signs an Article 9 security agreement. If all the parties agree to this arrangement, should they be allowed to divide and treat the property in this manner? What is the impact or binding nature of their arrangement on third parties? Do they need to do anything more to properly bind third parties, and, if so, what would you recommend?

(b) Assume instead that Veronica buys the property from Betty and takes a transfer of everything under the warranty deed. In this exchange, she borrows $500,000 from Big Bank and gives it a first mortgage lien on the property. She pays the other $2.5 million in cash. Six months after the deal, Veronica approaches Commercial Credit and offers to give it an Article 9 security interest in the entire building in exchange for an extension of a revolving line of credit not to exceed $2 million. In the event of a default on both loans and a foreclosure by Big Bank, should it be bound by the severance of the building from the land as attempted by Veronica and Commercial Credit?

C. DRAGNET AND CROSS-COLLATERAL CLAUSES

FISCHER v. FIRST INTERNATIONAL BANK

Court of Appeal of California, Fourth District, 2003
109 Cal. App. 4th 1433, 1 Cal. Rptr. 3d 162

AARON, J. . . . Plaintiffs Karl and Pamela Fischer appeal from a summary judgment order and final judgment in favor of defendant First International Bank (FIB or the bank). . . .

The Fishers' appeal presents the following question: When a bank enters into a written loan agreement that specifies the collateral for two different loans, and does not state that the loans will be cross-collateralized against each other, may the bank subsequently enforce a broadly worded "dragnet" clause contained in the fine print of a standard form deed of trust securing one of the loans? On the particular facts of this case, we conclude that the trial court erred by granting summary judgment in defendants' favor on this issue. . . .

In 1989, Karl and Pamela Fischer purchased two contiguous commercial lots located at 2102 Main Street in Ramona, California, for $310,000. They took out a $707,000 construction loan from FIB and invested another $750,000 to construct a large family dining and recreation center on the property.

In 1998, the Fischers entered into negotiations with FIB for two additional loans: a takeout loan in the amount of $730,000 to pay off the existing construction loan (Loan #1) and an equipment loan in the amount of $325,000 (Loan #2). On September 14, 1998, FIB and the Fischers entered into a written agreement regarding the terms and conditions of the loans (the September Agreement). The agreement was drafted by FIB in the form of a letter to the Fischers signed by both a loan officer and a senior vice-president, to be countersigned by the Fischers. According to the loan officer, the September Agreement was intended to define the terms of the loans to the Fischers.

The September Agreement specified the identities of the borrowers, the dollar amounts of the loans, the purpose of each loan, the term of each loan, the interest rates, loan fees and packaging fees, the terms pertaining to prepayment and assumability, and the estimated closing costs. The September Agreement also included the following provision specifying the collateral for each of the two loans:

> *Collateral*:
> Loan #1: First deed of trust on commercial property located at 2102 Main Street, Ramona, CA

Loan #2: Second deed of trust on commercial property located at 2102 Main Street, Ramona, CA

Second deed of trust on single-family residence located at 14382 Blue Sage Road, Poway, CA

The agreement included express conditions pertaining to each of the loans. One of the conditions for Loan #2 was a "second deed of trust on the residential property located at 14382 Blue Sage Road, Poway, CA 92064." There was no such condition for Loan #1. . . .

The signed September Agreement contained no reference to cross-collateralization of the loans. According to the Fischers, they "specifically negotiated" the loan agreement so that their Blue Sage residence would not be collateral for Loan #1. This was one of their "main objectives" in negotiating the agreement.

On September 30, 1998, the Fischers went to the bank to sign final loan documents, including a deed of trust for their residence. They met with FIB Vice President Steve Pollett. The Fischers brought a copy of the September Agreement with them to this meeting. According to the Fischers, Pollett assured them that their home was collateral only for Loan #2, as stated in the September Agreement. The Fischers pointed out that the proposed deed of trust incorrectly stated that their home would be collateral for both loans. Pollett agreed that this was a mistake, and told the Fischers they did not have to sign the incorrect deed of trust because their home was not needed as collateral for Loan #1, but rather, only for Loan #2. The bank subsequently changed the deed of trust so that the definition of the word "note" referred only to the $350,000 loan for Loan #2.

According to Mr. Fischer, Pollett said that if the Fischers were to sell their Blue Sage residence, any equity from the sale would be used only to pay off the balance of Loan #2. . . .

The deed of trust signed by the Fischers for their Blue Sage residence stated in bold and capital letters that the deed was "GIVEN TO SECURE (1) PAYMENT OF THE INDEBTEDNESS AND (2) PERFORMANCE OF ANY AND ALL OBLIGATIONS OF TRUSTOR UNDER THE NOTE, THE RELATED DOCUMENTS, AND THIS DEED OF TRUST." On a separate page of definitions, the word "Note" was defined to mean "the Note dated September 30, 1998 in the principal amount of $325,000." The phrase "in the principal amount of $325,000" was inserted in larger print than the other definitions contained on the standard form. However, the word "Indebtedness" was broadly defined in the fine print as follows:

> The word "Indebtedness" means all principal and interest payable under the Note and any amounts expended or advanced by Lender to discharge obligations of Trustor or expenses incurred by Trustee or Lender to enforce obligations of Trustor under this Deed of Trust, together with interest on such amounts as provided in this Deed of Trust. In addition to the Note, the word

> "Indebtedness" includes all obligations, debts and liabilities, plus interest thereon, of Borrower to Lender, or any one or more of them, as well as all claims by Lender against Borrower, or any one or more of them, whether now existing or hereafter arising, whether related or unrelated to the purpose of the Note, whether voluntary or otherwise, whether due or not due, absolute or contingent, liquidated or unliquidated and whether Borrower may be liable individually or jointly with others, whether obligated as guarantor or otherwise, and whether recovery upon such Indebtedness may be or hereafter may become barred by any statute of limitations, and whether such Indebtedness may be or hereafter may become otherwise unenforceable.

The deed of trust also included a "Due on Sale" provision giving FIB the right to "declare immediately due and payable all sums secured by this Deed of Trust upon the sale or transfer, without the Lender's prior written consent, of all or any part" of the Blue Sage residence.

Finally, the deed of trust contained a provision stating: "This Deed of Trust, *together with any Related Documents,* constitutes the entire understanding and agreement of the parties as to the matters set forth in this Deed of Trust." (Italics added.) The phrase "Related Documents" was defined to "mean and include without limitation all promissory notes, credit agreements, loan agreements, environmental agreements, guaranties, security agreements, mortgages, deeds of trust, and all other instruments, agreements and documents, whether now or hereafter existing, executed in connection with the Indebtedness."

In 1999, the Fischers decided to sell their Blue Sage residence. . . . [T]he Fischers sold their home. After paying off Loan #2 through escrow, there was $125,000 left over from the sale.

. . . FIB demanded that any funds remaining from the sale of the residence be applied to Loan #1. . . .

According to the Fischers, they would not have sold their home if they had known that FIB was going to take the money that remained after the balance of Loan #2 was paid. The Fischers allege that they intended to use the proceeds from the sale of their home as working capital, and that without these funds, they were forced to sell their commercial property and business for below fair market value.

The Fischers filed suit against FIB . . . alleging breach of contract, conversion and misappropriation of money, breach of fiduciary duty, fraud in the inducement, negligent misrepresentation, breach of the implied covenant of good faith and fair dealing, and false promise.

The trial court granted summary judgment in favor of [FIB]. . . .

The trial court found that the dragnet clause contained in the deed of trust defeated all of the Fischers' causes of action as a matter of law. Finding no ambiguity as to the parties' intent regarding collateralization of the loans, the court applied the literal language of the dragnet clause and concluded that the bank had a right to apply the proceeds from the sale of the Fischers' residence to both loans. We disagree with the trial court's conclusion and find that there are triable issues of fact regarding whether the parties mutually agreed to cross-collateralization of the loans.

A "dragnet" clause (also known as an "anaconda" clause) is a clause stating that a mortgage secures all the debts that the mortgagor may at any time owe to the mortgagee. . . .

Courts in different jurisdictions have adopted widely varying approaches to broadly worded dragnet clauses that purport to apply to all existing and future debts and obligations. *See generally* Annot., *Debts Included in Provision of Mortgage Purporting to Cover All Future and Existing Debts (Dragnet Clause)—Modern Status,* 3 A.L.R.4th 690 (1981). In many states, a dragnet clause will not be applied to other existing debts unless such debts are explicitly described in the security agreement. . . .

At the opposite extreme are courts that view the literal language of a generally worded dragnet clause as conclusive evidence of the intent of the parties that the clause encompass all other debts. *See, e.g.,* Hamlin v. Timberlake Grocery Co., 130 Ga. App. 648, 204 S.E.2d 442, 444-445 (1974). . . .

In a number of jurisdictions, courts have adopted an approach somewhere between these two extremes. These courts examine a variety of factors to determine whether the parties intended the dragnet clause to apply to existing debts. . . . The factors these courts consider in assessing the intent of the parties include: (1) whether the dragnet clause is boilerplate; (2) whether the other debts are of the same kind as the primary debt; (3) whether the other loans are listed in the dragnet clause; and (4) whether the debt which the lender seeks to have included in the dragnet clause is otherwise fully secured.

California courts have taken an intermediate position with regard to the validity of dragnet clauses. . . .

Because a dragnet clause is one of the provisions "least likely" to be understood by a layperson reading the fine print of a deed of trust, California limits the enforcement of such a provision "to those transactions where objective evidence discloses the intention of the *debtor and the creditor* to enlarge the lien to include other obligations." 4 Miller & Starr, *California Real Estate* (3d ed. 2000) §10.12, com., pp. 50-51. The proponent of a dragnet clause bears the burden of establishing that the parties intended all existing or contemporaneous loans to be included within its scope. . . .

Applying these general principles, we do not find an objectively clear and unambiguous expression of mutual intent to cross-collateralize Loan #1 and Loan #2. Preliminarily, the presence of the dragnet provision would have been discernable to a borrower only by cross-referencing from the highlighted security provision to the fine print of a 177-word, two-part definition of the word "indebtedness" filled with legal jargon that would have been incomprehensible to the average layperson. The first part of the definition of "indebtedness" expressly referred only to the $325,000 note for

Loan #2. Yet, the second part purported to make the deed act as security for all other "obligations, debts and liabilities" in language so sweeping that it encompassed even debts "barred by any statute of limitations" or "otherwise unenforceable."...

In contrast to the deed of trust, the September Agreement did not include a dragnet provision that would have permitted cross-collateralization of the two loans. Significantly, the agreement was not silent on the subject of collateral; it specifically identified the collateral for each of the two loans and expressly stated that the business would serve as collateral for both loans, but that the Blue Sage residence would serve as collateral for Loan #2 only. Cross-collateralization was not a condition of either of the loans according to the terms of the September Agreement.

As with any contract, the September Agreement must be construed according to the "ordinary and popular" meaning of its language. . . . Because the September Agreement specifically addressed the subject of collateral and did not mention cross-collateralization, we believe that any layperson reading its plain language would have understood it to mean exactly what it said: that the Blue Sage residence would serve as collateral for Loan #2, but not Loan #1. The clear terms of the September Agreement would have precluded the bank from using the residence as collateral for Loan #1. . . .

. . . [W]e therefore conclude that the conflicting provisions of the September Agreement and the deed of trust create a triable issue of fact regarding the true intentions of the parties. At a minimum, the loan agreement creates ambiguity as to whether the parties mutually intended to permit cross-collateralization. Parol evidence is admissible to resolve this ambiguity. . . .

. . . Accordingly, we must reverse the judgment in the bank's favor. . . .

D. LEASES AS FINANCING DEVICES

Two commonly used arrangements that are likely to appear in a complex commercial real estate transaction are the *ground lease* and the *sale and leaseback.* Each of these two arrangements has its own tax and entity selection implications. For our purposes, however, we will focus on the use of these arrangements as tools to facilitate financing of a transaction. The basic idea behind each arrangement is that the project to be developed or managed (a mall or an office building, for instance) will be constructed on or transferred to a leasehold estate. If the project is one to be constructed, the developer will typically become the tenant on a long-term ground lease. If it is a completed project that is being sold, it is generally the current owner or operator of the project that sells the fee interest and remains in possession with use of the property as a tenant under a long-term leaseback arrangement.

1. Ground Lease

Two common situations lead to the use of a ground lease. The first is when a developer identifies land for a suitable development project but the owner refuses to make an outright sale of the fee ownership. An owner may want to keep control of the ownership of property for many reasons, but if she refuses to sell the fee a developer may still be able to negotiate a lease allowing the use of the property for a stated number of years.

The second situation involves the developer using the ground lease as a source of financing. Because the developer will acquire less than the full fee ownership of the property and will have to pay rent and be subject to lease restrictions on its use of the property, acquisition costs are lower than for an outright fee purchase.

The developer must make sure that the term of the ground lease is both long enough and stable enough in its duration to allow adequate amortization of the cost of any improvements to be constructed on the land. The terms of the lease will also have to be sufficient to provide an adequate return on investment to the developer. As a consequence, the fee owner and the developer will have to agree on terms under which both parties will share in the expected profit from the undertaking. For the developer to recoup investment costs on a major construction project, the lease will probably have to be long-term.

The ground lease must be made to fit correctly with other sources of financing. Probably construction lending will have to be secured by a mortgage that will have priority over the lease. This means that the fee owner under the lease must agree to subordinate the lease to any subsequently approved construction loan. If the lease is prior in time and is not subordinated, a default on the lease by the tenant developer could lead to a lease termination and the end of the tenant's leasehold interest. The construction mortgage would be unsecured because the estate that secured it is no longer in existence. Because the fee owner will want the deal to be marketable it will generally agree to a subordination provision in the ground lease. A condition of that subordination is likely to be that the fee owner approve of the terms and identity of the construction lender to which it will subordinate.

A great deal of commercial real estate is rental property. After entering into a ground lease, the developer as landlord will enter into subleases that allow tenants to occupy space in the contemplated improvements. Some of these subtenants are likely to obtain their own financing for purposes such as the purchase of tenant fixtures and improvements. Thus, there will be another layer of leases and potential creditors to deal with in the transaction. One of the issues to be addressed is the relationship between the fee owner and these subtenants. Generally, two documents are used to address this relationship. These documents relate to attornment and nondisturbance. The *attornment agreement* provides that all the subtenants must agree to attorn to or look to the lender if the lender should take over the project, primarily as the result of a default by the developer. The implication is that the subtenant cannot use the lender takeover as an excuse to change the terms of its lease with the developer. The *nondisturbance agreement* flows in the opposite direction, in that it obligates the lender to leave the subtenants undisturbed in their leases. Rents cannot be arbitrarily raised or terms changed simply because the lender takes over as the new landlord under a sublease. The nondisturbance agreement, as might be anticipated, is given by the lender only to key subtenant stores that are essential to making the property a success — in other words, the tenants that have market power. In contrast, all subtenants will be expected to enter into an attornment agreement.

The landlord generally views the ground lease as a passive investment. The landlord does not want an active role in ownership even though it technically owns the land. As a result, the landlord usually sets up the ground lease as a *triple net lease,* which means that all the normal costs of ownership are placed on the tenant (developer). The costs of property taxes, insurance, and maintenance are all shifted from the fee owner to the tenant under such an arrangement.

2. *Sale and Leaseback*

To develop a basic understanding of the sale-leaseback transaction, consider a simple example. Giovanni owns and operates a commercial investment company. One of his business assets is the five-story building that serves as his business headquarters. For simplicity, assume that the building is worth $1 million and that it is debt-free. As a result of financial losses from investments in international stocks and derivative issues, Giovanni finds himself in need of additional operating capital. One thing that Giovanni could do in such a situation is go to a lender and ask to borrow money against the equity value of his building. He would get a cash infusion for his business and would execute a mortgage in favor of the lender. He would then pay back the lender under the terms of the promissory note and mortgage agreement. As an alternative to this, Giovanni might offer an investor the opportunity to purchase the building. The sale, however, would be part of a complementary arrangement whereby Giovanni agrees to lease the building back from the new owner. In this way, Giovanni would sell the building but still have its use, so that he can continue to operate his business. The result is similar to the mortgage loan transaction, in that Giovanni gets a cash infusion from the sale, keeps possession of the property, and makes monthly payments. In the sale and leaseback arrangement, the monthly payments are for rent rather than a mortgage payment, but the rent payment will come close to being the same as a comparable mortgage payment for a similar amount of cash amortized over a similar term. At the end of the leaseback period, Giovanni will generally have the right to buy back the building at some nominal amount. However, the sale and leaseback arrangement implies a different relationship between the lender/investor and Giovanni than does the mortgage transaction. With the sale and leaseback, the lender becomes the owner of the property and the landlord under a long-term lease. This means that lease law and the implications of ownership and of landlord and tenant relations apply between the parties. Default remedies and other legal rights and duties may differ in such a setting when compared to the lender and debtor relationship of a standard mortgage transaction.

It is important to note that Giovanni could also have split his interest in the building and created two investment opportunities. He could have sold the fee simple land interest and leased back the use of the land on which the building sits, thus creating a ground lease, and he could also have sold the building separate and apart from the land, with its own leaseback arrangement. Sometimes by dividing a property into a variety of separate property interests you can enhance its value by making it possible to reach more types of investors who have different investment objectives and different amounts to invest. By properly structuring the sales and leases of the split estates in the property, it is possible that Giovanni can get more total cash than he would get by merely selling it as one complete unit (with or without a leaseback) or by mortgaging it out as collateral for a single loan.

No matter how the sale and leaseback is structured, it will tend to involve a long-term lease, and thus will be drafted with many of the same features and provisions as a ground lease. For income tax purposes, it is important that the lease make economic sense beyond merely being a disguised mortgage. This means that lease payments should not be exactly what mortgage payments would be if the deal were done as a loan instead of a sale and leaseback. It also means that the repurchase option for the tenant at the end of the lease should not be merely nominal. If the lease has independent economic merit, the buyer will get the tax benefits of ownership. If, however, the sale is merely a way of transferring tax benefits between the parties, it is likely to be ignored by the IRS. The analysis here is similar to that used under §1-203 of the UCC to determine whether a transaction structured as a lease of personal property or fixtures is really a lease or merely a disguised security interest. If it is really a security interest, the parties must comply with the relevant law despite the fact that they have labeled their transaction as a lease exchange.

E. COMMERCIAL FINANCING

The financing of commercial real estate development consists of two broad categories of lending activity. The first category, construction lending, includes funding for basic land acquisition, infrastructure development, and construction of planned improvements on the property (sometimes collectively referred to as "ADC" funding when the construction loan covers all three functions of **A**cquisition, **D**evelopment, and **C**onstruction). The second category of lending, permanent lending, involves long-term financing for a project after construction is complete. Construction loans and permanent loans differ in their structure and in the role that they play in facilitating commercial real estate activity.

1. Construction Loans

Construction loans are typically short-term loans in the range of 6 to 24 months. Although construction loans are subject to the usual market risk factors that affect all real estate loans, they carry especially high risk. The construction loan is funded in the expectation of success for a project that has not even been built. At the outset, a typical commercial real estate project exists as a developer's idea and is represented by drawings, architectural plans, legal documentation, and marketing data. A construction lender may be asked to lend $5 million, $50 million, $200 million, or more for a project that does not yet exist. There are several important risks involved in such an undertaking. First, the developer may borrow the funds and never complete the project. Second, the developer may complete the project but do so in a way that fails to comply with the original plans and specifications, so the completed project is substandard and has less value than anticipated by the lender. Finally, the project may be completed properly but turn out to have less appeal with consumers than originally anticipated, or market changes during the construction period may have lowered the desirability and value of the undertaking. In each of these situations, the construction lender is worried about the same things — namely, the value of the collateral for its loan and the likelihood of its being repaid.

In some respects, the lender's worst-case scenario is when the borrower defaults with the construction project partially finished. Imagine the trouble when a lender loans out millions of dollars for construction activity and ends up with an unfinished project that has a poorly constructed foundation and a substandard steel structure. It is conceivable that the property is less valuable in its current state than it was as vacant land. Despite the amount of money poured into such a project, the "improvements" may have to be substantially removed or redesigned to render the property useable or saleable. In other words, property may lose value at certain stages during construction, especially if work or materials going into the project prove to be substandard. In this and other situations, the construction lender is always concerned about getting the project completed in accordance with approved plans and specifications and about having access to sufficient collateral in the event of a developer default.

The construction loan requires careful evaluation and close supervision. Because there is no finished product, no office building or shopping center, to look at in evaluating the loan, a construction lender must have a staff of in-house experts capable of determining the viability of the developer's plans and specifications. The lender's staff must be able to review plans and specifications for construction and understand the marketing, economic, and accounting projections related to cost and profitability expectations. In essence, the construction lender must truly understand the details of the developer's "sales" pitch when she comes to seek funding for a particular project. In some ways, this expertise may help the developer, inasmuch as the lender takes a serious second look at the development proposal and may administer a healthy dose of reality to an overly enthusiastic entrepreneur. A construction lender must also be able to supervise the construction process throughout the term of the loan. Constant supervision is required to ensure that the money being extended is in fact being used for the approved purposes. This means that the construction lender has to keep track of construction progress and the rate and quality of production. It must be certain that dollars loaned are spent on the project in question rather than misdirected to some other location. It must also be able to determine that the money is being used to purchase and install materials of proper quality and in accordance with all approved plans and specifications as well as with all zoning, labor, and environmental regulations.

As a result of issues like those just discussed, construction loans are typically structured as recourse loans and are funded as *draw-downs* against the full loan amount. A *recourse loan* is one in which the borrower has personal liability on the promissory note in the event of a default. This is the standard case in a residential loan but is usually accomplished by indirect means in a commercial real estate transaction. A developer/borrower is usually some form of a limited liability entity such as a corporation or a limited partnership. The borrower, as such, will have only limited liability, even on a recourse loan. In such a case, the lender may want the ability to get at more than the limited assets of the development entity. It may seek additional financial guarantees from the developer entity or a related developer company. It is also likely to require *a personal guarantee* from the individual principal(s) who constitute the developer entity. The *loan guarantee* might be secured by a pledge of assets as further collateral for the loan to the development entity. In the event of a default, the construction lender could then foreclose on the real property, the construction materials, and the borrower entity assets, and also pursue any assets used to support the loan guarantees. This is a form of recourse loan in both the direct and indirect sense, because the loan documents themselves, including the note and mortgage, are typically of a recourse nature with the limited liability entity, and the additional and personal guarantees are executed as a side agreement between the parties so that the lender can reach assets beyond those used to capitalize the development vehicle. The lender thus receives the added benefit of recourse against the individual(s) behind the developer entity, but the developer is still allowed to act within a protective sphere of limited liability with respect to any other parties involved in the development project. Naturally, the use of a guarantee, as well as its scope, is highly negotiable and depends on a number of factors, such as the working relationship between borrower and lender and the market clout of each party.

In a *draw-down loan*, the full loan amount is not released to the borrower at the time of closing on the loan. While construction proceeds the lender makes periodic disbursements, which are called *draw-downs*. This establishes a correlation between the money disbursed and the value of improvements added to the property, while also making it easier for the lender to supervise the developer's compliance with the loan. A draw-down schedule might indicate, for instance, that $500,000 will be released at closing for purposes of preparing the land and pouring the building foundation. When this is accomplished within the agreed time frame and in accordance with the loan conditions, the developer will be entitled to a second draw of $500,000 to be used for placing the first floor of the building, and a third draw for accomplishing yet another phase in the construction plan, and so on until completion. In this way, the lender limits its loss exposure at any given time and makes it easier to supervise the progress of construction. Generally, if a developer fails to meet any of a series of conditions precedent to a draw, the lender will be excused from making any further disbursements or advances under the loan. Such an event would also normally be considered an event of default and trigger an acceleration clause making the entire construction loan immediately due and payable.

Construction loans also must deal with another problem, which is that the developer will generally have little or no actual income during the time period of this short-term loan. The developer may be building an income-producing property like an office building, an apartment building, or a shopping center, yet while construction is going on little (if any) income will be generated by the building. Consequently, the construction lender must deal with the fact that payments are not likely during the construction process. Instead, the developer will borrow the interest expense as part of the loan. Construction loans typically expire at the time scheduled for completion of construction. At this time, the borrower will not have cash on hand to repay the loan. To handle this problem, the borrower usually arranges to repay the construction loan by obtaining a permanent loan on the property.

For similar reasons the loan is likely to set out *performance standards* requiring a certain percentage of units, or a set amount of space, to be sold or leased in advance of funding the loan, and as prerequisites to additional draw-downs on the loan.

2. *Permanent Loans*

Permanent loans generally have a term that is anywhere between 10 and 30 years. Unlike the construction loan, therefore, the permanent loan is a long-term loan. As a long-term loan, the permanent loan embodies the risk related to a long time horizon. Compared to the construction loan, however, the risk factors are very different. To begin with, the project is completed by the time the permanent loan is made, so there is no need to supervise work production. The lender can look at a finished project and evaluate its construction quality, its income position, and its market viability. If the project involves tenants, the lender can review the number and quality of leases. Although a finished project being evaluated for a long-term loan raises issues of risk, the risk here is much different and much simpler to assess and control than the risk involved with actual development and construction.

Permanent loans require a different kind of supervision than do construction loans. At the completion of the project, all the people providing labor, materials, or services to the project should be fully paid. Thus, there should be little concern about unpaid bills and liens that could upset the priority of the permanent mortgage. A good title examination should be able to assess priority issues prior to any permanent funding. Supervision will be required, however, with respect to the operation of any income-producing property. The permanent loan will be paid back on a regular basis, usually monthly. These monthly payments are expected to be paid out of income revenue from the property. Therefore, the permanent lender may want to have access to continuing information about the financial well-being of the project, so that any early signs of a problem can be detected. In addition, it is not uncommon for a permanent lender to take a percentage interest in the cash flow from an income-producing property. This might involve a percentage of developer income over and above some set level. By sharing some of the revenue from a successful project, a developer may be able to lower its loan costs. This arrangement can provide a lender with extra revenue and profit from lending operations, but it also adds to the need to supervise the developer's accounting. For instance, how will the developer's expenses be figured and what will count as income? Will percentages be based on net or gross amounts, and what accounting standards will apply?

Sometimes a permanent lender structures the loan as a *convertible mortgage*. This is different from the residential convertible loan discussed in Chapter 15, under which an adjustable interest rate becomes fixed. Here it means that the permanent lender is given a set or predetermined option for swapping part of the mortgage debt for a given percentage of equity in the project. Thus, debt is converted into equity, much like the situation when convertible shares in a corporation are exchanged for common stock. The convertible mortgage can be a good deal for the lender if the project turns out to be very successful. It is advantageous to the developer if it helps to entice a lender into making a favorable loan.

The permanent loan is based on a finished project that is relatively easy to evaluate and that has a predictable cash flow. As a consequence, the permanent loan will often be structured as a *nonrecourse* loan. This means that the developer will not typically have to make any personal guarantee on the loan. Instead, the lender will take the property with its income stream as the sole collateral for the loan.

3. *Take-Out Arrangements*

Given the very different focus and type of risk associated with each of the two key categories of loans, it is not surprising that lending institutions tend to specialize and develop particular expertise. Although statistics on market shares by institution shift over time in response to various regulatory and market factors, general observations can be made. The high-risk construction loan business is dominated by commercial banks, savings and loans, and other major primary financial market participants. These lenders are joined by a variety of other institutions when it comes to permanent financing. Very active in the long-term and less risky permanent loan business are major insurance companies, like Aetna and Prudential, as well as pension funds like those of the United Auto Workers, the Teamsters, and Teachers Annuity. For these institutions, permanent funding is a stable long-term source of income flow with relatively low risk. For a developer, these institutions control billions of dollars in assets that can be tapped to capitalize a variety of real estate projects.

The process by which the permanent lender steps in to pay off the construction loan and roll the debt over into a long-term permanent loan is referred to as the *take-out.* Literally speaking, the permanent lender takes the construction lender out of the deal by replacing the construction loan and mortgage with its own and by paying off the mortgage debt in a process that refinances the obligation under the terms of the permanent loan. For the take-out to work effectively in practice, both lenders must carefully coordinate their loan documentation and transactional expectations. The two lenders must coordinate the timing for completion of the building so that money will be available when it is needed. They must also agree on what qualifies as "completion" of the building, so that there will be no disagreement as to when and if permanent financing conditions have been met.

There are essentially three types of take-out arrangements that can be considered by a developer and a lender: *lock-in, stand-by,* and *open-ended.* The *lock-in take-out* is one in which the developer obtains a firm commitment from a permanent lender to take over the construction loan by paying off the construction lender and rolling the debt into a long-term mortgage obligation. It is considered a firm commitment because the permanent lender legally obligates itself to make the anticipated loan on the terms and conditions stated in the loan commitment. However, if a term or condition of the commitment is not complied with, the permanent lender can legally refuse to fund the loan. Failure to fund the take-out when the conditions of the commitment are met can result in an action for breach against the lender.

The *stand-by take-out* is a loan commitment that the developer hopes will not have to be used. The stand-by commits a permanent lender to be prepared to fund a take-out if called on to do so, and, like the lock-in, it sets out terms and conditions that have to be met prior to the lender's having to fund. The stand-by is unlike the lock-in in that the lock-in is expected to be used and the stand-by is in place for use only if needed but is generally not expected to be used. To better comprehend a stand-by, consider the typical context in which it is used. Sometimes a project is planned and organized at a time when mortgage interest rates are very high. The developer may still want to go forward because a great deal of time and money may have been invested in preparing for construction. Perhaps a lot of work went into land acquisition or obtaining zoning approval, and the developer does not want to lose the opportunity to go forward. Also consider that the construction process may take 18 or 24 months, and the developer is expecting the market to change in its favor by the time construction is complete. To start the construction process and get a construction lender, the developer may agree to take loan terms from a permanent lender that it hopes it will not really have to live with for the long-term period after a take-out. Instead of getting a lock-in commitment with a permanent lender as a prerequisite to obtaining the construction loan, the developer may get a stand-by, which sets up a permanent loan take-out with an option to avoid it and seek an alternative source or deal for permanent financing in the event that interest rates drop. In the case of both the lock-in and the stand-by, the developer pays a substantial fee for getting a permanent lender to commit to funding a take-out, just as it must pay a similar fee to the construction lender for making the loan available. These fees are very similar in purpose to the fees and points paid by a homebuyer seeking a residential mortgage, as discussed earlier in this book.

The *open-ended take-out* is very different from the other two types. It basically means that there is no commitment for a permanent loan take-out of the construction loan. Instead, the developer and the construction lender proceed with the understanding that the take-out process remains open. The hope and expectation is that by the time it is needed, a source of long-term funding will be in place. If not, the construction lender may have to take over the project or reluctantly agree to roll its construction loan over into a longer-term loan until some other arrangement is made. The developer takes the risk that it may lose the project if it is unable to line up the permanent funding at a later date. An open-ended arrangement is used when the developer and construction lender feel that they can get a better deal by making successful progress on the project and lining up a permanent source of funding at a time when the value of the project is more readily assessable and when market conditions might be more favorable. A construction lender may also be less worried and willing to accept an open-ended arrangement when the developer is a very rich entity or when the proposed project has major tenants and user commitments in place even before construction commences. Such strong financial positions reduce the risk to the construction lender by increasing the probability of success for the project and reducing the risk that the developer will have insufficient assets in the event of a default.

It is important to note that some lenders do both the construction and permanent loan financing for a project. The documents they use, however, are likely to be drafted so as to be useable by others if the lender should decide to transfer its loan position to another party. Thus, the documents themselves generally are written as if the institutions were two different and unrelated parties, even when the initial transaction anticipates that the same or a related entity will make both loans. It should also be noted that the lender views its role here as part of a business deal. The lender looks at these loans as investment opportunities where it can earn fee income, interest, and perhaps a share in equity or income generated by a successful project. Thus, some lenders also act in a way that is similar to the developer. They may try to get involved in the transaction by putting in only part of the investment (mortgage) money and by getting others to co-invest with them. Thus, it is possible to see a lender commit to a $100 million loan when it intends to lend only $25 million. Such a lender will then have to get other lenders to agree to participate in the loan to cover the remaining amount. This would be very similar to a developer's trying to do a $100 million project, for which it seeks to borrow $70 million and needs to come up with $30 million in an equity contribution. Often the developer commits to the $30 million equity part of the transaction even when it does not have or does not intend to put that much into the project. In that case, the developer needs to find investors willing to participate in the equity investment. In return, the investors will enjoy some form of compensation from the finished project. When a lender engages in such an activity, it is generally referred to as a *lead lender* (the lender that puts the deal together). The selling of shares in the loan is called a *loan participation*. Just as a developer gets a return and fees for putting the deal together for equity investors, the lead lender gets a return and fees for putting the loan participation in place. Later in this chapter we will see this issue illustrated in the *Penthouse* case.

4. *Three-Party Agreements*

A commercial real estate project involves a close working relationship between the developer, the construction lender, and the permanent lender. The developer is charged with conceiving the idea for a project, getting equity investors, and putting the deal together. The construction lender takes on the high-risk funding of construction and must have expertise with respect to building practices and short-term money management. The permanent lender takes out the construction loan by paying off the construction lender and then rolls the developer's debt over into a long-term mortgage. Although the relationship is easily depicted as linear, with the construction loan being first relative to the permanent loan, the general case is that the permanent loan has to be arranged first. The economic feasibility of a project depends heavily on the costs of the permanent loan, and for this reason developers usually have to fix their permanent financing costs at an early stage in the development process. Moreover, a construction lender is not likely to agree to do its part unless it knows that a take-out is in place. Each party must work with each of the others, and all three are interdependent.

The written agreement that binds together the developer, the construction lender, and the permanent lender is the *three-party agreement*, which is sometimes also referred to as the *buy-sell agreement*. The three-party agreement is designed to spell out the conditions under which the various parties undertake to work with each other. Its primary legal objective is twofold. First, it is designed to put each of the parties in privity with each of the others; second, it is designed to give each party a right of specific performance against each of the others. Having privity is important when each party will be relying on documents, representations, and warranties that are related. Establishing privity in the three-party agreement avoids potential legal problems later on by eliminating a common contract defense based on a claimant's not having privity. It also means that the lenders do not have to go through the developer to reach each other; they are able to sue each other directly as a result of being in privity with one another.

The provision for specific performance is also important. It means that all parties can demand specific performance from any one of the others. Thus, the developer can seek specific performance against each of its lenders, and each lender can seek to use the same remedy if the developer attempts to switch to another lender. Likewise, each of the lenders can seek this remedy against the other with respect to the take-out obligation. If the permanent lender unfairly refuses to fund the take-out, the construction lender and the developer might seek specific performance. Reciprocally, if the developer seeks a permanent loan from a different lender (one offering a better deal, for instance), the permanent lender can seek specific performance. A developer might try to do this if interest rates drop during the course of construction and it can get a better deal elsewhere. The permanent lender may, in other words, be entitled to do the take-out in accordance with the deal that everyone thought looked good and desirable prior to commencement of construction. It must be remembered that specific performance is an equitable remedy, and the ultimate ability to get an equitable remedy will turn on the discretion of the court. Nonetheless, it constitutes a powerful bargaining chip between the parties and helps bolster the evidence of expectation and reliance among the parties. This makes the case for equitable recovery stronger while also enhancing the remedies at law for damages.

5. Coordination of Independent Loans

In thinking about the typical commercial lending process, it is probably best to think in terms of a circular rather than a linear process. Because of the interconnected nature of commercial lending, the permanent loan is not simply a loan that comes after a construction loan. As we have been discussing, these two loans, though serving different functions, are dependent on each other. Consequently, we should think of the coordination of commercial loans as a circular and nine-step process. These steps are: (1) a developer gets an idea for a project, lines up investors, and gets the process in motion; (2) there is a property acquisition contract or loan arrangement to acquire the land for the project; (3) a permanent lender is secured with a lock-in commitment; (4) a construction lender is secured with a construction loan commitment; (5) the three parties coordinate documents and execute a three-party agreement; (6) the developer closes on the construction loan and starts construction under a draw-down financing arrangement; (7) construction on the project is completed in accordance with the plans and specifications; (8) the permanent lender takes out the construction lender and closes on the long-term mortgage with the developer; and (9) the property is either sold off to other investors or begins producing income and enters into the property management phase. At this point, the process may start over as the developer gets an idea for a new project.

Problem 20C

Fletcher Inc. is a developer and it enters into commitments with Big Bank for a construction loan and Insure U for permanent loan financing on a proposed $100 million apartment building complex. In planning the project, Fletcher has engaged the Suzan Bee Architectural Design Co. to prepare all the drawings and specifications for the project. It has also hired T&J Construction to act as the general contractor for the actual construction work. About halfway through the construction phase of the development, Fletcher runs into financial problems and finds that it is unable to complete the project. Big Bank takes over the project and seeks to complete the project, with the expectation that finishing it will enhance its value and that the take-out will still be possible.

(a) When Big Bank takes over the project from the defaulting developer, Suzan Bee refuses to let it use the plans and specifications. Big Bank needs the plans and specifications so that it can properly finish the construction. Suzan Bee claims that they are the work product of her firm and the contract for use was with Fletcher and not Big Bank. Suzan Bee suggests that she might be able to turn over the plans if she gets a release from Fletcher and a professional fee increase of $30,000 for various items for which she claims she was originally underpaid in the deal with Fletcher. Big Bank wants to know whether Suzan Bee has a legitimate point and, if so, what Big Bank might have done to prevent such a problem when it structured its deal with Fletcher.

(b) When Big Bank takes over the project from the defaulting developer, it also hears from T&J Construction. T&J claims that other projects have opened up and it is getting offers to work for more money elsewhere. Suddenly the construction market is taking off, probably as a result of falling interest rates and a good long-term outlook for low levels of inflation. T&J claims that market conditions have changed and that its deal was with Fletcher. Now that Big Bank is in the picture, a new deal has to be worked out, as T&J has no contractual obligation to work for Big Bank. T&J wants to increase the general contractor's fee on the deal by 15 percent. When Big Bank objects, T&J says it is a cost of doing business, and Big Bank can either seek the added expense as damages from Fletcher or build it into the end price of the project by adjusting rents. Big Bank wants to know whether T&J's position might be correct and, if so, what it should have done to prevent this type of price change from happening when it takes over a project from a defaulting borrower.

(c) In both of the preceding situations, what happens if Big Bank has to pay more to complete the project? Will it be able to make Insure U take out the construction loan at a new higher amount that reflects the added expenses? Should Insure U be able to walk away from the take-out obligation (even if the amount stays the same) on the assertion that its obligation runs only to Fletcher?

(d) Assume that the construction loan is to run for 18 months, with a take-out to occur between December 1 and December 30 of the following year. Fletcher does not default on the construction loan, but the project is not complete by December 30. Should Insure U be able to avoid the take-out obligation on the ground that the completion date was not met and that such a date was a condition precedent to funding under its loan documents and its loan commitment? Should it make a difference if the $100 million project is substantially complete; everything is done with the exception of some interior door and carpet installation estimated to cost $35,000? The project is substantially complete except for work valued at $200,000? $500,000? $1 million? Should the reason for delay make a difference: a labor strike, bad weather, back-ordered supplies, etc.?

(e) Assume that the construction of the apartment building gets completed and Insure U does the take-out. Also assume that the building is in full operation and one year later the permanent loan is defaulted on and Insure U proceeds with a foreclosure to take over the project. Will Insure U's mortgage be sufficient as security for such things as rent deposits held by Fletcher or for insurance rebates and apartment services contract discounts payable to Fletcher? Is a real estate mortgage a proper way to secure such collateral?

TEACHERS INSURANCE & ANNUITY ASSOCIATION v. ORMESA GEOTHERMAL

United States District Court, S.D. New York, 1991
791 F. Supp. 401

KIMBA M. WOOD, District Judge. Teachers Insurance and Annuity Association of America ("TIAA" or "Teachers"), a New York corporation that is an institutional lender, brought this action against a prospective borrower alleging breach of a commitment letter agreement that "circled" a "blended" interest rate of 10.64% for a twenty-year loan of $25,000,000. After a sharp decline in interest rates rendered the agreement less advantageous to the borrower, the borrower took a negotiating stance allegedly designed to alter or scuttle the transaction, and finally refused to continue negotiating with TIAA, claiming that TIAA had "walked" from the deal. Plaintiff and defendant Ormesa each seek damages for breach of contract. . . .

I. Liability

A. Background and Origins of the Transaction

Defendant Ormesa Geothermal ("Ormesa") is a general partnership formed under the laws of California to construct a geothermal power plant in the Imperial Valley of California (the "Project"). . . .

The financing arrangements for the Project were complex. The Project contemplated the placement of three types of debt financings and the contribution of equity funding. With respect to the debt, the Project needed approximately $50,000,000 of interim or "construction" financing (the "Construction Loan") for the period during which the Project would be constructed. It then needed approximately $50,000,000 of long-term financing (the "Long-term Loan") to replace the Construction Loan when construction was completed. The Construction Loan and the Long-term Loan were to be 90% guaranteed by the United States Department of Energy (the "DOE"). At the time TIAA was negotiating the transaction at issue in this litigation (the "Transaction") with Ormesa the Long-term Loan was to have been 90% guaranteed by the DOE, and the Loan was to have been made through the issuance of two sets of notes, with the unguaranteed notes at a higher rate of interest. In addition to the Construction Loan and the Long-term Loan, the Project also needed approximately $10,000,000 of subordinated financing (the "Subordinated Loan"), to be funded at the time the Construction Loan closed. It would also require the equity contribution of LFC (the "Equity Contribution") at the time of the closing of the Construction Loan.

The construction lender on the Project was Bankers Trust Company ("Bankers Trust"). . . . As a condition to closing its Construction Loan, Bankers Trust desired a "takeout" commitment by a long-term lender, to provide the Long-term Loan to repay and thus replace or "take out" the Construction Loan. The collateral for the Construction Loan would also secure the Long-term Loan after it replaced the Construction Loan. Therefore, documents with respect to the Long-term Loan were drafted and negotiated concurrently with those relating to the Construction Loan and the Subordinated Loan.

B. ORMESA'S SEARCH FOR LONG-TERM FINANCING; THE COMMITMENT AGREEMENT

In the fall of 1985, Ormesa retained E. F. Hutton as its agent for the purpose of obtaining the Long-term Loan for the Project. The E. F. Hutton employees with principal day-to-day responsibility for the Transaction were Vince Castellano, and, after Castellano's departure from E. F. Hutton in August 1986, Gerald Gminski. . . .

Among the prospective lenders contacted by Castellano were TIAA and John Hancock Mutual Life Insurance Company ("John Hancock"), an insurance company that invests, inter alia, in debt securities obtained in private placements. Because the Ormesa loan was highly complex, requiring negotiation with several entities including the DOE, and because it required fixing the interest rate far in advance of funding, only sophisticated institutional lenders were likely to (and did) show serious interest in the transaction. For these reasons, Ormesa had to increase the interest rate from that contained in its original offer in order to interest investors. In late January 1986, TIAA and John Hancock each expressed a willingness to provide 50% (or approximately $25,000,000) of the total of approximately $50,000,000 for the Long-term Loan. The interest rate for the Long-term Loan was to be a blended rate (*i.e.*, the weighted average of (1) the interest rate on the 90% portion of the total debt, which was guaranteed, and (2) the higher interest rate on the 10% portion, which was non-guaranteed) equal to the sum of (a) the yield, on a date to be determined, on a hypothetical 13-year United States Treasury Note, plus (b) 150 basis points. (A basis point is 1/100 of a percent; thus, 150 basis points represents 1.50%.)

Ormesa offered the portion of the Long-term Loan that was to be guaranteed by the DOE (the "Guaranteed Notes") with "call protection," that is, an agreement that (1) the Guaranteed Notes could not be repaid prior to a certain time, and that (2) after that time, they could be repaid only with a premium intended to give a lender the benefit of its bargain over the term of the loan. This type of call protection is common in long-term lending to preserve for the lender the benefit of its bargain. Early in the negotiations, TIAA advised Ormesa that it wanted call protection not only for the Guaranteed Notes but also for the Non-guaranteed Notes, and Ormesa agreed to this.

Because TIAA and John Hancock were comfortable with complex transactions of this type, they found this transaction, on these terms, to be highly attractive.

On February 7, 1986, TIAA, John Hancock and Ormesa "circled" the transaction at a blended rate of 10.64%. When a financing is "circled," the parties orally agree that they will do the transaction on the specified terms, and the interest rate and certain other key economic terms are, by this oral agreement, fixed. It is the custom in the financial community that once the parties circle a deal, neither party tries to change the interest rate that has been agreed. . . .

On February 20, 1986, TIAA's Finance Committee approved the Long-term Loan and authorized TIAA to proceed with the Transaction. On February 26, 1986 John Hancock's Committee of Finance approved the Long-term Loan and authorized John Hancock to proceed with the Transaction. On February 24, 1986, TIAA sent a commitment agreement to Ormesa for signature, and on February 26, 1986, John Hancock did so. . . .

After John Hancock and Ormesa committed to the Long-term Loan, John Hancock committed itself to a "match funding," *i.e.*, it incurred "matched" obligations relying on the income it would receive pursuant to the Long-term Loan. As a result, John Hancock stood to suffer a substantial loss if its share of the Long-term Loan did not fund. Ormesa knew, no later than the end of June 1986, that John Hancock would suffer a substantial loss if John Hancock's share of the Long-term Loan did not fund.

Interest rates dropped precipitously between February 7, 1986, when the interest rate for this transaction was circled, and July 25, 1986. By July 25, the average of the levels of the 10-year and the 20-year Treasuries — the average used in fixing the original circled rate — dropped 197 basis points. Application of the lower rate would save Ormesa about $1,000,000 a year in interest. Ormesa was aware of this drop in interest rates, and its attempts to back out of the Transaction were motivated by the drop in interest rates. . . .

Ormesa decided that it was cheaper to defend and/or settle the litigation that Ormesa anticipated than to perform pursuant to the Commitment Agreement. This decision, and the actions Ormesa took to implement it, violated Ormesa's duty to negotiate in good faith. . . .

Call protection for the Long-term Lenders was an integral part of the Transaction; it was expressly provided for in the commitment agreements of both TIAA and John Hancock. . . .

. . . TIAA and John Hancock did not repudiate or withdraw from the Transaction, nor did they intend to do so. Indeed, they were trying to do exactly the opposite. The Transaction was an extraordinarily attractive one for them, at a level of 200 basis points above the then prevailing market, and John Hancock had match-funded the Transaction and would suffer a multi-million dollar out-of-pocket loss if it did not fund, as Ormesa was aware. TIAA and John Hancock were working to preserve the Transaction. . . .

Discussion

Ormesa's primary legal contention is that the commitment letter did not bind the parties to complete the transaction because it did not contain all the material terms of the contemplated loan: Ormesa contends that a mutually satisfactory resolution of those to-be-agreed terms would be required in order to bind the parties to complete the transaction.

Ormesa contends that it was further contemplated that once all material terms were satisfactorily negotiated, TIAA and Ormesa would execute loan documents that themselves would be subject to certain conditions that would have to be satisfied before the loan would be made, and that these conditions were never satisfied. Ormesa contends that the only binding agreement in the TIAA commitment letter was that Ormesa would pay certain TIAA expenses. . . .

Here the Commitment Agreement expressly said it was a "binding agreement":

> If the foregoing properly sets forth your understanding of this transaction, please *evidence acceptance of the conditions* of this letter *by having it executed* below by duly authorized officers of Ormesa Geothermal *and by returning one executed counterpart* to TIAA. . . . *Upon receipt by TIAA of an accepted counterpart* of this letter, *our agreement* to purchase from you and your agreement to issue, sell and deliver to us, . . . the captioned securities, *shall become a binding agreement between us.* (Exh. P-1 at 2, emphasis added).

Although there were many open terms to be negotiated, all of the crucial economic terms of the loan were set forth in the Commitment Letter, including the amount and term of the loan, the interest rate, the repayment schedule, the portion of the loan to be guaranteed by the United States government, the security for the guaranteed senior secured notes, the period during which the loan would not be callable, and prepayment penalties applicable thereafter. The language of the agreement suggests that the Commitment Agreement was intended to be, and was, a binding agreement. . . .

The parties' actions in the context of the negotiations . . . also suggest that the Commitment Agreement was intended to be, and was, a binding agreement. . . .

The open terms . . . were terms that customarily are left for later negotiation once the critical terms such as loan amount, term, interest, description of any security and guaranty, and prepayment penalties have been agreed. . . .

. . . Teachers' partial performance is merely one act among many that suggests that the commitment was viewed as binding. . . . Teachers partially performed its contract with Ormesa by committing $25 million of its funds to the transaction; the court rejects Ormesa's contention that because Teachers did not physically segregate these funds, there was no commitment of the funds by Teachers. . . .

It is customary for borrowers and lenders in transactions similar to the one at issue here to accord binding force to preliminary agreements similar to the Commitment Agreement.

I conclude that the Commitment Agreement was a binding preliminary agreement that obligated the borrower and the lenders to seek to effectuate a final loan agreement upon the agreed terms by negotiating in good faith to resolve the other terms customarily found in such agreements.

Ormesa breached its duty to negotiate in good faith to resolve the issues left open by the Commitment Agreement. By, among other things, insisting upon a lowered interest rate, Ormesa attempted to change and undercut terms that had been agreed to in the Commitment letter. . . .

II. DAMAGES

Under New York law, a party injured by breach of contract should be placed in the same economic position as it would have been in had the contract been performed. Teachers Insurance & Annuity Assn v. Butler, 626 F. Supp. 1229, 1236 (S.D.N.Y. 1986). TIAA is thus entitled to damages equal to the discounted present value of the incremental interest income TIAA would be expected to lose as a result of the breach.[6] Specifically, the lost interest income is measured as the difference between (a) the interest income TIAA would have earned had the contract been performed, and (b) the interest income TIAA would be deemed to have earned by timely mitigating its damages — *i.e.*, by making an investment with similar characteristics at the time of the breach. . . .

Using the assumptions adopted in this decision, TIAA's damages are $4,094,530 for the whole loan on a blended basis. . . .

The foregoing shall constitute the court's findings of fact and conclusions of law. Judgment may be entered accordingly.

Problem 20D

(a) In the *TIAA* case there is discussion of the lenders wanting "call protection" in their loan arrangements with the borrower. What is call protection, and what is it intended to accomplish? Why does a lender want such protection, and why should a developer agree to it? Draft a call protection provision that you might offer for use in a transaction such as the one described in the *TIAA* case.

(b) In the *TIAA* case we are told that John Hancock had "match-funded the transaction." What does this mean? Why is match-funding done?

6. The court rejects Ormesa's contention that the "payment of expenses" language in the Commitment Agreement limits TIAA to reimbursement of its expenses, rather than damages. The court finds that the "payment expenses" language has to do only with allocation of expenses to the borrower whether or not the loan closed, not with remedy for breach. *See* Walter E. Heller & Co. v. American Flyer Airline Corp., 459 F.2d 896, 900 (2d Cir. 1972). The court also finds that Ormesa failed to meet its burden of proving that TIAA failed to mitigate its damages. Ormesa claims that TIAA turned down loans at interest rates higher than that in the Commitment Agreement (10.64%), but does not indicate the nature, quality or risk of these investments, or the reason they did not eventuate. *See* Jenkins v. Etlinger, 55 N.Y.2d 35, 39, 432 N.E.2d 696, 698 (1982).

Problem 20E

The questions in this problem are designed to assist in organizing and understanding the following *Penthouse* case. This is a long case, but it includes all of the elements of a commercial real estate project and illustrates almost every point covered in this chapter and in the book. Use the questions in this problem to help you map out the various parties to the transaction and the development and financing entities. Identify the contract, title, and other points of contention, and clarify the conditions and the various financing relationships.

(a) What is the relationship between Penthouse and Boardwalk Properties, Inc.? What advantages are to be found for Penthouse in setting up such a relationship rather than just developing the project on its own?

(b) Penthouse sought to acquire property for a hotel and casino project in Atlantic City. What was it able to do in its process of acquisition, and what potential problems were presented by the land ownership arrangement? What special concerns should be raised when leased properties are involved? Think of this from the perspective of both a developer and a lender. What special problems might exist with respect to coordinating multiple parcels to function as one for purposes of a project like the one undertaken by Penthouse?

(c) What happens to the Penthouse project if one of the leased properties has a default on its lease? A default on a mortgage on the leasehold estate of the leased parcel? Could the leasehold estate be eliminated by a default or foreclosure, and what might be the consequence for Penthouse and for any lender to Penthouse?

(d) What general role does Queen City play in this transaction? Why might Penthouse use such a small lender to play this important role?

(e) What arrangement is made to govern the relationship between the construction loan and the permanent loan with respect to Penthouse and Queen City?

(f) Construction is already underway when Penthouse turns to outside funding for the project. What precautions should be taken by a lender when contemplating funding for a project that has already commenced?

(g) What is the loan participation arrangement and how is it structured for this deal? Why do some lenders agree to participate in another lender's loan? What is the role and responsibility of a lead lender to the participating lenders? Does a lead lender generally have the power to modify or change an agreement once it has entered into that agreement with the borrower? Do participating lenders generally have the right to object to the way the lead lender carries out its responsibilities? If one of five participating lenders has an objection concerning the conduct of a lead lender, what do you think it should be able to do? Unilaterally withdraw from the loan? Sue for breach? Force a default? What potential liability might attach to various actions undertaken by a participating lender?

(h) Why does Dominion agree to pick up $35 million of the loan and then do a subparticipation to Community?

(i) The funding agreement between the parties established a number of conditions precedent to making the loan. Who has what burden in completing or establishing satisfaction of each condition? What conditions were the source of trouble in this case?

(j) What arguments did Dominion raise as the basis for not having to fund the loan? What response was presented?

(k) How did anticipatory repudiation enter into the dispute? Could the lawyer for Dominion have predicted that this issue would be raised? What factors should a lawyer consider in assessing the merits of such a potential argument?

(l) Without the funding, what will happen to the Penthouse investment in this project?

(m) How were damages fixed in this case, at trial and on appeal?

(n) At the time, in March of 1984, when the loan participation started to unravel, what economic factor was at play in the market that influenced at least some loan participants to reconsider the economic viability of the transaction?

(o) What potential risk does a lawyer confront when participating in negotiations of the type in the *Penthouse* case? How can the lawyer best protect himself from potential liability in such a situation?

PENTHOUSE INTERNATIONAL, LTD. v. DOMINION FEDERAL SAVINGS & LOAN ASSOCIATION

United States Court of Appeals, Second Circuit, 1988
855 F.2d 963

ALTIMARI, Circuit Judge. Defendants-appellants Dominion Federal Savings & Loan Association ("Dominion") and Melrod, Redman & Gartlan, P.C. ("Melrod" or the "Melrod firm") appeal from judgments entered in favor of plaintiffs-appellees Penthouse International, Ltd. and its wholly-owned subsidiary, Boardwalk Properties, Inc. (hereafter referred to as "Penthouse"), and third-party defendant-appellee Queen City Savings & Loan Association ("Queen City"). After a three-week bench trial in the United States District Court for the Southern District of New York (Judge Kevin T. Duffy), the district court held that Dominion committed an anticipatory breach of its agreement to participate in a $97 million loan transaction. The district court awarded Penthouse approximately $128.7 million and awarded Queen City nearly $7.7 million (plus interest and costs) for the damages caused by Dominion's anticipatory breach. In addition, the court dismissed with prejudice Dominion's cross-claim against Queen City. After the court issued its opinion, it ordered that the Melrod firm be held jointly and severally liable for the Penthouse judgment, not on breach of contract grounds, but for fraud.

Dominion and the Melrod firm present several arguments on appeal. Dominion's principal contention is that the district court erred when it found that Penthouse carried its burden of demonstrating the existence of an anticipatory breach and that, in absence of the breach, Penthouse had the ability to perform its contractual obligations before the loan commitment expired. The Melrod firm argues that there is no basis in law or fact for holding it liable for the Penthouse judgment.

For the reasons that follow, we reverse in part, affirm in part and remand.

Facts and Background

Sometime after gambling was legalized in Atlantic City, New Jersey, Penthouse's President, Robert Guccione, conceived the idea of opening a Penthouse Hotel and Casino along Atlantic City's famed Boardwalk. To implement this idea, Guccione set about to locate prospective financiers and potential partners to assist in underwriting the construction project. Boardwalk Properties, Inc. was formed as a wholly-owned subsidiary of Penthouse for the purpose of handling Penthouse's affairs in connection with the hotel and casino project.

Initially unsuccessful in its efforts to obtain outside financing, Penthouse used its own resources to commence the project. Penthouse proceeded to assemble five contiguous plots of land along Missouri Avenue adjacent to the Boardwalk. Three of these parcels Penthouse held in fee simple and the other two were obtained through leasehold estates. The first leased property, on which was located a Holiday Inn Hotel, was obtained from the Boardwalk and Missouri Corporation, an entity controlled by New York real estate financier Harry Helmsley (the "Helmsley lease"). The second leasehold estate, which was then occupied by a Four Seasons Hotel, was obtained from Albert and Robert Rothenburg (the "Rothenburg lease").

Penthouse's construction plans included the use of the existing tower structure from the Holiday Inn, the rebuilding of the structure from the Four Seasons into a second tower and the construction of a seven-story building between the two towers. In these structures, Penthouse planned to house its casino, a 515 room hotel, a health club and other facilities. By June 1983, Penthouse had invested between $65 and $75 million into construction of the hotel and casino which was approximately 40 to 50 percent complete.

Although Guccione believed that the entire project could be financed with Penthouse's own funds when construction commenced, as time passed and costs escalated, it became apparent that it would be necessary to obtain outside financing. Penthouse then sought financing unsuccessfully from various sources. In or about April 1983, Penthouse retained Jefferson National Mortgage, a mortgage broker, to locate prospective lending institutions interested in providing Penthouse with construction and permanent financing for the hotel and casino project. As a result of Jefferson National's efforts, Queen City extended to Penthouse in June 1983 a $97 million loan commitment.

On June 20, 1983, Queen City issued to Penthouse (through Boardwalk Properties, Inc.) a commitment to lend Penthouse $97 million for construction and permanent financing in connection with the Penthouse Hotel and Casino project (the "Queen City loan commitment" or the "loan commitment"). The Queen City loan commitment was accepted by Penthouse on June 29, 1983. In the loan commitment, Queen City advised Penthouse that "your request for construction/permanent financing . . . with Queen City Savings and Loan Association . . . has been approved subject to the following terms and conditions [.]" The term of the loan was ten years with a construction phase in effect during either the first 24 months or until Penthouse received a certificate of occupancy from Atlantic City and permission to operate the casino. The interest rate was fixed at 14⅞% for years one through five and 15⅜% for years six through ten.

To secure the loan, pursuant to paragraph 6 of the loan commitment, Penthouse was required to deliver to Queen City a mortgage on the hotel and casino and the underlying properties. Thus, Penthouse was required to deliver a note secured by a "valid first mortgage lien on all real estate owned by [b]orrower covering the project site" and all improvements thereon and was required to provide a "valid first leasehold interest" in the Rothenburg and Helmsley leases and "a first mortgage covering the improvements thereon." Penthouse also was required to provide assignments of its interest in the leasehold estates to be effective in the event of Penthouse's default. Paragraph 6 required Penthouse to certify at closing that there were "no violations" of the Helmsley or Rothenburg leases.

Paragraph 14 of the loan commitment required Penthouse to represent and warrant 1) that there was no pending litigation that would affect title to the properties, the validity of the mortgage liens, the validity and non-violations of the leases, etc., 2) that the final plans and specifications for construction would satisfy and conform with local, state and federal regulations, and 3) that all necessary utilities (*i.e.*, water, electricity, sewer, telephone service and gas) were available to the full needs of the property and that "valid and enforceable agreements to supply such services have been entered into[.]"

Under the heading of "Commitment Expiration Date," paragraph 15 provided that the commitment would

> expire one hundred twenty (120) days after the date hereof (the "Commitment Expiration Date") unless mutually extended in writing by Lender, and upon such expiration Lender shall have no further obligation to Borrower, except as set forth in item 19 of the attached Conditions.

Paragraph 16 of the commitment, which was headed by the term "Closing," stipulated that the "[c]losing of the Loan ("Closing") shall be held . . . on or before the Commitment Expiration Date[.]"

Paragraph 17 of the loan commitment provided that an additional twenty enumerated "Conditions Prior to Closing" ("preclosing conditions") contained in a document attached to the commitment were incorporated as part of the commitment. Paragraph 17 also stipulated that "[l]ender's obligation to close the Loan [was] contingent upon the satisfaction of each of said conditions."

In relevant part, the preclosing conditions provided:

> . . . .
>
> 5. TITLE INSURANCE: There shall be furnished to Lender, at least 15 days prior to Closing, a current preliminary title insurance binder, issued by a title company initially approved by Lender. At Closing, a standard ALTA title policy shall be issued by such company insuring Lender's interest or lien in or on the Property subject only to such title objections as Lender shall approve. Such title insurance policy shall affirmatively insure the priority of the lien of the Mortgage. The title company insuring Lender's lien shall obtain reinsurance in such amounts and with such companies, as Lender may require. . . .
>
> 10. UTILITIES: The Lender shall be furnished with copies of all agreements for providing the utility services required for the operation of the Property, including without limitation thereto, agreements pertaining to water, sewer, and electricity and/or original current letters from the suppliers of such utilities stating that the utilities are available and are offered in sufficient quantities for the project.
>
> 11. PLANS AND SPECIFICATIONS: The written approval of all plans and specifications for the Improvements to be erected must be obtained from Lender. No change of any substance shall be made in the final plans and specifications without the prior written approval of Lender and all governmental authorities having jurisdiction.
>
> 12. CERTIFICATION BY ARCHITECT AND CONSTRUCTION MANAGER: Borrower shall deliver to Lender at Closing a certification by Borrower's architect and construction manager containing (i) a detailed listing of the then-current plans and specifications for the Improvements; (ii) a statement that said plans and specifications are complete documents for the construction of the Improvements and contain all details requisite for the completion, occupancy and operation thereof; and, (iii) a statement that said plans and specifications are in full compliance with all local, state and federal (if any) rules, ordinances and regulations governing or applying to the construction of the Improvements. . . .
>
> 16. CONSTRUCTION — CONTRACTS: Borrower shall submit, for Lender's approval, Borrower's contract with its architect, construction project manager and all major trade contractors. Lender may at its option require assignment of the aforesaid contracts or any of them. . . .
>
> 19. PARTICIPATION: Lender's obligation to complete the Closing is also contingent upon execution of a participation agreement between Lender and other lenders pursuant to which said other lenders will participate in making the Loan (through the Lender as "lead institution") at least to the extent of $90,000,000 on terms and conditions satisfactory to the Lender. Borrower

> acknowledges that it is Borrower's sole responsibility (either directly or through mortgage brokerage companies) to obtain such participants who are satisfactory to Lender, it being understood that Lender shall have no obligation to obtain such participants. In the event the aforesaid $90,000,000 participation agreements are not obtained, then Lender shall refund to Borrower the origination fees it received pursuant to Item 8 of the Commitment. . . .

The preclosing conditions also established that New Jersey law would govern the terms of the loan commitment and stipulated that Queen City's attorneys would have the final decision on whether the various preclosing conditions had been satisfied. Nowhere, however, did the commitment or the preclosing conditions provide that Queen City was authorized by the participating lending institutions to waive Penthouse's compliance with any of the terms of the commitment.

Once the loan commitment was in place, pursuant to preclosing condition 19, Queen City and Penthouse began searching for financial institutions interested in participating in a syndicate of lenders to underwrite the loan. Lending institutions that decided to participate in the syndicate (the "participants") would enter into a "Loan Participation Sale and Trust Agreement" (the "participation agreement"). Under the commitment, Queen City was designated to serve as the lead lending institution (the "lead lender") for the syndicate. Under the participation agreement, the participants would purchase from Queen City "undivided participating ownership" interests in the mortgage loan. Pursuant to the participation agreement, Queen City assumed various administrative responsibilities for servicing the loan. The agreement stipulated, however, that Queen City was to act, not as an agent, but as an "independent contractor" for the participants and would serve "as a trustee with fiduciary duties" in connection with protecting the rights of the participating lenders. In addition, the participation agreement contained an integration clause, provided that it could not be modified except by written agreement and established New Jersey law as the governing law.

By the fall of 1983, twelve financial institutions, including Queen City, had agreed to participate in the financing syndicate and had committed to provide a total of $62 million for the project. In mid-November 1983, Dominion expressed interest in providing Penthouse with financing and on November 14th offered directly to Penthouse a commitment to provide $40 million in financing for the project. Although Dominion's offer was never accepted, it did lead to Dominion's decision on November 21, 1983 to participate in the $97 million loan syndicate.

On November 21, 1983, a meeting was held at Penthouse's offices in New York City. In attendance at the meeting were representatives of Penthouse, including its Chief Operating Officer and General Counsel, David J. Myerson, and Penthouse's outside counsel for the loan transaction, Jay

Newman; representatives of Queen City, including its Senior Vice President, John E. Beahan, and Queen City's attorney, John J. Lipari; and representatives of Dominion, including its Executive Vice President, David A. Neal, and its outside counsel, William J. Dorn. At this meeting, Dominion agreed to participate in the loan syndicate to the extent of $35 million. Dominion's agreement to participate in the loan was embodied in three documents: two letter agreements exchanged between Queen City and Dominion and a third document which was a letter from Penthouse to Dominion. In substance, Dominion "accepted" all of the terms and conditions of both the loan commitment and the participation agreement except that the participation agreement was amended to include Dominion as "co-lead seller" for the syndicate. In addition, the loan commitment was modified at the meeting in a side agreement between Penthouse and Queen City to include as a preclosing condition that

> arrangements, reasonably satisfactory to [Queen City], shall have been made with the staff o[f] the Casino Control Commission to permit the opening of the casino and hotel, upon completion of construction, utilizing a trustee or fiduciary in the event the license to [Penthouse] . . . or any of its principals has not been granted.

Although it does not appear that Dominion entered into any written agreement with Penthouse directly, Penthouse did deliver to Dominion a letter indicating that it agreed to pay Dominion certain fees "[i]n consideration" for Dominion's agreement to participate "as a Co-Seller" for the syndicate. Penthouse also gave Dominion a check for $175,000 for fees it agreed to pay.

Also on November 21st, Penthouse and Queen City mutually agreed to extend the Commitment Expiration Date to December 1, 1983. This written extension was prompted by Lipari's observation that the 120-day condition of the commitment had expired and his belief that, in order to have a "valid commitment," it was necessary for Queen City and Penthouse to mutually extend the expiration date. In addition, Lipari discussed the timing of the loan closing with Newman and Dorn, and then, in a letter also dated November 21st, Lipari and Newman agreed that "we shall close th[e] loan no earlier than February 1, 1984 or later than March 1, 1984."

Once the loan commitment syndicate was complete, Penthouse and Queen City directed their efforts to closing the transaction. Toward that goal, Lipari and Newman maintained regular contact and Lipari held a series of "status meetings" during which representatives of Penthouse and Queen City reviewed the steps taken in connection with Penthouse's satisfaction of the preclosing conditions. During these status meetings, Penthouse sought alternate arrangements for satisfying some of the preclosing conditions. For example, although preclosing condition 10 required Penthouse to deliver copies of all agreements for providing utility services required for the operation of the hotel and casino and/or original, current letters indicating that the utilities would be available in sufficient quantities for the project, Penthouse sought to proceed without having fully satisfied this condition. Penthouse did not have agreements with some utility companies to provide certain essential services and it did not have written assurances that those services were available to meet the demands of the proposed hotel and casino. Similarly, Penthouse sought to proceed to closing without having fully complied with preclosing conditions 11, 12 and 16.

Penthouse's position in this regard was that, since the construction project was 40 to 50 percent complete, many of the requirements of the preclosing conditions could be satisfied through substitute arrangements. Thus, instead of providing an architect's and construction manager's certificate, as required by preclosing condition 12, Penthouse offered to provide a certificate from its project engineer and to allow Queen City's architect to examine the project. This substitute performance was necessary because, at that time, Penthouse had not retained an architect. In place of providing Queen City with copies of final plans and specifications for the project, as required by the preclosing conditions, Penthouse sought to provide Queen City with its original plans and specifications for the project, even though they were out of date due to changes in the applicable building codes and despite the fact that Penthouse had no final plans for the electrical or mechanical work on the project. Notwithstanding the modifications Penthouse sought, Lipari was satisfied that the transaction could close in light of Penthouse's proffered substitute performance. It does not appear, however, that Lipari sought Dominion's or the other participants' consent to a waiver of Penthouse's full compliance with any preclosing conditions.

After the second status meeting, Queen City sent Dominion and the other participants a letter stating in essence that substantial progress had been made toward satisfying the preclosing conditions and announcing that a "preclosing meeting" would occur sometime between February 1 and 8, 1984. It was later determined that the "preclosing meeting" would occur on February 9, 1984 at Penthouse's New York offices.

Once Dominion agreed to participate in the loan syndicate, it proceeded to attempt to sell in the secondary market sub-participation interests of its $35 million interest in the loan syndicate. Dominion's decision to subparticipate out its interest in the loan was motivated in part by the fact that its legal lending limit was $18.5 million. Thus, Dominion could not lend to a single borrower more than that amount. By letter agreement dated December 2, 1983, Dominion sold to Community Savings & Loan Association ("Community") a $17.5 million interest in its original $35 million participation interest. At that time, Community had not completed its underwriting analysis of the loan, and proceeded with this analysis in December 1983 and continued on through February 1984. In early February 1984, however, Community started to show some reticence with proceeding in the transaction.

As Penthouse and Queen City prepared for the "preclosing meeting" set for February 9, 1984, Newman received a letter from Commonwealth

Land Title Insurance Company regarding Penthouse's ability to furnish the mortgage security required by the loan commitment. This letter indicated that there were several objections to title on the Helmsley lease. That parcel was subject to two mortgages, the McShane mortgage and the Chase mortgage, which needed to be discharged or subordinated before Penthouse could furnish the required security. Unless the McShane and Chase mortgages were discharged or subordinated, if foreclosed upon, they potentially could wipe out the Helmsley lease and any security interest in that lease. The letter also raised title objections to the Rothenburg lease and pointed out that there was a declaration of encumbrances in connection with the parcels held in fee simple which had to be removed or modified. In addition to the title problems, it also appears that the Helmsley lease had to be modified before closing. Unless the lease was modified, the closing of the loan would violate its terms. The commitment required, however, that Penthouse certify, at closing, that there were "no violations" of that lease.

To resolve the various title problems and the problems with the terms of the lease, Newman knew that he would have to negotiate a discharge or subordination of the McShane and Chase mortgages, negotiate with Helmsley to obtain amendments to the lease and obtain a subordination of encumbrances in connection with the Helmsley leased property. Although Penthouse had made some initial contacts with Helmsley's representatives by February 9th, no agreement resolving these problems had been reached, nor had actual negotiations with Helmsley's representatives commenced. It is also unclear whether the holders of the Chase and McShane mortgages were willing to discharge or subordinate their liens because they apparently had not been contacted by February 9th.

On February 9, 1984, representatives of the parties to the loan transaction and the participants met at Penthouse's offices in New York City for the preclosing meeting. Among several others, Lipari was present to represent Queen City and Newman was there representing Penthouse. Penthouse's Myerson made sporadic appearances throughout the meeting. Dominion was represented by Philip Gorelick of the Melrod firm who had been brought into the deal on February 8th. At the meeting, after Penthouse made a presentation of a scale model of the planned hotel and casino, Lipari handed out some press clippings, copies of status reports and copies of draft loan closing documents. He then reviewed each of the preclosing conditions and described the progress made toward their satisfaction. Among the draft closing documents Lipari circulated was a standard, preprinted, six-page "Blumberg" form for a "plain language" mortgage and a standard, six-page, preprinted form for a "security agreement" for the furniture and fixtures. At the top of the Blumberg form appeared the admonition: "Consult your lawyer before signing this mortgage — it has important legal consequences." The draft mortgage included a rider requiring that Penthouse satisfy each of the preclosing conditions. Nowhere in the draft closing documents was there a provision allowing for preclosing conditions to be waived or modified.

After sitting through the meeting and reviewing the documents prepared by Lipari, Gorelick presented a list of items he wanted to review prior to deciding whether Dominion could proceed. He also indicated his belief that the loan transaction was not in a position to close, explaining that, in light of the unresolved title problems, problems with the leases, the unfulfilled status of some of the preclosing conditions and the inadequacy of the draft loan documents, he could not advise his client to proceed.

Gorelick gave the strong impression that the entire deal had to be overhauled. In giving this impression, Gorelick was less than tactful. He was particularly vehement about the inadequacy of the documents prepared by Lipari, which he described as "idiotic." To satisfy Gorelick's concerns, Queen City and Penthouse agreed to allow Gorelick and his firm to prepare appropriate closing documents and to review condition compliance in order to bring the deal to a close. Penthouse also agreed to pay the Melrod firm's fees while it focused its resources on the loan transaction.

After Penthouse and Queen City gave Gorelick and the Melrod firm responsibility for moving the deal toward closing, Gorelick immediately sought documents and information from Penthouse concerning all aspects of the transaction. Gorelick then drafted checklists of the documents and information he felt was necessary to review and communicated these checklists to Newman. Gorelick's checklists were very broad in scope and covered all facets of the hotel and casino project. Gorelick's initial requests for information regarding the transaction were communicated on February 9th, but were followed up by several additional requests later that month. Newman responded at length to these requests in letters dated February 29th and March 1st 1984.

Responsive to the problems with the Helmsley lease, Melrod lawyers prepared a list of proposed amendments to the Helmsley lease that they believed were necessary before closing. Gorelick insisted that Penthouse seek the proposed amendments from Helmsley and described each amendment as being "required." When, however, the proposed amendments were sent to Penthouse, they were accompanied by a cover letter from Gorelick's partner, Louis Trotter, that indicated that the proposed amendments reflected "a nearly final version of what the lender will be looking for and [would] certainly provide you with a jumping off point for your discussions with Helmsley."

To respond to an inquiry concerning the status of alternate licensing arrangements, which was required as a preclosing condition, Penthouse's attorney, Arthur S. Goldstein, sent the Melrod firm two letters. These letters addressed the status of Penthouse's license application and set forth the results of Goldstein's inquiries with the staff of the New Jersey Casino Control Commission ("CCC"). In the first letter, after providing an overview of the New Jersey Casino Control Act (the "act") and explaining in detail the license application process, Goldstein discussed the status of Penthouse's application. He stated that Penthouse had commenced the application process but that, at its request, the process had been suspended in September 1982 pending the outcome of Penthouse's efforts to obtain financing. As of February 1984, the application process had not been reactivated. Goldstein also explained that the financial institutions participating in the loan transaction would have to "qualify" under the act. Goldstein's prognosis as to the timing of licensing was that the whole process might be accomplished within a year.

More directly responsive to the status of the preclosing condition was Goldstein's second letter. The preclosing condition required that "reasonably satisfactory" arrangements be made with the staff of the CCC to permit the opening of the casino in the event that Penthouse did not obtain a license. In the second letter, Goldstein stated that he had discussed the matter with staff members at the CCC, but he explained that they had no authority to make binding decisions and that it would be necessary for Penthouse to submit a formal proposal. Nevertheless, based upon his informal discussions with the CCC staff, Goldstein opined that if Penthouse became unlicenseable, it would be necessary for it to completely divest itself of any "beneficial interest" in the casino. He suggested that this could be accomplished by using a trustee who would buy out Penthouse's interest in the casino. He also stated that this transaction would have to be structured in such a manner to insure that Penthouse would have no recourse against the casino in the event of default. After Goldstein set forth additional details of the proposed trusteeship and the buy-out transaction, he concluded by stating that his comments only reflected a "rough outline of what I believe to be a proposal that might be acceptable to the Commission."

In addition to the document and information exchanges, Gorelick and representatives of Dominion engaged in a series of meetings with Myerson and, subsequently, Guccione. At one meeting held on February 29, 1984, Myerson met with Gorelick and other Melrod attorneys to discuss the progress toward closing. Gorelick indicated that he was still in the process of revising his closing checklists and that until he had finished that analysis there was not much to discuss. At that meeting or shortly thereafter, Gorelick reminded Myerson that, since the loan commitment would expire on March 1, 1984, Myerson should submit a request for an extension of the commitment expiration date. Myerson refused, however, to make such a request. Myerson believed that the loan commitment could not expire unless and until Penthouse was presented with the closing documents.

Later in the day on February 29th, Myerson went to Dominion's offices in McLean, Virginia where he met with Dominion's President, David Neal, and a representative of Community, William J. Wienke, Jr. Neal explained that Wienke was present at the meeting because Community was a participant in the loan. During the course of the meeting, the parties discussed various aspects of the project. At the conclusion, however, Wienke expressed his concern about the delays in closing and told Myerson that he needed more information about the loan. Wienke then presented Myerson with a list of thirty-five items concerning the transaction and explained that "this is the kind of stuff that I need." Myerson said that he would review the matters raised in Wienke's list.

Also on February 29th, Gorelick, Wienke and Neal engaged in a telephone conference call to discuss the transaction. During this telephone conference, Wienke explained that he was "getting a bad feeling" about the transaction and inquired whether the commitment should be terminated due to Penthouse's failure to satisfy the preclosing conditions by the March 1st date. Gorelick advised against this and Wienke acquiesced.

In addition to Gorelick's work on the transaction, representatives of Dominion were sending information requests and other items to Penthouse directly. For example, on March 1, 1984, Dominion's Vice-President, James Winston Bray, sent Myerson a letter recapping the "areas of concern" which he felt "need[ed] particular attention." Bray stated that one matter he thought needed addressing — "to make the proposed financing for the project marketable" — was the existence of "[a] satisfactory management agreement, prior to loan closing, for the operation of the proposed hotel." Nevertheless, he prefaced his comments by stating that his concerns were not intended "to replace or diminish" the various other aspects of the loan transaction.

On March 6, 1984, Myerson met with Guccione and Dominion's Chairman of the Board, William L. Walde, at Guccione's home. Although Walde expressed Dominion's continued interest in financing the project, he raised concerns regarding Queen City's ability to serve as the lead lender for the transaction. Walde described Queen City as a small and inconsequential savings and loan and suggested that it was ill-equipped to handle a transaction of this size. Guccione said that he would speak to Queen City about Walde's concerns, but he also stated that he thought it would be unfair to remove Queen City from the lead position.

On March 14, 1984, Guccione flew to Washington, D.C. to meet with Walde. At that meeting, Guccione told Walde that Queen City would not relinquish its lead position, but he offered to compensate Dominion for the fees that it otherwise would have earned had it been the lead lending institution. Also at this meeting, Walde informed Guccione that he wanted to appoint a construction company, Sigal, to perform a long in-depth reevaluation of the structure, the steel and all the parts thereon. Guccione explained that he thought that this was unnecessary. Walde also requested that Penthouse designate a specific individual at Penthouse whose sole responsibility would be to address matters of concern raised by Dominion in connection with the loan transaction.

On March 15, 1984, Walde followed up the meeting with Guccione by sending him a letter summarizing the issues discussed which Guccione had agreed "to look into." One of the items for review was that "[t]he hotel manager [was] to submit to lender a hotel management program." On March 22, 1984, Dominion's Neal sent a letter to Guccione recommending that Penthouse engage Sigal to formulate a construction cost evaluation. Neal concluded the letter by stating that he felt that "this project has been allowed to drift without direction entirely too long. I sincerely hope that you will implement our recommendations . . . at the earliest possible time, the decision is, of course, entirely yours." Not long after the March 22nd letter, Penthouse broke off communications with Dominion and the Melrod firm and refused to respond to their telephone calls.

Beginning on March 20, 1984, the loan participation syndicate began to unravel. First, on March 20th, Community sent a letter to Dominion stating that it had "elected not to extend its offer to participate" in the loan. Then, on March 28, 1984, another participant, Shadow Lawn Savings & Loan Association, wrote to Queen City and indicated that in view of the fact that the loan commitment "has now expired" and because interest rates had changed, it had to meet with Queen City before it would "reconsider an extension" of its participation interest. In May and June 1984, several other participants sent notices to Queen City indicating their belief that the loan commitment had expired and that they were relieved of their participation commitments. Subsequently, after it was unsuccessful in obtaining alternate financing, Penthouse filed the instant action in June 1984.

Proceedings in the District Court and Its Decision

A brief review of the district court's docket sheet reveals that the instant litigation was hard fought with several discovery battles and other disagreements. The case proceeded to a bench trial on May 11, 1987 before Judge Duffy and concluded on June 1, 1987. A number of witnesses appeared for both sides and the record was supplemented by affidavits of witnesses who did not appear at trial.

Important to Dominion's defense to the anticipatory breach claim was its insistence that Penthouse was not in any position to close the loan by March 1st because it could not have satisfied various terms and preclosing conditions of the commitment by that time. To address this point, Dominion presented the testimony of an expert in real estate construction and permanent financing transactions, John C. Nelson, who was a partner in the New York City law firm of Milbank, Tweed, Hadley & McCloy. After setting forth the factual predicate upon which he based his opinion, Nelson opined that, in light of the various title problems (which were supported by the objections to title asserted by Commonwealth), the lack of agreements with certain utility companies, the absence of final plans and specifications, no final project budget, the lack of contracts with an architect, a major construction contractor and major trade contractors, and no agreement concerning casino licensing, the transaction was in no position to close any time from 60 days to six months from the February 9th preclosing meeting. When Nelson presented his opinion at trial, however, the district court asked him how long it would take to close the transaction if all of the preclosing conditions he had taken into account when formulating his opinion (*i.e.*, final plans and specifications, project budgets, trade contracts, etc.) had been waived. Nelson replied that the deal could close as soon as the papers were drawn up. He qualified his response, however, by insisting that a prudent lender would not waive the various conditions which the hypothetical question assumed were waived.

Also important to Dominion's case was the testimony of Melrod partner, Philip Gorelick. Because of his extensive involvement in the transaction, he was in the best position to present Dominion's perspective concerning the deal. The district court was not, however, receptive to Gorelick's testimony. After Gorelick had concluded his testimony on direct examination and began responding to questions on cross-examination, Judge Duffy called a morning recess. As the Judge was leaving the courtroom, he requested that the Melrod firm's attorney, Robert L. Tofel, join him in the robing room. When Tofel met Judge Duffy in the robing room, the judge handed him a copy of Volume 377 of the Federal Supplement and requested that Tofel read the first line in United States v. Tramunti, 377 F. Supp. 1 (S.D.N.Y. 1974) (Duffy, J.). That line reads: "John Spurdis is a liar." After reading the sentence to himself, Tofel looked at the judge. Saying nothing, Judge Duffy simply shrugged expressively. Tofel then said in essence that Judge Duffy had misread Gorelick. Tofel explained that Gorelick may have been obnoxious or aggressive but that he was not a liar. Again, Judge Duffy did not respond and simply shrugged.

On July 29, 1987, the district court filed its reported decision in which it held in favor of Penthouse and Queen City and against Dominion. *See* 665 F. Supp. 301 (S.D.N.Y. 1987). The district court held that Dominion's conduct during February and March 1984 constituted an anticipatory breach of the loan commitment. The district court began its analysis by reasoning that a party to a contract commits an anticipatory breach when it "indicates its refusal to perform unless entirely new or different conditions are first met[.]" *Id.* at 310 (citations omitted). The district court then found that Dominion's conduct on at least four occasions gave rise to an anticipatory breach. Specifically, the court found that 1) Gorelick's demand that Penthouse obtain amendments to the Helmsley lease, 2) Dominion's insistence that a hotel management agreement be entered into prior to closing, 3) Dominion's insistence that Penthouse hire Sigal to perform a construction cost evaluation, and 4) Dominion's insistence that it replace Queen City as lead lender, taken together, "amounted to an unambiguous refusal to close by Dominion," *id.* at 311, and thus constituted an anticipatory breach.

In response to Dominion's argument that Penthouse was not in a position to satisfy the preclosing conditions before March 1st, the district court found that, by the February 9th preclosing meeting, "all of the conditions precedent had been met, waived, or were in a position to have been met by the date set for closing the loan." *Id.* at 310. The district court specifically found 1) that the title and lease problems were "minor" and could be worked out during the "ongoing" discussions with Helmsley; 2) that Queen City had waived Penthouse's full compliance with preclosing conditions 10, 11, 12, and 16; 3) that Penthouse had satisfied preclosing condition 13; and 4) that arrangements with the Casino Control Commission were "easily within reach." *See id.* at 304-05, 310. The court failed to make factual findings or legal conclusions establishing Queen City's authority to waive any preclosing conditions on behalf of Dominion.

The district court explored Dominion's motive for committing the anticipatory breach and found that "[b]ecause of Community's withdrawal on February 29, . . . Dominion either had to stall the closing until the loan expired and then withdraw from its commitment, or breach its agreement." *Id.* at 310. According to the district court, Gorelick was employed to serve as "Dominion's hatchet man intent on destroying the deal," *id.* at 308, that "Dominion hired Gorelick to bully and intimidate the plaintiffs into delaying the loan until Community could be replaced or[,] failing that, to delay until the Commitment expired and Dominion was released from its obligation." *Id.* at 307.

The district court also carried forward its earlier, private attack on Gorelick's veracity. In its decision, the district court found that Gorelick committed "outrageous perjury" during trial. *Id.* at 306-07. Making reference to Gorelick's trial testimony, the district court stated

> [t]he decision as to the credibility of witnesses is properly left to the trial judge or to the jury because as finders of fact they are in a position to view the demeanor of the witnesses.
>
> Gorelick took the stand and attempted brazenly to lie to the court. During cross-examination, the crucible of truth, Gorelick continuously shifted uneasily in the chair, sweated like a trapped liar, and the glaze that came over his shifty eyes gave proof to his continuing perjury. His total lack of veracity was shown not only by his demeanor but by the shady practices he seemingly reveled in. He charged needless and exorbitant fees, Joint Exh. 41, for work that was intentionally unproductive. While representing the bank he demanded a $150,000 "bonus" from the borrower if the loan closed, an arrangement Gorelick never disclosed to his bank-client.

Id. at 306 n.1. Thus, the court made a specific factual finding that Gorelick committed perjury during his trial testimony.

After reaching its decision on the liability issue, the district court considered the damage question. The court first determined that Penthouse was entitled to various out-of-pocket and "carrying" expenses. Then, the court turned to the question of whether Penthouse was entitled to recover the profits it would have made had the construction been completed and the hotel and casino become operational. Applying the rationale of Perma Research & Development v. Singer Co., 542 F.2d 111 (2d Cir. 1976), the court determined that Penthouse's lost future profits over a ten-year period could be properly awarded. Accordingly, the district court held that Penthouse was entitled to recover damages in the amount of $129,904,455, $112,083,583 of which was for the lost future profits.

Also in its decision, the district court concluded that Queen City should prevail on its counterclaim in the third-party action: "Having held that Dominion breached its agreement, I must also find it liable to Queen City for that breach." 665 F. Supp. at 312. In addition, the court concluded that Dominion should lose on its third-party claim against Queen City because "[t]here [was] a total failure of proof that Queen City breached any duty owed to Dominion." *Id.*

After the court issued its opinion, Penthouse submitted its proposed judgment to the district court. In the proposed judgment, Penthouse did not name the Melrod firm as a judgment-debtor for the lost profits award. To correct what it perceived as a discrepancy, the district court sua sponte conformed the pleadings to the proof and held that the Melrod firm was jointly and severally liable for the entire Penthouse judgment. The court explained that the Melrod firm was liable for the Penthouse judgment because its conduct amounted to active fraud. The district court did not, however, make any factual findings concerning what acts or omissions allegedly perpetrated by the Melrod firm gave rise to the court's conclusion that it committed fraud. Nor did the court explain how a judgment for lost profits which resulted from an alleged anticipatory breach of a loan commitment could also serve as the basis for a fraud judgment.

After amending its original decision, the district court entered final judgment on October 2, 1987 and awarded Penthouse $128,682,830.80, held Dominion and the Melrod firm jointly and severally liable for that judgment, awarded Queen City $7,652,352.91 plus interest and dismissed Dominion's claim against Queen City with prejudice. Subsequently, in a memorandum and order dated December 2, 1987, the district court denied the defendants' motion for a new trial. 678 F. Supp. 61.

Discussion

Dominion and the Melrod firm raise several arguments on this appeal. Dominion contends that the district court erred in concluding that its conduct amounted to an anticipatory breach of the loan commitment and that the court erred in concluding that Penthouse was ready, willing and able to perform its obligations under the loan commitment. Dominion also argues that the district court applied an incorrect legal standard when it awarded Penthouse damages for its lost future profits and that the court erred when it dismissed its claim against Queen City. The Melrod firm challenges the judgment entered against it on fraud grounds, arguing, inter alia, that because such a finding was not supported in law or fact, the district court erred in sua sponte holding Melrod jointly and severally liable for the Penthouse judgment.

For the reasons that follow, we reverse the judgments entered in favor of Penthouse and Queen City, affirm the dismissal of Dominion's cross-claim and remand with instructions that judgment be entered in favor of Dominion and the Melrod firm.

I. Dominion's Appeal of *Penthouse* Judgment

A. Preliminary Matters

At the outset, Dominion argues that the loan commitment expired by its own terms on March 1, 1984 and contends that, after that date, Dominion, Queen City and the other participating lenders were under "no further obligation" to proceed with the mortgage financing. Dominion therefore suggests that the March 1st date has crucial significance in part because it would constitute the date on or before which the parties would have been required to perform and/or satisfy their obligations under the loan commitment.

At the November 21st meeting, the parties understood that the commitment had expired by its own terms. A written extension of the expiration date was therefore necessary to have a "valid" commitment as of the date Dominion agreed to participate. The parties then mutually extended the expiration date to December 1, 1983, but they simultaneously agreed that the "closing date" for the loan would occur "no earlier than February 1, 1984 or later than March 1, 1984." Aside from these agreements, the parties entered into no other arrangements with respect to further extensions of the expiration date or the closing date. . . .

What we must resolve is whether, when the parties agreed to close the loan "no later than March 1, 1984," they intended on extending the expiration date to March 1st. We believe they did. Reading the expiration date clause together with the clause regarding the closing date leads us to conclude that the parties must have intended to extend the expiration date when they agreed that the closing would occur no later than March 1st. Any other construction of these documents would leave the parties agreeing to close the loan after the commitment had expired which would make no sense. . . .

In view of the above, we conclude that not only was March 1st the closing date, but also that the commitment expired on that date. We acknowledge that the parties' conduct in continuing to negotiate after March 1st may be consistent with an implied extension of the expiration date. We observe, however, that Penthouse and Queen City had allowed the commitment to expire by its own terms once before. Thus, we do not believe that our conclusion here is at odds with the parties' expectations. In holding that the commitment expired on March 1st, we simply construe the terms of relatively unambiguous documents. The parties bargained for a loan commitment that remained open only for a stated duration and we are not at liberty to construe that agreement in a manner inconsistent with its clear language.

B. EXISTENCE OF AN ANTICIPATORY BREACH

We now turn to the district court's factual findings and legal conclusions concerning the existence of an anticipatory breach. The district court determined that "Dominion's representatives' conduct and statements amounted to a clear refusal to proceed to closing unless conditions beyond those required by the Loan Commitment were first met." 665 F. Supp. at 310. As examples of Dominion's "clear refusal to proceed," the district court relied on 1) Gorelick's insistence on the proposed amendments to the Helmsley Lease, 2) Dominion's alleged insistence that a hotel management agreement be in place prior to closing, 3) Dominion's alleged requirement that Penthouse hire Sigal, and 4) Dominion's alleged demand that it replace Queen City as lead lender. Pointing out that three of the four examples the district court took into account when it found that an anticipatory breach occurred all took place after March 1st, Dominion argues that the district court erred as a matter of law by considering Dominion's post-March 1st conduct. In addition, Dominion contends that, when only its pre-March 1st conduct is taken into account, it is clear that it did not by word or conduct commit an anticipatory breach. We agree.

"Ordinarily no action for damages or for restitution can be maintained until the time for performance has come and there has been an actual failure to perform." Miller & Sons Bakery Co. v. Selikowitz, 8 N.J. Super. 118, 73 A.2d 607, 609 (1950). Nevertheless, "where . . . one party [to a contract] either disables himself from performing, or prevents the other from performing, or repudiates in advance his obligations under the contract, and refuses to be longer bound thereby, communicating such repudiation to the other party," the nonbreaching party "is not only excused from further performance . . . , but may at his option treat the contract as terminated for all purposes of performance, and maintain an action at once for damages occasioned by such repudiation, without awaiting the time fixed by the contract for performance by the defendant." Dun & Bradstreet, Inc. v. Wilsonite Products co., 130 N.J.L. 24, 31 A.2d 45, 47 (1943) (*quoting* O'Neill v. Supreme Council American Legion of Honor, 70 N.J.L. 410, 412, 57 A. 463, 464 (1904). . . .

In recounting the evidence concerning Gorelick's conduct at the February 9, 1984 preclosing meeting, the district court found that "[t]he overwhelming evidence shows that Gorelick's demands were equal to a demand that the deal be completely done over[.]" 665 F. Supp. at 307. Subsequently, the court found that

> [t]hroughout February and March, Dominion, through the Melrod firm, continued to make requests for more information which Newman described as "never ending." . . . Dominion further demanded numerous changes in the way the entire deal was to be structured, the parties involved, and other changes not required by the Loan Commitment.

Id. at 309. When, however, the court sought to provide specific examples of the "changes not required" by the commitment, the only one that occurred before March 1st was Gorelick's demands concerning amendments to the Helmsley lease. The evidence established that Gorelick did in fact insist that the proposed amendments were "required." Thus, the issue we confront is whether Gorelick's insistence on the proposed amendments represented a demand for performance for which Dominion had no right and whether his insistence amounted to a "definite and unequivocal refusal" by Dominion to fulfill its obligations under the agreement unless this condition was met.

It is undisputed that, unless amended, the Helmsley lease would have been violated by the closing of the Queen City deal. Because the loan commitment required that there be "no violations" of that lease at closing, it is clear that some amendments were necessary to satisfy the terms of the loan commitment. To this end, the Melrod lawyers submitted a list of proposed amendments to Penthouse. Even though Gorelick insisted that each proposed amendment was required, when the proposed amendments were sent to Penthouse, Dominion's position was equivocal. Trotter's cover letter indicated that the amendments represented what Dominion would be "looking for" and would provide Penthouse "with a jumping off point" for its negotiations with Helmsley. Thus, Gorelick's statements that the proposed amendments were required clearly were qualified by the statements made in Trotter's cover letter.

In addition, we observe that the list of proposed amendments was just that—a proposal. With the proposed amendments, it was contemplated that Penthouse would then engage in negotiations with Helmsley. As indicated in Trotter's letter, the proposed amendments constituted a starting point for the negotiations with Helmsley, but they did not represent Dominion's "final" position. Viewed in this light, we are persuaded that the district court clearly erred when it found that Gorelick's insistence on the proposed amendments gave rise to an anticipatory breach. New Jersey consistently requires that the breaching party in these cases make a "clear and unequivocal declaration" that performance would not be forthcoming and Gorelick's conduct in this regard falls short.

Nevertheless, we are left with the court's general finding that Dominion refused to perform unless the entire deal was restructured. As pointed out above, most of the specific instances of conduct cited by the court occurred after March 1st and thus are not relevant to our inquiry. We do confront, however, the district court's finding that Gorelick demanded at the February 9th meeting that everything in connection with the deal be "completely done over." We observe that Gorelick was so adamant in this regard that the parties allowed him to assume responsibility for drafting the closing documents and reviewing condition compliance. Thus, it is arguable that his demands at the February 9th meeting were sufficiently clear and unequivocal to give rise to an anticipatory breach if his refusal to proceed was unjustified.

When Gorelick attended the February 9th meeting, he only recently had been brought into the deal. He was there to represent his client's interests in connection with its agreement to participate in a $97 million construction and permanent financing transaction, of which more than a third was to be funded by his client. At the time of the preclosing meeting, the parties contemplated closing the transaction within a few weeks—by March 1st at the latest. At the meeting or shortly before, Gorelick discovered that there were significant problems affecting title and problems with the Helmsley lease and yet there were no active negotiations to resolve those problems. Gorelick also learned that Queen City intended on closing the transaction without insisting that Penthouse comply fully with all of the preclosing conditions. In addition, he received draft loan documentation which, in his judgment, was amateurish and substandard for a transaction of this magnitude.

While we do not pass upon the reasonableness of each of Gorelick's objections, we note that Nelson's expert testimony fully supported Gorelick's position that the transaction was not in a position to close any time in the near future. We also note that although the district court found that some of Gorelick's objections were unreasonable, it did not find that most of his concerns were unfounded. Gorelick attended the preclosing meeting in order to ensure that the interests of his client were protected. In so doing, he insightfully observed serious problems with the transaction and promptly raised his objections. Gorelick's insistence on marketable title in the face of the objections reported by the title company all by itself would justify his position that the deal was in no position to close and thus cannot, as a matter of law, constitute an anticipatory breach. Coupling the title and lease problems with Penthouse's failure to establish that it was in a position to fully satisfy all of the preclosing conditions, we conclude that Gorelick properly refused to proceed unless his concerns were addressed. We therefore conclude that the district court clearly erred when it found that Dominion committed an anticipatory breach of its agreement to participate. Accordingly, we reverse the judgment entered against Dominion.

C. PLAINTIFFS' ABILITY TO PERFORM

As part of this damages action for an alleged anticipatory breach, Penthouse bore the burden of establishing its willingness and ability to perform all of the obligations under the agreement. . . .

That the plaintiff must establish its readiness and ability to perform does not mean that it is required to tender performance. After the occurrence of an anticipatory breach, "[i]t is no longer necessary for the plaintiff to perform or tender performance." . . . Nevertheless, the plaintiff must demonstrate that it had the willingness and ability to perform "before the repudiation and that the plaintiff would have rendered the agreed performance if the defendant had not repudiated." *Id.*

In the instant case, the district court found that "at the time of the preclosing meeting, all of the conditions precedent had been met, waived, or were in a position to have been met by the date set for closing the loan."

665 F. Supp. at 310. Thus, it found that Penthouse was ready, willing and able to proceed by the time of the alleged anticipatory breach. In challenging this conclusion, Dominion argues that Penthouse had not met and could not have met its obligations to convey valid mortgages and to satisfy certain of the preclosing conditions and that the district court's findings in this regard are clearly erroneous. Dominion also argues that the district court erred in concluding that certain conditions had been waived, contending that Queen City had no authority to waive preclosing conditions. Dominion concludes that, when properly viewed, the evidence demonstrates that Penthouse was in no position to satisfy the preclosing conditions on or before March 1st and thus failed to establish that it was ready, willing and able to proceed. We agree.

Despite the fact that Penthouse and Queen City never argued at trial that any of the preclosing conditions had been waived, the district court determined that Penthouse's full compliance with preclosing conditions 10, 11, 12 and 16 had been waived as a result of Lipari's meetings with Penthouse during the January 1984 status conferences. The district court's waiver finding was integral to its determination that Penthouse was ready, willing and able to perform by the closing date because, in the absence of a waiver, it is clear that those material preclosing conditions were not and could not have been satisfied by March 1st. Penthouse offered at trial no evidence to contradict Nelson's opinion that it would have taken at least 60 days, and more than likely 6 months, from February 9, 1984 for Penthouse to comply with all of the preclosing conditions. Nelson's prognosis changed only after the district court inquired as to how long it would have taken to close if the unsatisfied preclosing conditions had been waived. Although he bristled at the suggestion that those preclosing conditions would ever be waived by a prudent lender—let alone an institutional lender—he testified that, assuming a waiver, the loan could have been closed as soon as the papers were drawn up. In the face of this testimony, we must squarely decide the propriety of the district court's waiver finding. This inquiry requires, in turn, that we examine whether Queen City had the authority in the first instance to waive Penthouse's compliance with preclosing conditions. We conclude that it did not.

Before we inquire into Queen City's authority to waive compliance with preclosing conditions, we must examine the nature of Dominion's agreement to participate. On November 21st, Dominion entered into an agreement with Queen City whereby it agreed to participate in the lending syndicate to the extent of $35 million. That agreement was embodied in several documents which, in turn, incorporated the terms and conditions of both the Queen City loan commitment and the participation agreement. When construing Dominion's agreement, we read these documents "together as one instrument, and the recitals in one may be explained or limited by reference to the other." Schlein v. Gairoard, 127 N.J.L. 358, 22 A.2d 539, 540-41 (1941); *see* Schlossman's, Inc. v. Radcliffe, 3 N.J. 430, 70 A.2d 493, 495 (1950). Applying this rule, we therefore look to the terms of both the loan commitment and the participation agreement when examining whether Queen City had the authority to effect a waiver of preclosing conditions.

The loan commitment provided that

> [a]ll title questions and all other legal matters relating to or arising out of the Loan shall be subject in all respects to the approval of the Lender's counsel . . . and the decision of the Lender's counsel as to whether all conditions of the commitment have been met shall be final.

The commitment also provided, however, that "[l]ender's obligation to close the loan is contingent upon the satisfaction of each of [the preclosing] conditions." Reading these two provisions together, we conclude that, although Queen City had the final word on whether the preclosing conditions had been satisfied, Penthouse nevertheless was required to satisfy each of the preclosing conditions. Thus, Queen City was granted essentially administrative authority to oversee the manner in which the preclosing conditions were satisfied, but it was not empowered to waive Penthouse's compliance with the preclosing conditions.

The participation agreement further limited Queen City's authority in connection with the administration of the loan transaction. It expressly provided that its terms could not be modified except by an agreement in writing. Thus, Queen City was not empowered to modify the terms or conditions of the participation agreement without obtaining the participants' prior approval. In addition, when the participants entered into the agreement with Queen City, they only authorized Queen City to act on their behalf in the capacity of an independent contractor; Queen City was not authorized to act as their agent. To this end, Queen City was given discretionary power as to the means and manner of contractual performance, *see, e.g.*, Errickson v. F. W. Schwiers, Jr. Co., 108 N.J.L. 481, 158 A. 482, 483 (1932), but was not empowered to make material changes that rendered the participants less secure. Even if we were to conclude that Queen City was authorized to act as agent for the participants, it would not have been empowered to waive or alter material terms "or otherwise to diminish or discharge the obligation of the third person [.]" *See* Restatement (Second) of Agency §51 comment C (2d ed. 1979).

In view of the above, it is clear that Queen City was not authorized expressly or inferentially in the commitment or the participation agreement to modify the terms of the commitment by waiving Penthouse's full compliance with preclosing conditions. In addition, when Dominion was first informed concerning the full extent of Penthouse's proposed substitute performance for preclosing conditions 10, 11, 12 and 16, Gorelick objected. Then, after the Melrod firm was given responsibility for reviewing condition compliance and Gorelick transmitted his various checklists, it was made clear that Dominion expected that Penthouse would comply with the terms of each preclosing condition. Thus, there could be no implied waiver of these conditions here, either. We therefore conclude that the district court erred when it found that Queen City waived Penthouse's full compliance with preclosing conditions 10, 11, 12 and 16. Because Queen City could not waive these conditions in the first place, it could not accept Penthouse's substitute performance without first obtaining the participants' approval.

Sound national banking policies support the conclusion we reach here. As amicus curiae Federal Home Loan Bank Board points out:

> the proposition . . . that a lead lender may, without consulting participating lenders, waive or modify significant conditions of a loan to the detriment of participants, seriously undermines the Bank Board's supervisory policies concerning safe and sound underwriting of participation purchases and is completely at odds with the Bank Board's policy that loan participants must satisfy themselves that the participation is a loan that the participating association would make itself.

If a lead lender has this authority . . . , the Bank Board's supervisory control regarding underwriting of participation purchases is rendered more difficult or impossible and the FSLIC fund is exposed to inordinate risk. A savings and loan association's independently and prudently underwritten participation in a loan could be changed into an entirely reckless act if fundamental terms and conditions of the loan are altered prior to closing by the lead lender on its own initiative and without consulting the participant. This would make it very difficult, if not impossible, for a participant to assure prudent underwriting or participations.

While we do not necessarily find that these policy considerations by themself are binding if the parties had agreed otherwise, they certainly militate against the district court's unsubstantiated and erroneous finding that Queen City had the authority to waive various essential preclosing conditions.

As a separate matter, Dominion contends that the district court's other findings that bore upon Penthouse's ability to perform were erroneous. The district court found that the outstanding title and lease problems were "minor," 665 F. Supp. at 310, and that "the entire matter could have been resolved in time to close the deal before March 1, 1984." *Id.* at 305. The district court also held that, although licensing discussions with the Casino Control Commission "were to resume after the closing, . . . it appeared an arrangement with the Commission was easily within reach." *Id.* Dominion argues that, notwithstanding the court's characterization, the title and lease problems were not minor and that there was no evidence to support the court's conclusion that those matters could have been resolved by March 1st. With regard to its finding concerning the licensing arrangements, Dominion contends that it supports the view that Penthouse could not have satisfied this preclosing condition before closing and that the court's characterization that these arrangements were "easily within reach" is belied by the evidence. We agree with both of Dominion's contentions.

Turning to the court's findings concerning the title and lease problems, we are compelled to conclude that the district court clearly erred when it characterized these matters as being "minor." Unless these problems were resolved, they absolutely would have prevented Penthouse from delivering the title required in the commitment. Likewise, unless the Helmsley lease was modified, Penthouse could not certify that there were "no violations" of that lease. Thus, in view of the gravity of these problems, Penthouse knew that they had to be resolved by the closing date. We therefore cannot conclude that they were "minor."

In addition, the district court's characterization of the title and lease problems as "minor" presupposed that several contingencies could and would occur to resolve them before closing. . . .

The absence of ongoing negotiations undermines the district court's finding that the title and lease problems could have been resolved before March 1st, and no evidence in the record indicates that negotiations would have commenced by March 1st, let alone be concluded by that date, to resolve the problems with the lease and title.

In addition, Penthouse failed to establish that it was working toward clearing up the problems posed by the McShane and Chase mortgages. Those mortgages had to be subordinated in order for Penthouse to provide the security required by the commitment and Penthouse apparently had not even made contact with the holders of those mortgages.

With regard to the court's finding concerning the status of the alternate licensing arrangements condition, we note that the district court overlooked the fact that this was a preclosing condition. Because the court found that those arrangements could have been made after closing, it is clear that Penthouse did not carry its burden to demonstrate its ability to perform this condition before closing.

In view of the foregoing, we conclude that Penthouse failed to carry its burden at trial to demonstrate that it was ready, willing and able to perform its contractual obligations at any time before March 1st. Accordingly, the judgment in favor of Penthouse is reversed. . . .

D. DAMAGES

Having found that Penthouse failed to establish the essential elements of its anticipatory breach claim, we need not address the merits of the district court's award of lost future profits. . . .

II. Dominion's Appeal of Queen City Judgment

A. ANTICIPATORY BREACH CLAIM

. . . .

In view of our determination that the court erred in concluding that Dominion committed an anticipatory breach and that Penthouse was ready, willing and able to proceed by March 1st, we reverse the judgment entered in favor of Queen City. Because Dominion's conduct did not amount to an anticipatory breach, it is not liable to Queen City on the counterclaim. Likewise, because Penthouse did not establish that it could have satisfied the preclosing conditions before March 1st, Queen City is also precluded from recovery against Dominion.

B. DISMISSAL OF DOMINION'S CROSS-CLAIM

Dominion contends that the district court erred when it dismissed with prejudice its third-party claim against Queen City. Dominion predicated its theory of Queen City's liability on the argument that, if Queen City did in fact waive four preclosing conditions, in so doing it breached its fiduciary duties owed to Dominion and the other participants. Because, however, we conclude that no waiver occurred — because Queen City had no authority to waive conditions — it follows that Queen City is not liable for any purported waiver. Accordingly, we affirm the district court's dismissal of this claim.

III. THE MELROD FIRM'S APPEAL OF PENTHOUSE JUDGMENT

A. BACKGROUND

Nowhere in the district court's reported opinion did it find that Dominion or the Melrod firm committed fraud. The entire decision was devoted to a discussion of Dominion's alleged anticipatory breach and the damages resulting therefrom. There was no suggestion that Gorelick and the Melrod firm were to be held liable for the Penthouse judgment. In addition, while the district court made findings concerning Dominion's alleged undisclosed intent and Gorelick's purported role as "hatchet man," we observe that the court found no fraud or misrepresentation concerning the November 21st agreement and made no other specific findings with regard to subsequent events or statements suggesting that fraud was committed. . . .

Having concluded that Penthouse does not prevail on the merits of the fraud claim, it is unnecessary to pass on the several other arguments raised on this appeal. Nevertheless, we are quite concerned by the district court's conduct during the robing room incident as well as by its perjury finding. Suffice it to say that we believe that ex parte communications between the district court and only one of the litigants are rarely, if ever, looked upon with favor, even if intended to impart advice to a fellow member of the profession. With regard to the perjury finding, we are somewhat surprised by its presence in the court's decision. If the court viewed Gorelick's testimony as incredible, that is its prerogative as the trier of fact in a non-jury case, but unless perjury is at issue in a case, such a finding is not necessary once the trier of fact finds the witnesses' testimony incredible. The perjury finding here, however, was not only unnecessary but also was erroneous since it was not based upon clear and convincing proof. *See* Barr Rubber Products Co. v. Sun Rubber Co., 425 F.2d 1114, 1120 (2d Cir.), *cert. denied*, 400 U.S. 878, 91 S.

Ct. 118, 27 L. Ed. 2d 115 (1970). Accordingly, we specifically reverse that finding.

Conclusion

In view of the foregoing, we reverse the judgments entered against Dominion and the Melrod firm in favor of Penthouse and against Dominion in favor of Queen City, affirm the dismissal of Dominion's cross-claim, and remand to the district court for the purpose of entering judgment in favor of Dominion and the Melrod firm and against Penthouse and Queen City dismissing the complaint and the related cross-action.

Table of Cases

Principal Cases are in Italics

Index